From Mount Hooly to Princeton

Andrew Hook is Emeritus Bradley Professor of English Literature at the University of Glasgow. Earlier in his career he taught in the English Departments of both Edinburgh and Aberdeen universities. Since his retiral in the 1990s he has lectured and taught at a range of American colleges and universities. He is a Fellow of both the British Academy and the Royal Society of Edinburgh. His scholarship is distinctive in that it focuses on all three of English, Scottish and American literatures. His books include *Scotland and America, A Study of Cultural Relations 1750-1835* (Blackie, 1975, 2nd edition, Humming Earth, 2008), *F. Scott Fitzgerald, A Literary Life* (Palgrave, 2002) and Penguin editions of Scott's *Waverley* (1972) and (with Judith Hook) Charlotte Bronte's *Shirley*. He regards *From Mount Hooly to Princeton* as much a personal as a scholarly work.

From Mount Hooly to Princeton

A Scottish-American Medley

Andrew Hook

K&B

Kennedy & Boyd,
an imprint of
Zeticula Ltd,
Unit 13,
196 Rose Street,
Edinburgh,
EH2 4AT,
Scotland.

http://www.kennedyandboyd.co.uk
admin@kennedyandboyd.co.uk

First published in 2020

The following chapters have previously been published, and are reprinted with permission.

'The Writers' Conference Revisited' was published in Angela Barrie & Eleanor Bell, *The International Writers' Conference Revisited: Edinburgh, 1962*, Cargo. 2012, pp. 202-204.

'Braveheart, Rob Roy and Sir Walter Scott' was published in *The Newsletter of the Eighteenth-Century Scottish Studies Society*, no. 10 (1996), 14-16.

'Scott in America' was published in the *Bulletin of the Edinburgh Sir Walter Scott Club* 2005, 3-12.

'The Glasgow Renaissance: A Personal View' was published in the *Contemporary Review*, January 1988, 28-31.

A large proportion of the material in various sections of this book derives from the author's contributions to the *Scottish Review*, and is reprinted with their kind permission.

The remainder are lectures given at a variety of conferences.

Paperback ISBN 978-1-84921-189-5

Remembering Judith, Sarah, and Caspar.

Cherishing Nathaniel, Diane, and India.

Preface

Not so long ago, Alasdair Gray published a book called *Of Me And Others*. In his Foreword he says he 'thought this book would turn out to be a ragbag of interesting scraps'. However, he goes on to argue that despite the diverse range of material it contains – essays, reviews, reminiscences, obituaries – his book 'has the unity of a struggle for a confident culture, a struggle shared with a few who became good friends and thousands I have never met'. In other words, *Of Me And Others* is about all of us. I make no such claim for this 'Book of Allsorts'. Given the striking diversity of the material it contains, academic and non-academic, 'a ragbag of (I hope) interesting scraps' is a perfectly plausible description.

The 'scraps' focus on the following topics or themes: my early life, my professional life in the academic world, the past and present world of both Scotland and America, and the educational, literary, cultural and political life of both these countries. It is focusing on these different areas that has in the end determined the series of sections that provide the book's structure. The book also contains unpublished papers I have delivered at academic conferences and, perhaps 'scrappiest' of all, a substantial body of material which derives from the contributions I have been making to the online magazine *The Scottish Review* since its inception in 2008. Given the centrality in all of this of my professional life, I hope a quick survey of its outlines may help the reader in navigating the different areas of the book.

An undergraduate in the Edinburgh English Department, after graduation I was lucky enough a few years later to be awarded a Visiting Fellowship to the Princeton University Graduate College. Gaining my PhD in 1960, in session 1959-60 I had taught Freshman English at Duke University in Durham, North Carolina. Returning to the U.K, in 1960-61, I taught briefly at Magee University College in Londonderry, and Trinity College, Dublin. The rest of my U.K. career was (roughly) made up of ten years in the Edinburgh English Department (including a year back at Princeton in the 1960s), ten years in the Aberdeen department, and almost twenty years as Bradley Professor of English at Glasgow University. In the years that followed I returned regularly to the USA. First as a Visiting Research Professor at Princeton in 1999-2000, then as the Gillespie Visiting Professor at the College of Wooster in Ohio in 2001-02.

In following years, three times I spent a semester teaching at Dartmouth College in New Hampshire, and I ended my teaching career with a semester at St. Thomas University in Minneapolis-St. Paul. During my spells in the US, I gave visiting lectures at a range of other colleges and universities.

As the Contents page indicates, I have attempted to divide up the book's material into more or less coherent sections. Some of these were easy to identify — such as one focusing on autobiographical material. But I quickly found that autobiography often involved matter that spilled over into other sections – such as American universities or the politics of contemporary America. So I have to ask the reader to be generous over the arbitrary nature of the placing of some material. Again, written over many years, some topics and references inevitably recur in different contexts. This means that an element of repetition does occasionally occur — as for example Professor Trevor-Roper's comments on Scottish history and historians, or accounts of John Witherspoon's role in America. With an apology, I felt it better to let these comments stand.

Finally, I wish to thank Dr David Cunningham for his invaluable help in creating this book. Without his editorial expertise, a dream would never have become a reality. Islay McLeod, the current editor of *The Scottish Review*, has also been unfailingly helpful. My publisher has throughout been a key figure in making it all happen.

Contents

Illustrations

Part One

Pages of Autobiography.

Initially my intention was to limit this section to accounts of my boyhood years: growing up in Wick, visiting my Gloucestershire relatives, holiday periods in Glasgow and elsewhere. Leaving it at that would have would have underlined the point that this was in no sense going to be a book detailing the story of my private life. However, my professional life was another matter. I recognised that many of the topics and themes I do plan to address emerge from the pattern of my academic career. That being so, I decided it would be appropriate in the autobiographical section to include accounts of later periods in my life – such as times spent in American colleges and universities. Such accounts go on to include material that could well have appeared in subsequent sections. But the way they illuminate my overall experience I feel justifies their appearance here.

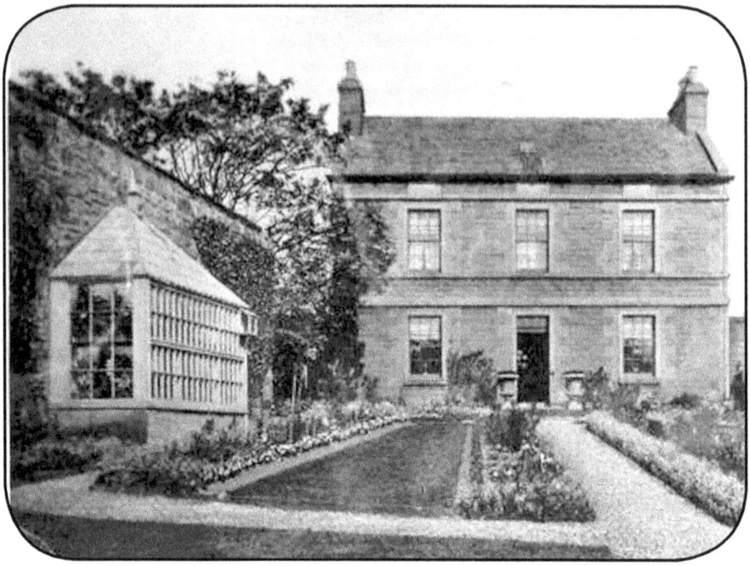

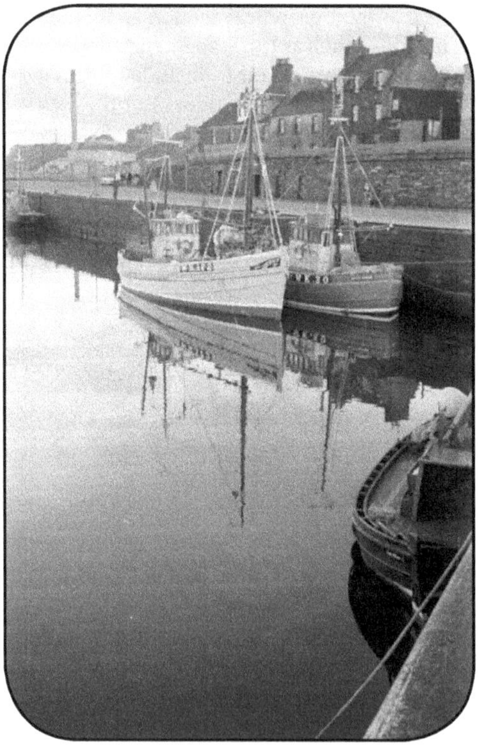

Top: Mount Hooly House

Left: Wick Harbour, 1965

1 Mount Hooly House

Born in Wick in 1932, I lived in Mount Hooly House, Shore Lane, until 1949. As the photograph shows, Mount Hooly was not really part of Shore Lane. The green iron railings at the bottom of the large garden, and the heavy iron entry gate, did form part of the lane, but the path from the gate, past lawns and flowerbeds, to the house's front door was, as you can see, a long one. Like the two grand flowerpots on either side of the door – always there in my memory – Mount Hooly was built on quite an imposing scale.

My family, on the other hand, could in no way be described as grand. My father, employed by the GPO, was a wireless operator in Wick Radio station. My mother was never in paid employment after her marriage. So how could they have afforded to buy such a large house? Part of the answer at least is that they didn't. As a boy growing up, it seemed the most natural thing in the world, but looking back I suppose the arrangement was a relatively unusual one: until the end in 1949, Mount Hooly was shared with my maternal grandparents. So I guess a pooling of resources between the two generations was what made the purchase of such a large house possible.

Still I suspect the house must have been available at a bargain price. In all the years I grew up alongside my maternal grandfather he never seemed to have a job. Apparently he had retired successfully from full-time work at a relatively early age! As a young man he had begun a career in the one industry that had made Wick into a thriving boom town around the end of the nineteenth century. This was the period when Wick had become the most successful herring-fishing port in the U.K. Vast millions of fish were caught and processed through the summer fishing season. Each year the town's population was swollen by the influx of fishing crews and all those associated with the herring industry: the mass of women gutting the newly-landed fish; those involved in the curing and packing of the catch; coopers making the barrels in which they were stored; boat-builders and rope and net-makers; fish merchants and fish salesmen. The Old Pulteney distillery produced three thousand litres of whisky per week – most of it for local consumption. In the years before the Great War the sea's rich harvest of the 'silver darlings' had transformed the town's economic prosperity. My grandfather (after whom I was named) used to regale us with stories about these great days. He said you could walk across Wick Bay – outside the actual harbour – without getting your feet wet – on the decks of the mass of herring fishing boats so tightly moored together. And given that, as early as the 1860s, over eleven hundred boats were operating out of the port, it could even have been true! Even as late as the 1930s I remember seeing the foreign fish-buyers from the Baltic states tasting the raw herring before deciding whose catch to buy.

However, Grandad's actual experience of the herring fishing industry appears to have been limited to one season in which he followed the movement of the herring from the Western Isles around the north coast to Caithness. At that point my grandmother put her foot down and insisted there would be no more fishing trips away from home for her husband. At least that was the story I picked up from my mother, and I certainly recall my grandmother as the stronger personality of the two. From then on Grandad seems to have got by doing little more than odd jobs. He certainly worked for a spell in a local grocery shop, but within my memory span, he simply helped to keep Mount Hooly in good order – cutting the grass on the lawns, growing potatoes in the back garden, that kind of thing. His spell as a seagoing fisherman probably remained the most exciting part of his life. Growing up, I was a regular frequenter of Wick's Public Library (like that in so many Scottish towns – endowed by Andrew Carnegie). But one of my duties was to bring home reading matter for my grandfather. And the subject was always the same, the sea. Grandad read endless books about sailing ships, the Cutty Sark, Thermopylae, and the other tea-clippers racing across the Indian Ocean, stories of shipwrecks, and tales of fantastic endurance by crew members cast adrift and miraculously surviving. No fiction – just real-life stories of adventures at sea. The only poem he seemed to know off by heart was Felicia Dorothea Hemans' 'The Boy stood on the Burning Deck' (Casabianca).

II

When my family acquired it in 1933, Mount Hooly House was not in what could be described as a fashionable area of the town. On the northern side of Wick River, it was above but close to the oldest part of the original town, and not far from the harbour area. In the early nineteenth century, Wick had benefited from the work of the British Fisheries Society, which had been set up with the express purpose of developing the potential of a new fishing industry – based specifically on herring – in small coastal towns in the Scottish

Highlands. The harbour was designed and built by Thomas Telford in 1803. Subsequently it was expanded by Thomas Stevenson (father of Robert Louis), and James Bremner, a local naval architect, harbour builder and ship-raiser. After 1803, on the south side, a whole new section of the town was planned and built on a gridiron plan – as opposed to the random and unplanned shape of the town to the north. Lord Pulteney was then Governor of the Fisheries Society, so the new development was designated Pulteneytown. With its small but neat artisan-style houses, Pulteneytown must have had its attraction in the nineteenth century. But with the decline of the fishing industry in the twentieth century, it became increasingly unfashionable. By then the better-off section of Wick's population was living on the edges of the town, well away from the harbour areas both north and south. So Mount Hooly, despite its size, must have been available in 1933 at a reasonable price. Its past history, however, had been somewhat different.

My family acquired the house after the death of the previous owner – an Isabella Bruce – who died in August 1933. The local newspaper, the *John O'Groat Journal*, reported that 'Miss Isabella Bruce of Mount Hooly House, only daughter of the late Mr Charles Bruce, an estimable Wick lady... passed away on August 15th, 1933. Miss Bruce had numerous friends, and every year she purchased about 100 copies of our Christmas Number, which she posted with her compliments and good wishes, to her correspondents in all parts of the world'. In fact the Bruce family was one of considerable standing in Wick society. Charles Bruce, Isabella's father, was born in 1826 and lived until 1897. A bailie in the town, Charles Bruce was well-known for his intellectual and cultural interests. A member of the Edinburgh-based Society of Antiquaries of Scotland, he had a special interest in local history and antiquarian research and appears to have built up in Mount Hooly House his own collection of antiquities relating to northern Scotland.

By becoming a bailie in Wick, Charles Bruce was maintaining a tradition of public service in his family. His father William Bruce, who owned a drapery business in the town's Bridge Street, had served two incumbencies as Provost in 1836-38 and again in 1839-43. In recognition of his service to the town, the Wick and Pulteney subscription library presented him with his portrait in August 1841. In fact the subscription library had been William Bruce's brainchild almost two decades earlier. Recognizing that there was a demand from young men (it does sound as though initially at least it was an all-male membership) for the availability of good reading material,

Bruce came up with the idea of such a library. The forty original members soon grew to two hundred. Born in 1795, the ex-provost died at the age of 56 in 1851. At the time, his widow announced to the public that the drapery business would remain open, but she herself died only four years later. By then the business may well have been in the hands of their son, Charles Bruce.

Before turning to my own memories of life in Mount Hooly House, I have to admit that gaps remain in my own knowledge of the house. Specifically, when was it built and by whom? Does the name provide us with any kind of clue? I'm now convinced that the word 'hooly' is indeed one of several variant spellings — hellie', 'halie' — of the word 'holy'. More significantly the location 'mount hooly' comes up in relation to the career of the early Pictish saint — Fergus. As is the case with the lives of many early saints, documented evidence about Fergus and his career is in short supply. He probably lived in the early eighth century and worked as a Christian evangelist in the Buchan area of northeast Scotland. However, his evangelising activity appears to have brought him as far north as Caithness, and he probably established centres for Christian services in two locations: at Halkirk, a village between Thurso and Wick, and in Wick itself. This is why Fergus in the sixteenth century was adopted as the patron saint of the royal burgh of Wick. Even more interestingly, these two centres of Christian activity in Halkirk and Wick were located at Mount Hooly/Halie. There is some disagreement over the precise location in Wick of this original Christian church. A case has been made for 'the western end of the town', but it has also been suggested that this pre-Reformation church stood 'near the east end of the town at a place called Mount Halie'. In other words, Mount Hooly House, built in the early nineteenth century, was so-named, precisely because it stood very much within the area of St. Fergus's original Christian foundation.

Who would have been aware of this association? Who could have been sufficiently impressed or moved by it that, when it came to naming the new house built high above harbour and shore, they chose to memorialise the old Mount Hooly name? Well I think it's not impossible that the Bruce family, with their known interest in history and culture, were responsible. After all Charles Bruce's documented serious interest in antiquities must have come from somewhere. He could well have been developing an interest he inherited from his father. So there's a perfectly plausible case to be made for the view that William Bruce was responsible for choosing to call his new, impressive house, Mount Hooly.

In some respects, my personal memories of Mount Hooly House are surprisingly sketchy. Considering I spent the first fifteen or sixteen years of my life living there, surely I ought to remember every detail? But I don't. Perhaps just being the place where I lived, I somehow took it all for granted. Still some facts do stand out. The house was big with many rooms. The gardens both back and front were huge. And around the house itself there was a series of outbuildings: a coal-house, a washhouse, a workshop, and other small sheds. Outside the main back door on Braehead, I remember my father built a small wooden garage for our family car – a ten horse-power Hillman Minx, registration number ST 9147.

The house's many rooms included an old-fashioned kitchen with a huge, old black-leaded iron range. However, the range was rarely used: a new gas-cooker had been installed in the 1930s – which must have made life, and meal-making in particular, a great deal easier for my mother and grandmother. Directly above the kitchen, and reached by a narrow wooden stair, was a small room which in our time had become the 'toy-room' for my brother and myself. Clearly in the past it would have been the bedroom of the kitchen-servant whose job would have been each day to light the old range and get family breakfast underway.

Elsewhere on the house's three floors was a range of rooms: sitting room, dining room, drawing room – which I remember as being virtually never used – and various bedrooms, exactly how many I can't say. Certainly, I eventually had my own room on the second floor. For some reason my visual memory of the various outbuildings around the house is more vivid than my recollection of the interior. Next to my father's workshop was my grandmother's chicken run where at least half a dozen hens kept us in fresh eggs. On the house's gable end nearby was a dovecot for our family of all-white homing pigeons. The washhouse contained a large, old-fashioned, coal-fired boiler and a mangle big enough to deal with blankets. At spring-cleaning time once a year it would be fired up and the house's bedclothes laundered. And there was a kind of pantry where my grandmother every year prepared her own large haunch of salt pork.

At the rear of the house was a large vegetable garden. The main crop every year was made up of potatoes. But my father's Gloucestershire origins were no doubt reflected in his determination to grow a wider range of vegetables. Each year he constructed a wooden frame in an effort to get runner beans to grow – usually without a great deal of success. His pickled onions, on the other hand, were always great. Making his own 'pop' was another annual event – a sweet, non-alcoholic fizzy drink decanted into lemonade bottles with push-down tops which were then stacked in the house's roomy cellar. (Wine – or drink of any kind – I never saw except ritually at New Year.) Memorable, however, was the year Dad got the pop ingredients slightly wrong: in the middle of the night the house was wakened up by the sound of shattering glass as bottles began to explode under the fizzy pressure from within.

Thinking of that fine cellar now, I wonder whether the Bruce family in the nineteenth century filled it with bottles of claret or port or sherry? I'd like to think so. What that family would never have done would have been to use their cellar as a place of refuge. After 1939, when Wick soon found itself on a war footing, that is exactly what, early on at least, the cellar became. The air-raid siren would go off and we would dutifully take our places in the cellar. I suspect that as such warnings became pretty routine, we began not to bother – but the story of Wick in World War II is one that requires a fresh start.

2 Wick, Identity, and the War

Wick is a small town of a few thousand people in the far north-east of Scotland. From time to time its name appears on the BBC weather report but these days it makes little or no impact on the national consciousness. It's where I was born — an early Christmas present in 1932. But in terms of the Wick of that time, my parents were rather an odd couple. Despite living and working at the very top of Scotland, beyond the Highlands, my father was an Englishman from Gloucestershire. In the nineteenth-century his family had been local church-builders, but his own father had moved with *The Times* and in the early years of the twentieth century had left churches for the new world of motor-cars, garages, petrol pumps and repairs.

This grandfather, who died comparatively young in the 1930s, was never a presence in my life, but his widow — my 'Nan-in-Stroud' — was another matter, as we shall see. First though, how had my father, an Englishman from Gloucestershire, ended up in Wick?

Well he was among those seventeen-year-olds who passed themselves off as eighteen in order to join up in World War I. Originally he served in the Royal Artillery — once in a blue moon he would make a joking remark about Vimy Ridge or 'Wypers' (the troops' version of Ypres) or 'Blighty'(England), and I regret never having pressed him to tell the whole story of his war experiences. What I do know is that some stage he was gassed — something that probably contributed to the chronic bronchitis he died of at a relatively early age — and subsequently sent back to France. At this stage he apparently transferred out of the Artillery and moved to the Royal Flying Corps where he trained as a wireless operator. Morse code and wireless telegraphy rather than romantic dog-fights over the Western front. But this final part of his war experience was to become the source of Corporal Hook's job for life.

When the war ended my father, unlike his brothers, chose not to return to the family business in Gloucestershire. Instead, capitalizing on his wireless telegraphy skills gained during the war, he took a job with the coastal radio service of the General Post Office (GPO). After early postings in Wales and the west of England, it must have been something of a shock when in the early 1920s he found himself dispatched to Wick Radio in the most distant and remote part of the U.K. Did he know anything at all about Scotland? Not to mention its furthest north-east comer? I have no idea, but if the notions and attitudes of the other members of his family I came to know are anything at all to go by, then the answer has to have been no. For all of them Scotland was and remained another country. So I expect it was for my father in the 1920s. But he was a sociable and adaptable man. Within a short time he had acted out a familiar pattern by meeting and marrying a local girl whose name happened to be the same as the northernmost headland of the British mainland.

So we were a Wick family. Growing up I had no sense at all that the Gloucestershire connection made any difference. I was who I was and that was it. True enough there were summers when we made the long odyssey from Caithness to Gloucestershire in our Hillman Minx. (My father shared enough of his family background to always be a car person, expert at maintenance and repairs.) I remember little of these trips except the initial worry of having to negotiate the steep climbs at Dunbeath and particularly Berriedale with its frightening hairpin bend. Would we make it unscathed? We always seemed to, but it was a relief to be over the Ord, that test left behind.

After that I remember very little until the journey was broken at Warrington in the south of Lancashire where we could stay with relatives. My uncle-on my mother's side-was a GP there, a brusque and jocular figure not wholly unlike Dr Cameron in Dr Finlay's Casebook. (And as it happens I'm sure I remember my uncle saying that he knew A. J. Cronin when he was studying medicine at the University of Edinburgh.) The doctor's large house, complete with consulting rooms and his own pharmacy, was something of an adventure in itself. As I indicated above, the Wick house I grew up in — Mount Hooly — was large with an extensive front garden, with lawns and large flowerbeds, as well as a big back garden for potatoes and vegetables, various outhouses and a garage which my father built himself. Nonetheless the Warrington way of life was subtly different. I sensed a living standard and a comfort level higher than I knew at home. Almost certainly what it was about was that GPs were substantially better off than radio operators. Still Warrington had its drawbacks. In those days tanning was one of its main industries and the result was a permanent, heavy smell that made Kirkcaldy's linoleum seem comparatively innocuous.

Gloucestershire — and specifically Ebley village, near Stroud — was nothing like this. It was a high, walled garden, an orchard heavy with the scent of apple and other fruit trees. It always seemed to be warm and still and I had never known anything like it. The garage was there, the petrol pumps and cars, but later there was something new. Again it was something I had never seen: television sets. On display one or two would be working: black and white cricket matches, England v. the West Indies in the days of the three Ws — Weekes, Worrell, and Walcutt. But all of this was incidental. The reality of the Gloucestershire experience was my Stroud grandmother despite the fact that she had died well before the television days. Why was she so important? Because she was the difference. There after all was a difference, and she was it. My mother supplied the clue. Somehow in Stroud we children had to be careful, less free and easy. In Wick, even in comfortable Warrington, it never even crossed our minds that we might offend anyone. But here it was different. Looking back, I am sure that what was involved was the great divide. The wife from the distant north of Scotland, never able to be familiar with her in-laws, having to cope with the intimidating, elderly Englishwoman, the head of a large and expanding family. No wonder that she was nervous, a bit fearful, and that her fears were passed on to us. My Nan at home was a familiar, reassuring figure; my 'Nan-in Stroud' an intimidating one. So there at least the divide was real; Wick and Gloucestershire could not always be so easily accommodated.

But let me not exaggerate. It is only looking back that I understand my mother's attitude; and at the time I had no awareness of its having anything to do with Scotland and England. But that I'm sure now was at least a factor, exacerbating the normal tension between wife and mother-in-law. That there really was a cultural gap — not one necessarily involving superiority or condescension or anything of the kind, simply an assumption of difference, of almost foreignness — the attitudes and opinions of my father's family made clear at a much later date. But I believe that for most of his life my father, for so many years the odd man out, the Englishman in Wick, was successful at overcoming it. Yet at the very end, when he was in hospital in Edinburgh for the last time, his mind wandering, he began to say things about the Scots and the English which riveted me with their suggestion of long-suppressed pain and persecution. Just for an instant or two an abyss of prejudice and ill-will seemed to open up in front of me. But if that is what it was, it was too late for any kind of exploration to be made.

There had been times when my father struck local people as something of an eccentric. One occasion in particular sticks in my mind. It happened early in the war. As well as the family house in Wick we owned a small farmhouse in the country a few miles along the north coast from John o'Groats. The Huna house had been built by my great-grandfather Dunnett, and had never been modernized. There was no running water; no electricity; and only the most primitive form of sanitation in an outhouse. Yet the house itself was solid enough with a large kitchen containing an open hearth for burning peat, with a box-bed in the opposite wall, as well as another bedroom and a kind of pantry where the pails of water carried two at a time in a square wooden frame from the well across the fields were kept. There were unused farm buildings at the back, and a kind of rough kitchen garden, with flagstone walls, covered the area between the front door and the passing main road. In the summer of 1940, my father decided he should dig an Anderson shelter in the front garden of the Huna house. (The Wick house was well-provided with a deep cellar.) An Anderson shelter in a farmhouse on the remote northern coast of Scotland?

What mad eccentricity was this? That was certainly the view of most of the locals who sometimes would watch from the roadside as my father worked away with pick and shovel. But my father was no fool. He had been in World War I – not that many years ago. He knew what high explosives could do. North across a couple of fields beyond the main road lay the sea. And a few miles across the Pentland Firth were the Orkneys. Orkneys' Scapa Flow was one of the British Navy's most important bases. But its defences had already been penetrated. In October, 1939, a German U-boat had torpedoed and sunk the anchored battleship the Royal Oak with the loss of hundreds of British lives. And there had also already been German bombing raids on the naval base. At night in Huna we could sometimes see the dark sky criss-crossed by the beams of Scapa's searchlights. My father's thinking must have been that during some such raid the lights on our side of the firth might accidentally or intentionally become the target. But the shelter was never finished. I remember it as a forlorn, half-built warning. Perhaps after 1940 my father decided the danger from the air had passed.

This was certainly not true of Wick where, despite its remoteness, the war had come much earlier than for most of the U.K. First there were reports of the loss of the *Rawalpindi*, and later of the *Jervis Bay*. These were both smallish passenger liners requisitioned by the Admiralty and converted into lightly-armed merchant cruisers in the early days of the war. Their job was to help protect British merchantmen convoys in the Atlantic from German submarine and surface vessel attack. In November, 1939, the ex-P&O liner *Rawalpindi*, escorting a convoy, found herself confronting the two

German battle-cruisers *Scharnhorst* and *Gneisenau* in the Atlantic between Iceland and the Faroe Islands. Hopelessly outclassed and out-gunned, the *Rawalpindi* could only try to gain a little time while the convoy under escort scattered. When she went down, three of the four Caithness men on board were lost — the first of the forty or so Wick and Caithness seamen who would die in the war. Almost exactly a year later the losses on board the Jervis Bay would be heavier. Escorting a convoy out of Halifax, Nova Scotia, in November, 1940, the Jervis Bay in mid-Atlantic engaged the pocket-battleship *Admiral Scheer* in another heroic but equally hopeless attempt to defend the merchant ships she was escorting. This time of the eighteen Wick and Caithness men among her crew, nine were killed. The news of such losses travelled fast.

Much more surprising were the civilian deaths that occurred equally early in the war. Wick would surely have struck most people as one of the last places in Britain to be a likely target of German bombing. But the truth was different. Mount Hooly house stood high on the north side of the town, from the back commanding an excellent view down to and across Wick harbour which had been developed and extended by the Stevenson family in the nineteenth century. (RLS himself spent some time in the town but the experience was clearly an unhappy one. 'Subarctic Wick' he described as 'one of the meanest of man's towns... on the baldest of God's bays,') In fact Wick had become more and more of a boom town in the later decades of the nineteenth century and in the years before World War I. My grandfather Dunnett often spoke of how he remembered being able to walk across the bay — not miraculously on the water but on the decks of the closely-packed herring boats all there for the hugely rewarding fishing season. For years the silver darlings ruled.

Of course, by my time in World War II these great days were long gone — though there would still be drifters in the harbour and sometimes stacks of herring barrels on the quay. In any event, early in the war — it was the first of July, 1940 — I remember all too clearly standing at the foot of the large potato garden at the back of our house looking out across to the harbour-side area where a huge plume of black smoke was rising in the air. The preceding bang had been loud and clear and we had run to see. A German plane had dropped two bombs — aiming at the harbour perhaps? Or was it simply lost, unable to find its target, and getting rid of its bombs before returning home? Whatever the case, the bombs fell in the late afternoon in the middle of a busy street. No fewer than fifteen men, women, and children were killed, and many more injured.

Was this attack big news nationally? Or censored perhaps? I just don't know. But I do remember that thick black smoke spiralling up against the sky. It has been suggested that this was the first daylight bombing raid on Britain in World War II.

Perhaps it was... But there were more raids to come.

One of my very earliest memories is of being taken to see inside the Old North School, very close to where I lived. This was the primary school I would have been expecting to attend a year or so later. It was an old, presumably Victorian structure, and I recall feeling it was a drab and dreary and uninviting place. This no doubt was why it was decided to build a brand-new school — the New North School — which was completed just before the outbreak of the war. Built on the northern edge of the town, alongside Wick's small airfield, the gleaming New North should have been my school. It never was.

With the coming of the war, Wick's airfield suddenly became strategically very important as a centre of operations for Coastal Command. Large numbers of air-force personnel arrived in the town and there was a problem over accommodation. Our house was one of those that became a billet for RAF officers. But the new school building was too good to miss. In no time it was taken over as the headquarters of the expanding air operations. (As a result, much of my primary education took place in church halls and other temporary locations.) But the importance of the airfield ensured that Wick remained a target. Only a few months after the harbour bombing, in October, 1940, German aircraft launched a night-time raid. One bomb fell on the bungalows of Hill Avenue, close by the airfield, killing three people including a school classmate of my brother's. German bombers returned the following summer and this time I happened to be outside in the late evening in a neighbour's garden and saw a German plane zoom past with the bright flashes of tracer bullets coming from or at it.

As the tide of war slowly turned, Wick ceased to be a target. The air-raid siren continued to go off with some frequency, and one never stopped being a bit fearful until the all clear was sounded, but there were as I remember no more bombs. Later on though there were nights when the sound of aircraft approaching and landing seemed to drone on all night. These were nights, I now understand, when British bombers, flying out of East Anglia and the south of England to attack Germany's cities, were diverted north on their return journeys to avoid possible German interception. Hence a time came when I became an avid listener of BBC radio's reports of yet another thousand bomber raid over Germany's cities...

Yet there were summers away from Wick when the war seemed a world apart. My father had been posted to the remotest north-west coast of Sutherlandshire to operate a tiny, temporary radio station, located south of Cape Wrath and north of Kinlochbervie, designed to work with the endless Atlantic convoys crucial to the conducting of the war in Europe. I spent two idyllic summers in that unspoiled area of deep sea-lochs and beautiful, empty, sandy beaches – empty, that is, except for the flotsam and jetsam washed in from an Atlantic Ocean at war. Sutherland, of course, was only a temporary posting, and our family base remained in Wick. With the war over, however, it was not long before my father's job took him permanently south. Edinburgh became the family base, and my own time at school in Wick was drawing to its close.

As I have indicated, in none of these early years was I particularly conscious of who or what – in national identity terms – I was. Scottish? British? Anglo-Scottish? The question just did not arise. It was never an issue. Yet I have to admit that in my sixth-form, pre-university year at an Edinburgh college, I did stand (and win) as the Scottish National Party candidate in the school's mock-election. The choice of party, I suspect, had more to do with expectations of victory than political ideology. Certainly as a student at Edinburgh University, despite the exploits of those who in my first year stole the Stone of Destiny in London, I took no part in nationalist politics. Cultural nationalism, on the other hand, did make some impact. MacDiarmid, Sydney Goodsir Smith – it was hard not to be broadly on their side. But kilts and the political movement – that was another matter. Perhaps it was a vague sense of my mixed background which kept me firmly on the side-lines, but in fact I think I was still in denial that the issue of national identity had any kind of personal relevance. I was who I was – end of story. In fact, it was only post-university that it was brought home to me that indeed I did apparently possess a national identity – and then only because it was forced upon me. In the early, traumatic days of National Service I was taken aback, stunned really, to hear myself called 'jock'. For the very first time I was made to realize that there were plenty of people out there who saw me – whatever I thought – as no more and no less than just another run-of-the-mill Scot. End of their story. Did I like that? Not a lot. I felt better, I think, two years later, when, sitting across the table from a battery of Oxbridge dons being interviewed for a postgraduate fellowship to study in America, I heard the Master of Balliol asking me was I really from Wick...

3 The Bombing of Wick

You will recall my writing about growing up in Wick, in the far north of Scotland, during the Second World War. That my home town, only a few miles south of John O'Groats, could ever have been subjected to attack by the Luftwaffe I assumed would come as a surprise to most readers, so I did my best to reconstruct the experience. I described how, in the late afternoon of the 1st of July, 1940, I heard a loud explosion, rushed out into the vegetable garden at the back of our house, and saw a pillar of black smoke rising from the harbourside below and across from me. Two bombs, it turned out, had fallen on a busy street. In what was one of the earliest daylight bombing raids of the war, no fewer than fifteen men women and children had been killed, and many more injured. I went on to speculate that the bombs had been aimed at the shipping in the harbour – or that failing to find its real target, the German plane had simply been dumping its bombs before heading home.

I now know that these speculations were entirely wrong. *Scotland from the Sky* by James Crawford is a beautifully produced book published by Historic Environment Scotland in association with a BBC documentary of the same name. Published in 2018, what the book provides is a history of aerial photography from its beginnings early in the twentieth century up to the present day. It emerges that a crucial element in that development was a military one. From the period of the First World War on, spying from the air grew increasingly important. And the German military were as aware of it as the British.

In the summer of 1938, Germany's Lufhansa civilian aircraft toured the Scottish coastline, ostensibly to map out new routes for the airline, but in fact, using concealed cameras, involved in photographing key strategic locations. With the outbreak of the war in 1939, German aerial spying on potential bombing targets intensified. The Forth Bridge was photographed, and likewise such targets as Clydebank shipyards, Grangemouth oil refineries, aircraft engine factories and other industrial sites. But 'Target Scotland' ranged across the length and breadth of the entire country including the Highlands and Islands. Including, it turns out, Wick's small airfield on the north side of the town and less than a mile from the harbour.

The proof is irrefutable. On page 20 of *Scotland from the Sky* appears a reproduction of a German aerial photograph of Wick, with the location of the airfield clearly identified as a target by a pencilled cross. What had occasioned the July, 1940 bombing raid? It's impossible to know for certain but it is at least possible that by then German intelligence had learned that the RAF had decided to make the Wick airfield — with its nearby, fortuitously recently-completed brand new New North School — the headquarters of Coastal Command. The July bombing missed its target but in October, 1940, the Luftwaffe tried again. This time a night-time raid probably did some damage: at least one bomb struck Hill Avenue, very close to the airfield, destroying a bungalow and killing three people, one of them a school classmate of my brother. However, the airfield at Wick and Coastal Command continued to play significant roles up to the end of the Second World War.

Nothing makes up for the loss of life that resulted from these bombing attacks on Wick, but within months of that second raid the airfield made possible what may be seen as an act of retaliation. According to James Crawford, on 21st May, 1941, a Spitfire took off from Wick on a reconnaissance mission. Piloted by twenty-year old Flying Officer Michael Suckling, it refuelled in Shetland then headed for Bergen in Norway. In a remote fjord, and from a height of 25,000 feet, the pilot spotted a large German warship which he was sure was the *Bismarck* — Germany's largest and most powerful battleship. Having successfully photographed the *Bismarck*, within an hour Suckling was landing in Wick and developing his aerial photographs. Almost immediately he was back in the air, aiming to deliver them himself to Coastal Command in London. Running out of fuel, he landed in Nottingham and went on to London by car. The rest is history.

The *Bismarck* in the following days tried to escape into the north Atlantic, pursued by the aircraft and ships of the British navy. The so-called 'Battle of the Denmark Strait' on 24th May, 1941, saw the sinking of the *HMS Hood* but two days later, on May 26-27, the British battleships *Rodney* and *King George V* were finally able to sink the *Bismarck*. The Wick that had paid a price after being targeted by Germany even before the war began, went on to contribute to its eventual defeat.

4 Boys' Weeklies

The shock of recognition is not a phrase to be used lightly, but I experienced the phenomenon recently reading the interview with Jimmy Reid in *The Scottish Review* 288. Asked about his childhood reading, Jimmy replied 'I started off reading Robert Louis Stevenson. I never read a kids' book in my life. Unless it was comics like the Hotspur and the Wizard'. That might have been my answer too. The proof is sitting on the shelves here in my study: neat Nelson Classic editions of *Treasure Island,* with my inscription 'April 1945 Glasgow', followed by *The Master of Ballantrae,* '6th April 1945 Glasgow' and *Travels with a Donkey in the Cevennes,* '16th April 1945 Glasgow'. Even more fascinating for me is the great man's reference to the *Hotspur* and the *Wizard.* But Jimmy, I don't think you're right to call them 'comics'. The *Dandy* and the *Beano* were comics; but when Jimmy and I were growing up the *Hotspur* and the *Wizard* — and *Adventure,*the *Rover,* and the *Skipper* — were something else: boys' weeklies or boys' papers. The distinction is a simple one. The five D.C. Thomson boys' weeklies I've listed did not tell their stories graphically. Unlike comics, their serial stories were told in standard English narrative prose. Words, not pictures, were their narrative medium.

Some of their stories I still remember. 'Red Circle' in the *Hotspur,* set in an English public school with 'forms', a Lower Fourth, the 'Remove', and probably a 'tuck shop'. Perhaps that it was so unlike the school I actually attended made it more, not less, interesting. (After all J.K. Rowling has pulled off the same trick with Hogwarts!) Or better still, the serial in the *Wizard* about Wilson, the supreme athlete. I remember his out-racing a huge, smoke and fire-breathing, iron monster to warn the inhabitants of the nearest town — only to learn that while he had been in another time or place, the railway engine had been invented. But my individual memories are not the point.

D.C. Thomson of Dundee began publishing *Adventure, Rover,* and the *Wizard* in the 1920s. *Skipper* and the *Hotspur* followed in the early 1930s. And their basic format of serial prose narratives remained unchanged until the late 1950s. Hence a whole generation of children — admittedly mainly boys — grew up reading a weekly diet of adventure stories in one or more of these boys' papers. The point is they were accustoming themselves to reading narrative prose — so as they grew older the move to more mainstream fiction (Robert Louis Stevenson) was an easy one. In more recent times, particularly in the USA, 'composition' — how to teach students to read and especially write — has become a mushrooming academic subject. You can even earn a PhD in it. But for all the expertise and teaching techniques such study has led to, I remain convinced that wide reading from an early age is the best preparation for learning to write well. When students ask me about how to improve their writing, I still tell them to read more.

So, like Jimmy Reid, I belonged to the generation in which the boys' weeklies I've been describing continued to flourish. But everything changed towards the end of the 50s. After various amalgamations and re-launchings, the form of the weeklies became fundamentally different. American comics and strip cartoons had begun to dominate the market. D.C. Thomson decided to go with the flow and replace texts in narrative prose with comic-strip graphic illustration. An era had ended. Am I being merely fanciful in seeing a connection between this change in boys' reading habits and the emergence of concerns about a decline in their ability to read and write effectively — concerns that are still with us today? In his monumental *British Children's Fiction in the Second World War* (2007), Owen Dudley Edwards suggests that had the Thomsons realised that the change from text to strip could have ill consequences in educational terms for their child audience, they might not have gone ahead — but he thinks the possibility was never put to them. However Edwards does believe that the transformation of the boys' weeklies into 'comics' created a literacy gap between children whose families could afford books and those who could only afford comics. Perhaps all of us of Jimmy Reid's generation have reason to be grateful that, while we were growing up, the *Hotspur* and the *Wizard* were there to be read.

5 The Sporting Class

Melvyn Bragg's current BBC 2 series on *Class and Culture* has reminded me of my own first encounter with upper class Britain and what its power could bring about. Growing up in Caithness, I was always aware that in the summer months it was a common experience to catch a glimpse of those we referred to as the 'sporties'. Driving over the country roads in what we called their shooting brakes ('estate cars' I think is today's term), we knew they were toffs visiting the county's landed estates for the hunting, shooting, and fishing available across the empty moorlands of Caithness. But the notion that I could have any contact with these people never even crossed my mind. They could well have been men – and women – from some notional Mars.

One summer in the late 1940s, however, all that changed. Back then, Wick did not have a lot to offer its young people in the way of entertainment. As a result, Rosebank was for many of us a hugely important spot. In the middle of the town, it had a bowling green (used of course exclusively by those we regarded as old men), an eighteen-hole putting course, and, most important of all, three hard tennis courts. For my social set of High School boys and girls, Rosebank's tennis courts and clubhouse were a big deal. We could meet there, sit around, chat, drink lemonade, and play tennis. In the long summer days, Rosebank was the place to be.

I was known as a keen and reasonably good player. One May or June day I was told that two girls, dressed for tennis, had booked a court and were asking whether I'd be willing to play with them as they were in need of practice. Surprised, and a bit puzzled, I thought why not. In a moment I was on the court with them, noting their white dresses and good rackets. I don't think they even told me their names. All they wanted to do was knock up with me for a few minutes. Then I had a spell of serving to them, so that they could practise their returns. Finally, a third girl joined us, and she and I played a set against the other two. I don't remember who won. That was it. I didn't mind. I'd had a free game with decent enough players, and I'd had a decent enough time. Afterwards someone told me they thought the girls were visiting Stirkoke House: a kind of lodge on a landed estate a few miles outside the town.

That was that and I thought no more about it. However, a week or two later in June, the Wimbledon Championships began. BBC television was covering the opening days, and I was able to watch the black and white pictures. Suddenly I couldn't believe what I was seeing. There they were arriving at Wimbledon all set to play: my two playing companions from Rosebank. Thinking about it, I suppose it must have been the Girl's Championship in which they were competing. But all the same — there they were, playing at Wimbledon, the most prestigious event of the tennis year. Why them? Certainly not because of any outstanding sporting talent. The answer had to be concerning who they were, not what they were. They were the right kind of people from the right kind of background. Wimbledon was for young ladies. As late as the 1940s, social class — not sporting class — was what really counted.

6 Glasgow

1944. I am an eleven-year-old living in Wick. My radio operator father has just become a ship inspector stationed in Glasgow. (He certifies that shipping entering or leaving the Clyde is equipped with radio equipment that functions up to the standard required by U.K. regulations.) So that summer Glasgow it will be for the full length of the school holidays. We live in a flat in Kenmure Street, Pollokshields. What is it that made that holiday so memorable? The warm, sunny weather. Was the south always like this? The public library just down the street. I was a dedicated reader.

Of what? That summer it was westerns. I couldn't get enough of them. Sometimes two in one day – and a reminder from the library that a book could not be returned on the day it had been borrowed. Cricket. My father had played so I was anxious to follow in his footsteps. Clydesdale Cricket Club at Titwood was within walking distance. Soon I was in a team: Clydesdale Minors. In one match I scored 28 runs and held a sky-high catch. The result was promotion to Clydesdale Juniors. Alas I never again made it into double figures. Finally there was 'Buffalo Bill'. Desperate to see the film, I am allowed for the very first time to travel alone into the city to go to the cinema. What an adventure! The stars are Joel McCrea and Maureen O'Hara.

The stand-out moments? Little Big Horn and Custer's last stand. I was not disappointed.

A summer to remember. A Glaswegian now for almost 40 years, I'm not sure I recall a better one.

7 The Writers' Conference, 20th-24th August 1962

I have to admit that my memories of 1962, and my involvement with that year's International Writers' Conference at the Edinburgh Festival, are limited at best. Fifty years are a good excuse for forgetfulness. At the time I was twenty-nine years old, and had just completed my first year as an Assistant Lecturer in Edinburgh University's Department of English Literature. I had no involvement whatsoever in the creation of this conference. I remember it as the brainchild of two people: John Calder, the London-based, Scottish publisher of avant-garde European literature, and the American Jim Haynes, the owner of Scotland's first paperback bookshop in Charles Street (now demolished), near Edinburgh's George Square into which the university was expanding. Sonia Brownell, George Orwell's widow, I was eventually told, was brought in at an early stage because of her many contacts within the contemporary literary scene. I had never met John Calder whereas, as a recent graduate of an American university, and committed to the development of the teaching of American literature at Edinburgh, I had become one of Jim Haynes's many Edinburgh friends. When Jim invited me to become the editor of a publication linked to the forthcoming writers' conference, I naturally consulted my colleagues in the English Department. No one suggested I should refuse, but equally no one seemed very enthusiastic. I don't think I even told my head of department — Professor John Butt. In any event I did agree to take the job on, and the 128 page *The Novel Today, Programme and Notes* which was finally published, is the real memorial of my involvement in the writers' conference.

In 1984 Jim published a kind of scrapbook autobiography called 'Thanks for Coming!'. (Yes, there I am listed among the several thousand people for whom the book is written.) Reading it carefully now, I discover I wasn't first choice for the role of conference book editor! In February, 1962, writing in the Edinburgh Evening News, Magnus Magnusson describes the background to the decision to hold a waiters' conference at the Festival that year. John Calder, identified as the original architect of the proposal, had set up a small committee in Edinburgh to organize and administer the event. Its members were Jim Haynes, the journalist and BBC producer W. Gordon Smith, Neil McCallum — an Edinburgh-based novelist and advertising agent — and Alex Neish, a writer and assistant editor of the magazine *Scotland*. Neish had been tapped as the editor of the 120 page publication that would introduce the writers and serve as a conference programme. He was an obvious choice. As a student at Edinburgh University he had edited two rather avant-garde publications *Jabberwock* and *Sidewalk*. He was an enthusiast for European and American experimental writing, and had somehow managed to publish in *Jabberwock* what turned out to be the first chapter of William Burroughs's *The Naked Lunch*. Just the kind of figure to produce the kind of programme the organizers had in mind.

So what happened? I don't know. In 2010 Neish was interviewed in RealityStudio, a kind of online journal for fans of William Burroughs. Asked about the Writers' Conference, he said he did not attend it. He was abroad at the time. And later in the interview it emerges he had gone to South America to pursue a rather different career in business. But clearly he had been on board early in 1962. Did he fall out perhaps with the organizing committee? The decision to take off for South America does sound a rather sudden and unexpected one.

What is clear is that the basic contents of the programme/brochure – reflecting what was proposed for each of the five days of the conference – had already notable contributors: for example, Malcolm Bradbury on contemporary English novelists; David Daiches on Scottish literature; Raymond Williams on commitment; Denis Donoghue on censorship. It throws fascinating light on the overall state of international fiction in the early sixties. (How many literary critics or scholars were writing about West Indian, African, Indian, and even American fiction in 1962?) And it represents a major contribution to any assessment of what was engaging the literary world in that day and age. Like the conference itself, the publication appeared on the brink of the sixties cultural explosion that would define the entire postwar artistic world. If literary historians are looking for a significant archive of the setting within which that cultural and political transformation occurred, this is it. At a price of Five Shillings (25p), *The Novel Today* was quite a bargain.

In today's academy our masters tell us our research and publications should have 'impact' – contributing to the big society out there. On those grounds *The Novel Today* should have got my professional career off to a flying start. And there is an odd sense in which it did. A year or two later I was happy to agree to the reprinting of my own contribution to the 'Commitment' topic in a book edited by two American scholars, James B. Hall and Barry Ulanov, called *Modem Culture and the Arts* (1967). My little essay appeared in a section called 'The Word Arts: The Novel' and my companion contributors were Henry James, Joyce Cary, Jose Ortega y Gasset, George Orwell, and Alain Robbe-Grillet. I suspect I never flew so high again! Thank you 1962 and *The Novel Today*.

8 The Glasgow Renaissance

In recent years Glasgow has become a quite extraordinary place in which to live. I arrived in 1979 and was quickly made aware of a pattern of change in the city's life the implications of which long-term residents had scarcely begun to register. Looking for a house to buy, I was frequently told by local friends that there were whole streets and areas near the University, in the West End, where I wished to live, which were strictly off-limits. When I actually looked at these streets and areas what I found confronting me was not decadence and decay, urban neglect and shabbiness, but attractive rows of Victorian flats or terraced houses, light and bright in their newly stone-cleaned splendour, sometimes complete with art nouveau motifs in doors and windows. My well-intentioned colleagues had clearly been talking of a Glasgow of the past – and of their own past, ten or twenty years ago, when for the middle and professional classes desirable Glasgow living meant a house in the suburbs, in Bearsden or Milngavie on the north side of the city, or Giffnock or Newton Mearns on the south.

It is the physical transformation of its inner-city housing, which today provides the most striking evidence of Glasgow's urban renewal. In street after street the stripping away of a century of grime has revealed a creamy stone with a lightness of texture which seems able almost to float the buildings free from their own mass and volume. But it is not only stone-cleaning that is in question. In the post-war years, a massive programme of slum-clearance in Glasgow, just as in other cities, replicated and extended the devastation produced by war-time bombing. Now a combination of Housing Associations and private sector housing development is slowly filling Glasgow's gaunt and gaping urban spaces with decent red-brick houses which, if of no architectural distinction, at least put to flight the dereliction of the past. Even in the heart of the city the pattern recurs. Abandoned ware-houses and office-buildings are being converted into flats making inner-city living an attractive proposition for the young and socially mobile; as a result, increasingly in Glasgow it is smart to live in the city, not out of it.

All in all, the lessons of the post-war past have been learned. Demolition and site-clearance are out of fashion; renovation and restoration are the order of the day. And it works. Even along the derelict and neglected banks of the Clyde – once the dynamo of the city's economic life — progress is being made. The new Scottish Exhibition Centre, the Garden Festival development for 1988, and new blocks of private housing, are beginning to bring the river area back into the living city. Of course Glasgow still has an enormous housing problem: but its focus is in the vast post-war housing estates, miles from the city centre, not in the inner city itself. The restoration and revitalization of the city's streets cannot solve the problems of Easterhouse, Drumchapel, and the rest, but Glasgow is proving that inner city renewal can be a great deal more than a pious dream.

Glasgow's physical renaissance, however, is in one sense only a mirror of its spiritual one. In the 1940s F.L. Matthiassen called his book about America's literary culture in the 1850s *The American Renaissance* and as a result laid himself open to the rebuke that the notion of a 'renaissance' could not apply to a new country such as the United States. No such charge can be made against the idea of a Glasgow renaissance. We all know that in the nineteenth century Glasgow was the second city of the Empire, and that its driving enterprise and industry had brought it much wealth and economic strength. The outward evidence of that power, and the sense of Victorian self-confidence that accompanied it, are permanently preserved for us now in such structures as Gilbert Scott's University building, dominating the city from its site on Gilmorehill, the splendid Kelvingrove Art Gallery directly below, and the marvellously Italianate City Chambers presiding over George Square in the city centre.

But Glasgow's wealth was created on the back of an urban working-class whose community — of poverty and deprivation — was constantly threatened by the divisiveness of religion and race. In that situation lay the seeds of the fate that overtook Glasgow in the hard times of the twentieth century. Then it was that the city's rich cultural tradition of painting and architecture, of art and design — a tradition still flourishing at the turn of the century with Charles Rennie Mackintosh and the city's major contribution to art nouveau — was forgotten, replaced by an urban image of a quite different kind.

Then it was that Glasgow became identified everywhere as an archetype of twentieth-century urban alienation: the city seen as a waste land, a physical and spiritual desert, characterized by squalor, decay, and violence. This is the Glasgow of the Gorbals slums and its razor-gangs; the Glasgow crudely but vividly evoked by Long and McArthur in *No Mean City*. This is the Glasgow that made workers in the Ministry of Defence recoil with horror some years ago at the suggestion that they should be moved from London to Glasgow as part of a government decentralization scheme. But this is the Glasgow which contemporary Glasgow is at last repudiating. On the face of it, Glasgow's self-promoting advertising campaign with its familiar slogan — Glasgow's Miles Better — seems to fit all too depressingly into that strain of cosy, self-congratulatory, inward-looking sentimentality, which has recurred so often in Scottish culture since its successes in the eighteenth and early nineteenth centuries. Yet the reality is different. The campaign has been a remarkable success. The logo and its stickers blossom everywhere. And its message has somehow proved to have nothing in common with a standard Scottish self-indulgent complacency. Symbolically, Glasgow's cars carry the message in a variety of European languages — French, Spanish, Italian, German and several more: local wit goes international. The whole campaign has been a gesture, a creative moment, a cultural statement, and, as such, an appropriate symbol of the Glasgow renaissance.

It is appropriate because the Glasgow renaissance has not occurred in a climate of economic recovery. Glasgow has not solved its long-established and deep-seated economic problems. Not that there has been any lack of trying. Immense effort and energy have indeed gone into schemes for economic revival, and some progress has been made. GEAR (Glasgow Eastern Area Renewal) has become a model of its kind, widely studied as an imaginative solution to the problems of inner-city economic decay. Bringing together investment from the local authority, from national government through the Scottish Development Agency, and from the private sector, GEAR has been remarkably successful. In ten years some £500 million has been spent in one of the most economically and culturally deprived areas of the city, with £200 million of that sum coming from private investment.

New flats and houses have been built; old tenement buildings have been cleaned and restored; small factories and work-shops have been built; grass and trees grow. Self-respect has been restored to an apparently hopeless and abandoned urban area. But even the success of GEAR is a qualified one. Tested on the most sensitive of social barometers — level of unemployment — not a great deal has been achieved. According to the Scottish Development Agency, GEAR has created four thousand new jobs, but that figure does not begin to match up to the number of jobs lost through the apparently irreversible decline in Glasgow's traditional industries. In the city as a whole, unemployment figures remain stubbornly high, well above the national average. On the vast post-war housing estates, unemployment among young people in particular is a way of life. Yet, in the face of such a massive problem with its potentially dangerous consequences (think of Belfast), the renaissance is real. The life of the city is buoyant; one's sense is of energy and vitality, not of depression and defeat.

The West End, for example – how right I was choosing to live there in 1979 – provides urban living at its exhilarating best. With its varied population, ethnically diverse, and a recognizable community of actors and writers, painters and musicians, students and academics from the University, media people from BBC Scotland and Scottish Television, its German beer and Italian restaurants, its all-day bars and shops open half the night, the West End offers more than a hint of bohemia, without any damaging sense of apartness from ordinary living. (The area incorporates much of the Hillhead parliamentary constituency: Roy Jenkins's seat until even he was swept away in the avalanche which was Labour in Scotland last June.) Urban life here is something to be enjoyed, not endured. And it is a similar affirmation that lies at the heart of the city's cultural life.

When the announcement came through that Glasgow was to be European city of culture in 1990 the city took the news in its stride. There was satisfaction: a sense of something achieved, a job well done, rather than any kind of embarrassed self-consciousness. What lay beneath that reaction, though, was a feeling that at last the old image of Glasgow, the Glasgow of urban violence and decay, had been publicly, officially, internationally, repudiated. Glasgow's smile was indeed better.

We have known it for some time. Art and music and drama and writing have become very central to the contemporary Glasgow experience. For whatever reason, in recent times the Scottish cultural pendulum has swung from the east to the west. There is much that is tiresome about the alleged rivalry between Glasgow and Edinburgh. The two cities are less than an hour apart; many people live in one city and work in the other. The East-West divide is often more of a myth than a reality: Scotland is a small country, and its cultural life, its artists, actors, and writers, cannot afford to be divided into two hostile camps. And yet it is impossible not to feel that in recent years there has been a change of focus. When I was an undergraduate in Edinburgh in the 1950s, reading English Literature, my friends and I never doubted that if there were any serious Scottish writers they were centred in Edinburgh. Milne's Bar, the Abbotsford, Rose Street – these were the places to be. I doubt if this is so now.

Of course the Edinburgh Festival still brings to Scotland's capital its annual injection of artistic and intellectual excitement; but for the other forty-nine weeks of the year it is in Glasgow that the mainstream of Scotland's cultural life is to be located. What is in question is not a single art form – not even Glasgow painting or Glasgow writing; nor a single institution – Scottish Opera, Scottish Ballet, the Scottish National Orchestra, the Citizens Theatre or the splendid Burrell Collection, already Scotland's major tourist attraction. Rather it is a spirit of creativity manifesting itself in a tremendous range of artistic forms from film and television, through poetry, fiction, and drama, music and painting, to pop groups and stand-up comics. Inevitably some names and places stand out. Bill Forsyth, whose films at their best catch the flavour of west of Scotland humour; Alistair Gray, offering us a post-modernist vision of urban Glasgow; William Mcllvanney whose novels – including his crime thrillers – provide disturbing analyses of some of the harsher aspects of west of Scotland life and culture, and are already much imitated in prose and film; the rich and diverse school of younger Glasgow painters, of whom Stephen Campbell is only the most famous in international terms; Giles Havergal's Citizens Theatre, resolutely internationalist in its ethos; the Tron Theatre, providing a stage, under its young and gifted Artistic Director Michael Boyd, for new writing from Scotland and elsewhere; inevitably the Theatre Royal, the home for Scottish Opera that Edinburgh signally failed to provide; Sauchiehall Street's Third Eye Centre, an exciting combination of bookshop, exhibition and performance space; individual women writers such as Liz Lochead and Marcella Evaristi, amazingly versatile in the modes in which they work, but always verbally *brilliant* and with a profoundly feminist sense of the tragi-comedy of life. But all of these are supported by, and help to support, a richness of artistic activity, both popular and experimental, which shows no sign of losing strength. John Byrne's widely-acclaimed television production, *Tutti-Frutti*, perhaps hints at the sources of strength in Glasgow's contemporary culture; an unselfconscious readiness to draw on local and regional strengths in language, expression, and attitude, linked to an emotional directness and honesty which confounds parochialism or provincialism in any limiting sense. The Glasgow renaissance should indeed continue to produce smiles-– of better and better aesthetic satisfaction.

9 A Scot at Princeton

A small room filled with a long table behind which sat a battery of Oxbridge dons wearing their black academic gowns. I remember very clearly the presiding Master of Balliol's first question: looking up from his pile of papers, 'Was I really from Wick?' he asked. Well, yes, but that was quite a long time ago. After Wick High School came Edinburgh's Daniel Stewart's College, followed by Edinburgh University. Success there had meant a big decision. Should I proceed straight on to postgraduate study? Or should I get national service out of the way? The latter was the choice I made. A mistake because national service would be abolished during my second army year... ? Yes, but perhaps not. The Intelligence Corps sent me to Langeleben, on the border between West and East Germany, where we listened in to the routine radio activity of the armies and navies of Russia, Poland, and East Germany. But my daily contribution to the safety of the West and the preservation of democracy was normally parcelled up by lunch-time and I had the rest of the day to read books borrowed from the American library in Brunswick.

When I returned to Edinburgh eighteen months later, Professor Renwick was not at all encouraging when I told him I was proposing to take up my Vans Dunlop scholarship to pursue research in American literature. Much better, he told me, to take the job in the National Library of Scotland he was sure he could get for me. But Faulkner and Hemingway and Fitzgerald were much too exciting for me to agree. So in no time I was off to Marcus Cunliffe's and Geoffrey Moore's recently-established and ground-breaking Department of American Studies in Manchester. But after a single year (with Malcolm Bradbury as a fellow student) the message I received was loud and clear: if I was serious about research in American literature I had to get myself across the Atlantic to an American university — the more prestigious the better. There were a range of teaching assistantships, scholarships and fellowships to apply for; I was a well-qualified student from an ancient Scottish university; just go for it. I did. And here I was sitting opposite the Master of Balliol and his fellow-berobed scholars.

It was years later before I began to understand what was really going on that day. The awards I had applied for — tenable at Harvard, Yale, or Princeton — were theoretically open to any graduate of any British university in any subject. The interviewing committee was thus supposed to be able to cover any .possible discipline. Did that include American literature? In fact it was the panel itself that was being tested. 'Mr Hook', I was asked, 'What is your opinion of Joseph Hergesheimer?' Needless to say that was not a name with which I was familiar.

Years later I discovered that Hergesheimer was a novelist who had a short-lived vogue in the 1920s — probably when the questioner had been an eager undergraduate keeping up with the currently fashionable. I mumbled something about being more interested in other American novelists such as Faulkner and Hemingway. After a short silence a neighbouring don managed to remember the name of another American author: 'Well, Mr Hook, what do you think of T.S. Stribling?' By an enormous stroke of good fortune, Stribling was a name I'd come across in the context of the Southern literary renaissance in the 20s and 30s. I even knew he'd written a novel called *The Forge* (though of course I had not read it). Thus I was home and dry this time with my insistence on the importance of Southern writing in the period — with Faulkner rather than Stribling being the key figure. What other questions I was asked I no longer recall — but I'm sure none of them had anything to do with American literature, old or new. Much later at Princeton I learned that history and the pressure for change had probably helped to get me there. The Jane Eliza Procter Fellowship I had been awarded had been established in the late 1920s. But since its inception, and despite its U.K-wide terms of reference, only Oxbridge graduates had been its recipient. It was time for a change. That change was me.

As Procter Fellow elect, I quickly learned that I had gained a new status. Back in Edinburgh after my year at Manchester, and preparing for my transatlantic expedition, I was surprised to receive a summons from Chas. H. Stewart, Secretary to the University of Edinburgh. Throughout my undergraduate years his august name had regularly appeared on official communications, but meeting him was never in question. Things were different now. One day I found myself shepherded into his grand office, seated in a comfortable chair, and handed a glass of sherry. What was going on? The University of Edinburgh, it emerged, was ready to do its best for one who had chanced to become its ambassador to Princeton. Extraordinarily, I learned that a modem version of nineteenth century letters of introduction would be dispatched on my behalf to friends of Edinburgh in Princeton. And in due course one of these at least bore fruit: in my years at Princeton's Graduate

College I was from time to time entertained to Sunday lunch by a local family with Scottish ties who lived in splendid style in the town's exclusive Battle Road. Clearly it was to a new world that I had been given access.

So how did the brave new world strike a young Scot whose previous educational experience had occurred in two large, urban British universities? Well it was immediately obvious that Princeton the place and the university were one and the same. The small town circled around the university campus. At its heart was Nassau Hall, an elegant and impressive building whose neo-classical architectural style reflected its eighteenth-century origins. But the surrounding ivy-clad buildings, set among tall trees, leafy paths, and well-kept lawns, were hardly classical at all. Instead nineteenth-century Gothic dominated, with courts and archways, towers and quadrangles in an imitation Oxbridge college style. I had stepped back into a scholarly world which I knew of but had never experienced. And this impression was underlined when I finally settled into my rooms in the university's Graduate College.

Early in the twentieth century, when Princeton first committed itself to the creation of a college for the exclusive use of the new kind of student who, post graduation, had decided to go on to further study and research – there was a long drawn-out argument over where it should be located. It was James McCosh, the Scottish clergyman and professor of philosophy – who assumed the Princeton presidency in 1868, and was ultimately responsible for the transformation of what had become a small, Presbyterian college into a major university – who understood that postgraduate study would become an essential element of the modem, expanded, educational institution he was determined to create.

Woodrow Wilson, McCosh's pupil, and for a time his successor, argued that the new graduate college should be built in the middle of the existing campus; the air of scholarly commitment and dedication, which he believed would characterize the new college, would in his view have a beneficial effect on young undergraduates perhaps not always recognizing the true nature of the intellectual life on offer around them. Wilson's opponents argued the opposite case: the best way to underline the new college's dedication to the life of the mind was to have it physically removed from the distractions of undergraduate life and behaviour. This was the view that prevailed. Princeton's new graduate college – its tower modelled on that of an Oxford college – was built on an elevated site outside the existing campus. I soon discovered that life inside echoed its outside appearance: Procter Hall, where our evening meal was served, had a high table; we students were required to wear gowns; and the Dean of the Graduate School pronounced a Latin grace before we could eat.

If all this rigmarole represented a new world for me, my fellow students in English simultaneously struck me as a new and formidable bunch. Gone were the scruffy lot of Edinburgh undergraduate days. My new Contemporaries, in their white, button-down shirts, bow-ties, tweed jackets, and brown Oxfords, were all too clearly scholars in the making. Sophistication was the keynote. And intellectual sophistication above all. To observe and listen was distinctly intimidating. How could I possibly survive in this academic hothouse? My national service in the T Corps hardly compared with their Fulbright years in Rome or Vienna or London. My Edinburgh and Manchester seemed a poor second to their Harvard and Yale. I felt like an amateur surrounded by professionals and really did wonder whether I could possibly keep up and compete with these people.

But of course there was an upside to all of this. The intellectual life I was experiencing at Princeton, inside and outside the seminar rooms in McCosh Hall, was hugely exciting. These graduate students in English were there to do well and get ahead; they were one hundred percent committed to their subject; they were well-read and well-prepared so that seminar discussion was provocative and stimulating; academic exchange really did take place. Such excellent students were matched by outstanding faculty: in my time the Princeton English Department boasted major critics and scholars such as D.W. Robertson, G.E. Bentley, Willard Thorp, Carlos Baker, Lawrance Thompson and R P. Blackmur. The whole experience amounted to academic life at least approximating what ideally it is supposed to be. Certainly nothing in the rest of my academic career in Britain and the US would get closer to that ideal.

By my first Christmas I was beginning to feel that perhaps after all I would be able to hold my own In fact I was beginning to realize I was not without a few advantages of my own. First and foremost I was a native of the country that had produced 'English Literature'. It had not taken me long to identify a strong sense of anglophilia in the Princeton world. 'Englishness', whether in speech, clothes, architectural style, or academic background, seemed always to command respect. The fact that I was a Scot from Edinburgh did not seem to matter. What did was that as a Scottish graduate I already possessed an MA degree. For all Americans an MA is a postgraduate degree. In my early days at Princeton I explained repeatedly the exact status of my MA; but the point that mine was a first degree never seemed to register. So eventually I simply began agreeing I had my MA and accepted whatever advantage that gave me. Then there was the fact that my Edinburgh undergraduate degree had included substantial study of Anglo-Saxon. Despite majoring in English, Americans did not encounter Old English until they reached graduate level. So once again I had the advantage... But in the end I think it was the general, residual feeling that as a Brit. I had a kind of inside track on English Literature that explained Princeton's willingness to let me proceed to the research element of the doctoral programme ahead of the normal timetable.

Research on what became a pressing issue. American literature had brought me to Princeton. Some Americans I met found this difficult to understand. As I've already hinted, in the British academic world of the 1950s American literature remained less than familiar territory. To find American literature treated with similar scepticism within the US was more of a surprise. But then again I did meet Americans at Princeton who regarded the South as a foreign country, were more than familiar with London, Paris or Rome, but were rather proud of never having been west of the Mississippi. Willard Thorp, on the other hand, my mentor in the English Department, was one of that small band of literary scholars who, in the period between the two world wars, had undertaken the task of making American Literature and American Studies acceptable areas of study within the academy. Willard, it emerged, had a very clear idea of the research he wanted me to undertake – and it did not involve Faulkner, or Hemingway, or Fitzgerald, or any other modem American writer. He wanted me to work on Princeton's, and America's, eighteenth-century links with Scotland.

The university's Firestone Library possessed the Witherspoon Collection that no literary scholar had worked on. Now here I was, a Scot, an Edinburgh graduate, just the person he had been waiting for. At this point I have to say I knew nothing about Witherspoon, nothing about Princeton, and nothing about Scotland and America in the eighteenth century. That there was even a connexion was news to me. Professor Thorp of course assumed that as a graduate of a Scottish university I was well versed in Scottish literature. But that too was not exactly true. The Edinburgh curriculum had occasionally glanced at Scottish writers: Henryson and Dunbar as 'Scottish Chaucerians', Burns and Scott in the Romantic period, Carlyle in die nineteenth century. But I had never been exposed to a formal course in Scottish literature – a point on which I maintained a discrete silence. In no time the issue was settled: I would pursue the research topic the professor had in mind. Looking back, I see that he was right. I might have had something useful to discover about Faulkner or one of the other recent novelists. (In fact, a little later, I was able to meet and talk to Faulkner.)

He had come to the Princeton campus to read from *The Sound an the Fury*, talk about writing, and meet both undergraduates and postgraduates. I was lucky enough to be responsible for his entertainment one evening at the Graduate College. We talked about Scotland and he amazed me by saying he had visited Gatehouse-of-Fleet. I have puzzled over this for years and it is only very recently that I've come to believe the visit must have been in 1950 when the aircraft he was flying in to Stockholm, to get his Nobel Prize for literature, touched down and stayed over in Prestwick. But the truth was that neither Faulkner nor any other of the novelists I had in mind were suffering from critical or scholarly neglect, whereas the topic of Scotland and America, in academic terms at least, was almost a virgin field.

Scotland and America it was and I have never regretted it. Pursuing the subject I learned a great deal about crucial, formative years in the history of both countries: post-Union Scotland, and the new republic of the United States in the eighteenth century. Princeton, it emerged, was indeed a largely Scottish creation. Established to train Presbyterian clergy, the College of New Jersey, as it then was, was generously supported by the Church of Scotland. Nassau Hall itself was built largely with Scottish money. The college's early years in the 1750s and 60s were distinctly precarious; in under twenty years it was headed by five presidents (including Jonathan Edwards) none of whom lived long enough to get the institution properly up and running. It was John Witherspoon, the Edinburgh University-educated minister of the Laigh Kirk in Paisley, who changed all that. Witherspoon was the college's president from 1768 to 1794; under his direction the small, struggling college became a major player in America's educational, religious and political life.

An ardent patriot, Witherspoon trained a generation of young Americans who would become clergymen, teachers, writers, judges, congressmen, senators, and governors in the new republic of the United States. James Madison, framer of the Constitution, and fourth president, was his favourite pupil. In the nineteenth century the college's status declined as it became caught up in a long-running dispute between exponents of hard-line and more moderate Calvinism. Exactly a century after Witherspoon, another Scot, James McCosh, as noted above, was appointed college president. And McCosh succeeded just as Witherspoon had done: it was under McCosh's direction that the college began to take the shape of the modem Princeton University.

In my years at Princeton my feeling was that its Scottish heritage had been largely forgotten. Only the charismatic figure of Ernest Gordon, the Presbyterian chaplain, kept the Saltire flying. For most Princetonians my Scottishness, if recognized at all, was of no significance, while the kind of recognition I occasionally did receive made me feel uncomfortable. The writers Allen Tate and his wife Caroline Gordon, for example, loved my accent and insisted I read Burns aloud to them. I of course was too polite to say I was intrigued by their Southern accents. Inevitably, while I researched away in the Firestone Library on my Scottish-American topic, as any Scottish visitor to the US still tends to do, I met quite a number of people who claimed to be of Scottish descent.

But few of them had the slightest idea that America's debt to Scotland amounted to a great deal more than boatloads of immigrants. Even in recent years when Senator Trent Lott persuaded the US Senate to honour the Scottish-American connection with the establishment of a national day of celebration, the title chosen was National Tartan Day and the day selected was April 6, the supposed date of the Declaration of Arbroath. Why? Because the relevant Senate resolution insisted that America's Declaration of Independence was actually based on the medieval Scottish document. The truth is that the immensely significant Scottish-American relationship has very little to do with tartanry or romanticized history — but that is another story.

In any event, I like to think that my research at Princeton has at least helped to change things to some degree on both sides of the Atlantic. My 1960 thesis became my 1975 book *Scotland and America 1750-1835;* since the 1970s America's debt to eighteenth-century Scotland has gained growing recognition within some intellectual and academic circles. Today it is no surprisc to find American scholars suggesting — or even assuming — that the Scottish Enlightenment played an important role in the intellectual and cultural life of the new republic, that American education, American philosophy, American science, and even American politics, had a distinctly Scottish coloration. Princeton itself has recently erected on its campus Alexander Stoddart's fine statue of John Witherspoon. Could thc university do more to honour its Scottish origins? I think so. It could become the first leading American university to institute a programme in Scottish Studies that would include investigation of the intellectual and cultural world out of which its most distinguished presidents emerged.

And on this side of the Atlantic? Well in recent years there have been growing indications that some Scottish historians, alongside commentators, journalists, and writers, have begun to take a serious interest in post-Union eighteenth-century Scotland. A new more outward-looking, internationalist Scottish history very much involving Scotland's role in the British Empire, in America, in the rise of the modem, industrialize world, has finally begun to emerge in post-devolution Scotland. I thought it of some significance that in his speech at the opening of the new session of the Scottish parliament in Edinburgh in 2004, the presiding office, George Reid, made reference to the Edinburgh of David Hume and Adam Smith while failing to mention the Jacobites in Holyrood House in 1745. Perhaps Scotland is at last beginning to reposition itself, becoming less preoccupied with Bannockburn, Mary Queen of Scots, the Covenanters, Bonnie Prince Charlie, and the other totemic areas of traditional Scottish history, while growing more aware of its role and achievements in the Atlantic world of which it is part. In this new context today's Scot at Princeton would have good reason for feeling very much at home.

10 Dartmouth and the State of the Union

I have recently returned to Glasgow after a term's teaching of English and American literature at Dartmouth College in Hanover, New Hampshire. Founded in 1769 – and thus older than all but two of England's universities – Dartmouth is a member of that elite group of private American universities known as the Ivy League. However it is unique in retaining its original 'college' title: all the Ivy League institutions (except the relative newcomer Cornell University) began life as 'colleges' but in the nineteenth century 'university' became the preferred title indicating expansion especially into postgraduate education and research. Why Dartmouth chose a different path is not entirely clear. History certainly played a part. Back in 1815, the college president, a Presbyterian and Republican, was removed from office by a majority of the Board of Trustees who were Congregationalists and Federalists. The ousted president appealed to the state legislature and was reinstated as the head of a new corporation called 'Dartmouth University'. However, the case went all the way up to the U.S. Supreme Court where in 1819 the arguments led by the college's most famous graduate – Daniel Webster – prevailed, meaning that the original Board of Trustees regained control of the institution. Thus for at least the rest of the nineteenth century the term 'university', in a Dartmouth context, would have been an unwelcome reminder of past controversies. On the other hand Dartmouth's retention of its 'college' title in the twenty-first century signals its continuing commitment above all to undergraduate teaching. Despite having both a small but excellent Medical School and – in the Tuck School of Business, the first-ever American business school – Dartmouth, unlike the rest of the Ivy League, has chosen not to develop postgraduate programmes leading to the award of doctoral degrees.

Dartmouth owes its name to the second Earl of Dartmouth who, while holding the governmental office of secretary for the colonies, obtained the college's original charter from George III. But as was so often the case with the development of higher education in the American colonies, Scotland had a substantial input into the establishment of the new college. The Earl of Dartmouth's support for the new institution was largely a result of his deeply religious nature. Known as the 'Psalm-singer', the pious earl admired the work of Eleazar Wheelock who around 1750 had established Moor's

Indian charity school in Lebanon, Connecticut, with the aim of providing a Christian education for Native Americans. In 1765, Samson Occum, a former student at the school who had become a successful preacher, travelled through England and Scotland raising funds for the expansion of the school and its removal to Hanover, New Hampshire. The Earl of Dartmouth became president of the board of trustees supervising the money raised by Occum's trip, but the Society in Scotland for Propagating Christian Knowledge (SSPCK) made the largest contribution to the £10,000 raised. The first result of the successful campaign was the building, on the new Hanover site, of Dartmouth Hall, a handsome classical-style structure, quite like Princeton's Nassau Hall which had similarly been paid for by funds collected at the doors of Scotland's Presbyterian churches one Sunday in 1754.

Within the last decade, Dartmouth's Scottish link has been renewed even if on a somewhat modest scale. Each autumn term a group of Dartmouth students, accompanied by a faculty member, comes to Glasgow University to study English and other subjects in the Faculty of Arts. At the same time a Glasgow English Department lecturer goes to Dartmouth to teach a couple of literature courses. (Given that tuition, room and board at Dartmouth now costs over $40,000 a year, it is perhaps not surprising that no Glasgow students make it to Dartmouth.) 2006 was the second time I had arrived in Hanover as Glasgow's representative and, as I had done in 2003, I began my classes by telling the students both of their college's founding debt to Scotland and how it might be repaid by their signing up for the study abroad programme at the University of Glasgow. (In fact what really makes the Glasgow programme flourish is the revelation that, rather than twenty-one as in the USA, the legal drinking age in Scotland is eighteen: Glasgow's West End pubs have gained legendary status on the Dartmouth campus.)

I am regularly asked how American students compare with Scottish ones. Not an easy question to answer. Sometimes I'm inclined to say that in fact there's not much difference – students are just students wherever they happen to come from. American students can be bright, responsive, committed – but so can Scottish ones. Scottish students can be dull, predictable, disengaged – but so can American ones. Undoubtedly there are American students for whom the college experience, however expensive, is less about the life of the mind than about sex, alcohol, fraternities, and having a good time. But equally there are not a few Scottish students, supported by grants or loans, who spend more time in the Union and the pub than in the lecture hall or the university library. What I would say is that the students at a relatively small college such as Dartmouth – the total enrolment is only around five thousand – are a much more homogeneous bunch than the students at a large, metropolitan university such as Glasgow. To start with, Dartmouth students are overwhelmingly in the same eighteen to twenty-two age range; mature students are conspicuous by their absence. Then family background by and large places them all in the same American middle-class. Given the huge cost of an Ivy League education this is hardly surprising. Of course there are awards, loans, campus jobs, and even a 'needs blind' admission policy. But for poorer American families as a whole a Dartmouth-style education remains well out of reach. As a result, the student body is essentially a well-to-do, economically secure one, and I would guess that the majority of students take it for granted that their Dartmouth education will do much to ensure that their own economic future will be equally secure.

However there is one area in which diversity rather than homogeneity does characterize Dartmouth's student population. Like every comparable American college or university, Dartmouth goes to great lengths to find as many qualified students from as wide a range of racial or ethnic minorities as possible. Of course until the 1970s, Dartmouth, like all similar institutions, admitted only men; since then, despite the opposition of at least some alumni, the number of women admitted has grown to roughly half the total intake. The percentage of ethnic minority students is nowhere as high, but one nonetheless meets on the campus substantial numbers of Asian-American, African-American, Hispanic, and perhaps not surprisingly given the college's origins, some Native-American students. Diversity in terms of race and diversity – not to mention gender – has become such a necessity in American higher education that no college or university can afford to be seen to be neglecting the issue in terms both of student body and teaching faculty.

So much so that a recent challenge to this orthodoxy has been greeted with shocked disbelief. Walter Benn Michaels, a well-respected professor of English at the University of Illinois, has recently published a book entitled *The Trouble with Diversity: How We Learned to Love Diversity and Ignore Inequality* in which he argues that liberal America's preoccupation with racial equality, however well-intentioned, has led educationally to increasing social injustice and inequality. The statistics support such a view. A mere three percent of students at the top 150 American colleges come from families in the bottom quartile of national family income. On the other hand, in Ivy League style colleges, the percentage of students from the top quartile has in recent years risen to almost half. The result is that, as a reviewer in the New York Review of Books put it, 'there are very few poor students at America's top colleges, and a large and growing number of rich ones'. Hence the middle-class environment of Dartmouth is in no way exceptional. According to Michaels, the liberal left's obsession with affirmative action as a way of correcting America's history of racial oppression and segregation has actually led to a damaging neglect of the bigger problem of economic injustice suffered by the poor of all races. In relation to education, says Michaels, it is time to redirect reforming energy away from the race issue to the economic one. Such views remain highly controversial, but my own experience does confirm the view that the diversity of the student body in an elite American college in no way extends to the inclusion of a significant number of working-class students.

Of course no one would suggest that even the issue of race and diversity in higher education in America has been successfully resolved. During my term at Dartmouth that issue proved to be very much alive. Given the college's origins in a school dedicated to the education of Native Americans, it is no surprise that in the not so distant past Dartmouth's sporting teams were known as the 'Indians', with the result that stereotypical 'Indian' images and icons frequently appeared among the paraphernalia associated with the college. Today's Dartmouth has officially turned its back on such a problematic tradition, even though it has proved difficult to find an acceptable replacement for the 'Indian' description. What happened during my term, however, shows that the underlying issue involved in all of this remains a highly sensitive one. Several incidents of an apparently minor nature, involving thoughtless behaviour in fraternity houses and an offensive cartoon on the cover of the Dartmouth Review, a student magazine well-known for its conservative views, revealed very clearly the tensions that can still exist beneath the surface of the most liberal campus. That college fraternities should have been involved was almost inevitable. Dartmouth, like so many other American colleges and universities, is deeply ambivalent over the campus fraternities and sororities that remain the focus of undergraduate social life. Selective and exclusive, these organizations, many of them national in scope, often seem to promote behaviour, attitudes and values incompatible with the aims of a liberal education. In any event, all the campus groups devoted to respect for diversity, equality of treatment, and tolerance of minority values, were suddenly up in arms about what was seen as the disrespect being shown to Native Americans on the campus. Statements were issued, demonstrations organized, speeches made, all calling for the rejection of intolerance and affirmation of the college's policy of racial and ethnic diversity. At the largest demonstration, held outside Dartmouth Hall, I estimated about seven or eight hundred people turned out to listen to a succession of speeches denouncing what had occurred and affirming Dartmouth's role as an inclusive and welcoming community. The crowd included faculty as well as students, and the best speeches were made by members of the college administration. Nevertheless, almost at the end of term, the Dartmouth president felt it necessary to publish a very long statement on the college website, deploring what had happened and insisting yet again on Dartmouth's absolute commitment to equality within diversity. As I was leaving Hanover, one issue remained unresolved: should Dartmouth cancel an ice-hockey match with a Dakota university which still retained its Native American mascot?

These campus shenanigans, however interesting and revealing, were far from being the dominant political reality during my Dartmouth term. For all of America, and so for me, throughout every month, every week, every day, there was only one, overwhelming political issue – the war in Iraq. People often ask me about the differences between living in Scotland and living for lengthy periods in the US. Well as of now the answer is simple. America and Americans are preoccupied with Bush's war to an incomparably greater degree than is the case here. Returning home in January last, I was stunned by the difference. In the U.K, the war is no longer front-page news. It is possible to sit through BBC One's Six O'clock News and hear no mention of the war at all. Even in the quality papers news from Iraq is normally tucked away in the inside pages. Television coverage in the form of film reports from within Baghdad (or even Basra where the Brits are supposed to be in charge) has become a relatively rare event. As I write all our news media are providing us with endless coverage of a bird 'flu outbreak in Suffolk which has killed not a single person; meantime bombings in Iraq which kill five, ten, twenty, fifty Iraqis merit no more than a sentence or two. The contrast with the US could not be greater. Iraq is never off the front page. All the 24 hour news services – CNN, Fox News, MSNBC – carry reports from their own correspondents in Iraq on a daily basis; PBS and the mainstream networks NBC, CBS and ABC invariably include Iraq updates in their evening bulletins; newspapers such as the *New York Times* and the Washington Post provide daily news coverage, return editorially to the subject again and again, and constantly print columns by their major journalist contributors — many of them powerful figures on America's political scene — on the latest developments concerning Iraq. Last December, a day or two after the number of American military killed in the Iraq conflict passed the three thousand mark, the *New York Times*, over five or six pages, published passport size photographs of every one of the last thousand casualties. Likewise, several TV news programmes, including Public Service Broadcasting's highly-regarded and nation-wide Jim Lehrer's Newshour, regularly display, in complete silence, the photographs, names, places of origin, and ages of the latest Pentagon list of servicemen and women killed in action.

President Bush repeatedly tells America it is a country at war. This is patently absurd. Since the outrage of 9/11, the vast majority of Americans have gone on living and behaving exactly as they have always have done. Not even the incredible cost of the war — $250,000 a second — yes, that's right — half a million dollars every two seconds — is having any recognizable impact upon individual Americans. The Bush tax-cuts remain in place. Apart (of course) from the countless thousands of Iraqis, the only people affected by this war are the American military and their families. (Any attempt to take Bush at his word by reintroducing the draft across America — as suggested by veteran New York Democrat, Charles Rangel — would bring this war to an end within weeks...) But the fact of the war, as a consequence of the kind of media attention I have described, remains the one over-riding political reality in America today.

The war in Iraq dominated the November, 2006 midterm elections, which saw a decisive switch in the balance of power in American politics. The Democrats took control both of the Senate and the House of Representatives. The win in the Senate was razor-thin. In the House, on the other hand, despite the fact that years of gerrymandering over constituency boundaries by both parties had seemingly made it extraordinarily difficult for seats to change hands, the Democratic victory was decisive. The reason was the Iraq war. Throughout the campaign the Republican Party struggled to persuade voters that local issues and individual candidacies should determine their choices. Except in a few seats where, ironically, Republicans lost because of egregious corruption scandals, the electors disagreed. The only issue that mattered was the war — and the way to protest the war was to vote Democratic. The result was that Republican incumbents who, in a normal year, would have comfortably retained their seats, lost. My own state provides a perfect illustration. New Hampshire is traditionally a rock-solid Republican state. But in 2006 the state's two mainstream Republican congressmen were defeated by their Democrat challengers. Even more extraordinarily, New Hampshire's own state legislature switched from Republican to Democratic control for the first time since the 1870s. In adjacent, but traditionally more liberal Vermont, a left-wing 'Independent' candidate (who will vote with the Democratic caucus) was elected to the Senate with a handsome majority. In the run-up to this election most political analysts and commentators had doubted that the Democrats could possibly win control of the Senate. To do so would mean winning in such states as Tennessee, Missouri, Montana and Virginia — all of them in recent times distinctly 'red' in their allegiance. In fact, by narrow majorities, the Democrats won all but Tennessee. The point is that only the Iraq war explains such unexpected outcomes. Gay marriage, stem-cell research, anti-Darwinism — none of these now traditional evangelical Christian Republican issues were powerful enough to prevent enough Americans from voting against the war by denying control of Congress to President Bush and his supporters.

So what will happen between now and the next presidential election in November, 2008? It is impossible to say. Lame-duck or not, the president remains in control of American foreign policy. And the early signs hardly suggest that Bush is paying much attention to his defeat in November. Last December Washington, the American media, and many ordinary Americans waited breathlessly for the release of the Iraq Study Group report. The rumour was widespread that this bipartisan group, the brainchild of the elder Bush and his buddies, had been set up to provide the younger Bush with an honourable way out of the Iraq quagmire. What happened? As if in a version of some Greek tragedy, the son killed off the father. There would be no diplomatic involvement of Iran and Syria; there would be no draw-down in the number of American troops actively involved in the war. In no time at all the White House leaks were on the contrary all about a possible increase in American troop levels in order to bring 'security' to Baghdad and Anbar province. This is the policy now in place. More troubling still, what last autumn was a scarcely credible rumour that the Pentagon had in place a plan to strike Iran has in recent weeks been taken more and more seriously. As a result of investigative articles in the New Yorker by Seymour Hirsch no one now doubts that such a plan exists, and that it has the backing of elements within the Bush administration. Is it conceivable that Bush will decide that attack is the best form of defence?

Voter disillusionment with the Iraq war has led to Democratic control of Congress. Does this mean that the Democrats can respond to their supporters by bringing the war to an end? Almost certainly not. I cannot believe they will use their power to choke off the money needed to pursue the war: the patriotic argument that 'our boys' have to be supported no matter what will prove irresistible. More to the point perhaps is the fact that their majority in the Senate depends on the vote of former vice-presidential candidate Joe Lieberman. Now Lieberman was actually defeated by an anti-war candidate when he ran for re-election in the Democratic primary in Connecticut. Nonetheless he chose to run in the November election as an 'independent' Democrat and, with the support of many Republican voters, retained his seat. His views on the war reflect those of what is easily the most powerful foreign policy pressure group in America: the Jewish lobby. Thus Lieberman is an unswerving supporter of the Israeli government's policy in the Middle East, a consistent critic of Iran and Syria, and a senator unlikely to vote against the Iraq war. During my term at Dartmouth there were several illustrations of just how powerful the lobby for which Lieberman speaks actually is. In March, 2006, two political scientists at Harvard wrote an article in the *London Review of Books* (it had been turned down by the *Atlantic Monthly*) arguing that the pro-Israel lobby in Washington was able to exercise disproportionate influence over American foreign policy in the Middle East. The result in the American media? Outrage, rebukes, refutations, and, more disturbingly, recurring suggestions of anti-Semitism. A few months later, in October, 2006, Tony Judt, the distinguished, British-born modern historian at New York University, planned to deliver a lecture at the Polish consulate on 'The Israel Lobby and American Foreign Policy' — but at the last minute he discovered his lecture had been cancelled because of pressure from the powerful Jewish Anti-Defamation League. Subsequently 114 American intellectuals (no doubt including many of Jewish background) wrote a letter to the *New York Review of Books* protesting that decision. A point had been made nonetheless. Finally in recent weeks former president Jimmy Carter has felt the full force of Jewish pressure-group politics. Carter chose to call his latest book *Palestine: Peace not Apartheid.* That title alone was enough to infuriate the American Jewish lobby. Possibly Carter intended to provoke — if so he succeeded admirably. Once again the American media rang with accusations of prejudice and even anti-Semitism. How could Carter dare to draw a parallel between Israel and South Africa? What such controversies suggest is the continuing strength of the pro-Israel lobby within America's society and culture.

So without Lieberman's support (and in March 2007 he has just voted with the Republicans to defeat a Democratic proposal for a fixed timetable for the withdrawal of American forces from Iraq) can anti-war Democrats have any hope of meaningful resistance to the executive power of the White House? Despite this early setback perhaps there is a glimmer of hope. A handful of more liberal Republican senators have occasionally shown themselves willing to defy the president — this, for example, is why Bush could not get John Bolton confirmed as American ambassador to the UN. Again several of these senators were ready to speak out strongly in favour of the Iraq Study Group report. How they vote on foreign policy issues in the months to come could prove decisive. Finally there is the question facing all those senators up for re-election in November, 2008. Will they be prepared to go on supporting American involvement in a war which over sixty percent of their constituents want to see ended? I shall be back at Dartmouth College this September in what will surely be exciting times. By then the next presidential campaign will have moved up several gears and, as always in American politics, New Hampshire, with its early primary elections for both Republican and Democratic candidates, will be a key state. The debate will be fast and furious between all the candidates – McCain or Giuliani or Romney on the one side, Clinton or Edwards or Obama on the other — but who can doubt that the war in Iraq will remain the crucial issue?

11 My Sentimental Journey

I have just returned from my own sentimental journey to the far north of Scotland. I was returning to Wick, where I was born and brought up, to John O'Groats, which I visited regularly as a boy, to Huna, a few miles away along the coast where my great-grandfather once owned a small farmhouse, to Canisbay churchyard, where my maternal grandparents are buried and a gravestone memorialises other members of my family, to the Castle of Mey, and finally to Dunnet Bay.

We travelled up the A9 – now certainly much improved with long stretches of dual carriageway — and stayed overnight in one of a rather soulless complex of hotels in Aviemore. Then on to Inverness and northwards, on a much less busy A9, through small but quite attractive little towns like Golspie and Brora, over the Ord at Berriedale, and finally into Caithness. (In the old days, travelling south from Wick in the family car, Berriedale, with its fearsomely steep hairpin bend, was the one frightening moment on the entire trip.) My home town was now almost within reach.

I had lived in Wick until I was sixteen. How many years had passed since my last visit? At least thirty or forty. So my arrival now was not without an element of trepidation. I have no surviving relatives, but how much will the town have changed? How will I feel seeing the house in which I grew up? We got off to an excellent start. The apartment we had hired turned out to sit above Wick River in the centre of the town. Particularly when the incoming tide filled the river estuary, the view was splendid. But it was mid-afternoon on a Saturday, and I was anxious to get out and about. We were only yards from Bridge Street, in the town centre, and the first thing I noticed was that the Station Hotel was no longer there. (It turned out that the building was now some kind of old people's home.) Then almost next door was the church that my family used to attend — but that building too had been transformed — it had become a graceless furniture store. Walking along Bridge Street and turning into the High Street, everything seemed different. None of the shops I remembered were there. Of course there were familiar names – but only in the sense of local examples of chains one would find in any town in the U.K.

But now the key moment had almost arrived. Near the end of High Street, Shore Lane runs up to the left. It is quite steep and at its foot there used to be a Congregational church — but it too I see is now some kind of commercial emporium. My house stood at the top of Shore Lane. Walking up, it seemed shorter than I remembered. Then there I was – standing at the front gate of Mount Hooly House. But it was in no way the house I remembered. That house had a long path through beautiful lawns and large flowerbeds up to a front door flanked by large flowerpots. There was a glasshouse in the garden and a side area of strawberry beds. All gone. There was nothing to see but overgrown grass. The house itself was clearly empty. The sense of desolation and abandonment was overwhelming. We were able to walk around the house but the back was in even worse condition than the front. This early nineteenth-century mansion house which, long before becoming my house, had been built and owned by a provost of the royal burgh of Wick, is in desperate need of restoration.

It was sad to see my family home in such disrepair, but it quickly became clear that there was little in contemporary Wick to cheer me up. The outer harbour was empty. The inner section did have a number of yachts and pleasure boats, but there was little evidence of the fishing industry that had once made Wick famous. More disturbing still was the number of houses and properties in the town's streets that were empty and boarded up: the effect was dismal indeed. Such new buildings as there were — including a new hospital near the town centre — were wholly unattractive. Rosebank, with its tennis courts, bowling green, and putting course — where I and my school friends had spent so many happy hours — was shut down and looked neglected. The two cinemas of my time — the Pavilion in the High Street (where every Saturday morning I used to watch an episode of Flash Gordon) and the Breadalbane in Pulteneytown – proved to no longer exist. A vast, ugly car park, down by the river, served a Poundland shop. But there were few cars and equally few customers — which reinforced the sense I already had that, on a late Saturday afternoon, the town's streets were surprisingly empty. Next day, on the outskirts of the town, on our way to John O'Groats, we passed a large Tesco store. So perhaps Wick is just another example of how the fashion for out-of-town shopping has sucked the life out of our streets.

The only entirely positive experience I had during my return to the town in which I grew up proved to be one concerning the past. Wick Society's Heritage Museum is a splendid example of this kind of institution. Here Wick's past at least comes vividly to life. Three generations of the local Johnston family were photographers of

Wick. Their work, from the 1880s on, provides an amazing insight into what the port that had become the hub of Europe's herring fishing industry was like. My grandfather often spoke of how he remembered before 1914 being able to walk across Wick Bay — not miraculously on the water, but on the decks of the closely packed herring boats. The museum photographs show exactly what he meant — the hundreds of fishing boats jammed tightly together. Then there are pictures of the fishermen themselves — alongside the women whose job it was to gut the fish, the coopers who made the barrels into which the catch was packed, the fish-curers and buyers. Shot early in the twentieth century, film sequences bring to life every aspect of the industry and the period when the vast shoals of 'silver darlings' had brought booming prosperity to Wick.

However the museum is about much more than the herring industry. The life of the town as it used to be is evoked by material of all kinds. For me however, the most surprising and moving moment came when I saw some radio equipment. Why was it there? Because in 2000 Wick Radio, which had begun operating in 1908, was finally closed down. So my father's workplace was now part of Wick's past. Strange to think he could even have used the equipment I was looking at....

John O'Groats, which I visited regularly in my youth, is famous only because of its location as the northernmost habitation in the United Kingdom. The landscape around it is flat and treeless like so much of the county of Caithness. The seascape however is another matter. On the shore of the Pentland Firth, which stretches between the mainland and the Orkneys, one looks out on the stormy meeting point of the North Sea and the Atlantic Ocean. The island of Stroma is a few miles offshore, the smaller island of Swona is just in view, and on the horizon the outline of Orkney is clearly visible. Duncansby Head, jutting out into the Firth, is a short distance to the east. (Dunnet Head, some miles to the west, is in fact the northernmost tip of Great Britain's mainland.)

Inevitably John O'Groats turns out to be not at all as I remembered it. The strikingly gothic John O'Groats hotel, with its two lofty towers, is still in place, but now the hotel is surrounded by all the familiar trappings of a modern holiday resort: a large car park, gift shop, cafés and other eating places, and an information centre. At the centre of the tourist area is a large white signpost indicating how far John O'Groats is from Land's End, Edinburgh, Orkney and Shetland, and New York. Fair enough no doubt. One thing however, did disappoint. In my day John O'Groats was mainly its lovely sandy beach. Many a time I walked there, searching for 'groatie buckies' – tiny pinkish seashells of special delicacy which were much prized. Now that beach has gone, replaced by a small jetty surrounded by only layers of rocks and boulders. No doubt it is progress to be able to take a ferry from John O'Groats to Orkney, but a price has been paid.

It was time to move on to Huna, a few miles along the coast. It was here that my great-grandfather had built the little farmhouse that my family had inherited and used for brief visits or holidays. The house had no running water or electricity. Peat fires and oil lamps were the order of the day. Water had to be carried in buckets from a well a field away – and of course the only toilet was in an outhouse. But the beach where I played so freely was near at hand. Of course I was anxious to see if the house was still there. And once again I was disappointed. The cottage on the site was clearly modern. Huna too had changed. The one little shop had gone – replaced by a phone booth and a letterbox. The lifeboat shed I remembered was still there, but entirely ruinous. Even in my time the lifeboat itself had already gone, but the railed slipway from the shed's door down into the sea was then still functional. Small motor boats from Stroma, only three or four miles away, would use it to land catches or pick up supplies. But here too a major, and saddening change had occurred. The slipway was still there, but a warning notice now indicated it was not safe to walk on. Looking over to Stroma, it used to be easy to see the island's single road, its scatter of houses, and its cultivated fields. Now there was nothing to see. Stroma's last inhabitants left in 1962. Is anyone out there thinking of buying Stroma and bringing it back to life?

My sentimental journey was almost at its end. Fighting a powerful wind – the legacy of Hurricane Ophelia – we managed to locate the family gravestone in Canisbay churchyard. The saddest name it bears is that of my cousin Alistair, lost at sea in the Royal Navy in 1944 at the age of nineteen.

The same wind was responsible for the great waves rolling in on the vast stretch of Dunnet beach – surely its miles-long sands, dominated by the grandeur of Dunnet Head, are on a scale scarcely matched anywhere else in Europe. However, with the Castle of Mey closed, it was time to return to Wick and prepare for the long drive south. (I know there are people for whom the north begins at Watford; for me in Wick, all of the U.K. was the south.) Robert Louis Stevenson visited Wick in 1868 to inspect the work that his family firm had carried out on the town's harbour. He did not relish the experience, describing Wick as 'one of the meanest of man's towns', on the 'coldest of God's bays'. In a letter to his mother he wrote – 'Certainly Wick in itself possesses no beauty: bare, grey shores, grim grey houses, grim grey sea...' Well Mount Hooly House was neither grim nor grey, and growing up in Wick was not at all the dismal experience that Stevenson implies. And in fact some readers may know that not so long ago Wick regained its world-leading status – not this time for the herring fishery, but for the world's shortest street! In 2006 the *Guinness Book of Records* announced that Ebenezer Place in Wick was exactly that. The street's one door leads into Mackay's Hotel No. 1 Bistro. We had dinner there and enjoyed the one outstanding culinary moment of our entire trip: its rhubarb and gin soufflé was a triumph of delicacy and flavour. What a pity that my home town struck me as falling a long way short of matching that achievement.

Part Two

Scotland and America.

Having done well in my final Honours exam in English literature at Edinburgh University in 1954, gaining a first-class degree, I was awarded funding to proceed to postgraduate research. What I had to decide on was the area in which I would work. As an undergraduate, I had greatly enjoyed and admired the fiction of twentieth-century American authors — the generation in particular of Hemingway, Fitzgerald, Faulkner and Dos Passos. I felt that was the area in which I might work. However, when I mentioned this to Professor Renwick, then head of the Edinburgh English Literature department, he was far from enthusiastic: the status of American literature in academic terms was still uncertain. In 1954, two years of national service was still a requirement for men of my age. If I proceeded straight away to postgraduate study, I would be granted a deferment until my studies were complete. I thought about deferring, but decided it would be better to get national service over and done with. The result was two years in the British army's Intelligence Corps, largely spent on the border between east and west Germany, listening in to Russian military communications. However, I had plenty of spare time to get on with my reading of American literature, happily made easy by the presence of an American library in the nearby city of Braunschweig.

Post-national service, in 1956 I took up my postgraduate award and went off to the University of Manchester to join what was then the only programme in American Studies available in the U.K. Focusing on American history and American literature it was run by Professor Marcus Cunliffe and Geoffrey Moore. However, their advice was that if I was proposing to make an academic career in American literature, I had to get myself across the Atlantic and study there. Taking their advice, I was lucky enough to be awarded a Jane Eliza Procter Fellowship at Princeton University's Graduate College. (Subsequently I gathered I was the first non-Oxbridge appointee since the fellowship was established in 1921-22, but it was only very recently that I was intrigued and moved to learn that in 1938 one of the Procter Fellows was the brilliant Alan Turing.) Enrolling for the PhD, I had to decide on a dissertation topic with Willard Thorp, head of the Princeton English Department. He had no doubt what it should be. Princeton's Firestone Library contained the Witherspoon Collection. Witherspoon was the Scot responsible for effectively establishing in the eighteenth century what would become Princeton University. Like Witherspoon, I was an Edinburgh graduate. Willard said he had been waiting for the right person to come along to work on Witherspoon and the cultural connection between Scotland and America in the eighteenth century. I was just that person. How could I refuse? Scotland and America it was, and that subject would remain a major research interest throughout my academic career.

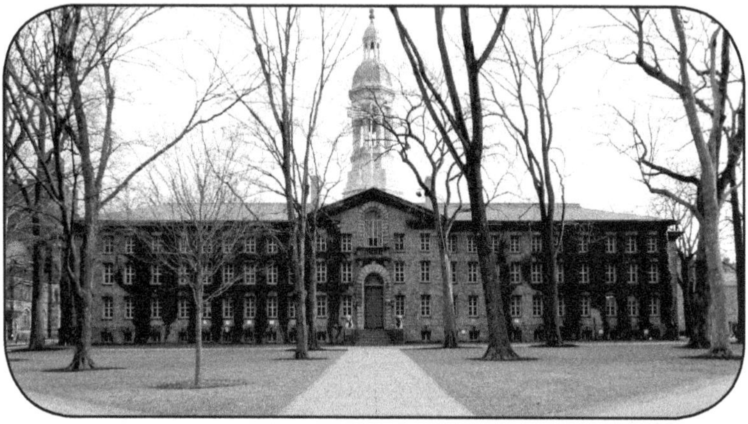

Nassau Hall, above, and the Graduate College, Princeton

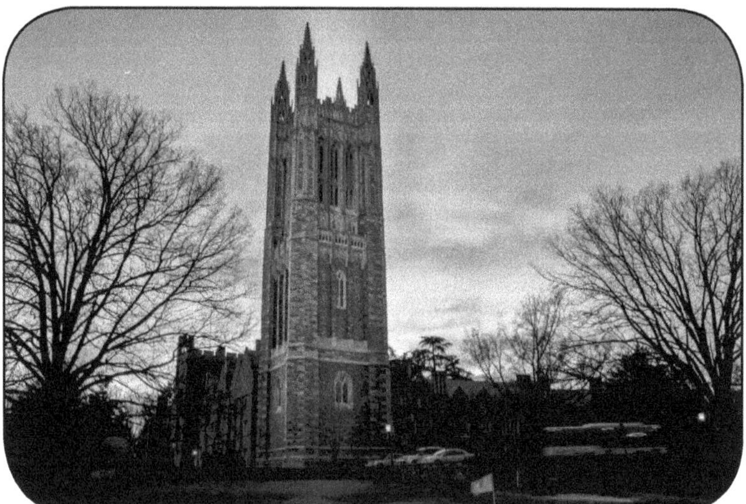

1 Glasgow and the American Revolution

I must begin by admitting to some sense of disappointment over this paper. When I undertook to write it I had in mind the possibility of unearthing fascinating new material from the range of archival sources available in the city: Glasgow University's own Library, its Archives, the Mitchell Library, etc. But I had reckoned without the diligence and thoroughness of several earlier scholars in the field including in particular William Brock, Emeritus Professor of Modern History at Glasgow University. Most of you will know Professor Brock's *Scotus Americanus: A survey of the sources for links between Scotland and America in the eighteenth century*, which was published in 1982. That survey inevitably pays considerable attention to the topic of Glasgow and the American Revolution. Indeed I came increasingly to feel, whenever I called up an item from our Special Collection, that William Brock had been there before me: he was a kind of ghostly presence making it clear that all this had been looked at already.

My first problem, then, is the absence of exciting new material. But there is also a second, more serious problem. This conference's theme is Glasgow and the Enlightenment. What I had hoped to do was to talk about Glasgow and the American Revolution within that specific context. But the conjunction of Glasgow, Enlightenment, and Revolution is not one that lends itself to easy scholarly investigation and documentation. Is there any necessary connexion between the elements that make up this particular trinity? And even if there is, what is the nature of the evidence that can be adduced to demonstrate it? In the familiar words of a recent US presidential candidate, where's the beef?

Obviously what I have in mind here is the contrast between talking about Glasgow and the American Revolution in a general, wide-ranging way, and talking about the topic in specific terms of intellectual and cultural history. The former case is a relatively straightforward one. The historical record that documents the impact of the American Revolution upon Glasgow's economic and political life in particular is by now reasonably clear and reasonably well-known. Hence there is no need for me to rehearse in detail the familiar story of the rise of Glasgow in the tobacco trade with the American colonies, nor indeed to dwell on the effect the Revolution had upon this crucial trading link between the Clyde and the Chesapeake Bay. In this area the work of such economic historians as Jacob Price and Thomas Devine has been outstanding.[1] More letter-books, more ledgers and account-books of the Glasgow tobacco merchants may yet turn up on both sides of the Atlantic, but there is no reason to believe that such discoveries will significantly alter our present understanding.

Briefly, the picture is as follows. From quite early in the eighteenth century, the Atlantic trade had been a growing source of wealth for Glasgow merchants; and in the immediate pre-Revolutionary period the tobacco trade had become a hugely important element in Glasgow's booming economic life. Hence, in the long dispute between Great Britain and her American colonies, economic self-interest inevitably meant that the Glasgow mercantile community spoke always for reconciliation and compromise. Glasgow was doing extremely well out of the status quo; change could only be for the worse. As a result, up to and even beyond the point when the Revolution had begun, Glasgow was one of the few places in the United Kingdom where war with America was openly opposed. However, once it became clear that reconciliation was impossible, and that the war would be fought to a finish, then Glasgow shifted its ground: its economic investment in the colonies would be best protected by a quick British victory in the war. Glasgow then would do all in its power to achieve that end.

As I say, this story is by now sufficiently familiar. Almost equally familiar is the new orthodoxy concerning the economic consequences for Glasgow of the American Revolution. The Revolution did disrupt the tobacco trade which was never to return to its pre-Revolutionary prominence. However, Glasgow's trading economy suffered a set-back, not a catastrophe, as a result of the American War. A few commercial houses did fail, but most did not. The majority of Glasgow merchants with investments in the American trade seem to have been shrewd enough to weather the Revolutionary storm. And the losses incurred as a result of the initial disruption of the American trade were not long in being made up. During and after the war, Glasgow's commercial life would continue to flourish.

The economic consequences for Glasgow of the American Revolution are thus reasonably clear. Of the political consequences much the same is true. Historians argue that the origins of the campaigns for changes within the Scottish eighteenth-century political settlement all date from the period of the American War. What the war did was to increase political awareness within

Scotland as whole, and in Glasgow in particular. As we have seen, powerful elements within Glasgow's social and business elite actually opposed government policy at the time of the outbreak of the Revolution. The lack of effectiveness of such opposition may well have been a factor in making the notion of political reform seem attractive. Certainly by the end of the war with America, discontent in Glasgow, and elsewhere in Scotland, over the existing political arrangements was clear. Meikle notes Professor John Millar's opposition to a loyal address from Glasgow on the occasion of Pitt's accession to power in December 1783, and equally, Glasgow's support for the subsequent Fox-North coalition at a time when most 'loyal' Scots remained hostile.[2] In April 1783, the *Caledonian Mercury* printed a letter suggesting that 'the spirit of liberty had taken a northern turn' and in May 1784, the paper reported, 'never was there a period when the spirit of party ran so high'.

It is thus in this period that the Scottish campaign for reform in the system of parliamentary representation, both at burgh and county level, begins. The Yorkshire Committee for reform was already in existence. The Committee specifically recognized the need for reform in Scotland and in return the Yorkshire Committee gained Scottish support. Its resolutions indeed were sent to two leading figures of the Scottish Enlightenment — Adam Ferguson and Gilbert Stuart — but their response was less than enthusiastic.

Ferguson and Stuart's equivocation over the cause of parliamentary reform may be seen as a continuation of the Scottish Enlightenment's general stance over the political issues raised initially by the American question and subsequently by the Revolution itself. As you will be aware, various Enlightenment luminaries, including Hume, Smith, and Karnes, expressed opposition to government policy towards the American colonies; but only John Millar seems to have remained a staunch adherent of the colonists' cause once hostilities had begun. But beyond the political postures adopted by individual Scottish thinkers, is there a wider, more general sense in which the Scottish Enlightenment may be seen as being involved in the American Revolution? And if there is, what is Glasgow's role within that wider context? Is there in fact any meaningful alignment between Glasgow, the American Revolution, and the Scottish Enlightenment?

Here one must say immediately that the position is much less clear than in the areas of economics and internal politics which I have just been glancing at. The question of the specific contribution of the Scottish Enlightenment to the ideological background of the American Revolution remains unresolved. At the very least, however, that contribution was greater than used to be generally recognized. And the general thrust of Garry Wills's arguments – whatever one may say about specific points of detail – would have been greatly strengthened had he been able to place his particular argument in the context of that wider Scottish intellectual and cultural contribution to colonial America which many of us present here have helped to demonstrate and define. Because he lacks a knowledge of that pattern of Scottish-American intellectual relationships, Wills allows his arguments often to appear merely eccentric: the case his books make seems to exist in a kind of intellectual vacuum. And it is this that helps his opponents to reject his arguments. The basic point, however, remains. The Scottish Enlightenment was a widely available source for a range of ideas that fed into the thinking of those Americans who eventually saw the Revolution as the only possible way of resolving the issue of what were or were not the rights of Americans. In the creation of that intellectual climate, Glasgow's professors played a full part – Francis Hutcheson, Adam Smith, Thomas Reid, and John Millar among them. Did Glasgow then create the American Revolution? Hardly. Enlightenment ideas, like Enlightenment professors, are not the possession of any one city.

Glasgow has no absolute claim either to the ideas or to the professors, but equally Glasgow certainly has a share in both.

Glasgow's export of ideas along its trans-Atlantic trading routes may well have helped to fuel the American Revolution. Glasgow's import of news from America may well have helped in a minor way to spread enlightenment in Glasgow. There can be no doubt that Glasgow's economic investment in the American colonies meant that the city took a keen interest in all aspects of the Anglo-American dispute from its very beginning. There was a demand for news from America – as well as from London – and as a result the ships carrying tobacco to the Clyde from the Chesapeake Bay frequently also carried news. From the 1760s on, *The Scots Magazine*, and the Scottish newspapers, regularly reprinted lengthy extracts from the American press on the topic of the dispute with the mother-country. When war broke out access to American opinion on the state of affairs was no longer so easy, but the demand for news of the progress of the conflict intensified. Local businessmen founded the Morning Club meeting in a tavern in Currie's Close on the east side of the High Street in the merchant city. Club members assembled before breakfast to read the newly arrived newspapers from

Edinburgh and London in search of news about the American War and the affairs of Parliament. The existence of the Morning Club is a specific example of the way in which the American Revolution can be seen as stimulating political debate within Glasgow.

Debate and discussion — particularly within the context of a network of clubs and societies — have always been recognized as playing a central role in the spread of Enlightenment ideas in Scotland. Thus the Morning Club is only a minor example of a familiar phenomenon recurring throughout all of Scotland's urban centres in the eighteenth century. Other Glasgow social institutions with perhaps closer links to the Enlightenment included the Literary Society and the Hodge-Podge Club.[3] The Literary Society was very much dominated by professors from the university though the odd Glasgow merchant does appear in the list of members. The case of the Hodge-Podge Club, admittedly more convivial in its nature, is different: at least twenty-five Glasgow merchants were members. What has to be kept in mind in this connexion is the fact that the Glasgow merchant community became a living demonstration of the view that enlightened liberal values in education could and should have a practical application: Brock tells us that no fewer than 36 of the 166 tobacco merchants identified in Glasgow between 1740 and 1790 matriculated at Glasgow University; and there is good evidence that an additional substantial number of merchants attended classes in the university without matriculating.[4] The evidence does suggest that Glasgow's mercantile community was well-educated and therefore in no way unfamiliar with those values, attitudes, and opinions, associated with the Scottish Enlightenment.

It is this percolation of Enlightenment values down into the professional and mercantile middle class that lies behind Glasgow's increased political awareness traditionally seen as being sparked off by the American Revolution. In the debates over parliamentary reform in the 1780s in Scotland the influence of the philosophers of the Scottish Enlightenment is clear. The ideas of Hume and Smith, reinforced and extended by those of liberals like John Millar and Dugald Stewart, undoubtedly created a climate in which reforming ideas could flourish. Meikle tells us that in their pamphlets making the case for change, the proponents of reform quote Hume and Smith as well as Locke, Montesquieu and Machiavelli.

The point I am making then is this. Even if it is true that Glasgow's original concern over the dispute between Britain and the American colonies, like its intense and continuing interest in the outbreak and progress of the war with America, was based overwhelmingly on the ground of economic self-interest, nonetheless, the diffusion of enlightenment values in Glasgow ensured that the larger political, ideological, and philosophical issues involved in the American Revolution did not go unnoticed. Some at least of the occasional material printed in Glasgow during the war with America lends credence to this point of view. In 1778, William Thom, Minister of Govan, who must have been a member, like John Witherspoon before him, of the popular or evangelical party within the Church of Scotland, was still able to publish his strongly pro-American sermon, *The Revolt of the Ten Tribes*, originally delivered on December 12th, 1776. More significant, however, is the publication by John Bryce in the Saltmarket in 1783 of the United States Congress's pamphlet *A Collection of the Constitutions of the Thirteen United States of North America*, originally printed in Philadelphia by order of Congress at the end of 1780. The Scottish edition contains a prefatory set of 'Verses on the Constitutions' which are of real interest. Let me quote some lines:

> But now, behold, a set of new-born states (Their western shores the vast Atlantic beats) whose constitutions have no other plan, nor aim than this, the happiness of man.

The echo of the Declaration of Independence is clear, but the basic error in geography makes it clear that the poet in question, was more familiar with American ideas than with the physical reality of the United States. However, the verses now become of still greater interest. The poet asks of the new United States, 'Whence they their institutions drew?' and goes on to attempt an answer:

> Perhaps their wisdom's borrowed from the store
> Of civil policy in ancient lore;
> From Him who knew to form a warlike race;
> Or Solon who excell'd in arts of peace:
> Perhaps they've culled from states of modern days
> Whate'er was best and most deserving praise:
> Perhaps, in fine, they've search'd Utopian schemes
> From Grecian Plato's down to David Hume's.

The final poetic answer is that the American constitutions derive from none of these sources; instead they are directly inspired by the goddess of liberty. What is interesting, however, is the way in which this Glasgow poet approaches the subject of the new American constitutions from within a framework which is very much that of the Scottish Enlightenment. The references to 'civil policy', the 'arts of peace' and the classical allusions to Lycurgus and Solon, not to mention David Hume, all underline the point. The poetry may be undistinguished, but the enlightenment emphasis is clear. Perhaps it is not going too far to suggest that the existence of these verses demonstrates that there were those in Glasgow in the 1780s who were prepared to see in the successful conclusion of the American Revolution an endorsement and vindication of Enlightenment values.

A prose reaction to the American Revolution which in a somewhat similar fashion sees the success of America in the context of the spread of Enlightenment values – with an emphasis this time on the economics of Adam Smith – appears in Thomas Tod's pamphlet entitled *Consolatory-Thoughts on American Independence* published (admittedly) in Edinburgh in 1782. The sub-title of the pamphlet is 'Shewing the great Advantages that will arise from it to the Manufacturers, the Agriculture, and Commercial Interest of Britain and Ireland' and this is the emphasis that appears in the nicely rhetorical peroration from which I quote:

> Perhaps this strange and unaccountable American war has been appointed as the means of great and glorious revolutions through the world. Perhaps that happy day now dawns, when the horrid shackles of slavery are to be knocked off millions of our fellow-mortals; when the bolts, the locks, and doors, which, from prejudice or wrong ideas, ignorantly shut up commerce, are now about to burst open like floodgates, and allow trade and manufacture to run in their natural channel, through all nations where they are found most necessary and profitable; and when that universal communication in trade may be the means of circulating the knowledge of religions and philosophy through the dark and ignorant corners of the earth, whereby this age may yet be a glorious era in the future page.

The reference here to the abolition of slavery is particularly fascinating, but to see the American Revolution as an impetus to the sweeping away of ignorance, prejudice, and wrong ideas, and to the dissemination even in the dark and ignorant corners of the earth of a fuller knowledge of religion and philosophy, is certainly to identify it with the spread of Enlightenment on a universal scale. One recognizes, of course, that such views were not necessarily shared by all of those in positions of power, or authority, or influence either in Glasgow or Edinburgh. But at least these passages I have been quoting allow us to say that there were those who, at the time, did recognize a link between the Enlightenment – in Glasgow and elsewhere – and the American Revolution.

Finally, one should at least raise the question of the longer-term consequences of the Revolution upon Glasgow's relations with America. Did the Revolution, as has sometimes been argued in the context of Scottish-American relations in general, mark the end of an era? Did the discord and disruption produced by the American War mean that the old relationship between Glasgow and America could never be renewed? Brock accepts the view that as far as Scotland as a whole was concerned, 'the Revolution caused a radical change in the relationship between Scotland and America'. The Revolution, he writes, 'closed a chapter in Scottish-American relations'. And he includes Glasgow in this accounting. On the other hand, Professor Brock does recognize that 'the years after independence saw a strengthening of intellectual links' between Scotland and America, and that 'cultural contacts increased rather than diminished after independence'.[5] Perhaps the best that one can say is that the Revolution altered the relationship between Glasgow and America but did not end it. Glasgow lost something of its economic and financial dominance – but as a source and focus of intellectual and cultural ideas and civic values, Glasgow would remain a significant force for most of the nineteenth century. That is the story that Bernard Aspinwall tells in *Portable Utopia*.

1. Jacob M. Price, 'The Rise of Glasgow in the Chesapeake Tobacco Trade, 1707-1775, ' *William and Mary College Quarterly*, 3rd Series, XI (April, 1954), 179-99, and T.M. Devine, *The Tobacco Lords, A Study of the Tobacco Merchants of Glasgow and their Trading Activities 1740-90*, Edinburgh, 1975.
2. H.W. Meikle, *Scotland and the French Revolution*, Glasgow, 1912, and Dalphy I. Fagerstrom, 'Scottish Opinion and the American Revolution,' *William and Mary College Quarterly*, 3rd Series, XI (April, 1954), 255.
   Meikle, op. cit., pp.4-5.
3 Garry Wills, Inventing America: Jefferson's Declaration of Independence, New York, 1978 and *Explaining America: The Federalist*, London, 1981.
4. For details of the Morning Club, the Literary Society and the Hodge-Podge Club, see John Strang, *Glasgow and its Clubs*, London and Glasgow, 1857.
5 W.R. Brock, *Scotus Americanus*, Edinburgh, 1982, p.19.
   Meikle, op. cit., pp.15-16.

2 Scotland and the South in the Eighteenth Century: Some Notes and Issues

I

To begin I have two issues. The first is somewhat abstract and theoretical; the second is immediate, practical, and unavoidable. The first is this: is it appropriate to talk of the South in the eighteenth century? Did the South even exist in the eighteenth century? Virginia, the Carolinas, Georgia, and intermittently East and West Florida existed as colonies or states in the eighteenth century in the southern section of North America, but did they compare the South? Probably not. The inhabitants of these regions, including their Scottish inhabitants, do not appear to have thought of themselves as Southerners. By the revolutionary period Virginia and the rest were beginning to recognize that their needs and ambitions were not always identical to those of New England and the more northern states, but even then it is doubtful if a clear sectional identity – the South – was generally recognized. My own inclination is to agree with those who argue that the South only came into existence when the slavery issue in the early nineteenth century drew the slave-holding states into a new Southern sectional unity. So our Eighteenth Century Scottish Studies conference theme should perhaps have been not Scotland and the American South, but Scotland and the southern colonies and states in the eighteenth century...

You may well feel that this first issue is not worth lingering over; that cannot be your reaction to my second issue. This is what it is. What is the theme of Scotland and the American South – and from here on I plan to use the conference's anachronistic wording – meant to include? What kind of material is relevant? Such recent scholarly titles as *Scottish Highlanders in Colonial Georgia, Scots in Georgia and the Deep South 1735-1845*, and *Carolina Scots, An Historical and Genealogical Study of Over 100 Years of Emigration*, make it clear that the most obvious focus of attention is Scottish eighteenth-century immigration into the South. But when we talk of the Scots in Virginia or the Carolinas or Georgia whom do we mean? Or rather whom should we mean? Those who left Scotland to settle in America? or those plus other native-born Scots who came to America as sojourners – soldiers, merchants, clerks, administrators, tutors and teachers – and remained for a number of years before returning home? or, and here is the central issue, should we include those Scots who had emigrated to Ulster before they or their descendants emigrated to America? Should the Scots in the South, that is, include the Ulster Scots, or, as they were long described in American historiography, the Scotch-Irish? If the answer is yes, then the story of Scotland and the American South becomes an altogether different and bigger story. Ulster Scots in America, that is, greatly outnumbered native-born Scots. Traditional estimates of the number of Ulster Scots emigrants from Ireland up to the outbreak of the American revolution arrive at a figure of 200,000 plus – a total four or five times larger than that for native-born Scots immigrants. Further, these are America-wide estimates, while all scholars agree that the vast majority of Ulster Scots, having arrived in Philadelphia and other Chesapeake Bay ports, headed west and south populating the Delaware, Susquehanna and Cumberland valleys in Pennsylvania, turning south into the Shenandoah valley in Virginia, pushing further south into the frontier of the Carolinas, Georgia and eventually Tennessee. Despite the existence of substantial numbers of Scottish Highlanders in North Carolina and Georgia, and of Lowland Scots in and around the coastal towns of Virginia and the Carolinas, it's hard to argue that native-born Scots immigrants showed any particular preference for moving into the American South.

So should we be concurred with Scots only, or Scots plus Ulster Scots? Older scholars inclined towards the view that the two groups should be regarded quite separately. James Leyburn, for example, writing in 1962, suggested that

> A clear distinction should be made between colonists from Scotland and those from Ulster, for the two have often, to the complete distortion of events, been thought identical.

And again:

> Scots in America from the first showed traits clearly different from those of the Scotch-Irish. Scots were seldom explorers, Indian fighters, or frontier traders; they played only a minor role as pioneers, preferring to settle in the east and to carry on business enterprises.

In fact some Scots in the South certainly were frontier traders and the Highlanders in North Carolina and Georgia clearly were pioneers, but Leyburn's generalization may still be a tenable one. Maldwyn Jones points out that in the eighteenth century, while the term 'Scotch-Irish' does occasionally occur, those so described were much more widely and generally called 'Irish' not 'Scotch' – and seem to have no objection to such a designation. It was only in the middle of the nineteenth century, with the huge influx into the USA of post-famine Catholic Irish, that Americans of Protestant Ulster origin began to insist that they were not 'Irish' but 'Scotch-Irish'. Another argument against the view that Scots and Ulster Scots should be regarded as a single ethnic group invokes the movement of history itself. The original Scots settlers in Ulster arrived in the early seventeenth century. New immigrants continued to cross from Scotland to Ulster almost to the end of that century. What this means is that the great majority of eighteenth-century emigrants from Ulster to America were several generations away from their Scottish origins. Why would they continue to regard themselves as Scots? Many historians suggest they didn't. Rather the Ulster Scots had acquired a distinct and individual identity, their values, attitudes, manners the product of the local circumstances and particular conditions in which they found themselves in the north of Ireland. More specifically, what the Ulster Scots were in terms of character and behaviour was largely determined by the fact they were a colonizing group who had dispossessed an indigenous population who still surrounded them. These were the background circumstances that in turn made the Scotch-Irish in America almost ideal pioneers and frontiersmen. But these were also the circumstances that made the society and culture of Ulster quite remote from that of Scotland.

Despite these arguments, some scholars now argue that it is a mistake to make a complete separation between Scots and Ulster Scots. Their case focuses above all on religion. What Scot and Ulster Scot had crucially in common was Presbyterianism. Whatever local factors or circumstances might have kept Scot and Ulster Scot apart, they were not enough to sever the bond created by shared Presbyterian beliefs and a shared Presbyterian heritage. In the particular circumstances of arrival in a new country, Presbyterianism provided immigrants from both Scotland and Ulster with a common identity, and an existing structure of institutional support which could only have had a unifying influence. This argument from a shared Presbyterian tradition between Scot and Ulster Scot is a weighty one, but it is not decisive. Maldwyn Jones argues that 'Scots and Ulstermen were often joined in the same synods and sometimes merged their identities in a common Presbyterianism. But there was less interaction than might have been supposed, since the two groups tended to settle in different regions. The differing patterns of settlement also explain why it is possible to question Presbyterianism staying power as the binding element keeping

Scots and Ulster Scots together. the constant movement west and south of the vast bulk of Ulster Scot colonists created a problem that the existing Presbyterian synods found difficult to solve – the provision of an adequate supply of ministers to care for the ever-growing number of mobile newcomers and their growing families. The Presbyterian tradition insisted on a well-educated clergy, and the American synods were determined to maintain that tradition. For much of the eighteenth century American Presbyterians relied on the Scottish universities to provide them with trained clergy – but the available number never matched the demand. And even when the Presbyterians succeeded in establishing their own educational institutions such as the College of New Jersey, the problem of matching supply to demand remained. The result was that in the frontier areas of the west and south where so many of the Ulster Scots and their families were locating, the gap created by the absence of Presbyterian clergy was increasingly filled by Baptists and circuit-riding Methodists whose education level was not an issue. Thus it can be argued that at least in the later eighteenth century the Presbyterian tradition was ceasing to be the defining characteristic of the Scotch-Irish in the American South.

II

That then is my second issue. Clearly there are good arguments on both sides of the question, but my own indication is to see the story of the Scots in the American South as remaining separate from that of the Ulster Scots. But that is partly because I have always been sceptical of the idea that the scale of immigration into America from Scotland or northern Ireland should be seen as the decisive or key factor in determining Scotland's impact upon America. At the outbreak of the American revolution no more than one in ten Americans were of Scots or Scotch-Irish origin. But that is not the main point. In the work of the many scholars who have in recent times worked on the variety of ways in which eighteenth-century Scotland contributed to the formation and development of American society and culture before and after the revolution, there is little suggestion that Scottish emigration was the fey factor. What is true of America as a whole is also true of the American South. The Scottish contribution to the eighteenth-century South is a question of ideas and ways of thinking, of trade and commerce, of religion and education. The Scottish Enlightenment may well have found its most receptive American audience in cities such as Philadelphia, New York and Boston, but it was in the College of William and Mary in Virginia that, as we shall see, Jefferson became the favourite pupil of William Small, the enlightened Scot who 'fixed the destinies' of his life.

So let me move swiftly to brief notes on these different areas of Scottish influence on the South. Trade and commerce. Virginia, the Carolinas and Georgia were as likely, or even more likely, to be importers of Scottish influence in all of its forms because these colonies were very much part of Scotland's Atlantic trading network. Tobacco was a key export in the economics of these colonies and as we know for much of the eighteenth century Scottish merchant houses played an increasingly important role in the development of the tobacco trade. Robert Pringle's successful career as a merchant in Charleston, as revealed in his published Letterbook, may readily be seen as epitomizing the mercantile link between Scotland and the South. An emigrant from the Edinburgh area early in the century, Pringle independently and for periods in partnership with other Scots, succeeded in building up a many-sided trading enterprise. Equally involved in the import and export of manufactured goods and natural resources – rice in particular – his correspondence clearly reveals the extraordinary range of his commercial contracts and business dealings on both sides of the Atlantic. He was in regular contact above all with London, where his merchant brother was located, but also with Boston, New York, Hull, Antigua and St. Kitts. But in the six or so years covered by his Letterbooks he was also wheeling and dealing from time to time in Newport, Philadelphia, Barbados, Jamaica, Bahamas, Madeira, Lisbon, Limerick, Amsterdam, Rotterdam, and Hamburg. The one surprise, perhaps – particularly given his obvious self-identity as a Scot – is the absence of any contact with Glasgow on any other Scottish seaport. But if Pringle had no involvement with the Scottish-American tobacco trade, he did have a substantial role in the native Indian trade. That trade with the Indians in the Carolinas was dominated by fellow-Scot Alexander McGillivray, but Pringle certainly had a major involvement in the importing to Charleston of the kind of material goods that trade with the Indians required.

An early president of the Charleston St Andrews Society, Pringle's business success allowed him to become a substantial landowner, an assembly representative, and finally a judge in Charleston. One of his sons would study medicine at the University of Edinburgh. In the business period of his career, Pringle emerges from his letters very much as the entrepreneurial Scot on the make. But however far his eye is focused on the main chance for self-advancement, he seems always to have been ready to help out those he called his 'countrymen' – and needless to say his countrymen are not Americans but fellow-Scots. But in this, as in most respects, Pringle seems to embody the characteristic outlook and attitude of the Scottish trading community in the South and elsewhere in the eighteenth century.

Religion. One of today's best known police detectives has suggested that 'John Calvin was much more the inventor of our Southern homeland than Sir Walter Scott'. *Intruder in the Dust* in particular indicates that William Faulkner is another Southern writer who seems to share James Lee Burke's opinion. So the impact of Calvinism on Southern manners and moves, from whatever source, particularly in frontier and rural areas, is clearly a major area for investigation. But it is a mistake to imagine that Scotland's religious contribution to the American South concerns only Presbyterian Calvinism. The impact of the Scottish Episcopal church on eighteenth-century America deserves closer attention than it has received. In Virginia in particular, the Scottish Episcopalian tradition appears to have been especially important. James McLachlan's figures indicate that in the century between 1681 and 1780, 443 university graduates emigrated to the Chesapeake Bay colonies, the great majority to Virginia and Maryland. Of the 443, 171 were Scottish universities graduates, 58 from Glasgow, 58 from Aberdeen, 51 from Edinburgh, and only 4 from St Andrews. Of the rest 153 were Oxbridge graduates. Of the 171 Scots graduates, 138 were clergymen: 23 Presbyterian and no less than 115 Episcopalian. What this means is that for much of the eighteenth century, between thirty and forty percent of Virginia's Episcopal clergy were Scotsmen. But it was not only in Virginia that Scottish Episcopal clergy found employment. John Fraser, and Edinburgh graduate, officiated in East Florida in 1769, while the Rev John Kennedy practiced as both clergyman and schoolteacher in the same section from 1777 to 1781. William Gordon was an Episcopalian minister in Mobile, West Florida in the period 1767 to 1775, while James Seymour, a graduate of King's College, Aberdeen, emigrated to Georgia in 1771 and served as an Episcopal clergyman from 1773 to 1782.

Scottish religious influence in America everywhere goes hand in hand with Scottish educational influence, and this is certainly the case with the eighteenth-century South. but at least in Virginia it is Scottish Episcopalianism rather than Presbyterianism that is in question. The College of William and Mary, founded at Williamsburg in 1693 is America's second oldest university. Its originator and first president was James Blair, an Aberdeen graduate. Like most of the college's early faculty, Blair was an Episcopalian. As commissary for the Bishop of London in Virginia, he was for over half a century the most powerful clergyman in the colony, and in the opinion of some scholars its leading and most influential intellectual figure. William Small, another Aberdeen graduate, taught at the college in the period 1758-64 and famously included among his students Thomas Jefferson. In his *Autobiography* Jefferson would write that it was Small who fixed the destinies of his life and there is good evidence that the teacher-pupil relationship between Small and Jefferson was a particularly close one. A typical product of the Scottish Enlightenment, Small on his return to England would lecture at the Royal Society and became a member of the famous Birmingham Lunar Society; his relationship with the youthful Jefferson perfectly illustrates how Scottish Enlightenment thinking came to play a major role in the shaping of American culture. But the college at which Small taught, and over which Blair had presided, had other important Scottish links. Born in 1693, Robert Dinwiddie was an Arts student in Glasgow University in 1707. His father was a successful merchant and his brother was twice Glasgow's Lord Provost. Robert himself became one of the many Scots involved in the administration of the British Empire. Having originally served in the West Indies, in the period 1751-58 he became lieutenant-governor of Virginia, effectively being in charge of the running of the colony. Much of his energy was devoted to trying to persuade Virginia and the other colonies to spend money on raising forces to defend the western frontier from French encroachment, but he recognized the importance of the College of William and Mary and did everything in his power to support it, becoming a major benefactor of the college library. The intricate nature of Glasgow's ties with Virginia in the educational field is illustrated even more clearly by the example of the Rosse family. Andrew Rosse was professor of Humanity at Glasgow from 1706-1735. One of his sons, also called Andrew, became a merchant in Virginia. A second son, George, succeeded his father in the chair of Humanity for the period 1735-54. George's younger brother John became one of his students, subsequently emigrating to Maryland as an Episcopalian clergyman. At least seven more of Professor Rosse's students migrated to the Chesapeake Bay area of the colonies, four as merchants, three as Episcopal clergy. A generation later, this Scottish-American link in education was still in place – the Rev John Rosse's son matriculated at Glasgow in

1774. The Rosse family's links with Virginia may well be not at all untypical. Certainly there is clear evidence that Scots graduates, like Small and Rosse's students, regularly found employment in the eighteenth-century South as clergy, schoolteachers, and tutors. Hence no doubt the frequent comment that Virginian students pronounced their Latin with a Scots accent. As another, if somewhat less direct, source of Scottish educational influence on the south, one might point to John Witherspoon's College of New Jersey. Under Witherspoon, perhaps the most influential of all American Scots, the college became attractive both to non-Presbyterians and to students outwith New Jersey – and from the Southern colonies in particular. That most distinguished of all of Witherspoon's pupils, James Madison was an Episcopalian from Virginia. And in time graduates of the College of New Jersey would be prominent in the establishing of new educational institutions in the South – such as Hampden-Sydney College or Washington College.

Culture. Any investigation of the Scottish contribution to the culture of the South in the eighteenth century inevitably take us back to the argument over the Scots and Ulster Scots. If the latter are included then there is a Scottish dimension to almost every aspect of the Southern way of life outside that of the oldest, settled, urban areas. In Grady McWhinney's terms, 'cracker' culture is by definition of Scottish origin. Ulster Scots are excluded, then the general Scottish influence on the eighteenth-century South has much less to do with Scottish immigrants. Virginia, the Carolinas, Georgia, east and west Florida are simply to be seen as receptive to the same Scottish influence as affected the mid-Atlantic and more northern states. As Richard Beale Davis put it in his study of Virginia's intellectual history: the writers of Jeffersonian Virginia were as much influenced as other Americans by the Scottish school of rhetoricians, aestheticians, and common-sense philosophers... By 1800 Blair's *Lectures on Rhetoric*, Lord Kames's *Elements of Criticism*, and Reid's works were widely used in schools and especially in colleges, along with Hartley, Adam Smith and Hume.

Similarly, according to Davis, the literary circles of Richmond, Virginia 'over their bowls of punch discussed *Ossian, The Scottish Chiefs*, the *Edinburgh Review* and the works of Scott'. And what was true of Richmond was almost certainly equally true of Charleston and Savannah. Indeed given the prominence of Scots in its political economic, educational, and social life, the eighteen-century South may well have been exceptionally receptive to the complete range of Scotland's transatlantic cultural exports.

3 *Indian Captive, Indian King, Peter Williamson in America and Britain* by Timothy J. Shannon

This is a remarkable book about an even more remarkable Scotsman. In June 1758, the Aboyne-born Williamson appeared in the streets of Aberdeen, dressed in the full regalia of a native American chief, ready and eager to tell the story of how as a young boy in Aberdeen, he had been kidnapped and sold into slavery in America. In the book he had written describing his experiences – copies of which he had with him to hawk in the streets — he tells of his fate as an indentured servant in Pennsylvania; his becoming a soldier in the Seven Years War; his capture and torture by the Indian allies of the French; and his experience as a French prisoner-of-war. Appalled above all by Williamson's insistence that his kidnapping had been made with the full cognizance of the city's merchants, within days the local magistrates had him arrested and imprisoned. They dismissed his whole story as nothing but lies, and banished him from the city.

The book Williamson had written in the months after his arrival back in the United Kingdom and discharge from the army in 1757, was called *French and Indian Cruelty.* Only a hundred pages long, it was a work of popular literature, a version of the well-established captivity narrative, designed above all to appeal to and entertain a mass audience. The first edition appeared in York in 1757 where Williamson as a strolling player was staging his act as an Indian chief. After his banishment from Aberdeen, a second edition appeared in York in 1758. Subsequent editions were issued in Glasgow (1758), London (1759), Edinburgh (1762), and Dublin (1766). In every case, these editions coincided with Williamson appearing and performing in his Indian costume. But his book long outlived Williamson: versions of it appeared in no fewer than eleven editions in the nineteenth century.

At bottom what Professor Shannon's book consists of is a meticulous analysis of the story *French and Indian Cruelty* purports to tell. His is a rigorously academic book but one written in the very best tradition of academic work which can appeal to the general reader. It is a work of literary detection as exciting and absorbing as any thriller. There is none of the endless theorising which is the bane of so much academic writing today. Instead there is shrewd and careful analysis of all the evidence available to evaluate the central elements of the story Williamson tells: his 'kidnapping', his life in Pennsylvania, his Indian 'captivity', his experience as a soldier in the Seven Years War, and his return to the United Kingdom and banishment from Aberdeen. Remember the city magistrates dismissed Williamson's tale as nothing but a pack of lies. Shannon invites the reader to join him in determining whether they were right or wrong.

How exactly is the modern scholar able to do this? Largely as a result of Peter Williamson's own behaviour. Banished from Aberdeen, he soon settled in Edinburgh. Clearly making a good living from the income from his performances and the sale of his popular book, in 1760 in the city's High Street he opened the significantly named American Coffee Shop, where he no doubt continued to perform and sell more copies. More significantly still in terms of the existence of Shannon's book, in January 1760, Williamson launched a lawsuit against the city magistrates of Aberdeen. In the course of his book, Shannon frequently reminds us that the events he is describing are occurring in the heyday of the Scottish Enlightenment. Yet as he sees it, it is the Scottish Enlightenment seen from the bottom up rather than the top down. He is right to do so. Williamson was the son of a tenant-farmer in Aberdeenshire. He had arrived back in the United Kingdom as a penniless ex-soldier. He had no social status or wealthy supporters. Yet here he is able to raise an action in the Court of Session, Scotland's highest civil court, against the ruling magistrates of one of Scotland's major cities. It is impossible to believe that a person with his background could have been able to do as much even a single generation earlier.

Williamson proved to be a formidable legal adversary. He went about preparing his case by accumulating a large body of testimonies from witnesses concerning his identity and the events surrounding his transportation across the Atlantic in a vessel called the Planter in 1743, Then there are further depositions about his joining the British army and aspects of his service. All this material survives in the court records, and it enables Professor Shannon to build a detailed and convincing account of what actually went on in Williamson's life. He concludes that while it was true that Aberdeen merchants were regularly involved in illegally transporting young people as indentured servants to the American colonies, Williamson exaggerates when he claims he was 'kidnapped' on board the Planter. Then his claim in the early editions of his book that he was only eight years old when dispatched to Pennsylvania is certainly false — all the evidence suggests he would have been thirteen or fourteen. His service in the British army in America, leading up to his capture by the French, is well-documented, and Shannon regards this as the most reliable section of the book. But, crucially, various other elements in Williamson's account of his American experience just do not add up, and are almost certainly pure fiction. Thus most importantly of all, Shannon dismisses the writer's account of his Indian 'captivity' as 'a bald-faced lie' — and the evidence he provides in support of this conclusion is totally convincing.

French and Indian Cruelty turns out to be a mixture of truth and falsehood. Williamson did not hesitate to pretend that he himself had witnessed and suffered the horrific cruelties that native Americans were regularly accused of perpetrating during the Seven Years War: the scalping of the dead and alive, the burning at the stake, and other forms of torture. He clearly knew full well that this was the kind of material that would make his book a best-seller. And he was right. It's worth remembering that here in the middle of the eighteenth century Williamson was helping to establish what for the following two centuries would become the stereotypical image of those who in my childhood we still called 'Red Indians' — the war cries, war dances, tomahawks, scalping knives, moccasins, powwows, wampum, headdresses and so on.

However, the veracity of *French and Indian Cruelty* was not at issue in the case Williamson had raised over his treatment by the Aberdeen magistrates. It finally came before the Court of Session in January, 1762. The presiding judge was none other than Henry Home, Lord Kames, that major contributor to the Scottish Enlightenment. On February 2nd, Kames ruled in Williamson's favour, and ordered the Aberdeen magistrates to pay him £100 in damages and also meet his legal expenses. Encouraged by this success, Williamson soon launched a second lawsuit, this time suing the Aberdeen merchants involved in the voyage of the Planter and seeking £1000 in damages. This case dragged on for several years but in 1768 the Court of Session once again ruled in Williamson's favour, awarding him £200 in damages. Relaxing in what Robert Fergusson in one of his poems calls 'Indian Peter's coffee-room' — and which James Boswell records visiting in December, 1774 — Peter Williamson must have felt very much the Indian king.

4 The Scot who argued with a President

Rupert Murdoch is a force in the land. A media mogul rather than a politician, he still manages to wield enormous political power. Prime ministers and party leaders defer to him. His support for particular policies, parties and politicians is sought – almost at any price. Our coalition government is apparently willing to agree to his complete takeover of TV's BSkyB, thus in the long run adding a televisual arm to the political influence he already exercises through his ownership of *The Times*, *The Sunday Times*, the *Sun*, and *The News of the World*.

Of course Murdoch is far from the first newspaper tycoon to wield political influence. He is simply the current front runner in a tradition that runs from such figures as William Randolph Hearst in the USA to Lord Beaverbrook and Robert Maxwell in the U.K. However, I'd like to suggest that none of these media heavyweights ever matched the achievement in the world of international politics of a nineteenth-century Scottish editor.

That editor was Francis Jeffrey. Born in 1772, Jeffrey attended the famous Edinburgh High School, and went on to study at Glasgow, Edinburgh, and Oxford universities. A law student, he was admitted to the Scottish bar in 1794. However, the event that changed his life occurred a few years later: the founding of the *Edinburgh Review*. The *Review* was the brainchild of Jeffrey and three of his liberal-minded young friends. The first number appeared in October 1802, and, in the words of Henry Cockburn, Jeffrey's first biographer, its 'effect was electrical'. In no time at all, the *Edinburgh Review* became a hugely influential force in Britain's literary and political culture. Whiggish in its politics, the Review set new standards in what a literary journal could be. Right-wing rivals would soon appeared, but through the early decades of the nineteenth century, the Edinburgh's prestige and power were undiminished.

Jeffrey had married in 1801. Devoted to his wife, he was deeply shocked by her unlooked-for death in 1805 and felt he could never find happiness again. However, in 1810, he met Charlotte Wilkes, a young American on a tour of Scotland. Their relationship developed and Jeffrey came to feel that domestic happiness could be his once again. Hence in late August, 1813, Jeffrey sailed from Liverpool to New York with the intention of making Charlotte his wife. However, there was one little local difficulty: Britain and the USA were in the middle of the War of 1812 (sometimes called 'the forgotten war'). Jeffrey, that is, arrived in America as an enemy alien.

That status proved to have no effect upon his reception. The American cultural world had long venerated the *Edinburgh Review*, and so saw in its editor, Francis Jeffrey, what a contemporary commentator called, 'the incarnation of mental vigour, wit, knowledge, and pleasantry, which, under the name of the *Edinburgh Review*, had been their chief intellectual repast for several preceding years'. From 1802 onwards, articles from the *Review* had been reprinted in American journals and magazines, and soon the *Edinburgh* was being reprinted in full in both Boston and New York. Just as in the U.K, the *Edinburgh Review* had become a cultural touchstone in the USA.

In November,1813, Jeffrey, now successfully married, left New York *en route* to Washington. The famous editor was feted everywhere he went. In both Philadelphia and Baltimore he was wined and dined by the local intelligentsia. But it was in Washington itself that his reception was truly amazing. Soon after arriving in America's new capital city, he was introduced to James Monroe, then Secretary of State in President Madison's administration. (Monroe would succeed Madison as America's fifth president.) A long discussion followed about the rights and wrongs of the ongoing war between Britain and the USA. Next day Jeffrey dined in the White House with President Madison and after the meal found himself engaged with the president in a second lengthy dialogue over the War of 1812.

In the pages of the *Edinburgh Review*, Jeffrey had argued powerfully against the policies of the British government that had led to the outbreak of hostilities. He regarded it as a disaster that the only two free nations in the world (most of Europe of course being in thrall to Napoleon) should be fighting each other. The true cause of the war, he argued, was nothing other than deep-seated, disreputable, anti-Americanism on the part of the Brits. But here in Washington, as it were in the hands of the enemy, Jeffrey chose to argue cogently in favour of the British position on such immediate issues as the prevention of American trade with Napoleonic France, and the impressing by the Royal Navy of British seamen serving on American vessels.

But in truth the really astonishing thing is that these long discussions with Monroe and Madison ever took place at all. Jeffrey was not a statesman, an ambassador, or any kind of representative of the British government. He was simply the editor of a literary journal published three thousand miles away in Edinburgh, Scotland. But for several hours he had the ear of the leaders of a nation with which his was at war. Rupert Murdoch: you will never have it so good!

5 Scottish and American Studies

Billy Kay's Radio Scotland series on the history of the Scottish universities reached programme three (out of seven) on September 28th, 2011. Called 'American Enlightenment', it focused on the influence of our universities on college education in America in the eighteenth and nineteenth centuries. A minor contributor, I failed to mention that the Scottish contribution to the American curriculum included our invention of American Studies.

Yes — I'm perfectly serious. Two distinguished Scots wrote books in the late nineteenth century which clearly point forward to the creation in the twentieth century of the new academic discipline eventually called American Studies. John Nichol's *History of American Literature* appeared in 1882; James Bryce's *The American Commonwealth* in 1888. The authors were close friends as students at both Glasgow and Oxford universities. Nichol, the first professor of English literature at Glasgow, was in today's terminology an historicist critic. He believed that American literature should be understood not as a supplementary offshoot of English literature, but as a product of the distinctive national culture of America. Bryce's classic text is an equally pioneering work, focusing on America's constitutional history, but having much to say about the characteristics of American society and culture.

In today's Scotland, however, it is Scottish Studies, not American Studies, that has been hitting the headlines. Alasdair Allan, the awkwardly-titled Scottish Learning Minister — and of course the sponsor of the plan to introduce Scottish Studies into the Scottish schools' curriculum — has just told the Edinburgh parliament that he has found £150,000 to continue the Heritage Education Travel Scheme which makes it possible for school children to visit such heritage sites as the new Burns Museum, Stirling and Edinburgh castles, Bannockburn and New Lanark. Newsnight Scotland has also recently addressed the Scottish Studies topic. However, as the three invited expert participants were all agreed that the plan to introduce Scottish Studies was an excellent one, it was left to the presenter, Gordon Brewer, to suggest there might be an issue to be debated. And as it happens, the final programme in Billy Kay's series will return to the topic as it will include discussion of the role of Scottish Studies in our universities.

Of course we are still waiting to hear how exactly the study of Scottish heritage, history and culture will be introduced to our school curriculum, but in the meantime I'm wondering whether, in the context of our growing recognition of the original links between Scottish and American culture – of which Billy Kay's 'American Enlightenment' is only the latest example – our nascent Scottish Studies programme has anything to learn from the development of American Studies.

American Studies only became an accredited subject in most American universities after the Second World War. At the heart of the new discipline was the study of American history and American literature. These were subjects which themselves had struggled for recognition within the American academy. Why? Essentially because everything American in intellectual and cultural terms had traditionally been seen as only an offshoot from, or a supplement to, the Anglo-European academic mainstream. Hence the pioneering scholars of American history and literature had to demonstrate that the American republic was something entirely new and different – definitively not a replica of the European counties from which its population had come.

This is the origin of the key academic doctrine of American exceptionalism. American exceptionalism argued that the USA is a special case, a country unlike all others. Remember the Pilgrim Fathers believed that what they were building in New England was God's own covenanted country, the biblical 'shining city on a hill'. Even more important for the doctrine of American exceptionalism was the successful outcome of the American Revolution. What the founding fathers of the United States of America had created was indeed a new country, based for the first time in human history on the principles of liberty, democracy and the rights of man. The Old World had been decisively rejected in favour of the New. Such was the view of America, however qualified or corrected, around which the new discipline of American Studies was structured. Hence it is no surprise that in the post-war period the US government was more than willing to support the development of American Studies across the European academic world. American money was available through agencies such as the United States Information Service to fund professorships and lectureships and build up American libraries. (There were American libraries in London, Edinburgh and Liverpool, and as a national serviceman I had access to one in Brunswick, West Germany.) The Fulbright programme made it easy for students and scholars to travel to the US, and for American academics to become visiting professors in Europe. This kind of state-sponsored support for ostensibly purely academic matters reached a scandalous high when it was revealed in 1967 that the English literary magazine *Encounter* was being funded by the CIA.

A decade or two on from 1967, however, everything changed. American Studies underwent dramatic re-definition. Academics began to question the basic notion of American exceptionalism. The emergence of 'theory' was destabilising conventional orthodoxies in every subject including history and literature. American exceptionalism was an obvious target. Exceptional for whom? White, Protestant, middle-class men perhaps. But what about everyone else? Women? African Americans? Non-Anglo-Saxon immigrants? Minorities of whatever kind? With the emergence of a range of new academic subject-areas in American universities and colleges — gender studies, women's studies, African American studies, Chicano studies, Asian American studies, queer studies — the whole idea of American exceptionalism was utterly rejected. So much so that today's scholars of American Studies have effectively argued their own subject out of existence. In the current academy American Studies has transmuted itself into transatlantic or transnational studies, seeing the American experience in relation to, rather than distinct from, other parts of the world. Does this narrative have any relevance to the Scottish Studies about which we will be hearing a great deal more? Judge for yourself — or let's wait and see.

6 Scotland and America Revisited

In Tom Gallagher's recent, wide-ranging account of Scotland's relation with America, there is much with which I agree. On some points of detail, however, he is wrong. John Witherspoon did not found the College of New Jersey (later Princeton University). When he arrived in Princeton from Paisley in 1768 he was in fact the college's sixth president. Among the previous five was the New Englander Jonathan Edwards, America's greatest theologian, but neither Edwards nor any of the others remained in office long enough to get the new college, founded in 1746, firmly up and running. It was Witherspoon who made the difference. In the twenty-six years of his presidency, he transformed a small, struggling institution into a major centre of higher education in America. However, great admirer as I am of Witherspoon and his achievement – indeed I like to think that my own work has helped to win him recognition as among the very greatest of Scots-Americans – I feel that Professor Gallagher overstates his role in the making of the American Constitution and its system of government. Among the most intellectual figures in the Continental Congress, and the only clergyman to sign the Declaration of Independence, Witherspoon certainly played an important role in the political debate. But it is his favourite pupil at the College of New Jersey – James Madison – not Witherspoon himself, who deserves most credit for establishing the federation of the USA. It may well be true that it was through Witherspoon that Madison (who would be America's fourth president in 1811-17) was exposed to the thinking of such Scottish Enlightenment figures as Hutcheson, Hume, and Kames, but if credit is to be given to Witherspoon, as it were at one remove, then Professor Gallagher should have mentioned William Small, professor of natural philosophy at the College of William and Mary in Virginia. A young man, recently graduated from Marischal College, Aberdeen, his head full of the newest ideas in Enlightenment thinking, Small's favourite pupil was Thomas Jefferson. And of course it would be Jefferson who would become the major framer of the Declaration of Independence in 1776.

Then Professor Gallagher rightly draws attention to the level of support for the loyalist side in the American War shown by Scots both in the colonies and back home. Some readers may even recall my writing at some length on this topic in the context of the outburst of anti-Scottish feeling in the US over the release of the so-called Lockerbie bomber. But in fact it was not only in some English towns that support for the North administration's policy towards the colonists could not be found. In the period leading up to the outbreak of the Revolutionary War, neither Edinburgh nor Glasgow were willing to dispatch to London the normal addresses of loyalty in support of royal policy. The west of Scotland in particular was doing so well out of trade with the colonies that it was felt that war should be avoided at all costs. It was only when hostilities had actually begun, that the two Scottish cities became willing to fund the raising of new Highland regiments in the hope that this would help to bring the conflict to a speedy conclusion.

On the issue of more recent Scottish attitudes towards the US there is little in the way of hard evidence, so subjective generalisations are the order of the day. Certainly for those of us of the CND generation – as we demonstrated at Dunoon or elsewhere – anti-Americanism was almost an automatic reflex. But I think back to World War II and wonder about ordinary Scots' attitudes then. That was a time when the Clyde was full of American troopships and freighters. I still remember my father returning from his official inspections of such vessels, his pockets full of cartons of Lucky Strike pressed upon him by generous GIs. Surely versions of this kind of personal lend-lease were happening everywhere? An academic colleague, who grew up in Bathgate, once told me that for the working-class in the west of Scotland, America meant the 'grand ole opry' (which still flourishes in Glasgow) and the Mormon Church. Legacies perhaps of that wartime world?

My own view is that the deep-seated problem in the contemporary Scottish-American relationship is the dominance on both sides of the Atlantic of the Homecoming/Gathering image of Scotland. When I asked my Dartmouth students, who had signed up for a course in modern Scottish fiction, what they knew about Scotland, their answers were sadly predictable. In this post-*Braveheart* world, William Wallace has good name recognition. (I share Tom Gallagher's fears over what 2014 and the Bannockburn celebrations will be like.) And *Trainspotting* continues to reverberate. Otherwise it was only clans, kilts, whisky, haggis, and Burns night. Professor Gallagher writes of the need for serious media programmes about the careers of Witherspoon, Carnegie, and other Scots-Americans. Well I'm familiar with attempts to make such programmes, but funding is hard to come by. The Scottish diaspora in the US has bought into the Scotland of the clan, Highland Games, and the ‘kirkin’ of the tartan. I see no prospect of change until a more educated vision of Scotland becomes available, and that in turn will only happen when Scottish Studies gains at least something of the status of Irish Studies in American college education. Alex Salmond and Jack McConnell in recent years have both delivered speeches at Witherspoon’s Princeton. When will a flagship programme in Scottish Studies be established there? Pressed, the university does not dismiss the idea – but asks who is the donor producing the funding? Perhaps Tom Gallagher should approach Craig Ferguson . . .

Part Three

Scottish History and the Scottish Enlightenment

One of the most striking features of recent Scottish history is the amount of attention being paid to the Scottish Enlightenment of the eighteenth-century. Not so long ago eighteenth-century Scottish history seemed to be about little more than Bonnie Prince Charlie and Flora Macdonald. Now it is more likely to be about Adam Smith and David Hume. How this change in what is defined as Scottish history came about is explored in this section. But the impact of Scottish Enlightenment thinking was felt not only in Scotland itself, but across the western world as a whole — and nowhere more than in the newly-created United States of America. Thus to study Scotland and America inevitably involves recognising just how significant the influence of the Scottish Enlightenment was on many of the principal founding fathers of America.

Today, however, the Enlightenment is once again under attack. In the later seventeenth and eighteenth centuries, the proponents of the new thinking that became the Enlightenment were regularly assailed by committed upholders of traditional religious belief. In the end, however, the enlightened values of rationality, common sense, justice and democracy, prevailed, and helped to shape the future course of human society. In recent times all this has changed. The emergence of identity politics, the neo-liberal economics of the post-Thatcher and Reagan world, and the fashion for 'deconstruction' in various forms within the academy, has led to a Trumpian world in which 'facts' and truth are seen as having no basis in reality and are determined merely by the power of those who define them. Addressing the graduates at the 272nd Commencement ceremony at Princeton University in June this year, President Eisgruber warned his audience that they were 'moving into a world in which civic norms crucial to our shared political life are fraying. Your generation's ability to address the world's problems will depend on, among other things, your capacity to nurture and repair such norms. If ever there was a time when quiet, everyday virtues such as civility, truthfulness, due process, and moderation could be taken for granted, that day is gone'. President Eisgruber is describing precisely the threat to the values of the Enlightenment I have been recognising. He ends by asking the graduating students to live and speak up for those 'civic virtues' which are 'the indispensable foundation for any democratic society'. How right he is.

In this section I am aware that identical points, references and allusions recur in only marginally different contexts. No doubt the repetition accurately reflects my own preoccupations and biases! I am particularly pleased to be able to publish here the paper I gave at an international conference which I dedicated to Judith, my late wife and wonderful scholarly colleague.

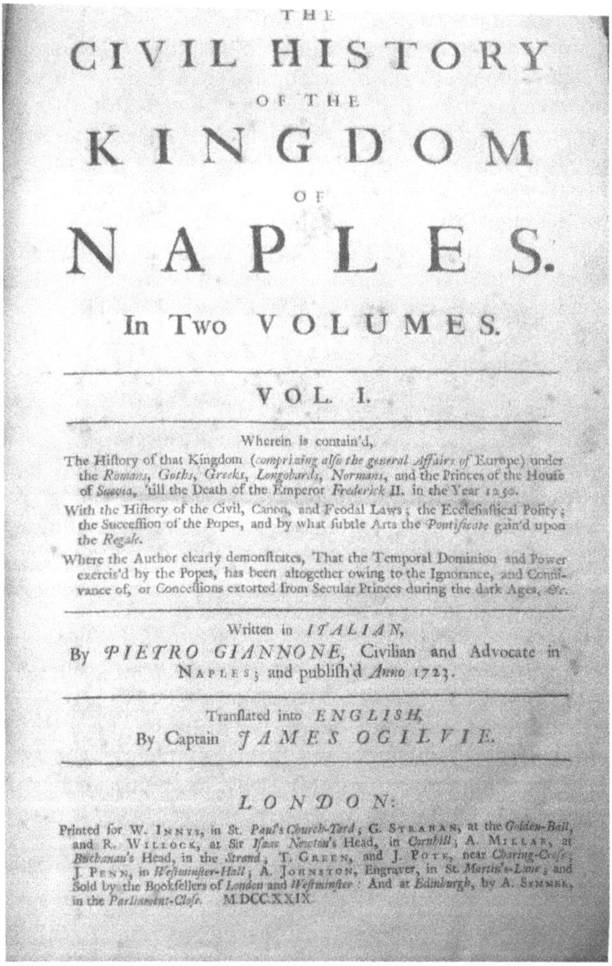
THE

CIVIL HISTORY

OF THE

KINGDOM

OF

NAPLES.

In Two VOLUMES.

VOL. I.

Wherein is contain'd,

The Hiſtory of that Kingdom (*comprizing alſo the general Affairs of* Europe) under the *Romans*, *Goths*, *Greeks*, *Longobards*, *Normans*, and the Princes of the Houſe of *Suevia*, 'till the Death of the Emperor *Frederick* II. in the Year 1250.

With the Hiſtory of the Civil, Canon, and Feodal Laws; the Eccleſiaſtical Polity; the Succeſſion of the Popes, and by what ſubtle Arts the *Pontificate* gain'd upon the *Regale*.

Where the Author clearly demonſtrates, That the Temporal Dominion and Power exercis'd by the Popes, has been altogether owing to the Ignorance, and Connivance of, or Conceſſions extorted from Secular Princes during the dark Ages, *&c.*

Written in *ITALIAN*,

By *PIETRO GIANNONE*, Civilian and Advocate in NAPLES; and publiſh'd *Anno* 1723.

Tranſlated into *ENGLISH*,

By Captain *JAMES OGILVIE*.

LONDON:

Printed for W. INNYS, in St. *Paul's Church-Yard*; G. STRAHAN, at the *Golden-Ball*, and R. WILLOCK, at Sir *Iſaac Newton's* Head, in *Cornhill*; A. MILLAR, at *Buchanan's* Head, in the *Strand*; T. GREEN, and J. POTE, near *Charing-Croſs*; J. PENN, in *Weſtminſter-Hall*; A. JOHNSTON, Engraver, in St. *Martin's-Lane*; and Sold by the Bookſellers of *London* and *Weſtminſter*: And at *Edinburgh*, by A. SYMMER, in the *Parliament-Cloſe*. M.DCC.XXIX.

1 Adam Smith

The original *Edinburgh Review* was published in 1755. Only two issues appeared but its contributors included three major figures of the Scottish Enlightenment: William Robertson, Hugh Blair, and Adam Smith. The preface to the first issue makes the attitude of these Scottish literati to contemporary constitutional arrangements perfectly clear. The Union of 1707 had led to a significant degree of 'improvement' in Scotland. 'What the Revolution [of 1688] had begun, the Union rendered more compleat'. But Scotland has still a lot to learn: 'If countries have their ages with respect to improvement, North-Britain may be considered as in a state of early youth, guided and supported by the more mature strength of her kindred country'.

I quote these passages because they help to explain why the Scottish nationalist movement was for so long reluctant to celebrate the broadly philosophical and intellectual achievements which so transformed Scotland's international standing in the second half of the eighteenth century. Scotland's Golden Age had been seen as owing everything – or at least almost everything – to the Union with England. The Enlightenment was apparently no more than a 'North British' achievement. So not something that Scottish nationalism could afford to get excited about. But that was yesterday. Today is very different. Modern scholarship, much of it deriving from England and America, has in the last few decades been underlining just how major was the achievement of the Scottish literati in the eighteenth century, and how important their contribution to the philosophical and intellectual life of the modern world has actually been. Cultural nationalists have finally come to recognize that there is nothing to lose, and much to gain, by celebrating the Scottish Enlightenment. World-renowned figures such as David Hume and Adam Smith bring immense prestige to their native land.

It is within this context that I want to share with readers some views of Adam Smith that strike me as relevant to our ongoing debate about the constitutional future of Scotland and the United Kingdom. The text in which these views are expressed, however, is not Smith's most famous work *The Wealth of Nations* (1776) but rather his earlier philosophical work, *The Theory of Moral Sentiments* (1759).

In the section of *The Theory of Moral Sentiments* called 'Of the Character of Virtue,' Smith has quite a lot to say about how states are organized and constituted. In his view states are composed of 'different orders and societies, each of which has its own particular powers, privileges, and immunities'. The 'particular distribution' of these rights between the orders and societies determines 'the constitution of that particular state'. I think it is reasonable for us to regard England, Scotland, Wales, and Northern Ireland as making up the 'orders and societies' of the United Kingdom. Smith then argues that although the different orders and societies are ultimately subservient to the state, their members are reluctant to agree to any change or diminution of their 'powers, privileges, and immunities'. And this may be a good thing. Why? 'It checks the spirit of innovation. It tends to preserve whatever is the established balance among the different orders and societies into which the state is divided; and while it sometimes appears to obstruct some alterations of government which may be fashionable and popular at the time, it contributes in reality to the stability and permanency of the whole system.'

Smith moves next to consider the nature of patriotism. It involves, he suggests, two different principles: 'a certain respect and reverence for that constitution or form of government which is actually established', and secondly 'an earnest desire to render the condition of our fellow-citizens as safe, respectable, and happy as we can'. In normal times these two principles 'lead to the same conduct'. 'But in times of public discontent, faction, and disorder, those two different principles may draw different ways...' Then 'even a wise man' may be disposed to think that some change is necessary in the established constitution or form of government. In such circumstances, however, Smith feels it requires 'the highest effort of political wisdom to determine when a real patriot ought to support and endeavour to re-establish the authority of the old system, and when he ought to give way to the more daring, but often dangerous spirit of innovation'.

Smith seems prepared to admit that there are times when constitutional change is necessary. But if so, it has to be led by someone of outstanding, patriotic character. He must be strong enough 'to prevail upon his own friends to act with proper temper and moderation'. Doing so, 'he may re-establish and improve the constitution, and from the very doubtful and ambiguous character of the leader of a party, he may assume the greatest and noblest of all characters, that of the reformer and legislator of a great state; and, by the wisdom of his institutions, secure the internal tranquillity and happiness of his fellow-citizens for many succeeding generations'. Clearly this is for Smith the ideal outcome, but in what follows he appears to cast doubt on the likelihood of such a leader emerging.

'Amidst the turbulence and disorder of faction', it frequently happens that those in favour of constitutional change become fanatical in pursuit of their goal. 'The madness of fanaticism,' says Smith, replaces 'the love of humanity', the 'real fellow-feeling with the inconveniences and distresses to which some of our fellow-citizens may be exposed'. He analyses this development as follows. 'The leaders of the discontented party seldom fail to hold out some plausible plan of reformation which, they pretend, will not only remove the inconveniences and relieve the distresses immediately complained of, but will prevent, in all time coming, any return of the like inconveniences and distresses. They often propose, upon this account, to new-model the constitution, and to alter, in some of its most essential parts, that system of government under which the subjects of a great empire have enjoyed, perhaps, peace, security, and even glory, during the course of several centuries together.'

Smith goes on to argue that the members of the discontented party become 'intoxicated with the imaginary beauty of this ideal system, of which they have no experience...' In response, their leaders pander to them, even becoming 'the dupes of their own sophistry', acting 'as if they were under the common delusion'. The outcome is failure. 'The violence of the party, refusing all palliatives, all temperaments, all reasonable accommodations, by requiring too much frequently obtains nothing; and those inconveniences and distresses which, with a little moderation, might in great measure have been removed and relieved, are left altogether without the hope of a remedy.'

Finally, Smith discriminates between the statesman 'whose public spirit is prompted altogether by humanity and benevolence and who respects the established powers and privileges 'of the great orders and societies, into which the state is divided', and 'the man of system' who 'is apt to be very wise in his own conceit' — too convinced, that is, of 'the supposed beauty of his own plan of government'. A statesman, Smith concedes, may require some 'idea of the perfection of policy and law' to direct his political vision. 'But to insist upon establishing, and establishing all at once, and in spite of all opposition, every thing which that idea may seem to require, must often be the highest degree of arrogance. It is to erect his own judgment into the supreme standard of right and wrong. It is to fancy himself the only wise and worthy man in the commonwealth, and that his fellow-citizens should accommodate themselves to him and not he to them.'

How far Adam Smith's comments are relevant to our current constitutional debate – and if they are, what their implications might be — readers will of course decide for themselves. But surely given Smith's status and international recognition as one of Scotland's most distinguished and admired intellectual luminaries, his opinions deserve to be part of our ongoing constitutional discussion.

2 John Dos Passos, Thomas Jefferson, and the Scottish Enlightenment

His father the son of a Portuguese immigrant, his mother from a well-established Maryland family, John Dos Passos is hardly the twentieth-century American author one would have imagined having an interest in Scotland, not to mention Scotland of the eighteenth century. Meeting the poet Archibald MacLeish in the company of Gerald and Sara Murphy at Antibes in the 1920s, he felt that MacLeish had 'a Scottish charm which was hard to resist'.[1] But that Dos Passos himself might have had a Scottish connection of any kind whatsoever is, one would have thought, highly unlikely. It's true that when he was seven or eight, in 1903 or 4, he had visited Scotland with his charismatic father, the Commodore. In his 'informal memoir' called *The Best Times* (1968), he recalls a childhood image of his father's hands:

> We are fishing for salmon on a Scottish lake. A storm of rain and wind has come up and the boat is half swamped and I'm only a tiny bit scared because his hands look so quiet and powerful as he pulls for the shore. [2]

However, unless one counts a sighting of Rockall, far west of the Hebrides, when he was crossing the Atlantic en route to Copenhagen in 1928, he seems never to have revisited Scotland in person.

Imaginatively, however, the situation was different. Consider this passage from early in *Manhattan Transfer* (1925), arguably the first truly Modernist novel in American literature:

> Ellen in her new dress of Black Watch plaid mummy'd bought at Hearn's walked down the asphalt path kicking her toes in the air. There was a silver thistle brooch on the shoulder of the new dress of Black Watch plaid mummy'd bought at Hearn's. Elaine of Lammermoor was going to be married. The Betrothed. *Wangnaan nainainai*, went the bagpipes going through the rye.
> The man on the bench has a patch over his eye. A watching black patch. A black watching patch. The kidnapper of the Black Watch, among the rustling shrubs kidnappers keep their Black Watch.[3]

What we have here, in a form of stream of consciousness, is a mass of Scottish literary and cultural allusions: Black Watch tartan, a Scottish thistle brooch, the wail of bagpipes. Three major Scottish writers are referred to: the Sir Walter Scott of the

Bride of Lammermoor and *The Betrothed*; the Burns of 'Coming Through the Rye'; and the Robert Louis Stevenson of *Kidnapped* and *Treasure Island*. In *The Best Times*, Dos Passos recalls that the first book his father gave him was Captain Marryat's *Mr Midshipman Easy*, and that Ballantyne's *Coral Island* was another early favourite. A student at Harvard, in 1914 he listed Stevenson among authors he'd been reading, and soon afterwards comments on Henry James's essay on Stevenson in *Notes on Novelists* (1914), describing it as 'excellent' but 'rather unsatisfactory there is not enough red-bloodedness & feeling to the essay to properly express Stevenson'.[4] A year later, he writes enthusiastically about Stevenson to a Yale friend: 'you must read the Inland Journey (he means *An Inland Voyage*) and *The Travels with a Donkey* – They are two of the books one can read forever, and still want to read again!'[5] Much later in *Manhattan Transfer*, the grown-up Ellen refers again to Burns: 'They are walking up the Mall in Central Park. "Looks like he had a boil on his neck," says Ellen in front of the statue of Burns. "Ah," whispers Harry Goldweiser with a fat-throated sigh, "but he was a great poet."'[6] I think it's fair to assume that it is Harry here who is voicing the view of the author. Stranger perhaps is Dos Passos' choice of the less familiar 'Scotland's burning' rather than 'London's burning' in the well-known 'pour on water, pour on water' jingle which floats around Stan Emery's consciousness sa he drunkenly sets the fire that kills him.

Dos Passos was writing Manhattan Transfer in the early 1920s. The evidence is there in the text to show that from this early in his career he was not unfamiliar with major aspects of the Scottish literary tradition. But it would be another thirty years – in the 1950s — before he seriously immersed himself in the culture of eighteenth-century Scotland. Doubleday published his *The Head and Heart of Thomas Jefferson* in 1954. That is the year in which the William and Mary College Quarterly published its issue devoted to the Scottish-American theme which, in my view at least, marked the beginning of a more general, serious study of that subject-area. (It was also the year in which Mossner's *Life of David Hume* was published.) My point is that when Dos Passos began to take a serious interest in the era of the Scottish Enlightenment he was up there with the earliest academic investigators of the period.

Dos Passos of course had established his reputation as an important American novelist long before 1954. In the 1920s and 30s, with such works as Manhattan Transfer and the great USA trilogy, completed in 1936, he was recognized at home and abroad as a major figure alongside such contemporaries as Fitzgerald, Hemingway, and Faulkner. Again in this first half of his career, he was identified, like so many other contemporary artists and intellectuals, as politically a man of the left. Disillusioned by events in the Spanish Civil War, however, he began to move away from that left-leaning position. His second trilogy, *District of Columbia*, completed in 1949, reflected this ideological shift and was not well-received. In any event by then he had begun to write non-fictional narratives, all of them focused on the early years of the American republic. Increasingly hostile to contemporary politics and political ideologies of both left and right, in Europe and America, Dos Passos appears to have become convinced that the best times had actually occurred in the period when the new USA was in the process of being created.

Given such an attitude, Dos Passos's decision to write a book about Jefferson comes as no surprise. He had begun to read seriously in early American history by the end of the 30s and the first fruit of this research was *The Ground We Stand On*, published in 1941. Preparatory work for his study of Jefferson began in the late 40s, but as noted above, the book did not appear until 1954. Of course, like many professional writers, Dos Passos usually had various projects in hand at the same time, so there is no suggestion that work on Jefferson occupied most of his time throughout these years. But it is nonetheless clear that he did recognise the need to undertake serious research – including research on the Scottish Enlightenment – as he prepared to write his book on Jefferson. Why the Scottish Enlightenment? Because inevitably he had read Jefferson's Autobiography and noted the extraordinary tribute he pays there to William Small, his Scottish teacher at the College of William and Mary. In fact on p.85 of *The Head and Heart of Thomas Jefferson* he quotes the whole astonishing passage in full, and goes on to gloss it by providing the reader with the fruits of his research on Small, Marischal College, Aberdeen, Dr John Gregory, the Scottish Enlightenment, and Scotland's intellectual life in the eighteenth century in general. What had he read? Well in September, 1951, in a letter to his friend Edmund Wilson, he described his recent research:

> Recently I've been reading about various Scottish characters in the mid-eighteenth century; largely through Lord Kames' letters and the memoirs of an entertaining clergyman named Alexander Carlyle. Hume and Robertson and Reid and Adam Smith seem to have managed to differ about fundamental matters without bitterness

> and to have entertained each other at various meeting places with hair splitting and claret and sharpened each others wits no end. I always found the Dr Johnson legend rather repulsive, but while that eminent bore was booming at the Thrales, the Scotch seem to have been really using their heads.[7]

There is much that is interesting here. Dos Passos assumes Wilson's familiarity with the Scots literati; he is confident of their intellectual superiority over Dr Johnson; and there is an implied contrast between the sociability of the Enlightenment figures even when they disagreed, and the bitterness of the ideological divisions in the contemporary world.

On the issue of Dos Passos' research, the 'Notes on Reading' section of the Jefferson book is rather less forthcoming on his Scottish sources. 'For the Scottish Enlightenment', he writes, 'the most amusing guide is Alexander Carlyle, a gregarious clergyman who left numerous memoirs'. 'For Dr Small', he continues, 'and the Birmingham circle of which he was for a while the center the best source is Muirhead's two books on James Watt'.[8] However, in the list of thank yous at the very end of the book, he includes 'W. Douglas Simpson, Librarian of the University of Aberdeen, for looking up the record of Dr. Small's degrees'.[9] Of course it is clear that Dos Passos read widely in the existing scholarship on Jefferson and his life, as he was in direct contact with such figures as Julian Boyd, Lyman Butterfield, and Dumas Malone. So no doubt his account of the Scottish Enlightenment was also indebted to secondary sources he chooses not to mention.

Perhaps in concluding the key question to ask is this. How satisfactory and how accurate an account of eighteenth-century Scottish intellectual and cultural history did readers of *The Head and Heart of Thomas Jefferson* in the 1950s actually encounter? Well my view would be a pretty positive one. Writing of Jefferson's Scottish schoolteacher, the Rev William Douglas, Dos Passos speculates that from Douglas the young Jefferson 'must have picked up some inkling of the intellectual energy of Scottish ways of thinking'.[10] Clearly his research had persuaded Dos Passos that Scotland was indeed a land of learning. In all he devotes about seventeen pages of his book to describe William Small and provide an account of the Scottish Enlightenment. Most of the major figures at least get a mention: Hutcheson, Leechman, Hume, Smith, Robertson, Kames, the Gregories, Cullen, Black, Watt, the Ramsays, John Home, James Macpherson, the Adam brothers. The Select Society and the Wise Club are referred to. The tone is set by this style of generalization: 'During the years when Small was getting his education between Dundee and Aberdeen the Scottish intelligence was entering into a great period of energy and brilliance.'[11] And Dos Passos goes on to argue that the sources of this intellectual flowering included Knox's system of public education (which he compares favourably with that of New England), the Union of 1707, and specifically its opening up of the Atlantic trade to Scottish merchants. He argues that this economic development encouraged the growth of a spirit of free enquiry and investigation, particularly within the universities, which supplanted the more dogmatic attitudes of earlier generations. 'For the new generation in Scotland', he writes, 'the professor was taking the place of the clergyman as the venerated figure'.[12] He sees Small as just such a professor and insists that it was through his close friendship with Small that Jefferson was introduced to the world of Enlightenment thinking. 'Young Jefferson', he suggests, 'had application. He had energy and vast curiosity, but it is not in the nature of the human brain to make something out of nothing. Small presented the materials his faculties needed to work on. It took the contagion of intellectual enterprise to start Jefferson's well-equipped mind to working. In his walks and talks with Small he established a connection with the main currents of the adventurous intellect of Europe which was not to be interrupted throughout his whole long life'.[13] Small was a man 'who knew what the first rate men of England and Scotland were thinking'.[14] At the famous dinners in Governor Fauquier's residence, accompanied by Small and George Wythe, Jefferson would have listened to discussion of 'Adam Smith's recently published theory that sympathy, the faculty for feeling other people's ills as pain, was the mainspring of human behavior, or Lord Kames' essays on the morals of the law' – or 'Black's work on heat and gases'. [15]

Thus in the mid-50s, Dos Passos was providing an account of Jefferson's early exposure to the Scottish Enlightenment which suggests he would have been much less surprised by Garry Wills' arguments in *Inventing America*, a generation later, than the great majority of American academics appear to have been. Bearing in mind the idea that Dos Passos was able to anticipate the work of later scholars, let me end on a personal note. At the ECSSS conference in Williamsburg in 2006 I argued that the College of William and Mary's failure to become a major American educational institution in the later eighteenth century was a direct result of its refusal to make William Small its president. In 1954 Dos Passos suggested that Small made his decision to return home to Britain because he was 'tired of the chills and fevers of Williamsburg and of the blank hostility and incomprehension which met his efforts to turn William and Mary into a real university on the Scottish pattern'.[16] Precisely my point in 2006.

1 John Dos Passos, *The Best Times*, London, 1968, p.148
2 Ibid., pp.11-12.
3 John Dos Passos, *Manhattan Transfer*, Boston & New York, 2000, p.54.
4 *The Best Times*, p.14 & Townsend Ludington, *The Fourteenth Chronicle, Letters and Diaries of John Dos Passos*, Boston, 1973, pp. 9, 22.
5 *The Fourteenth Chronicle*, p.24.
6 *Manhattan Transfer*, p.202.
7 *The Fourteenth Chronicle*, p.596.
8 John Dos Passos, *The Head and Heart of Thomas Jefferson*, New York, 1954, p.419.
9 Ibid., p.420.
10 Ibid., pp.25-26.
11 Ibid., p.89.
12 Ibid., p.91.
13 Ibid., p.100.
14 Ibid., p.101.
15 Ibid., p.110.
16 Ibid., p.279.

3 Pietro Giannone's *Civil History of Naples*, Jacobitism, and the Scottish Enlightenment

For Judith Hook (1941-84)

I

Pietro Giannone's *Storia Civile del regno di Napoli* was published in Naples in 1723. *The Civil History of the Kingdom of Naples*, translated into English by Captain James Ogilvie appeared in London in 1729 (Volume One) and 1731 (Volume Two). However, it would be almost another two and a half centuries before Giannone's major historical study, and Ogilvie's translation, made a significant impact on Scottish historiography.

It was in 1967 that Hugh Trevor-Roper, Regius Professor of History at Oxford, acting like a border reiver of old, crossed into Scotland and delivered a lecture which set alight the field of Scottish history. If one of the tasks of distinguished professors, of history or any other subject, is to provoke discussion and debate, then Trevor-Roper's foray into Scottish history was an outstanding success. The occasion was the second International congress on the Enlightenment, and the professor's subject was the Scottish Enlightenment. But before providing his analysis of the Scottish Enlightenment and its origins, he drew attention to his subject's neglect by contemporary Scottish historians in language more likely to ruffle than to soothe Scottish feathers. The problems surrounding our understanding of the Scottish Enlightenment are problems 'from which modern Scottish historians turn impatiently away'. 'They', Professor Trevor-Roper continues, 'prefer to reiterate their atavistic war-cries: to remember Bannockburn, or to debate, for the thousandth time, the admittedly very debatable virtues of Mary Queen of Scots'.[1] Remarks such as these, allied I suspect to his strong emphasis in the body of his paper on the narrow-minded intolerance, and defensive nationalism, of the Presbyterian Church of Scotland for most of the seventeenth century, led many Scottish historians to the hasty conclusion that they had nothing to learn from the Oxford professor. And some at least saw in Professor Trevor-Roper's remarks confirmation of their own dark suspicions: students of the Scottish Enlightenment were somehow by definition wrong-headed, confused, perhaps not really Scottish historians at all.

Some ten years after 1967, a leading Scottish academic historian wrote as follows: 'It is the fashion for some nowadays to adulate

A

LIST of the NAMES

OF THE

SUBSCRIBERS.

N. B. *Those mark'd* [*] *are for Large Paper.*

* THE Most Honourable my Lord Marquis of *Annandale*
* The Right Honourable the Earl of *Airly*
* The Right Honourable the Earl of *Aberdeen*
* The Right Honourable the Earl of *Abington*, 2 Copies.
* The Right Honourable my Lord Viscount of *Arbuthnot*

Alex. Arbuthnot, of *Findowry*, Esq;

* *John Arbuthnot*, M. D.

Mr. *Robert Arbuthnot*, Banker at *Paris*

* Captain *George Arbuthnot*
* Mr. *John Arbuthnot*, of *Paris*, 2 Copies
* Captain *Aslaby*, of the 4th Troop of Guards
* Mr. *Alexander Alexander*, Banker at *Paris*, 3 Copies

Sir *Tho. Ashton*, of *Ashton* in *Cheshire*, Baronet

* Captain *Alexander Abercromby*, of *Glasbaugh*
* Captain *James Abercromby*, of Col. *Montague*'s Regiment
* Captain *James Agnew*

Sir *Robert Abdy*, Baronet

* Sir *John Anstruther*, Baronet

John Aitkine, Esq;

* *Henry Archer*, of *Oakley* Park in *Shropshire*, Esq;

B

* His Grace the Duke of *Beaufort*

Right Honourable the Earl of *Burlington*

* The Right Honourable my Lord Viscount *Bulkly*
* The Right Honourable my Ld. *Binny*

Right Honourable Lord *Balhaven*

* The Honourable *James Bertie*

Sir

eighteenth-century "Enlightenment" with an uncritical devotion that is the very reverse of enlightened, and their folly to proceed on the assumption that rational thought was virtually unknown before 1 January 1700. Indeed, for some devotees of the cult the intellectual tradition of Scotland dates only from 1 May 1707....'.[2] It requires no great act of historical deconstruction to see the significance of the dates mentioned in this passage: scholars of the Scottish Enlightenment, we are asked to believe, are obsessed with the eighteenth century, and exclusively with the history of post-Union Scotland. Such a statement demonstrates perfectly the accuracy of Colin Kidd's recently expressed view of the highly ambivalent place occupied by the Scottish Enlightenment in what he calls the 'patriotic canon' of Scottish history:

> ... being so intimately associated with Union, Anglicisation and the assimilation of Scots to North Britishness, the Scottish Enlightenment sat uneasily in the patriotic canon.[3]

But in the particular instance of Professor Trevor Roper's 1967 paper, the point to remember is that he quite simply makes neither of the assumptions that the so-called devotees of the eighteenth-century Enlightenment are accused of in the passage quoted earlier. He does not argue that the Scottish Enlightenment is to be seen merely as a consequence of the Treaty of Union of 1707, he *does* argue that the origins of Enlightenment in Scotland are to be found in the several decades prior to 1700.

Looking back now, with the hindsight provided by the passage of more than a quarter of a century, I believe that one can see in Professor Trevor-Roper's address to the second International Congress on the Enlightenment a piece of historical scholarship of the very greatest significance, authority, and eventual influence. On the incidental point of the relative neglect of the Scottish Enlightenment by modern Scottish historians, Trevor-Roper was correct. Even today it is doubtful whether the Scottish History shelves in most libraries suggest that the Enlightenment attracts historians as much as those more familiar and obsessively-debated episodes and areas which relate disconcertingly to what Colin Kidd calls 'the debased canon of Scottish history which still dominates the national memory'.[4] Of the topics and events which compose that 'debased canon' none are more prominent than Jacobitism, the '15 and the '45. But, as it happens, the main thrust of Professor Trevor-Roper's 1967 lecture, the story it is concerned to tell, is one which rescues Scottish Jacobitism from Bonnie Prince Charlie and

Butcher Cumberland. The title of the conference, of which this paper is part, is: 'Jacobitism, Scotland and the Enlightenment: Focus on the North'. Such might very well have been the title of Trevor-Roper's paper. Because the core of his argument about the Scottish Enlightenment is very much that the origins of Enlightenment in Scotland are to be found, in the late seventeenth and early eighteenth centuries, in the Jacobite, Episcopalian culture of Scotland, and the north-east of Scotland, in particular. There is no need for me now to rehearse the arguments — they have passed successfully into the mainstream of Scottish Enlightenment studies and debate. Indeed the pioneering work of 1967 is still being developed and expanded; but 1967 itself remains a crucial date in the fuller mapping of the Scottish Enlightenment.

II

As illustrations of the Jacobite, Episcopalian contribution to the Enlightenment of early eighteenth-century Scotland, Professor Trevor-Roper offers first the library of Lord Panmure — it is the library, he says, already, 'of a gentleman of the Enlightenment'[5] — and second, Ogilvie's translation of Giannone's *Civil History of Naples*. Perhaps I should explain that this second illustration has long held a peculiar fascination for me. My late wife, Judith Hook, herself an eminent Italian historian, owned a copy of Ogilvie's two volumes. For years the lengthy list of subscribers to the publication, printed in the prefatory material, has intrigued me. The occasion of this conference, I felt, was an opportunity to look again: particularly since nothing seemed to have been added — except as it turned out by the author himself — to what Professor Trevor-Roper said in 1967. This in itself is distinctly surprising. Surely the existence of Ogilvie's translation raises a number of significant historical questions. Why should a Scot in 1729 have been publishing a translation of a major work by a contemporary Italian historian, an exponent of the 'civil history' destined to become so characteristic of Enlightenment culture? What was the audience for such a work? Did it, like so much of the literature of the period, have any political or ideological significance? And, of course, why did it receive the support of so many Scots, from the counties of the north-east of Scotland in particular? These strike me as questions well worth asking and trying to answer; and indeed the closer one looks at them the more intriguing they become.[6]

The first fact to note in the search for answers is that among his contemporaries in Italy, Pietro Giannone was a highly controversial figure. His *Civil History of Naples*, when it was published in 1723, quickly caused outrage. Why? Because his work by the very nature of the kind of history it represented, spoke for change and reform, for progress and enlightenment. Inevitably then his writing was seen as a threat to the established, traditional, Catholic authorities in Naples. As a historian, that is, Giannone was revolutionary in that he treated ecclesiastical history on the same basis as political history; but as an advocate of reform, he directly attacked those 'feudal' traditions and values in Naples which stood in the way of enlightened change. Quite specifically, as the title page of Volume One of the Ogilvie translation announces, he questioned 'the Temporal Dominion and Power exercised by the Popes'. Thus the Papal authorities in Rome soon joined with their Neapolitan allies in bitter denunciation of Giannone. Soon thereafter the author was excommunicated, and his work, deemed scandalous and seditious, was publicly burnt. Before long, Giannone was forced to flee for his life from Naples, finding refuge for a number of years in Vienna. His subsequent life and career are not my concern here. Let me just say that as the reputed author of a second, still more subversive work — *Il Triregno* — which remained unpublished — Giannone remained a marked man in the eyes of the Papal authorities. Returning to Italy in the 1730s, he was once again threatened and pursued. This time he found refuge in Geneva; eventually, however, he made the mistake of entering Catholic Savoy; there he was betrayed, and the rest of his life was spent in various Italian prisons. Having recanted his alleged heresies he was allowed to study and write; but not of course to publish. In the end, the secular rulers, whose rights ironically he had defended against the temporal power of the church, were unwilling or unable to protect Giannone from the exercise of that same power directed against his own person.

III

What then were the circumstances in which Giannone's revolutionary historical study of Naples became available to British readers in 1729? One thing only is clear about these circumstances — that they were and are obscure. To begin, Captain James Ogilvie, Giannone's translator, remains almost totally unknown. An eighteenth century biography of Giannone suggests that Ogilvie was a British naval officer who had corresponded with Giannone about his translation of the Italian's famous work. Other colourful details are included in this account, but it is unconfirmed by any kind of documentary evidence, and is probably to be discounted.

More reliable — and more suggestive — are the details concerning himself that emerge from the dedicatory and prefatory material that Ogilvie includes in his translation. At the opening of the Dedication, he alludes to 'the Change of my Circumstances' and assigns the 'Date of my Misfortunes' to the 'fatal Year that involved so many in irretrievable Ruin'. The generosity of Lord Grandison had redeemed him from these misfortunes, and thus his first volume is dedicated to him; the second volume was to have been dedicated to Lord Falkland, with whom he tells us he had travelled in Italy, but Falkland having died, Volume Two is dedicated to his son. Significantly, Falkland was a lifelong, committed, active Jacobite; his brother-in-law, Lord Grandison, from an Anglo-Irish background, may well have also been a Jacobite sympathizer. Does this not make it highly probable that the 'fatal year' that 'involved so many in irretrievable ruin', which Ogilvie refers to, was 1715, when the first serious Jacobite rebellion was defeated? If so, then it would appear certain that Ogilvie's own sympathies were with the Jacobite party, and there is supporting evidence for this in the only other literary endeavour that he is known to have undertaken. Captain Ogilvie is named as the translator in 1735 of an historical work in French by an exiled Scottish Roman Catholic priest, Robert Monteth. Monteth's *History of the Troubles of Great Britain*, covering the period, particularly in Scotland, from 1633 to the Restoration of Charles II, and celebrating the Scottish campaigns of Montrose, was a work of straightforward Stuart political propaganda. Ogilvie's association with it hints strongly once again at Jacobite political sympathies.

Ogilvie's translation of Giannone was of course published in London (as well as in Edinburgh), and when one looks at the London context in which Ogilvie appears to have been working, the Jacobite thread in the story reappears. In London Ogilvie seems to have been encouraged and supported in his undertaking by two friends, one English, one Scottish. The Englishman was Richard Rawlinson who appears to be the key figure in making possible and promoting Ogilvie's endeavour. Rawlinson was an antiquary who had travelled widely throughout Europe, including in the early 1720s an extended visit to Italy. Lord Dacre, in his recent paper, describes him as 'in politics a high Tory, in religion a non-juror... in loyalty a Jacobite'. Indeed in Rome he had paid his respects to the Stuart court in exile there. Significantly he was also in Rome at the time when the *Civil History of Naples* was condemned by the Papal authorities, and he subsequently collected material relevant to the Giannone controversy. Again, in 1728, Rawlinson published in England a translation of the Frenchman Nicolas Lenglet de Fresnoy's popular work, *Méthode pour étudier l'histoire*, which contained a brief account of the Giannone affair. Rawlinson adds the comment that 'a proposal has recently been published for a translation by Captain Ogilvie'. This proposal could perhaps have emanated from Ogilvie's second major promoter in London — the Scotsman, Archibald Bower.

Bower, born in Dundee, became a Jesuit and spent the first part of his life teaching Latin and Greek in Italy. However, in 1726 he returned to England, and having declared himself disgusted by the activities of the Inquisition, was received into the Anglican church. In London in 1730 he became the editor of a new, progressive literary periodical, *Historia Literaria*, which aimed to provide reviews of valuable books published throughout Europe. The review lasted for four years, and did provide accounts of quite a number of books by authors of importance in the development of the Enlightenment. But chief among these — and the book given the longest review — was Giannone's *Civil History of Naples*. Indeed the first four issues of *Historia Literaria* were devoted to Giannone's work, which Bower praised as 'the most perfect history of Naples that is extant in any language'. By the time these comments were appearing, the first volume of Ogilvie's translation of Giannone, published by Andrew Millar — inevitably yet another London-based Scot — had already appeared. In other words, Rawlinson, Bower, and Ogilvie seem almost certainly to have worked together to promote Giannone's work in England. What is clear, however, is that Giannone himself had no direct involvement in the matter; neither he nor any of his friends had any knowledge of this, the first translation, of his *History*. When he finally received a copy of Ogilvie's work — he was in Vienna at this time — he was predictably delighted. Delighted that his work was appreciated in a country where science and literature were flourishing; delighted too that the translation had received support from such distinguished sources as are indicated by the lengthy list of Ogilvie subscribers. The contrast between the banning and burning of the book in Italy — not to mention its author forced to live in exile in Vienna — and this truly grand reception in England, could, for Giannone, hardly have been more dramatic.

How, then, had it come about? What could have induced Ogilvie, Rawlinson, and Bower to collaborate as they appear to have done? The one factor that appear to link these men is their participation in the Jacobite culture of early eighteenth century England and Scotland. Was the Giannone translation then some kind of Jacobite venture?

What does the list of subscribers tell us? Who were these people who were willing to pay out good money to support the publication of a controversial, pioneering work of the Italian Enlightenment? The list of subscribers amounts to some 346 names. Of these some 64 are members of the aristocracy: Dukes, Marquesses, Earls, Viscounts, Barons, Baronets. The rest are army officers — no less than 50 of these — merchants, lawyers, academics, — including four from Cambridge — bankers, doctors, and other professionals. Most striking is the Scottish bias in the list. Exact figures are of course impossible to arrive at, but around half of the 346 subscribers appear to be Scottish, the great majority from the north-eastern counties of Scotland. The list, that is, is particularly strong in Arbuthnots, Ogilvies, Grants, Gordons, Gardens, Forbes, Grahams, and Hays. Graduates of King's College and Marischal College, Aberdeen, all also well represented: thirteen or fourteen subscribers are from Marischal, four from King's. Almost all the army officers are Scots, largely from the 7th Hussars, also known as Brigadier-General Ker's Dragoons — the Brigadier-General himself is a subscriber.

The list of subscribers thus emerges as heavily weighted towards gentry, soldiers, and Scots. But description of the list is easier than its interpretation. Given the account provided above of the probable origins and context of Ogilvie's translation, does the list in any way support the view that a Jacobite tendency is indeed involved in the promotion of Giannone's *History* in England and Scotland? Or, to put the question more bluntly, is the subscription list dominated by Jacobite sympathizers? At first glance, an historian might well decide that the list simply reflects a good cross-section of those in early eighteenth-century England and Scotland who might be expected to support a learned endeavour of the kind represented by Ogilvie's translation. The list, that is, mirrors the ideological divisions within English and Scottish culture in this period. Thus Sir Robert Walpole is a subscriber, as are others identified with the Whig oligarchy such as the Earl of Macclesfield and the Archbishops of Canterbury and York. Closer scrutiny of the list, however, begins to suggest a different interpretation. Despite the presence of some Whig grandees, there does seem to be a preponderance of well-known Tories and Jacobites. The extremely heavy representation of gentry from the north-east counties of Scotland, with their undeniable history of support for the Jacobite and Episcopalian causes, is particularly telling. But Lord Dacre also identifies a range of individual subscribers, resolute in their support of the Jacobite cause. These include Colonel Cecil, the Jacobite agent in England;

Alexander Alexander and Robert Arbuthnot, both Jacobite bankers in Paris; John Gordon of Glenbucket who had fought in the '15 and would be 'out' again in the '45; Lord Lansdowne, a Jacobite émigré; Sir John Hinde Cotton, MP for Cambridgeshire and an open Jacobite; Pope's friend Dr John Arbuthnot and his brother; and Sir John St Aubin, MP for Cornwall, a long-term enemy of the Whig establishment. Given the political sympathies of most of the Scottish gentry from the northern counties, the crucial roles of the Stuart adherents Rawlinson and Bower, and the clearly Jacobite sympathies of the Ogilvies in general as well as the probable active Jacobite background of Captain James Ogilvie himself, then the case for the Jacobite tendency seems to be a strong one.

Nonetheless, a degree of scholarly caution may be in order. Presumably it would be a mistake to assume that all of those who agreed to support Ogilvie's translation of Giannone were alert to all the nuances, political or ecclesiastical, of doing so. One suspects that many of the Scottish subscribers may well have responded more in a spirit of local patriotism: here is a reputable form of Scottish cultural activity going on in London which deserves to be supported by other Scots. The eighteenth century was not going to lack later examples of such Scottish solidarity in literary matters. Then there is the interesting case of David Verner. Verner, who appears in the subscribers' list, was a regent at Marischal College in Aberdeen – but Verner owed his appointment to the government commission of 1717 set up to purge the College of all of those who had supported the Jacobite cause in 1715. Hence it is hardly likely that Verner would have subscribed had he recognized any pro-Jacobite implication in so doing. Verner indeed seems to had had an interest in historical studies as part of a progressive and liberal university education: hence it is probably safe to assume that his interest was purely in Giannone as an exemplary modern historian.[7] At the end of the day my own feeling is that Ogilvie's translation of Giannone did originate among a group of Jacobite sympathizers – and that as a result the word did go around in Jacobite circles in Scotland and England that this was an enterprise worth supporting.[8] But on the face of it there were also obvious reasons why good Hanoverian Whigs might well have been interested in Giannone's History – and the subscription list confirms that indeed they were.

IV

By 1729, when Ogilvie's translation of Giannone appeared, the Neapolitan scholar had long been resident in Vienna, driven out of Naples and Italy by the implacable hostility of Church and Pope.

Defending, then, the rights of secular rulers to resist interference from the Catholic church in all matters of state, Giannone might well have gained sympathy and admiration from Protestant administrations in northern Europe. Certainly the Whig parties in England and Scotland, determined above all to resist Catholicism in every form, could readily have recognized in Giannone a victim of typical Papal tyranny and old-fashioned Catholic despotism.

But if there is any kind of truth in this view, why on earth should Jacobites in Scotland and England have had the slightest interest in promoting Giannone's work? The paradox may, however, be more apparent than real. In the first place, Giannone himself always maintained he was a good Catholic. He had no quarrel of any kind with the spiritual role of the Church. His objection was only to the social and political power it had acquired – its interference in matters which were properly those of the state and civil authority, including freedom of thought. Thus British High Tory non-jurors, or Roman Catholic sympathizers, had no reason to discount Giannone on purely religious grounds. On the contrary, many might easily have experienced a sense of fellow-feeling with the Neapolitan author, as victims themselves of another form of Papal injustice. The Jacobite movement in Britain has little reason to thank the Papacy. Many Jacobites believed that their sacred cause had been betrayed by Rome's determination to pursue its own purely temporal aims in a wider European political context. Equally, since the period of the Glorious Revolution, Jacobites, and particularly those in Scotland, had felt themselves the victims of a régime in which state policy was driven by the narrow, sectarian beliefs of an intolerant church. Their inclination then may well not have been to exchange one form of clerical despotism for another; in so far as Giannone's posture could be seen as one of resistance to the 'ultramontane' ambitions of the Papacy, then Scottish Jacobites in particular might well have felt themselves on his side. Finally, one further factor could have played a part. After the Union of 1707, Scottish Jacobitism to some degree tapped into Scottish national feeling. Like Scotland, Naples was an ancient, independent kingdom which had lost its freedom to more powerful neighbours – Spain or Austria. The parallel with post-Union Scotland is suggestive at least, and it might easily have been registered by those Scottish Jacobites who saw themselves as defenders of ancient Scottish rights and liberties.

V

What, finally, of the role of Ogilvie's translation of Giannone in the history of the Scottish Enlightenment? Is it possible, for example, to find in Giannone a model for the kind of historical writing which would bring such distinction to Scottish letters later in the eighteenth century? Do Hume, Robertson, Smith, Ferguson, and the rest owe anything to Giannone's *Civil History of Naples*? Modern historiographers are clear in recognizing in Giannone a crucial figure in the development of the kind of philosophic history that flourished during the Enlightenment. But this point does not seem to have been noted at the time. Certainly Robertson knew Giannone's work and cites it in his summary of Neapolitan history in the first volume of his *History of Charles V*; and we also know that Adam Smith bought *The Civil History of Naples* for Glasgow University Library when he was quaestor between 1758 and 1760: the eighteenth-century library catalogue lists both the original Italian and Ogilvie's translation of the work.[9] But it is only with Edward Gibbon that a British historian emerges who acknowledges a major debt to the work of Giannone.[10]

In this situation, the significance of Ogilvie's translation for the Scottish Enlightenment is simply the fact that it happened. The appearance in 1729 of such a translation has to be an event of some sophistication in Scottish intellectual history, but like all other events it can only be explained in terms of its historical context. And with that point we are back, as Professor Trevor-Roper recognized in 1967, within the world of Scottish Jacobite and Episcopalian culture at the end of the seventeenth and early eighteenth centuries. Readers of *Waverley* will remember that Scott allows the old Jacobite, the Baron of Bradwardine, to stand as representative of a Scottish literary tradition embracing both Latin and the vernacular. In addition to the classics, the Baron reads Blind Harry, Barbour, Lindsay, and Allan Ramsay; but also the Latin poetry of George Buchanan, Arthur Johnstone, and Johnstone's anthology of Scottish Latin poets, the *Deliciae Poetarum Scotorum*. As so often, Scott's sense of history is perfectly accurate. The survival of Scottish Latinity and classical scholarship into the eighteenth century is closely associated with both Jacobite and Episcopalian traditions. Colin Kidd summarizes the inter-connexions, and the link with the north-east, in these terms:

> The flourishing of the classics in Scotland was associated with the Episcopalian civilisation of the northeast. After the Glorious Revolution, Scottish Episcopalianism was virtually synonymous with Jacobitism. In the early seventeenth century, Aberdeen, always more Episcopalian and conservative than the other cities of Scotland, was renowned both for its learning and its Latinity.[11]

This then is the context into which Captain James Ogilvie's translation of Giannone's *Civil History of Naples* fits. Aberdeen, Jacobitism, Episcopalianism, even Latinity, are the relevant terms. The translation represents a late flowering of those political and religious, intellectual and cultural traditions, in the north-east of Scotland, that did much to prepare the ground for the Scottish Enlightenment.

1 Hugh Trevor-Roper, 'The Scottish Enlightenment,' *Studies on Voltaire and the Eighteenth Century*, 58 (1967), p. 1637.
2 William Ferguson, *Scotland's Relations with England: A Survey to 1707*, (Edinburgh, 1977), p. 242
3 Colin Kidd, 'The canon of patriotic landmarks in Scottish history,' Scotlands, 1 (1994), p. 13.
4 Ibid, p.7
5 Trevor-Roper, op.cit. p.1652
6 Lord Dacre himself, at least, has remained interested in such questions. In September, 1993, he contributed a paper entitled 'Pietro Giannone and Great Britain' to an international conference on Anglo-Italian Studies. The paper, to be published in the *Historical Journal*, contains the fruits of his latest research on the Ogilvie translation. In what follows I owe a huge debt of gratitude to Lord Dacre for allowing me to see a pre-publication copy of his paper.
7 For Verner's interest in historical studies, see Paul B Wood, The Aberdeen Enlightenment, (Aberdeen, 1993), p.60.
8 Much the same seems to have been true in 1735 over Ogilvie's translation of Monteth's *History of the Troubles of Great Britain*. This volume too contains a list of subscribers – around 238 in all. The great majority this time are clearly Scots – presumably attracted by the focus on Scottish history. More intriguing is the overlap between the names in this list and those who subscribed for the Giannone translation. Around forty names appear in both lists, and a great many more seem to come from the same families. In other words, the subscribers to Ogilvie's translation of a work of Jacobite history are very much of a kind with those who supported his translation of Giannone.
9 See W. R. Scott, *Adam Smith as Student and Professor*, (Glasgow, 1937)
10 The fullest account of Gibbon and Giannone is contained in John Robertson, 'Gibbon and Giannone,'
11 Colin Kidd, 'The ideological significance of Scottish Jacobite Latinity,' in Jeremy Black and Jeremy Gregory (eds.), *Culture, Politics and Society in Britain, 1660 – 1800*, (Manchester and New York, 1991), p. 115.

4 Scottish History

In the current issue of the University of Edinburgh Journal, Owen Dudley Edwards has been writing at some length about the teaching of Scottish history in the university. Owen notes the irony that while in the eighteenth century William Robertson, principal of the university, had become the greatest of contemporary historians, it took the Faculty of Arts until 1894 to establish a Chair of History. Robertson had launched his career as historian with his immensely successful History of Scotland (1759), but in 1894 the teaching of Scottish history was not what the founders of the new history chair had in mind. Then, and for most of the coming century, an honours degree in history meant a degree in British history which in turn meant a degree in English history. In fact a bequest led to the founding of a Scottish history chair not long afterwards (in 1901 Peter Hume Brown became its first occupant), but Owen's point remains that subsequently Scottish history, even in Edinburgh, remained something of a sideshow, something outside mainstream history.

As it happens, the first generation of scholars in the Scottish universities teaching Scottish literature faced a situation very similar to that confronting their colleagues in Scottish history. English literature was mainstream, while Scottish literature was no more than a tributary. Could a professional career based on academic expertise in Scottish literature alone be assured? The reality was that it could not – which makes it all the more remarkable that a handful of individuals were prepared to continue working in the field of Scottish literature despite the possibility that doing so would not enhance their career prospects.

Where the early generations of scholars in Scottish history and Scottish literature differed, however, was crucially over the definition of their subject and its chronology. Scottish literature had flourished while Scotland was an independent kingdom in the Middle Ages. The Union of 1603, followed by that of 1707, and ever-increasing closeness in Anglo-Scottish relations, inevitably produced changes in Scottish literature – but these were largely positive in terms of new subject matter and new forms of literary production. Scottish history proved to be a very different case.

From an academic point of view, popular Scottish history had always been a problem. A handful of episodes and individuals had come to dominate what most Scots recognized as their history:

Wallace, Bruce and the Wars of Independence in the medieval period, Mary Queen of Scots and John Knox in the sixteenth century, the persecution of the Covenanters and the Massacre of Glencoe in the seventeenth, the Jacobite rebellions and Bonnie Prince Charlie in the eighteenth. In this popular, totemic Scottish history, in the nineteenth century the Highland clearances seemed to be more important than the Industrial Revolution. Rather than rewriting this version of Scottish history, the first generation of academic Scottish historians created a new version of Scottish historiography in which Scottish history ended in 1707.

To be fair, these historians were largely traditionalists in the sense that they were preoccupied with issues involving politics and the exercise of power. Newer forms of history — social, economic, cultural and intellectual — were not their concern. Therefore 1707 did indeed mark the end of history – because in the post-Union situation power was exercised from London alone. Scottish history had disappeared into British history — and British history largely meant English history. So Scottish historians were no longer interested, and had little or nothing to say about Scotland in the eighteenth century and after.

This it is that best explains the issue raised by Roger Emerson in his recent book — *An Enlightened Duke: The Life and Times of Archibald Campbell (1682-1761), Earl of Ilay, 3rd Duke of Argyll* — which received the Saltire Society's award for the 2013 Book of the Year in Scottish history. Emerson tries to explain 'why Argyll has had no biography', and of course the question is certainly one that needs to be asked. Rather than some kind of minor aristocrat who dabbled in politics and took an interest in a range of subjects addressed by the eighteenth-century Enlightenment, Argyll, from the 1720s until his death in 1761, was beyond question the dominant figure in Scottish affairs — and a powerful player in English politics. For almost four decades, that is, Argyll exercised major influence over almost every aspect of the public life of his native country. Supervising day-to-day Scottish politics, but also contributing to the development of Scottish commerce and industry, Scottish agriculture and science, the Scottish universities and Scottish culture, no other figure did so much to define the nature of Enlightenment Scotland. But it has taken until now to write his biography.

In his survey of existing scholarship — such as it is — on Argyll, Emerson does suggest that the provinciality of English historians should not be under-estimated. On the other hand he is equally ready to point out that 'Scottish historians too have paid him little attention'. From my point of view, this is the heart of the matter. Mainstream Scottish historians have always been ambivalent about post-Union Scottish history. It is this, alongside their somewhat old-fashioned notion of the nature of history itself, that best explains their lack of interest in eighteenth-century Scotland.

It is possible to go even further and suggest that for much of the twentieth century, Scottish historians were dismissive of eighteenth-century Scotland. In 1976, for example, the Oxford historian, Hugh Trevor-Roper, wrote of the Scottish Enlightenment that it is 'very unpopular in departments of Scottish history in the universities of Scotland'. Lest this opinion be dismissed as that of a prejudiced Oxbridge outsider, here is the opinion — a year later — of a very Scottish insider. In 1977 Tom Nairn wrote that 'if Scottish nationalists have ever been really united on one thing, it is their execration and denunciation of Enlightenment culture'. Of course not all Scottish historians have necessarily been Scottish nationalists, but on the other hand it is impossible to believe that the strongly nationalist William Ferguson of Edinburgh's Scottish History department was a unique figure. What is beyond question is that most Scottish historians had no interest in the Scottish Enlightenment of the eighteenth century.

The academic study of Scottish history did in the end change. But Scottish History departments were not exactly in he forefront of new developments. Edinburgh's Nicholas Phillipson, a leading figure among the new generation of Enlightenment scholars was, until his retiral, a member of the department of Modern History, not of Scottish History. In fact the new history of eighteenth-century Scotland has been the work of scholars outside Scotland. J.H. Burns at University College London included material on the Scottish Enlightenment in his political theory courses from around 1970. A group of scholars at Sussex University — Donald Winch (who had previously taught at Edinburgh), John Burrow, and Stefan Collini — joint authors of *That Noble Science of Politics* — also engaged in Scottish Enlightenment studies. But ultimately it was from Oxbridge that the major impctus in dcvcloping such studies emerged.

Writing about Trevor-Roper four or five years ago, I recalled the immense furore in the 1960s in Edinburgh University occasioned by the talks by Cambridge's Duncan Forbes (on Hume as historian) and Oxford's Trevor-Roper (on the Scottish Enlightenment). Such interventions in Scottish history by English academics were not exactly warmly welcomed. Nonetheless new approaches to Scottish history did begin to open up. Once described by a Scottish historian in 1987 as a school of anti-nationalist fifth columnists, Nick Phillipson and John Robertson, Colin Kidd and Hugh Ouston, for example, helped to make the Scottish Enlightenment the distinguishing feature of eighteenth-century Scotland in the context of a wider, international world. (Today's Scottish nationalists have performed a necessary u-turn here: a post-Union phenomenon or not, everyone now agrees that the Scottish Enlightenment is something to celebrate. Alex Salmond happily lectures on Adam Smith at Princeton University.) Equally Scotland's pivotal role in the Industrial Revolution, and the extraordinary scale of Scotland's contribution to the administration and defence of the British Empire, have come to be generally recognized.

However our new understanding of the Scottish eighteenth century remains largely the work of scholars from outside Scotland. American historians, for example, continue to play a leading role. In fact the only association of scholars in the field – the Eighteenth Century Scottish Studies Society, now twenty-five years old – was created by a group of American academics, and today Americans still make up the majority of its members. That the author of the first biography of the third Duke of Argyll should turn out be from New England thus should hardly be a surprise. But in the current climate of increasingly fervent cultural nationalism perhaps there are dangers here that need to recognised. Back in 1987, commenting on the furore over Trevor-Roper and the Scottish Enlightenment, Richard Sher, soon to become one of the founding fathers of the ECSSS, wrote: 'The literati of the Scottish Enlightenment are as much a part Scotland's national heritage as Mary Queen of Scots and John Knox, and efforts to discover a sense of national identity which do not take this fact into account are bound to fail'. One hopes that those who look forward to a newly independent Scotland will continue to share this view.

5 The Invention of Scotland

The Invention of Scotland, by Hugh Trevor-Roper, was published by Yale University Press in 2008. It's a posthumous work, its author having died in 2003. If nothing else, the book certainly confirms Trevor-Roper's reputation — especially north of the border — as a hugely controversial English historian. Having served in British intelligence during the Second World War, in 1947 he published the immensely successful *The Last Days of Hitler*, quickly established himself as a leading figure among English academic historians, and went on to enjoy a highly successful career holding plum posts at both Oxford and Cambridge universities. In 1979, near the end of his teaching career, he was elevated to the peerage by Mrs Thatcher as Lord Dacre of Glanton (in Northumberland). Ironically, however, it was Hitler once again that brought him out of the ivory tower of historical scholarship and back into the full glare of popular publicity. In 1983 he was asked by *The Times* newspaper to assess the authenticity of what were claimed to be newly discovered Hitler diaries. The noble historian chose to validate publicly what soon proved to be totally fabricated material. Here in Scotland not a few historians and cultural commentators must have been far from unhappy to witness this humiliating fall from scholarly grace. Why? Well the reason is hinted at by the subtitle of *The Invention of Scotland*: 'Myth and History'.

From his boyhood years in Northumberland, Trevor-Roper was very familiar with Scotland. For a brief period he went to school in Dunbar; he knew the border country – Hadrian's wall, border keeps and castles — very well; as a boy he was an enthusiastic reader of the poems and novels of Sir Walter Scott. In 1959 he and his wife — a daughter of Earl Haig — bought a country-house outside Melrose, and long vacations from Oxford and Cambridge were regularly spent there. Yet Trevor-Roper was quintessentially an English and Oxbridge man. Then his war-time experience had not encouraged him to think well of nationalism in any form. So perhaps it is no surprise that in the 1960s and 70s he was alarmed by the rise in Scotland of cultural and political nationalism, calls for greater Scottish devolution, a parliament in Edinburgh, and all the rest. As a committed unionist, believing that both Scotland and England had benefited greatly from the settlement of 1707, he felt strongly that the threatened separation of the two countries would be a disaster for both. And as an historian, he was ready and willing to come to the defence of the constitutional status quo.

Attack, however, was typically Trevor-Roper's mode of defence. And nowhere was this more true than in the case of the issue of Scotland. In the distinguished professor's opinion the case for Scottish nationalism was based not on any kind of historical reality, but on a series of romantic myths about their past that too many Scots accepted as facts. Thus he planned to publish a book which would demolish these dangerous and distorting myths embedded in traditional Scottish historiography. Material already existing in essay form from the 1960s would be developed and expanded in the 1970s to complete the work of historical deconstruction. However, like many other of Lord Dacre's major historical projects, the book on Scottish history was never completed. Thus *The Invention of Scotland* is not a work seen approvingly through the press by its author. (The text though is almost one hundred percent Trevor-Roper's own.)

So what are the Scottish myths against which the English historian's salvoes are launched? They are three in number: the Political Myth, the Literary Myth, and the Sartorial Myth. The Political Myth focuses on the great humanist scholar and poet George Buchanan whose works in the sixteenth century argued that the Scottish people always had the right to depose and replace their king. The Literary Myth concerns James Macpherson who in the eighteenth century published what he said were translations of the works of Ossian, a major Celtic bard of third century Scotland. The Sartorial Myth centres on tartan and the kilt and their role in defining Scotland's national identity. Writing in an accessible, lively, and even entertaining style, Trevor-Roper takes over two hundred pages to make his deconstructive case. But does *The Invention of Scotland* succeed in its fundamental aim? Does it demonstrate, in the words of the historian's literary executor 'the obstinate readiness of the Scots to prefer fictitious accounts of their past to true ones'? Or does it —as Jeremy J. Cater, the book's editor, suggests — refute 'the attempt by Scottish nationalists to arouse atavistic tribal loyalties in support of their cause through appeal to a fraudulent romantic vision of their country's history'? Well, not quite –at least in my opinion.

In the first place, reading the sections on the second two 'myths' in particular, images of hammers and nuts do begin to rise in one's mind. Trevor-Roper goes to extraordinary, detailed lengths to make his case against Macpherson and tartan. The essays have a driven intensity of flavour that seems disproportionate to the actual subject-matter. But there are more serious problems. The essay on George Buchanan is both learned and persuasive. I'm persuaded that Buchanan's argument that ancient Scottish history proves that it was acceptable for kings to be deposed and replaced does indeed suffer from the fatal weakness that the ancient Scottish history, and even the kings in question, are nothing but fictions. But is that the end of the story? Trevor-Roper makes it abundantly clear that in the sixteenth century Buchanan was recognised across Europe as a humanist and Latin poet of unrivalled status. So surely it was his own personal commitment to the view that monarchs could be overthrown that mattered — not the 'mythic' arguments he used to support his position.

Something similar is wrong with the essay on Macpherson. Trevor-Roper does not choose to recognise the essentially political nature of the debate in England and Scotland over the authenticity of Ossian. In the 1760s the English were in a panic about a North British take-over of the U.K.in political and cultural terms. To denounce Macpherson as a hoaxer was a useful counter-attack. For the vast majority of readers across Europe and America, however, the authenticity issue just didn't matter. To prove that Macpherson was less than honest in no way changes the reality of Ossian's enduring appeal to the new Romantic sensibility everywhere. And as far as the kilt is concerned, the professor's worries about 'invention' and historical false consciousness have been overtaken by recent developments. Tartan today is mainly a fashion statement. The young men who hire out Highland dress for some formal occasion are not making a point about their membership of a clan — or even about their Scottish identity. Hardly surprising given that they may well be from England...

Despite these possible shortcomings in the posthumous *Invention of Scotland*, Hugh Trevor-Roper remains a key figure in contemporary Scottish historiography and cultural debate.

6 Literature and Union

Literature and Union, Scottish Texts, British Contexts (2018) is something of a cat among the pigeons book. In fact there are two cats: its editors (who are also contributors) Colin Kidd, professor of modern history at St Andrews University, and Gerard Carruthers, professor of Scottish literature at Glasgow University. The 'pigeons' are those whom Professor Carruthers, in the closing sentences of the book, calls the Scottish 'literary intelligentsia' – meaning the scholars, critics, and writers who make up the current literary establishment of Scotland.

Kidd and Carruthers have put together this important collection of essays in the belief that the well-established and widely accepted view of the fundamental nature of Scottish literature and its history is a seriously misguided one.

The book is made up of 16 chapters and just who their authors are provides a clue as to what it is that the editors see as the crucial flaw in the current critical understanding of Scottish literature. Strikingly, in a book about Scottish literature, only eight of its 15 contributors are literary scholars – the other seven are historians. Historians have such prominence here because a misunderstanding of Scottish history is the source of the problem that the book sets out to challenge and remedy.

In an opening introductory chapter entitled – not I think particularly helpfully – 'Union and the Ironies of Displacement in Scottish Literature' – Colin Kidd sets out the basic reasons why a reassessment of the role and meaning, or meanings, of the Union of 1707 leads to a challenging of the current orthodoxy over the history and focus of Scottish literature. So I feel there is no better way of clarifying for the reader exactly what this book is about than by quoting at some length from what Professor Kidd says.

'Traditionally', he writes, 'literary historians have assumed that Scottish writers became nationalistic and defensive after the Union of 1707, which induced an 18th-century crisis of identity and the emergence of a vernacular renaissance in Scots championed by Allan Ramsay, Fergusson and, of course, Burns. These assumptions are questionable. Party identities – Whig-Presbyterian and Jacobite-Episcopalian – were, if anything, stronger than national identity, and certainly more ubiquitous in Scottish literature until the 20th century'.

Hence 'in place of the dominant existing mode of literary interpretation that assumes a close relationship between Scottish literature and Scottish nationhood, this project will challenge received ideas about the "national" basis of the Scottish literary tradition'. Rather 'in this volume, we shall look at the way in which union influenced Scottish self-fashioning in the fields of poetry and the novel' and 'contrary to the assumed run of literary analysis – Scottish writers reshaped English culture and identity'.

Professor Kidd is also prepared to offer explanations for the dominance of such mistaken views on the Union in current literary critical discourse. The meaning of nationhood is the heart of the matter. Ever since the appearance of Benedict Anderson's influential book *Imagined Communities,* the notion that nationhood is some kind of given historical reality, fixed and essentialist, has been increasingly questioned. Postmodern theorising is equally hostile to any unqualified endorsement of the concept of nationalism. But Scottish literary scholars have taken little or no account of such developments. Thus their own emphasis on a questionable notion of nationhood, and the salience of the Union, has 'been back-projected willy-nilly onto the past'.

Scottish politics is also involved. Since its origins in the 1920s, the SNP has always enjoyed the support of major Scottish writers. Hugh MacDiarmid, Neil Gunn, and Compton Mackenzie, for example, were early members. Nothing has changed in recent times, and like myself, Colin Kidd was much struck by how far, during the 2014 referendum debate, 'Scottish writers were outspoken in their commitment to a future outside the Union'. And the same was true of Scottish scholars – including many good friends of mine – in the fields of Scottish literature and history. Just how far this phenomenon was due to a commitment to political nationalism or cultural nationalism, or a combination of the two, is hard to say. But it is abundantly clear that a commitment to Scottish independence necessarily means a rejection of the Union of 1707.

MacDiarmid and the rest were outspoken in their condemnation of the Union, seeing it as a lethal threat to traditional Scottish culture. That view prevailed in subsequent years. It was articulated in the clearest of terms in the devolutionist manifesto published by the Campaign for a Scottish Assembly in 1988. Of Scottish culture, it said, 'Since the Union, the strength of that culture has fluctuated but there is no ground for any claim that, overall or even at any particular time, it has benefited from the Union'. Therefore 'the Union has always been, and remains, a threat to the survival of a distinctive culture in Scotland'.

The reference here to 'any particular time' hints that the post-Union cultural achievements of Adam Smith and David Hume might – mistakenly – be seen as worthy of celebration. In recent years the SNP has come round to the view that the 18th-century Scottish Enlightenment is indeed worthy of celebration – but that in no way alters its view of 1707.

What this volume of essays attempts to do is to show that the essentialist-nationalist, negative view of the Union of 1707 can be corrected by a more synthetic, less confrontational, either-or approach. The contributors seem largely to be comfortable with such an approach. To my mind the one exception is the essay entitled 'England's Scotland' by St Andrews University's excellent poet and scholar, Robert Crawford. In his text he argues that three works by Shakespeare, Samuel Johnson, and Virginia Woolf agree in depicting Scotland in a deeply negative light – and he makes much of the fact that major English writers rarely, if ever, choose to locate their stories within a Scottish context – so England's Scotland remains a very dismal place. Perhaps so, but if one chooses to look at accounts of Scotland, particularly after the emergence of the Romantic movement, by writers from a range of nationalities including English, the result would surely be very different.

In any event, the rest of the contributors appear to go along with the view that the post-Union Anglo-Scottish relationship should not be seen reductively as either 'synthetically British' or 'antithetically Scottish'. There are other more nuanced, more complex alternatives. The nature of this more rewarding approach is set out – in somewhat theoretical terms – by David Goldie near the opening of his essay called 'Unspeakable Scots'. Literary culture, he writes, should be seen as 'a dynamic system: not a dialogue between two relatively well-defined subject positions... but a dialectic in which the subject positions themselves are dissolved, reformed, made discontinuous by their encountering of each other and their products; a model that insists that all subject positions and notions of identity are contingent and contextual rather than fixed and essential'.

This notion of hybridity, of the dissolving and reforming of Scottishness and Englishness and Anglo-Scottish identity after 1707, keeps emerging as the basic, conceptual underpinning of this book.

However let me end by making it clear that this is not an academic text weighed down by theoretical gobbledygook. These essays are the outcome of impeccably solid historical research. Over and over again they open up new areas of research – on a strikingly broad range of topics. Major works of the established literary canon are all here – *Humphry Clinker*, *Waverley* and other Scott novels, *The Private Memoirs and Confessions of a Justified Sinner*, the poetry of Ramsay, Fergusson, Burns and James Thomson – the author of 'Rule, Britannia'.

But there is much that is unfamiliar: 18th-century representations of the English John Bull and the Scottish Sister Peg, the statuary of Robert Burns, the plethora of 19th-century magazines published by Scottish churches, the dominance of Scottish editors, journalists and literary agents in 19th-century London, the Scot responsible for establishing the Royal Historical Society, the major literary figures in 19th-century Presbyterian Ulster. And a great deal more.

What such topics perhaps indicate is that – in a book that frequently draws attention to a range of ironies in the post-Union Anglo-Scottish relationship – the essays that make up the main bulk of the book are, ironically, much less controversial than its central argument. However, such concepts as Professor Carruthers' 'Jacobite Unionism' and Professor Kidd's 'banal unionism,' meaning 'a union so well established as to need no defence or justification,' are bound to provoke responses.

Indeed it seems inevitable that there will be defenders of the current orthodoxies in the study of Scottish literature who will be determined to rebut the challenge this book represents. What is not in doubt is that *Literature and Union* is a major work pointing up new directions in Scottish literary studies.

Part Four

Scott and Scottish Romanticism.

My career as a teacher and researcher in university English departments has at least one unusual feature: I have found myself able to lecture and publish on three separate literatures – English, Scottish and American. When I was working on Scotland and America at Princeton, my thesis supervisor assumed that as a graduate of Edinburgh University I would be well-versed in Scottish literature. This in fact was not exactly true. I had some knowledge of Scottish writing. In my medieval English course, some Scottish poets were quite prominent: in particular, the so-called 'Scottish Chaucerians' (and the name itself could not have been more telling) William Dunbar and Robert Henryson. But as for the rest, as was normal at the time, while figures such as Ramsay, Thomson, Boswell, Burns, Scott and Stevenson were mentioned from time to time, there was no actual course in Scottish literature. In other words, in working on my dissertation involving Scottish and American writers in the eighteenth and early nineteenth centuries, I learned a lot quite quickly. My other Scottish credential involved Scott himself. Early in the 1970s I was lucky enough to be invited by Penguin Books to publish an edition of a Scott novel of my choice. At that point Scott's reputation was not exactly flourishing. Of all the Waverley Novels only *The Heart of Midlothian* seemed to be critically admired. I opted instead for Waverley itself which Penguin published in 1972. Reprinted several times, I like to think it did something to encourage new readers of Scott and thus contribute to the gradual recovery of his reputation that has occurred more recently.

My teaching career at Edinburgh, Aberdeen and Glasgow focused mainly on American literature. At all three universities I set up or developed formal courses on American writers. In fact, at Edinburgh my title became 'Lecturer in American Literature' as a result of funding from the American State Department which at that time was promoting a major scheme to facilitate courses in American Studies across European universities. Thus I did in the end write quite extensively on such figures as Fitzgerald, Hemingway, Faulkner and

Dos Passos, as well as on many major nineteenth-century American writers.

Needless to say, despite my Scottish and American interests, English literature remained central to my career. Less so perhaps in terms of research and publication, though I did work on the Bronte sisters and once was urged to publish a book on Charlotte Bronte. With Judith Hook, I did edit for Penguin paperback, Bronte's often neglected but excellent historical novel Shirley (1974). Rightly or wrongly, I suspect that in today's climate it would be almost impossible for a literary scholar to range as widely over different national literatures as I found myself able to do.

In the section that follows the focus is largely on Scott, though often in an international context. I recognise that the writer discussed in the section's final piece has little in the way of a debt to Scott – but few Scottish writers are more 'romantic' than R.B. Cunninghame Graham.

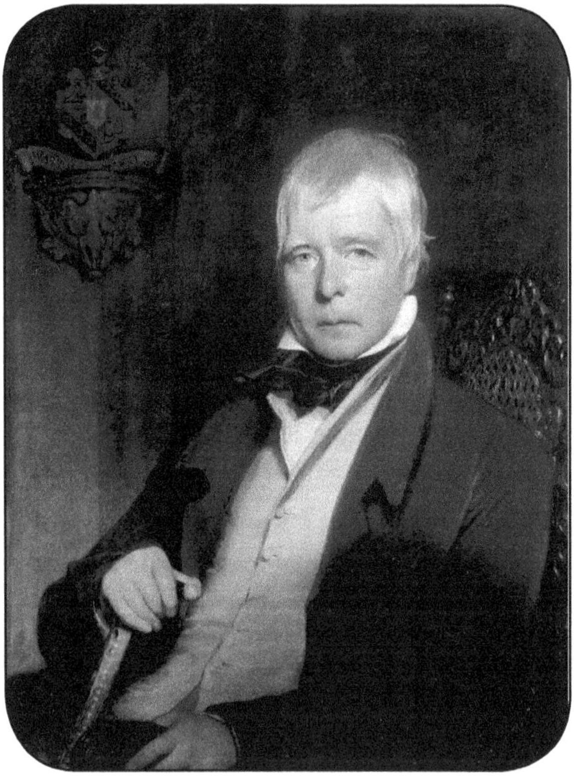

1 The Reputation of Sir Walter Scott

Appalled by one of the names nominated by Scottish Television in its search for the greatest Scot of all time, Kenneth Roy wrote movingly in a recent issue about the four contributors to a similar search, initiated by the Review itself ten years ago, who have subsequently died. Among them was the poet and broadcaster Maurice Lindsay who chose Sir Walter Scott as his nomination for the accolade. Kenneth then quotes Allan Massie's suggestion that 'no one reads Scott any more', tells us that Scott 'is in the nadir of his reputation', and asks 'Does anyone know why?'

Well the answer is that no one does, because the assumption upon which the question itself is based is just plain wrong. Scott's reputation is years and years away from its lowest point. That occurred in the first half of the twentieth century when the author of the Waverley Novels was dismissed as just one of those once-admired eminent Victorians whose work was now seen as dull, boring, conventional, long-winded, and – worst of all — intellectually wanting. But that was then, not now. Scott's reputation has been on a steep upward track for several decades. The great Marxist critic Georg Lukacs wrote admiringly of Scott's key role in the creation of historical fiction in the 1930s, but his work did not become available in English until the 1960s. By then our own luminary David Daiches had ridden successfully to Scott's rescue. Daiches' essay 'Scott's Achievement as a Novelist', originally published in 1951, and widely reprinted, set in motion the radical restoration and re-evaluation of Scott's defining contribution to English and Scottish fiction which is still ongoing. Where literary critics and scholars alike, in the pre-1950 period, felt able to ignore and dismiss Scott unread, such a stance is impossible today. Across the academic world in Europe and America, Scott's crucial role in the history of the novel is once again universally acknowledged. Year on year book-length studies of Scott's achievement continue to appear from university presses; the flow of scholarly articles and conference papers shows no sign abating; the University of Wyoming will host the next major Scott conference in 2010; plans to virtually reinvent Abbotsford, Scott's Borders home, are well-advanced. But most significantly of all, in Edinburgh in early December a reception will be held – Scottish media please note — to celebrate the completion of the magnificent Edinburgh Edition of the Waverley Novels published by Edinburgh

University Press. (Okay, I played a small part in this project but it's still magnificent.) All twenty-eight Scott novels will now be available in an edition produced in accordance with the highest possible standards of contemporary, editorial scholarship. Originating in the 1980s and produced by a team of editors from a range of universities and countries, this edition is a work of exemplary professionalism. It is an achievement that should be recognized as a highlight of Scotland's contemporary cultural landscape.

All very well, I can imagine Kenneth and other readers responding, but what about the common reader? Despite what you say about Scott's rising reputation, does anyone other than scholars (and students) actually read him? Well compared with his vast, world-wide readership in his own day, the answer no doubt is not so very many. But even here there are signs of improvement. My own Penguin English Classics edition of *Waverley* appeared in 1972; it has never been out of print and is currently in its third cover design. Penguin is also now producing paperback versions of ten titles from the Edinburgh Edition, and paperback editions of other Scott novels are available from a range of publishers. Once the Great Unknown (because he published his novels anonymously), perhaps Scott did become the Great Unread. Is that true today? I don't think so.

Anyway Scott's reputation and importance will surely continue to rise in the changing climate of post-devolution Scottish history. Scottish commentators and historians are continuing to think again about the importance of eighteenth-century Scotland in relation to questions of social and political change, national culture, and national identity. In such a context no writer is more relevant than Sir Walter Scott. That is why the Scottish government's programme of excellence in education should include the reintroduction of Scott to Scottish schools. Okay not *Waverley* or *The Heart of Midlothian*, but why not a brilliant short story such as 'The Two Drovers' or 'The Highland Widow'? I bet Maurice Lindsay would agree.

2 Scottish Literary Romanticism and Its American Reception

In 2002 Murray Pittock delivered the British Academy's annual Chatterton lecture choosing as his topic 'Robert Burns and British Poetry'. When Professor Pittock was asked to repeat his lecture at the Royal Society of Edinburgh, I was asked to make a brief comment at the lecture's conclusion. I did so by focusing on a point when Murray, looking for explanations of Burns's current academic neglect, suggested that one reason is 'the overlooked Britishness of Romanticism'. While agreeing with this perception but also exploiting the licence of a mere commentator, I suggested he could have gone further and pointed to 'the overlooked Scottishness of British Romanticism'. Murray has told me that this observation was at least one of the triggers that set in motion the idea of the conference in which we are all now taking part. So let me begin by sketching my general sense of the Scottishness of British Romanticism which I believe the traditional historiography of Romanticism in Britain has more or less overlooked.

The orthodox account of English Romanticism sees the Preface to the *Lyrical Ballads* (1798) as marking the defining moment for the emergence of Romanticism. Wordsworth and Coleridge then become the first generation of the Romantic poets, to be succeeded by the second generation of Byron, Keats, and Shelley. With Blake as a kind of unheralded herald, these are the major poets who define the Romantic period in English literature. Of course in more recent times this conventional view has come under severe revisionist pressure from different perspectives – most tellingly, no doubt, from a feminist perspective with the rehabilitation of a range of Romantic women poets and writers. But despite such changes, the Scottish dimension of Romanticism remains largely unexamined and unexplored.

Yet the case for the Scottish origins of British Romanticism is a strong one. It is Scottish history and geography, Scottish society and manners, Scottish landscape and scenery, and Scottish popular culture of ballad and song, that from early in the eighteenth century begin to reflect, and help to create, the ideologies of the Romanticism that would challenge the hegemony of classical literary values throughout Europe around the opening of the nineteenth century. From the eighteenth century, that is, Scottish writing exhibited characteristics that could appeal to the tastes and sensibilities of a new audience responding to what would be ultimately identified as European Romanticism. The history of Scottish literature in the eighteenth century – particularly in terms of readers' response – makes this point clear. Scottish writers who were successful enough at appealing to audiences in their own time were even more successful at appealing to the audience for the new Romanticism. As the eighteenth century went on, that is, a group of Scottish texts became increasingly popular as the movement towards Romanticism gathered force. The literary critical quality of some of these texts may be disputable but the fact of their popularity is beyond question.

In chronological terms the first important text is Allan Ramsay's pastoral drama *The Gentle Shepherd* (1725). Successful when it was first performed in the 1720s, Ramsay's work was at the height of its fame and popularity in the period 1780-1820. It was then that the majority of its some 120 editions were published and it was then that most of its 160 or so separate productions in Scotland, England, and America occurred. This publication and theatrical history makes it clear that *The Gentle Shepherd* enjoyed its greatest vogue when the new Romanticism was winning popular approval – despite the fact that the work had also appealed when neo-classical literary values still prevailed. In form and content *The Gentle Shepherd* is conventionally classical. A pastoral drama concerning the lives and loves of shepherds and shepherdesses, it is written throughout in rhyming couplets. The shepherd of the play's title is 'gentle' in the sense of being of gentle birth; his beloved turns out to be equally highly born. Their birth explains their superior qualities. The plot of the play hinges on the return from exile of a nobleman, a supporter of Charles II, at the time of the Restoration in 1660. The Scottish peasantry rejoice at the restoration of their old master; good times are returned, old buildings restored, the land re-cultivated . The good life is seen to lie in a recreated past, not a revolutionary future. The politics of the play are Tory, aristocratic, and Jacobite. A similar conservatism pervades the ideas of the piece: the values of reason and common sense take precedence over those of feelings and passion.

How could such a work continue to grow in popularity long after neo-classical values were no longer dominant? The answer is that The Gentle Shepherd included a potentially Romantic strain which a changing sensibility could register and bring to the fore. The play displayed the way of life of a part of rural Scotland which appeared increasingly remote from modern, sophisticated society. It seemed to take seriously the feelings of simple people. Its language had the natural spontaneity of an unpolished vernacular. And perhaps most importantly, the play included versions of about twenty traditional Scots songs. Incorporating this folk material, Ramsay was both catering to, and helping to create, for the unaffected simplicities of traditional Scottish popular culture. Thus *The Gentle Shepherd* simultaneously looks backward to Augustanism and forward to Romanticism. There may be a clue here to the future success of Scottish literary romanticism in general.

3 *Braveheart*, *Rob Roy* and Sir Walter Scott

This year the films *Braveheart* and *Rob Roy* have been introducing large audiences world-wide to the heroes of Scotland's past. But what today's audiences have been enjoying, courtesy of Hollywood, is no more than a reprise of an old song. Around two hundred years ago, both Wallace and Rob Roy were already emerging as popular icons, heroic figures very much to the admiring taste of the public of the day. The taste that Wallace and Rob Roy appealed to was the taste for romanticism, and it is worth remembering that no group of writers in the eighteenth and early nineteenth centuries did more than the Scots to create, diffuse, and cater for the new romantic sensibility. At the opening of the eighteenth century Scotland was a remote region on the northern fringe of Europe distinguished only by its poverty, backwardness, and religious fanaticism. A hundred years later and a miraculous transformation had occurred: Scotland had become a focus of international attention as an archetypal land of romance. It was the work of Scotland's own writers, that is, from Allan Ramsay's *The Gentle Shepherd*, through Home's tragedy *Douglas*, to Macpherson's *Ossian*, Burns's poetry, and, above all, Scott's Waverley Novels, that moved Scotland to the centre of the romantic map of Europe. With her sublime landscapes, her folk culture of ballad and song, and her valorous and zealous people, Scotland early in the nineteenth century became a kind of living embodiment of the ideology of romanticism, for a few decades replacing Italy and Greece as the new 'classic ground' of European culture.

Nowhere was the impact of this Scottish literary romanticism more evident than in the area of Scottish history. Scottish history, that is, was inscribed in Scotland's romantic identity. As a result, a handful of figures and episodes from Scotland's past soon acquired quasi mythic status: Wallace and Bruce and the struggle for Scottish independence; Mary Queen of Scots and her exquisitely tragic fate; the massacre of Glencoe; Bonnie Prince Charlie and the doomed Jacobite risings of 1715 and 1745; Rob Roy, the Scottish Robin Hood of the eighteenth century. Today's *Braveheart* and *Rob Roy* demonstrate just how enduring the appeal of this romantic vision of Scottish history can be. And in this sense nothing has changed since the novels of Scott were being devoured by a readership throughout the Western world on a scale unequalled by any successful writer before or since.

Scott in fact never chose to base a novel on the life and times of Wallace. His characters frequently pay tribute to the greatest of Scottish champions, but there is no Waverley novel about Wallace. (In *Tales of a Grandfather*, the history book Scott wrote for his grandson, there is a vivid anecdotal account of Wallace and Bruce and their campaigns.) But an explanation for the absence of a novel is not hard to find. Scott was very familiar with the work which was more responsible than any other for the heroic mythologizing of William Wallace throughout Europe and America: Jane Porter's novel *The Scottish Chiefs*. A bestseller when it appeared in 1810, a standard read throughout the nineteenth century, and still being reprinted in the first half of this century, *The Scottish Chiefs* and its success may well have encouraged Scott to launch his own career as a novelist a few years later. In any event, *The Scottish Chiefs* purports to describe the life of Wallace and the struggle for Scottish independence that triumphs with Bruce at Bannockburn. But Porter's novel is quite ahistorical. William Wallace emerges here as nothing more than a type of ideal, eighteenth-century gentleman. Scott recognized exactly this. Jane Porter suggests that Scott sent her some kind of commendation when her novel appeared, and he may well have done so. But his true feelings about the book are described by James Hogg. In his *Familiar Anecdotes* of *Walter Scott*, Hogg reports a conversation on the subject of Wallace and *The Scottish Chiefs*. Scott, Hogg tells us, 'had a great veneration for the character of Sir William Wallace' and he 'had often heard him eulogize it.' But when *The Scottish Chiefs* appeared he told Hogg he was much disappointed by it: 'I am grieved about this work of Miss Porter!' said Scott, 'I cannot describe to you how much I am disappointed..'. Her Wallace was far from being his Wallace: 'It is not safe meddling with the hero of a country; and, of all others, I cannot bear to see the character of Wallace frittered away to that of a fine gentleman'.

This mistake at least Mel Gibson's meddling avoids: the Wallace of *Braveheart* is a democratic hero, a man of the people rather than a fine gentleman. But in other crucial respects Gibson's Wallace remains a Wallace in the Jane Porter tradition. The film Wallace may not be a fine gentleman, but he is learned in both Latin and French. Both film and novel Wallaces are compelled into action, not by any commitment to the political freedom of Scotland, but by the murder of their wives. Mel Gibson's Wallace's apparently extraordinary involvement with the French wife of the future Edward II is matched by Jane Porter's Wallace's intrigue with

Edward I's Queen Margaret. Jane Porter seems to link Wallace's fate with the doomed enterprise of the eighteenth-century Jacobites, while the film's tartan army bears a surprising resemblance to the conventional portrayal of Bonnie Prince Charlie's Highland army. In the end both Jane Porter and Mel Gibson settle for epic scenes of battles, sieges, and violent derring-do, rather than troubling their audiences with the finer points of historical accuracy or analysis. Scott would rightly regard both texts as Romances, rather than versions of the *historical romance*, combining historical realism with excitement and adventure, which he himself tried to write.

Rob Roy of course he did write. But Michael Caton-Jones and Alan Sharp's film has nothing at all to do with Scott's novel. What Sharp has done is take over the character, whose legendary status as a kind of heroic freebooter had been enormously boosted by Scott's 1818 novel, and recreated him in significantly more heroic guise. Sharp's excellent script is full of verbal energy and a nice line in bawdy eighteenth-century humour. The contrast between the eighteenth century's aristocratic culture – with its high formality of dress and speech – and an underlying reality of grossness and squalor is beautifully exploited in a variety of ways. Despite this, what a comparison of the two *Rob Roy* texts brings out is the relative simplicity of the essentially romantic attitudes and values that the Hollywood version celebrates. The contrast here between the two texts is quite exact. From the opening episode of the film what is made clear is that the driving force behind Rob Roy's actions is his sense of personal honour. He recovers the cattle stolen by the Highland reivers, and kills their chief, because he has given his word to Montrose that his cattle will be protected. All of his subsequent actions are of a piece with this opening. When he tries to explain to his young son what he is doing, it is a notion of a man's honour that he tries to get across. Offered a way out of his own and his clan's difficulties if he will bear false witness against Argyle, he of course refuses to do so whatever the cost. And the final challenge to a duel – defeat in which would destroy both family and clan – has to be accepted. Scott's Rob Roy is equally in his way an honourable man, but Scott's novel in no way endorses the un-complex code of honour the film is committed to. Scott balances Rob Roy against an alternative hero – Bailie Nichol Jarvie. Jarvie, a Glasgow merchant, is a more modern hero than Rob Roy reflecting in his person all the economic, political and social changes in eighteenth-century Scotland that make Rob Roy appear a figure from the past. Jarvie, unlike the corrupt factor Killearn in the film, is an honest businessman, but one who rejects utterly the old notion of individual honour:

> I maun hear naething about honour — we ken naething here but about credit. Honour is a homicide and a bloodspiller, that gangs about making frays in the street; but Credit is a decent honest man, that sits at hame, and makes the pat play.

For all his expression of such sentiments, Nichol Jarvie is no kind of craven or mean-spirited coward: however canny, he is also brave and ready to act unhesitatingly out of a deep sense of personal loyalty and friendship. These are qualities which he shares with the man who, significantly, turns out to be his cousin: Rob Roy. But as the quoted passage indicates he also understands how the world of high 'honour,' to which Rob Roy belongs, may all too readily descend into uncontrollable violence and lawlessness: a perception that Scottish history hardly contradicts. Recent contributors to *The Herald* have seen in Scott an artist with a wider vision, a more encompassing range of human experience than appears in the work of acclaimed Scottish writers of today. It is just that wider range and complexity, evident here, that Hollywood's recent Scottish romances, for all their entertaining virtues, fail as works of art to achieve.

4 Scott and the Middle Ages

In *Huckleberry Finn* it is no accident that the wrecked steamboat on the Mississippi River that threatens the lives of Huck and Jim is called the 'Walter Scott'. Chapter 46 of the largely autobiographical *Life on the Mississippi* makes it clear that Mark Twain regarded Scott as the very worst of wreckers. Scott, he tells us, 'did measureless harm, more real and lasting harm, perhaps, than any other individual that ever wrote'. How had he done this? Through his 'enchantments' which had set the world 'in love with dreams and phantoms; with decayed and swinish forms of religion; with decayed and degraded systems of government; with the sillinesses and emptinesses, sham grandeurs, sham gauds, and sham chivalries of a brainless and worthless long-vanished society'. According to Twain, 'the genuine and wholesome civilization of the nineteenth century' has been 'confused and commingled with the Walter Scott Middle Age sham civilization'. And nowhere has this been more true than in the American South. In fact Scott has had such a wrecking influence on the South, and 'so large a hand in making Southern character,' that he is 'in great measure' responsible for the Civil War itself.

Unsurprisingly, given such issues as slavery and states' rights, historians have largely disagreed with Twain over the causes of the American Civil War. But a recent article in the *New York Times* suggests that the view that Scott had a malign influence on the American South retains considerable plausibility. Professor Cynthia Wachtell's article – 'The Author of the Civil War' – cites Twain's views, and in a general sense at least, endorses them. As evidence she offers examples of poems by forgotten Southern poets, and other kinds of writing, which, produced during the war, appear to impose an allegedly Scott-inspired, romantic and chivalric gloss upon the actual horrors of the civil conflict. She quotes, for example, a soldier writing 'I have read all of Sir Walter Scott's novels within the last month'. (If true, he could not have done much soldiering in that month....)

Let me make it clear that I agree entirely that Scott's fiction was enormously popular in the American South. But then Scott's novels were enormously popular everywhere – including the American North. Where I do take issue with Twain (and Professor Wachtell) is over their assumption that the Waverley Novels are above all concerned to promote a totally fraudulent account of the Middle Ages. According to Professor Wachtell, Scott presented his readers with 'a highly idealized depiction of the age of chivalry'; held 'a romantic conception of combat'; and, 'over the course of many volumes', 'glamorized the Middle Ages'. In fact he did not. Of the twenty-seven Waverley Novels, only seven have any kind of connection with the Middle Ages. And in only one of these – *Ivanhoe* – can chivalry be seen as taking anything close to centre stage. In the two Scottish novels with a Middle Ages setting – *The Fair Maid of Perth* and *Castle Dangerous* – one looks in vain for glamour of any kind. In the Crusader novels, chivalric values, as represented by Saladin and Richard the First, exist alongside political intrigue, treachery and betrayal.

Yes, *Ivanhoe* does treat of knights and their ladies, of chivalry and knightly codes and values. But does Scott present the reader with a 'highly idealized' picture of the medieval world, or a 'romantic conception' of knightly combat? A reading of the actual text suggests not. Take the famous description, early in the novel, of the jousting tournament at Ashby-de-la-Zouche. (Versions of this event were apparently re-enacted in the South in the nineteenth century.) Scott's account is grippingly entertaining. But it is not a simple-minded celebration of chivalry. Politics and ethnicity involving Normans and Saxons are crucially involved. And even more importantly, Scott is fully aware of the cost being paid for chivalric display. How else does one read the paragraph with which he closes his account of the chivalric deeds of this dramatic day?

> Thus ended the memorable field of Ashby-de-la-Zouche, one of the most gallantly contested tournaments of that age; for although only four knights, including one who was smothered by the heat of his armour, had died upon the field, yet upwards of thirty were desperately wounded, four or five of whom never recovered. Several more were disabled for life; and those who escaped best carried the marks of the conflict to the grave with them. Hence it is always mentioned in the old records, as the Gentle and Free Passage of Arms of Ashby.

Mark Twain himself could hardly have written of chivalry's finest hour with a more telling irony.

5 Home's *Douglas* and Macpherson's *Ossian*

Two hundred and fifty years after *Douglas*'s initial publication, (the play was first performed in December 1756 in Edinburgh's Canongate Theatre), two issues arising from Home's tragedy remain of abiding interest. The first concerns Scottish religious and cultural history, the second, theatrical history inside and outside Scotland from the mid-eighteenth to mid-nineteenth centuries. The first, that is, focuses on the religious controversy that from the beginning surrounded Home and his play, while the second attempts to explain why it is that *Douglas* held its place on the international stage for almost a whole century following its initial production. My paper will be mainly concerned with this second question, but in terms of the history of the Enlightenment in Scotland it is the first that is the more revealing.

The *Douglas* controversy can be readily seen as a significant turning-point in the struggle for power within the Church of Scotland between the Moderates and their Popular Party opponents. From a broader perspective that very struggle can be seen as symbolizing the contest between the proponents of ongoing, progressive Enlightenment values, and those fearful of the undermining of traditional religious habits of mind. Initially the Moderates seem to have been caught off-guard by the strength of the hostility occasioned by the staging of Home's play. On the political front in Edinburgh, Home's friends among the literati seem to have worked to ensure that the new play would have the support of the North British establishment. In London, Garrick may have felt able to turn down *Douglas* for Drury Lane, but Home's trip to the metropolis did gain for him such powerful London-Scottish friends as Sir Gilbert Elliott and the Earl of Bute. Prior to the first Edinburgh staging of *Douglas*, however, no attempt was made to avert potential criticism from within the Church of Scotland. Predictably enough, such criticism emerged from the moment of the first production and soon developed into a storm of religious outrage and fury. Home's critics were offended on two fronts. First, that a Church of Scotland minister should have written a play at all, thus associating himself with all the kinds of immorality traditionally linked to actors and the world of the theatre; and secondly that the play he had written was itself full of fundamentally unchristian attitudes and behaviour: characters swore oaths and prayed on stage, while raging against the gods and their fate, and even committing the sin of suicide. So battle was joined in succeeding months in a series of pamphlets focusing either on the specific case of Home and '*Douglas*', or on the general issue of the morality of stage performances. At first the traditionalists in the Church seemed to be gaining the day. John Home himself took the easy way out of resigning his charge in the parish of Athelstaneford in East Lothian. His friend and supporter Alexander Carlyle, however, was forced to appear before the Presbytery of Dalkeith and try to defend his behaviour as a theatre-goer. Reprimanded by the Presbytery, Carlyle appealed to the Synod of Lothian and Tweeddale where his behaviour was defended by fellow-Moderates including William Robertson. The Synod expressed its displeasure at his conduct but refused to endorse the Presbytery's public condemnation. Furious at this decision, the Presbytery appealed in turn to the General Assembly of the Church of Scotland. However, in May, 1757, that appeal was rejected by a substantial majority. The Assembly went on to debate the general issue of the morality of stage plays and theatrical attendance, but once again it was the Moderates who prevailed. The *Douglas* controversy thus ended with a significant repudiation of Calvinist rejectionism by Scotland's most prominent and powerful public body. And few commentators can resist pointing out that less than a generation later, in 1784, almost all the ministers attending the General Assembly that year flocked to the great actress Mrs. Siddons performing in an Edinburgh theatre.

Before leaving this topic, however, I'd like to draw attention to a minor aspect of the controversy which nonetheless tells us much about the nature of the Scottish Enlightenment: the close friendship between David Hume and Presbyterian clergymen like William Robertson, Alexander Carlyle and John Home. In fact the issue of the relationship between Home and the allegedly atheistical philosopher became a major subtext of the *Douglas* controversy. After all David Hume was planning in 1757 to dedicate his religiously contentious *Four Dissertations* to the 'Author of *Douglas*'. So it is not surprising that this relationship should have been in the sights of John Maclaurin – son of Colin and no friend of the Moderates – in *The Philosopher's Opera*, one of his several satirical contributions to the controversy. In this excerpt Mr Genius (David Hume) engages in dialogue with Satan:

Mr Genius: You have read my books then, Sir?
Satan: Yes, Sir, with great delight.
Mr Genius: Why, then, Sir, you are convinced, I suppose, that there

is God, no devil, no future state; that there is no connection betwixt cause and effect; that suicide is a duty we owe to ourselves; a duty we owe to our neighbour; that the tragedy of *Douglas* is the best play ever was written; and that Shakespeare and Otway were a couple of dunces. This, I think, is the sum and substance of my writings.
Satan: It is, Sir.

David Hume was indeed one of *Douglas*'s greatest admirers and defenders, and Maclaurin is not wide of the mark in suggesting that the philosopher did regard his namesake as a dramatist superior to Shakespeare or any other modem British writer. Was this then the general contemporary view, and does it explain *Douglas*'s amazing theatrical success over the following hundred years?

I think not. Home was the author of six tragedies. Five sank without trace. Only *Douglas* remained a hit. So the Home/ Shakespeare comparison is fanciful at best. How then, despite the famous first night shout of 'whaur's your Wullie Shakespeare noo', does one explain *Douglas*'s success? What was it about the play that allowed it, alone of Home's works, to hold its place in the classic repertory of British theatre for so long? Dramatic scholars and theatrical historians have struggled to answer this question.

Much of *Douglas* is standard eighteenth-century dramatic fare. The play's modem editor, Gerald Parker, makes it clear just how unexceptional much of its language, structure, and even content, is.

> The classical unities of time, place, and action are observed. The long declamatory and expository speeches are written in familiar eighteenth-century language and style. The emphasis throughout falls on the pathos and sentiment that can be wrung from the events depicted. Nothing here is new or original.

Maybe so, but of course the more one emphasizes the play's conventionality, the more difficult it becomes to explain its enduring success.

Written and produced in the neo-classical world of the mid-eighteenth century, why did *Douglas* continue to hold the stage through the high Romanticism of the early nineteenth century?

There can be no argument over the scale of *Douglas*'s success. Published in Edinburgh in 1757, and with two separate editions in Dublin in the same year, *Douglas* is designated a bestseller in Richard Sher's *The Enlightenment and the Book*. Around 75 editions would follow. First published in America in Philadelphia in 1790, another ten editions would appear by 1821. Amédée Pichot would publish a French translation in 1822, and an Italian translation would appear in Genoa in the same year. The play was performed in Philadelphia as early as 1759 and as late as 1825 the *New York Literary Gazette* was referring to it as 'one of the best modem tragedies'. It became a favourite acting vehicle for most leading British actors: Mrs Siddons, Mrs Crawford, John Philip Kemble, Henry West Betty, John Howard Payne, Charles Kean, Edwin Forrest. Both the play's publishing and theatrical history, that is, confirm that this conventional, sentimental eighteenth-century drama enjoyed an enduring success far beyond anything achieved by any of the works of contemporaries such as Thomas Otway or Nicholas Rowe. Once again the question is why?

From the beginning there were those, like David Hume and Hugh Blair, who saw something fresh in Home's play in its successful combining of the classical and the pathetic or sentimental. Subsequently some literary historians have argued that the play succeeded because it had a 'pre-romantic' quality; its medieval setting, its descriptions of wild nature, its brooding melancholy, afford the play a Romantic or Gothic atmosphere that allowed it to appeal to the emerging Romantic sensibility. Gerald Parker, however, rejects this view. He suggests that 'the so-called "gothic" or "romantic" elements found in this play do not appear to be of any greater significance in the history of English drama than those which can be found earlier in Rowe, Ambrose Philips, Edward Young and James Thomson'. Parker then, denying that there is anything in *Douglas* which clearly separates it from the standard theatrical productions of its period, has no explanation for the play's enduring success other than that it provided desirable acting roles for famous performers. In my view what Parker fails to register is the key to *Douglas*'s success; its Scottishness. Its Scottish dimension is what sets *Douglas* apart, and it is the Scottish context of the potentially Romantic elements present in the play that best explains why audiences and readers in the Romantic period responded so enthusiastically to Home's work.

Douglas is set in a somewhat vague medieval past when Scotland is under attack from a Danish host. But there are references to specific Scottish locations and landscapes; the Grampian Mountains, Edinburgh, the Lothians, the Bass Rock, Lorn, the river Teviot. The main characters — Randolph, Young Norval, John of Lorn — belong to a distant but heroic society and age when individual valour and honour are simple but admirable spurs to action. Above all, perhaps, the mood of the play, enhanced by the descriptions of wild and melancholy scenes and landscapes, is one suggestive of the inevitability of loss and suffering in human life. In other words, *Douglas* contains within its conventional framework materials of a kind that readily blend into the immensely popular Ossianic world that James Macpherson would begin to create within three years of the play's original production.

Home and Macpherson were to become close friends. In fact it is no exaggeration to say that without Home there would have been no Ossian. Of course I have in mind here the familiar story of the two men meeting in Moffat in 1760 and of the key role apparently played by Home in persuading Macpherson to begin producing translations of the traditional Gaelic poetry he had described in his conversations with the playwright. Hence emerged the 'Death of Oscar' and the 'Fragments of Ancient Poetry' which electrified Home and his North British friends in Edinburgh including Hugh Blair, Adam Ferguson, Alexander Carlyle, and David Hume. As far as Ossian is concerned the rest is history. But is it possible that Home and *Douglas* was an influence on Macpherson at an earlier date? In question here is Macpherson's 1758 poem 'The Highlander'. Here is Fiona Stafford on key elements in both 'The Highlander' and the earlier poem 'The Hunter':

> "In both The Highlander and The Hunter, Macpherson examines the idea of the prince raised in obscurity, proving his worth through deeds rather than merely inheriting his power. In both, the military interest of Scotland being close to defeat but emerging victoriously is mingled with a romantic tale of love and marriage".

Obviously the parallel here with the story of *Douglas* is far from exact. But the similarities are certainly striking, and all the more so when one recognizes that the external threat o Scotland comes in both works from Scandinavia. Fiona Stafford is interested in finding sources for 'The Highlander' in Gaelic ballad traditions. Is it not possible that Home's *Douglas* was another, readily available source?

Even if the idea that Home's triumph with *Douglas* helped to point Macpherson towards the creation of a specifically Scottish mytho-poetic world in which literary success could be achieved is discounted, the link between Home and Macpherson remains an important one. In 1769 Home clearly believed that the reading-public's taste for Ossian could be exploited to guarantee theatrical success; in that year he wrote *The Fatal Discovery* – which is no more than an expanded and dramatized version of Fragment IX of Macpherson's *Fragments of Ancient Poetry*. *The Fatal Discovery*, however, was at best only a minor success. Scott described the play in 1827 as 'written in the false gallop of Ossianic composition to which we must avow ourselves by no means partial'. My own view is that *The Fatal Discovery* was a partial failure because the public already knew the Ossianic play it wanted to see and read — and that play was *Douglas*. *Douglas*'s popularity coincides exactly with the popularity of Ossian. It has to be borne in mind that Ossian was not an instant success everywhere in the 1760s. It took time — almost a whole generation — for the Ossianic vogue to begin its sweep across the whole Western world. Like the Romantic movement it helped to create, Ossian was at the height of its fame and influence in the early nineteenth century. *Douglas*, I believe, was carried along on that Ossianic wave. The settings, the landscapes, the sentiments, the Scottish historical background, the emphasis on martial heroism and valour, and on the inevitability of human loss and suffering, all blend easily into the seductive world of Ossian. This is the explanation of *Douglas*'s enduring success.

Scott reviewed Henry Mackenzie's *Life and Works of John Home*, published in 1825, in the *Quarterly Review* in 1827. Very long and anecdotal, the piece is not one of Scott's most incisive. However, he does provide corroborative evidence of *Douglas*'s continuing fame late in the 1820s. The 'celebrated tragedy of *Douglas*', he tells us, 'retains the most indisputable possession of the stage'. Home is 'that rarest of all writers in the present age — a successful tragic author'. His 'chef-d'oeuvre, *Douglas*, is known to everyone, and his other dramatic labours are scarcely known at all'. Scott comments that the final outcome of the *Douglas* controversy 'was a considerable increase of liberality on the part of the churchmen', and as we have seen, he mentions the Ossianic background of *The Fatal Discovery*. However, the greater part of his account of Home amounts to a retelling and elaborating of the stories concerning the author's life Mackenzie had included in his edition. At the end of his long essay, Scott acknowledges the limitations of his work in a manner that deflects criticism with professional skill: what Mackenzie has written, he says, amounts to no more than 'old-fashioned Scottish gossip, which, after all, in a literary journal of the present day, sounds as a pibroch might do in the Hanover Square concert-rooms'.

6 "Ossian" MacPherson as image maker

James Macpherson is the black sheep of Scottish literature. Immensely successful in terms of popularity, his work translated into every major European language, a potent influence on the Romantic movement in Western culture, Macpherson has been despised and reviled as few other writers — even Scottish writers — have been. The pattern was set almost from the moment in 1760 when he published what he said were *Fragments* translated from the Gaelic of the ancient Scottish bards of whom Ossian, son of Fingal, was only the most famous. Immediately the battle-lines were drawn. In England and Scotland there were those who accepted Macpherson's work at face value: exciting proof of the existence of an ancient Scottish bardic tradition of grandly heroic and epic stature. Equally, there were those who refused to believe a word of it: Macpherson was a charlatan, an impudent imposter and forger, his Ossianic poems no more than a gigantic literary hoax. Almost inevitably, for the next hundred years or so Ossian in Scotland and England meant above all the continuing argument over the authenticity of Macpherson's work.

To be identified as a supreme literary forger is, one might think, bad enough (even if, largely unhelpful on the authenticity issue, Macpherson was happy to amass a considerable fortune). But the charge brought against Macpherson by all Scottish cultural historians and commentators is still heavier. He is guilty of something worse than personal dishonesty: cultural bad faith. Everything that is corrupt and debilitating, sham and distorting, in the Scottish cultural tradition — everything, that is, that is summed up by the Scottish Tourist's Board brand image of Scotland — may be traced back, it is implied, to James Macpherson and the kind of Scottish literary romanticism he did so much to create and diffuse.

There is truth in the charge. All the most compelling and popular romantic images of Scotland and the Scots do indeed originate in the literary romanticism of eighteenth and early nineteenth century Scotland. But the question that needs to be faced is this. Is Macpherson to be held responsible — any more than Burns and Scott after him — for the path followed by Scottish culture in the years after he had written? A society and a culture take from a work of art what they want to take, find in it what they want to find. James Macpherson may or may not have intended to impose upon Scotland a new, romantic and sentimental identity, but if he succeeded in doing so it was because his work found in Scotland, England, the continent of Europe, and America, a willing and receptive audience. Scottish cultural historians just cannot go on dismissing Macpherson because of the largely irrelevant fraudulence issue. And, ironically, those who wish to link the element of the ersatz in Macpherson's Gaelic epics to the debilitating effect of his influence on Scottish culture, may unwittingly be conniving at the kind of English cultural imperialism which, in other contexts, they are all too eager to deny.

The point is this. Macpherson, Ossian, and the Ossianic controversy, did not emerge in some kind of decontextualized heaven where the issues involved were objectively assessed by disinterested, unprejudiced, pure-minded scholars and critics. Quite the reverse. From the very beginning, Macpherson's *Ossian* was caught up in the bitter factionalism of contemporary English politics. Even more significantly, the Ossianic material appeared at a time when that factionalism was expressing itself in a particularly violent and virulent form in the specific context of Anglo-Scottish political relations.

James Macpherson was born in 1736 in Ruthven, Inverness-shire – where the surviving remnants of the Jacobite army assembled after Culloden. Having attended both King's College and Marischal College in Aberdeen, and probably the University of Edinburgh, he became a schoolteacher and tutor. His literary ambitions were demonstrated by the publication of 'The Highlander', a poem in heroic couplets, in 1758. However, 1759 was the critical year, when he was taking the waters, in Moffat. Probably through Adam Ferguson, a pillar of the Scottish Enlightenment, he was introduced to John Home. Home's tragedy, *Douglas* (1754), had recently demonstrated the immense potential, in terms of audience appeal, of a literary work set in a remote Scottish past, amid wild and melancholy landscapes, with characters of an unpolished but heroic kind.

Macpherson clearly understood the lesson that *Douglas* had to teach. He showed Home what he said were translations of fragments of Gaelic poetry. Home in turn showed the poems to his friends among the Edinburgh literati: William Robertson, Lord Elibank, David Hume, Lord Hailes, and, most important of all, the man destined to be Macpherson's most influential advocate, Hugh Blair, Professor of Rhetoric and Belles-lettres at the University of Edinburgh. As a result, *Fragments of Ancient Poetry* was published in Edinburgh in 1760. The reception of the slim volume in Edinburgh was predictably enthusiastic; but in England the poets Gray and Shenstone, and Horace Walpole, were equally positive. Macpherson now moved quickly to exploit his success. After a tour of the western Highlands and Islands he said that he found an ancient epic poem by Ossian, a third century Celtic bard, on the subject of the deeds of Fingal.

It was now that Macpherson made what was perhaps a fatal mistake. He accepted the patronage of the Earl of Bute and, in December, 1761, allowed *Fingal, An Ancient Epic Poem In Six Books,* to be published in London by the Scottish publisher, William Strahan. The problem was that, by 1761, the Earl of Bute was well on his way to becoming the most hated man in England. For a number of years he had been tutor to the future George III, and it had long been felt that this Scotsman exercised undue influence over the king-to-be. When George succeeded to the throne in 1760, and Bute was appointed First Lord of the Treasury in the new administration, the opposition's worst fears seemed to be confirmed. Bute was now in a position to run the country in the interests of his native land, and, in a torrent of abuse, this he was immediately accused of doing. According to George III's opponents, prime-ministerial power and patronage were everywhere being exercised in favour of Scotland and the Scots; the wealth of England was being plundered by hordes of ravenous Scotsmen; jobs for the boys now meant exclusively jobs for Scottish boys. Worse still, Bute, whose family name was Stuart, was believed to be, like most "Scotchmen", a crypto-Jacobite, and therefore a major threat to the traditional liberties of Protestant Englishmen.

Bute's actual period in power was extremely brief — no more than eleven months — but for at least the following decade it was the unshakeable conviction of all those opposed to the successive governments of George III that he remained the power behind the throne: with all that that implied for Anglo-Scottish political relations. As the 1760s went on, Macpherson's identification with Bute and his successors became ever more complete. In the period 1763-66 he was made secretary to Governor Johnstone of Florida, and on his return to London he quickly emerged as one of the most active and reliable hack-writers and polemicists engaged by the government to answer the opposition's attacks. In the early 1770s he was active in the defence of Lord North's American policies and, as 'Scaevola' and 'Musaeus', even engaged in exchanges with the famous Junius. For his unswerving allegiance to successive administrations he was finally rewarded with a seat in the House of Commons which he held until his death in 1796.

Literature and politics are then interwoven in the pattern of Macpherson's career. The one cannot be understood if the context of the other is ignored. That Macpherson was a Scottish writer meant, in the 1760s, that he was going to be in trouble; that his work should have been praised in Smollett's (another Scot, of course) pro-government *Critical Review* was more than enough to ensure a hostile reply; that he should finally emerge as a faithful adherent of Bute and his successors in government made it inevitable that he should face a massive onslaught from all those determined to oppose in every possible way the policies of the ministers of George III. Fundamentally, this is why, in England and Scotland, 'Ossian' came to mean primarily the 'Ossianic' controversy. For Macpherson's political opponents the authenticity argument was a gift from the gods. How better put down this latest in the line of upstart Scotchmen? How better embarrass his supporters? The strategy worked. In England and Scotland the debate ran and ran.

Move out of the context of Anglo-Scottish political relations and the picture alters dramatically. In France, Italy, Germany, in Europe generally, and in America, 'Ossian' meant, above all, a new, exhilarating and liberating poetic experience. Of course the controversy was perfectly familiar in all these countries; but the point is that no one seemed to care. It was the prose-poems that mattered, not their precise status. I would not wish to imply by this that *Ossian*'s impact in Europe and America was everywhere the same. The ripples produced on the contemporary sensibility by Macpherson's work were initially small; as time passed, however, they grew larger and larger until at last the vogue for Ossian became a great wave sweeping across Europe and America.

The Ossianic vogue is at the heart of the emergence of the new romantic sensibility; Macpherson's work both helps to create, and is sustained by, the new romanticism. Thus *Ossian*'s impact in Germany, a cradle of romanticism, begins to occur several decades before its power is felt in France, a country where romanticism had a harder struggle tto establish itself. The earliest German translations of fragments of Macpherson appeared in 1762; a complete translation was made by Michael Denis in 1768-69. Not all German readers were satisfied that Denis had caught much of the spirit of the original, but his translation was nonetheless immensely influential. From the 1770s Ossian was a potent force in German culture. Most of the major German writers were admirers: Herder, Klopstock, Lessing, Schiller, Novalis, Burger. And Goethe's decision to make the protagonist of his famous novel, *The Sorrows of Young Werther* (1774), an *Ossian* enthusiast – the text of the novel contains lengthy excerpts from Goethe's translations of the Songs *of Selma* – both reflected and helped to increase *Ossian*'s European vogue.

In Italy a translation of Macpherson's work appeared amazingly early: that by Melchior Cesarotti published in Venice in 1763. But that original Cesarotti edition had little impact. It was only in the 1780s and 90s, with the republication of Cesarotti's translation in Bassano, that the Italian vogue for *Ossian* really got underway. It was at its height in the early decades of the nineteenth century when editions of Cesarotti appeared in almost every major Italian city: Venice, Pisa, Florence, Milan, Naples. As a result *Ossian* became a key work in the emergence of Italian romanticism.

Again a complete French translation of *Ossian* appeared relatively early: that of Letourneur in 1776-77. But French enthusiasm for the Ossianic world did not really kindle until the early years of the nineteenth century when romantic writers and theorists, such as Madame de Stael, Lamartine, and Chateaubriand, found in *Ossian* an authentic articulation of the kind of sensibility that fascinated them. *Ossian's* French vogue is best symbolized by the enthusiasm of a single reader: Napoleon himself. Throughout all his military campaigns, the poems of Ossian remained Napoleon's favourite reading. In conversation with Lady Malcolm, wife of the naval commander of St Helena, in 1816, he expressed his continuing admiration for Ossian and asserted that it was his influence that had brought the poems into such vogue throughout Europe:

> It was I – I made them the fashion. I have been accused of having my head filled with Ossian's clouds.

Clearly there is an element of exaggeration here, but Napoleon's enthusiastic patronage of the poems was inevitably important. Paintings commissioned for the imperial apartments at the Quirinal in Rome in 1812 included Ingres's 'The Dream of Ossian', while Malmaison, the Empress Josephine's Parisian house, was also decorated with paintings of Ossianic heroes and heroines. Bernadotte, whom Napoleon made King of Sweden, named his son Oscar – he was later King Oscar I of Sweden – as a gesture of respect towards Napoleon's admiration for the Ossianic hero. In fact Oscar and Malvina became popular Christian names in various European countries, and in the end translations of *Ossian* appeared not only in German, French and Italian, but in Spanish, Dutch, Danish, Russian, Swedish and Polish.

In America the Ossianic vogue got underway in the 1790s. The first American edition dates from 1790; between that date and 1823 another eight editions appeared. Thomas Jefferson had been an enthusiastic reader as early as 1773: he decided that Ossian was the greatest poet who had ever lived, and, like a true son of the Enlightenment, wrote to Edinburgh for a grammar and a dictionary that he might learn the language of the original. But it was another twenty years or so before an American versifier of an extract from *Ossian* could assume that "the source whence I draw, is in every library". 1796 saw the production in Boston and Charleston of a theatrical work based on Macpherson's writings: *Oscar and Malvina: or, the Hall of Fingal.* A *Grand Scottish Heroic Spectacle.*

Such an American spectacular reminds us that the Ossianic fashion was everywhere expressed in a wide range of artistic forms: Ossianic plays and melodramas in Scotland, France, Germany and Italy; settings of songs from *Ossian* by Schubert, Brahms, Weber and a variety of other less famous composers; at least two operas; a great range of paintings on Ossianic subjects in France, Germany, Scotland and other countries. In the early nineteenth century the Ossianic world had become part of the permanent romantic landscape of Europe and America.

The depth and pervasiveness of *Ossian's* impact throughout the western world seem abundantly clear. What exactly was it that all these enthusiastic readers responded to in Macpherson's prose poems? They responded to the vision of a strange, remote, exotic ancient world, peopled by grandly heroic characters who move with a kind of stately dignity across wild and barren landscapes of mountains, crags, rivers, seas, clouds and mists. What particular enterprises these characters are actually engaged in is not always very clear: plot lines are not one of Macpherson's stronger points. But every episode involves battles or epic contests of valour and heroism; victory or defeat are equally worthy of celebration.

Most of all what contemporary readers responded to was the consistent mood or tone of the poems. *Ossian* is pervaded by sentiments of regret and melancholy; it communicates a sense of elegiac sadness at the loss of home and country, loss of fame and reputation, loss of life – at the fading and failing and passing away of all the brightest things in the days of man.

> Why openest thou afresh the spring of my grief, O son of Alpin, inquiring how Oscur fell? My eyes are blind with tears; but memory beams on my heart. How can I relate the mournful death of the head of the people! Prince of the warriours, Oscur my son, shall I see thee no more!

> He fell as the moon in a storm; as the sun from the midst of his course, when clouds rise from the waste of the waves, when the blackness of the storm inwraps the rocks of Ardannider. I, like an ancient oak on Morven, I moulder alone in my place. The blast hath lopped my branches away; and I tremble at the wings of the north. Prince of the warriours, Oscur my son! shall I see thee no more!

This above all is the note of Ossianic gloom and melancholy which seems to have captivated Europe.

Macpherson was a colleague and friend of most of those learned Scots *literati* who were his contemporaries. And in the debate over the authenticity question they generally rallied to his defence. But ironically Macpherson's Scotland was not their Scotland. The new Scotland, the North Britain of enlightened Progress and Improvement had nothing in common with the 'Grand Scottish Heroic Spectacle' that Macpherson was concerned to evoke and make familiar to so many readers everywhere. In the end Ossian represented a challenge to the new, material civilization of Lowland Scotland and to the intellectual and cultural hegemony it had so brilliantly established; Ossian was a kind of Highland counter-attack, an attempt to impose upon Scotland, as her truer and more traditional self, a romantic, Celtic image created out of the wild grandeur of her Highland scenery, and the heroic simplicity of a poetic Highland past.

And it was to this mythopoetic vision of Scotland that romantic Europe was responding at the end of the eighteenth century; early in the nineteenth that vision would be reinforced and expanded by still more powerful literary forces. Perhaps it is true that it would have been better for Scotland, and the future of Scottish culture, had it never happened. The fact is that it did. Our cultural historians should cease trying to wish it away and make a greater effort to understand how it came about. They could do worse than make a start with James Macpherson.

7 Scott and America

Commenting on Scott in 1864, the young Henry James wrote that the popularity which he had enjoyed forty years earlier 'has in no measure subsided'. Today's undergraduate students are hardly likely to regard Scott as a 'popular' writer, much less a hugely important and massively influential one. To get their attention I have often used the tactic of beginning by declaring that Scott is the only author who has been responsible for establishing an industry and starting a war. The industry is obvious enough. When Dr Johnson and Boswell set off on their tour of the western Highlands and the Hebrides in 1773 they were going boldly where almost no one had gone before. But when Scott began publishing his narrative poems and the early Waverley Novels a transformation occurred: his first enthusiastic readers were determined to see first-hand the scenes and settings of his works and very soon the Scottish Tourist Industry, created by Scott, was well and truly launched. Scott's war I shall come to later: it is a war very relevant to the title of my talk, but it is not the first transatlantic war that caught Scott's attention.

Sir James Mackintosh, that life-long friend and admirer of America, remembered how as a schoolboy in the days of the American Revolution he had set up an impromptu House of Commons composed of fellow scholars, and delivered the speeches of Burke and Fox attacking the policies of Lord North's administration. Had Walter Scott been a member of Mackintosh's House of Commons we know of one schoolboy at least who would have risen to the defence of North and his policies. From Scott's *Memoirs* of his early life we learn that as a boy he took a lively interest in the progress of the war in America, and that his sympathies were not in the least engaged by the patriotic struggle of the colonists to free themselves from the control of a Hanoverian king. On the contrary. Scott records that he waited hopefully to hear of Washington's defeat 'as if I had had some deep and personal cause of antipathy to him*. General Washington was not able to oblige the youthful Scott's expectations in this matter, but Scott's revenge, as it were, was nonetheless complete. Where the might of British arms failed, Scott's pen triumphed. The United States established in successful defiance of the British Crown was in turn conquered by Walter Scott. And nowhere in the world was Scott's conquest so complete and enduring.

If there is more than a little amusement in the picture of the youthful Scott waiting hopefully for news of the defeat of the country that was subsequently to idolise him, there is something positively ironic about Scott's initial reception as a writer in America. That Scott was to find in America one of his largest and most enthusiastic audiences has always been recognised; much less well-known is the story of Scott's inauspicious introduction to the American literary scene. A girl called Joanna Graham was a childhood friend in Edinburgh. In 1780 her mother, Isabella Graham, a widow, had set up a private school in the city and among her friends and patrons was Scott's mother. Presumably it was this friendship that led to Joanna Graham and Walter Scott coming to know each other. In any event Joanna left Edinburgh for New York with her mother in 1789. Mrs Graham's decision to return to America, where she had briefly resided previously while her husband was alive, was arrived at partly through the influence of John Witherspoon, that most distinguished of Scottish-Americans, president of the College of New Jersey at Princeton, whom she had met in Edinburgh in 1784. In New York Mrs Graham opened a school for young ladies which was one of the earliest of such establishments to be set up in America. In due course Joanna Graham married another exiled Scot in New York and became Mrs Divie Bethune, her husband being a successful merchant and philanthropist. Whether or not Scott maintained any kind of contact with the Graham family after their removal to NewYork I am unable to say; the chances are no doubt that he did not. But he does not seem to have forgotten Joanna completely.

When Scott's first major poetic work – *The Lay of the Last Minstrel* – appeared in 1805, among those who received a presentation copy of the poem was Mrs Divie Bethune of New York. Through this happy circumstance a number of the New York literati were enabled to read the poem at a time when its author's reputation was yet to be made. As was of course the normal procedure with any new work that had been deemed worthy of publication in Britain, the question was raised whether the poem merited republication in New York. After due deliberation the coterie of critics decided that the answer was no. The poem, they decided, was 'too local in its nature' to have universal appeal. One can fairly assume that this opinion was one that this particular group of Knickerbocker literary *savants* would subsequently have dearly liked to forget. As it was, not all American publishers were impressed by their decision; David Longworth printed the first, introductory section of the poem in the *Belles-Lettres Repository* of 1805; the whole poem appeared in Philadelphia later in the same year; New York fell into line in the following year, and 1806 also saw publication of the poem at Charleston, South Carolina; publication followed at Philadelphia again in 1807 and 1810; at Boston in 1807 and 1810; at New York in 1811; at Baltimore in 1811 and 1812; and at Savannah, Georgia, in 1811. The pattern established here with the *Lay of the Last Minstrel* was of course repeated with each of the narrative poems that followed it: extensive and repeated American republication followed hard on the heels of the appearance of a new Scott poem in Britain. And collected editions of Scott's poems were soon making their appearance in America. Hence three years before the publication of *Waverley*, Scott's popularity in America was already so great that a writer in the *American Review* could remark that,

> No poetical works, not excepting even those of Cowper and Burns, have been more widely circulated or read with more avidity in this country, than those of Walter Scott, who is now as a poet, on the highest pinnacle of fame and popularity. The 'Lay of the Last Minstrel' belongs to every private library, and is familiar to the memory of almost every man among us, who has the most inconsiderable pretensions to literature.

The writer goes on to state that five thousand copies of the *Lay of the Last Minstrel* had been sold, and already, only a year after its initial publication, four thousand copies of *The Lady of the Lake*. Even if these figures do not strike us as particularly impressive – they do make it clear that Scott's narrative poems, however local their nature, did enjoy a substantial vogue in America.

The Lay of the Last Minstrel itself in fact won immediate and widespread critical approval on its appearance in America. It was first praised in the *Literary Magazine*, a periodical then edited by the novelist Charles Brockden Brown. In 1805 a contributor to the magazine wrote of the *Lay:* 'there has just fallen into my hands a poem, which has given me so much pleasure that I cannot forbear calling the attention of your readers to it'. It is 'a very beautiful and entertaining poem, in a style which may be justly deemed original, and which affords evidence of the genius of the author'. In fact these sentiments are not all entirely what they seem: the second part of the quotation is evidence of a direct crib from the *Edinburgh Review*'s notice of the poem which had appeared shortly before. The *Port Folio*, probably the most respected of the

American literary periodicals at the opening of the nineteenth century, proceeded more straightforwardly: it simply reprinted in its columns a large part of the *Edinburgh*'s article. As early as 1807, then, the *Port Folio* was able to refer to Scott's 'honourable name' as 'now perfectly familiar to every lover of poetical description'. And finally, in the following year, 1808, in the course of a laudatory notice of *Marmion*, Scott is recognised in the *Port Folio* as the newest in a long line of distinguished Scottish poets:

> Scotland has long been eminently distinguished for the splendour of her poetical reputation. Drummond of Hawthornden, Hamilton of Balfour [Bangour], Thomson, Beattie and Burns have glorified their country by the most brilliant colours of imagination. To these *time honoured* names we may now add that of Walter Scott, who in every respect is most certainly their compeer.

Substantial and widespread as it clearly was, Scott's vogue as a highly-praised poet, in America as elsewhere, was soon eclipsed in its scale by the amazing response to Scott the novelist. Exact figures for the numbers of copies of the Waverley Novels produced in America are of course impossible to arrive at. In 1823, in a speech entitled *Discourse concerning the Influence of America on the Mind,* C. J. Ingersoll asserted that 'nearly 200,000 copies of the Waverley novels, comprising 500,000 volumes, have issued from the American press in the last nine years. Two years later, in 1825, John Neal, the Baltimore novelist and critic, subsequently author of a series of articles on American literature in *Blackwood's Magazine*, wrote that 'half a million of the great Scotch novels, we dare say, have re-issued from the American press. They are read by everybody – everywhere – all over the states'. During his travels in North America between 1828 and 1831 James Stuart, grandson of the philosopher Dugald Stewart, noted that copies of Scott's works were to be found 'even more frequently than Mr Cooper's novels, wherever we go in this country'.

The immense popularity of the Waverley Novels with the American reading-public was echoed by a chorus of critical praise. Dissenting voices were few and far between. For a brief period the *Port Folio* went through an anti-Scott phase, arguing that *Waverley* was too poor a work to be attributed to Scott. But within a few years it fell into line with the rest of the American periodicals, expressing a boundless enthusiasm for each successive new work by Scott. Everywhere the pattern of review was the same: a few introductory pages, mostly of praise, then many pages of extracts from the work in question. Phrases such as 'the wealth of his imagination', 'the reach and majesty of his power' are typical of the American critical reaction to Scott: he 'stands upon an eminence, to which approaches have been made, but no one has placed himself by his side'. If anyone at all shared Scott's lofty eminence, it could only be Shakespeare: 'the novels of Scott, have become in fact, a literature of themselves', announced the *Southern Review*, 'and we know not if his writings were expunged, what deeper injury could be inflicted on English literature, except sentence of oblivion were passed on Shakespeare himself'.

This enthusiasm for Scott in America inevitably had many ramifications. The American public apparently had an inexhaustible appetite for anything connected with the author of the Waverley Novels. A favourite area of investigation and explanation was the background material which Scott had drawn on for individual novels. Articles about the 'Originals' of characters and settings appearing in the novels clearly had a wide appeal. In 1818 the editor of the *Analectic Magazine*, introducing an article called the 'Original of the Black Dwarf', commented on this enthusiasm for everything connected with the Waverley Novels:

> The public feeling is alive to all that issues from the prolific genius of the author of Rob Roy, etc. and connects with whatever is illustrative of his works, the eagerness of curiosity and the attention of interest.

Americans displayed 'the eagerness of curiosity and the attention of interest' in relation to another aspect of Scott: the cloak of anonymity under which *Waverley* and its successors was produced. Once again American interest in the question was almost obsessional. Among the many suggestions made on the problem of the true authorship of the Waverley Novels more than one linked the novels with a North American author.

In 1819 the *Analectic Magazine* pronounced all such suggestions worthless: 'With respect to the disputed parentage of these novels, we are positively informed, that the many stories of their transatlantic origin, so confidently circulated in the United States are destitute of all foundation'. Only a year before, in discussing *Rob Roy*, the same magazine, largely on the flimsy evidence of the use of the word 'wig-warn', and in earlier writings of the term 'the plantations', had cheerfully attributed the authorship of the novels to a Dr Greenfield who had visited America some years before. A much more popular attribution was to Walter Scott's brother, Thomas Scott, who lived in Montreal. Professor John Griscom, an American chemist who travelled in Britain and Europe in the period 1818-1819, and who studied for some months in Edinburgh, mentions the canvassing of this idea, and a comment in the Philadelphia *Literary Gazette* a year or two later in 1821 confirms the popularity of the suggestion:

> he Quarterly Review, a few years ago hinted, that the merit of authorship belonged to a *brother* of Walter Scott, living beyond the Atlantic, and the same idea has been more than once expressed in our newspapers. We understand that at Montreal, the place of residence of Mr Thomas Scott, the fact is universally believed.

In his book of reminiscences called *Old New York*, written about the middle of the nineteenth century, J.W. Francis, for long a member of the literary circles of New York, recalls hearing arguments in favour of the view that the true author of the Waverley Novels was Scott's brother in Canada. According to Francis, Charles Mathews, the English comic actor, in the course of a visit to New York, was the first person 'who gave a pretty decisive opinion that Scott was the author of the Waverley Novels'. Mathew's decisive opinion was given five years before Scott's own public admission at the Ballantyne dinner in 1827, at a time when, again according to Francis, 'we in New York were digesting the argument of Coleman, of the Evening Post, and his correspondents, who attempted to prove that such could not be the truth, and that a Major or Col. Scott, of Canada, was the actual author'. Quite clearly the idea that Thomas Scott could be the author of the Waverley Novels was taken perfectly seriously.

Before turning to the question of why Scott was so much to the American taste I wish to mention one other area of evidence, rather different in its nature from what has gone before, which reveals the power and pervasiveness of Scott's impact upon America. This is the effect Scott had on the American view of Scotland. Scott consummated a literary and cultural tradition which converted Scotland into the most romantic country in Europe. Nowhere was this development registered more clearly than in America; for many Americans Scott endorsed, confirmed, and authenticated what they had long suspected – that Scotland was beyond compare as the land of romance. As such, Scotland exercised a peculiar fascination, and American travellers in Europe almost invariably at some point in their European journey visited the northern half of the United Kingdom. What they saw, where they went, how they responded, all reflected their enthusiasm for Scott above all else. Walter Scottland was indeed the main object of their visit; Walter

Scottland was no less than a new classic ground. The point is made over and over again by different American visitors. Calvin Colton, an American journalist and economist, between 1831 and 1835 served as European correspondent of the *New York Observer*. Of Scottland Colton wrote:

> The genius of a single man has consecrated those wide regions, as modem classic ground, and the history of that country as a classic legend. Italy and Greece have at this moment, if possible, less interest in the eye of travellers for their classic associations, than the land which gave birth to Walter Scott.

Orville Dewey, an American cleric who travelled through part of the Scottish Highlands in the summer of 1833, reiterates the theme. In Glasgow on July 20, he described the tour he had just completed:

> From Edinburgh, I have come round through the Highlands to this place. Every step of the way has been on classic ground; the beautiful windings of the Forth with the Grampian Hills on the north; Stirling Castle; the wild grandeur of the Trossachs; Ben Nevis and Ben Venue; and the haunted waters of Loch Katrine, every rock and headland garlanded with romance; the haunts of Rob Roy, the Lennox country, and the soft scenery of the Leven.

But it was not only Americans writing and thinking about their own first-hand experience of travel in Scotland who tended to conceive of Scott and his influence in precisely these terms. American critics and commentators too were peculiarly alive to this particular dimension of Scott's achievement. A writer in the *North American Review* in 1831 noted both the transformation wrought by Scott on the face of Scotland and the impetus his writings had given quite literally to travels in the Scottish Highlands: 'a hundred years ago, the Highlands of Scotland were as little known as the Rocky Mountains', but Scott's pen 'has thrown them open as completely as a thousand military roads, and travellers will wander over them in all generations to come'. The tone of such comments is almost religious in its reverence. And indeed some commentators did make explicit use of religious imagery: Scotland is a new holy land, and Scott's admirers visit his homeland as literary pilgrims.

That Scott's reception in America was consistently enthusiastic and that his impact was correspondingly deep and wide are evident enough. Less obvious is any satisfactory explanation of Scott's success. Of course a large part of Scott's appeal in America must have been identical with the appeal felt by readers in Scotland, England and throughout all of Europe. The universality of Scott's success clearly indicates that there was much in his work that appealed to contemporary readers whatever their place of origin. What precisely it was has never been definitively identified. Scott's romanticism obviously played a major part, and the Waverley Novels do exhibit central characteristics of the whole romantic movement. But these are not enough on which to convict Scott of uninhibited romanticism, and hence in turn, to identify his romanticism as the source of his triumph. Scott's romanticism, as we all now recognise, is in fact hedged around with reservations, ambivalences, limitations, uncertainties. It is almost as likely that these inhibitions about the world of romance were the secret of his success as that it was his romanticism alone that explained it. The period 1814 to 1832 – the period that spanned the writing of the Waverley Novels – was a period of social and political counter-revolution in Europe. On the face of it the writer to be idolised in such a period is hardly likely to have been an exponent of revolutionary romanticism. On the whole it seems much more probable that Scott succeeded precisely because his romanticism, with its undoubted popular appeal, was in the end unthreatening because removed to the safety of the past.

But still one is not entirely satisfied. To appeal to social and political history to explain the Scott phenomenon, seems to leave *literary* history itself too much out of account. Perhaps it is dangerously easy to dissolve literary movements into broader socio-political terms. Existing explanations of the Scott phenomenon in America exhibit such dangers all too clearly. And here we finally arrive at Scott's war. The most popular account of the reasons behind Scott's American success derives ultimately from some remarks by Mark Twain, in chapter 46 of *Life on the Mississippi*, in 1883, to the effect that Scott was responsible for the American Civil War. Scott's romantic nationalism, his celebration of bogus aristocratic values, his advocacy of medieval notions of chivalry and nobility, had, according to Twain, inspired the South with a set of misguided notions about its self-identity, what it believed in, and what it represented.

Subsequent commentators have offered somewhat modified versions of Twain's thesis. The recurring suggestion is that Scott's American success owed most to the fact either that conservative Southern society shared the aristocratic principles and virtues his work was seen as celebrating, or that at least these were the values the South most admired. In other words Scott's appeal in America is best understood in terms of the nature of Southern society. Now it is perfectly true that some of the more extreme manifestations of the Scott vogue in America occurred in the Southern states. It was in the South, for example, that quasi-medieval tournaments, modelled on that described at Ashby in *Ivanhoe*, became a common form of popular entertainment. Southern plantations and Southern children did frequently owe their names to Scott's novels. But in the end the sociology of the South is hardly adequate as an explanation of Scott's appeal in America. How does one explain the fact that it was not only in the South that Scott was enthusiastically received in America? There is no hard evidence that Scott was read in Charleston or New Orleans with any significantly greater enthusiasm than in Boston or New York. Perhaps the South did respond to certain aspects of Scott's work with peculiar fervour; perhaps it is even true that the reading of Scott encouraged the South towards certain notions of its own social and cultural identity which had previously remained less well-defined. But it is equally clear that Scott appealed in parts of America which in no way shared the social structure of the South.

What best explains Scott's American appeal is something much less glamorous than Twain's socio-political account. It is instead literary history in a remarkably traditional sense. The basic weakness in Twain's case, and in that of the modem commentators who have either tried to disprove his contention or in a modified form agree with it, is its lack of a truly historical perspective. Almost without exception all of these commentators treat Scott in America as a wholly isolated phenomenon; as if Scott had arrived in America like some meteor from outer space. The American reading public one gathers, responded ecstatically overnight to what was literally a Great Unknown. But was Scott in fact a kind of literary bolt from the blue as far as America was concerned? Is it true that Scott emerged from no literary context, that no preparation had been made, no trail been blazed? The answer of course is that it is not true. And I mean a great deal more than that the success of the narrative poems smoothed the way for the Waverley Novels. The first half-dozen or so Waverley Novels, all of them concerned with periods in the Scottish past, rocketed Scott to a position of unparalleled fame and admiration in America not because they represented something unfamiliar and unknown, but because they represented the consummation of a Scottish literary tradition which had long been welcomed and admired in America. Ramsay's *The Gentle Shepherd,* Home's *Douglas*, Beattie's *The Minstrel*, Macpherson's *Ossian,* Burns and the whole tradition of Scottish ballad and song, all of these were read and admired in America, and all helped to make Scott possible. Therein lies a key to his success – in America and perhaps elsewhere.

What of Scott's influence on American literature? His influence was in fact, as we might guess from his immense popularity, considerable – both on individual American writers and on the general context of America's literary culture. In connection with this second area Scott did much to help the creation of a situation in which American literature could finally come into existence. Since the end of the Revolution Americans, facing constant European cultural condescension and disparagement, had been calling for the establishment of a national literature; Scott did as much or more than anyone else in showing America how to do just that. Once again it is Scott's Scottishness, and his relation to Scots writing in general, that is in question here. At the beginning of the eighteenth century Scotland was seen as a poor, backward, culturally dependent nation; by the time of Scott she was the proud possessor of a national literature, enthusiastically read and admired throughout most of Europe and America. Her writers had given her a cultural and national identity and self-definition. How had it been done? Scottish writers had turned back to their own land, its history, traditions, legends; they had written about their own countryside, its mountains, rivers and glens; they had written of the customs and manners of their own people. And in all these areas Scott's own contribution was of course pre-eminent. The message for America was obvious; and it was recognised. For a period in the 1820s and 1830s there was what one scholar described as a 'romance ferment' in America. What Scott had done for Scotland through the Waverley Novels, American authors by writing about American manners, American scenes, American history, should do for America. Scott was repeatedly offered as both example and model.

The appearance of James Fenimore Cooper's novel *The Spy* in 1821 was the signal for a flood of American romances cast in the mould of the Waverley Novels. Cooper's novel was praised precisely because it seemed to have much in common with Scott's historical romances. As John Neal put it in 1825, *The Spy* 'was, at least, an approach to what we desire – a plain, real, hearty, North American story; a story, which, if we could have our way should be altogether American – peculiarly and exclusively so, throughout: as much American to say all, in a word, as the Scotch novels are Scotch'. The vast majority of these American romances of the 1820s and '30s now remain unread. Doubts about the availability in America of suitable material for historical romances, which had been commonly expressed before the appearance of the Waverley Novels, soon began to be expressed again. The romance ferment itself began before long to die down. But there cannot be the slightest doubt that Scott, and the Scottish writers who had preceded him, did much to point the way forward for the development of a genuinely national American literature.

The key figure in that development was James Fenimore Cooper. Throughout his career, and much to his own chagrin, Cooper was widely known as 'the American Scott'. And the nick-name, offensive or not to its bearer, was not without its justification. The Scottish-ness of Scott has much in common with the American-ness of Cooper: the choice of settings and themes, the concern for manners and modes of life uncharacteristic of the civilised present and its social structures. But the influence of Scott on Cooper is probably even more specific. In Cooper's handling of the major theme of his Leather-stocking novel series, the clash between primitivism and civilisation, between frontier and society, between settlers and native Americans, there is an obvious link with Scott's exploration of the contrast between the way of life, the customs and manners of the Scottish Highlander, and those of progressive, modem Scotland and England. The Highland line becomes Cooper's frontier. And in Cooper too there is much of Scott's ambivalence over precisely where the author's sympathies lie; perhaps one senses in the end in both authors a major collision between head and heart. Like Scott, Cooper is intellectually a conservative, an upholder of the traditional values of civilised society – law and order, enlightenment, rational moderation and tolerance and the rest; but like Scott again he is emotionally drawn to another world, in this case a freer, more individual, independent world, not anarchic, but without the constraints inevitably imposed by civilised society. Cooper saw Scott as a rival, if possible to be outdone; at the same time it is clear that Scott helped Cooper tremendously to see more clearly what his true subjects were.

It is tempting to end on this positive note of Scott's beneficient influence on James Fenimore Cooper and the development of a national American literature. But – during all the years of my work on Scotland and America I have been conscious of the danger of focusing exclusively on the positive side of Scottish influence upon America: the approach that suggests it is only the good things in American life that have a Scottish origin. With that danger in mind, let me end by referring to a more troubling Scott legacy to American life and culture. I have already referred to Mark Twain's view that Scott's influence on the American South was malign. The images of human conduct and manners his work created, accepted by Southerners as models for their own behaviour, led the South, Twain suggests, to self-destruction. Romantic Scottish images, that is, moved the South to violence and civil war.

Now the Ku Klux Klan was founded in Pulaski, Tennessee, on December 24, 1865. John C. Lester, the moving spirit in the creation of the new organisation, tells us that the term 'Klan' was included in the title because its founders were 'all of Scotch descent'. Most accounts of the origins of the Ku Klux Klan concentrate on the Greek dimension of the title, but the Scottish connotations may be of greater significance. As everyone knows, the Klan quickly became the main focus of white resistance to Reconstruction in the post-Civil War South. To achieve its aims, it employed violence and terror, elaborate rituals, and above all, secrecy. The Klan, then, offers a powerful parallel to the Vehme or Secret Tribunal of fifteenth-century Germany, as that organisation is fully described in the Old South's favourite novelist's *Anne of Geierstein*. Unquestionably Chapter 20 of Scott's exciting novel provides an elaborate description of a secret society which both in its methods and rituals, and in the reasons and justifications for its existence, provide an uncanny likeness to the Ku Klux Klan, Scott's character Philipson is forced to appear before the Secret Tribunal in a subterranean vault, lit only by torches borne by men muffled in black cloaks, and wearing cowls 'drawn over their heads, so as to conceal their features'. Set out on an altar are a coil of ropes and a naked sword 'the well-known signals and emblems of Vehmique authority'. Elaborate oaths are sworn binding adherents of the order to unquestioning loyalty and obedience. Probably most significant of all is Scott's explanation of the Secret Tribunal's rise to power:

> Such an institution could only prevail at a time when ordinary means of justice were excluded by the hand of power, and when, in order to bring the guilty to punishment, it required all the influence and authority of such a confederacy.

And Scott continues:

> In no other country than one exposed to every species of feudal tyranny, and deprived of every ordinary mode of obtaining justice or redress, could such a system have taken root and flourished.

The availability of such passages in a popular Scott novel, justifying as they appear to do extra-legal action in the name of justice itself, must at the very least have contributed to the cultural context out of which the Invisible Empire of the Klan emerged. The suggestion is not that *Anne of Geierstein* is the source of the Klan. But it is hard not to believe that a great many Southern readers of the novel found in it a peculiar and reassuring relevance to their own situation.

The *Braveheart* version of Scottish history has been widely exploited by the South's neo-confederate, reactionary groups to further their own unpleasant agendas in the 1990s. So perhaps we should not be too surprised to learn that their predecessors in the 1860s could have similarly exploited a work by the novelist whose vast American popularity, James reminds us, had by then in no way subsided.

8 Scotland and South America:

The Role of R. B. Cunninghame Graham

In recent years, and particularly since the bicentenary of the American Revolution, British and American scholars have been paying increasing attention to Scotland's contribution to the formation and development of the countries of modem North America. There is now widespread scholarly agreement that Britain's American colonies, and subsequently Revolutionary and post-Revolutionary America, experienced a distinctive Scottish imprint in terms of economics, politics, religion, education, and intellectual and cultural life; nineteenth-century Canada in a variety of ways was even more indebted to Scotland and the Scots. Scotland and South America, on the other hand, is a story waiting to be told. Presumably near the beginning of that story would stand the ill-fated Darien scheme: Scotland's costly attempt in 1698, promoted by William Paterson, founder of the Bank of England, to create a Scottish American colony to rival those of England. Established in the southernmost area of Central America, where it was violently opposed by the Spanish and cold-shouldered by the English, Darien hardly survived for a single year. The severe damage to the Scottish economy that this failed investment in the Americas entailed would play a significant part in bringing about the Treaty of Union between Scotland and England in 1707 involving as it did the abolition of Scotland's independent political identity.

The narrative of Scotland and South America would also note the appearance in 1777 of William Robertson's *History of America*. For much of the eighteenth century only fellow-Scot David Hume rivalled Robertson, Principal of Edinburgh University, as the major historian of the period. In its first eight books Robertson's history focused on the discovery of America and the Spanish conquest of Mexico and Peru. Only in 1796 were books 9 and 10 on Virginia and New England added. A key figure in the Scottish Enlightenment, Robertson's histories are written in the spirit of the new historiography that reflected wider Enlightenment values.

One has to move on from the Scottish Enlightenment of the eighteenth century to the later nineteenth century, however, to find the man who has to be seen as easily the most flamboyantly important figure in any account of the connexion between Scotland

and South America: R. B. Cunninghame Graham — or 'Don Roberto' as he liked to be called. In the notes to his play *Captain Brassbound*, George Bernard Shaw — one of Graham's many literary friends — included a long and vivid pen portrait of Graham:

> 'I have not made him the hero of my play, because so incredible a personage must have destroyed its likelihood — such as it is. There are moments when I do not myself believe in his existence. And yet he must be real; for I have seen him with these eyes... The man is on public record too... He is a fascinating mystery to a sedentary person like myself. The horse, a dangerous animal whom, when I cannot avoid, I propitiate with apples and sugar, he bestrides and dominates fearlessly, yet with a true republican sense of the rights of the four-legged fellow-creature... He handles the other lethal weapons as familiarly as the pen: medieval sword and modern Mauser are to him as umbrellas and Kodaks are to me. His tales of adventure have the true Cervantes touch of the man who has been there... He is, I understand, a Spanish hidalgo: hence the superbity of his portrait by Lavery (Velasquez being no longer available.) He is, I know, a Scotch laird. How he contrives to be authentically the two things at the same time is no more intelligible to me than the fact that everything that has ever happened to him seems to have happened in Paraguay or Texas instead of in Spain or Scotland.'[1]

Shaw's own brand of rhetorical wit is much in evidence here, but the picture he provides does highlight central features of Graham's character and personality. Graham was never less than a larger-than-life figure. He was a man of action who became both a public man, and a man of letters. He was indeed a 'Scotch Laird' because he inherited the extensive lands and estates of his father's ancient family in an area on the very edge of the Scottish Highlands. But he also had Spain in his blood: his mother's mother was Spanish with an Italian background, and from this grandmother the young Graham heard tales of Spain and Latin America as well as having lessons in spoken Spanish in an accent he never lost. Shaw's implication that nothing ever happened to Graham in Spain, or even in Scotland, is not quite accurate, but if to Shaw's Paraguay and Texas are added Argentina, Uruguay, Brazil, and Mexico, then it is true that the decisive, formative experiences of his life — what made him the kind of man he became — did occur in the Americas rather than in either of his native lands.

Like most boys from his landowning, gentry class, Cunninghame Graham was sent for his education to a major English public school — in his case, like that of another minor Scottish aristocrat, Lord Byron — to Harrow. But after school the issue arose of a suitable career for Graham to follow – the family finances were in an uncertain condition largely because his father, as the result of a head wound incurred while on military service in Ireland, was in the process of going mad. There were traditions of both army and navy service in his family, but the young Graham had something else in mind. Influenced by his Spanish background he wanted to become one of those Englishmen, Irishmen, and Scotsmen whose aim it was to make their fortune in South America. Overcoming the objections of his family, Graham left for the River Plate on the first of three separate visits to South America in May, 1870. In a symbolism not inappropriate to the nature of his South American experiences as a whole, he arrived to find himself in the middle of an anarchic civil war.

This is not the place to rehearse in detail Graham's South American life, but the briefest of sketches is essential. From one point of view Graham's South American visits were a failure: he never did make his fortune. He did not settle down as a rancher or a cattle dealer; he did not establish a successful export – import business. His entrepreneurial attempt to buy horses cheap in Uruguay and sell them dear in Brazil – after herding them for hundreds of miles – brought only a modest profit. He failed to convince London financiers and investors to take a chance on the unstable political and social conditions in the republics of South America. Nonetheless, his four years' experience of life there was quite extraordinary. And what he saw and heard and did he never forgot. The Argentina he encountered in 1870 was a place of near-anarchy. Rival bands of revolutionary gauchos looted and pillaged and burned. Random violence and brutality were endemic. Graham himself may only have survived by agreeing to ride along with one such band. This he could do because he had quickly adapted to the gaucho way of life: he had become a brilliant horseman, and could use the lasso and the bolas like a native. Fully aware of the incompatibility between the gaucho life-style and the demands of ordered society, he was not ready to judge or condemn the gauchos – rather he found much to admire in their independent life and the fearless skills which he had learned to emulate.

Having almost died from a typhus fever attack, he returned to Britain where his mother noted that despite all he had endured and all the violence and mayhem he had witnessed, he was still possessed by a 'craze for South America'.[2] Graham's second visit in the 1870s was mainly to Paraguay – a Paraguay still in chaos after its suicidal war against the Triple Alliance of Brazil, Uruguay and Argentina. Interested in the development of mate plantations, Graham traversed the country noting the decaying monuments of the old Jesuit influence in the region in the ruined plantations, baroque church-fronts, and thinly-populated villages. In Paraguay too the original Indian inhabitants were still a presence and often a threat. Graham's third visit to South America occurred in 1876 – when the plan was made to buy and sell horses between Uruguay and Brazil. It was in this period that Graham is rumoured to have been captured by a band of Indians – and may have escaped in the manner of a Hollywood film hero. In fact Graham's story is exotic and colourful enough not to require such legendary additions. His experiences in South America taught him unforgettable lessons about life and its complexities: about Indians and gauchos, about horses and horsemanship, about violence and cruelty, about the conflict between the natural world and civilization, about the European presence in the New World, about change and decay. A young man rather than a grave philosopher, Graham was no doubt not without his own prejudices and limitations as an observer of South America. Waiting in a town in Brazil he called Cruz Alta to get rid of the remaining cavalry horses bought in Uruguay, he developed a strong antipathy towards Brazilians:

> Of all the people in the known world the Scotch not excepted the Brazilians are the most despicable, mean, thievish mendacious lot of brutes I ever came across. Cruz Alta of itself is lovely but the pomposity of the people surpasses all belief.[3]

But what is so characteristic of Graham is the reference here to 'the Scotch not excepted'. The Brazilians may be a bad lot but Graham's own people are clearly close runners-up.

What is clear, however, is that Graham's South American experience fed directly into his future career both as public figure and as man of letters. As his most recent biographers put it: his 'South American exploits stocked his brain with remembered situations and remembered sensations for the rest of his life. The memories stay relatively constant; what changes is their significance'.[4] What never changes is his memories' vividness. The volume of Graham's writings about South America is such that the impression is created that he spent most of his life there. In fact that impression hardly exaggerates the importance of the South American years. To quote his biographers once again: 'His writing was constantly nourished with South American memories, his outlook on life directed by South American experience'.[5] After South America, Graham always looked at Scotland, England and the rest of Europe, with something of an outsider's eye. His perspective was individual, purely his own. Of course countless young Scots had left home usually to make their way in India or elsewhere in the British Empire. But for most of them the subaltern experience was essentially a reinforcement of the values they had brought from home. Graham's perspective remained much more distant and detached, much less confident of the worth of the kind of progressive change which his own presence in South America was paradoxically helping to bring about.

The first, formative, phase of Graham's life thus ended with his return from South America in 1877. Soon, recently married, he would be back in Texas and Mexico. But within a few years, influenced at least in part by the continuing financial difficulties of the family's Scottish estates, and recognizing that he had failed to establish himself in any kind of profession, he decided to embark on a career in British politics. Defeated in his first attempt to win the parliamentary seat for North West Lanarkshire in 1885 on behalf of the Liberal party, a year later he had a second chance and this time defeated his Tory opponent by a narrow margin of votes. The election campaign he waged was both eloquent and colourful, and the policies he advocated indicated the nature of the parliamentary career he would subsequently pursue: he argued in favour of Home Rule for Ireland; he advocated the passing of a bill to restrict the working man's labour to a maximum of ten hours a day; and he was happy to be endorsed as a candidate by the Scottish Land Restoration League, a group much influenced by Henry George's radical work *Progress and Poverty* (1880) which had argued that the solution to the hardship endured by the working-class under capitalism was a single tax on the ownership of land. Once elected to Westminster Graham was soon regarded as a thorn in the flesh by the Liberal party leadership and most of its parliamentary members. In the House of Commons he became the leading radical voice, while outside of parliament he came to know William Morris and the leaders of the various groups pursuing Socialist principles. He campaigned tirelessly on behalf of the 'have nots,' the oppressed both at home in Britain and in countries overseas. He spoke eloquently in favour of justice and freedom for all – including freedom of speech and assembly; and he condemned the excesses both of capitalism and imperialism. Two moments in his public life will adequately suggest the role he came to play in Britain's political culture towards the end of the Victorian era.

The first occurred on the original 'Bloody Sunday' – 13 November 1887. The occasion was a planned protest meeting in Trafalgar

Square in central London, originally over the imprisonment of an Irish M.P., a militant leader of the Home Rule campaign. But other issues were soon involved – for example, the execution in Chicago of the anarchists allegedly responsible for the Haymarket bombings of the year before, and, even more provocatively, the British Government's decision to deal with the situation by banning all public meetings in Trafalgar Square, thus in the eyes of the protesters denying them their democratic rights of free speech and free assembly. Graham was a hundred percent behind the protesters. Having failed to persuade the Home Secretary to drop the ban on the meeting, Graham appeared in Trafalgar Square intending to make a speech. The opportunity did not arise, however, as the authorities acted with brutal efficiency to suppress the protest meeting; a huge body of police, backed up by Foot Guards and cavalry, soon dispersed the marchers. Graham was among the 300 arrested, his head bloodied by a blow from a policeman's truncheon. Subsequently found guilty of unlawful assembly, he was sent to prison for six weeks. To most of his conventional parliamentary colleagues, the whole incident simply confirmed their view that Graham was a crazy, revolutionary radical. Inside and outside of Westminster, he himself insisted that he was a revolutionary only if it were revolutionary to wish to improve the living conditions of London's poor and to work for a more democratic form of British government.

The second indicative moment concerns America's original inhabitants – not this time the Indians of South America, though Graham was well aware of their history and fate too, but the Lakota Sioux of North America. In November and December 1890, and in January, 1891, the London *Daily Graphic* published three letters from Graham responding to the reports the paper carried on the final confrontation between the Sioux Indians and the U.S. Army at Pine Ridge, North Dakota. Graham's letters are masterpieces of irony, outrage, and anger; the barbarity of the events, and the hypocrisy that surrounds them, are denounced with equal power. For Graham the whole episode is an example of imperialistic *real-politik* of the most brutal and indefensible kind. In the third and final letter he actually links the American Indian's way of life with that of the Scottish Highlander before his final defeat at Culloden in 1746: 'It is as ridiculous to expect an Indian to love work as it would have been to expect a Highlander of the time of the '45 to take to type-writing rather than cattle-lifting as a means of subsistence'.[6] But the letter's ending is even more bitterly ironic:

'It seems a pity, too, to waste so many good Indians who might have been so advantageously used to turn honest pennies for enterprising showmen, if no other method of utilising them occurred to the great American Republic. However, I may be permitted to make my moan over the women and children at least, for I doubt much if they had committed any weightier crimes than the unpardonable one of living'.[7]

Graham's three letters on the Indian question make his potential as a writer abundantly clear. And it was in fact in the 1890s, when he was already more than forty years old, that he began the literary career which would extend on up to his death in 1936. Having begun to write articles and essays for contemporary newspapers and magazines, he published his first book, an idiosyncratic tourist guide to his native district of Scotland, in 1895; by the end of his life he would be the author of some thirty books in all. Yet it is difficult to decide how accurately he is to be described as a professional author. Writing never received his undivided attention; and he appears to have been careless about such matters as proof-reading, checking quotations, foot-noting, and the rest. There is a touch of the Byronic gentleman scribbler about him. And of course although he lost his seat in parliament in 1892, he in no sense lost his interest in the political life and affairs of the country. Nonetheless, his writing quickly won him the attention and admiration of many of the leading literary artists of his time: W.H. Hudson, George Bernard Shaw, Edmund Garnett, Joseph Conrad, Ford Madox Ford and Ezra Pound among them. Graham's work remains unjustly neglected today, perhaps because so much of it is difficult to categorize: often it is hard to tell whether what he is writing is fiction, memoir, sketch, essay, reminiscence, autobiography, history or whatever. The boundaries between these forms seem to be disregarded — or they seem to flow in and out of each other within a single work. Despite this problem — if that is what it is — Graham's writings do represent a significant contribution to Scottish literature, English literature, and perhaps, as his biographers argue, Argentinean literature.[8]

As this last category indicates, when Cunninghame Graham did begin to write, his South American experiences provided him with his most fertile source of material. Indeed of his later books the majority either concern America or provide biographies of major figures in the history of nineteenth century South America. These books may not have been definitive, but to readers unfamiliar with the classic works of Robertson and Prescott, they must have contained much that was new and illuminating. Most striking, perhaps, is Graham's defence of the role of the Roman Catholic church in the early stages of the European conquest of South America: probably unjustly, he accuses earlier historians such as Robertson and Prescott of a Protestant bias against the Roman church. The source of Graham's attitude probably lies in his personal experience of Paraguay in particular; the conditions he witnessed there were so bad that the vestiges that remained of the old Jesuit – dominated Paraguay convinced him that for the Indian population in especial, the older, church-dominated Paraguay, was superior to the modern one. As early as 1901 Graham had written about the Jesuits in Paraguay in the seventeenth and eighteenth centuries – in a book he chose to call *A Vanished Arcadia*. In any event, it is true that in his early writings in general, South American material predominates over Scottish, Spanish, or any other kind.

Nevertheless, throughout his life, 'Don Roberto' always regarded himself as a 'Scotchman'. Thus it was inevitable that in his writing Scottish topics and themes would sometimes be juxtaposed with South American ones. In fact, given that so much of his writing about South American is elegiac in tone, registering the passing away of earlier ways of life – of the gaucho, of the Indians, and the fading of the old freedom and openness of the limitless pampas – it is perhaps surprising that he does not write more often about possible parallels between the changing face of South America and the transformation of the Scottish Highlands in the post-Culloden period.

In both regions older values and older ways of life prove helpless in the face of the march of materialism, commercialism, and what is called civilization. But then Graham was not a Highlander, and he was deeply hostile to the kind of kitsch tartanry which he felt had defaced Scottish culture in the Victorian period. Indeed Graham remained deeply ambivalent about Scotland, Scottish traditions, and the Scottish character in general. This ambivalence is clear in one of his earliest collections of stories and sketches – *The Ipane* – published in 1899.

The Ipane contains four pieces that reflect on Scotland and the Scottish character. The 'S.S. Atlas' recounts Graham's transatlantic crossings aboard a dirty, rusty, Glasgow freighter with a west of Scotland crew. With the *Faerie Queene* for reading-matter, he contrived to survive the two-way crossing, but among the most vivid passages is that describing the behaviour of the Scottish crewmen at Hogmanay: 'they had smuggled liquor on board with the result that on New Year's Eve all were soon hopelessly drunk'. The ship had to be sailed by the officers alone, helped by Graham and one or two Spanish emigrants.

Two other pieces – 'A Survival' and 'Salvagia' – contain more direct assaults on Scottish society and its traditions. 'A Survival' includes an indictment of the 'kailyard' school of nineteenth-century Scottish literature which Graham contends has promoted a distorted view of the Scots to the outside world: '...today a Scotchman stands confessed a sentimental fool, a canting cheat, a grave, sententious man, dressed in a "stan o' black," oppressed with the tremendous difficulties of the jargon he is bound to speak, and above all weighed down with the responsibility of being Scotch'.[9] Then follows an entertaining romp through the history of Scotland's relations with England, including a sympathetic account of the pre-Culloden Highlander: 'I object' writes Graham, 'to the assumption that the douce, gawky, three per-centling of the kailyard has quite eclipsed the pre-Culloden type. In remote places it still remains in spite of education, kodak, bicycle, cheap knowledge and excursion trains; it lingers furtively without a reason, but perhaps that of disproving Darwinism'.[10] But characteristically the story Graham tells at the end of the piece of one such survivor from the past is a story of decline and failure. 'Salvagia' is a still blunter attack on an aspect of Scottish life that Graham frequently condemns: the tradition of Scottish Presbyterian Calvinism. For Graham this harsh and austere Scottish religion is characterized by 'much faith and little charity'.[11] He sees it as responsible all too often for the least attractive aspects of the Scottish character: its hypocrisy, its suppression of feeling, its subordination of women. This is a cold, dehumanizing religion and it produces a society with similar characteristics:

> 'Stony indeed the country, stony the folks, the language, manners and all else pertaining to it. Even the Parameras outside Avila, when every boulder is a tear that Jesus wept, is not more sterile'.[12]

Or, as Graham puts it in an earlier passage:

> In every house a picture of Dr Chalmers flanked by one of Bunyan, and a Bible ever ready on a table for advertisement, as when a minister or charitable lady calls, and the cry is heard of "Jeanie, rax the Bible doon, and pit the whisky-bottle in the aumrie."[13]

In the fourth *Ipane* piece Scotland and South America are juxtaposed.

'Heather Jock' is a colourful description of the life of an itinerant pedlar from the west of Scotland who entertained his clients by a kind of bells and dance performance of the traditional song 'Annie Laurie'. Graham appears to have some respect for this figure who has chosen to live outside the conventions of normal society. However this account of Heather Jock's life co-exists with the report of his death which Graham learns of in a letter he receives in South America – and that death in turn exists in the context of another one. The rider who has brought Graham his letters seems disconcerted and perturbed, even if he is as polite as ever. Where, asks Graham, is his brother who usually rides with him when he is delivering his letters? Killed by the Indians at a level crossing is the answer. Graham makes no attempt to find any meaning in the deaths so curiously linked except to say that at the funeral celebrations for the dead brother,

> 'above the neighing of the horses shut in the corral for fear of Indians, I seemed to hear the jangling of the dead fool's bells, and listen to the minstrelsy, such as it was, of the hegemonist of Bridge of Weir.'[14]

However, Graham's most extended treatment of the Scotland and South America theme occurs not in *The Ipane* but in a book called *Charity* published in 1912. 'San Andres' is a sketch concerning Scottish Highland immigrants who had come to an outlying settlement in the province of Buenos Aires some time in the post-Culloden period of the eighteenth century. The sketch is organized around attitudes towards the dead and what Graham asserts is the ancient Scottish notion that too much grieving for the dead is a bad thing because it denies them rest. What follows is a vivid account of this group of 'Scoto-Argentines,' their 'patriarchal manners', 'grave sententiousness,' 'belief in fairies and the second sight', 'the natural good manners both of the gaucho and the Highlander'. Among these people were some who still spoke Gaelic, or 'even those whose fathers once had spoken what they called *el guelico*'. But the focus of the story is on the chief of the settlement Don Alejandro Chisholm, and the legendary love between his daughter Saturnina and her husband Anacleto. The inevitable death of his beloved wife occurs when Anacleto is far away on the southern frontier. When he learns what has happened he grieves for week upon week, but is finally warned by Don Alejandro to stop: 'We cannot call her back to us alive. To pain the spirit by our selfishness, that would be cowardly'. This is the tradition from the ancient Scottish past to which Anacleto finally accedes: 'No, it would be cowardly to break her rest, Don Alejandro says so; he had it from his father, who spoke *gaelico,*' he slowly lit a cigarette and in the last rays of the light, watched the smoke curl up in the air, blue and impalpable'. Earlier in the sketch Graham had characteristically written that the old San Andres settlement 'no doubt not long ago has turned into a town, with modern improvements, electric lights and drains, beggars and churches...' [15] Similarly, no doubt, the links between Scotland and South America have taken and will take new forms in the 20th and 21st centuries, but in any account of that connexion, the role of R.B. Cunninghame Graham is certainly both an important and honourable one.

1 Quoted in Cedric Watts and Laurence Davies, *Cunninghame Graham, A Critical Biography,* Cambridge, 1979, p!33.
2 *Ibid.,* p. 21
3 *Ibid.,* p. 31
4 *Ibid.,* p. 32
5 *Ibid.,* p. 35
6 See John Walker (ed.), *The North American Sketches of R. B. Cunninghame Graham,* Edinburgh 1986, p. 31.
7 *Ibid.,* p. 32.
8 Watts and Davies, *op. cit., p. 37*
9 R. B. Cunninghame Graham, *The lpane,* London, 1899, p. 162.
10 *Ibid.,* p. 163.
11 *Ibid.,* p. 191.
12 *Ibid.,* p. 194.
13 *Ibid.,* p. 191
14 *Ibid.,* p. 187
15 For these quotations see John Walker (ed.), *The South American Sketches of R. B. Cunninghame Graham,* Norman, 1978, pp. 126-34.

Part Five

F. Scott Fitzgerald.

Scott Fitzgerald has always been one of my favourite writers. While I was at Aberdeen, Robin Gilmour, the general editor of a book series called Modern Fiction, published by Edward Arnold, invited me to contribute a volume on Scott Fitzgerald. The series aimed to provide short introductions to major twentieth-century novelists. The book, with an opening chapter on 'Fitzgerald and the American Dream' followed by five chapters covering in turn each of Fitzgerald's novels, duly appeared in 1992. A decade later, a second series called 'Literary Lives', edited by Richard Dutton, and published by Palgrave Macmillan, invited me to write *F. Scott Fitzgerald, A Literary Life*. Focusing on the author's literary career, the book was published in 2002. Most of the material in this section consists of papers I read at annual conferences of the Scott Fitzgerald Society in America.

One such conference took place in Asheville, North Carolina, in 1998. Asheville was the site of the Highland Hospital, where Fitzgerald's wife Zelda was treated for her psychological problems over a number of years. In 1948 she died in a fire in the hospital. Those attending the conference included two of Zelda Fitzgerald's granddaughters, and they were present at the placing of a memorial plaque honouring Zelda on the spot where the long-demolished building in which she died had stood. I have the clearest memory of Eleanor and Cecilia explaining that their mother Scottie had prevented them from knowing anything about who their grandparents were for as long as possible while they were growing up.

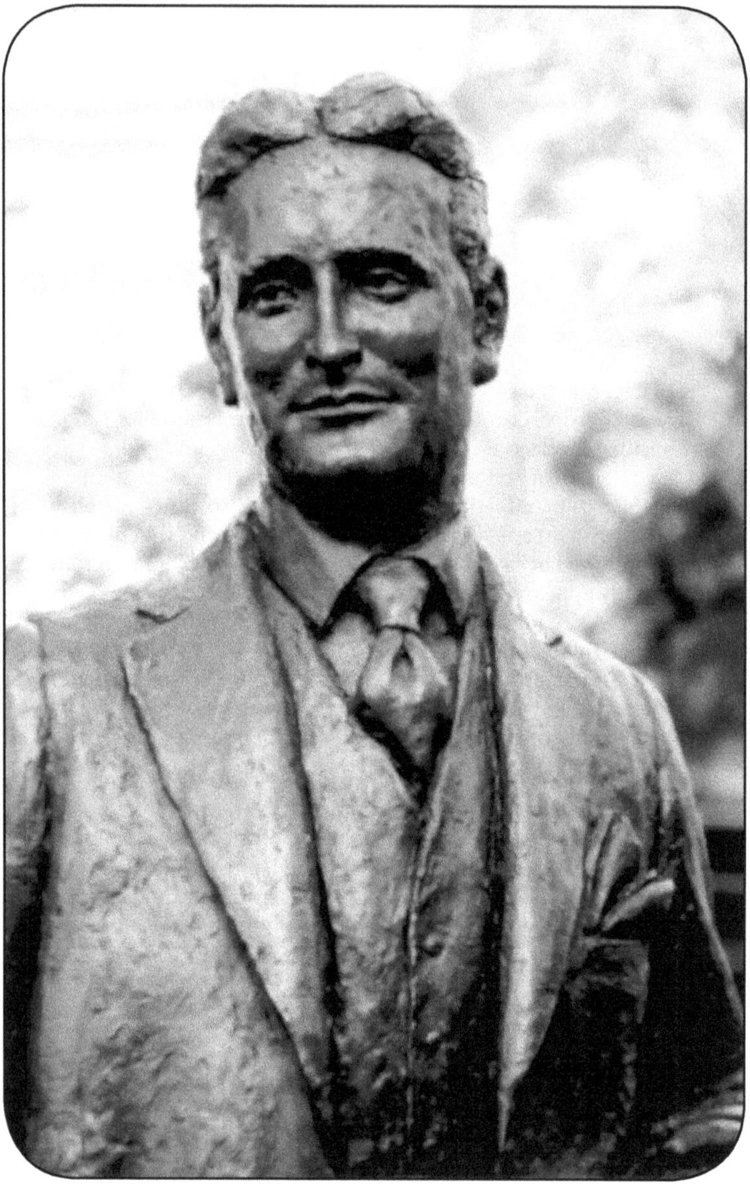

Scott Fitzgerald

1 Fitzgerald and Provence

The Fitzgeralds' first visit to Europe occurred in the summer of 1921. The version of *The Beautiful and Damned* that would be serialized in *Metropolitan Magazine* having been sent to Harold Ober in April, and with Zelda already pregnant with their daughter Scottie, the couple sailed in the *Aquitania* from New York to Southampton in the first week of May. In the course of the next two months they visited London, Oxford, and Cambridge as well as Paris, Venice, Florence and Rome. Given the future frequency and duration of their European visits, it comes as something of a surprise to recognize that this first trip was not a success. Of the cities visited, only Oxford appears to have impressed them. At least in London their old friend the Irish writer, Shane Leslie was on hand to take them on an exciting night-time tour of the docks area – and Lady Randolph Churchill had them to lunch with Winston Churchill. But both France and Italy they disliked intensely. The problem almost certainly was their sense of isolation. Accustomed to a supportive social circle of friends and acquaintances – and indeed to their Jazz Age celebrity in America – in France and Italy they were unreceived and unknown, their isolation intensified by the fact that English was their only language. The role of anonymous tourists was clearly one not at all to their taste. In any event, his sense of frustrated rejection by Europe led Fitzgerald to write a letter to Edmund Wilson from Paris in July, 1921, that one suspects he must subsequently have regretted:

> God damn the continent of Europe. It is of merely antiquarian interest. Rome is only a few years behind Tyre and Babylon. The negroid streak creeps northward to defile the Nordic race. Already the Italians have the souls of blackamoors. Raise the bars of immigration and permit only Scandinavians, Teutons, Anglo Saxons and Celts to enter. France made me sick. Its silly pose as the thing the world has to save. I think it's a shame that England and America didn't let Germany conquer Europe. It's the only thing that would have saved the fleet of tottering old wrecks. My reactions were all philistine, anti-socialistic, provincial, racially snobbish. I believe at last in the white man's burden. We are as far above the modern Frenchman as he is above the Negro.... We will be the Romans in the next generation as the English are now. (L, 346)

There can be no excusing such outlandish ravings. Clearly Fitzgerald is in the darkest of moods leading him to transfer the angry discontents he is feeling on to the world around him. All one can say is that a year or two down the line he had the good sense partially to redeem himself by reinscribing similar racist attitudes into the language of the bullying and hypocritical Tom Buchanan in *The Great Gatsby*.

Almost exactly three years later, in the early summer of 1924, the Fitzgeralds decided to leave Great Neck, Long Island, and return to Europe for the second time. Behind this decision lay no notion of the irresistible pull of European high modernism. The Fitzgeralds had no idea even of sampling again the European culture which they had found so distasteful in 1921. Nor were they fleeing from the puritanical restrictiveness of conventional American morality in search of the freedom and excitement of post-war Paris. The decision was a purely financial one. Unable to begin to live within their income in America, they hoped and believed that their dollars would stretch a great deal further in France or Italy. And in a general sense they were right. Their house in Long Island had rented at $300 a month; the equivalent figure for the Villa Marie they eventually rented in Provence was $79.

With money in hand from a burst of story-writing that had cleared off his debts earlier in the year, Fitzgerald at last felt able to get down to serious work on his third novel. After a week in Paris — interviewing nannies for Scottie — the Fitzgerald's left for the French Riviera, — which Fitzgerald called 'the hot, sweet South of France – and in 'How to Live on Practically Nothing a Year' described as irresistibly romantic:

> When your eyes first fall upon the Mediterranean [he wrote] you know at once why it was here that man first stood erect and stretched out his arms toward the sun. It is a blue sea; or rather it is too blue for that hackneyed phrase which has described every muddy pool from pole to pole. It is the fairy blue of Maxfield Parrish's pictures; blue like blue books, blue oil, blue eyes, and in the shadow of the mountains a green belt of land runs along the coast for a hundred miles and makes a playground for the world. The Riviera! The names of its resorts, Cannes, Nice, Monte Carlo, call up the memory of a hundred kings and princes who have lost their thrones and come here to die, of mysterious rajahs and beys flinging blue diamonds to English dancing girls, of Russian millionaires tossing away fortunes at roulette in the lost caviar days before the war.

In fact the villas of Cannes, Nice and Monte Carlo proved either too large or too small for the Fitzgeralds to rent, and it was only by chance that they came upon St Raphael:

> Then one morning just five weeks after we had left New York we got off the train at a little town that we had never considered before. It was a red little town built close to the sea, with gay red-roofed houses and an air of repressed carnival about it; carnival that would venture forth into the streets before night. We knew that we would love to live in it...

And soon they did:

> Within an hour we had seen our home, a clean cool villa set in a large garden on a hill above town. It was what we had been looking for all along. There was a summerhouse and a sand pile and two bathrooms and roses for breakfast and a gardener who called me milord.

Fitzgerald settled down in this villa to write *The Great Gatsby* in a mood of high creative excitement. In May 1924, he wrote to his friend Thomas Boyd insisting that his current isolation in Provence was exactly what he needed: 'I hope to God I don't see a soul for six months. My novel grows more and more extraordinary; I feel absolutely self-sufficient...' (LL, 68)

In June 1924, he told Carl Van Vechten:

> We are living here in a sort of idyllic state among everything lovely imaginable in the way of Mediterranean delights. Unlike you I have only an occasional lust for the exotic streets of the metropolis — at present I am content to work and become excruciatingly healthy under Byron's and Shelley's and Dickens' sky.

And at this time Maxwell Perkins at Scribners received very much the same message: 'We are idyllically settled here and the novel is going fine...' For perhaps the only time in his life, in the following weeks and months in Provence, Fitzgerald let nothing, absolutely nothing, stop him from allowing a work of sustained creative power steadily and consistently take shape under his hand. For once Fitzgerald's commitment to his art proved stronger than his commitment to anything else; in this one period not even Zelda could break the spell. Significantly, however, it was in these weeks that the Fitzgerald's marriage faced its most serious threat. While Fitzgerald worked steadily at his novel, Zelda became romantically involved with a young French military aviator, Edouard Jozan. At first Fitzgerald seems not even to have noticed what was going on; his writing alone had his full attention. It is almost as though at some level he needed and wanted Zelda out of his way; getting on with his novel undisturbed was the only thing that mattered. Did he perhaps for a time choose to ignore Zelda and Jozan? Did the demands of his art for once shut out what was happening in his life? If so, the situation was one that could not last. The end came in mid-July. Fitzgerald's *Ledger* entry reads: 'The Big crisis — 13th of July'. Briefly there was talk of divorce, but in a week or two the whole matter seemed to blow over. The Fitzgerald marriage — and the writing of *Gatsby* — went on. Later, however, in his *Notebooks* Fitzgerald recorded: 'That September, 1924, I knew something had happened that could never be repaired'. How far Fitzgerald had got with the writing of *Gatsby* when this episode occurred is not clear; in any event such interruption as Zelda's behaviour caused was short-lived, but it could well be that in due course its consequences contributed to the note of elegy and loss that would eventually characterize the finished novel. At the end of August, Fitzgerald told Perkins: 'It's been a fair summer. I've been unhappy but my work hasn't suffered from it. I am grown at last'. (FP, 76) What is implied is that coping with the Zelda — Jozan affair has been a maturing experience for Fitzgerald the man; but there is a later *Notebooks* entry which at least raises the possibility that for a time the creative intensity of the artist blotted it out:

> I can never remember *The Times* when I wrote anything — *This Side of Paradise* time or *Beautiful and Damned* and *Gatsby* time, for instance. Lived in story.[12]

Despite his determination to get on with his novel, Fitzgerald however, did not live in complete seclusion in Provence in the summer of 1924. There were trips with Zelda to the more fashionable resorts such as Cannes, Monte Carlo, and Antibes. It was probably on such a trip in August to Cap d'Antibes that the Fitzgerald's met the couple who would prove their closest friends in France — Gerald and Sara Murphy. The Murphys clearly impressed the Fitzgeralds as Americans of considerable cosmopolitan glamour and style; not rich, they nonetheless lived well, maintaining houses both in Paris and Cap d'Antibes, and both were actively involved in the world of art and culture. Fitzgerald would make use of his relationship with both Murphys in the long-drawn-out writing of *Tender is the Night*, and the Murphys' Villa America would always be a central focus of Fitzgerald's Provençal experience.

In yet another attempt to economize on living expenses the Fitzgeralds left France for an hotel in Rome around the beginning of December 1924. Back in 1921 they had found little to choose between France and Italy: both countries were unappealing and unrewarding. Now Fitzgerald felt differently: the French Riviera was a great place to be (perhaps because his writing had gone well there) but Italy remained as unattractive as before. In January 1925, he wrote Ober from Rome telling him 'I hate Italy and the Italians so violently that I can't bring myself to write about them for the *Post*...' This degree of alienation from a country that earlier generations of American artists and writers had found irresistible is difficult to account for. Admittedly the Rome Fitzgerald was living in was the Rome of Mussolini, but there is nothing to suggest that contemporary Italian politics were the source of Fitzgerald's prejudice. Getting himself beaten up by Italian policemen in a drunken escapade presumably did little to make him feel better about Italy and Italians, and soon matters were made worse by both Fitzgeralds falling ill in the wintry cold of Rome. By early February they had decided they should move further south to Capri, in the search for warmer weather. Despite all these problems, the final revision of *Gatsby* was successfully concluded.

For the publication of *Gatsby* in April 1925, the Fitzgeralds returned to France and decided to remain in Paris. One of the first persons they sought out was Ernest Hemingway, whose early work Fitzgerald knew and admired and whom he had been recommending to Maxwell Perkins for the previous six months. Fitzgerald was convinced that Hemingway had a brilliant future, and felt that Perkins should make ever effort to recruit him as a Scribners author: an outcome finally achieved the following year, largely as a result of Fitzgerald's unstinting effort. In any event, with *Gatsby* proving a great critical success, if not a commercial one, Fitzgerald had wholly changed his mind about France: 'I've gotten to like France' he told Edmund Wilson. That summer the Fitzgeralds spent all of August in Antibes, leading a life of extravagant and gaudy good-timing. As Fitzgerald put it wittily in a letter to John Peale Bishop in September:

> There was no one at Antibes this summer except me, Zelda, the Valentinos, the Murphys, Mistinguet, Rex Ingram, Dos Passos, Alice Terry, the MacLeishes, Charlie Brackett, Maude Khan, Esther Murphy, Marguerite Namara, E. Phillips Oppenheim, Mannes the violinist, Floyd Dell, Max and Crystal Eastman, ex-Premier Orlando, Ettienne de Beaumont — just a real place to rough it, an escape from all the world. But we had a great time.(L, 379)

The Fitzgeralds continued to have a great time in France for the following six months or so. Somewhat unexpectedly, the Broadway stage version of *The Great Gatsby* was proving a big success — and earning Fitzgerald a substantial amount of money; an edition of the novel was about to be published in London; a French translation was underway; and the follow-up collection of short stories – *All the Sad Young Men* – was selling quite well in the US. In March, 1926, having left Paris and rented a villa in Juan-les-Pins, Fitzgerald wrote to Maxwell Perkins in a mood of almost serenity:

> With the play going well & my new novel growing absorbing & with our being back in a nice villa on my beloved Riviera...I'm happier than I've been for years. It's one of those strange, precious and all too transitory moments when everything in one's life seems to be going well.

In fact such a moment would never recur in the rest of Fitzgerald's life.

The Fitzgeralds' third visit to Europe occurred just over two years later in the summer of 1928 – but this time there was no visit to Provence. Zelda Fitzgerald had begun ballet lessons in Philadelphia and was determined to pursue her training by studying under Egorova, a leading Russian ballet teacher in Paris. Fitzgerald's progress with his new post-Gatsby novel was more or less at a standstill, but he was able to fund the transatlantic trip by the success of the highly autobiographical 'Basil Lee' stories. Over the summer in Paris Fitzgerald saw something of James Joyce and Sylvia Beach as well as Thornton Wilder and John Peale Bishop. And it was at this time that he enthusiastically recommended the young French writer André Chamson to Maxwell Perkins:

> Really, Max you're missing a great opportunity if you don't take [him] up. Radiguet was perhaps obscene – Chamson is absolutely not – – he's head over heels the best young man here, like Ernest and Thornton Wilder rolled into one.

But Fitzgerald spent most of the summer in the by now familiar disorganized and disruptive way. Two evenings-out ended with him spending the night in Parisian jails. Little or no progress was made on his novel, and when the Fitzgeralds returned to the US in September, 1928, they brought with them a Paris taxi-driver, theoretically employed as a chauffeur-butler, but really little more than Fitzgerald's drinking partner.

In the spring of 1929 the Fitzgeralds decided to return to France for what would prove to be their fourth and final visit. One motive was Zelda's desire to resume her ballet lessons under Egorova. Probably another was Fitzgerald's hope that his blocked work on his novel would benefit from a return to its geographical location. The Fitzgeralds would remain in Europe for the next two and a half years but in all that time Fitzgerald's progress on what would be *Tender is the Night* would continue to be painfully slow. Neither in Paris nor in his now favourite Provence did he find the new source of creative inspiration needed to get the novel moving towards completion. After spending April and May 1929 in Paris, the Fitzgeralds left for what would be their last extended stay in Provence, renting a villa in Cannes. Fitzgerald repeatedly assured both Maxwell Perkins and Harold Ober that living economically in Cannes he would free up time to make progress on his novel. But in the event this did not happen. Fitzgerald did work on the Saturday Evening Post style stories which were his main source of income – it was at this time that his price for a single story peaked at an all-time high of $4000. The novel however remained stymied. In October 1929, the Fitzgeralds returned by car to Paris, driving all the way through Provence in their small Renault. Back in Paris Fitzgerald was interviewed by an American journalist and his paper published the following account:

> Describing the French Riviera as "the most fascinating amalgamation of wealth, luxury and general uselessness in the world," Scott Fitzgerald, famous and still youthful American novelist, has returned to Paris after a short sojourn in Nice. He was accompanied by his wife and little daughter, "Scottie Jr" and will remain here until he has finished his latest book – the first in two and a half years. That's the why of my now novel," said Mr Fitzgerald. "It's about the Riviera, and that's all I can say about it today."
>
> The young author of *This Side of Paradise* and half a dozen other best sellers didn't give the reporter a chance to ask questions. "As I said on leaving Nice, "he continued, "I have nothing to say about the Hoover Administration, the I'm Alone case, Prohibition in America, Col. Lindbergh or why I live abroad."
>
> He consented, however, to confide a bit of Riviera scandal. "The American artists' colony at Cagnes-sur-Mer is having a lot of trouble with the town postmaster," he laughed. "Their cheques from home haven't been arriving fast enough, and you know what life is for Bohemians when cheques stop coming from home. Anyway, I hear they're going to have the postmaster fired for holding up their letters."

The humour here is probably wryer than it would have appeared to most contemporary newspaper readers. No American Bohemian was more reliant on the arrival of cheques from home than Fitzgerald himself – though in his case 'home' usually took the form of his agent Harold Ober.

What in conclusion did his experience of France and Provence mean for Fitzgerald? At the very least it meant an extended cultural experience for a middle-western American boy whose values and instincts, despite his familiarity with Princeton, New York, and the more culturally sophisticated east coast of the US, remained by and large those of an old-style, more traditional America. Clearly Fitzgerald did mature enough to overcome his initial hostility to everything European, but it is equally clear that he never experienced any kind of Jamesian identification with European culture. Fitzgerald was always an American in Paris – or Antibes or St Raphael or wherever. The same is true of his fictional use of France and Europe. *Tender is the Night* often beautifully evokes the landscapes and colours and sights of Mediterranean France; but the local culture is always seen from the viewpoint of the visiting American. The novel brilliantly registers the rather brittle style and manners of expatriate Americans in Europe in the 1920s, but there is no suggestion of American manners being wholly Europeanized. And in commercial terms at least, there is evidence that Fitzgerald could not afford to allow European attitudes and values too great a prominence in his work – not, that is, if he wished to bring his readership along with him. For example, 'On Your Own', a highly competent and one would have thought marketable story, was rejected by the Saturday Evening Post, Redbook, Collier's, College Humor, Pictorial Review, Good Housekeeping and Woman's Home Companion, and in the end found no contemporary publisher. Drawing on Fitzgerald's own experience of his return to America in 1931 to attend his father's funeral, the story focuses on a woman protagonist returning from Europe to America in a similar situation. The story does however suggest that the woman's European experience has gained her a sophistication of manners that is lacking in America. And that recognition seems to be the reason why the editors of America's mass-circulation magazines turned it down. In fact it was just at this point in the early 1930s that Fitzgerald's old facility at turning out stories automatically snapped up began to break down. And it is significant that one of the complaints of the magazine editors, reported by Harold Ober, is that too many of Fitzgerald's recent stories have unfamiliar European settings. Could he not write some American stories – by which they meant 'stories laid on this side of the Atlantic?'

Provence for Fitzgerald meant Gerald and Sara Murphy and the Villa America, meant Hemingway, meant the romance and colour and glamour of the Mediterranean of Cannes and Nice and Monte Carlo, meant St Raphael and the writing of *The Great Gatsby*. But like all of Fitzgerald's paradises, Provence was a fallen world offering at best but a transitory escape from the tensions and problems of both Fitzgerald's life and his art.

2 The Fitzgeralds and the South today

Zelda Fitzgerald used to be known – if she were known at all – only as the wife of Scott Fitzgerald. Those who took a greater interest in her finally tragic life were of course aware that at different times she had attempted to become an artist in her own right: as dancer, painter, and writer. But there was general agreement that in all three artistic fields she had achieved little or no success. As a ballet-dancer she had one offer to dance professionally – which she turned down; as a painter the work she exhibited in her lifetime made little or no impact; and even as the author of one novel, one play, eleven short stories, and a dozen articles or sketches, her literary career never really took off. Today, however, the situation is very different. For reasons that I shall discuss below, Zelda Fitzgerald is widely recognized as an important and significant figure in her own right. Zelda is Zelda – not simply Mrs Scott Fitzgerald – and Zelda has a story to tell just as interesting as any of those told by the man she chose to marry. And, as we shall see, this new recognition extends even into the South today.

Scott Fitzgerald's case is different. His status as a classic American author of the twentieth century remains broadly unchallenged. His readership extends worldwide, while *The Great Gatsby* has infiltrated the modern world's cultural consciousness as only a handful of other titles have done. But in relation at least to today's literary academy, I am inclined to think that the reputation reversal is more or less complete: Zelda Fitzgerald now excites more interest and enthusiasm than Scott Fitzgerald. Younger scholars and critics care about Zelda in a way that they do not about Scott. That, at least, is my impression.

I suggested above that the new interest in Zelda Fitzgerald is evident even in the South. In fact, if there is any such new interest, it would be surprising if the South were not involved. Because of course Zelda is very much the Southern half of the Fitzgerald equation. Every aspect of Zelda's background rooted her exclusively in the South. Born in Montgomery, Alabama, in 1900, Zelda belonged to a family with impeccable Southern, Confederate, credentials: her maternal grandfather was briefly a United States Senator for Kentucky, and a nominee for the Vice-Presidency of the country; subsequently he became a successful lawyer and planter, very much a member of the South's ruling class. Zelda's father's family were equally identified with the South's ruling oligarchy: Anthony Sayre's uncle was the builder of the White House in Montgomery occupied by Jefferson Davis during the Confederacy, while his mother's brother was a U.S. Senator for Alabama for thirty-one years. Sayre Street in Montgomery was named for the family. The Zelda Sayre then, whom Scott Fitzgerald met in Montgomery in 1918, was a Southern girl by birth, by family background, by education – she attended a public high school in Montgomery – and by every other aspect of her experience up to her initial encounter with Fitzgerald. Indeed the powerful impression that Fitzgerald made upon her had much to do with the fact that he was *different* – a handsome, blond, elegantly-uniformed, soldier from the exotic North. If Fitzgerald had been just another Southern boy from Auburn or Georgia Tech rather than a Northerner from Princeton, it is probable that Montgomery's most flamboyant Southern belle would hardly have noticed him.

In fact, however, Scott Fitzgerald did not arrive in Camp Sheridan, outside Montgomery, like an adventurer in a foreign land. He had always been aware of his own links with the South and may even have been inclined to exaggerate them. The young Fitzgerald's place in the better-off section of St. Paul society in Minnesota was largely secured by the wealth of his mother's industrious Irish family. His father's business career, on the other hand, had ended more or less in failure. Yet in terms of manners and personal style, the young Fitzgerald seems to have admired his father rather than his clearly unstylish mother. Preferring his father's social graces to his mother's, he was leaning towards the Southern aspect of his inheritance – because Edward Fitzgerald's family had its roots in Maryland where it was distantly related to established, aristocratic families such as the Scotts and the Keys. Scott Fitzgerald could then with at least some justification see himself as sharing in Southern traditions and Southern values. Certainly he learned much about the Civil War from his father's stories, became strongly Confederate in his sympathies, and came to value notions of honour and good manners in a distinctly Southern sense. His decision to attend Princeton University may well have been influenced by his recognizing that Princeton was easily the most 'Southern' of the Ivy League colleges. None of this could have been known to Zelda when she first met Fitzgerald in 1918 – part of his appeal was precisely, as I've suggested, his exotic, non-Southern, status. But it does help to explain why the South does emerge as a theme in the writings of *both* Fitzgeralds.

What is surprising about the Southern writing of Scott and Zelda is how much it has in common. Certainly when either writer is trying to evoke the quality of Southern life, the atmosphere of the South, the experience of Southern towns or countryside, Southern days and Southern nights, what one says is hardly distinguishable from the other. Perhaps though one should not be surprised: given Zelda's involvement in Scott's writing, his concern for her critical opinions, and their closeness as husband and wife, perhaps it was inevitable that, particularly in areas of to some degree shared experience, there should be a carry-over from the writings of one to the other. In any event the descriptive emphasis in both writers' evocation of the South is remarkably similar: they return again and again to the same images, the same ideas – the somnolent heat of the South, the vivid colours of its flowers and trees, the indolence of its way of living, and the stasis and timelessness of its seasons, its streets and landscapes. Consider these examples:

> Under the gathering twilight the town was unexpectedly attractive. The sidewalks were peopled by vividly dressed, overpainted girls, who chattered volubly in low, lazy voices, by dozens of taxi-drivers who assailed passing officers with 'Take y'anywhey, Lewtenant,' and by an intermittent procession of ragged, shuffling, subservient Negroes. Anthony, loitering along through the warm dusk, felt for the first time in years the slow, erotic breath of the South, imminent in the hot softness of the air, in the pervasive lull of thought and time.[1]

Or this:

> We drove through pinewoods heavy with lichen and Spanish moss, and between the fallow cotton fields along a road white as the rim of the world. We parked under the broken shadow of a mill where there was the sound of running water and restive squawky birds and over everything a brightness that tried to filter in anywhere – into the lost nigger cabins, the automobile, the fastnesses of the heart. The South sang to us – I wonder if they remember.[2]

Or this:

> The Southern town slept soundless on the wide palette of the cotton fields. Alabama's ears were muffled by the intense stillness as if she had entered a vacuum. Negroes, lethargic and immobile, draped themselves on the depot steps like effigies to some exhausted god of creation. The wide square, masked in velvet shadows, drowned in the lull of the South, spread like soft blotting paper under man and his heritage.[3]

Or this:

> The solid South stretches away for miles from Jeffersonville, long clay roads climbing slow hills covered with straggling pines, broad,

blank cotton fields, isolated cabins in patches of sand, and far off in the distance the blue promise of hills.[4]

The first two passages are by Scott Fitzgerald, the second two by Zelda. But the South that is present in all four seems very much of a muchness. At some levels at least, the Fitzgeralds' vision of the South was a shared vision.

In terms of the South's ultimate meaning for the two writers, however, it is possible to see significant differences. With the passing of time, and the changing nature of his relationship with Zelda, Scott Fitzgerald's view of the South became less romantic, more disillusioned. In an early story, 'The Ice Palace' (1921), which explicitly explores the North-South theme, the scales are tilted very much in favour of the South. The point of view is that of the Southern girl Sally Carrol Happer engaged to Harry Bellamy from St. Paul, Minnesota. The visit she makes to the North with Harry disorientates her. Where the South she knows is a land of warmth, indolent, easy-going, with a strong sense of the past and history, the North is all coldness, energy, and newness. Northern manners, too, brusque and direct, strike the Southern girl as lacking in warmth and gallantry. Temporarily trapped in the Ice Palace, she escapes, breaks off her engagement, and returns to the South.

In *The Beautiful and Damned* (1922), however, the vision of the South is already different. The novel charts the decline and fall of its protagonist, Anthony Patch, and the Southern section, occurring towards the end, is no exception to that general movement. Anthony enrols in the U.S. Army and is sent to a camp in South Carolina for his military training. Once in town he meets a girl called Dorothy Raycroft — a very ordinary Southern girl with none of the sophistication, beauty, or social status of his wife Gloria — and drifts casually into a relationship with her. Fitzgerald means us to see this affair as further evidence of Anthony's loss of control over his life, of his moral weakness and irresponsibility. But what is significant is how the Southern setting is used to reflect Anthony's moral decline. The affair, we are told, is the result of Anthony's 'increasing carelessness about himself'. [5]

But the South itself seems to encourage such carelessness; the heat, the indolence, the dream-like quality of moon-lit nights, seem to invite a surrender of responsibility:

'In town the streets were in a sleepy dream again, and together Anthony and Dot idled in their own tracks of the previous autumn until he began to feel a drowsy attachment for this South — a South, it seemed, more of Algiers than of Italy, with faded aspirations pointing back over innumerable generations to some warm, primitive Nirvana, without hope or care.' [6]

In the heat of the Southern countryside, Anthony would talk to Dot, we are told, 'in a sleepy monologue, in a conversation of no significance, of no replies'. [7] The South's complicity in Anthony Patch's moral dissolution is made abundantly clear.

Fitzgerald's disillusion with the South is further signalled in the short story 'Gretchen's Forty Winks' (1924). Gretchen is a Southern girl married to a man determined to get ahead in the world of advertising. Gretchen is more interested in a good time than in business success — to her husband's chagrin. For much of the story the reader seems to be invited to share Gretchen's dislike of her husband's single-mindedness; but in the end Roger is vindicated, and Gretchen is humbled. Northern vigour and determination, that is, triumph over Southern self-indulgence.

The South's final chapter is written in *The Last of the Belles* (1929). After this story Fitzgerald never returns to the Southern theme. As the title suggests, the story has a distinctly elegiac feel. The narrator returns to Tarleton, Georgia, fifteen years after he had been stationed there during the war, and recounts his relationship with Ailie Calhoun, the town's most beautiful Southern belle. He remembers her as a Southern archetype:

'She had the adroitness sugar-coated with sweet, voluble simplicity, the suggested background of devoted fathers, brothers and admirers stretching back into the South's heroic age, the unfailing coolness acquired in the endless struggle with the heat. There were notes in her voice that ordered slaves around, that withered up Yankee captains, and then soft, wheedling notes that mingled in unfamiliar loveliness with the night, [8]

The climax of the story comes with the narrator's acknowledgement that he has always himself been in love with Ailie. She turns him down, however, thus allowing the story to sustain its sense of the fading away of the romance and glamour of the past: 'in another month Ailie would be gone, and the South would be empty for me for ever'. [9]

Of course it is impossible to read this finely poised story without seeing in it Fitzgerald's vision of the South interpenetrating and modulating with his vision of Zelda. The Zelda of 1929 is clearly not the glamorously romantic figure of 1918. But Zelda's own South was not the one that Scott thought he recognized. For Zelda Sayre the meaning of the South was above all narrowness, limitation and restriction. The familial and social structures of the South were incompatible with the free spirit; for a young woman in particular, the South meant immutable rules of conduct limiting and circumscribing individual freedoms. For Zelda Sayre to become Zelda Fitzgerald was to strike a blow for freedom; to marry Scott Fitzgerald, and escape to New York, was a way out of the prison of the South.

In her autobiographical novel *Save Me the Waltz* (1932), Zelda provides an account of her growing up in Montgomery. As a child and young girl Alabama Beggs suffers no kind of actual oppression – her family love and protect her. Yet Zelda emphasizes the constraints that surround Alabama's life, the expectations that she is meant to fulfil: that she should agree, for example with her sister Joan's decision to make a 'sensible' marriage. As she grows up Alabama comes to feel 'the sense of suffocation that seemed to her to be eclipsing her family, her sisters, and mother'.[10] She indicates repeatedly her desire to be different, not to conform; hence her readiness to become 'the wildest one of the Beggs' [11] In marriage to David Knight she believes she has found her route to freedom; in bed in the Biltmore Hotel in New York after her wedding she feels she has arrived there: 'No power on earth could make her do anything, she thought frightened, any more, except herself'. [12] In fact Alabama's escape from the South proves to be much more problematic than she imagined – just as Zelda herself had recognized well before 1932.

In 1929 she wrote and published a story called 'Southern Girl' which is unmistakably her version of the story her husband wrote at her instigation and called 'The Ice Palace'. Once again the atmosphere and life-style of Jeffersonville are vividly evoked, and the story is narrated from the point-of-view of a local girl. Its theme of course is the contrast between North and South. Harriet runs a boarding-house in Jeffersonville; Dan from Ohio arrives there with his fiancee Louise. Dan responds positively to Southern manners and the Southern way of living; he breaks off with Louise and becomes engaged to Harriet. But when Harriet goes north to Ohio to visit Dan's mother, she feels completely out of her depth; where Louise – who is still around – appears entirely at her ease with Dan's well-to-do mother, and the social round of country clubs, Harriet feels that the freedom of her Southern manners makes her seem wholly out of place: 'She felt foreign to herself in finding herself so foreign to the others'.[11] Soon Dan breaks off again and marries Louise. But this is not the end of the story. In a final twist — which I feel reveals Zelda's own ambivalence over the possibilities of escaping or not escaping from the South — Harriet meets an architect from Ohio; runs away and marries him; and ends up living with his mother aping in every detail the kind of life she would have had had she married Dan. The impossibility of escape becomes possible after all.

Save Me the Waltz ends rather differently. Alabama Beggs' marriage to David Knight does allow her to escape from the South to New York and then to Europe. She is free — but free to be or do what? Her role as wife and mother she finds unfulfilling; but she struggles to find an identity that is simply her own. Only when she determines to master the art of the ballet-dancer does she truly become free. In real life Zelda turned down her one opportunity to become a professional dancer; in the novel Alabama accepts; succeeds; and then falls ill in a manner that destroys her career. The novel ends with Alabama returning to her hometown where her father is dying, and these closing pages are full of a rich sense of childhood, of family tradition, of memory, of history and the past. In a manner hauntingly prescient of Zelda's own return in the final years of her life to Montgomery and North Carolina, Alabama returns at the last to the South from which she had sought to escape. To some readers today that return will seem like a failure — a failure to find herself as artist and individual; to others it will be seen as a mature recognition of the individual's need to confront and come to terms with her past.

My title links the Fitzgeralds to the South today. In a moment I shall try to show that the South has recently shown increased interest in both Fitzgeralds, but what of the more general position? As I suggested earlier, my view is that while Scott Fitzgerald continues to be read and recognized as widely or even more widely than ever, in the American literary academy he does not excite particular interest. The Princeton centenary conference in 1996 was as interesting for the people who were not there and for the papers that were not presented as for those which were. The case with Zelda is precisely the reverse. Scott Fitzgerald does seem to suffer from the handicaps of being dead, white, and male, Zelda shares two at least of these attributes but she has the immense advantage of being female — and a female who struggled to be dancer, painter, and writer. It is the rise of feminist criticism that has led to the renewal of interest in Zelda Fitzgerald — not simply as the wife of Scott Fitzgerald but as an artist in her own right.

This is a development wholly to be admired: it is never too late for justice to be done. On the other hand, feminism frequently has its own agenda into which the individual text or author has to be fitted, and Zelda has not always avoided such a fate. A recent book-length study is entitled *Zelda Fitzgerald and the Failure of the American Dream for Women* (1991). Like other feminist accounts, this one suggests that Zelda was the victim of a series of familial, social, Southern, and American, patriarchal assumptions about the expected role of women both before marriage and after it. The difficulty is that the biographical evidence does not suggest that Zelda was ever prepared to be victimized by anyone's assumptions about anything. If she was a Southern belle she was a Southern belle very much on her own terms.

In her brilliant and ground-breaking 1970 study, *Zelda: A Biography*, Nancy Milford lets us read some of a note written to Zelda by her mother, which Zelda in turn enclosed in a letter to Scott. Here is what her mother said in 1919: 'Zelda: If you have added whiskey to your tobacco you can substract your Mother.... If you prefer the habits of a prostitute don't try to mix them with gentility. Oil and water do not mix'. [13] If there is a case to be made for the view that Zelda Fitzgerald was driven mad by a culture which could not allow her the freedom to be what she wanted to be, then the non-passive, non-victimized, tobacco-smoking and whiskey-drinking Zelda has at least to be fitted in to the final picture. There is a deep irony in the feminist vision of Zelda as the very conventional woman-victime which she herself daringly refused to be.

Finally let me return specifically to the story of the Fitzgeralds in the South today. It begins in the fall of 1971 when Scottie Lanahan Smith came down from Washington D.C. to Montgomery, Alabama, to dedicate a very small park, with a fountain, to the memory of her parents Scott and Zelda Fitzgerald. In the fashionable Cloverdale area of Montgomery, the park was quite close to the house at 913 Felder Avenue where Scottie had lived with her parents for nine months in 1931-32; the memorial park itself was devised by Milo B. Howard, the Alabama state archivist, and a Nimrod T. Frazer. Scottie often seems to have found her role as the daughter of famous parents a difficult one; certainly she did everything she could to protect her own children from over-exposure to the legend of their grandparents. Her own attitude seems neatly summed up by a remark she made to a friend, John Napier, after her return to Montgomery on a more permanent basis in 1973. Colonel Napier had seen her talking to two air-force officers on the veranda of her house in Gilmer Street — he asked who they were; Scottie's reply was devastatingly dismissive — 'Daddy-worshippers'. But the fascinating point is Scottie's own decision to return to her mother's hometown. She seems to have been much impressed by the warmth and cordiality of her reception in Montgomery when she came for the ceremony in 1971. Having decided to buy a house in the city, she was soon spending six months there, six months in Washington. After her divorce from Smith, she spent more and more time in Montgomery, participating in the cultural life of the city, working, for example, with Mrs John Napier, on the restoration of the original White House of the Confederacy. And it was in the house in Gilmer Street, in June, 1986, that Scottie died. Perhaps like Zelda before her, it was in the South that she finally recognized and accepted her own identity.

It was Scottie's death that led more or less directly to the next chapter in the Fitzgerald-Montgomery story. In the same year, 1986, the house the Fitzgeralds had lived in in Felder Avenue in the early thirties fell vacant. Soon there were rumours that the house — built early in the 20th century — was to be demolished to make way for condominiums. At this point Julian and Leslie McPhillips, who lived down the street from the Fitzgerald house, decided to buy it with the intention of converting part of it at least into a Fitzgerald Museum. Julian McPhillips' interest in the Fitzgeralds dated from his own student days at Princeton, and in December 1986 he told the *Alabama Journal* that Montgomery should be proud of its links with the Fitzgeralds. If the idea of the Museum could be successfully pursued, then it would celebrate these links — 'People may have a greater claim to F. Scott, but no one has a better claim to Zelda' said McPhillips — as well as preserve the memory of the late Scottie Smith. The Scott and Zelda Fitzgerald Museum Association was duly formed, and in October, 1987, the press reported that the Alabama Historical Commission had named the house in Felder Avenue an historic landmark. In December of that year the Museum Association held an open house to promote the Museum idea — and sponsored a lecture by Matthew Bruccoli to go with it. On May 4th, 1989, the scheme finally came to fruition with the grand opening of the Scott and Zelda Fitzgerald Museum. The day was celebrated with a Great Gatsby Bash, a jazz-band, and bathtubs of beer and wine. Today the museum flourishes with Al Norris as Executive Director, Julian McPhillips as President, Leslie McPhillips as Vice-President, Amy Strickland as Secretary-Treasurer, a Board of Directors of 18 Montgomery citizens, and

Honorary Board Members including surviving descendants of the Fitzgerald family. The growing collection includes a library of books by and about the Fitzgeralds, memorabilia of Zelda's family and her childhood; portraits and photographs of the Fitzgeralds and their homes at different periods in their lives; and a body of material by and concerning Scottie. The Fitzgeralds have finally come home again to the South.

1 F. Scott Fitzgerald, *The Beautiful and Damned* (Penguin Books, 1966), p. 261.
2 F. Scott Fitzgerald, 'The Last of the Belles' in *The Crack-Up With Other Pieces and Stories* (Penguin Books, 1965), p. 102.
3 Zelda Fitzgerald, *Save Me the Waltz* in Mathew J. Bruccoli, (ed.) *Zelda Fitzgerald, The Collected Writings* (Abacus, 1991), p. 181.
4 Zelda Fitzgerald, 'Southern Girl' in Bruccoli, *op.cit.,* p. 299.
5 *op cit.,* p.264
6 *ibid,* pp 274-5
7 *ibid,* p.275
8. *op. cit.*,p.92
9. *ibid,* p. 109
10 *op.cit.*, p.32
11 *ibid.*
12 *ibid*, p.44
13 Nancy Milford, *Zelda Fitzgerald* (Penguin Books, 1974), p. 52.

3 Scott Fitzgerald's Hollywood Fiction

I

Three times in his career Fitzgerald moved to Hollywood hoping that success as a screen-writer for films would solve his ever-present financial difficulties. The first occasion was in 1927; the second in late 1931 and early 1932; and the third lasted from 1937 until his death in 1940. The initial 1927 visit established a pattern that the subsequent visits confirmed: Fitzgerald achieved little as a screen-writer, and his financial position remained as problematic as ever. In 1927 the script that Fitzgerald eventually produced was turned down; thus the $12,500 he would have received – on top of the $3,500 original advance – never materialized. Such disappointments came to characterize Fitzgerald's relations with Hollywood. Yet it has to be said that in a sense Hollywood treated him quite generously. At the beginning of his third and final visit in 1937-38, when he was under contract to MGM, Fitzgerald's status as a major American writer was certainly in considerable decline, yet the studio was still prepared to pay him $1250 per week. Certainly it is difficult to see how he could have survived at all in the last two years of his life without the fees he picked up as a freelance writer in Hollywood.

Ending up with only a single screen credit to his name, Fitzgerald did not succeed in creative terms in Hollywood. Yet in terms of his own life as a writer of fiction the Hollywood years, as everyone knows, were in no way wholly unfruitful. Much of the last year of his life was spent working on a new Hollywood novel. In September 1939, he produced a lengthy synopsis of the novel which would remain unfinished at his death on December 21, 1940, but which Edmund Wilson would publish as The *Last Tycoon* less than a year later in October 1941.

Fitzgerald approached the writing of this new novel in a mood rather like that which had preceded the writing of *The Great Gatsby*. He was determined once again to recover lost ground, to show what he could do, to reassert his position as a major novelist. While at work on the novel, he wrote in his *Notebook*:

> 'I want to write scenes that are frightening and inimitable. I don't want to be as intelligible to my contemporaries as Ernest who as Gertrude Stein said, is bound for the Museums. I am sure that I am far enough ahead to have some small immortality if I can keep well.' [1]

To confirm his claim to 'some small immortality,[1] and perhaps enlarge it, was what he was aiming at in writing *The Last Tycoon*.

Gatsby had been written with the clear intention of forcing Fitzgerald's critics to recognize that he was a serious artist. Hence it was perhaps inevitable that, of all his books, it was *Gatsby* that was in the forefront of his mind when he came to compose *The Last Tycoon*. In October, 1940, he wrote to Zelda telling her his room was covered with charts describing the characters and their histories, just as it had been when he was working on *Tender is the Night;* however, the novel itself is 'more on the order of *Gatsby*'.[2] A week later, again to Zelda, he developed the comparison: 'I am deep in the novel, living in it, and it makes me happy. It is a constructed novel like *Gatsby,* with passages of poetic prose when it fits the action, but no ruminations or side-shows like *Tender*. Everything must contribute to the dramatic movement'.[3] These comparisons and contrasts with his earlier novels make it absolutely clear that Fitzgerald knew exactly what he was aiming at in *The Last Tycoon*. As early as 1933, in a letter to John Peale Bishop, he had described *Gatsby* as a 'dramatic' novel while *Tender is the Night* was a 'philosophical, now called psychological' one.[4] More recently, in a Hollywood letter of 1937, he had been even more explicit about the different types of novels he had already written. His novels, he wrote, 'have alternated between being selective and blown up. *Paradise* and *Gatsby* were selective; *The Beautiful and Damned* and *Tender* aimed at being full and comprehensive'. [5] what the letter to Zelda suggests is that *The Last Tycoon* will fall into the 'selective,' 'dramatic,' category of *Gatsby*, rather than the 'full and comprehensive' category of *Tender is the Night*.

Fitzgerald's remark to Zelda that the new novel made him happy reflects his confidence in the quality of what he was writing. He did not believe that the novel would necessarily be popular or successful, but he knew it was good. As early as October 1939, when he had just begun to write, he wrote to Scottie describing the work as 'a labor of love' which is 'maybe great'. [6] Later he told Edmund Wilson that his novel was good because 'I am trying a little harder than I ever have to be exact and honest emotionally'. [7] Another comment to Zelda indicates that his confidence in the novel related to his understanding of how what he was writing represented his artistic strengths: 'It is a novel *a la Flaubert* without 'ideas' but only people moved singly and in mass through what I hope are authentic moods'.[8] Flaubert of course suggests supreme stylistic precision, language used at its most aesthetically satisfying level, while the reference to the absence of 'ideas' — in the sense of detachable, abstract, philosophical themes — means only that Fitzgerald now understood that his artistic vision articulated itself always by way of the individual, responding consciousness rather than through any consistent set of abstract philosophical notions. After writing *The Beautiful and Damned* Fitzgerald seemed characteristically to blame himself for having paid too little attention to the 'general scheme' of the book: now he recognized that in his kind of fiction people and moods were more central that any kind of philosophical scheme or plan. The precise nature of the people and moods explored in *The Last Tycoon* seems also to be related to Fitzgerald's renewed confidence in the quality of what he was producing. And here again the example of *Gatsby* appears to have been very much in his mind. In September 1940, he wrote to Gerald Murphy that the new novel was 'as detached from me as *Gatsby* was, in intent anyhow'. [9] It is as if he suspected that one of the reasons he had wrestled so long with the writing of *Tender is the Night* was that there was just too much of himself and Zelda in the detail of that novel. He would not repeat that mistake. The new novel would be characterized precisely by its detachment from the everyday problems of its author's life. Is it the case, then, that *The Last Tycoon* is the work of a new Fitzgerald? After all it was only a year or two earlier that Fitzgerald had announced to the world that it was his precise intention to become an entirely different kind of writer.

The so-called 'Crack-Up' articles were written towards the end of 1935 and published in 1936. In three autobiographical essays Fitzgerald tries to account for the kind of disintegration he feels has overtaken his life. Initially he describes an overwhelming sense of anomie, a loss of confidence in everything in which he had once believed, even the disappearance of any faith in his own identity — 'there was not an "I" any more'. [10]

But it is in the third and final essay that Fitzgerald arrives at conclusions specifically concerning his role as writer. He says he had sought isolation for one reason only:

> 'I only wanted absolute quiet to think out why I had developed a sad attitude towards sadness, a melancholy attitude toward melancholy and a tragic attitude toward tragedy — *why I had become identified with the objects of my horror or compassion.*' [11]

He recognizes that 'identification such as this spells the death of accomplishment'. What was needed for survival was 'some sort of clean break'. He decides he will 'continue to be a writer' because that was his 'only way of life,' but he 'would cease any attempts to be a person — to be kind, just or generous'. [12] And the conclusion of the essay is a reiteration of the principle that the death of the man means the survival of the writer:

> 'I have now at last become a writer only. The man I had persistently tried to be became such a burden that I have 'cut him loose' with as little compunction as a Negro lady cuts loose a rival on a Saturday night.' [13]

Just before writing *The Crack-Up* Fitzgerald had of course finally completed *Tender is the Night*. And I would argue strongly that the autobiographical essays are highly relevant to what Fitzgerald was attempting to do in the work of fiction. Fitzgerald believes that his personal difficulties all flow from a confusion of the roles of man and writer: Dick Diver's fatal error is the confusion of the roles of man and psychiatrist. But rather than his past writing, do the *Crack-Up* articles illuminate the Hollywood fiction? In other words, is *The Last Tycoon* the work of the new 'writer only' Fitzgerald who is announced at the end of the autobiographical essays?

The artistic stance that Fitzgerald was telling himself to adopt in the dark days of 1936 was certainly one that encouraged him towards greater objectivity in his writing. *The Last Tycoon* does, as we shall see, reflect an attempt to achieve just such a goal. But there is no way in which the novel can be read as showing at any level Fitzgerald ceasing to be a man and becoming, in the sense that the *Crack-Up* defines the phrase, a writer only. What *The Last Tycoon* does reveal, however, is Fitzgerald's continuing awareness of the problems inherent in the roles of man and writer and the consequent tensions between the demands of art and life.

Yet if the 'writer only' Fitzgerald is not present in *The Last Tycoon,* he does emerge elsewhere in the final phase of Fitzgerald's Hollywood fiction. In the last year of his life, Fitzgerald's bread and butter writing consisted of seventeen stories for *Esquire* magazine, all concerning the same central figure, and now published in a single volume called *The Pat Hobby Stories.* Pat Hobby is a 49-year-old, increasingly out-of-work Hollywood screenwriter struggling to survive in a world where success is the only value that counts. The stories are sardonic, cynical, mordantly amusing. Pat Hobby himself, in the 1920s briefly the owner of a house with a swimming pool, is a has-been; broke, seedy, amoral, always with an eye on the main chance, but always losing out. In writing these stories, despite their superficial humour, Fitzgerald clearly draws upon a great deal of his own bitter disillusionment with Hollywood. On one level, this is the dark side of Hollywood that *The Last Tycoon* largely ignores.

On a deeper level, however, the Pat Hobby stories may be seen as an extended metaphor for the artistic self-definition that

Fitzgerald announced at the end of the *Crack-Up* articles. Through the character of Pat Hobby — whom Fitzgerald himself described in a letter to Arnold Gingrich, editor of *Esquire*, as 'a complete rat' [14]— Fitzgerald created, and simultaneously repudiated, the kind of artist figure he had insisted he would become. In the language of *The Crack-Up*, Pat Hobby has precisely ceased 'any attempts to be a person — , to be kind, just or generous'. He is interested in nothing but his own survival, and is constantly scheming, usually unsuccessfully, to try to ensure it. However, there is nothing to suggest any hope for Hobby's career as a screenwriter. Such reader sympathy as he evokes is directly related to the impression that he is never going to be other than a failure. If Pat Hobby is an image of the man who has become 'the writer only,' then Fitzgerald's ultimate rejection of such a role could not be more clear.

While the Pat Hobby stories reflect Fitzgerald's rejection of the cold-blooded artist role that the *Crack-Up* articles had ended by endorsing, *The Last Tycoon* does seem to reflect a new associated emphasis on authorial detachment. This is most evident in the narrative method that Fitzgerald chooses. Once again he goes back behind *Tender is the Night,* with its narrative looseness, to the tighter narrative structure of *The Great Gatsby*. *The Last Tycoon* is narrated by Cecilia Brady, a character in the novel whose role is quite similar to that of Nick Carraway in *The Great Gatsby*. Like Nick, Cecilia is involved in the action of the novel — which is at least in part about her — but she is not the main focus of attention. In so far as she is more than half in love with Monroe Stahr, the last tycoon himself, she is more involved, less detached, than Nick Carraway is with Gatsby, but there are advantages in this situation. If the main focus of the novel is intended to be Stahr's relationship with Katherine, the girl who seems to be the reincarnation of his dead wife, then to have the story told by a young, female character, herself deeply attracted to Stahr, nicely complicates the point of view and works against any kind of excessive sentimentality. Admittedly the text as it exists makes it clear that Fitzgerald was having some difficulty with Cecilia as narrator — but it was the kind of difficulty that the use of an internal character narrator creates for most authors. How can such a narrator be realistically allowed to know all that is needed to get the story told? The difficulty in Cecilia's case is over the scenes between Monroe Stahr and Kathleen; as it stands the text here allows her to drop out of sight, and the narrative seems to become the author's own.

Fitzgerald indeed has to revert to clumsy reminders to the reader of Cecilia's role: 'This is Cecilia taking up the narrative in person' and 'This is Cecilia taking up the story'. Of course, if Fitzgerald had survived to complete the novel, there is every possibility he would have found a way round the difficulty which such phrases clearly reflect. What is not in question is that Fitzgerald had thought out Cecilia's role as character-narrator with considerable care. Telling the story five years after the event, perhaps from a sanatorium bed, her character is to mature and develop as a consequence of the story in which she is caught up. (The parallel with Nick Carraway in *Gatsby* is again apparent.) Also, by making her the daughter of a Hollywood business mogul, Fitzgerald allows her to be simultaneously an insider and an outsider in Hollywood terms, and thus ideally placed as a narrator-observer. In Fitzgerald's terms she is 'all at once, intelligent, cynical but understanding and kindly toward the people, great or small, who are of Hollywood'. Writing to Kenneth Littauer, the editor of *Collier's Magazine* whom he hoped would accept *The Last Tycoon* for serial publication, Fitzgerald explained that by using Cecilia as a narrator he hoped 'to get the verisimilitude of a first person narrative, combined with a Godlike knowledge of all events that happen to my characters'. [15] But that combination — a difficult one to achieve — is not quite successfully present in the text at least as it survives.

Fitzgerald's plan for *The Last Tycoon* was that it should be like *Gatsby* not only in its narrative structure but in its scale. It was to be some fifty thousand words long, divided, as *Gatsby* was, into nine chapters. But the evidence suggests that in the end *The Last Tycoon* would not have paralleled the extraordinary poetic economy of *Gatsby*. The published fragment is already over forty thousand words long, and only about half of the outline plan has been covered. If one assumes that the rest of the material required similar treatment in terms of length, then *The Last Tycoon* might easily have ended up twice as long as Fitzgerald had originally projected. One may not be wholly convinced by the development of plot and action in the later stages of the novel that Fitzgerald outlined — there may be too much in the way of murder and blackmail — but that is not to say that simply by becoming longer *The Last Tycoon* was running out of control. There is no evidence of this in the published section. On the contrary, *The Last Tycoon* might easily have finally brought together the best of Fitzgerald's poetic suggestiveness, his lyricism, and mythopoetic imagination, with his detailed emotional honesty and depth of inner exploration of individual character.

II

In writing *The Last Tycoon,* Fitzgerald, as in all his fiction, drew heavily upon his own experience. Thus he acknowledged that the figure of Monroe Stahr, the novel's protagonist, was based on Irving Thalberg, the Hollywood producer who became head of production at Universal at the age of twenty and died when he was thirty-seven. Fitzgerald greatly admired Thalberg whom he knew only slightly; the impression the producer created though, he noted, was 'very dazzling in its effect on me'. Yet Stahr is not of course simply Thalberg; Fitzgerald noted at the same time that Stahr contained 'much of myself'.[16] Similarly, there is no doubt that for the character of Kathleen Moore, with whom Stahr falls in love, Fitzgerald drew upon his own relationship with Sheilah Graham. But in this case in particular the degree of formal control, and the distancing resulting from it, that Fitzgerald achieves over the material, however personal in its origins, is such that the link with his own life is irrelevant. In *Tender is the Night* the relationship between Dick Diver and Nicole is sometimes blurred by its uneasy parallel with the lives of Scott and Zelda. In *The Last Tycoon* the relationship between Stahr and Kathleen is in comparison pure and crystalline; life is entirely subdued by art. The role of the screenwriter in Hollywood is another area of *The Last Tycoon* where Fitzgerald clearly draws upon his own — less than happy — experience. But once again the objectivity of art is much in evidence: rather than any kind of special pleading on behalf of the talented writer exploited by the Hollywood production machine, Fitzgerald seems to sympathize with Stahr's toughness towards the writers he employs. In all these cases, *The Last Tycoon* shows Fitzgerald in complete artistic control of the material out of which he was fashioning his novel.

I have already suggested that the artistic strengths of *The Last Tycoon* in no way mean that Fitzgerald has become the coldly detached kind of writer he said he would become in the conclusion to the *Crack-Up* articles. Equally, however, his own concerns over the roles of man and writer, present throughout his writing career, are in no way absent from the text of his last novel. Indeed in *The Last Tycoon* the relationships between art and life, the artist and the man, are as problematic as ever.

The story of *The Last Tycoon* has both a public and a private face. This is something new for Fitzgerald, whose earlier novels had always focused on the private lives of their characters. The protagonists of the two first novels choose to reject the public world: it is too corrupt or unfulfilling for them to be part of it. Gatsby has a public existence but what it is, is deliberately kept shadowy and mysterious. With Dick Diver, Fitzgerald at last portrays a character with a profession; but what the novel is concerned to show is the manner in which Dick gradually abandons his profession. Thus there is not a great deal in *Tender is the Night* about Dick's actual work as a psychiatrist.

With *The Last Tycoon,* it is different. Monroe Stahr's work as a film producer is as central to the novel as his affair with Kathleen Moore:the protagonist's public and private roles now interact and illuminate each other. The novel is as much concerned with Stahr's role in the studio — his direct involvement in film-making, the decisions he makes, the authority he wields, and the challenge that begins to be made against him — as it is with his private relationship with Kathleen.

Fitzgerald wants to persuade the reader that Stahr really is a star of Hollywood, an heroic figure, by showing him in action He is defined by his work. He is offered for our admiration on account of his professionalism, the way in which he in on top of his job. He is efficient, decisive, purposeful, knowing what he wants to achieve, refusing to allow himself to be diverted by the scheming or silliness of those around him. In a series of convincing scenes Stahr is shown demonstrating these qualities as he gets on with his job. Yet Stahr does have something in common with earlier Fitzgerald heroes such as Gatsby and Dick Diver. Like them, Stahr is able to impose himself upon others; like them, he has a kind of personal charm and charisma that make others rely on him; like them, he sorts out other people's problems — he is the one who can salvage a reputation, stop a rumour in its tracks, re-direct a career. The difference, however, is that Stahr's kind of individual concern is used to sort out others working lives. Once again it is as though Fitzgerald wants to accord moral authority to a kind of professionalism — as though he had gone back to Conrad, and perhaps Hemingway, in linking moral integrity to purely professional skill and judgment.

Stahr, however, is presented as much more than just a successful Hollywood film producer. He is a businessman, dealing in millions of dollars, wholly aware that Hollywood is a world of commercial materialism. But Stahr is also an artist. Fitzgerald rejects the idea that the commercialism of Hollywood means that its products have nothing to offer the world of culture and art; *The Last Tycoon* mocks the kind of writer who thinks that his art is too pure to be sullied by contact with film makers. Stahr's concern is with the quality of the films he makes; money, pure commercialism, never determine his decisions. In *Tender is the Night,* Dick Diver the psychiatrist is an artist by analogy. In *The Last Tycoon* no such analogy is needed: as a maker of films, Monroe Stahr is an artist in his own right —

an artist whom Fitzgerald invites us to admire for his dedication, professionalism, and personal integrity.

Yet inevitably this means that *The Last Tycoon* will continue to explore Fitzgerald's own central concerns with the problematical relationship between the artist and the man. Successful as a Hollywood film producer, what kind of a man is Stahr? With his wife dead, Stahr's life seems to revolve exclusively around his film-making. He is the dedicated artist, with no life outside the studio. Is this indeed why he is so successful? When Cecilia lets Stahr know that she would be happy to marry him, he replies, 'Oh, no ... Pictures are my girl. I haven't got much time ... I mean any time'. [17] Later it emerges that he had not 'lost his head' even over Minna, the beautiful star he had married: only when she was dying had he been in love with her. As a young man 'emotional sprees' (p.117) had never attracted him, and he had grown up, learning humane lessons, but never giving himself with any kind of total emotional commitment. Even at a moment of emotional climax in the novel, when it appears that by simply speaking out, declaring himself to Kathleen, he can win her, he hesitates and does not speak: 'but something else said to sleep on it as an adult, no romantic'.(p.139) There is a sense then in which Stahr, unlike Dick Diver, is a portrait of the artist who does not allow the complexities and commitments of living to interfere with the dedicated pursuit of his art.

But of course there is no way in which 'the last tycoon' can be seen as the type of coldly dehumanized artist figure Fitzgerald had declared himself as choosing to be in the *Crack-Up* articles. In a brilliant and haunting early scene Kathleen Moore literally floats into Stahr's life after an earthquake tremor causes a flood in the studio lot. With an extraordinary shock of recognition Stahr sees in the face of this unknown girl a reincarnation of that of his dead wife: 'An awful fear went over him, and he wanted to cry aloud. Back from the still sour room, the muffled glide of the limousine hearse, the falling concealing flowers, from out there in the dark — here now warm and glowing'. (p.33) But characteristically Stahr does not cry aloud; and when he hears a voice that is not Minna's voice, he does not even speak. However, in the days that follow, while his public life as film producer goes on as before, he pursues Kathleen out of the deepest kind of need. Fitzgerald handles their affair with a delicacy that is artistically perfect; the emotional honesty he aims at is triumphantly achieved, and as a result nowhere in his fiction is the movement of a personal relationship rendered more persuasively. The effect inevitably is to humanize Stahr; pictures after all are not his girl. As a film maker he continues to fight for what he believes in; but as a man he accepts his commitment to the world of experience and feeling.

Not even Monroe Stahr, however, can win. He is ill, probably dying, and his enemies in the studio are plotting against him. All Fitzgerald's outlines of the story make it clear that Stahr will die – and that his relationship with Kathleen will be used against him. Not even in *The Last Tycoon* will Fitzgerald allow art or the artist to triumph over the complexities of life and living.

III

Among Fitzgerald's many notes for *The Last Tycoon* occurs this intriguing comment on his own position as writer: 'I am the last of the novelists for a long time now'.[18]

What exactly he meant is far from clear. A growing awareness of the passing of time, accompanied by a deeper sense of the movement of history itself, is manifest in Fitzgerald's artistic career. Writing now after the outbreak of the Second World War, perhaps he is acknowledging that his friend John Dos Passos had been right to remind him back in 1936 at the time of the *Crack-Up* articles that he could only go on writing as long as 'the murderous forces of history' would allow. In any event a sense of 'lastness', an elegiac feeling of the passing away of things, is strongly present in *The Last Tycoon*. (Fitzgerald had not made up his mind about the title of his last novel: *The Last Tycoon* is merely a version of a possible title which Edmund Wilson chose to adopt.) In *The Beautiful and Damned* Fitzgerald describes a visit that Anthony and Gloria pay to the home of General Robert E. Lee in Arlington, near Washington. Gloria is appalled by the way in which the mass of tourists seems to demean the house, take away its historical meaning. The values of 1860 are disconnected from those of 1914. Similarly, in the opening sequence of *The Last Tycoon,* Cecilia and two of her fellow-passengers, their aeroplane grounded by a storm in Nashville, Tennessee, go to visit the Hermitage, the home of President Andrew Jackson. Later we learn that Schwartz, the passenger whose Hollywood career has ended in failure, stays behind at the Hermitage in order to shoot himself. Fitzgerald seems once again to be consciously juxtaposing the American past, an older traditional America – the America of houses which contained 'the old American parlour that used to be closed except on Sundays' (p.142) – against a newer, rawer, more frightening America. Monroe Stahr, under pressure from big business on the one side, organized trade unions on the other, seems to belong to that older, more heroic America. But of course the point is that Stahr cannot survive. And here once again Fitzgerald's life and art play off against each other with the deepest kind of irony. Fitzgerald never managed to find a way of reconciling the demands of art and the demands of life. The best he could do was to confront the problem by writing about it, as he continues to do in *The Last Tycoon*. But the novel also continues his career-long meditation on the meaning of American history. That meditation is summed up in this passage from his notes for *The Last Tycoon:*' I look out at it – and I think it is the most beautiful history in the world. It is the history of me and of my people ... It is the history of all aspiration – not just the American dream but the human dream and if I came at the end of it that too is a place in the line of the pioneers'. The sense of the ending of things, so richly present here, and so reminiscent of the closing sentences of *The Great Gatsby*, is made infinitely more poignant by the fact of Fitzgerald's death before he could come to the end of *The Last Tycoon*. But what we recognize now is that Fitzgerald's art had achieved by then more than enough to ensure that the ironies of his life would not have the last word.

1 See M.J. Bruccoli, *Some Sort of Epic Grandeur*, (London, Sydney, Auckland, Toronto, 1981), p.488.
2 Andrew Turnbull, (ed.), *The Letters of F. Scott Fitzgerald* (Penguin Books, 1968), p.145.
3 *Letters*, p.146.
4 *Letters*, p,383.
5 *Letters*, p.571.
6 *Letters*, p.77.
7 *Letters*, p.369.
8 *Letters*, p.149.
9 *Letters*, p.450.
10 F. Scott Fitzgerald, *The Crack-Up with other Pieces and Stories*, (Penguin Books, 1965), p.50.
11 *The Crack-Up*, p.51-52.
12 *The Crack-Up*. p.53.
13 *The Crack-Up*, p.55.
14 F. Scott Fitzgerald, *The Pat Hobby Stories*, (Penguin Books, 1967), p.13.
15 See Bruccoli, *Some Sort of Epic Grandeur*, p.477.
16 See Bruccoli, *Some Sort of Epic Grandeur*, p.466.
17 F. Scott Fitzgerald, *The Last Tycoon* (Penguin Books, 1960), p.86. All subsequent references are to this edition.
18 See Bruccoli, *Some Sort of Epic Grandeur*, p.467.

4 The Enduring Gatsby

Directed by the Australian Baz Luhrmann, and starring Leonardo DiCaprio and Carey Mulligan, the latest (2013) film version of Scott Fitzgerald's *The Great Gatsby* opens in the US on May 10th, in the U.K. on May 16th. But the new film is only one among a quite extraordinary range of artistic productions testifying to the enduring appeal of both Fitzgeralds. *Z: A Novel of Zelda Fitzgerald* by Theresa Anne Fowler was published a few weeks ago. Two more novels are due to appear soon: *Beautiful Fools* by R. Clifton Spargo, and *Call me Zelda* by Erika Robuck. (I know nothing of Ms Robuck, but by echoing the opening sentence of *Moby-Dick* – 'Call me Ishmael' – she is obviously taking quite a gamble.) Yet another untitled novel is also in the stocks. *The Great Gatsby Musical* opened in a London theatre last August, and *Zelda at the Oasis*, a new play by P.H. Lin, premiered in New York in December. Meanwhile, 'Gatz', which involves a group of actors reading the complete text of *The Great Gatsby* in a single session, has recently packed in audiences around the world including New York, London and Los Angeles.

The multiple ironies at the heart of this amazing Fitzgerald-fest would not be lost on Scott and Zelda. In Jazz Age America, after the success of the twenty-three year old Fitzgerald's first novel – *This Side of Paradise* – the newly-married Fitzgeralds quickly became archetypes of the new phenomenon of glamorous celebrities. Indeed the first half of Fitzgerald's career, in all its early brilliance and success, seemed to echo the economic boom of 1920s America. A second novel – *The Beautiful and Damned* – followed in 1922 and, like its predecessor, sold close to 50,000 copies. Two collections of short stories also sold well.

In the midst of this narrative of success, the Gatsby story is a very different one. Published in 1925, *The Great Gatsby* was in one sense a triumph. Fitzgerald had finally written a book that got him what above all else he wanted: recognition that he was a major American novelist. The fellow-writers and critics whom he most respected were unanimous in their praise: *Gatsby* was a great book. In terms of sales, though, the story was very different. However hard it is for us to understand – given what the future was to bring – *The Great Gatsby* was a huge disappointment for Fitzgerald in terms of sales. An initial print run of 20,870 copies was eventually sold out; a second printing of 3000 copies followed, but years later some of these remained unsold. In other words *Gatsby* at the time sold only half as well as the previous two novels. (William Collins, Fitzgerald's British publisher, decided against reprinting the novel – because 'the atmosphere of the book is extraordinarily foreign to the English reader, and he simply would not believe in it'.)

It would take Fitzgerald almost ten years to finish another novel: *Tender is the Night* finally appeared in 1934. By then its author's life, like that of much post-1929 Wall Street crash America, had descended into deep depression. For the rest of his short career, Fitzgerald would struggle professionally and personally. Zelda's mental breakdown meant she was constantly in and out of hospitals and clinics; his own alcoholism was a growing problem. And the days when he could earn an amazing $4000 for a single story in the *Saturday Evening Post* were long gone. When he died in Hollywood in 1940 at the age of 44, effectively unemployed, and with the text of a new novel – *The Last Tycoon* – only half completed, he believed he was a forgotten man. And in terms of readership he was right: royalties from his novels had dwindled away to next to nothing.

Yet extraordinarily it took only a few years for a dramatic transformation to occur. Launched perhaps by his fellow-Princetonian Edmund Wilson's edition of *The Crack-Up* in 1945, containing essays and letters by Fitzgerald, as well as tributes from contemporary authors, the forgotten man of 1940 was soon re-emerging as a major figure in America's literary culture. *The Great Gatsby* above all was quickly recognized as a classic American text – required reading in every American high school and college. In no time it was selling at least 300,000 copies every single year.

With the immense publicity surrounding the new *Gatsby* film, that figure will undoubtedly be surpassed in 2013. Two new paperback editions have already appeared. One tied to the film has a flashy cover which features DiCaprio and the other stars in the film. Scribners are printing 350,000 copies of this edition, and significantly Walmart stores across the US will stock it alone. However the top selling title on Amazon in April was the rival paperback edition which reproduces the cover of the original 1925 edition. (Copies of the first printing of that edition with the original cover sell for as much as $150,000.) Francis Cugat's cover features a strange, deep blue, shadowy vision of two eyes and bright red lips looming over a gleaming New York cityscape. (Fitzgerald may have drawn on this image in describing the eyes of Doctor T.J. Eckleburg brooding over the novel's valley of ashes between West Egg and the city.) At the moment – before the actual opening of the new film – the version with the 1925 cover seems to be winning the sales battle. Coming up on the outside, however, the e-book version of *Gatsby* may in the end outsell both paperback editions. By the end of 2013 may the total sales of *The Great Gatsby* exceed one million? It's not impossible. This side of paradise indeed for Scott Fitzgerald.

5 Filming *The Great Gatsby*

In some ways Baz Luhrmann's film of *The Great Gatsby* (2013) is everything that Fitzgerald's novel is not. Where the novel is short and lean, the film is long and ample. The film is as loud, brash, and extravagant, as anything that has ever been written about the so-called 'Roaring Twenties' or Jazz Age America. It's true of course that Fitzgerald's protagonist emerges as an archetype of that fast and furious 20s world. But while he might well have made this film, Gatsby does not write the book.

As I indicated in a previous article, Fitzgerald was bitterly disappointed in 1925 by the failure of his novel to become any kind of bestseller. On the other hand he was partially mollified by the book's largely favourable critical reception and delighted by the new level of prestige and status as a writer its success brought him. None of this, however, made him change his mind over a basic problem: even favourable reviewers and readers had failed to see what his book was really about. Writing to Carl Van Vechten thanking him for his positive and perceptive review, Fitzgerald said that while others had been complimentary, 'only three or four seemed to have cared to notice what I was driving at and whether or not I approached realizing my intention'. In a letter to his friend Edmund Wilson, he went further: 'of all the reviews', he wrote, 'even the most enthusiastic, not one had the slightest idea what the book was about'.

As it happens, Baz Luhrmann's 'Gatsby' remains remarkably faithful to the text of the novel. The film's dialogue, for example, rarely diverges from Fitzgerald's in the book. Equally we encounter the novel's characters, locations, and events more or less exactly as they are in the novel. But does this mean that the director has, as it were, passed Fitzgerald's test, and shown that he cannot be included among those lacking the slightest idea of what the novel is about? Unfortunately I think not.

Most of the principal actors in the film do well. Leonardo DiCaprio, giving one of his finest performances, is excellent as Gatsby; Carey Mulligan is sufficiently appealing as Daisy; Joel Edgerton is effectively overbearing as Tom Buchanan. Tobey Maguire's Nick Carraway, however, is a disaster, and the source of the film's major weakness. Carraway of course is crucially the novel's narrator. It is his story we read. Now it's true that at the outset of the novel Nick tells us that he had returned from his venture into the world of New York, a deeply disillusioned and morally offended man: 'when I came back from the East last autumn I felt that I wanted the world to be in uniform and at a sort of moral attention forever...' But this hardly justifies Luhrmann's opening the film with Carraway being treated in some kind of psychiatric clinic – and only writing down his memories of his involvement with Gatsby on his doctor's advice.

This clumsy attempt to explain Nick's dual role as a participant at the heart of the events he is also narrating is only a minor flaw. A major one is Tobey Maguire's version of Nick Carraway's character. For most of the film Maguire's Carraway comes over as naïve to the point of simple-mindedness, caught up in a sequence of events he finds entirely baffling. A look of blank vacuousness rarely leaves his face. Fitzgerald's Carraway may sometimes struggle to understand Jay Gatsby and his behaviour, but his mind is never vacant. Regrettably, that is exactly what Maguire's appears to be.

Many of the mass of current commentators on the book and the film, including Jay McInerney in the recent BBC 2 Culture Show Special on Fitzgerald, have been insisting on how much of Fitzgerald himself has gone into the creation of Gatsby. And of course there is some truth in this view. But it is far from the whole story. There is equally as much of Fitzgerald in the character of Nick Carraway. Near the end of the novel's second chapter, when he finds himself caught up in the deeply unpleasant party in Tom Buchanan and his mistress Myrtle Wilson's secret apartment in New York City, Carraway describes himself as 'within and without, simultaneously enchanted and repelled by the inexhaustible variety of life'. This is exactly Fitzgerald's own position. As a man of the rumbustious, postwar, 1920s, seeking and celebrating every kind of new, uninhibited freedom, Fitzgerald was determined to experience everything life had to offer. (Hence his wonderfully imaginative understanding of James Gatz's determination to remake himself as Jay Gatsby.) But as an artist and writer, Fitzgerald knew his role was to stand back from life and experience, to preserve the detachment necessary for the transformation of observation into art. Like Carraway in the novel, Fitzgerald himself had to live simultaneously within and without the world around him.

Unfortunately, the bemused Carraway of the film can provide the audience with little or nothing in the way of understanding the true significance of Gatsby's life and behaviour. In the film, Gatsby's parties are no more than raucous extravaganzas. The alternatives behind the material excess – the alternatives of hope and aspiration, of romantic readiness or romantic gesture — supplied by Fitzgerald's lyrical prose, simply disappear. More seriously, without an informed and informing narrative voice, the film's audience is in the end denied any suggestion of the wider resonances that transform this tale of a 1920s bootlegger in pursuit of a lost love into an elegiac and classic commentary on the whole history of America, and the tragic limitations of all human aspiration. This is the sixth attempt to make a film out of *The Great Gatsby*. There remains room for a seventh.

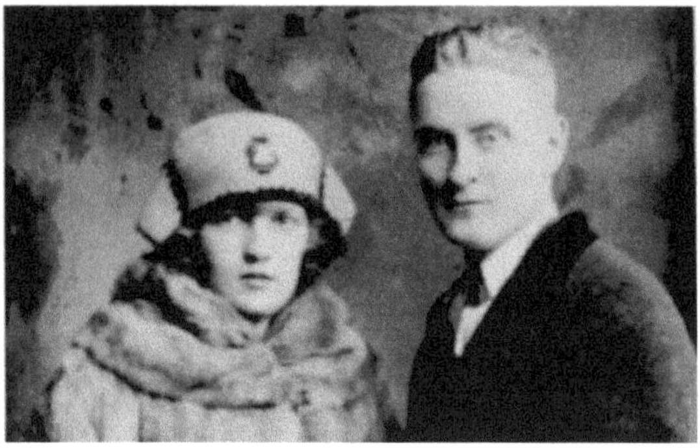

Zelda and Scott in 1921

Part Six

U.K.and US universities.

Over a long career in a range of British and American universities, I have to record that my experience has been an overwhelmingly positive one. I regard myself as extremely lucky to have been able to lead such a rewarding and fulfilling professional life. I have found the academic world almost always a welcoming one. In both countries, faculty and students have seemed to work together to make the university experience a genuinely life-enhancing one. From time to time one finds oneself talking to someone who in the past was one's student. It's good to hear that one's lectures or tutorials did have an impact!

Given all this, it's hardly surprising that since retiring from full-time teaching, I have paid close attention to what has been going on in the university world today. I'm fully aware of the danger of sentimentalising or romanticising the past, but I'm afraid that my sense is that my own university career spanned the best of times. The university world has become a harsher one than in the past. In some of the pieces that follow I try to point up the kind of changes that have led me to such a conclusion.

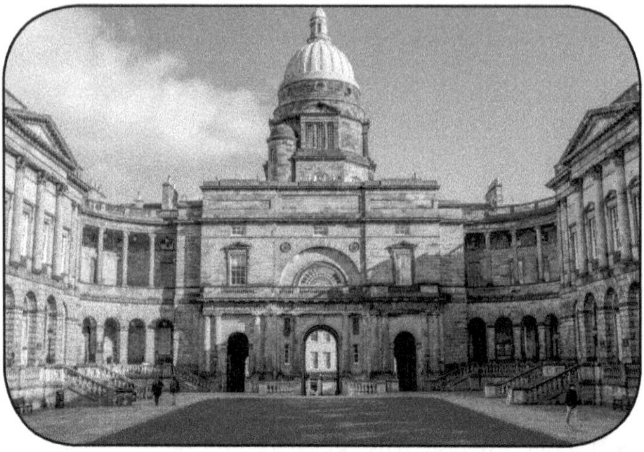

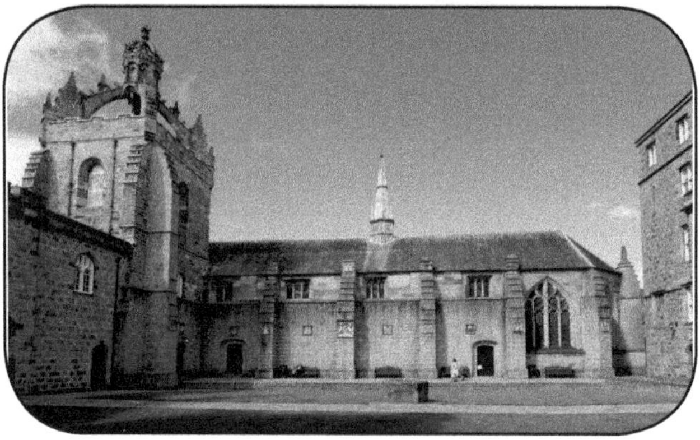

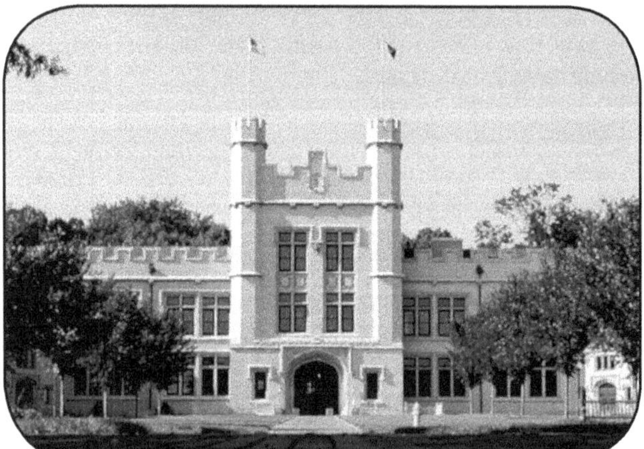

From top: Old College, Edinburgh University; King's College Chapel, Aberdeen; Kauke Hall, College of Wooster

1 John Maclean: Princeton's Professor of Chemistry

Soon after beginning work on this paper, I learned that John Maclean's son – John Maclean Jr, initially professor of mathematics, subsequently professor of ancient languages, and from 1854 to 1868, tenth president of the College of New Jersey – had written a memoir of his father's life. I was delighted to find that the research annexe of Glasgow University library contained a copy of this work which I duly ordered up. When it arrived my delight was still greater. It turns out that Glasgow's copy was the personal gift of President Maclean and that it arrived bearing the following handwritten inscription: 'Presented to the University of Glasgow, with the best wishes of the Author' and signed 'John Maclean, Princeton N.J. May 19th, 1885'. I found it both extraordinary and moving that I had in my hand, here in Glasgow, a book handled and signed in Princeton by the son of the John Maclean who had chosen to leave Glasgow for the United States in 1795. 1795, 1885 and the present seem suddenly linked together to a quite remarkable degree; past and present are, for once, within touching reach of each other.

Of course there is nothing surprising in John Maclean Jr's decision to send a copy of his book about his father to Glasgow University. The Macleans were originally a Glasgow family. John Maclean himself was born in Glasgow in 1771. His father, yet another John Maclean, practised surgery in the city, having previously been a doctor in the British army. However, both John Maclean's parents died relatively young and a George Mackintosh became his guardian. Charles Mackintosh, George Mackintosh's eldest son, and John Maclean became lifelong friends, and among their shared interests was the study of chemistry. However their careers were to follow different paths. Mackintosh, despite remaining enough of a scientist to become a Fellow of the Royal Society, chose business and commerce rather than the academy, and became rich and famous as the inventor of the waterproof fabric necessary for the manufacture of the raincoat – or mackintosh as it is still frequently called. Maclean was educated initially at Glasgow Grammar School (which became the High School of Glasgow in the nineteenth century) and then at Glasgow College which he entered at the age of twelve. Glasgow University's matriculation records identify him as a member of Professor William Richardson's class in Humanity in 1783. His son's memoir suggests he would also have studied Mathematics, Natural Philosophy, and Chemistry. However, these are subjects for which students were not required to matriculate so unfortunately no class lists survive. What we are certain of is that Maclean was an active member of the university's Chemical Society. This was basically a student club, established with the approval of the college authorities in 1782 or 83. It met once a week in the class room of either Professor Thomas Reid or Professor John Millar, and several of the papers that the young John Maclean read at the society survive. The Chemical Society appears to have disappeared around 1794 or 95 – significant years as we shall see both in Maclean's own life and in Scotland's social and political life in general.

In his student years Maclean's original intention seems to have been to follow in his father's footsteps and qualify as a surgeon. In 1790 Dr Alexander Stevenson certified that John Maclean had taken Glasgow College courses in the Theory and Practice of Physics, Botany, Anatomy, and Midwifery probably in the years 1786-7. Lectures on Surgery would have been part of the course on Anatomy. After 1787 Maclean left Glasgow for Edinburgh probably to attend the lectures of Joseph Black, formerly a pupil of William Cullen's in Glasgow, and his successor as professor of chemistry in Edinburgh. Black by then had of course become recognized as one of the period's outstanding chemists. After Edinburgh Maclean went on to pursue his studies both of surgery and chemistry in London and Paris in the years between 1787 and 1790. Back in Glasgow in 1790, Maclean became known as a leading exponent of the new 'French' chemistry developed by Lavoisier, Berthollet, and others. However in 1791 he was admitted to the Faculty of Physicians and Surgeons of the city of Glasgow by the then president Dr Robert Cleghorn, and in the following years began to develop his medical practice in the city. Why then, in 1795, did he decide to emigrate to the United States?

His son's Memoir offers a clue. Writing of his father's period in Paris and his mastery of the French language, he goes on:

> Not only did Dr. Maclean embrace the new system of Chemistry, as developed and taught by the French Savans of this period, but he appears also to have entertained views on the comparative merits of the monarchical and republican forms of government, which eventually led him to emigrate to the United States.[1]

Entertaining views on the comparative merits of monarchical and republican forms of government probably hardly does justice to the young Maclean's politics in the heady early days of the French Revolution. When exactly Maclean was in Paris we do not know, but it could easily have been within months of the storming of the Bastille. Nor is it likely that it was only when he reached France that he developed his radical views on desirable modes of government. Maclean had been a student in Glasgow University in the 1780s – a period when he must have heard a great deal about the rights of man and the case for major reform of the British political system. Writing about Irish students studying divinity in Glasgow around this period, I noted that no fewer than ten Glasgow-trained Irish Presbyterian ministers were active supporters of the United Irishmen movement in 1798. Like them, Maclean in Glasgow would inevitably have experienced an intellectual world in which discussion and debate about the need for radical social and political change and reform was not at all uncommon. Even if he did not take any of the classes of Thomas Reid or John Millar or John Anderson or Archibald Arthur or George Jardine – all of whom were ready to support the ideals and aims of the early French revolutionaries – he could hardly not have encountered something of their views. One wonders indeed whether the student Chemical Society, supported by Reid and Millar, did not reflect a kind of youthful radicalism of its own.

Disappearing around 1794 or 1795, the Chemical Society might well have been a victim of the clampdown on every form of challenge to the status quo in society imposed in these years by the Scottish government. The trial of Thomas Muir in 1793, and the transportation of all five 'Scottish martyrs' in 1794, made it clear just how dangerous it had become for Scots to profess reformist principles of any kind. Whether Maclean was in danger of persecution by the authorities in Glasgow is not clear. Michael Durey in his book *Transatlantic Radicals and the Early American Republic* [2] says Maclean, whom he describes as 'the brilliant young physician', may well have been a member of the Glasgow branch of the Friends of the People organization. If this were the case he would undoubtedly have come under suspicion , and it would explain why he found in this period that his professional prospects had seriously declined. Among his Glasgow friends was John Craig Millar, son of Professor John Millar and married to a daughter of William Cullen, whose own son was a Whig lawyer very active in the movement for reform. Another Whig lawyer, and deeply committed to liberal, reform principles, Millar too would soon decide on emigration to America. Maclean seems to have been contemplating the move from early in 1794.

In September of that year, Mrs Anne Grant of Laggan, author among other works of *Memoirs of an American Lady*, wrote to her friend Mrs George Mackintosh referring to John Maclean as follows: 'Did I tell you what pleasure it gives me to find that your friend and favourite Dr. Maclean had given up that wild scheme of going to America?' She goes on to admit how much she had enjoyed her own early experience of America but that 'the alterations which the last twenty years have brought about in that country', and her own changed views, would make it impossible for her to return.[3] What she means of course is that for a Tory like her, the independent United States, rather than the desirable place of refuge it was for liberal-minded Scots, was a wholly unacceptable location. In any event, Maclean had not changed his mind about America.

A little over six months later, in April, 1795, he left Scotland for New York. In his son's words, he had decided 'it would be better for him to settle in this country, the political sentiments of which were fully in accord with his own: and in which he would have as wide a field for scientific research and usefulness, as he could possibly have anywhere else'. Having adopted the motto "Ubi libertas, ibi patria", and believing that 'his idea of true liberty could be realized most readily and happily under our Republican form of government', he soon decided to become an American citizen[4].

Unlike some of the British radicals who arrived in the US at this time, Maclean seems not to have become engaged in the American political scene. When his son was twelve years old and an 'ardent Federalist', he remembers asking his father about his political views. Someone had described Maclean as a Democrat but asked about this he had said 'he was a British but not an American democrat' adding that as a foreigner by birth, 'he deemed it his duty not to take an active part in any merely political contests'[5]. One senses a slightly bland tone to this exchange but there is no evidence to suggest that Maclean in America engaged in any kind of political activity. Equally there is nothing to suggest that his political principles ever changed.

Early on in Princeton he met Wolfe Tone and his family, who had rented a farm nearby in 1795. When the United Irishmen movement was crushed in 1798, and Wolfe Tone executed, he remained a helpful and lifelong friend of Matilda Tone. Again, once in America he remained in touch with his fellow Scottish exile, John Craig Millar. The Millars had crossed the Atlantic at almost exactly the same time and they would visit Maclean in Princeton late in 1795. Maclean and Millar clearly had much in common. Active in the movement for liberal reform in Scotland, denied advancement in their respective professions as a result, both had chosen exiled in a country whose form of government they admired. But their fates in their new home would prove very different. John Craig Millar and his wife left Philadelphia for western Pennsylvania where they hoped to establish a new community for Scottish emigrants in particular. But soon afterwards, working on his land, Millar suffered from heatstroke and died. Maclean, on the other hand, left Philadelphia for Princeton where he would enjoy a successful career of scientific usefulness.

Landing in New York in April or May 1795, Maclean soon left for Philadelphia. The medical establishment of that city was aware of his impending arrival. Richard Millar, professor of materia medica in Glasgow, had written on his behalf to Dr Caspar Wistar, an Edinburgh graduate in 1786, and now a leading figure in Philadelphia's medical world and a professor at the university of Pennsylvania. Millar recommended Maclean as a friend who, after 'going thro a course of education of the most liberal kind' had successfully established himself as a surgeon in Glasgow. He goes on to say that 'In chemistry he is particularly eminent, especially in the French or Pneumatic Chemistry; indeed in the new Chemistry, for extent & accuracy of information, I know not any man of this Country with whom he may not come in competition'.[6]

Soon after his arrival Maclean met another Edinburgh medical graduate who held an even more distinguished position in Philadelphia's intellectual life – and who I suspect was a key figure in sustaining what one might call the Scottish dimension of Philadelphia's enlightenment world. This of course was Benjamin Rush, graduate of the College of New Jersey, signer of the Declaration of Independence, and a leading figure in almost every aspect of Philadelphia's social and cultural activity. Rush had played a crucial role in persuading John Witherspoon in 1768 to leave his church in Paisley and assume the presidency of the College of New Jersey in Princeton. So perhaps it is no surprise to learn that it was Rush, aware of Maclean's distinction in the new chemistry, who suggested that he leave Philadelphia for Princeton. Initially in Princeton Maclean joined Dr Ebenezer Stockton in carrying on a medical practice, but it is clear the college authorities were well aware of the scientific qualifications of the newly-arrived young Scotsman. Samuel Stanhope Smith, who had succeeded his father-in-law John Witherspoon as college president in 1793, had invited Maclean to deliver a course of lectures in chemistry in the college within weeks of his arrival. Clearly the idea behind this arrangement was to allow Maclean to show what he could do as a lecturer and teacher. Just how well he succeeded in impressing the college president and trustees is shown by the letter he received from Samuel Stanhope Smith a few weeks later. Dated at Nassau Hall on October 1st, 1795, it begins:

> Sir, the trustees of the College are desirous of establishing a professorship of Chemistry in the institution and have directed me to convey frankly and distinctly in writing their sentiments on this subject. They have full confidence in your qualifications for the office, and have accordingly elected you professor of chemistry with an appointment of £100…' [7]

It is clear from the letter than £100 was rather less than the salary Maclean had hoped for, and this no doubt explains why for the next two years he was allowed to continue to practice as a doctor in Princeton. However, the situation changed when Walter Minto, professor of mathematics and natural philosophy in the college and another Scot, died in October 1796. Maclean was invited to take over the teaching of natural philosophy, while President Smith took on instruction in mathematics. Then in April, 1797, the college's board of trustees appointed Maclean professor of mathematics and natural philosophy with a salary of £250 per annum, with the direction that 'Chemistry and Natural History be taught as branches of Natural Philosophy'[8]. At this point Maclean gave up his local medical practice – and it is worth remembering he was still a young man in his twenties. In 1804 the college appointed an Andrew Hunter to teach mathematics and astronomy, but he left in 1808, and from then on until his own resignation in 1812, Maclean remained responsible, with the help of some college tutors, for all the science teaching at the College of New Jersey.

Why then did Maclean resign his position in 1812? College politics seems to be the answer. He had always played an active part in the administration of the college, including issues involving student behaviour and discipline. A letter survives in which Maclean writes to Ashbel Green – who would succeed Samuel Stanhope Smith as college president – describing in vivid terms the so-called student rebellion of 1807 with its walkouts, threats of damage to buildings, and employment of townspeople as guards. This event, which was serious enough to lead to the suspension of teaching in the college for a considerable period, seems to have triggered changes in the college structure that Maclean probably did not agree with.

Whatever the reason, in the autumn of 1812, John Maclean accepted an appointment as professor of natural philosophy and chemistry at the College of William and Mary in Williamsburg. He remained in Williamsburg through the following year but then his health gave way. He returned to Princeton, was forced to resign from his William and Mary chair, and died in February, 1814, aged forty-two.

How important a figure in the history of chemistry is John Maclean? The answer has to be that in terms of original research and publications he is at best a minor figure. In his Memoir Maclean Jr does ask why, given his outstanding abilities, his father did not achieve more as what he calls a 'Discoverer'.[9] The answer he supplies is one that still resonates today. As a full time teacher and administrator, he suggests, Maclean just did not have the time and opportunity to pursue original research. However, on one occasion at least John Maclean did make an impact upon the wider scientific community of the day. In the course of 1796 he made a substantial contribution to the ongoing debate over Joseph Priestley's theory concerning what he called phlogiston – a hypothetical substance which Priestley argued was present in all combustible materials and released during burning. Lavoisier and other French chemists had already disputed this theory, but in 1796 – by which time, like Maclean, he had left Britain for the more congenial shores of the United States – Priestley defended his theory in a pamphlet called 'Considerations on the doctrine of Phlogiston and the Decomposition of Water'.

Soon afterwards Maclean published what appeared as 'Two lectures on Combustion supplementary to a course of lectures read at Nassau Hall' in which he argued against Priestley's position. In the period that followed the controversy ran on with contributions from a range of scientists appearing in the New York Medical Repository in particular. Maclean, however, chose not to reply to those who challenged his arguments. He had sent a copy of his lectures to Dr Cleghorn, then lecturer in Chemistry at Glasgow, and seems to have accepted the advice he received in response. Cleghorn clearly agreed with Maclean on the phlogiston issue, but insisted that it was a mistake to become embroiled in a public dispute with Priestley. 'In the dispute', he writes, 'your character as a Chemist and Philosopher has lost nothing; but still I wish you had not entered into it... By declining controversy, Newton shewed his superior sagacity'.[10] Maclean made no further public contribution to the phlogiston dispute.

My guess is there were those in Glasgow, Philadelphia and elsewhere, who would have expected Maclean's early brilliance to have led to a more major contribution to research in the field of chemistry. But if he fell short in this sense, he succeeded in another. In the history of the teaching of chemistry in the US, Maclean is clearly a major figure. On the occasion of Joseph Priestley's centenary in 1874, Benjamin Silliman Jr, professor of chemistry at Yale, gave an address on 'American contributions to chemistry' which included the following statement:

> Of the public seminaries of learning other than medical institutions where chemistry was taught from a separate chair, and as a distinct branch of the college curriculum of instruction prior to 1800, we find but one, and that distinction belongs to Nassau Hall, Princeton, New Jersey.[11]

In fact it seems that some form of instruction in chemistry was given by contemporaries of Maclean at Harvard, Columbia, and Pennsylvania, but perhaps not as a distinct branch of the college curriculum. In any event, Benjamin Silliman Sr, who had been appointed Yale's first professor of chemistry in 1802 despite his lack of expertise in the subject, confirms Maclean's importance as an inspirational figure in the teaching of chemistry. Silliman, who spent six months in Edinburgh in 1805-06 pursuing his study of chemistry with Professor Thomas Hope, wrote as follows:

> At this celebrated seat of learning (Princeton), an eminent gentleman, Dr John Maclean, resided as professor of chemistry, etc. I early attained an introduction to him by correspondence, and he favored me with a list of books for the promotion of my studies... I also passed a few days with Dr Maclean in my different travels to and from Philadelphia, and obtained from him a general insight into my future occupation; inspected his library and apparatus , and obtained his advice respecting many things. Dr Maclean was a man of brilliant mind, with all the acuteness of his native Scotland; and a sparkling wit gave variety to his conversation. I regard him as my earliest master in chemistry and Princeton as my starting point in that pursuit. [12]

The accuracy of Professor Silliman's account of his debt to Maclean is confirmed by letters preserved in the Princeton University library. From the first of these letters, dated December 1st, 1801, it is clear that Timothy Dwight, the Yale president, had learned of Maclean's teaching of chemistry in Princeton and had contacted President Samuel Stanhope Smith about what was involved in setting up such a course. President Smith passed this query to Maclean who replied at some length. The main thrust of

Maclean's letter is that chemistry is a subject requiring laboratory-style experiment and demonstration:

> 'I am of opinion it is impossible for me to require even a slight knowledge of chemistry without either making experiments or seeing them performed, and that to become proficient in the science it will require much practice as well as extensive reading.'

The letter also includes a list of some nine titles of works on chemistry with which students would need to be familiar. Subsequent letters are addressed to Professor Silliman at Yale. Writing in August, 1803, Maclean refers to the fire which had badly damaged Nassau Hall the previous year, indicating that his room — 'for philosophical and chemical experiments' — would not be ready until the following January by which time new apparatus would also have arrived. From this letter it's clear that Silliman had sent Maclean an account of the chemical apparatus he had now assembled at Yale and was asking Maclean whether it was sufficient for the teaching of a course. Maclean says it is, but goes into some detail over what might be added and how it is important not to bewilder students with over-complex experiments.

In a letter of February, 1804, Maclean explains to Silliman that his room is still not finished so he is unsure whether he can go ahead and teach his course. Clearly Silliman in Philadelphia had been thinking of coming up to Princeton to sit in on Maclean's class, but without his laboratory and apparatus there would be little point. In a letter of 1810, Maclean responds to two invitations form Silliman; he would be pleased to visit Silliman and his colleagues at Yale were it in his power to do so, but because he has had little time in the last year and a half to devote to his work in chemistry, he does not feel able to accept an invitation to contribute to a new edition of Henry's "Chemistry". (William Henry's *Elements of Experimental Chemistry*, originally appearing in 1799, had been frequently republished as a standard chemistry textbook.) By 1810 of course, Benjamin Silliman's position as professor of chemistry at Yale was well-established. But his debt to his predecessor at Princeton is abundantly clear. [13]

One other point about Maclean's legacy as a teacher of chemistry remains to be made. In his course he seems to have stressed the practical applications to which a knowledge of chemistry could lead. Like Franklin he seems to have asked — 'what signifies Philosophy that does not apply to some Use?' Then again the commercial and manufacturing success of his old friend Charles Mackintosh, who had shared his early enthusiasm for chemistry, may well have been something that he never forgot. In any event, given his early training in medicine and surgery, it is not surprising that he should have emphasised the importance of chemistry in medical education. But he appears also to have insisted on how a knowledge of chemistry could contribute both to the development of agriculture and to areas of manufacturing. This is an emphasis in the study of chemistry that he may well have passed on to both the Sillimans. Benjamin Silliman Jr would go on to play a key role in the emergence of the oil industry in the United States. John Maclean would no doubt have been proud to know that his son would become the tenth president of the college in which he had pioneered the teaching of science in general and chemistry in particular. But he himself deserves to be remembered as one of the Scottish founding fathers of Princeton University.

1 John Maclean, *A Memoir of John Maclean M.D.*, The Princeton Press, 1885, p.13.
2 Michael Durey, *Transatlantic Radicals and the Early American Republic,* University of Kansas Press, 1997, p.75.
3 John Maclean, op. cit., pp. 14-15.
4 Ibid., p. 15.
5 Ibid., p. 14.
6 Manuscript letter in the John Maclean Collection, Princeton University Library.
7 Manuscript letter in the John Maclean Collection, Princeton University Library.
8 John Maclean, op. cit., p.20.
9 Ibid., p. 35.
10 Ibid., pp. 31-32.
11 William Foster, 'A Century Old Chemistry Notebook', Journal of Chemical Education, Vol 2, No 3 (March, 1925),p.165.
12 Ibid., pp. 164-5.
13 For the quotations from these letters by Maclean, see William Foster, 'Some Letters by Doctor John Maclean', Journal of Chemical Education, Vol 6, No 12 (December, 1929), pp. 2105-2114.

2 The Ivy League

Last April, Lord Sutherland of Houndwood delivered the annual Sir Malcolm Knox memorial lecture at St Andrews University. A former vice-chancellor of both the universities of London and Edinburgh, Lord Sutherland is perhaps best known as the architect of the scheme for the comprehensive care for the elderly which the Scottish government – unlike Westminster – continues to implement. His theme at St Andrews was the future of the Scottish universities. His central point was one with which I strongly agree: that the Scottish government was failing to face up to the scale of the funding gap the universities were facing as a result of the policies of the U.K. administration. 'Without significant injection of taxpayers' money or charges of one kind or another to the recipients' (i.e. student fees), the Scottish universities, he argued, will cease to be adequately resourced. The suggestion that increased philanthropy, and larger contributions from the business sector, could fill the gap, was unrealistic. Efficiency savings of course could be made, but again not on a scale to provide a solution.

To find a way forward, Lord Sutherland turned to an idea that has been widely touted by government spokesmen. The Scottish universities should move towards providing a private university education modelled on that represented by the Ivy League universities in the USA. As I suggest, Lord Sutherland's is far from being the only voice arguing that the Ivy League is the touchstone to which British universities in general should aspire. That the eight American universities in question are world-class in terms of both teaching and research is not in question. They occupy lofty positions in most of the relevant world league tables, their teaching faculties are rich in Nobel Prize winners, their share of the research income provided by both the American government and private sources is huge. But as a model for Scottish or English universities is the Ivy League any more realistic in financial or any other terms than the Scottish government's funding suggestions which Lord Sutherland rejects?

The eight institutions that make up the Ivy League, with their founding dates are as follows: Harvard University (1636), Yale University (1701), Princeton University (1746), Columbia University (1754), University of Pennsylvania (1755), Brown University (1764), Dartmouth College (1769), and Cornell University (1865). The Ivy

League institutions, that is, have been around for substantially longer than the vast majority of British universities. Of all the contemporary English universities, only Oxford and Cambridge predate the nineteenth century! (Scotland of course with its four ancient universities fares rather better.) But why does this matter? Because the endowment wealth that can deliver vast investment income to supplement fees and other sources of income cannot be created overnight. Harvard, Yale, and Princeton's endowment billions were created over centuries of accumulation. Except for a handful of Oxford and Cambridge colleges, the British universities have almost nothing comparable in terms of endowment income. And without that income the Ivy League would not exist.

Then again the Ivy League universities can rely on a contemporary source of income that just doesn't exist in Scotland or England: the extraordinary generosity of their alumni. The sheer scale of their alumni giving is difficult for us to grasp. In 2007 Princeton launched a five-year programme to raise 1.75 billion dollars. By March 10 this year – despite the economic downturn – $1.47 billion had already been raised from alumni and friends: 58,624 of them. And this campaign exists alongside, and in addition to, the permanent 'annual giving' system through which millions of dollars are raised for the university every year. How is it done? Well again in part because the tradition of alumni giving in the Ivy League is an established, historical fact of life. The tradition goes back at least as far as the late decades of the nineteenth century – that is when alumni associations began to be created in every American city or region. Then one other factor, peculiar to the entire American college and university system, makes it easier to make alumni giving a permanent reality: the system of student class identity. All American students beginning their studies this fall will be identified at the institution they are entering as the Class of 2015. And they will always retain that class identity. Alumni associations use that identity to facilitate fund-raising: classes compete with each other over the amount they contribute. In the Ivy League – and probably in most of America's private colleges and universities – the majority of graduates will participate in annual giving. Year after year.

This is not a league in which Scottish graduates compete – and it's difficult to imagine them ever doing so. (The British Treasury could help them to make a start though by making all financial gifts to educational institutions fully tax allowable.)

Finally there is the issue of student admissions. The Ivy League universities as private institutions receive no direct federal or state funding. Hence their annual tuition fees make even £9000 a year sound like a bargain. Around $50,000 per year is the going rate. So they are the exclusive preserve of the richest families in America? In fact they are not. (Think Michelle Obama at Princeton, her husband at Harvard). Most operate a 'needs blind' admissions policy. What this means is that funding is available to make it possible for any student from whatever financial background to accept an offered place. Hence the student body at an Ivy League school reflects the diversity of American society at large. Princeton received 27,115 applications to enter the Class of 2015: 74% of that number sought financial aid. (Of the 2,282 offered admission 22% are Asian-American, 9.8 % are Hispanic or Latino, 9.1% are African-American, 5% are multi-racial, less than 1% Native American. And the university expects that 60% of the incoming class will receive financial aid.) Obviously the 'needs blind' admissions policy does work; but only because the institution has the resources to pay for it. A Scottish Ivy League, however, inevitably lacking such resources, would undoubtedly become an upper class preserve. Surely not an outcome that Lord Sutherland would favour.

3 Princeton and Scotland

A few years ago Princeton honoured one of its most distinguished presidents — the Scotsman John Witherspoon — by placing a grand, life-size statue on a plinth directly across from the entrance to the university chapel. But Princeton's debt to Scotland and the Scots in fact predated Witherspoon's accession to the presidency in 1768. When the Presbyterian Synod of New York decided in 1746 that it was necessary to establish an educational institution to train new ministers, funding was a major issue; Britain, and Scotland in particular, were quickly identified as likely sources of financial support and two emissaries were dispatched on a fund-raising mission. Scotland provided them with their principal success. The General Assembly of the Church of Scotland agreed to a collection being made 'at all the church doors in Scotland' and the very substantial sum of £3200 was raised. This was the money that paid for the building of the magnificent Nassau Hall — designed of course by another Scot, Robert Smith of Philadelphia.

So Scottish money played a major role in making the College of New Jersey, as it then was, into a physical reality. Previously located in Elizabeth and Newark (the homes of the first two presidents), the college's early years had been distinctly precarious. The move to Princeton, and the completion of Nassau Hall, ensured its continued existence, but the short-lived incumbencies of its early presidents meant that its long-term future remained uncertain. The arrival of John Witherspoon, from the Laigh Kirk in Paisley, Scotland, as sixth president changed everything. Remaining in office until 1794, Witherspoon transformed the struggling college he took over into a major player in the educational, religious and political life of America. Back in Scotland Witherspoon had been a leader of the hard-line Calvinist party within the Church of Scotland, but there was nothing dogmatic or illiberal about his leadership of the college he headed: Anglican and other non-Presbyterian students were admitted and students from outside New Jersey welcomed. The curriculum he developed was essentially modelled on that of the Scottish universities he himself had attended — hence Witherspoon was a major conduit of those Scottish Enlightenment ideas that were to play so important a role in moulding the intellectual and cultural life of pre-and post-Revolutionary America. One of the two Scottish-born signers of the Declaration of Independence, Witherspoon educated a generation of young Americans who were to play leading parts in the new republic: one president (James Madison), one vice-president (Aaron Burr), 10 cabinet members, 21 senators, 39 representatives, 12 governors, 33 judges, and 56 state legislators. By the time of his death in 1794, the Scottish clergymen turned American patriot had established the Princeton college as one of his adopted country's major educational institutions.

Witherspoon was succeeded as president by his son-in-law Samuel Stanhope Smith. But in the early decades of the nineteenth century the college became increasingly caught up in controversies over how far the educational experience it offered should remain strictly in line with traditional, orthodox Calvinist assumptions. The result was a period of stagnation and even decline: Princeton was losing its national status and in danger of becoming a provincial backwater. In the years immediately after the Civil War its enrolment declined to no more than 200 students. It was in these problematical circumstances that Princeton turned once again to Scotland for an answer to its problems.

In 1868, uncannily exactly one hundred years after the arrival of John Witherspoon, the college trustees appointed James McCosh, another Scottish clergyman and scholar, to the presidency. And exactly as Witherspoon had done, McCosh revived and transformed the college during the twenty years of his incumbency. As dedicated a Presbyterian as his Scottish predecessor, McCosh was nonetheless open and responsive to the new intellectual currents of the nineteenth century. Accordingly he restructured the institution he had taken over: history, political science, psychology, modern languages and electrical engineering were added to the curriculum; the study of science including natural history, chemistry, physics and geology, was greatly expanded; the faculty grew from a mere sixteen to forty, while the student body increased from 264 to 604.

McCosh went on fund-raising missions throughout the country; he raised money for new buildings on the campus; he encouraged the establishment of the first alumni associations; he campaigned for alumni representation among the trustees; and he placed a new emphasis on sport as an essential part of undergraduate life. And it was McCosh who initiated the campaign to have the college change its name to Princeton University – with all that that implied about its new status and identity. Thus it was under its second Scottish president that Princeton began to recover its original status as a national academic institution while also beginning to take the shape it retains today. As early as 1871 McCosh was able to arrange the attendance at the Commencement exercises of what in the recent past had become a sleepy Presbyterian college of the president of the United States, the Secretary of War, both New Jersey's senators, and the state governor.

Inevitably McCosh had his opponents, who argued that the changes he was introducing meant an undermining of Princeton's Presbyterian traditions. But with the passage of time McCosh's own pupils began to emerge as leaders of alumni associations and even as young faculty members — thus ensuring that his modernizing strategy prevailed. In 1896, two years after his death, the College of New Jersey finally became Princeton University.

In the early twentieth century the most significant inheritor of McCosh's vision of Princeton was Woodrow Wilson. Not a Scot (though his grandfather Thomas Woodrow was born in Paisley and graduated from Glasgow University in 1819) Wilson had been a pupil of McCosh before joining the faculty as professor of political science and subsequently becoming a reforming president in the period 1902-1910. But even without Wilson, Princeton's massive debt to Scotland and its two Scottish presidents is abundantly clear. It is above all to Witherspoon and McCosh that Princeton owes its lofty standing in the educational hierarchy of the United States. Accordingly, the campus's new statue of Witherspoon is a fitting tribute to his various achievements. Still more appropriate, however, would be the establishment of a course of study within the university focusing on the intellectual and cultural traditions of the country which produced him, and of which he is such an outstanding exemplar. In the American academy today, Irish Studies flourish in a wide range of universities and colleges. Where are comparable courses in Scottish Studies to be found? The answer is that, despite the putative existence of 20 million Americans of Scottish descent, Scottish Studies hardly exist. Yet this is a time when Scottish life is being transformed by the creation of a new Parliament (the previous one having been abolished by the Treaty of Union in 1707); when Scottish art and culture are vibrant and challenging; when Edinburgh has just been declared UNESCO's first City of Literature; and when a new Scottish history is emerging focusing on the eighteenth century and the world-wide influence of the Scottish Enlightenment. What better time to create a new School of Scottish Studies? And where better to establish it than in the Princeton of John Witherspoon and James McCosh?

For details of James McCosh's presidency I am indebted to J. David Hoeveler's excellent book, *James McCosh and the Scottish Intellectual Tradition* (1981).

4 John Witherspoon

'Who is the Scot who made the greatest impact upon the United States' is a question that is often asked. The commonest answer is of course Andrew Carnegie. The Dunfermline–born Carnegie made an enormous fortune in iron and steel in the period Mark Twain dubbed 'the gilded age' — the time after the American Civil War when laissez-faire American capitalism, turning the US into the world's largest industrial nation, created extraordinary wealth even if most of it remained firmly in the bank accounts of a handful of enormously successful entrepreneurs: the Rockefellers, J.P. Morgan, J.J. Hill, the Vanderbilts, Frick, Gould, Mellon — and Andrew Carnegie. So how did they make their money? By not allowing their belief in Social Darwinism — the survival of the fittest in a fiercely competitive economic world — to be ameliorated by any notion of wider social welfare or communal good. Popularly known as the 'robber barons' these men were more than ready to live up to that title — and Andrew Carnegie was a leader of the pack. Of course in the latter part of his life Carnegie became an immensely generous philanthropist – his native country benefited as we all know in the shape of the Carnegie Libraries which were established in almost every Scottish town. But it is hard not to think that there was an element of guilt over how it was amassed, in Carnegie's ultimate readiness to give away so much of his fortune.

My candidate for the greatest American Scot you will gather is not Andrew Carnegie but rather the subject of this brief talk: John Witherspoon. Born in 1723 in Gifford, East Lothian, and dying in 1794 in Princeton, New Jersey, Witherspoon during his lifetime was a relatively well-known Scot – but not in his native land a particularly admired or celebrated one. After his death he soon faded out of the national consciousness. In America, as we shall see, there were good reasons for him to be remembered and indeed celebrated, but even in the US he is not exactly a nationally admired or revered figure. So how can I possibly claim that he deserves to be recognized as Scotland's greatest contributor to the emergence of America as the world power we acknowledge it is today?

Having studied at the universities of Edinburgh and St Andrews, and distinguishing himself in opposing the Jacobite rebellion of 1745, Witherspoon was installed as the Church of Scotland minister in Beith in Ayrshire later that year. In 1758 he moved to the more distinguished parish of the Laigh Kirk in Paisley. By then he had become a leading light in the so-called Popular Party of the Church of Scotland meaning that he was a leading figure among those clergy resisting the attempts by the so-called Moderates in the church who wished to move away from strict adherence to all the tenets of traditional Calvinism. This meant that by the time he left Paisley for the new world of New Jersey he had an established reputation as a fine theologian, a powerful preacher, and a formidable controversialist.

It was in 1766 that representatives from the College of New Jersey arrived in Paisley offering Witherspoon the opportunity to become president of that College. The institution had been established in 1746 by the Presbyterian synods of New York and Philadelphia basically to provide well-and locally-educated clergy for the Presbyterian Church in America. The Church of Scotland had supported the idea of the college, even setting aside a Sunday when that day's collection across the country was handed over to the college's representatives on a fund-raising mission in Scotland. However, the early years of the college proved very uncertain. None of the first five figures selected as college president survived in the post for more than two or three years. Their early deaths meant that the college never enjoyed a firm hand able to guide and direct its development. Thus when its fifth president died in 1766 its survival as an academic institution was by no means certain. Facing this situation the college's trustees looked to Scotland for help. John Witherspoon was identified as a powerful figure able to overcome the various divisions within the Presbyterian Church in America and well-equipped intellectually to lead an academically ambitious institution. But Witherspoon took a lot of persuading. His wife in particular was reluctant to leave her native land. However, the college representatives finally got their man and Witherspoon took up his position in Princeton New Jersey in 1768.

And what a man he turned out to be. In the twenty-six years of his presidency Witherspoon transformed the struggling College of New Jersey into one of America's major academic institutions, overshadowing the older Episcopalian College of William and Mary in Virginia, and challenging Harvard and Yale for supremacy. The quality and public careers of his graduates tell the astonishing story. Witherspoon taught one future American president – James Madison – and one vice-president – Aaron Burr. But among the rest were 10 future members of presidential cabinets, 21 US Senators, 39 members of the House of Representatives, 12 state governors, 56 state legislators, and 33 judges. From the beginning Witherspoon had recognized that his college would have to be more than a training ground for Presbyterian ministers. What was needed was an education in civic humanism – the training of young men to contribute to the growth of every aspect of a virtuous, polite, and civil society.

In other words what Witherspoon brought to America from Paisley were the educational values of the Scottish Enlightenment. The curriculum he established at Princeton was clearly modelled on that of Glasgow and Edinburgh universities. What became known as the Scottish common-sense school of philosophy, and the distinctively Scottish study of rhetoric, lay at the heart of the new curriculum, and very quickly these areas of study were taken up, not only at Princeton, but at all the other major American universities. For almost two generations, the standard American college curriculum remained deeply indebted to the specific Enlightenment of Glasgow and Edinburgh. Scottish teaching methods, Scottish textbooks, and Scottish philosophy in particular, permeated American universities, colleges, and seminaries. And John Witherspoon was indisputably a key figure in making this happen.

Witherspoon's contribution to the development of the USA, however, went far beyond his role as an academic teacher. He arrived in New Jersey at a time when the debate over the future direction of the American colonies was growing in intensity. The colonists' demand for more control over their own affairs was met by the British government's attempts to impose more authority from the imperial centre in London. The gap between these conflicting visions of America's future was becoming increasingly wide and bitter. One issue concerning many colonists was a religious one. It was widely believed that George III and his government was about to make the Anglican Episcopal Church the established Church of America. This was a notion that both frightened and angered Presbyterians, Congregationalists, Methodists, and all other Christian sects. One suspects that Witherspoon as a good Presbyterian would have shared their sense of outrage, but whether or not this was the case, the president of the college of New Jersey soon emerged as a leading figure supporting the local, patriotic side in the dispute with the mother country. As a result in 1776 he was elected to the Continental Congress as part of the New Jersey delegation. He was soon invited to take up the post of Congressional Chaplain, and served in Congress from 1776 to 1782. In 1776 he was the only active clergyman to sign the Declaration of Independence.

Only two Scots signed that document – Witherspoon and the lawyer James Wilson. Subsequently Witherspoon remained a hugely active member of Congress, serving on around 100 committees and taking part in all the institution's major debates. He helped draft the original Articles of Confederation and argued successfully that the state of New Jersey should ratify the new American Constitution.

What proves John Witherspoon's firmness of mind and personal integrity, in his politics as elsewhere in his life, is that siding with the patriots in the struggle for American freedom, he was choosing alienation from the vast majority of fellow-Scots both in the American colonies and at home. Whatever Burns suppers, St Andrews Societies and National Tartan Week Scots would like to believe, the evidence is overwhelming that in the Revolutionary period most Scots in America, and their countrymen in the United Kingdom, remained loyal to the government of George III. As a result, it is no exaggeration to say that at that time the Scots – or rather the 'Scotch' — became the most vilified ethnic group in America. 'A free exportation to Scotchmen and Tories' became a common Revolutionary toast. Even that great democrat Thomas Jefferson succumbed to the widespread anti-Scottish prejudice. In his first draft of the Declaration of Independence Jefferson complained that George III was sending over 'not only soldiers of our common blood' but 'Scotch and foreign mercenaries to invade and destroy us'. It was Witherspoon who made Congress delete this hostile reference to his fellow-countrymen. He also did his best to rebut the denunciations of the Scots that were echoing around the colonies. In a pamphlet called 'An Address to the Natives of Scotland Residing in America' he argued that the Scots were the victims of an anti-Scottish campaign, and that they had been dissuaded from supporting the patriotic side by its association with John Wilkes, notorious for his anti-Scots campaigns in England. But this was one battle Witherspoon failed to win.

Finally there is one other reason why I feel that Witherspoon deserves to be recognized as the greatest of all Scottish-Americans — his influence on the Founding Fathers of the new United States of America that emerged after the successful conclusion of the American Revolution. I mentioned earlier that Witherspoon taught one future American president –James Madison. In fact Madison was his favourite pupil, and Madison went on to become a key figure in all the debates over the exact forming of the American Constitution. Through Witherspoon's philosophical teaching at the College of New Jersey, Madison was familiar with the ideas of major thinkers of the Scottish Enlightenment such as David Hume, Francis Hutcheson, and Lord Kames, and it was these Scottish philosophers who became the shapers of Madison's own thinking on the fundamental political issues involved in the creation of the new American Constitution itself. I'm afraid I see no reason to believe the now popular idea that America's Declaration of Independence was somehow modelled on Scotland's Declaration of Arbroath. But Scotland does have a claim to the invention of America —-through the debt of the Founding Fathers to the philosophical ideas of the Scottish Enlightenment. In making that Scottish-American alliance possible, no figure played a larger part than the former minister of Paisley's Laigh Kirk — John Witherspoon.

5 Alex in Princeton

Like Scotland's first minister, I was recently in Princeton, New Jersey, attending an event organized by the town's Center of Theological Inquiry. Somewhat to my surprise, the CTI turned out to be a wholly independent institution distinct from both its distinguished neighbours: Princeton University and Princeton Theological Seminary. A kind of theological think-tank, established in 1978, CTI's current Director is a Scot — William Storrar — who chooses to define 'theology' in decidedly liberal terms.

Professor Storrar had invited around 25 scholars in different disciplines, to come to Princeton in the first week of April 2013 to take part in a symposium on the Adam Smithian theme of 'The Wealth and Well-being of Nations'. The participants came from a range of countries — the majority from the US, but others from France, Germany, South Africa, and the U.K. Scotland was well represented by a group from Glasgow Caledonian University including Pamela Gillies, its principal and vice-chancellor, who had chosen to support the symposium.

The first day consisted of a book festival in the Center's Luce Hall – named after Henry Luce, publisher of *Time* and *Life* magazines, whose foundation had been a major contributor to the establishment of the CTI. The format was a discussion between Sally Magnusson, of BBC Scotland, and the authors of three recent books: *Adam Smith, An Enlightened Life* by Nicolas Phillipson; *Francis Jeffrey's American Journal, New York to Washington 1813*, edited by myself and Clare Elliott; and *A Floating Commonwealth, Politics, Culture, and Technology on Britain's Atlantic Coast, 1860-1930,* by Christopher Harvie. Sally Magnusson was characteristically generous in her ability to bring out what was of greatest general interest in all three books.

In the following days the symposium was structured around three presentations by the authors of published or forthcoming works addressing the issues involved in any analysis in today's world of the wealth and well-being of nations. Nicolas Phillipson, however, began proceedings by providing an eighteenth-century, Scottish Enlightenment, context for the contemporary debate by describing Smith's analysis of the relevant moral and economic factors in first *The Theory of Moral Sentiments* and subsequently *The Wealth of Nations*. Smith never uses the term 'well-being', but his emphasis on economic self-interest in *The Wealth of Nations* does not negate that on virtue, friendship, sentiment and imagination, as essential elements of civic society, in the earlier *Theory of Moral Sentiments*.

The first contemporary analysis came in the form of the opening chapter of a forthcoming book by Angus Deaton, a professor of economics and international affairs at Princeton University, originally from the Scottish Borders. His book is entitled *The Great Escape* and is about how in the modern world vast numbers of people have escaped from the poverty and premature death that was the norm in earlier centuries. For many 'life is better now than at almost any time in history'. They are better off, healthier, and live longer. But at the same time in the world at large, massive inequality prevails. Millions 'still experience the horrors of destitution and of premature death'. Deaton's book 'tells stories of how things got better, how and why progress happened, and the subsequent interplay of progress and inequality'.

As an inexpert 'general reader' what strikes me about Professor Deaton's chapter is that indeed it 'tells stories'. *The Great Escape* is of course the title of a well-known WWII film about the escape from Germany's Stalag Luft III of 250 Allied prisoners of war. The professor makes deft use of the arc of the film to bring home the human reality behind the issues involved in the escape from poverty and death of many in the contemporary world – but also behind the increased inequality between the escapees and the millions left behind trapped in deprivation. In the opening chapter of his book, Professor Deaton continues to expand on these themes in a lively and accessible style.

The symposium's following session was led by Joao Biehl, professor of anthropology at Princeton University, and author of the book *Will to Live*. Published in 2007, the book focuses on a range of issues surrounding the treatment of HIV/AIDS in Brazil, the first developing country to adopt an official policy of making antiretroviral drugs universally available to all who need them. As the author puts it, his book 'moves between a social analysis of the institutional practices shaping the Brazilian response to AIDS and the stories and lives of people affected by it'. For the reader unfamiliar with the scholarly language of the social sciences, it is that second dimension concerning the lives and stories of actual individuals that is the source of the book's enormous and moving power. Again and again we listen to the voices of individual people telling in their own words the story of their lives as HIV/AIDS sufferers. And we not only hear them – but in a series of photographs taken over a space of years, we add faces to their voices. The result is that the world of academic analysis and discussion remains embedded in people's actual daily lives.

The penultimate session was led by Cam Donaldson, Yunus professor of social business and health at Glasgow Caledonian University. Readers may recall that Muhammad Yunus, awarded the Nobel Peace Prize in 2007 for his pioneering work in establishing 'micro' banks lending tiny sums of money to the poorest members of Bangladeshi society to set up small business enterprises, visited Glasgow in 2008. Glasgow Caledonian followed up his visit by creating the Yunus Centre for Social Business and Health, made up of a team of scholars from different disciplines working together on research programmes exploring two 'Yunus' themes: microcredit, health and well-being, and 'social enterprise', health and well-being.

The paper that Cam Donaldson and members of his research team presented at the CIT symposium focused on that second theme: 'social enterprise' or 'social business'. The basic notion appears to be that the best way forward to improve the health and well-being of the poorest and most deprived members of any society — including our own — is through community-based programmes in business enterprise which are not profit-led. The paper that followed – the work of the team of researchers — was rigorous and detailed in describing the nature of social enterprise — how it might be defined, developed and assessed. Academic and scholarly, the paper's language and expression remain throughout those of the professional social science researcher. For the non-expert reader, this can become something of a challenge. For public and private money to be invested in the social enterprise schemes that the Yunus Centre researchers describe, minds and hearts have to be won over. I suspect that MPs, MSPs, editors, commentators, and business leaders need to come on board. To my mind at least, this would be more likely to happen, were Cam Donaldson and his excellent team to come up with a way of humanizing their programme — of illustrating in immediate, individual terms how social enterprise could transform and enhance the health and well-being of actual, deprived communities.

The symposium's final session on governance, wealth and well-being, was somewhat disrupted by preparations for, and the actual the arrival, of Mr Salmond. Words of greeting and welcome — and books — were exchanged, and in no time we were bussed off to hear the first minister deliver his speech on 'Adam Smith and the Wealth and Well-being of Nations' to a Saturday afternoon audience of three or four hundred in an auditorium on the Princeton University campus.

It was an effective, polished and well-judged performance by an astute and experienced politician. There were a few good jokes; the tone throughout was confident – but measured rather than triumphalist. Before turning to his central theme – that the economics of *The Wealth of Nations* should be read alongside, not against, the morality of *The Theory of Moral Sentiments* – Mr Salmond paid due tribute to the links between Princeton and Scotland, and between Scotland and America more generally, in the eighteenth and nineteenth centuries. I was disappointed, however, to hear the first minister apparently endorse the popular myth that the Declaration of Independence was somehow modelled on the so-called Declaration of Arbroath. Again Mr Salmond or his speech writer managed to confuse William Small from Aberdeen, Thomas Jefferson's teacher at the College of William and Mary, with James Blair, also from Aberdeen, the college's first president many years earlier.

In a question and answer period, the first minister handled various questions involving the politics of independence with deftness and humour. Hence it was no surprise when the chairperson, bringing the event to a close, suggested that if the referendum vote were taken in the hall that afternoon, the result would be a resounding Yes. I suspect she was right. Certainly Mr Salmond's visit to the Center of Theological Inquiry and Princeton University left his personal well-being in good shape.

6 Irish Students at Glasgow University in the Eighteenth Century

This paper is essentially made possible by the volume *Matriculation Albums of the University of Glasgow 1728-1858*. The work of W. Innes Addison, Registrar of the University, published in 1913, the book contains a record of every student who matriculated in the period covered and includes the following information: the year of matriculation, the class in which matriculation occurred, and such personal details as the student's father's occupation and place of residence. Addison also supplies brief notes on students' future careers when he was able to identify these. Unfortunately, however, detailed as these albums are, they do not allow us to identify every student who attended Glasgow University. And the reason is simple: matriculation was not a requirement for attendance for anything approaching all students. Certain categories of students did have to matriculate but these were only a) 'gown' students in the Faculty of Arts who intended to proceed to graduation, and b) students who desired to vote in the election of the university rector. And even in these categories Addison tells us that the requirement was not rigidly enforced. For all other students matriculation was optional. In the Faculty of Arts the 'gown' classes included only Latin, Greek, Logic, Ethics, and Physics so these are the classes for which matriculation lists exist. Hence for such significant subjects as Divinity, Medicine, Law and Mathematics there are none. Again, matriculation did not have to occur in the first year of study. If it did, then the matriculation class would be Latin; if matriculation occurred in the second year of study the class would be Greek; in year three Logic; in four Ethics; and in five Physics. So the matriculation albums do not tell us how many students attended the University of Glasgow, nor how many students were present in any given class. It is not until 1843-44 that anything like a complete record of the entire student body at Glasgow begins to be recorded.

Despite the limitations, the matriculation albums do provide a major amount of information about the Glasgow student body in the 18th Century. They reflect only a sample or a selection of all the students, but there is nothing to suggest that the sample is not a representative one. Matriculated students, for example, come to Glasgow from the city itself, from its neighbouring counties, from the rest of Scotland including the Highlands and Islands, from

England and Wales, from Ireland, but also from the Americas, from the West Indies, and even from Russia. The albums, that is, provide a snapshot of the student body as a whole.

What then do the albums tell us about student numbers at Glasgow in the 18th century? In 1728, the first year for which figures are available, 53 students matriculated; in 1800, 103. Of the 53 in 1728, 6 were Irish; of 1800's 103, 12 were Irish, i.e. in the period the number of Irish students matriculating doubled but the percentage of Irish remained much the same. In fact over the period as a whole Irish matriculated students averaged around 13% of the total. This average, however, disguises the fact that there were years in which the Irish percentage was distinctly higher. In the 1760s and 1770s, for example – for reasons which I shall address later – the percentage figure shot up. In 1761 out of 82 matriculated students 29 were Irish; in 1762 out of 101, no less than 37 were Irish; in 1771 out of 115, 35 were Irish; in 1779, out of 99, 22 were Irish. In these decades, that is, the Irish percentage is sometimes as high as a third of the total.

The major question, of course, is do these figures in any way reflect the situation in the Glasgow student body as a whole? Was it the case that in the 1760s or 70s, say, Irish students ever amounted to a third of the total student population? That would surely be an astonishing figure – but in 1764 Thomas Reid suggested that Irish students did indeed amount to a third of the total. The difficulty we face is the absence of firm evidence of Glasgow student numbers in the eighteenth century. The album evidence suggests that student numbers remained relatively static up to 1760. Up to that year the highest number of students who matriculated in a single year was 81 in 1739. 82 matriculated in 1761, and between then and 1800 the number never fell much below that figure – except for 72 in 1782 – and in the majority of years the number climbed to 100 and above, with 1789's 141 being the highest single year. These figures then at least suggest that after remaining fairly stable in the first half of the eighteenth century, Glasgow's numbers began to expand from the 1760s onwards. In 1758, the English traveller Henry Wyndham reported that the Glasgow College was attended by 'about three hundred' students; the early scholar, Henry Gray Graham, suggested that the student body in 1750 amounted to 400.[1] As early as 1702, Principal Stirling had asserted the college had 400 students which 'included a large number from Ireland'.[2] In 1764 Thomas Reid believed there were between four and five hundred students of whom one third were Irish.[3] But in his autobiographical novel *Cyril Thornton* (1827), Thomas Hamilton, who matriculated at Glasgow in Professor Young's Greek class in 1803, writes: 'The session [of the college] had now commenced, and nearly two thousand students crowded its halls'.[4] These figures are of course anything but conclusive. But if for the sake of argument we accept the 400 figure for the 1750s, then the proportion of matriculated to non-matriculated students would be around 14%. My interest though is in Irish students at Glasgow so a final difficulty is over whether or not Irish students would matriculate in average numbers. In fact, as we shall see, there is some reason to believe that many Irish students may well have been among those most likely to matriculate. Whatever their precise numbers, Irish students made their presence felt at Glasgow from at least the opening of the eighteenth century. So much so that all accounts of the Glasgow College make reference to them.

Principal Stirling's 1702 remark acknowledging the presence in Glasgow of a large number of Irish students has just been cited. Such an emphasis on the Irish presence is reiterated through the eighteenth century and beyond. In *Peter's Letters to his Kinsfolk* (1819), J. G. Lockhart provides a lively sketch of the Glasgow college at the opening of the nineteenth century. Describing late-comers at Professor Young's Greek class – a class in which Lockhart himself had matriculated in 1805 – he evokes two representative figures from the class: a Scottish Highlander and 'some tall awkward Irishman'.[5] As late as 1856, a lengthy article in *Fraser's Magazine*, providing a detailed account of the Glasgow college, states that the student body included 'men in considerable number from the north of Ireland'.[6]

Fraser's specifies men from the north of Ireland and there is no doubt that indeed the majority of Irish students at Glasgow in the eighteenth century came from the Protestant counties settled by the so-called Ulster Scots. However one must remember that a university education was not available within Ireland to Irish Presbyterians from any part of the country, and this must explain the presence at Glasgow of many students from Dublin and a wide range of Irish counties outside the north. Similarly Irish students are as diverse in their status and family background as Scottish students, but it is still true that a clear majority of the students from the northern counties are taking courses in the Arts as a prelude to studying Divinity and qualifying as Presbyterian ministers. Addison records twelve Moderators of the Synod of Ulster and the General Assembly of the Irish Presbyterian Church between 1742 and 1800 who had studied at Glasgow.[7] It is these ministry-bound Irish students who seem to set the tone of the Irish presence in Glasgow in the eighteenth century.

So what was that tone? What impact did the Irish students make? How in general were they regarded? How did they behave? Inevitably one can only answer such questions in tentative fashion. Such evidence as is available is limited and often subjective. But it is provocative and interesting nonetheless. The Ulster Divinity students, for example, seem often to have been from poor backgrounds – with the result that they were often looked down upon by Glasgow students who were from a socially higher class. Frances Hutcheson's letters made it clear that he often acted as a kind of banker for his Irish students, even loaning them money of his own.[8] Again Glasgow undergraduates were required to wear a red gown, and one memoirist remembers that in his day (1811) the large influx of Irish students wore gowns – clearly second or third hand – that were so old that 'the scarlet hue was sometimes scarcely discoverable'.[9] Thomas Hamilton's account of the Irish students at the beginning of the nineteenth century reflects the familiar class prejudice: the Irish, he writes, were 'of the very lowest order of people, who came generally in a state of miserable destitution, to qualify themselves in the speediest and cheapest manner for the functions of the Ministry'.[10]

Perhaps their poverty was a factor in making the Irish students at Glasgow into a clearly segregated group, but poverty was far from being their only shared characteristic. Such evidence as we have suggests that the Irish students were more than most, prone to falling into modes of conduct that the wider public even today continues to believe to be the very type of student behaviour: neglecting their studies, spending too much time in pubs and taverns, staying out too late, antagonising local people by their unruly and noisy behaviour, and generally seeing their time at university as an opportunity to break free from all the disciplines and restraints of conventional society. Why should the Irish students have been particularly eager to act out this stereotype? A contemporary commentator – himself a former Glasgow student and at the time of writing a Moderator of the Synod of Ulster – attempts to provide answers. Having crossed over from Ulster to Scotland, Irish students have left behind the restraining influences of family and familiar society; as the moderator puts it: 'they are left with little check or control over them'. Then again because 'they seldom brought letters of introduction,' they are entirely on their own, left to their own devices, when they reach Glasgow. Hence their inclination to stay together as a distinct, separate grouping: 'they had no acquaintance, and they kept almost entirely to themselves'. The moderator insists that this sense of a separate, unassimilated identity, carried over even into their college classes: 'even, in the Divinity Hall, they generally sat, in a back place, by themselves, and formed little acquaintance with the other students'. And he comes back to the point that the Irish students were dangerously free from any kind of check or control: 'Besides what they did there was unknown to their parents and guardians here; and, from what I have heard, I have no doubt that many of them fall into practices very dangerous to them'.[11]

Earlier in the century, Frances Hutcheson himself had hardly been less critical of the behaviour of his fellow Irish students. Arriving in Glasgow in 1730 to take up his philosophy professorship, Hutcheson, we are told, brought no less than eighteen or twenty of his old Dublin pupils with him. And there can be no doubt that, as his first biographer put it, he 'had a warm corner in his heart for students who had come like himself from Ireland'.[12] But for all that, and despite his willingness to provide a previously unheard of degree of pastoral care for his students, and particularly for his Irish students, Hutcheson was all too aware of the frequently problematic behaviour of the Irish students at Glasgow. His letters to his old friend Thomas Drennan in Ulster make the point abundantly clear. Irish students are guilty of neglecting their studies through idleness, drinking, vanity, and foppery: 'our countrymen,' he writes, 'very generally have such an affectation of being men and gentlemen immediately and of despising everything in Scotland, that they neglect a great deal of good, wise instruction they might have here'. 'I am truly mortified,' he goes on, 'with a vanity and foppery prevailing among our countryman, beyond what I see in others; and a sauntering forsooth which makes them incapable of any hearty drudgery at books'.[13] In another letter he refers to the Irish students' drinking problem: 'The wretched turn their minds take is to the silly manliness of taverns'.[14] Perhaps he was remembering such cases as that of Joseph Paine from County Meath who in 1734, according to the university records, was twice fined 'for staying out and drinking late;' or of Eph Cuthbert from Dublin who in the same year was fined for 'drinking at unseasonable hours'. Certainly Hutcheson came to feel that the Glasgow intake from Dublin College were a particularly rowdy lot. A James Stuart 'from Dublin College' is identified as a bad influence and described to Drennan as leading 'some people you wish very well to, into idleness and drinking'. 'We almost constantly suffer,' Hutcheson continues, 'by such as come from Dublin College. I never desire to see one of them'.[15] Other letters refer to the cases of John Blackwood and Robert Haliday, both taking his own class in 1739. Their behaviour is such that good students, he tells Drennan, try to steer clear of them: some good Edinburgh law students, he writes, 'dreaded contracting acquaintance with Blackwood and Haliday in particular'. Blackwood was one of those addicted to 'the silly manliness of taverns' and he was 'a bad sight this way to lads of smaller fortunes, tho' otherways of a fine temper'.[16] Just as well perhaps in that he would in due course become a member of the Irish parliament as Sir John Blackwood, second Baronet of Ballyleedy. Haliday from Belfast was one of those, in 1741, 'idling away his time' in taverns, mocking the folly 'of bookish studious lads,' but perhaps Hutcheson's strictures had effect because by 1744 Haliday is reported to be 'doing very well'.[17]

Glasgow students in general gained themselves quite a reputation in the eighteenth century for a certain boisterousness of behaviour. James Wodrow described them as 'tumultuating'.[18] And from what has already been said, it is clear that the Irish students in Glasgow must have contributed to that reputation. In 1769, for example Marcus Wainwright from Tipperaray was we are told 'rebuked with severity' for being engaged in what was called a 'scuffle' with another student. But Irish boisterousness was not all about drinking and fighting. Their sense of freedom seems sometimes to have carried over into the lecture room. Hutcheson's biographer suggests that many of the professors 'used to dread the high spirits of the Irish students, who, less under restraint than the rest, seemed to have endeavoured to shock the sober people of Glasgow'[19] Perhaps it was this kind of Irish student behaviour that made Thomas Reid so critical on his arrival from Aberdeen in 1764. The 'stupid Irish teagues' he had to cope with in Glasgow may well have been a good less douce than the Aberdonians he was accustomed to. In any event his letter of December, 1765 to his old friend Andrew Skene of Aberdeen makes his displeasure abundantly clear:

> The most disagreeable thing in the teaching part is to have a great Number of stupid Irish teagues who attend classes for two or three years to qualify them for teaching Schools or being dissenting teachers. I preach to these as St Francis did to the fishes. I don't know what pleasure he had in his Audience, but I should have none in mine if there was not in it a mixture of reasonable Creatures... I have long been of the Opinion that in a Right Constituted College

there ought to be two Professors for each Class. One for the Dunces and another for those who have parts...[20]

The matriculation albums show that in Reid's first year at Glasgow of the 18 students who matriculated in his class, 13 were Irish; in the following year (1765) of the 11 who matriculated, 9 were Irish. Of 1764's 13 Irish students, five went on to become ministers in the Irish Presbyterian Church, while 3 of 1765's 9 followed in their footsteps. And we also know that the 1764 class contained at least one potential Irish trouble-maker: William Grant from the city of Cork. In 1767 Grant was complained against 'for breaking a sedan chair' – the change was not sustained – but a few months later he was fined three guineas by the university for fighting a duel.

So far Irish high spirits and boisterousness have been presented in a largely negative light. Both Hutcheson and Reid seem to suggest that the new sense of freedom that the Irish students discovered at Glasgow college led mainly to idleness, drinking, and neglect of their studies. But this is only part of the story. Relations between students and faculty at eighteenth-century Glasgow were frequently strained. As we have noted, Frances Hutcheson's willingness to engage with his students on a personal level was exceptional. Staff-student relations were usually wholly formal and distant. No doubt this is one reason why student squibs and skits, mocking and satirizing their teachers, were not uncommon. But there were occasions when the confrontation between faculty and students centred on more serious issues, and when this happened, Irish students appear to play a very prominent role. More than once in the eighteenth century, the voices speaking up on behalf of student rights and privileges, and calling for liberty and freedom, were distinctly Irish. A major issue arising early in the century concerned the election of the College Rector. Traditionally both faculty and students had been involved in this election, but after 1688 and the new order then established, the faculty had become the sole participants in the electoral process. However around 1716/17 – and the issue would run for at least the next ten years – some students began to demand the restoration of their voting rights. In 1717 nine students raised a court action against the conduct of Sir John Maxwell, the then Rector, hand-picked by the faculty. Among the nine students was none other than Frances Hutcheson himself. There was some support for the students among the faculty – including that of Gershom Carmichael, then still a Regent. The court case dragged on but was eventually lost. However in 1722 in

Dublin two Glasgow Irish students – James Arbuckle and John Smith – produced a pamphlet which rehearsed the dispute and the various ramifications that surrounded it. According to *A Short Account of the late Treatment of the Students in the University of G — —-w*, students had been disciplined for staging two plays – Addison's *Cato* and Nicolas Rowe's *Tamerlane*. Both plays enjoyed considerable popular success in the early eighteenth century, largely because of the political significance of their contrasting civic virtue with tyranny and corruption. The college faculty might well have seen the plays as representing an attack on them, and given that the performance of *Cato* included a prologue by Arbuckle and an epilogue by an English student, Thomas Griffiths, they were probably right. The college authorities had also cracked down on student clubs and societies – particularly the Trinamphorian of which Arbuckle and Smith were leading members. According to them, the faculty saw the club as 'a set of Latitudinarians, Free-thinkers, Nonsubscribers, and Bangorians, and in a Word, Enemies to the Jurisdictions, Powers and Divine Authority of the clergy'. The student case was based on an appeal to Liberty – the freedom from tyranny apparently gained after 1688. Smith, we are told, had 'very early interested himself in the Liberties of the College, while yet only a Student of Philosophy'. Arbuckle, yet another life-long friend of Thomas Drennan in Ulster – and so presumably known to Francis Hutcheson – was a poet in his own right (Allan Ramsay was another friend) and had played a prominent part in all the student disputes with the faculty.

Despite losing out in the Scottish courts, the student protestors refused to give up. In 1722 they decided to look for help in Parliament itself. Here again Francis Hutcheson almost certainly played a crucial role. Now teaching in his academy in Dublin, he had come to know powerful figures in Dublin's society including Robert Molesworth. In any event it was Viscount Molesworth, who had seats both in the Irish parliament and in Westminster, who agreed to support the Glasgow students' petition to Parliament. However, before the petition could be considered, Parliament was dissolved and new elections held. In fact Molesworth lost his seat, but a false report reached Glasgow that the man who had clearly become the college students' hero had been re-elected. The students decided to celebrate this success with a large bonfire in the High Street just outside the college. The faculty was outraged by such conduct, and clearly tried to clamp down on the student demonstration. Gershom Carmichael – who by now had apparently changed his mind over the legitimacy of the student cause – appeared in the High Street and ordered the bonfire to be extinguished. The students refused and a melée ensued: burning sticks from the bonfire were thrown; windows in the houses of the Principal and other professors were broken. Most serious of all Carmichael and John Smith – by now a student in the Divinity school – confronted each other and engaged in some kind of wrestling match. Inevitably Smith and others were made to appear before the faculty accused of misconduct. The outcome was that Smith was expelled for assaulting a regent. Smith, however, was clearly not a man to be easily intimidated. He appealed to the Court of Session against his expulsion. In the course of the case the Lord Advocate remarked:

> Mr Smith is an Irishman, and if he, and his Irish Brethren take the liberty to put on Bonfires when they think fit, others may do it upon very unlawful occasions.

Smith unsurprisingly saw these references to the Irish as a racist attack on those who were 'Britons transplanted' and were in fact effective upholders of the 'British Protestant Interest'. This case too dragged on for several years, but in 1726 the penalties imposed on Smith were revoked. By then he had left Glasgow and become a publisher in Dublin. With extraordinary appropriateness, the first book that Smith and his partner William Bruce published was Frances Hutcheson's *An Inquiry into the Original of our Ideas of Beauty and Virtue.*[21]

The 1722 fracas in no way ended the student movement for restoration of their voting rights in the rectorial election. In 1726 the campaign was being led by yet another Glasgow Irish student – William Robertson. Once again the faculty tried to defend their privileged position by disciplining the student protest leader: Robertson was expelled from the college. Molesworth was again appealed to and this time his influence led to the reinstatement of Robertson within a year. At this point the Glasgow faculty appear to have given up the struggle. The right to vote in rectorial elections was restored to matriculated students. The faculty continued to be able to vote but their number was so few that the position of Rector soon became what it remains to this day – a student appointment.

A second example of Glasgow-Irish political activism occurred later in the eighteenth century. The occasion this time was Professor John Anderson's long-running dispute with the majority of his academic colleagues over various aspects of the organization and running of the Glasgow college. Sometimes supported by Thomas

Reid and the astronomy professor Alexander Wilson, Anderson had long been calling for a Royal Commission to investigate the college's affairs. Bitterly opposed by the rest of the faculty, Anderson did have supporters both among the student body and the townspeople of Glasgow. Among these was Alexander Humphreys, a medical student originally from Armagh. In 1785 Humphreys was accused of publishing a defamatory account of Dr Taylor, a Glasgow minister, and Dr Meek, then Dean of the Faculty. Taylor and Meek had written to the Glasgow newspapers rebutting the charges against the university that Anderson supporters had published in the city. Humphreys' paper was an abusive rejoinder. Having refused to appear unattended before the faculty on a charge of 'subscribing certain Publications injurious to this University,' he was deprived of his 1777 MA degree. These 'certain publications' may well have included a pamphlet called *The State of the Facts* which had attacked the faculty and its proceedings. The minister Taylor subsequently raised a court action in which he claimed that John Anderson was the real author of Alexander Humphreys' defamatory paper. Taylor's action was successful and he was awarded £250 damages.[22] Humphreys incidentally had matriculated in Thomas Reid's Ethics class in 1774.

The examples of the disputes over the rectorial election and John Anderson's critique of the university suggest that the Irish students at Glasgow were inclined to adopt an anti-establishment, anti-authoritarian stance. But before pursuing this idea I want to look more closely at the significance of eighteenth-century Glasgow University in the history of Irish Presbyterianism. As we have already seen, easily the most readily identifiable group of Irish students at Glasgow were those qualifying for the Presbyterian ministry. Around 1760, however, these students became the focus of a significant dispute involving academic standards and the university curriculum. Many years earlier Frances Hutcheson, once again taking a special interest in the welfare of fellow Irish students, had persuaded faculty colleagues to make special provision for students who had attended Irish academies of the kind he himself had run in Dublin. The arrangement meant that such Irish students could gain an Arts degree after two years' attendance at Glasgow. Presumably this concession meant a reduction in the time it took for candidates for the Presbyterian Ministry to qualify – and this in turn would have meant a reduction in the cost of doing so. However, over the years opposition began to grow over this Irish privilege; it was argued that the Irish students were inadequately prepared for their university courses; and that two years' attendance was not enough to merit the award of the MA degree.

Action was finally taken in May 1764, when a new statute was enacted saying that no 'foreign student' (which actually meant no Irish student), who had not attended another university, could obtain a Glasgow degree until they had completed two full sessions at the university and had taken certain specified courses. These were Natural Philosophy, Moral Philosophy, plus another philosophy and a language course. Additionally certain set texts had to be read and studied – texts by Homer, Virgil, Livy, and Xenophon. Mathematics could be added, but was not a requirement. Some years later, in 1771, it was decided that other subjects taken would not be included on the graduation diploma but would be recorded on separate certificates. These developments suggest that one could argue that it was the presence of the Irish students at Glasgow that made the university think seriously, perhaps for the first time, about what the curriculum for a degree in Arts should include. Which is not to say that issues over professorial payments, and the usual personality clashes, were not also involved.

In the end the changes introduced in 1764 proved less than enough to satisfy the critics of the old Hutcheson-engineered provision for Irish academy students. In 1772 the Bishop of Down and Connor complained that Glasgow's two year Arts degree graduates were not good enough to be admitted to holy orders. Not to be outdone, the Irish Presbyterians and synods agreed – a two-year degree was not good enough for the ministry. Soon the Irish House of Commons was ready to pass a motion formally excluding two-year degree holders from admission to orders. Glasgow University responded by saying it would reconsider the whole issue. The argument dragged on for another decade but finally in 1782 a new regulation was passed by the faculty: no foreign students who had not studied at another university would be admitted to degrees any quicker than Scotsmen. Only John Anderson and Thomas Reid dissented.[23] A postscript to this story is that it explains why, from the mid-1760s on the great majority of matriculated students in Glasgow's Physics class were from Ireland: Physics had become a requirement for their Arts degree. And the change in regulation also explains the dramatic rise in the percentage of Irish in 'gown' class matriculations in the 60s and 70s.

The controversy over the two-year degree for Irish students had an impact upon the internal structures and regulations of Glasgow University. The fact that the great majority of its clergy was trained at Glasgow throughout the eighteenth century had a major external impact upon the development in that period of the Irish Presbyterian Church itself. That church, like the Church of Scotland, was characterized throughout the eighteenth century by an ongoing struggle between two bitterly opposed camps or parties. The division between the two sides was both theological and philosophical, and the outcome of the struggle between them was the same in both Scotland and Ireland. As the century went on, at least at the ministerial and assembly level, the Moderates or New Lights gradually gained the upper hand over the proponents of old-style, hard-line, traditional Calvinism. Hence by 1751, the Moderates had gained control of the Synod of Ulster. How had this come about? James Seaton Reid, the nineteenth-century historian of Irish Presbyterianism, had no doubt the answer lay over the water in Glasgow. The Moderates, he writes

> had been long struggling against the votes of orthodox majorities, but agencies had meanwhile been silently in operation, which eventually secured for them a paramount influence. Of these, the most important was the collegiate education received by candidates for the ministry. Professor Simpson, of Glasgow, had inoculated his students with those principles which led to the separation of the Presbytery of Antrim; and so remiss were the judicatories of the Church of Scotland, that even after the mischievous character of his teaching had been fully demonstrated, he was permitted, year after year, to continue his theological prelections.

However, Reid is convinced that it is not Simpson who is the main culprit:

> But of all those who filled chairs in the Scottish universities during the first half of the eighteenth century, no one was more influential in moulding the minds of young men preparing for the sacred office than Dr Frances Hutcheson, Professor of Moral philosophy in Glasgow. This gentleman who... was the son of the minister of Armagh, had, at an early period of life, relinquished the principles of his amiable and excellent father.

Reid's own sympathies are clearly not with the Moderate party, but he is in no doubt about attributing its success to the subversive influence of a Scottish university education upon the minds of trainee ministries:

> The theological training to which Irish students were subjected in the University of Glasgow amounts, to great extent, for the steady progress and ultimate ascendency of New-light principles in the

> Synod of Ulster. The orthodox majority endeavoured to exclude error, by passing resolution after resolution enforcing subscription to the Westminster formulary; but the moderate party did not deem it necessary to excite public alarm by opposing these impotent arrangements, for they knew that the attendance of the candidates for the ministry on the lectures of the Scottish professors would silently accomplish a theological revolution.[24]

Such a thesis raises the question of why those whom Reid describes as 'the orthodox majority' did not seek to provide an alternative educational route for potential Irish Presbyterian clergymen bypassing Glasgow and its harmful influence. Such a possibility did in fact arise in the 1790s. When the Foxite Earl Fitzwilliam was made the Irish viceroy, he supported a proposal that new institutes of higher education should be established both for Irish Catholics and Irish Presbyterians. The scheme led to the founding of Maynooth, the Roman Catholic seminary in Dublin, but the Presbyterian college did not materialize. It would be 1852 before the Presbyterian College would be established in Belfast. Before that, however, the so-called 'orthodox majority' among Irish Presbyterians had solved the problem of providing an education for entrants to the ministry which was in line with their principles by taking control of the Belfast Academical Institution around 1815. With the support of Castlereagh, the powerful British foreign minister, the Ulster New Lights had initially seemed likely to retain control, but on this occasion they were out-voted. 'From this period,' writes Reid, 'the majority of the Irish students ceased to frequent the Scottish universities'.[25]

The notion of an anti-establishment, anti-authority tradition among Irish students at Glasgow in the eighteenth century has already been mooted. For most of the century that tradition defined itself by boisterousness in the classroom; a commitment to the defence of student rights; a readiness to side with those within the university who were critical of the status quo; and more generally in a tendency towards idleness and self-indulgence rather than studious application and sobriety. However, it is possible to argue that in the closing years of the century that tradition emerged in a much more serious and politically explosive form. 1798 saw the outbreak of the Irish rebellion led by the Society of United Irishmen. The heartland of the United Irishmen was Presbyterian Ulster, and the Society's ideology favouring freedom and the rights of man was based on the radical principles of Revolutionary France. Glasgow University soon found itself touched by the Irish rebellion; in June 1798, the university authorities received a list of 19 students expelled from Trinity College Dublin for being members of treasonable societies; if any of their numbers applied to study in Glasgow, they were not to be admitted.[26]

On another level, however, Glasgow was already deeply involved in the 1798 rising. At least 10 Irish Presbyterian ministers who had trained in Glasgow supported the United Irishmen movement. One – Archibald Warrick – was executed in October, 1798. Three others – Samuel Barber, William Dickson, and Sinclare Kelburn – served prison sentences. Four others – Thomas Ledlie Birch, William Sinclair, Charles Wallace and James Hull – fled or were allowed to flee to the United States. One – Reuben Rodgers – was restored to his charge in 1803. And Arthur McMahon, who ironically had been the future Lord Castlereagh's tutor in classics, fled to France and enjoyed a successful career as 'General Mack'. Another Glasgow-Irish student who participated in the rebellion – Overstreet Grogan – was beheaded on Wexford Bridge on June 28, 1798.

Of the Irish Presbyterian Ministers listed, one studied under Francis Hutcheson; one under Adam Smith; two under George Jardine; one under James Clow; one under John Anderson; and three under Archibald Arthur. These of course are the classes in which their matriculation is recorded, but we can be certain that all these future ministers would have studied Ethics and Moral Philosophy during their Glasgow years under Hutcheson, or Smith, or Reid or Arthur. As we have seen, traditional Calvinists saw the Glasgow experience as indoctrinating Irish divinity students with New Light principles. May it not be the case that it was from this Glasgow philosophical tradition that these ten Presbyterian ministers at least learned to sympathize with social and political ideals of a potentially more revolutionary kind? Thomas Reid and Archibald Arthur, alongside George Jardine, John Anderson and John Millar, were certainly ready to support the aims and ideals of the French revolutionaries. Thomas Drennan, as noted above was Francis Hutcheson's long-time Ulster friend. William Drennan, Thomas's son, received his MA from Glasgow in 1772, and William Drennan was one of the founders of the Society of United Irishmen. Drennan then – who apparently was also the first to use the phrase 'the Emerald Isle,' – may stand as an archetype of the Irish student at Glasgow University in the eighteenth century.

1 See Andrew Hook & Richard Sher (eds.) *The Glasgow Enlightenment* (East Linton, 1995), pp. 10, 17.
2 See James Coutts, *A History of the University of Glasgow From its Foundation in 1451 to 1909* (Glasgow, 1909), p. 173.
3 *Ibid.*, pp. 314-15.
4 Thomas Hamilton, *The Youth and Manhood of Cyril Thornton*, ed. Maurice Lindsay (Aberdeen, 1990), p. 37.
5 J. G. Lockhart, *Peter's Letters to his Kinsfolk* (Edinburgh, 1819), III, 182.
6 See *Fraser's Magazine*, CCCXVII (May, 1856), p. 506.
7 W. Innes Addison, *The Matriculation Albums of the University of Glasgow From 1728 to 1858* (Glasgow, 1913), p. 546.
8 See A. T. Q. Stewart, *A Deeper Silence, The Hidden Origins of the United Irish Movement* (London, Boston, 1993), p. 99.
9 See David Murray, *Memories of the Old College of Glasgow* (Glasgow, 1927), p. 477.
10 *Cyril Thornton, op. cit.*, p. 37.
11 See William B. Scott, *Francis Hutcheson* (Cambridge, 1900), p. 69.
12 *Ibid.*, p. 69.
13 *Ibid.*, p. 69
14 *Ibid.*, p. 73.
15 *Ibid.*, p. 71.
16 Addison, *op. cit.* p. 21.
17 Scott, *op. cit.*, p. 72, Addison, *op.cit.*, p. 21.
18 See Murray, *op. cit.*, p. 488.
19 See Scott, *op. cit.*, p. 69.
20 Thomas Reid, *The Correspondence of Thomas Reid*, ed. Paul Wood, (Edinburgh, 2002), pp. 45-6.
21 For accounts of this episode, see Stewart, *op. cit.*, pp. 82-9, and Murray, *op. cit.*, pp. 489-90.
22 See Coutts, *op.cit.*, pp. 290-94.
23 *Ibid.*, pp. 307-09.
24 James Seaton Reid, *History of the Presbyterian Church in Ireland* (Belfast, 1867), III, 293-4, 301.
25 *Ibid.*, p. 434.
26 Coutts, *op. cit.*, pp. 304-05.

7 Student Life Today

A new academic year is about to begin. In the streets around our universities there is a lively sense of bustle and energy as freshers arrive full of expectation and excitement while old hands anticipate an even better year than the last one. I always find this time of year an inspiriting one: the feeling of youthful hope and shared commitment is an infectious one. But all the same worries remain. Looking back from a lifetime of involvement in universities in Edinburgh, Aberdeen and Glasgow, I ask myself whether today's institutions are doing everything they should to ensure that the student experience is as rich and fulfilling as it should be? I worry about two areas of student life in particular where it seems to me that the current generation of undergraduates experience a much tougher time than their peers did in the past. The two areas are employment and accommodation. Let me discuss each in turn.

EMPLOYMENT. A student in the early 1950s, I worked one Christmas sorting parcels in Edinburgh's GPO. After that, one summer I spent six weeks working for the Forestry Commission on the banks of Loch Ness. (The job involved cutting bracken growing up around recently planted trees.) Living at home, and in receipt of a grant of around £40 per year, I can say I was under no real pressure to find paid employment. All my effort went into being a full-time student.

Half a century later, how student life has changed! No doubt many of my peers worked for at least a portion of all our vacations. But that was it. Term-time was term-time, and no one dreamed of trying to combine full-time study with a job. I really don't know when that ceased to be true, but for years now a large percentage of students have had to do exactly that. For them studying has to be organised around waiting tables or pulling pints or some other way of earning money. Only a handful of universities – Oxford, Cambridge, Durham, Warwick — have banned term-time working by their students. Precise statistics are not available, but probably 50% of all U.K. students do take on term-time employment — working on average 15 or 16 hours a week.

Have university administrators and teachers really taken on board the significance of this change? I'm not persuaded they have. Again serious investigation of the situation is limited, but such research that does exist comes to the wholly unsurprising conclusion that students who do not have to work during term perform better than those who do. Only 62% of working students are as likely to earn a First or Upper Second class degree as their non-working peers. Many Scottish students work during term-time despite the fact that for now at least they are not required to pay fees. For students who do have to pay fees — and some at the Scottish universities are already in that situation — the pressure to combine study with work can only increase. Are we in fact heading to a situation where in fact the great majority of undergraduates are only part-time students? If so, attention needs to be paid to that new reality.

More disturbing still, however, are the circumstances in which students seeking employment are placed. In the current economic climate, the competition for jobs is unusually acute. In the services sector, even experienced workers, who would normally expect to be in full-time employment, are now forced to accept part-time or 'zero hours' contracts. What his means is that the cards are stacked even more against young, untrained students. Also there are a great many of them. In Glasgow's three universities the total student population is approximately 50,000. That figure includes postgraduate students, and of course not all undergraduates find themselves needing to work. But as we have seen, it is clear that a very large number do. Employers in the so-called 'service' industries are thus in a position to benefit from a very large pool of bright young people, all desperate to find some kind of employment. It is no surprise then that 'zero hours' contracts are very much the norm. Many students work for agencies that supply bodies to help with serving food and drink — often after only an hour or two's training — at one-off events such as corporate functions, pop-music gigs at Hampden Park, or racing at Ayr or Hamilton. But they have no idea how often they will be called upon or how many hours work will be involved. Travel for such events is not always paid for, and of course payment is invariably at the minimum hourly wage scale. Bosses don't always behave well, but in a situation where the supply of labour greatly outweighs demand, complaining is not a good idea and tends not to happen.

Students working as waiters face other problems — even at quite upmarket locations. Shifts can begin at 5pm. and go on until the last diner is prepared to leave — however late that is — even 2am. But while serving fancy meals, the waiters themselves are not provided with food of any kind. And if they take, say, a half-hour break, that time is deducted from their pay. The problem once again is that the employer holds all the cards. There is no trade union they have to answer to. Students need the job — and so accept conditions that workers in regular employment would never assent to.

ACCOMMODATION. In this area too, students find themselves very badly placed. In different towns and cities, more and more students compete for what is a limited stock of rented accommodation. So landlords — like employers — hold all the cards. There is no incentive for them to update or improve the properties they own. They just don't need to. Their impulse is rather to turn every room into a bedroom, and equip flats with the barest minimum requirements for an HMO (Houses in Multiple Occupation) property. And as I understand it, their behaviour can be quite ruthless. Deposits are a particularly contentious issue. Landlords and agencies frequently make it as difficult as possible for deposits to be reclaimed. A regular piece of sharp practice is for large sums to be kept back for so-called 'cleaning' fees. The new Letting Protection Service is supposed to ensure that deposits are handled appropriately — which implies that the authorities do at least recognise there is a major problem in this area. But whether this new service will remedy the unfair situation in which students regularly find themselves remains to be seen. Then again flats often turn out to have broken or dodgy boilers, stoves, showers, windows — but students often find it very difficult to get landlords or agencies to sort out such problems. As a result they can be left without heating or hot water for weeks on end. Clearly something needs to be done to protect student tenants from being exploited by indifferent and uncaring property-owners.

ACTION. In the brave new world of strict business efficiency imposed on all our universities, I know there will be those arguing that there is no need for institutions to become more involved in such areas as student employment and accommodation. Let market values rule. I would argue on the contrary that universities do indeed have a responsibility for the well-being of the students who keep them in business! There are steps that should be taken. Universities Scotland (the representative body of our higher education institutions) should be required to gather statistics on the scale of employment currently undertaken by full-time, undergraduate students. At least we would then know the size of the problem that needs to be addressed. Then all our universities should be required to provide their students with comprehensive information about their rights as employees and tenants. A student ombudsman would be an excellent idea. The existence of such a figure on every campus might go some way to redress the balance between struggling students and all too powerful employers and landlords.

8 Universities Today

A few weeks ago I wrote in the *Review* (September 17) about how many of today's university students are being taken advantage of, outside the classroom, by landlords and employers. Since then the topic of the universities, within the classroom, has become a lively and even contentious one within these pages.

This has encouraged me, a retired academic, to return to the question of our universities and have my say on where I think we are. Previous contributors have disagreed with each other, but they are mostly in agreement on one basic point. All is not well in our university system. There may be arguments over the nature of the problem. But problem there is. (Perhaps I should make it clear that in referring to 'our' system I'm referring to all of the U.K.)

My view is that the origins of that problem go back to the days of the most controversial figure in our modern political history. Despite being a graduate of Somerville College, Oxford, Mrs. Thatcher was no friend of the universities. In the early 1980s she pushed through massive cuts in university funding. (Oxford retaliated by denying her an honorary degree in 1985.) The legacy of the Thatcher cuts is still with us.

Their initial introduction led to administrative panic in many universities. At the time I was teaching at the university of Aberdeen. Senior administrators there – like those at many other institutions – responded badly, rushing to push through severe limits on departmental budgets, demanding early retirals by older faculty members, and refusing to make new appointments. All of this with little consultation or discussion with members of staff. The inevitable result was the emergence of a 'them and us' situation. Administrators and faculty were on now on opposite sides; trust was lost.

Soon after this I happened to move to Glasgow University, where I found a very different situation. A recently-appointed Principal succeeded where many others failed. Facing equally stringent cuts in resources, he kept all sections of the university united in attempting to come to terms with the new financial situation. At least in Glasgow, in difficult and demanding circumstances, it was possible to feel we were all on the same side.

The problems were real, however. When I arrived my Department of English Literature had I recall 25 full-time members of staff. By the mid-1980s – at a time when student numbers were still rising – that figure had fallen to 16. (It would be almost ten years later before these losses were made up.) At that time I was fully committed to the idea that our students in Junior and Senior Honours should have a weekly one-on-one tutorial with a full-time member of staff. (The Oxbridge model.) As Department head, I struggled for several years to maintain this system of tuition. Three GTAs (Graduate Teaching Assistants) were appointed to help with the teaching of tutorial groups for first and second year students. (Incidentally their number today is over twenty and such students now rarely experience tutorials taught by full-time faculty members.) But the individual tutorial system for Honours students came under increasing pressure. By the end of the 80s it had become clear to me that maintaining such a system was doing the department a disservice. Increasingly it was taken to mean we were over-staffed – and so that in tough financial circumstances we could not possibly expect to be allowed to appoint new members of staff. In the 1990s, seminars replaced individual tutorials.

Mrs. Thatcher's so-called 'reforms' of the university system were based on the same ideology as lay behind her government 's drive to privatise as much as possible of what had been the public sector. The aim was to create a new model of competitiveness between universities. In the past the external examiners' system was intended to ensure that degrees from all the British universities were more or less of equivalent value: a First was a First whether it was from Aberdeen or Exeter. In the post-Thatcher period, as more and more universities were created to educate more and more students, this always somewhat idealistic notion was effectively abandoned. The new reality would be a league table of competing universities and, crucially, a new system of treasury funding was created to enforce it.

As before, teaching would be funded according to the number of students admitted. But a new accountability would be assured by the creation of TQA (Teacher Quality Assessment). Research funding, however, would be distributed according to an institution's success – or lack of it – in the new RAE (Research Assessment Exercise). TQA never made much impact and characteristically was soon quietly forgotten. The RAE on the other hand quickly became the driving force behind radical changes across the entire university sector. Success in this competition over major funding became the only thing that mattered. Early on I was in favour of RAE. But in no time at all it became a self-serving, dangerously divisive monster, doing much more harm than good.

The rise of the RAE more or less coincided with another fundamental change in our universities which continues to disturb so many of those who work in them: the imposition upon institutions dedicated to teaching and research of an administrative and organisational model (with its own peculiar language) deriving from the world of corporate big business. A university, we gather, is just a business like any other. Hence free-market rules – customer satisfaction, income generation, public relations – become the order of the day. With the backing of successive governments, university administrators up and down the country have come to share this flawed vision of what a university is.

What has been the result? One is the reinforcing of the view that students come to universities for essentially vocational reasons. Of course it's true that from their earliest, medieval foundations universities have had a 'vocational' function – providing society with well-educated clergy, doctors, and lawyers. But in the past that professional training had a strongly philosophical foundation. In the Scottish tradition, it was normal for lawyers to combine their legal qualification with an MA degree; similarly it was not uncommon for doctors to combine their medical training with an Arts degree. The situation is very different today. The universities have more or less become complicit with this instrumental view of education. As one commentator puts it, 'universities are expected to deliver not just education but jobs'. He is right. Many universities are all too ready to suggest that 'employability' is a hallmark of their degrees.

A second result is the endless repetition by government ministers and their spokesmen that the principal justification for funding universities is the contribution they make to the success of the national economy. Teaching and research matter because they help us in the global race for economic success. With ever-increasing frequency we are told that university courses should somehow be relevant to the world outside the traditional ivory towers. Not to be outdone, business leaders say they are more than willing to work more closely with the universities. The content of courses could and should be debated and scrutinized to ensure that they produce students who meet the needs of the outside world.

But endless repetition, by voices inside both government and the universities themselves, of the view that the primary function of teaching and research is the servicing of the national economy does not mean that it is true. I am in no way persuaded that students spend three or four years at university simply to take up a place in the workplace of existing society. The difference between a university education and a vocational education used to be clear-cut. The problems that arise when that distinction is blurred are perfectly illustrated by the various exchanges over the teaching of journalism that have appeared in the Review. (See the issues on 26 September, 1 October, and 15 October.) But with the transformation in recent years of large numbers of former polytechnics and colleges of education into universities, such blurring has undoubtedly occurred, effectively consolidating the view that all higher education is instrumental in job and wealth creation. What is the result? A growing decline in the teaching and availability of what used to be mainstream subjects in the arts and humanities.

That decline has been accelerated by the system of university funding introduced by the present government. Funding for courses in science, technology and medicine is protected. (Justified inevitably by the standard national economy argument.) But courses in the arts and humanities are funded only on the basis of student demand. Those of us who argued from the beginning that this change could only mean an inevitable decline in the availability of subject areas and courses (and of teaching posts) are already being proved right. A.C. Grayling was recently quoted saying 'universities...have closed or are closing humanities departments left, right and centre, and are losing academics who teach English or history.... A lot of the former polys ... have had to do this, reconfiguring themselves as colleges that teach vocational courses'. Of course Grayling will be accused of exaggerating the situation in order to bolster the existence of the New College of the Humanities, *The Independent* undergraduate college of which he is the Head. But there can be no disputing the recently published evidence of the staggering decline in the teaching of modern languages in our universities. In 1998, 93 institutions offered single honours degrees in modern languages. Now 56 do so. 11 universities have closed down all their language courses. Significantly the speed of decline has quickened since 2007. Since then the number of universities offering degrees in French or German has fallen by 29%; in Spanish by 36%. Only 2.4% of honours students are studying a language. It would be interesting to have similar research on what is happening to such subjects as philosophy, history and English literature.

The decline in the teaching of the humanities in the U.K. is paralleled by an equally worrying decline in the USA. The current president of the American Council of Learned Societies recently said: 'College is increasingly being defined narrowly as job preparation, not as something designed to educate the whole person'. National federal data suggests that humanities majors now represent only 7% of the total. Only 15% of Stanford University students study the humanities – at Harvard humanities majors have declined by 20% over the last decade. Princeton is establishing a new first year course designed to increase enrolment in the humanities.

Does all this matter? If you share the view that the university experience has contributed to, and helped to define, the quality and values of our society and culture, the answer is that indeed it does.

9 The Future of the Universities

On December 9th I spent much of the afternoon watching the BBC's 24 Hours news coverage of the parliamentary debate and the student protest march over the tuition fees issue in England. It was instantly clear what the TV producers regarded as the big story. Snippets of speakers in the House of Commons debate were swamped by hours of coverage of banner-waving students milling around Parliament Square where they were 'kettled' by ranks of Metropolitan Police in full riot gear. Individual incidents such as the mounted police charge against what seemed to be a relatively small number of protesters (shades of Peterloo!) were run over and over again. Intrepid BBC reporters risked everything to get statements from students about what exactly they were protesting about. For me one student reply stood out. Why? Because of course what she said chimed with what for me is the most challenging and even frightening aspect of what our coalition government is planning to do over the funding of the university system.

In my view, both politicians and media commentaries alike have allowed the issue of higher fees, and what that will mean, to dominate the universities debate to the exclusion of all other issues. Of course the issue of fees — and the related question about access to a university education being open to students from every kind of background — are hugely important concerns and deserve to be hotly debated. But what has been called the biggest change in the provision of university education in a hundred years involves a great deal more. Asked why she was protesting, my favourite student said not for herself — she was completing a degree in journalism – but for her younger sisters. They would be facing a situation in which student choice would be hugely limited. No arts and humanities she said. Absurd? Way over the top? I've no doubt that would be the response of many — probably most — viewers. At a previous protest I glimpsed a banner saying 'Save Our Humanities'. What are these students talking about? How can the humanities possibly need saving? What is a university if it is not an institution dedicated to the study and passing on of that vast range of human knowledge we conventionally call the humanities?

Well as it happens I have beside me a statement issued on the morning of the tuition fees debate by Sir Adam Roberts, President of the British Academy. It is called 'The Continuing Challenges

Facing Higher Education'. Bear in mind that the British Academy was founded near the beginning of the twentieth century to provide for the arts and social sciences a national institution of equivalent scholarly prestige and authority to that represented in science and medicine by the Royal Society founded in the seventeenth century. (In Scotland we have the parallel Royal Society of Edinburgh, founded in the eighteenth century, bringing together outstanding scholars in all academic disciplines.) The obvious point I am making is that Sir Adam knows what he is talking about. He is not a politician, nor is he a servant of politicians. He speaks in the name of the institution he heads — though he accepts that not all its members will agree with everything his statement contains. And he speaks with authority. So what does he say?

Sir Adam insists that at the core of the Browne Review — which provides the 'highly controversial' basis of the coalition's proposals — is 'the dramatic withdrawal of direct public funding for university teaching in England, and the new funding mechanism proposed to replace it'. (The new mechanism is of course the rise in tuition fees to as much as £9000 a year.) The result will be that 'direct public support of higher education teaching in England will fall by some 70% between now and 2014-15'. Sir Adam goes on to consider the impact of this dramatic change on those subject areas with which the British Academy is concerned. 'The humanities and social sciences,' he writes, ' are widely seen as particularly threatened by the planned changes, and not without reason. The Browne review identified as priority areas science, technology, medicine and healthcare, but did not mention the humanities and social sciences (save "strategically important language courses"). And public funding is to be withdrawn almost entirely from humanities and social sciences, but only partially from other subjects'. I should say that when David Willetts, the universities minister, was challenged on this point in the Commons debate, he insisted that there was 'no bias against arts and humanities'. One wonders then why there is a bias in favour of science and the other protected subjects.

In his statement Sir Adam is confident that despite these far-reaching changes in funding, the humanities and social sciences will continue to flourish in our universities. (I am more pessimistic). But he does go on to emphasise major areas of concern: 'We need to ensure that vital expertise in certain vulnerable but important subject-areas is not unwittingly a casualty. There is a need for vigilance about threats to provision of particular subjects'. And 'certain valuable disciplines may starve'. Sir Adam's language is judiciously sober. But what he is saying is that if the teaching of the entire range of subjects in the arts and humanities is to be denied public funding, and therefore become wholly dependent on the choices of fee-paying students, then the survival of subjects with limited appeal-— however crucial they may be to sustaining our centuries-old civilised values and culture —-cannot be guaranteed. In other words the student protester and the President of the British Academy turn out to have quite a lot in common.

Exactly one week later the Scottish government has finally published its green paper on the future of higher education in Scotland. One thing at least we can be sure of – there will be no students rioting in the streets of Edinburgh. By highlighting its commitment to no tuition fees for Scottish students, the SNP administration has made sure of that. But what is positive about the green paper? Very little. This is at best a holding and at worst a dithering document. Its favoured policy of dramatic increases in the fees paid by non-Scottish students entrenches further a clearly discriminatory procedure. And as is the case with almost all the other tired old fund-raising options in the paper, it would almost certainly fail to produce anything like the sums of money required to fill the funding gap produced by the U.K. government's savage cuts in the universities' teaching budget. My own guess is that in the end all the Scottish political parties will find themselves adopting the 'some form of graduate contribution' option. But meantime at least the English universities know what the future holds. The Scottish universities still do not. Are the humanities and social sciences threatened in Scotland as they are in England? I strongly suspect they are. Our only option is to wait and see.

10 The Plight of the English Universities

On March 1st, David Willetts, Minister of State for Universities and Science, visited the British Academy and delivered a speech entitled 'The Arts, Humanities and Social Sciences in the Modern University'. Fully aware that the coalition government's policies on the universities have been widely seen as a threat to the arts and social sciences in particular, the minister had come to the institution which is, as it were, the public face of these academic disciplines, with the intention of rebutting such criticisms. Thus he began by insisting that he fully recognized the 'ongoing significance in our intellectual life' of the humanities and social sciences. In fact he was ready to endorse the summary of their importance that had been provided by the Academy's president, Sir Adam Roberts: 'The humanities explore what it means to be human: the words, ideas, narratives and the art and artefacts that help us make sense of our lives and the world we live in; how we have created it and are created by it. The social sciences seek to explore through observation and reflection the processes that govern the behaviour of individuals and groups. Together they help us to understand ourselves, our society and our place in the world'. And the minister goes on to underline the importance of these disciplines in his own words: 'Quite simply', he tells us, 'the humanities and social sciences are essential to a civilised country. They bring deep fulfilment to us personally. They often give meaning and shape to our lives'.

The rest of the minister's speech is intended to correct the 'misunderstandings' that have led to criticisms of the government's policies on the universities and specifically on the place within them of the arts and social sciences. But does he really engage with these criticisms? Unfortunately not. He argues at length that the change in funding method cannot be seen in any way as reflecting a bias against the arts and social sciences. He underlines the point that there will be no reduction in the support for research in these areas. He admits that he too at first had doubts about the relevance of 'impact' (the new buzz word in assessing the value of research proposals) – but is now persuaded by pilot schemes that 'impact' can and should be assessed. And in the final section of his speech – on the integrity of the university – he claims to offer challenges to the arguments of his critics such as Stefan Collini, the distinguished Cambridge intellectual historian.

Willetts's challenges, however, are decidedly weak. He chooses to defend the idea of students having 'a stronger consumer voice'. 'This sort of consumerism' he says will have no damaging impact. Some students he insists 'go to university as a route to a job'. (Collini does not deny this.) And finally he takes issue with his critic's views on the impact of the government's changes on the future of the universities. Willetts agrees that universities are 'very special places indeed'. Communities of a very special kind. Collini's deepest fear, he suggests, is that the university as an institution like this 'is at risk of unravelling'. The minister is right. Collini does fear such an unravelling. Why is he wrong? Mr Willetts does not tell us. His final comment is merely 'I am an optimist'.

But what really gives the Minister of State for the Universities' game away is his deployment here of the language of the business world: 'consumerism' and 'consumer voice'. With these terms we are back to the essence of the Browne report which provided the basis for the government's entire policy on the future of higher education. Mr Browne was formerly Chairman of BP. A businessman through and through. No surprise then that his report was permeated by the values and principles of the world he belongs to. Market forces, competition, consumer choice, value for money, future earning power, and all the other shibboleths of the world of business studies, form the basis for all the changes in the university sector which his report proposes – and which the coalition government has uncritically accepted. It is the enthusiasm with which the government has endorsed this transformation of the university into just another business which has dismayed and appalled so many of us. This is what at bottom Stefan Collini and many others have objected to – and this is the major challenge with which Mr Willetts simply refuses to engage.

To regard a university as just another commercial enterprise raises a whole range of questions. But I want to focus on just one dimension of the business model – because it is the one which I seriously believe in the long term will do permanent damage to our universities and what they stand for. It is the dimension that Mr Willetts specifically chooses to defend: giving students 'a stronger consumer voice'. In this brave new educational world, a university will only be able to teach those subjects and courses that students elect to pay for. The Browne report, endorsed by the government, is perfectly explicit about all of this. 'Our proposals put students at the heart of the system', says Browne. 'Our recommendations ... are based on giving students the ability to make an informed choice of where and what to study.' 'Students', Browne declares, 'are best placed to make the judgement about what they want to get from participating in higher education.' Really? As Stanley Fish, a leading American public intellectual, put it in an excoriating review of the report in the *New York Times*, 'the obvious objection to the last declaration is, "No, they aren't; judgement is what education is supposed to produce; if students possessed it at the get-go, there would be nothing for courses and programs to do". Exactly. Who would defend the idea that high school students should be the arbiters of what they are taught in their classes? Universities should be funded in such a way that they can go on teaching and researching the range of subject-matter that our culture and civilisation have over the centuries regarded as helping to define our selves and our world. To regard our universities as commercial enterprises, and our students as consumers, is to transform university education in a radically damaging way. If economic considerations rule OK, who, as Stanley Fish puts it, is going to invest in 'medieval allegory, modern poetry, or Greek history?'

Until now, the provision of higher education, and of university education in particular, has been regarded as a public good. The Browne report acknowledges 'the value of learning to students', and 'the significant contribution of higher education to the quality of life in a civilised society'. But for Browne the true 'value ' of learning turns out to be 'improved employability, and 'quality of life' really means 'a proven path to higher earnings'. A university education turns out to be about private benefits rather than anything to do with the public good. This is the philosophical principle that underlies the government's new funding mechanism for our universities. Carried through, it will do an immense amount of harm and very little good.

An addendum. How 'student/consumer' choice will work is already evident in the case of London Metropolitan University. Okay, I accept both that London Metropolitan is not an average university and that it has been facing particular problems of its own. But the fact remains that its vice-chancellor has just announced that it will close down almost 400 undergraduate courses: rather than its current 557 courses, in the future it will offer only 160 – needless to say the 160 enrolling most students. As far as I know, the Minister of State has not commented on this development. No doubt he remains optimistic about the future he has plotted for our universities. It is an optimism I and many others find very hard to share.

11 The Plight of the Scottish Universities

For the first time in my life I am tempted to vote Tory. Why? Because in the run-up to the May election, Annabel Goldie and her party are the only Scottish politicians facing up to the problem of funding the Scottish universities. As by now we all know, the coalition government in Westminster has cut the teaching budget in much of the university sector by between 70 and 80 percent. The consequent huge loss in income is to be compensated for (in England) by a tripling of tuition fees up to a maximum of £9000 per annum. (And to the government's chagrin, the majority of English universities appear to be ready to charge the full £9000 or something very close to it.)

But as we also all know, Scottish students at the Scottish universities pay no tuition fees. So where do the Scottish universities find the income stream necessary to keep them on a level financial footing with their English counterparts? Well in the days of the £3000 tuition fee paid by students in England, the difference was made up by the generosity of the Scottish parliament. Money was found from somewhere to keep the Scottish universities as well-resourced as the English ones.

All well and good then. But now is another matter. Many of us in the university sector find it hard to believe that the next Scottish government will be able to find the huge sum of money required to match the income stream in England arising from the £9000 tuition fee level. The Scottish Tory party, as I say, has recognized the problem, and proposes that Scottish students pay what in its manifesto it calls, in typically tortuous politics-speak, 'a graduate contribution facilitated through income-contingent loans'. But the Scottish Labour Party, the Scottish Liberal Democrats, and the SNP, all disagree. Scottish students will continue to pay nothing. So how do these parties propose filling the funding gap created by the Westminster cuts?

A scrutiny of the manifestos of all three parties suggests that basically they have no idea. The Labour Party insists there will be 'no up-front or back-end (sic) tuition fees for Scottish university students'. And it promises 'a root and branch review of Scottish higher education' involving 'improving governance and efficiency'. But that's it. The SNP offers us a vote-catching one-liner: 'Access to further and higher education should be based on ability to learn and not ability to pay'. But its manifesto tells us nothing about how this free education will be funded. The Liberal Democrat manifesto goes even further, promising not only to preserve free university education for Scottish students in Scotland, but also proposing the scrapping of fees paid by Scottish students enrolled in English universities. And this, we are told, will be achieved 'without cutting university income'.

In other words, all three parties are guilty of making promises, costing a vast amount of money, without providing even the slightest indication of where and how that money will be found. Once upon a time — i.e. a few months ago — Scottish Labour seemed to be moving towards accepting some form of graduate tax. Not any longer. Clearly the party was unnerved by the SNP's promise to maintain free university education for Scottish students by coming up with what it bizarrely called a Scottish solution to a Scottish problem. Effectively what that boils down to is a huge increase in the fees paid by students from England, Ireland, and Wales studying at a Scottish university.

The truth is that all these politicians are gambling with the future of our universities in the hope of winning a few votes. All of them talk endlessly about how wonderful our universities are, and how their world-wide reputation has to be maintained. That reputation is already threatened. A glance at any of the many league-tables about the international standing of universities makes this clear. The Scottish universities are not exactly prominent. Edinburgh usually makes it in the 25th to 50th area. But that's about it. If the parties likely to form the next Scottish government stick to their current (under)funding principles for our universities, then I greatly fear they will inevitably slide further and further behind in terms of their reputation across the world.

12 "Appointment of Vice-Chancellor"

Universities are currently much in the news. Fees? Capped or uncapped or none at all? A graduate tax? Low interest loans? High interest loans? Access for the under-privileged? 20% cuts in income? 40%? A two-tier system? One could go on and on. Universities facing such turmoil and uncertainty, one would have assumed, would be determined to impress the public with their intellectual rigour, their commitment to the maintenance of the highest standards of academic excellence. Would that it were so.

Have you heard of the University of Chichester? Neither had I. In our defence I'd suggest that in recent years so many institutions have become universities that it has become almost impossible to keep up: Bournemouth, Chester, Derby, Lincoln, Worcester, Cumbria, Bedfordshire, Gloucestershire, Northampton – the list continues to grow. But of course I would agree that it would be the worst kind of intellectual arrogance to imply that my ignorance of Chichester, or indeed of any of these new institutions, has anything whatsoever to do with their value as sites of higher education. Any one of them could be a Cambridge or Harvard in the making. Not, however, it seems Chichester.

I say that because of the advertisement recently appearing in the educational press inviting applications for the post of Vice-Chancellor at the University of Chichester. The accompanying job description is written in such an appalling form of market-directed officialese as to be beyond belief. Orwell once again would be spinning in his grave.

After an opening, self-congratulatory sentence about how the university provides an 'excellent student learning experience', the advert runs as follows:

> Benefitting [*sic*] from a scale that allows for the building of a truly collegial environment, [*I think this means the university is small*] and with very real opportunities afforded to it as a distinctive and differentiated University [*what in the world is a 'differentiated university'?*] at a time of rapid change in the liberalising external environment, [*what can this possibly mean?*] the University remains ambitious and highly determined. [*To do what exactly is not revealed.*]

The following paragraph describes the university's location near the South Downs National Park and its closeness to the towns of

Chichester and Bognor Regis, and goes on to insist on its 'prudent financial approach', 'whilst also exploring innovative models of organisational efficiency and shared service delivery'. (*One wonders about what services are being shared and indeed with whom?*)

The advert's final paragraph goes on:

> "The Board of Governors is now seeking to appoint a Vice-Chancellor who will develop the vision to promote and build on the University's strong foundations and ethos, [*is it possible to build on an ethos?*] powerfully invigorate its brand proposition, [*I'm not making this up!*] elevate its research profile and foster the collective strengths of the staff. [*Perhaps the 'staff' are a tug of war team?*]

And then the final sentence:

> The successful applicant will lead the University through the challenges ahead and engage dynamically and creatively with the local community and its regional and national partners.

After what has gone before, the grammatical ambiguity of that final phrase comes as no surprise. But once one has worked out that it is the university, not the local community, that has regional and national partners, what exactly this dynamic and creative engagement is all about remains totally obscure.

I suspect that this advertisement has been 'outsourced' to some kind of educational recruitment agency. But even if that is so, the university has no excuse for allowing it to appear. The first job of the new V-C should be to rewrite his or her job description in the simple, accurate, and lucid English which anyone working in a university should surely have the ability to deliver.

13 Campus Problems

Two recent reports will be giving university vice-chancellors and principals cause for concern. The first appeared in the *Guardian* newspaper and focused on the issue of sexual misconduct on campuses. This is hardly a new problem but the *Guardian* enquiry revealed that the number of women students today who are prepared to report that they have felt victimised in sexual terms by lecturers and tutors is worryingly high. The report suggested that the issue had reached 'epidemic levels in the U.K'. Within hours of its appearance in the paper sixty more women made contact alleging they had suffered sexual harassment. Responding to a freedom of information question, 120 universities revealed that between sessions 2011-12 and 2016-17, they had had to deal with 169 allegations of sexual misconduct by academics and non-academics. However, most observers agree that this figure greatly under-represents the true scale of the problem as it takes great strength of will for a student to make a formal complaint. Finally, the problem is hugely exacerbated by the fact that not all universities seem to have any established system for dealing with, or helping students who find themselves in this position.

I began my teaching career in the 1960s. Relationships between members of staff and students were certainly always possible, but they did not appear to happen that often and there was never any suggestion of compulsion. To my knowledge, no student ever made a complaint. One certainly knew of faculty members — often quite senior ones — who had married students, but there was never the slightest suggestion that this was anything improper about such an outcome. Of course it's always possible I was simply too naïve, unaware of what was going on — and there could well have been cases in which students did indeed feel an element of compulsion — but I can only report on what seemed to me to be the case.

In subsequent decades however, things did begin to change. Student numbers expanded greatly and more importantly changes in society at large — in particular the emergence of the women's movement — meant that sexual issues began to be more widely and openly discussed. I don't remember exactly when but somewhere around the 1980s I, like many of my colleagues, began to leave my office door open when I was meeting with individual students. Nothing was ever said explicitly. It was not a formal policy. It just seemed a sensible thing to do in a changing climate. A 'just in case' scenario. In the years that followed – when I became department head — no student came to me complaining of having suffered any form of improper sexual conduct by a member of staff. Again, I'm perfectly aware that this does not mean that such conduct never happened — the difficulties facing a student making such a complaint are crystal clear. But I can only report what actually happened — or did not happen.

The situation today is very different. Sexual abuse in a range of forms has become an all too familiar topic. Reticence about it is no longer the norm. That it should be occurring on university campuses comes as no surprise. But that it should be on the scale suggested by the *Guardian* investigation means that authorities need to take action of some kind. What kind of action? I really don't know. Clearly there is no easy solution. What I would say, however, is that it is now impossible for universities not to have in place systems or arrangements which make it possible for individual students to find help, comfort, and support over this kind of problem. Concern for a university's reputation should never mean that sexual misconduct is covered up rather than effectively dealt with.

The second issue I wish to discuss is also one that is difficult to resolve. It has arisen as a consequence of developments in computing and IT. Early in my career, a student's degree result depended almost exclusively on their performance in degree examinations. However, the view that this reliance on performance on three-hour examination papers did not always deliver a just outcome for all students, gradually brought about change. Performance in essays submitted as course work began to be recognised as part of the final assessment. Such essays were of course written by students in their own time, and so they were able to make use of existing scholarship in compiling them. The danger of plagiarism — the passing off of another's work as one's own — was always there, but tutors knew their students well enough to feel they could usually detect it.

In recent years, however, there have been major changes in the way students submit their work. They no longer sit down and write their essay. Rather they are typed on their laptop or computer. They can then be printed out and handed to a tutor for correction and return. However, I believe this is not always the procedure. Work can simply pass between computers without having any paper existence. Equally students now access existing scholarship not by going to the library shelves, but by going online. And it is what is available online that is causing a new and worrying problem.

With a click on their keyboard students can access a wide range of so-called 'essay mills'. Typical examples are U.K. Essays, based in Nottingham, OK Essay in Sheffield, and Oxbridge Essays based in London. However, the government agrees there are at least 100 such 'mills' in operation, while some investigators suggest there could be as many as 1000. All of them offer the same kind of service: 'model' essays on any subject in any area and at any academic status –from GCSE or 'A' levels to PhD Even the required mark can be designated – say an essay worth a 2.1 grade in an Honours course. What is required of the student? Payment of course: anything between £106 for a piece of 'B' grade GCSE course work to £82,238 for a PhD thesis. How many students are willing to pay up? Well U.K. Essays says it had 16,000 customers last year and used 3500 researchers to produce the goods.

Who are these students? No doubt there is a scattering from across the whole range of university students from those coping with their first year of study to struggling postgraduates. But it may well be the case that the majority are overseas students whose first language is not English. It is argued that they are likely to be studying in, say, engineering or the hard sciences. They are paying extremely high fees in our universities, so the pressure to succeed is intense. Asked for written work of any kind, employing the essay mills 'models' may well be understandably tempting.

But whatever the truth is concerning the categories of student willing to pay for this kind of assistance, our universities are clearly facing a major problem. Old-fashioned plagiarism is not the issue. In fact the majority of U.K. universities already employ a software system called 'Turnitin' which detects that kind of cheating. But the essay mill writers do not plagiarise – what they write is indeed their own work. The issue is what happens to it when a student buys it. Potentially the problem is on a scale far beyond anything that traditional plagiarism represented.

So what can be done? Jo Johnson, the current universities minister, recognises there is a problem. He accepts that what he calls 'contract plagiarism' is a threat to academic integrity. Apparently new guidelines on how to respond to this campus problem will be published before the beginning of the next academic year. It will be fascinating to see just how rigorous the new form of guidance will be.

14 Glasgow University Union

Founded in 1885, Glasgow University Union has long boasted an outstanding reputation as a centre of debating excellence. Many World University Debating Championships and *Observer* Maces have been won. Men who went on to become major political leaders earned their spurs and the tricks of their trade in Glasgow debating: John Smith, Donald Dewar, Menzies Campbell, Charles Kennedy — the roll call is an impressive one.

In recent weeks, however, the union's proud tradition has come under fire. Eight debaters from British universities (twenty-seven had originally participated) had reached the final of the union's Ancients debate. Among the eight were two women debaters — one from King's College, Cambridge, the other from the University of Edinburgh. Both were highly experienced and highly successful exponents of the art of debating. But after the event, both complained they had been subjected to a totally unacceptable level of blatantly sexist heckling and booing which they insisted had nothing whatever to do with the normal level of robust and hard-hitting exchanges in parliamentary debating. Their complaints soon reached the national press – including the *Daily Telegraph* and the *Daily Mail*– and inevitably the rights and wrongs of the women's case soon became a major issue both on and beyond the university campus.

In this context it's worth remembering the somewhat controversial history of Glasgow University's student unions. The 1885 Union was of course an all male affair. However, women students at the old Queen Margaret College established their own union in 1890, and in the early 1900s the Queen Margaret Union moved on to the university campus. For not far short of a century, that is, male and female students at Glasgow University attended — if they chose — segregated student unions. It was only late in the twentieth century that this disunion in student life began to come under pressure in a changing world. Not that either union was keen to abandon their segregated ways. The men's union in particular was deeply reluctant to give up its status and culture as a men's club — with all that that implied in terms of drinking and sexual attitudes and behaviour. But in the end the tide of history could not be resisted. The Queen Margaret Union opened its doors to male students in 1979; the Men's Union allowed women to join in 1980.

I think most observers would agree that the male membership of the two unions has remained quite distinct. Men who join QMU tend to be less conformist, more arty, probably leftist in their politics, whereas the majority who join the Men's Union are likely to be more sporty, more macho, outdoor guys. The latter sort – admittedly perhaps in extreme form — were clearly in evidence in the objectionable behaviour at the Ancients debate.

I want to be fair here. All accounts of the evening in question insist that only a small minority of the audience indulged in the sexist heckling. The two women debaters have been widely supported on the campus. Principal Muscatelli has written to them, apologising on behalf of the university and offering to meet them personally. He has also emailed the student body expressing his concern over what occurred and the damage it could do the university's reputation. A student protest march denouncing on-campus sexism and misogyny in any form was well attended. Condemnation has come in a joint statement from a range of student societies. Even the Union's own management has promised to take action against unacceptable behaviour at debates Support for the hecklers has been distinctly muted.

However support has come from a perhaps not wholly unsurprising source: the right-wing journalist Gerald Warner, himself a former Men's Union member. Writing in the *Spectator* magazine, Warner saw the whole affair as no more than an example of silly political correctness. The Glasgow debating tradition is a fine and admirably robust one; if women cannot take the heat they should stay out of the kitchen. Objections and complaints simply prove that 'the health-and-safety, equality-and-diversity, cellophane-coated culture' is 'spreading its Stalinist tentacles everywhere' making genuine debate 'unacceptable'.

I believe that Warner is quite simply wrong. Despite the existence of entrenched conservatives, the world does change. What may have been acceptable in debating in 1980 is not acceptable now. Sectarian and politically biased singing at Scottish football matches is unacceptable in a post-peace-process world. Augusta (and St Andrews) golf clubs cannot go on rejecting women. Gay men and women have the same rights as those who are straight — including, say, the right to debate in the Glasgow University Union without being heckled over their sexuality.

15 English Studies Today

A generation ago the central issue in English Studies was crystal clear. 'Theory' had emerged as the one topic confronting — and dividing — English Departments everywhere. Based on the work of a group of European scholars — Jacques Derrida, Robert Barthes, Paul de Man, Theodor Adorno, Walter Benjamin, and Michel Foucault, are among those most regularly cited – 'theory' seemed to offer literary studies a new and demanding intellectual rigour which would replace the mere opinionated subjectivity of past approaches. Theory became intensely controversial. In the 1970s and 80s and into the 90s, its exponents and opponents struggled to take or maintain control over how English was studied. More recently, however, that culture war has lost much of its intensity. Scholars and critics now can pick and chose whatever aspects of 'theory' they happen to prefer.

So if the theory war is over, what has taken its place? To my mind the answer is clear — even if no one could have predicted it in the post-theory world. The most striking aspect of the teaching and study of what we used to call 'English' is the rise and rise of 'Creative Writing'. Having joined the Glasgow University English Literature Department in 1979, I was surprised to learn that Honours students in their final year could chose to replace one of their nine final honours exam papers with a piece of creative writing of their own. In fact this option was very rarely taken up, but in my previous universities – Edinburgh and Aberdeen — no such option even existed.

I don't know when Glasgow instituted its creative writing option, but a decade before my arrival in Glasgow, the University of East Anglia had become the first British university to teach a course, and offer a postgraduate MA degree, in creative writing. Established by Angus Wilson and Malcolm Bradbury, both members of the university's department of English Studies, the East Anglia course soon gained a good reputation. The conventional position in British universities, however, remained — that literary study and literary creation were two entirely distinct activities. University English departments focused on the former, and had nothing to do with the latter. No doubt there were people who were aware that in the United States some English Departments had begun to teach creative writing: the hugely successful Iowa Writers' Workshop had been set up as long ago as 1936, and its participants and graduates made up an impressive list of major American poets, novelists, and dramatists. But even with the emergence of the East Anglia programme in 1970, in succeeding decades there was little sign that the conventional absence of such courses in the English departments of British universities was about to change.

The contrast with the present position could not be sharper. Today creative writing courses rule. So much so that in some institutions 'creative writing' has moved out of English departments altogether and gained wholly independent existence as a subject in its own right. For a time there was a debate over whether creative writing should be available (as at East Anglia) only as a postgraduate qualification, or whether undergraduates should be able to study it as part of their first degree. Next came an argument over whether it should be possible to obtain, not just an MA, but the ultimate accolade of a PhD in creative writing. Today, both in this country and the US, in almost all colleges and universities, creative writing courses are available for most students at every conceivable level.

To meet the demand for such courses, there has been a parallel, huge increase in the number of teaching posts in the area. In a recent year, the American Modern Languages Association reported that there were more appointments across America in creative writing than even in twentieth-century English literature. In fact creative writing has become the new main source of what used to be called 'patronage' for today's writers. Publish a novel, a book of short stories, a play or two, and the chances are that a part-time or full-time post teaching creative writing will guarantee you an income and a continuing role as an author. Outside academia, publishers, literary agents, and newspapers are offering writing courses of their own.

Why has creative writing boomed in this way? Student demand is the answer at the academic level. The funding of the humanities in our university system is now wholly determined by student choice. Once it was clear that creative writing was a popular option, it was inevitable that courses would be provided. Of course there is still a question over exactly why creative writing has proved so popular with contemporary students. Some have suggested that the dominance of 'theory' in the teaching of English departments is partly responsible: 'theory' had become a self-enclosed world, its texts more important than literary texts. At least in creative writing courses students study in detail actual stories by Hemingway or Fitzgerald or whoever. But there has to be a more comprehensive reason for the boom in creative writing. Has it to do with contemporary society's focus on the individual – on his or her right to self-expression? Is writing a possible route to celebrity status? Even if success cannot be guaranteed in career terms, creative writing seems to help to define and empower the individual.

What has triggered these speculations is two collections of contemporary Scottish writing: *Be the First to Like This: New Scottish Poetry* edited by Colin Waters, and *New Writing Scotland 32* edited by Gerry Cambridge and Zoe Strachan. The work of 38 poets appears in the first volume, 26 in the second. Clearly this is a good time to be a poet. The number of small publishers apparently willing to publish volumes of poetry is quite extraordinary. Never have there been more poetry competitions, prizes, and awards. Spoken-word events involving poetry in performance, music and film have become part of the contemporary cultural scene. (The editor of *Be the First* is an enthusiast for this development.) Those who take part in creative writing courses have good reason for hoping that success can actually lead to becoming a published writer.

Here is the evidence. Of the 38 poets in *Be the First to Like This*, as many as 14 are creative writing course graduates, while another eight have degrees in English or Scottish literature. They are 'new' in the sense that none have published more than two collections of poetry, and the great majority are under forty years old. In the Association of Scottish Literature volume, the proportion of creative writing graduates is not so high, but then they are not all 'new' and quite a number of contributors are teachers of creative writing. So are today's professionally-trained young writers any different to young writers in the past? It is a difficult question to answer. Is there emerging any kind of conventional orthodoxy about how to write a poem or story? (*New Writing Scotland 32*, like the previous volumes in the series, includes prose as well as poetry, and as before I remain unconvinced that the constant switching between genres does justice to either.) I suppose not, but perhaps certain trends or emphases are recognizable. Most of these young poets do indeed seem committed to the view that the essence of poetry is self-expression. Engagement with the world beyond the self is much less common. So what do they write about? In a poem called 'Bad moon', Claire Askew, one of only two writers who make it into both collections, comes to the not untypical conclusion that 'Nobody wants to read poems about this' – that is, about the unconventional 'bad' things the moon also shines down upon.

Roots and Fruits of Scottish Culture is a collection of papers on contemporary Scottish literature delivered at a conference in

France, attended mainly by European scholars, edited by Ian Brown and Jean Berton. At the conclusion of his summary introduction, Ian Brown writes:

> 'Contemporary Scottish literature continues to insist on the complexity of histories, myths, fictions and identities, and that these all include ambivalence rather than certainty, dark as well as light, and potential for corruption as well as genuine enlightenment.'

It strikes me that most of the young writers in these two anthologies have been encouraged to think and write along similar lines — with their emphasis tending to fall on the 'ambivalence', 'dark', and 'corruption'. The result for the ordinary reader may be a longing for a little more in the way of simple light — and the pleasure it can provide. In all, 82 writers are represented in *Songs of Other Places* and *Be the First to Like This*. Given such a huge number, and the brevity of individual contributions, I find myself unable to pick out any future Joyce or Yeats or Eliot. In conclusion, however, let me draw attention to what strikes me as the most fascinating, and perhaps the most important, piece that appears here. As it happens, it is not the work of a new or young Scottish writer. Christopher Whyte has a well-established reputation as a poet and translator working in both English and Gaelic. In *Songs of Other Places*, 'A Face That Won't Be Etched Along The Crest Of The Cuillin' is a poem in Gaelic, translated this time by Niall O'Gallagher, exploring in moving detail, Whyte's complex relationship with the most famous of modern Gaelic poets — Sorley MacLean. It is easily the longest poem in the volume, but the editors must have felt privileged to print it. The following passage comes in the poem's section 5:

> he reflects that no human authority
> at all can bestow the gift of new speech,
> the gift of a golden tongue and skilled words,
> that it's a fish, inhabiting the darkest
> waters, hiding the golden gleam of its scales
> until they are ready for the light.

No creative writing course can teach that golden gleam.

16 A Future for the Universities?

What is happening to our universities? I ask the question because it's one to which the media are paying surprisingly little attention. A recent *Newsnight Scotland* did turn to the issue, bringing together Alistair Sim, director of Universities Scotland, Iain Macwhirter, rector of Edinburgh University, and Murdo Fraser, deputy leader of the Scottish Conservative Party. This of course is the same Alistair Sim who last year assured us that the Scottish universities were in no kind of trouble and in fact were exceptionally well-placed to deal with any problems that might arise. Such blandness was not in evidence this time. His view was that in the situation created by the coalition government's financial cuts, the Scottish universities would have to require students to contribute to the cost of their education. Iain Macwhirter somewhat surprisingly argued that the Scottish tradition of free university education funded by the state should be maintained. (Had he forgotten that in an older Scottish tradition professors' salaries derived from the fees students paid to attend their classes?) Murdo Fraser of course supported the coalition government's view that students should be required to pay for the education that would bring them higher salaries in the future.

In England the argument is not over whether university students should or should not pay fees. They already do. The issue is over how high these fees should be. As we all know, the situation here is different. Scottish students pay no fees (like students from the European Union) whereas English students studying at a Scottish university pay around £1800 per annum. I am among those who were unhappy about this arrangement from the start. It has a hint of a dubious form of nationalism about it – the kind that led sometimes in the past to the argument that posts in the Scottish universities should not be filled by non-Scots. In any event, the change went through because the Scottish universities were assured by the Scottish government that funds would be made available to the SHEFC (Scottish Higher Education Funding Council) to offset the new stream of funding from tuition fees available to their English counterparts. The obvious question that now arises is the one which, as I've said, is at last beginning to receive some media attention. Given the current situation in which the Scottish government – and inevitably SHEFC – is going to have substantially less money to spend, how can the status quo possibly be maintained? English universities are going to have an income stream of up to £9000 per student. If the playing field in terms of scholarly status and international recognition is to remain a level one, the Scottish universities need to be provided with an equivalent source of funding. It is beyond belief that a Scottish government alone, whatever its make-up, will be in a financial situation to provide that level of funding.

So what is being proposed? Very little, so far at least. With next May's elections to the Edinburgh parliament very much in mind, the Scottish political parties are reluctant to commit themselves to policies that could be unpopular. The current Scottish Education minister, Mike Russell, is on record dismissing the idea that his government might introduce tuition fees. More recently on Any Questions, Roseanna Cunningham insisted her government was involved in ongoing discussions about other ways to fill the funding gap. (This is now the Scottish National Party's line: a spokesman says the party is leading a debate 'on finding a uniquely Scottish solution that fits our university sector'.) But pressed by David Dimbleby she refused to come up with a single example of what these other ways might be. The Labour Party is happy to denounce the coalition's tuition fees policy in terms of its negative impact on the access to university education of students from deprived backgrounds – but seems broadly to favour the introduction of some form of graduate tax. I'm not sure that the Scottish Labour Party has endorsed this position. With the May election looming, it may prefer to equivocate. The Scottish Liberal Democrats are in an even worse position. Do they go along with their colleagues in the coalition and break their promise of no tuition fees, or do they endorse their manifesto's graduate tax which Vince Cable now says is unworkable?

The real question is whether our universities can wait until after next May to learn how in the future they will be funded. I don't think so. Planning needs to start now. But alongside the question of funding, there is another issue of perhaps even greater significance concerning the future of our universities. And this is the issue that no one seems to be prepared to talk about. The Current Spending Review announced a 40% reduction in the Treasury funding of the British universities. When I heard David Willetts, the universities minister, talking about the implementation of this cut I was so amazed I decided I had misheard. I hadn't. The 40% is not to be spread evenly across the university sector. Teaching and research in science, technology, and perhaps some modern languages, will continue to receive Treasury funding. All other areas of study will not. So how will the arts, humanities, and social sciences continue to be funded? By the rise in tuition fees. So the survival at university level of a vast range of existing subjects of study and research will eventually be dependent on student choice. Popular subjects will flourish. Less popular ones? You tell me. Perhaps in the not too distant future the education which the great majority of British universities will provide will focus exclusively on jobs, salaries, and the national economy. The wider world of traditional scholarship and learning will become the preserve of a handful of older (and wealthier) institutions. If so, will any of them be in Scotland? But perhaps I'm wrong. Perhaps I've misunderstood. I hope I have. In that case it would be good if someone who really knows (Mr Sim?) would tell us what they expect the future of our universities to be.

17 More Universities?

Between 1987 and 1992 I had a role in CNNA (The Council for National Academic Awards) chairing that organisation's Committee for the Humanities. CNAA had been set up in1965 to supervise and validate the courses and degrees awarded by polytechnics and other non-university institutions such as colleges of higher education. Universities on the other hand, having been chartered to award their own degrees, were subject to no such external body. Only the system of external examining between universities guaranteed compatibility between the degrees awarded by different institutions. However, in the 1990s this distinction between the university and non-university sectors came under increasing pressure. The larger polytechnics in particular began to object more and more loudly to their being under the thumb of the professional staff and university professors who largely composed CNAA. In the end the government's ministry of education caved in, and in 1993 CNAA was abolished.

Major questions resulting from this abolition, however, remained unanswered. If universities and polys both had the right to award higher education degrees, what was the difference between them? No government was prepared to grasp this particular nettle. In the post-CNAA world, for an educational institution to become a university has had much more to do with organisational matters such as eligibility for HEFCE (Higher Education Funding Council England) support, and student numbers, than any consideration of the quality and range of courses being taught. What this means is that in recent years it has been pretty easy to acquire university status. As we all know, for many centuries England managed to flourish educationally with only two universities. In roughly the same period Scotland boasted five (King's College and Marischal College did not unite as the University of Aberdeen until 1860.) A few more universities were founded in the nineteenth century, and in the early post-Second World War period a group of so-called new universities were added: Keele, Sussex, East Anglia, Warwick, Lancaster, York, Essex, Kent, Stirling all emerged at this time. The scale of this expansion of the university sector was to prove as nothing compared with the explosion that followed in the post-CNAA period.

What is the position today? Across the U.K. there are now around 135 universities. Increasingly one senses that every medium-sized town feels it should contain a university. Universities with an initial 'B' include Bath, Bedfordshire, Birmingham, Brighton and Buckingham. Initial 'W' includes Warwick, West London, West of England, Westminster, Winchester, Wolverhampton, and Worcester.

How far there is any longer compatibility between the degrees offered by such a number of institutions is very much an open question. What is not is the fundamental change in the nature of our universities that has come into being in the post-CNAA period. Universities are now increasingly seen as commercial organisations – and most university administrations have happily colluded with the change. Students today are 'customers' and are to be treated as such. Value for money is what really counts. Scholarly teaching and research designed to encourage rational analysis and critical thinking in young minds are seen as relatively minor concerns.

Still more troubling for the university sector today is the boost to this commercialising direction of travel about to be imposed by the current U.K. government. The House of Commons has just passed a Higher Education and Research Bill that is being challenged by a number of amendments in the House of Lords. The Bill is dangerously misguided. It calls – can you believe it? – for the setting up of yet more universities. Why? Because that will increase competition for the enrolment of students and, as we all know, 'competition' can only be a good thing. Promoted by the Department for Business Innovation and Skills, the Bill's summary factsheet is headed by the following statement: 'The Higher Education and Research Bill will support the Government's mission to boost social mobility, life chances and opportunity for all, and enhance the competitiveness and productivity of our economy'. So an education bill is more concerned with social and economic change than with education itself.

The tone of the bill that follows is frequently one of self-congratulation. Here is an example of the kind of language it deploys and the future it envisages: 'new universities will drive more diversity and innovation, more choice for students, competitive pressure to drive up standards, and will mean that all students with the potential can access a high quality university place'. (High quality grammar perhaps deserves more attention.)

We learn that lightly regulated new universities, easy to set up and run, will challenge more traditional institutions. For example, new universities will be encouraged to offer degrees that can be completed in two years. Given that England is one of the few countries that allow undergraduates to complete an honours degree in only three years, this fast track proposal seems dangerously short-sighted and could damage the status worldwide of British higher education.

More troubling still is the Bill's implications in relation to the integrity and autonomy of all our universities. DAPs (degree awarding powers) and the University Title will be removed from the Privy Council and transferred to a new body called the OfS (Office for Students). Crucially membership of this body will ultimately be determined by ministers. We are assured the new body 'will operate at arms length from Ministers', but there is no guarantee that this will always be the case. Thus the principle of academic freedom is potentially at risk. The new OfS will also have responsibility over the funding and hence direction of academic research — so here too academic freedom will become an issue. 'The reforms', we are told, 'will also encourage providers to improve validation arrangements'. There will be 'rigorous tests for providers who want to enter the system and enable their students to receive funding; poor quality or financially unsustainable providers will not be allowed to enter'. Thus the OfS (Office for Students), according to a Department of Education spokesman, will have the effect of 'making universities rightly more accountable to their students so they get the best value for money'.

I suspect that the reference to money here gives the game away. The so-called 'new high-quality providers', who will find it easier 'to start up and achieve degree-awarding powers, and subsequently secure university status' will be driven above all by the profit motive. The question is do we really want to establish Trump universities in the U.K.? This is a bad bill. One can only hope that the government will pay attention to the amendments supported by the House of Lords, and thus make the best of a very bad job.

18 Fast Food Degrees

In our coalition's government mad stampede to force through a complete restructuring of higher education in the U.K, one proposal stands out as revealing the true awfulness of what is being demanded. Frequently endorsed by government ministers – and supported by the heads of 'private' colleges and universities (a sector that the government is determined to expand) this is the suggestion that all our higher education institutions should be considering the introduction of two-year degrees.

No other proposal reveals so nakedly what the imposition of a 'market forces' ideology on higher education really means. Seen as no more than corporate businesses, colleges and universities are being asked to implement the methodologies and procedures which apparently lead to profitable, economic success in the commercial world. Production lines have been hugely successful in upping outputs in factories, so why not adopt a production line approach to the delivery of higher education?

Let me try to be fair. For a small number of mature students, interested in improving their existing qualifications or acquiring a purely professional degree, there may just be a case for the occasional two-year programme. But for the vast majority of ordinary students, the idea of a two-year degree is dangerous nonsense. Students entering a university at the age of 17 and graduating at 19, their education completed? It's patently absurd. A university is not an 'A' level crammer's office block. Students do not come to university to be force-fed education like hapless geese. A university education happens as much outside the lecture room or laboratory as inside it. A university education is about having time to learn, to read, to think, about having the chance to engage with the world of knowledge and culture. A university education is about meeting new people, about encountering new ideas, new opinions, new ways of seeing the world. In the end it is about growing up. A fast-track, non-stop, two-year degree is incompatible with what a university is about.

One wonders how ministers and civil servants — most of them we can be sure having benefited from a (free) Oxbridge education — can even entertain the idea of such an educational travesty. What they need to remember in their Whitehall bubble is that the English three-year undergraduate degree, in the context of the world outside, is itself something of an anomaly. The much-touted, paradigmatic Ivy League degree in America is of course, like the Scottish universities Honours degree, of four-year duration. European university degrees are as long or even longer. Rather than piling pressure on school pupils with the creation of starred 'As' at 'A' level, the English system might well consider lengthening, not shortening, the standard undergraduate degree.

I cannot see the Scottish universities ever introducing two-year degrees. But is the future of our successful four-year Honours degree as secure as it ought to be? Our SNP government's insistence that the only way to maintain free university education for Scottish students is to make students from elsewhere in the U.K. pay up to £9000 a year is creating a major problem for our universities. What it means is that those institutions which recruit substantial numbers of non-Scottish, U.K. students – and in resource terms need to go on doing so – find themselves (given the four-year degree structure) becoming the most expensive places to study in the U.K. What can be done? The Principal of Aberdeen University has already announced that in his institution these non-Scottish students will be asked to pay the £9000 in their first three years – but the fourth year will be free. Will St Andrews, Edinburgh, and Glasgow follow suit? Or are their alternative solutions? Don't be surprised if the notion of a three-year Honours degree for 'A' level-qualified students in the Scottish universities is floated in the near future.

That would be a pity. The Scottish government needs to go back and think again about how our universities are to be funded.

19 What is happening to our universities?

At a time when our country's greatest achievements seem to belong exclusively to the past, in one significant area of our culture we apparently still stand out: our universities. Education ministers and their spokesmen never lose an opportunity to insist that British universities are the best in the world. In what follows I shall ask how true this claim is, and go on to argue more seriously that current practices and policies will inevitably lead to a decline in the status of our university system. I shall question in turn the growing number of our universities, the model on the basis of which they are now increasingly structured and run, the problem of grade inflation, and finally the implications of the introduction of two-year degrees.

So how good are our universities? The most frequently cited league-table of universities world-wide provides the following answers. We have four in the world's top 10 — Oxford (5th), Cambridge (6th), Imperial College London (8th) and University College London (10th) — and 18 in the top 100 including Edinburgh (18th), Glasgow (69th) and St Andrews (97th). Quite impressive if hardly earth-shattering. But the question I am asking concerns the future. Are the policies we are currently pursuing the right ones to maintain — never mind enhance — our positive reputation at the university level in higher education? The answer may well be no.

For centuries in the past England got by with two universities. In the same period Scotland had four. Today we have at least 154 and, as we shall see, are promised many more. In the past the system of external examining, in which faculty from one university were involved in the degree examinations of another, made it possible to argue that, say, a First class degree from Aberdeen was of equal status to one from Exeter. Few would argue that across the board the same is true today. In fact, with the emergence in 1994 of the so-called Russell group of 24 leading universities in teaching and research, the difference in quality and standing of institutions in the university sector was made quite clear. No doubt Russell group institutions will continue to do well in world standings, but it is all too likely that the recent explosion in the number of universities will in the end lead to a watering down of the prestige of U.K. university degrees in general.

A related issue is the currently much debated one of so-called grade inflation. The concern here is over the classification of final degree examination results. When I began my own teaching career in the early 1960s, students on the basis of their results were awarded a First, Second or Third class degree. However, there was a growing feeling that this arrangement was less than fair to those students who had done very well, narrowing missing a First. The answer was to divide the Second class into two categories: 2/1 and 2/2. In due course this change was made — with the assumption that the 2/2 would remain the standard mainstream award with the 2/1 being given to a relatively small body of candidates who had performed well above average. This has proved not to be the case. Grade inflation has meant that more and more students are awarded 2/1 degrees. And that in turn has led to the 2/2 result being regarded as a disappointingly poor one. Simultaneously there has been a huge increase in the number of students being awarded First class degrees. In 2016-17 in the U.K. as a whole 26% of students received a First. At the university of Wolverhampton Firsts were awarded to 28% of candidates, at the university of Surrey the figure was 41%. In that year, across all British universities, 70% of students received either a First or a 2/1. Does this really matter? I suspect that in the long term it will undermine the level of importance given to the class of degree with which individual students graduate. Perhaps in the end classification will be abandoned.

The problems created by grade inflation, and the growing number of universities, are minor compared with the issue to which I now turn. What I have in mind is the transformation of universities as centres of higher education into versions of big businesses. It is extraordinary just how completely a neo-liberal, free-market philosophy has taken over how our universities are structured, governed and run. The business world's values in terms of how money is raised and expended now dominate. Competition is seen as the crucial driving force behind university development. We've become accustomed to hearing students described as customers. And it is true that, apart from Scottish students at Scottish universities, students across the U.K. pay a high price (around £9000 a year) for the education they receive — and are encouraged to demand value for their money.

Only one aspect of this change to the university as just another free market enterprise has hit the nations' headlines: the salaries now being paid to vice-chancellors or principals. Readers will remember the outcry when it emerged a few months ago that the head of the university of Bath was being paid well over £400,000 a year. In fact six figure sums for the holders of such positions have become normal. Why? Because CEOs in the business world have long earned such salaries. But the impact of the change is being felt by all those working in the university sector, including both academics and administrators.

When I began my own career in the 1960s, securing an initial appointment was the major challenge. Even for holders of doctorates, the competition to gain an appointment was intense. But that hurdle crossed, one's career path was straightforward. Lecture and teach responsibly, research and write and begin to publish, and there was every reason to expect to build a secure career. That is no longer the case. With so many more universities there are inevitably more jobs. But it is increasingly common for appointments to be on short term contracts. Fluctuating student numbers can determine the size of departments. An initial appointment no longer guarantees a permanent job. Even more striking is that in the current climate a successful career is no longer built on significant research and publication. Now it seems that all faculty members are expected to be engaged in bringing money into their university. What this means is that it is no longer the quality of one's research that matters, but whether it gains large awards from the national or international research-grant awarding bodies. If projects involve sharing grants with other major universities so much the better. Money is what counts.

In relation to university administration, the business model has led to a substantial increase in the number of jobs in that area. Let me cite recent figures for Glasgow University which indicate that less than half of those employed by the university are engaged in teaching or research. Out of a 7219 total of employees only 3060 are teachers or researchers — 42%. 2347 — or 37% — are made up of management, professional and administrative staff. The rest are in non-academic areas. These figures may well sound quite surprising, but I suspect that what is true of Glasgow is almost certainly true of the university sector in general. What do so many administrators do? I don't know what the answer is, but some at least seem to spend their time trying to raise money — by increasing student numbers. Given that the income of most universities is now made up of student fees, this is hardly a surprise. In the case of the Scottish institutions, the push is above all to increase the number of overseas and postgraduate students, because they pay generously for their presence. Hence there are employees whose job it is to sell their university's attractiveness in relation to such students, emphasising the superior quality of the facilities of every kind they provide. On this basis we are now attracting very large numbers of Chinese students – and it even seems to be the case that Chinese money, or money from overseas tax havens, is helping to pay for quality housing and other facilities. Money talks here too. But there could be a future price to pay.

My final piece of evidence that our universities are in danger of losing the lofty prestige that over centuries they have gained, concerns the latest wheeze that Westminster educationalists are busily promoting: two-year degrees. I am astonished by the general lack of astonishment at a proposal that reflects an utter failure to understand what a university education is about. What it is not about is churning out quickie degrees so that students can pick up better paid jobs sooner than their less fortunate peers. Yet that is the basic argument advanced by those who support this absurd idea. The generally unrecognized truth is that even the current three-year honours degree in English universities is something of an anomaly: in world-wide terms a version of the Scottish four-year honours degree structure is far more common. (The three-year version no doubt reflects a belief in the superiority of English A levels – whether that superiority remains in place is an open question.) But the really damaging aspect of the two-year degree plan is the assumption that students choose to go to university because they believe a degree will get them a well-paid job. In all my almost forty years of university teaching I never met a student who mentioned money as the reason for their presence. I accept that taking courses and passing exams – which leads to a degree – is at the heart of the university experience. But it is about a great deal more. It's about growing up, becoming independent, meeting and getting to know new people, widening one's experience in all kinds of different ways. And above all it's about the opportunity to share in the world of knowledge and learning that universities have studied and promoted over long centuries. Today the so-called STEM [science, technology, engineering and mathematics] subjects are widely seen as more worthy of study – and perhaps in economic terms they are. But to suggest that the study of philosophy, history, literature, the arts, and the social sciences, should be limited or denied in a university makes no sense whatsoever. Back in 1605 Bacon announced he had taken all knowledge to be his province. If U.K. universities wish to lose such world-wide status as they presently retain, the road to follow is to abandon the study of the humanities – and, as a handful have done, start offering two-year degrees.

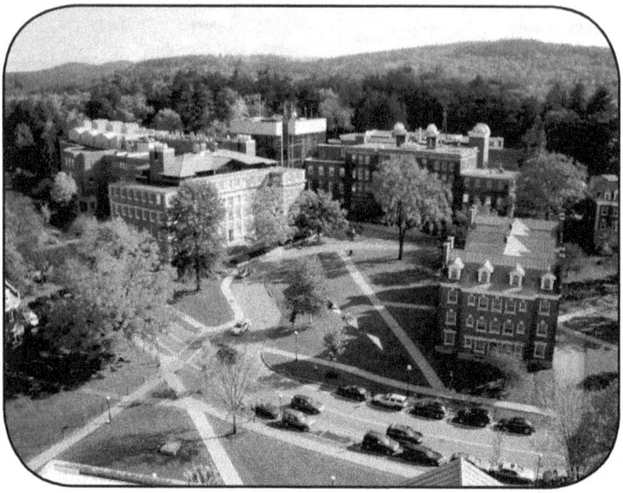

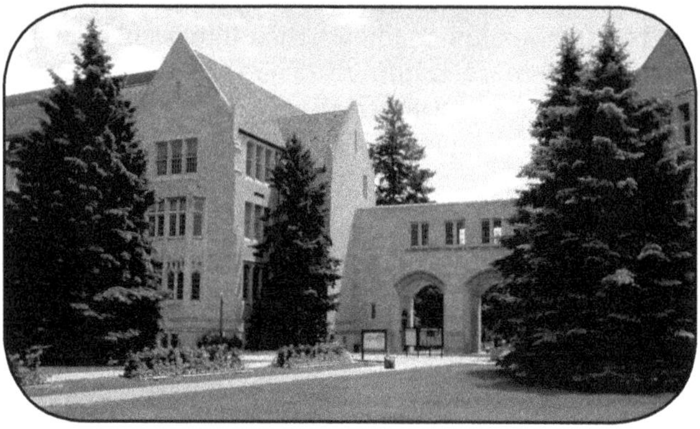

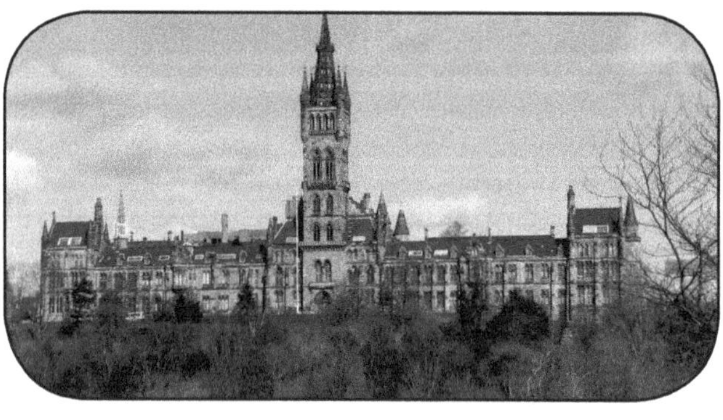

From top: Dartmouth College; St Thomas University; University of Glasgow

Part Seven

American and Scottish Politics.

Re-reading these pieces on the political world of Scotland and America in recent years has proved an intriguing experience. The big issues that emerge include the election of President Obama, the rise and rise of the Tea Party Republicans, the shooting tragedies in both countries, and the Scottish independence referendum of 2014. But the extraordinary thing that happens – to my mind at least – as one reads about such events, is how often one is reminded of still more recent events: the election of President Trump in the US, and the Brexit referendum in the U.K.

The relevance of so many of my comments on the state of American politics, to the coming election of Trump, seemed so striking that at one point I thought of heading this section 'The Road to Trump'. Drawing attention to such issues as the growing strength of Tea Party Republicans, the extraordinary influence of evangelical Christians on the Republican side, the success of pro-gun lobbying by the NRA (National Rifle Association) in so many state legislatures, and the consequences of the removal of all restraints on the level of funding in political campaigns, now helps to explain Trump's success in 2016. Likewise, reading my commentaries on the Scottish independence referendum, it is impossible not to be reminded again and again of aspects of the Brexit referendum, or for that matter of the calls for further referendums on both topics.

I make no claim to any unusual level of insight, but the way history has moved in recent days seems to give added resonance to this section of my book.

"A well regulated militia, being necessary to the security of a free state, the right of the people to keep and bear arms, shall not be infringed."

The 2nd Amendment to the United States Constitution, 1791

"Should Scotland be an independent country?"

Scottish Independence Referendum Question, 2014

"Should the United Kingdom remain a member of the European Union or leave the European Union?"

Brexit Referendum Question, 2016

1 Zealous Nation

Did you know that today's cadre of American air force pilots have to qualify not only with their wings but with born-again Christian credentials? Hard to believe? Easy to dismiss as a left-wing or, in contemporary American terms, a 'liberal' slur? If that is your view then you need to read the editorial in the *New York Times* of June 11, 2005, headed 'Zealots at the Air Force Academy'. The commanding general of the Colorado academy – the American equivalent of Cranwell – has just acknowledged that 'his campus is so permeated with evangelical proselytizing that it will take years to rid the institution of religious intolerance'. One campus chaplain is reported to have warned cadets 'not born again' that they will 'burn in the fires of hell', while the Lutheran chaplain who dared to complain of cadets being abused by 'systemic and pervasive' proselytizing has been quickly transferred to somewhere in Asia. Such religious intransigence and intolerance in the armed forces of all places will strike most of us as well-nigh incomprehensible (though those who planned and executed 9/11 would understand it perfectly well). But in today's America perhaps one should not be too surprised.

I have recently returned from a semester's teaching at a university in the Middle West, and have been thinking hard about what was different about the America I encountered in the first half of 2005. The University of St Thomas is located in St Paul, Minnesota – one of the 'Twin Cities' that make up Minneapolis St Paul. St Thomas is a Catholic foundation dating from 1875, and a Catholic atmosphere still pervades the campus: religious icons inside and outside the university classrooms and offices; buildings and halls of residence named for past bishops; quiet rooms for prayer and meditation; a line of seminarians (all men of course) processing with candles and banners in bitter, below-freezing temperatures to take part in some form of observance before a sandstone madonna outside the main university chapel. Not an atmosphere I was familiar with, and I have to admit that as I talked about American literature in the early twentieth century, noting in the usual way the loss of faith and the 'death of God' in the later nineteenth century, the devastating impact of World War I, and the emergence of the so-called 'lost generation' in the 1920s, I was just a bit aware that for some – perhaps most – of the bright young faces in front of me such religious doubts were entirely alien. Not of course that any of them spoke up to challenge Hemingway or Dos Passos or Fitzgerald or Wallace Stevens – or any other of the authors they were studying. They were all much too polite to do that. Reluctant to disagree with what they were reading or with each other, Middle West students at least seem to take the view that in a democracy all opinions are equally valid.

However let me hasten to make it perfectly clear that the religious atmosphere at a Catholic university in St Paul had absolutely nothing in common with that at Colorado's Air Force Academy. Outside speakers did come to the St Thomas campus to talk about questions of theology and faith, and – yes– about the Catholic Church's position on abortion, birth control, marriage and other controversial issues. But visiting speakers also included the extremely liberal comedian Al Franken (a Minnesotan native he is apparently thinking of running for political office) as well as anti-Iraq war campaigners. And when Anne Coulter, that most odious and vituperative of extreme right-wing Republican activists spoke in characteristically unpleasant fashion on the campus the university president issued a public apology to the university community over the offensiveness of her performance. Whatever may be happening elsewhere in contemporary American culture, universities like St Thomas continue to uphold the best American traditions of academic freedom and free speech.

How, then, does one explain what has gone on at the Air Force Academy? What has happened is a quite extraordinary change in the balance of power within America's social, political, and cultural life. My experience of the US extends back to the 1950s: from 1957 to 1960 I was a graduate student at Princeton University in New Jersey. Between 1960 and 2005 I have returned to America on numerous occasions for both short and extended periods. Friends regularly ask me about any changes I have noticed over so many years, and the question is one I have not always found easy to answer. One's personal experience is inevitably limited; my friends and contacts are almost all in the academic world; the country is so huge and diverse; different sections and regions have different characteristics, etc. etc. Pushed for a response, and to avoid more difficult issues, sometimes I mention cars: in the 1950s all Americans drove gigantic, tail-finned monsters – only the odd non-conformist made his point by opting for a Volkswagen Beetle. Slowly in the 60s and 70s medium and European-sized cars became more common – at first only in the eastern states, but gradually infiltrating the wide open spaces of the west. By the early 90s one could even believe that Americans were taking seriously the need to reduce exhaust emissions from their vehicles; but the sudden enormous popularity of SUVs showed what a delusion that had been.

But sometimes I have tried to think seriously about the larger issues. Have there been changes in relation to race? What about feminism, gender and all that? What about the temper, the general atmosphere or flavour of life in the society? Have there been noteworthy changes in these areas? Well, yes and no. Over race, for example, I think my answer is largely no. Of course there have been hugely important changes in the legal framework and in what is socially and culturally acceptable and what is not. Segregation in an institutional sense has gone. (In 1960, when I was teaching Freshman English at Duke University in Durham, North Carolina, the local cinema required whites to sit downstairs, African-Americans upstairs.) But has racial integration really been achieved? Every American university and college struggles to diversify its student body in terms of race and ethnicity; qualified African-American or Latino or native-American candidates are much sought after. But year after year in most institutions the percentage figures remain little above token levels. Only once in my experience have I encountered anything different: walking across a prestigious campus of the University of California it was impossible not to notice that there seemed to be as many Chinese-American students as white, Anglo-Saxon ones. The sociologists tell us that the African-American middle-class has expanded greatly in recent decades, and no doubt this is true. It is also true that on television and in the arts in general there is much greater ethnic diversity than was the case in the 1950s. (But even here there are qualifications: all black TV comedy shows are watched by an overwhelmingly black audience whereas all white shows, such as Friends, attract only a minority of black viewers.) For me the statistics that prove that American society remains crucially divided by race and ethnicity are those concerning crime. The United States has the highest rate of incarceration in the world (followed by Britain, China, France, Japan and Nigeria). But the ethnic make-up of those in prison in no way accurately reflects that of the country as a whole. A government report for 2004 shows that no less than sixty percent of jail inmates are from racial or ethnic minorities. Still more disturbing is the statistic that 12.6 percent of all black men aged between 25 and 29 are in prison; of Hispanics of similar age, 3.6 percent are in prison. The figure for white men? 1.7 percent. Such numbers point all too vividly to a continuing major problem within American society.

As far as gender is concerned, however, there has certainly been significant change. When Princeton – or the College of New Jersey as it then was – was founded in 1746 its student body was inevitably exclusively male. When I arrived in 1957 nothing had changed: all the undergraduate and postgraduate students were men. Duke University in 1960 had two campuses, one for men, one for women; and in all first year classes like mine, the sexes were taught separately. (My women students proved to be distinctly better than the men.)

All this changed, however, within little over a decade. By the mid-70s, Princeton, like all the previously all-male Ivy League universities, had begun to admit women. By now as many women are on campuses everywhere as men – and one suspects that if admission decisions were made exclusively in terms of pre-college grades, in many institutions there would be more women students than men. Certainly in the Humanities subject areas, just as in the U.K, women are in the majority. In 1957 my Princeton professors were of course all men. That too has changed utterly. Certainly in Humanities subjects at least, most colleges and universities are eager to employ as many women as men. The consequences are increasingly evident. In my academic generation, husband and wife academic teams were almost unknown; and if a wife did have a job – any kind of job – it was very much incidental to her husband's career. In today's America husband and wife academic teams are relatively common – and for a variety of reasons sometimes deliberately sought after by appointing committees. More striking still is the situation I've come across several times where it is the wife (or female partner) who occupies the full-time academic position while her partner finds whatever work he can as her career develops. A change indeed.

Looking back, and thinking outside such specific areas, I believe I can identify changes in the overall feel, the atmosphere of America in the different decades spanned by my visits. In the 1950s – Robert Lowell's 'tranquillized fifties' – America seemed stable, unified, fixed in the certainties of the Cold War. The impact of the Soviet Union's successful launch of the first sputnik seemed only to further the sense of an America united in its determination to catch up and overtake the Russians in space. When I returned to teach at Princeton in 1966-67 the atmosphere was very different. The Kennedy assassination had had a monumental impact, and soon the murders of Robert Kennedy and Martin Luther King reinforced the sense that an older America had gone forever. The Vietnam war was the new, overpowering reality. I remember different things:

the long, long list of academics (I was one) signing up on a page-length *New York Times* letter/advert protesting the continuation of the war; joining a rather small line of protestors outside Palmer Stadium in Princeton itself while the big Princeton v. Yale football game was taking place; most of all participating in the mammoth, simultaneous anti-war protests in New York and San Francisco in April, 1967. In New York the march was supposed to be from Central Park to United Nations Plaza. But the numbers were so huge that when the front of the march was already in the Plaza, many of us were still waiting to set off from Central Park. More astonishing still was the eerie silence in the streets through which we marched. The demonstration had taken over the city; it was as though no one else was there.

Returning to America in the mid-70s, I found a country changed again. I think the major cause was the defeat in Vietnam and the temporary loss of national confidence that flowed from it. Academic life had become more overtly politicized than it had been in the past. The result was a kind of ill-tempered souring of the intellectual atmosphere which to me at least seemed to reflect the loss of self-confidence in the wider society. The settled America of the 1950s now seemed permanently at odds with itself, much less sure of where it was heading. Was it perhaps to the further humiliation of the 'Iranian hostages' affair?

I was not back until 1989 by which time all seemed to have changed once again. Why? The Reagan factor perhaps, all that avuncular reassurance combined with a sense that the Cold War was being won, that the movement of history was once again flowing in America's direction? Anyway one had the strongest sense that the period of self-doubt was over. America was back on track. I was there in November, 1992, when Bill Clinton was making his first bid for the presidency. In Princeton people were queuing up to vote before the polls opened. The sense of excitement and anticipation was powerful. Compared to the elder Bush, Clinton seemed so youthful, dynamic, so eloquent and intelligent. Something of the Kennedy glamour, the Kennedy promise had apparently returned. The rest, disappointments and all, is (recent) history.

II

So yes, the America I found in 1957, when I disembarked from the Queen Mary in New York City, was a very different America from that I found on landing at Newark airport in January, 2005. Hardly a surprise you will say. But what is extraordinarily surprising is the nature of the change I found myself registering in my months in Minneapolis-St Paul. Something new and explicit was happening. Reading newspapers, watching television, talking to friends, it was unavoidably in your face. What was it? Exactly what the American Air Force Academy story encapsulates: the empowerment in most areas of American society of forms of fundamentalist, evangelical Christianity. Historians will of course argue that from the Great Awakening in the eighteenth century through the kind of camp-meeting revivalism that Twain satirized in Huckleberry Finn to John Brown abolitionism and the state of Tennessee's attempt to refute Darwinism in the 1925 Scopes trial, Christian fundamentalism has always been a power in the land. But most of us had agreed with H.L.Mencken that the Scopes trial had simply made Tennessee and the rural South look foolish Who in recent years would have dreamt of suggesting that the issue of Darwin would resurface in the twenty-first century?

It is now widely accepted that the younger Bush's electoral triumph in 2004 was largely based on so-called 'faith-based' issues. Even the 'war on terror' has a religious dimension. I was in Ohio on 9/11 and it was impossible not to register the religiosity in America's reaction. 'God bless America' signs were everywhere. No politician or government spokesman could comment without invoking the deity. (No one seemed to notice that the hijackers were equally convinced that God was on their side.) But beyond the politics of fear, the issues that produced the lines of voters at the polling-stations in Ohio and elsewhere in 2004 were essentially 'moral' ones: abortion, stem-cell research, gay rights and same-sex marriage. To protect America from such evils, millions of Americans were persuaded to vote against their own economic interests. In the early months after his re-election, the bills that Bush rushed through Congress were all paybacks to the big corporations which had contributed so much to his re-election campaign fund. A bill, for example, to change existing law in such a way as to make it much more difficult for ordinary consumers to sue large companies over malpractice of any kind; a bankers' bill to make it impossible for ordinary Americans to file for bankruptcy when overwhelmed by debt. This bill passed easily through Congress despite the fact that its opponents were able to show that the vast majority of Americans declaring themselves bankrupt did not do so because of credit-card debt, but because, lacking adequate medical insurance, the cost of medical care and hospital treatment had consumed all their financial resources. Bush's support for CAFTA (Central America Free Trade Agreement) and his proposals on the illegal immigrant issue are equally responsive to big business pressures. In fact one has to go back to the Harding, Coolidge, Hoover 1920s to find a time when the business sector had such influence on government policy.

But if the demands of big business have always dominated the Bush administration, what is new in the second term is the emergence into the open of the demands of the Christian right. If the business interest has got what it wanted by funding the Bush campaign, the Christian right, having provided the voting battalions, is now demanding its rewards. Science, medicine, education, culture, the law and government itself – all of these crucial areas within American society are suddenly under unprecedented pressure from well-organized and well-funded Christian lobbies.

As every schoolboy knows (at least every American schoolboy) the Founding Fathers of the United States insisted in their constitution on a total separation of church and state. Freedom of worship was not in question (nearly all the makers of the constitution were Christians of some kind) but there was to be no kind of state religion in the new republic. It is this venerable tradition that is now under attack. President Bush has sanctioned and encouraged so-called 'faith-based initiatives' over a wide range of social activities. What this means in practice is that huge sums of taxpayers' money are being channelled directly to religion-based providers of social services. Despite assurances to the contrary, church activities are being directly funded by the state. Money is available for programmes, run by churches, which combine social objectives with straightforward proselytizing. Religious tests are imposed on those who apply to work for the social programmes. Money is even available for the renovation of churches which undertake to provide social services.

Some will argue that the provision of social services, faith-based or not, has to be a good thing. But other forms of faith-based activity are surely indefensible. Thus today it is becoming increasingly common for pharmacists to refuse, on moral and religious grounds, to dispense emergency contraception – the so-called morning after pill in particular — and even birth control pills prescribed by a doctor. In Illinois and Mississippi legislation is already in place that allows doctors and other health-care providers to deny patients virtually any procedure that in 'conscience' they disapprove of. And President Bush continues to veto stem-cell research in the US because of pressure from Christian pro-life campaigners.

It is not only in the field of medical research that science is currently under attack in the US. As was noted above, the 1920s Scopes trial is being re-enacted in twenty-first century America. Evolutionary Darwinism is once again under attack from an anti-scientific, Christian fundamentalist perspective. In the states of Kansas, Pennsylvania, Georgia, and Ohio legislation is being debated that would restrict the traditional teaching of evolution; in counties in another nineteen states similar anti-Darwin campaigns are underway. The 'creationism' of a few years ago has been replaced by the notion of 'intelligent design' but the effect is the same: a challenge to Darwin's theory of evolution. (Only a third of Americans believe in evolution; a half believes that man was created only 10,000 years ago.) In Kentucky a born-again billionaire is about to build a Creation Museum at a cost of 25 million dollars. Most troubling of all is the degree of success being achieved by the anti-Darwin movement. Education authorities across the country try to avoid the 'E' (evolution) word. In various towns in the South showings of such perfectly conventional documentary films as Imax's Cosmic Voyage, Volcanoes of the Deep Sea, and Galapagos have been withdrawn because of pressure and complaints from creationist groups. And a survey by the National Science Teachers Association found that 31 percent of teachers feel under pressure to present creationism-related material in the classroom. Meanwhile the Justice Department in Washington apparently has a 'religious rights' unit to protect the interests of, for example, science students who reject the idea of evolution. Home-schooling – meaning the withdrawal of children from the public educational system – is increasingly common across America because it allows parents to protect their children from exposure to ideas out of step with their Christian fundamentalism. At higher education level new colleges linked to evangelical churchs and their ideology are being established.

America's popular culture is in no way immune to the Christian fundamentalist surge. The Left Behind series of novels by Tim LaHaye and Jerry P. Jenkins, now extending to thirteen volumes, has been enormously successful: over 62 million copies of these neo-Christian fictions focusing on the destruction of God's enemies and the triumph of his all-American, free-market, friends, have been sold. The 'rapture' of Armageddon is a unifying theme. The success of these works has to a degree been an underground one: the titles do not appear on the *New York Times* bestseller lists. But in the spring of 2005, the NBC television network ran a weekly mini-series called 'Revelations' which clearly represented the entry of a Left Behind perspective into mainstream American culture. Many public service television stations, on the other hand, recently felt obliged to withdraw a children's cartoon programme in which a bunny rabbit met a lesbian couple.

Science, education, popular culture — the newly emboldened and empowered religious right has been flexing its muscles in all these area. But most disturbing of all has been its increasingly successful interventions in the areas of law and government. What is going on is a successful erosion of America's constitutional division between church and state. In Washington today, among the most powerful lobbying groups is the National Association of Evangelicals, headed by Pastor Ted Haggard. The Association unites 45,000 churches and their thirty million members (more than a quarter of American voters). This is the constituency that brought Bush his second term and saved America from same-sex marriages. Haggard's own New Life Church, with 11,000 members, and able to seat 7,500 of the faithful, is located in Colorado Springs – within sight of the Air Force Academy. Every Monday the pastor talks directly to President Bush or his advisers.

In my months at St Thomas the news story the media pursued to the level of hysteria was that concerning the fate of Terri Schiavo. Not the Michael Jackson child molestation trial, not Iraq — though it is worth pointing out that, unlike in the U.K, Iraq features on all the mainstream news channels night after night — no, the biggest story arose from the proposal to allow a brain-dead woman in Florida to die by withdrawing her artificial life-support system. No sooner had the Florida courts, having listened to the legal and medical evidence, agreed to the husband's request that after eleven years in a vegetative state his wife be allowed to die, than the pro-life, religious right went into supercharged action. Exploiting the desire of Schiavo's parents to keep their daughter alive, it launched appeal after appeal in the Florida courts; hundreds of supporters picketed the clinic where Schiavo lay; prayer vigils were held around the country; and, worst of all, the lawyers and judges acting in the case were subjected to vilification and threats to the degree that they had to be provided with police protection. As if all this were not bad enough, both the House of Representatives and the Senate in Washington, under pressure from the religious lobbyists, rushed to pass special legislation to require further delays in the normal legal process. Not to be outdone, President Bush, in the full glare of publicity, flew up from Texas to sign the unprecedented Schiavo bill into law. The driving force behind these quite extraordinary political manoeuvrings was the egregious Tom DeLay, the Republican leader in the House of Representatives. DeLay believes his role is to bring a 'biblical world view' to American politics. Thus he told his supporters that 'one thing that God has brought to us is Terri Schiavo, to help elevate the visibility of what is going on in America'. Such shameless exploitation of an individual's life and death to further a radical, pro-life Christian agenda which implied that his 'liberal' opponents were somehow defying God and all that is good in the American way of life, was not limited to DeLay. In the Senate, the Republican majority leader Bill Frist, a doctor by profession, and a putative Republican candidate for the presidency next time round, was prepared to argue – on the sole basis of watching edited videos of Terri Schiavo – that the Florida doctors were wrong about her vegetative state. Frist, that is, clearly believes that if he is to succeed Bush, he has to keep onside with his religious constituency. As it happened, on this occasion these Republicans overplayed their hand. Opinion polls quickly showed that the vast majority of Americans felt that Congress should not have become involved in the Schiavo case. But that in no way alters the significance of the fact that the Republican right – and the majority of Republicans in both houses are now well to the right – felt the need to adopt positions in line with the demands of their religious supporters.

What the Schiavo case brought into the open was the readiness of Christian fundamentalists to coerce and intimidate even those constitutionally committed to uphold the laws of the US itself – the state and federal judiciary. In the wake of Congress's failure to overturn the decisions of Florida's state courts DeLay spoke ominously about unaccountable judges, whose rulings showed they were out of touch with the people, being made to pay for their decisions. But of course there are some judges who embrace DeLay's biblical ideals. In the course of 2005 two issues concerning the separation of church and state finally made their way to the Supreme Court. Both involved the display of the Ten Commandments in public contexts. Ludicrously enough, the first involved one of several thousand Ten Commandments monuments that Cecil B. DeMille distributed across America to publicize his 1954 blockbuster film of that name. This particular relic of that campaign now stands in the grounds of the state legislature Capitol building in Austin, Texas. The second case concerned the display of the Ten Commandments inside courthouses in Kentucky and Alabama. The Supreme Court's decision, by a five to four majority, was to allow the first display but ban the second: an outcome that indicates all too clearly how delicately balanced the court is, and how crucial Bush's likely opportunity to appoint at least two new Supreme Court judges in fact is. The pressure is on to appoint justices sympathetic to the religious right's agenda – on abortion, on stem-cell research, on same-sex marriages, on school prayers etc. etc. The leaders of the right-wing, free-market Christian movement know exactly what they want to achieve, and it does amount to a rolling back of America's long-established separation of church and state in the interests of a particular brand of uncompromising, biblical fundamentalism. It is a deeply troubling scenario and it is also one that a born-again President, and a Congress incorporating as many as two hundred self-styled born-again members, may find very hard to resist. The old Boston elite in the nineteenth century used to quip that one born in Boston had no need to be born again. But in the early twenty-first century, Boston's politicians are unlikely to be cracking that particular joke. John Danforth, a former Republican senator and UN ambassador, himself a clergyman, recently wrote in the *New York Times* that his party 'was becoming a political arm of the religious right'. In the make-up of today's Senate a handful of 'liberal' Republicans still exist and they have sometimes shown a readiness to buck the White House line. It may not be an overstatement to say that the future of America lies in their hands – and votes. Only with their help can the Democrats in the Senate effectively act as a check on the power of the White House and thus ensure that America is not stampeded by Christian zealots into what the critic and commentator Frank Rich has called 'McCarthyism in God's name'.

In his most recent novel, *The Plot Against America*, Philip Roth imagines a situation in which the anti-Semitic, fascist-sympathising Charles Lindbergh defeats Franklin D. Roosevelt in the 1940 presidential election. Roth does not draw any overt parallels between his imagined history and the current American political scene, but some readers will be tempted to make the link. Late in his novel, Roth has the anti-Lindbergh journalist Walter Winchell ask the question: 'And how long will the American people stand for this treachery perpetrated by their elected president? How long will Americans remain asleep while their cherished Constitution is torn to shreds by the fascist fifth column of the Republican right marching under the sign of the cross and the flag?' Of course this is fiction and no one is suggesting that the present American administration is headed by a Lindbergh look-alike. But on the other hand the links between today's Republican right, the cross, and the flag – and what that means for the interpretation of the Constitution itself – are more than enough to give many Americans, and non-Americans, good reason for pause.

2 Bad News

2011 has got off to a bad start. More4 has made the extraordinary decision to cut Jon Stewart's The Daily Show. Evenings at 8.30 from Tuesday to Friday will never be the same. (Monday at 8.30 was the so-called 'international' show made up of snippets from the previous week. Absurdly this is the only programme More4 will continue to broadcast.) A figure of 80,000 regular viewers has apparently been judged too few. 80,000 strikes me as quite a lot – and anyway there is the issue of quality as well as quantity. I'd bet my bottom dollar that that number includes nearly all of those who see themselves as our opinion makers, leader writers, political pundits, and of course experts and commentators on America today.

Because The Daily Show offers unrivalled insight into contemporary American politics and culture. Night after night the show mocks both the extremism of Fox News and the complacencies of the rest of America's daily news broadcasts. For more than ten years it has stood alone in providing the punchy political satire so sorely missing from America's countless other TV channels. And the role it plays is all the more necessary given that American current affairs programmes seem quite incapable of asking their politicians the hard questions which, say, Paxman's Newsnight interviews specialise in. For those of us of a certain age, the Daily Show and its impact are a reminder of what That Was the Week That Was represented in the U.K .in the early 1960s. In its lampooning of the cosy British establishment in uninhibited language and edgy style, That Was the Week blew us all away. For many Americans that is the impact The Daily Show seems to have. For many Americans but of course not for all. The makers of the programme insist it is only a comedy show. But for those on the right in American politics, its jokes are invariably at their expense.

In fact in recent weeks Stewart's politics have become a contentious issue. He himself continues to insist he is only a comedian. He denies that he is a journalist – and certainly not a journalist with an agenda of his own. He made lots of jokes about the egregious George Bush – but he makes jokes at the expense of President Obama too. However the impact of recent programmes has once again raised questions about the nature of the advocacy he engages in. A few weeks ago Republicans in the Senate prevented the passage of what became known as the 'first responders' bill. This was a bill to provide permanent health care for those emergency workers who were the first to respond to the devastation of 9/11. Many of those who, amid all the heat and smoke and dust and debris of the twin towers, struggled to do what they could to cope with that terrifying situation, have subsequently developed lung diseases and other health problems. The bill was designed to provide for them. But the Republicans argued the price was too high.

Stewart was outraged by this decision – and let his anger show. In savagely wounding programmes he showed us clips of a series of Republican senators shamelessly allying themselves with, and glorying in, the heroic and patriotic behaviour of the first responders. He invited on to his programme sick fire-fighters and first aid workers from New York to listen and respond. The impact was devastating. Within days the bill was somehow reintroduced and passed in the Senate. So was this 'advocacy satire' or – as those who suggest that Stewart is taking on the role of such great American commentators as Edward Murrow or Walter Cronkite – 'advocacy journalism'. I'm not sure it matters. The Daily Show matters enough for Jimmy Carter, Bill Clinton, Tony Blair, Gordon Brown, and President Obama to agree to appear on it. But it appears it does not matter enough for More4 to continue letting us see it. What an opportunity for the mandarins of the BBC to take advantage of More4's mistake and screen the programme. I wish I were more certain they will have the nerve to do so.

3 Campaigning in the USA

With Mitt Romney soon to be confirmed as the Republican Party's choice to challenge Barack Obama in November, the American presidential campaign is about to begin in earnest. Currently political commentators are obsessing over the question of who will Romney choose as his vice-presidential running-mate. Looming over the issue is what happened last time round: John McCain's fateful decision to pick Sarah Palin. Palin's admirers and detractors agree on one thing: once she was selected, she attracted more attention that the man who chose her. The Palin sideshow took centre stage. As a result the message for Romney is clear: play it safe, pick someone who won't end up embarrassing you. Romney will certainly act accordingly.

So who will be the challenger's choice? There is no obvious front-runner, while there are perhaps too many possible contenders. Names from the past pop up – Condoleezza Rice, Jeb Bush – only to drop out of sight. A range of Republican governors get mentioned – Daniels of Indiana, Jindal of Louisiana, Christie of New Jersey – and when asked they inevitably rule themselves neither in nor out. However in recent weeks two other names seem to keep cropping up: Senator Rob Portman from Ohio and Marco Rubio, junior senator from Florida. Portman is a party insider, admired by Republican professionals, and he calls himself 'a religious person'. He would be a safe pair of hands, but his name is not one that many Americans would recognize. Rubio's position is different.

Marco Rubio was elected to the Senate in 2010 with the support of Florida's Tea Party. Young and personable, he is, as his name suggests, from a Hispanic/Latino background. His parents were Cuban immigrants in Florida and so he can be identified with America's large and growing Hispanic/Latino ethnic minority. Such identification could be of crucial importance. Mitt Romney has a big problem with the Latino vote – which is already larger than that of African Americans. In order to ensure his nomination by a Republican base unsure of his conservative credentials, in the course of his campaign Romney moved decisively to the right over a range of issues. Hence over the hugely contentious problems of immigration into the US from Mexico and other Central and South American countries, and what to do about the millions of illegal immigrants who have been living and working in America for many years, he has expressed sympathy for the popular but highly discriminatory legislation being enacted in such states as Arizona, New Mexico, and Texas. The inevitable result is that opinion polls show him with miniscule support in the Latino community: a mere 14% against President Obama's 65%. An Hispanic with Tea Party support: it's easy to see why Romney might be tempted to have Rubio on the ticket. But the case is not an open and shut one. Most of America's Latino voters have nothing in common with Florida's well-established and successful Cuban Americans. Originally seen as refugees from the hated Castro's communist Cuba, these immigrants were welcomed in a manner denied to the vast majority of those arriving from Mexico and points south. Then Rubio has chosen not to support the so-called 'Dream' act which would allow some illegal immigrants to obtain permanent residency if they gain a college education or serve two years in the armed forces. So would Rubio's name on the ticket change Latino minds? Perhaps not. Still, a bet on Rubio for vice-president might prove profitable.

So in the coming months what kind of campaign are we going to witness? The omens are not good. Romney has won the Republican nomination by destroying his opponents — or rather having them destroyed for him. How? Through the use of 'Super PACs'. (Political Action Committees), and the overwhelmingly negative TV ads they fund. Super PACs made their appearance on the political stage as a result of the Supreme Court's decision in 2010 that legislation aimed at limiting the amount of corporate and trade union spending that could be used to influence elections was unconstitutional. Now there is no limit to the amount of money PACs can raise from their sponsors. Still more telling is another major difference between PAC commercials and traditional political parties' advertising: PAC material does not require any statement that it has been approved by the candidate it is supporting. Anonymity therefore encourages even greater negativity. This is why, in the words of one commentator, Super PACs have become the hit men of 2012.

By March 31st this year, Romney's main PAC (with the dotty title Restore Our Future), had raised 51.1 million dollars. By then the Obama-supporting PAC (Priorities USA) had banked a mere 8.99 million. Admittedly most of that Restore Our Future money has already been spent on winning Romney his party's nomination. But Romney has plenty rich supporters more than willing to pay up in order to ensure Obama's defeat. Another Super PAC — American Crossroads, allied to yet another fund-raising organization called Crossroads GPS (Grassroots Policy Strategies) — has already raised almost 100 million dollars to spend on Romney's behalf. Some American commentators are predicting that come November, the Romney campaign will have spent a billion dollars in its drive to dislodge Obama.

The Republican strategy will be to use Romney's personally endorsed TV commercials to highlight the positive side of their candidate's campaign, emphasising his business expertise and economic know-how. Meanwhile for almost six months America will be blitzed with endless Super PAC-funded, ruthlessly negative TV ads attacking, undermining and distorting President Obama's record, policies, and character. If in November the race is a tight one, money, not any principle of democracy, may well be the winner.

4 Republican Sharp Practice

In a recent article Alan Fisher agreed with other commentators in suggesting that most American voters have already made up their minds about whom they will support in November's election. At the time of his triumph in 2008, President Obama believed he could reach out and make the US a truly united country. Those of us who were sceptical about his — or anyone else's — ability to do any such thing, soon proved to be right. As Mr Fisher suggests, in the last four years, America has been as divided and polarised a nation as it has ever been in its history. The result is that the number of so-called 'independent' voters — those willing to be persuaded to vote for one or other of the candidates — seems to be smaller than ever.

It is this situation that explains Mitt Romney's choice of Paul Ryan as his running mate. In such a fractious and closely contested election, nothing is more important than getting out one's committed supporters. As the long drawn out primary contest showed, the Republican core vote remained unconvinced that Romney was really one of them. It has not been enough for Romney to disown past beliefs and policies regarded as dangerously liberal by Tea Party Republicans. However, by choosing Ryan (a man whose views only a few years ago would have been regarded as far-out and extremist even among Republicans) as his vice-presidential candidate, Romney clearly believes that the Republican base will have been transformed into his enthusiastic supporters.

But doing everything possible to guarantee that its own party loyalists turn out on voting day is only one half of the Republican Party's key strategy to ensure victory in November. It emerges that the other half is to do everything possible to prevent the Democratic Party getting out theirs. Crucial here is that the Republicans have complete political control in twenty-six states, and partial control in another fourteen. What they are doing in all these states is rushing to pass legislation that will undermine the Democratic vote. This is the real reason behind measures that will make it difficult for many ordinary people to exercise their democratic right to cast their ballot.

Republican strategists have identified different ways in which the restriction of the Democratic vote can be achieved. One is upping the level required for voter identification. (Republican legislators pretend this is needed to prevent voter fraud. In fact there is absolutely no evidence that voter fraud is even a problem.) Another is to make it much more difficult to authorise voter registration drives. (Such drives of course are aimed at minorities who are likely to vote Democratic.) Another is to drastically restrict existing provisions for early voting.

Proposed new legislation over voter identification usually means that would-be voters have to produce birth certificates or government-issued photo IDs — usually meaning driving licences. But there are large numbers of potential voters who do not carry such photo IDs. Who are they? The young, the very old, and ethnic minorities such as Latinos and African Americans. Apparently some 20% of these groups do not have photo IDs. No need to ask for whom they tend to vote. The Republican House leader in the key swing state of Pennsylvania recently openly assured his party that photo ID legislation would help Romney win the state.

In 2008, around 30% of American voters voted early. And Obama had a 10% lead among such voters. In a number of states Republican majorities are passing legislation to make it more difficult for Democrats to repeat this success. Thus in suburban Cincinnati, Ohio, voting will be possible in the evenings and over weekends. In the city itself, however, (which is 45% African American) early voting will end at 5 o'clock and not be available at weekends. In 2008, African Americans cast 31% of early votes. Early voting has been similarly restricted in Cleveland, Akron, and Columbus, Ohio cities with large African American populations. The Chair of the Franklin County Republican Party in suburban Columbus said he didn't think the state's early voting procedures should accommodate urban (i.e. African-American) voters: 'I guess I really actually feel we shouldn't contort the voting process to accommodate the urban voter-turnout machine'.

How significant will these legally-challenged Republican sharp practices prove to be? In tightly contested swing states such as Ohio, Florida, Pennsylvania and Colorado, they could conceivably make the difference between winning and losing. The current opinion polls give neither presidential candidate a decisive lead. And if President Obama is marginally ahead, we have to remember that in the vital closing weeks of the campaign, the enormous sums of money Republican Super PACs have in hand will be poured out country-wide, in a blanketing blitz of relentlessly destructive TV attacks on his person and policies. Is what we are now seeing really the kind of democratic process America's celebrated founding fathers had in mind?

5 The American Media

Back in the US in an election year I was immediately struck by two changes in the politico-cultural scene. First, the great *New York Times* is not what it used to be. It has become a diminished thing. Still a broadsheet of course, but not as broad as it once was. The slimline pages have room now for no more than six columns of print. It is hard not to feel that this change is somehow a sign of the times: the America of this more slender *Times* is not the expansive, heavyweight, self-confident US of old. The smaller format suggests a new austerity, a husbanding of resources, perhaps even a climb down into a more focused empiricism.

But all is far from lost. The *New York Times* remains a paper of record, and it is still a giant compared with the ever smaller fry of the British press. On a particular day in late April the paper contained an investigative piece on the behaviour of the mighty Walmart company in neighbouring Mexico. But what a piece! It consisted of column after column of continuous prose spread over several pages; the word count must have been three or four thousand at least. No British newspaper would be prepared to print anything of comparable length in a single issue. The article's chapter and verse set Walmart's insistence on the perfect probity of all its business dealings in the US against the malfeasance of its practices in Mexico: enormous bribes (some 24 million dollars) are being paid to Mexican officialdom to gain permission for the illegal opening of still more Walmart stores. Did the printing of this article have any effect? You bet it did. Next day Walmart shares fell by 5% – wiping millions of dollars off the company's value.

My second observed change represents only good news. Rupert Murdoch's Fox News, with its constant stream of unashamedly right-wing, anti-Obama reportage, no longer goes unchallenged in America. Day after day, hour after hour, MSNBC replies with equally barbed reporting on the behaviour of the Republican party and now its presidential candidate Mitt Romney. Fox's Bill O'Reilly, Sean Hannity, Greta Van Susteren, and Mike Huckabee continue to dominate the cable news channels in terms of viewing figures and remain (in my eyes) as aggressively biased and prejudicial as always. But MSNBC's Ed Schultz, Rachel Maddow (once a Rhodes Scholar), Luke Russert, and Melissa Harris-Perry (who taught at Princeton) answer back with energy and intelligence. They make up a quick-witted, younger team, and often make the Fox lot seem like grumpy old men. Of course it's worth remembering that the number of Americans who watch either of these programmes is really quite small: on a good day, Fox might approach two million viewers, MSNBC half as many. (America's population now exceeds 300 million.) But these cable news programmes, like the Russ Limbaugh-style shock-jock radio broadcasts, do seem to influence the tone of the wider political debate, and issues they take up often feed into more conventional TV news programmes.

What almost all commentators agree on is that in the recent Bush/Obama years American politics has become exceptionally confrontational and partisan; actual political debate has been effectively shut down. The Fox News v. MSNBC match-up is perhaps both a reflection of this development and a contribution to it. TV in the U.K. offers nothing comparable to these programmes. The BBC, ITV and Sky News stick to the view that the 'news' should be reported with journalistic objectivity and detachment. Government and opposition are as far as possible accorded equal exposure; the personalities of news commentators remain largely unobtrusive. I suspect that most of us think this is the way it should be – and recent events have made it no longer possible for Rupert Murdoch even to dream of introducing radical change.

The American cable news channels tend to turn politics into a kind of knock-about entertainment. British TV coverage of politics may sometimes seem stuffy and pedantic by comparison. But to watch these American programmes is to be struck by how repetitious and sometimes trivializing their coverage is. To fill in the endless hours of broadcasting, the same stories are repeated and mulled over by the successive presenters. Rarely is any new light shed. And political capital is sought in public figures' most casual comment, gesture, look, smile – or past history. Molehills quickly become mountains. Recently some researcher discovered that years ago the Romney family, setting out on holiday, were in the habit of carrying their pet dog in some kind of cage on the roof of their car. For days on end media supporters of Obama and the Democrats found purportedly witty ways of exploiting this ancient story. But then some Republican blogger discovered that in his personal memoir Barack Obama mentioned that as a boy he had eaten dog meat! This amazing revelation was thereafter also endlessly repeated. Perhaps there's something to be said for Lord Reith and Auntie BBC after all.

6 Republican or Democratic Toothpaste?

Two recent developments provide striking illustrations of what is happening in America's political culture today. The first concerns Senator Richard Lugar of Indiana, the second, Governor Scott Walker of Wisconsin. Richard Lugar has been a senator from Indiana since 1976. He has served six consecutive terms. Eighty years old, he is the senior Republican in the US Senate, and the ranking member of the Senate's Committee for Foreign Relations. But on May 8th this year (2012), losing a Republican primary election to Indiana's state treasurer, Richard Mourdock, his Senate career came to an abrupt end. Why? Because he was one of the dwindling number of Republican 'moderates' in the Senate. He had even been known to cooperate with Democratic colleagues across the aisle to get things done. Given the current make-up of the Republican Party, that was his undoing.

Today's polls indicate that only 23% of Republican supporters now describe themselves as 'moderates'. Ten years ago 62% of Republicans called themselves 'conservatives'. That figure now stands at 71%. Senator Lugar is thus a figure from the past, out of touch with today's Republican party. Hence his defeat by an opponent supported aggressively by the grassroots Tea Party, and generously financed by Super PACs from outside Indiana. A total of 4.6 million dollars was spent from such sources boosting Mourdock's finally successful campaign. Once again it appears that nothing counts for more in contemporary American politics than hard cash. (Incidentally the Democrats thought they'd no chance of defeating Senator Lugar. Against a new, more right-wing, candidate, they feel they are in with a chance.)

Scott Walker has been the Republican governor of Wisconsin since 2010. June 5th has just been announced as the day he will face a recall election after his Democratic opponents collected 900,000 votes — more than double the number required — to ensure that such an election would be held. So what has occasioned Governor Walker's recall? His determination to roll back a century of Wisconsin progressive history and take away collective bargaining rights from almost all of the state's public sector workers. However the trade-union-led challenge to his policies has transformed Walker into a champion of the politics of the Republican right nationwide. If he wins in Wisconsin, other Republican state governors will be encouraged to follow down the path he is blazing. As a result Walker too is benefiting from huge financial support from committed conservative donors such as the immensely rich brothers, David and Charles Koch. In the last three months, he has raised 13 million dollars whereas his Democratic opponent, Tom Barrett, the mayor of Milwaukee – whom he defeated in 2010 – has managed less than one million.

What has to be recognised, however, is that the controversial policies Scott Walker is trying to drive through in Wisconsin are part of a well-organized and well-funded national campaign to pass legislation everywhere in favour of pro-business, anti-Washington, policies. The American Legislative Exchange Council (ALEC), for example, funded by some of the world's largest corporations – Exxon, Mobil, Pfizer, Coca-Cola – provides Republican legislators with ready-to-go 'model legislation' that will reduce regulation, lower taxes, limit trade union power, and privatise everything from schools to prisons. Republicans in control of state legislatures simply adopt these bills and have them passed in their states. Only the market rules OK?

The Lugar and Walker cases indicate very clearly the direction in which American politics is heading. What is the result? An uncertain future in which Republicans and Democrats confront each other in an increasingly partisan and divisive manner. Last April, the *New York Times* columnist Thomas Friedman wrote an article headed 'Down With Everything' in which he argued that his country was moving from a democracy to a 'vetocracy'. His point is one that is shared by many other commentators and political experts. America's Founding Fathers created a system of checks and balances to ensure that no arm of government could amass too much power. But what has happened in the recent past is that the division of powers between the Presidency, Congress, and the Supreme Court, has been manipulated in such a way as to make it almost impossible for any important decision to be taken. The Founding Fathers did not conceive of a situation in which the nation's elected representatives would refuse to co-operate in any circumstance. Implacable division has replaced any kind of joint action. The result is Friedman's dangerous 'vetocracy'.

Would the re-election of President Obama in November make any difference? Not necessarily. Such an outcome could even reinforce division. What is required is fundamental change in the political process. The Senate's current filibuster rule – meaning that 60 votes out of a 100 are required for any legislation to be passed –

has to be amended. A simple majority of 51 has to be reinstated as the figure which allows most legislation to pass. The system of senatorial 'holds' — which, among other forms of disruption, allows a single senator to block legislation — has to be revised. The Supreme Court (hopefully with more liberal appointments made by the second-term Obama) has to look again at ways of limiting the amount of cash lobbies are allowed to spend on behalf of their employers, while also limiting the amount pressure groups can spend on influencing the outcome of elections. Finally in a situation where, as former Wisconsin senator Russell Feingold recently put it, Americans will soon be choosing between 'Republican and Democratic toothpaste', America's parties need to move towards the recognition that their primary duty is not to pander to their electoral base, but to attend to the nation's good. Without these or similar changes, it is hard to be optimistic about the future of American democracy.

7 US Elections 2012

Many of my American friends greeted Mr Obama's election to the presidency in 2008 with a mixture of great excitement, huge enthusiasm, and high hopes. They felt that, after years of disappointment and failure, their country had rediscovered its true identity. No comparable reaction has followed President Obama's re-election in 2012. Feelings this time have been much more muted. They are pleased at the outcome, but their mood is more one of relief and satisfaction than of joy or great expectation. Perhaps they are being too downbeat.

Obama's re-election was in fact a remarkable achievement. With unemployment running around eight percent, and the economy recovering extremely slowly from the crash of 2008, with a great many Americans no better off after four years of Obama government, and many of the high hopes of an Obama presidency unfulfilled, the election was one that the Republican Party might well have expected to win. After all in the 2010 midterm election they had swept to power in the House of Representatives, and were they not on course to take control of the Senate in 2012? The White House seemed to beckon.

So what went wrong? Once the polls closed, and the first results began to emerge, it became clear that the Fox News version of America and its discontents was lacking in reality. President Obama and his administration may not have got things right all of the time – but often enough to deserve respect and be given another chance to move on. The alternative was a great unknown. Which Romney would eventually occupy the White House? The ultra conservative of the election primaries, or the liberal Republican of the presidential debates? In the end America settled for Obama's four more years. His winning total of electoral votes was only two states down on 2008. The Republicans retained control of the House of Representatives, but with a much-reduced majority. In the Senate the Democrats actually improved their position. The Democratic success was surprisingly comfortable.

So from a Republican perspective what went wrong? I'd suggest that it is the outcome in the US Senate that provides the probable answer. As I noted above, after their success in the 2010 midterm elections, the Republicans fully expected to gain control of the Senate in 2012. The existing situation was that the Republicans held 45 seats, the Democrats 53 (including two 'independent' Democrats – Bernie Sanders in Vermont and Joe Lieberman in Connecticut). This time round the Democrats were defending 23 seats, the Republicans only 10.

The result? The Democrats lost one senator (in Nebraska) but gained three. The impressive Elizabeth Warren won back Ted Kennedy's former seat in Massachusetts; Joe Donnelly defeated Richard Mourdock in Indiana; Angus King, who ran as an independent but will caucus with the Democrats, won in Maine. The latter two results are particularly significant. I wrote some time ago about the situation in Indiana. The incumbent senator was the elderly Richard Lugar. Lugar had been re-elected several times and was universally expected to win again. However over the years he had sometimes been willing to co-operate with Democrats in the Senate to get things done. Tea Party hard-liners decided he was too liberal, forced a primary election, and with the help of large amounts of out–of-state money, got rid of him. So doing, they allowed a Democratic victory in a safe Republican seat.

The contest in Maine only occurred because the sitting Republican senator decided against running again. Olympia Snowe, a popular winner in the past, was a liberal Republican. She was retiring from the Senate, she said, because it had become hopelessly partisan. In other words she felt no longer at home in an increasingly right-wing Republican party. Maine voters appear to have agreed with her and cast their votes accordingly.

The same pattern of rejection of Republican extremism occurred in other senatorial races. Claire McCaskill's seat in Missouri had long been regarded as highly vulnerable; Republicans were certain that they would gain it. But Todd Akin, the Republican candidate, expressed views on rape and abortion of so extreme a nature that his defeat became almost inevitable. Exactly the same fate befell Richard Mourdock in Indiana – the candidate wished upon the Republican Party by the Tea Party-supporting Super Pac millionaires. His views too on rape and the 'right to life' proved too outlandishly extreme for the majority of voters.

So the 2012 Senate results deliver two positive messages for all of us who were concerned about the direction in which American politics appeared to be heading. First, Tea Party right-wing extremism has suffered a major setback. If it is to have a chance of returning to winning ways, control of the Republican Party has to be taken back by moderates and centrists. I know there are already voices arguing that Romney failed because he wasn't enough of a 'severe conservative'. Obama won the popular vote by only 2% – therefore the electorate, they argue, is as polarised as before. But this is misleading. The Republican popular vote included those who were persuaded by the Romney of the presidential debates and the closing weeks of the campaign – the pragmatic, business-like Romney who had apparently forgotten that he had ever been a 'severe conservative'.

Secondly, the Senate outcome suggests that big money doesn't after all always win. In Connecticut, the Republican candidate Linda McMahon spent 42 million dollars of her own money, but still didn't win. In a series of other states – Ohio, Virginia, Wisconsin – Super PACs spent millions upon millions of dollars attacking Democratic candidates. But to no avail. Indeed in Wisconsin Tammy Baldwin became the first openly gay candidate to be elected to the US Senate. Of course America should get back to finding ways of limiting the amount of money that can be spent on electoral races. But it is good to see that victory cannot always be simply bought.

8 Republican Manoeuvres

Jim DeMint, the Republican junior senator from South Carolina, recently announced that he is resigning from the US Senate. He is to take up the position of president of the Heritage Foundation, a very conservative Washington think-tank. In terms of promoting legislation or making things happen in the Senate, DeMint's senatorial career has not been an illustrious one. But he is well-known as a founding father of the Tea Party movement and so of the rightwards lurch of the Republican Party that helped it gain control of the House of Representatives in 2010, but ensured its defeat in the presidential election of 2012. His Republican PAC, the Senate Conservatives Fund, raised and spent $5.48 million in the 2010 and 2012 elections. However in the 27 races in which he was involved, his preferred candidate won only eight times. As a result, some Republican senators see him as largely responsible for the loss of winnable seats in Nevada, Colorado and Delaware in 2010, and in Indiana and Missouri in 2012.

American political commentators are offering different explanations for DeMint's decision to resign his Senate seat. The most cynical is money. A hugely successful fund-raiser for the causes he supports, his salary as a senator brought him around $174,00 a year; his predecessor as Heritage Foundation president earned $1.1 million. But presumably his motives are not quite so simple as this. His own explanation is this: 'I've decided to join the Heritage Foundation at a time when the conservative movement needs strong leadership in the battle of ideas'. What this means perhaps is that he suspects that the battle of ideas within the congressional Republican Party is being lost by neo-conservatives like him.

In a December 2012 *New York Times* article, the well-regarded commentator David Brooks listed what he sees as evidence of a new, more pragmatic Republican approach in the current political stand-off over crucial fiscal and budgetary issues. DeMint's decision to move from the Senate to an organization 'known more for ideological purity and fund-raising prowess than for creativity, curiosity or intellectual innovation', he sees as evidence of Tea Party supporters choosing to 'self-ghettoize'. And of course it is true that DeMint's was one of the loudest Republican voices protesting against any kind of cross-party agreement to prevent the US falling over the so-called 'fiscal cliff' on January 1st. Nonetheless, despite the stubborn opposition of DeMint and his Tea Party colleagues, a deal was finally done between the two parties to prevent that disastrous outcome. At the same time recent speeches by such leading Republicans as Senator Marco Rubio (a possible presidential candidate in 2016) and the Tea Party's favourite congressman Paul Ryan, at least hint at the emergence of a form of vote-winning 'compassionate conservatism' presumably anathema to the extreme right of the party.

So is the post-2012 Republican Party actually moving back towards the conservative centre in American politics? As it happens, the decision over who will replace DeMint in the Senate may help to clarify the answer to this key question. The post-resignation protocol means that the governor of South Carolina – the Republican Nikki Haley — gets to name a temporary successor to DeMint. That person will then be able to contest the seat in the 2014 electoral cycle. A clear front-runner for the position quickly emerged: Tim Scott who was elected in 2010 to the House of Representatives from the Charleston, South Carolina, district. Remarkably, Scott is the first African-American Republican to represent a South Carolina constituency since 1897. Should he be allocated the vacant Senate seat, he would become the first ever African American Senator from South Carolina, and the first from a southern state since the Reconstruction days of 1881. And he would be the only African American in the current Senate.

Nominating Scott, the Republican Party would be signalling its readiness to begin to move towards the diversification that most commentators see as essential if the party is ever to broaden its appeal to the range of minorities that increasingly make up the American electorate. On the other hand, if the widely favoured Scott is passed over, there will be no shortage of voices insisting that the Republican Party has learned nothing from its 2012 defeat, and remains the party only of its traditional white, male, base. On January 2nd, 2013, the Republican Party finally made its decision clear: in Washington on that day, Tim Scott assumed office as a Republican Senator from South Carolina.

9 Flying in America

Soon after I arrived in my friend's house in Florida he showed me – with great glee – the cover of a recent issue of the *New Yorker*. It depicted the inside of an airliner with passengers trying to stow their luggage into the overhead lockers. The main figure was a big man trying desperately to push home what was clearly the rear end of his car – two wheels of which were already blocking the passenger aisle. I looked at the cover, thought it was oddly funny, but certainly didn't share Bill's glee. The truth was I didn't really get it. And the reason I didn't was that I lacked any understanding of the context within which the cartoonist was working. A few more internal flights within the US changed all that – and perfectly illustrated the general principle that works of art, including comic ones, often depend upon a shared experience in their audience for their point to be communicated effectively.

My re-education began at the airport in Columbia, South Carolina. (A small airport but one of the most attractive I've ever encountered: surroundings with a carefully manicured landscape of grass and trees and water, and immaculately white buildings with striking blue glass – producing an almost elegant effect.) I checked in at the Delta desk. Did I have luggage to hand in? Yes, one bag. Very good sir, that will be 25 dollars. I was amazed. Crossing the Atlantic with United/Continental, and continuing to fly with them internally, there had been no question of paying for luggage. My travel agent had failed to mention anything about payment when organizing my Delta flight. Still, there it was. Another 25 dollars on my card.

It turns out that many of America's major airlines, facing increasing fuel bills in particular, are trying to balance their books by charging on internal flights for passengers' luggage carried in the aircraft's hold. What has been the result? An understandable increase in the number of passengers cramming their luggage into the kind of cases and bags which just match the dimensions for stowage in the overhead bins. The consequences in the case of an aircraft with a full complement of travellers are both obvious and inevitable: the bins are jammed and crammed to bursting point. One way of dealing with this problem is for an announcement to be made just before take-off suggesting to passengers that their carry-on luggage can be placed in the hold, without charge, with the proviso that it can be collected on arrival on the ramp outside the aircraft thus avoiding the delay of waiting at baggage reclaim.

Inside the aircraft the problem remains. Sitting in my seat waiting to leave Fort Myers for Newark and my connecting flight to Glasgow, I watched in horror as across the aisle yet another bulging case (with wheels) was trying to be stowed into an already full locker. A powerful, sweating man pushed and heaved, but the wheels of his case remained jutting out. He tried to force the lid shut again and again. I waited on edge, suppressing a groan, waiting for something to split or break – already imaging the consequences, the inevitable delays, missing my Glasgow flight... But with one final shove, the bin clicked shut. I was not the only one to sigh with relief. Seconds later a woman decides she has to recover something from her bag in the bin. The flight attendant remonstrates with her, advising her to leave well alone. But she insists and reopens the locker. Of course she is quite incapable of closing it. The attendant refuses to help. A burly passenger steps up and goes through the whole routine again: repeated almighty attempts to bang the lid shut. I hardly dared to look. But finally click shut it did. I made it to Newark on time.

Now the *New Yorker* cover with the man trying to stow his car comes completely alive for me. Comically but pointedly it hits the spot perfectly. This is flying today in the USA.

10 Death in Arizona

In recent days I've been contributing to a Facebook debate over the horrific shootings in Tucson, Arizona. And the first point I'd like to make is that its appearance on Facebook in no way prevents the discussion from being serious, searching and intelligent. The main point at issue is the rightness or wrongness of linking the twenty-two year-old Jared Lee Loughner's killing spree to the vitriolic and violent language and imagery which now characterises the confrontation between left and right in the US. Is Loughner to be seen as no more than a deranged loner, a mentally unstable individual, who regarded himself as a political terrorist, and finally acted upon his delusional obsessions? Or is it entirely legitimate to see a connection between his deadly behaviour and a political climate in which right-wing rhetoric in particular seems to be perilously close to promoting violence against those its exponents see as the enemy?

One contributor argues that there has been an unseemly rush to judgement in associating Loughner's lethal actions with the attitudes and opinions of some Tea Party members and commentators on the extreme right of the Republican party. 'The clamour to blame Palin', he writes, 'is a massive distraction and a form of political opportunism'. By 'a massive distraction' he means that the real issues raised by the tragic episode – and the ones we should focus on — concern gun control and mental health intervention. And indeed both of these should be major concerns. For anyone who is not living inside the gun culture of Arizona, it is barely credible that Loughner was able to walk into a store last November and buy over the counter, no questions asked, a powerful automatic pistol. This is a young man who had recently been suspended from college for erratic and inappropriate behaviour and told that he would not be readmitted until he had undergone a mental health check that showed he would not be a danger to himself or others. But then it is now lawful for anyone in Arizona over twenty-one to carry a concealed weapon in public without any kind of licence. Its legislature is even debating the notion that professors and students on college campuses should be allowed to carry concealed weapons — presumably so that they can defend themselves from mad assailants. Ironically of course, Congresswoman Giffords, Loughner's main target, supports the right of all Americans to bear arms, as the second amendment to the constitution is alleged to legitimise. Of course, fighting a Tea Party Republican in a very red state, the Democratic Giffords probably had little alternative. (However, on other major issues such as abortion, Obama's healthcare reforms, and the need for legislation to provide a road to citizenship for illegal immigrants, she is defiantly liberal.)

Whether or not it was merely 'political opportunism' for commentators on the left to raise the question of a link between this outrage, and the use of violently vituperative language by those on the right, is much more problematic. I'm inclined to think not. As more and more details begin to emerge, it is clear that this attempted assassination was a political act. Gabrielle Giffords was the target. She was shot first. It is only the other victims who were shot at random. Recovered from Loughner's house are materials saying 'I planned this'; 'Giffords'; and 'my assassination'. A well-known far right activist in Milwaukee — David Wynn Miller — is now saying that much of the material in Loughner's rambling videos comes from his website: he's 'repeating things I've said for years'. (Things about government's mind control, alternative realities, grammar and truth, the gold standard, etc.) So however mentally unstable Loughner was, his disturbed state of mind ran along political lines.

Trying to explain the violence itself, one 2011 Facebook contributor reminded us that 'political assassination is a tradition in America'. And it is hard to disagree. One British prime minister has been assassinated: Spencer Perceval in 1812. Four American presidents have been killed in office: Abraham Lincoln in 1865, James Garfield in 1881, William McKinley in 1901, and John F. Kennedy in 1963. There have been at least twenty other attempts to kill sitting or former presidents. One scholar investigating the role of violence in American politics has come up with a figure of 4381 deaths as a result of racial conflicts, labour disputes, bombings, riots, lynching, etc., in the twentieth century alone. Congresswoman Giffords' father, asked if his daughter had any enemies, replied "Yeah, the whole Tea Party." Given that Sarah Palin, on the day that the Obama healthcare bill finally passed, told her supporters, 'Don't retreat. Reload', he may well have a point.

11 America at the OK Corral

Lee County, in southwest Florida, boasts a strikingly modern general hospital. Entering through its gleaming glass doors, one finds oneself in a spacious atrium extending all the way up to the roof of the many-storeyed building. The ground floor, flooded in Florida sunshine, enjoys a grand hotel-like atmosphere with a colourful range of shops, cafes, services, and even a post office. For the European visitor there is only one jarring note. It takes the form of a notice, posted by the entrance doors, which reads: 'No Weapons Allowed in this Building'. No weapons in a hospital? Surely an unnecessary reminder? But this is Florida, an American state which, like the rest of the US, is in love with guns.

900,000 Floridians have a permit that allows them to carry a concealed weapon. Among them is the mayor of Tampa, Bob Buckhorn. In August this year, Tampa will host the Republican National Convention at which Mitt Romney will be endorsed as the Republican candidate for the presidency in November's election. To help ensure the safety of all those attending this Republican jamboree, Mayor Buckhorn (a Democrat) asked Florida's Republican governor, Rick Scott, to issue an executive order banning the carrying of guns in downtown Tampa for the duration of the convention. Governor Scott refused, insisting that such a temporary ban would 'surely violate' the American Constitution's Second Amendment concerning the right of citizens to bear arms.

Allow me at this point to insist that Governor Scott, like the National Rifle Association and the millions of Americans who share the governor's understanding of the Second Amendment, is utterly wrong. The Second Amendment exists in two forms. As originally passed by Congress, it reads: 'A well regulated militia, being necessary to the security of a free state, the right of the people to keep and bear arms, shall not be infringed'. In the version ratified by the different states, and authenticated by Thomas Jefferson, it reads: 'A well regulated militia being necessary to the security of a free state, the right of the people to keep and bear arms, shall not be infringed'. The comma-less second version makes it certain that Jefferson saw the right to bear arms as unequivocally linked to the maintenance of militias. Jefferson was the leader of the anti-Federalist party that aimed to limit the power and authority of the federal government. Hence it was opposed to the creation of any form of established church, a central bank, or a standing army – which explains the patriotic need to guarantee the existence of citizens' militias. Even with the inclusion of the comma, however, the Second Amendment, in the view of many Americans – and I agree with them – cannot be read as justifying the right to bear arms entirely independently of the militia context.

Nevertheless, there is no denying that it is Governor Scott's understanding of the Second Amendment that prevails in today's America. That is why the number of firearms currently existing across the USA is between 250 and 280 million – not far short of one gun for every individual citizen. But that last statistic is somewhat misleading. The most recent figure indicates that 47% of adult Americans have a gun in their house or on their property – while some of that number own more than one weapon. In 1993, as many as 57% of Americans owned guns. In the following years there was a downward trend, but the figure never fell below 40%. In more recent years the trend has been upwards, leading to the current 47%. A similar pattern emerges in the figures for and against gun controls. In 1993, 57% of Americans were in favour of gun controls; in 2009 that figure was 46%. In 1993, the figure for those who favoured the protection of the right to own guns was 34%; in 2009 it was 46%.

In the majority of American states, changes in the laws relating to the ownership, carrying, and use of guns have all been in the direction of more de-regulation. Florida, for example, has enacted a Stand Your Ground law. What this means is that a citizen may use force, even lethal force, in self-defence without any obligation to retreat first. The law provides a defence, or even immunity, from criminal charges or a civil suit, arising from such use of force. Half of America's states have already adopted the so-called 'Castle' doctrine – which says that there is no duty of retreat if one's home is thought to be in danger of attack. 'Stand Your Ground', 'Line in the Sand', and 'No Duty to Retreat' laws greatly extend the circumstances in which citizens are free to use attack as a form of self-defence.

While I was recently in Florida, the whole nation was suddenly engrossed by a case involving the Stand Your Ground law. On February 26th, George Zimmerman, the community watch coordinator of a gated community, encountered in disputed circumstances an unarmed, seventeen-year-old African-American called Trayvon Martin, and shot him dead. Zimmerman's defence will certainly invoke Florida's Stand Your Ground law. The NRA, which of course worked in support of the passing of that law, has already come out in its favour, describing self-defence as a 'natural right' which deters murderers, rapists, and robbers. In any event, Trayvon Martin's untimely death is but a single example of the terrifying total of gun-related deaths in contemporary America.

We are all familiar with the dire results of random shootings in American schools and colleges such as the 13 dead in Columbine in 1999, and the 32 dead in Virginia Tech in 2007. But nothing changes as a result. On February 27th, 2012, a Chardon High School pupil shot dead three fellow-students; on April 2nd, 2012, seven students were shot dead in Oikos, a Korean Christian university in California. On the rare occasions when crimes of this nature occur in the U.K, the call is always for tighter gun control laws. In today's America the most vocal lobby makes the opposite case. Students and professors on campuses would be better protected, we are told, if more of them carried concealed weapons – which they would be able to use in self-defence. At present 37 American states issue permits for the carrying of a concealed gun; some others allow a concealed gun to be carried without a permit. Only Illinois currently forbids handgun carrying in any form – and it is considering change. (Of course most states have long allowed the open carrying of guns.)

Hard to believe as it is – the carrying of a concealed gun has become so unexceptional across America that clothes manufacturers are beginning to cater for the habit. Trendy designers are rushing to make provision for doing so into a fashion statement. Men may no longer fear that their girl friends will complain about a lack of style in their gun-packing gear. The *New York Times* informs me that the old-fashioned, military 'tactical' look is being replaced by what is called 'concealed carry' or 'covert fashion' styles. Isn't it nice to think that today's potential shooters will be so much better dressed than the original participants in the gunfight at the OK Corral?

12 Gun Controls

I wrote some month ago about America's love affair with guns drawing attention to how, in recent years, state legislation in particular has made it easier for people to own and carry guns. The National Rifle Association and its supporters have been increasingly successful in arguing against any legislation that could be seen as infringing the right of American citizens to bear arms. Not any longer. In the wake of the dreadful massacre in 2012 in the elementary school in Newtown Connecticut, in which a young man used an automatic rifle to shoot six adults and twenty children aged between six and seven, President Obama has finally decided to act.

Congress will be asked to pass legislation controlling both what kind of weapons can be bought and who can buy them. The 1994 ban on the sale of Army-style assault weapons, the renewal of which the NRA successfully campaigned against ten years later, will be tightened up and reintroduced. Magazines will be limited to ten bullets. Background checks will become universal for firearms buyers, and there will be stricter scrutiny of buyers with mental health problems. Predictably the NRA is up in arms. (Naturally we assume this is only a metaphor. Unfortunately extremist fringe group supporters are already arguing that patriots should prepare for armed conflict to 're-institute the basic tenets of the Constitution'.) The organization's vice-president responded to the White House proposals in typically hyperbolic style: 'I warned you this day was coming and now it's here. It's not about protecting your children. It's not about stopping crime. It's about banning your guns...period'. (The organization's own reaction to the Sandy Hook school crime was the suggestion that every American school should have armed guards or armed teachers.)

It's highly improbable that a version of fortress America will be imposed on the American school system, but how good are the chances that the gun controls now favoured by President Obama will be passed by Congress? My guess is about fifty-fifty. At the moment public opinion polls are quite strongly in favour of the proposed legislation. But is that anything more than an emotional reaction to the Newtown outrage? The President's opponents will be hoping it is, and thus will try to delay any decision by Congress for as long as possible. The longer the debate drags on, the more likely the pro-gun lobby will be able to water down or even defeat the changes proposed.

The successes which that lobby has enjoyed in recent years proves just how powerful, well-funded, and well-organized it is. Many sitting members of Congress owe their seats at least in part to the financial help their campaigns received from the NRA. They will find it difficult to be seen to be favouring the introduction of new gun controls. Then consider what is already happening in some Republican controlled states. In Wyoming a bill has been introduced in the state legislature designed to block any federal government-supported legislation on firearms. Incredibly, any federal agent seeking to enforce, say, a ban on assault weapons, would face a five-year prison sentence. A similar bill has been filed in Tennessee, making it a crime to enforce federal gun legislation. Texas is jumping on the same bandwagon. In Mississippi, Governor Bryant, claiming that Washington has no jurisdiction over weapons made in Mississippi, has announced that his state will block all federal gun measures. Of course none of this madcap legislation is likely to be enacted or enforced. But it serves its purpose. It sends an unequivocal signal to pro-gun voters, pro-gun lobbyists, and the NRA, that these Republican legislators remain firmly on message.

It's also true that in recent years in the US there has been more in the way of deregulation of existing gun laws rather than any increase in gun controls. Nearly every state has now made it legal for citizens to carry guns concealed or unconcealed, with little in the way of background checks or permit requirements. The American Legislative Exchange Council, a conservative organization of state lawmakers, supported financially by the NRA, formulates these more permissive laws that individual states can pick up and proceed to pass into legislation. Five states now allow guns to be carried on university and college campuses. In Wisconsin it's legal for those sitting in the public gallery of the state assembly to carry guns. And the ALEC and the NRA are firmly behind the increasingly popular 'stand your ground' legislation that permits people to shoot and kill whomever they believe is threatening them.

More troubling still in the context of President Obama's decision to throw all his executive power behind the push for new and significant gun controls is the attitude of those many Americans who believe that the right to bear arms is the only ultimate guarantee of their individual freedoms. Republican Tim Donnelly in the Californian legislature goes so far as to suggest that gun ownership has God's approval. 'Guns', he says, 'are used to defend our property and our families and our faith and our freedom, and they are absolutely essential to living the way God intended for us to live'. When a duly elected representative of the people of California can articulate such views, perhaps it is not surprising that there is evidence of a growing tide of misinterpretation and dangerous misrepresentation of the new legislation the president has in mind. A hard core of gun lovers insist that a fascist, tyrannical president is determined to override the Constitution, invade their homes, and take away their guns. That this is nonsense doesn't appear to matter. A sheriff in a western state has announced in a published letter: 'I refuse to take firearms from law abiding citizens, and I will not turn law abiding citizens into criminals by enforcing useless federal gun control legislation'.

Of course, I know such views are not those of a substantial majority of ordinary Americans — including most of those who recently voted to give President Obama a second term. New York State has already passed new gun control legislation. Illinois, Connecticut, and New Jersey are moving in the same direction. California, which already has stricter controls than most states, is introducing more far-reaching proposals — specifically in relation to the sale of ammunition. The Governor of Colorado, reversing his previous position, is proposing universal background checks, and the use of the state's mental health system, in determining gun ownership. So there is some momentum in favour of new gun controls. But it is equally clear that there are those both inside and outside Congress who will never agree. Last Saturday, 19th January 2013, was declared Gun Appreciation Day, and thousands of people attended pro-gun rallies across a range of states. As this debate intensifies in coming weeks, one thing we can be sure of: those responsible for the president's safety will be on high alert. What I have called America's love affair with guns originates in the almost mythological status accorded to the Second Amendment to the Constitution. In a subsequent article I propose to look again at this legislation approaching it from a new (Scottish) perspective.

13 Gun Controls Again

Scotland has recently been remembering the day twenty years ago when Thomas Hamilton, carrying four loaded handguns, walked into the gymnasium of Dunblane primary school, and proceeded to shoot sixteen five-year-old children and their teacher, before killing himself. The reaction to that event in an appalled U.K.was swift. Two new laws were passed completely banning the private ownership of handguns. In the year after Dunblane there were 59 killings with such guns across the U.K. In 2014 that figure fell to 29. An editorial in *The Guardian* newspaper goes on to point out that, by contrast, in the USA twenty years ago, 13,252 people died from firearms injuries; the figure for 2015 was 13,393. The writer then alludes to a recent incident in which a mother – who happens to be an ardent believer in the right of American citizens to bear arms – was shot in the back while driving her car by her four-year-old son who found a loaded revolver on the seat beside him. To my mind it is patent that gun laws – meaning the absence of gun laws – represents a more despicable and terrifying blot on American democracy than racism, sexism or any other 'ism' you care to mention. Gun-related deaths are thirty-two times higher in the USA than in the rest of the civilized nations in the world. How has this situation come about? And why is a grief-stricken President Obama unable to do anything about it?

The key answer as we all know is the Second Amendment to the constitution of the United States. Not that you would guess it from the actual wording of that brief amendment which runs as follows: 'A well regulated militia, being necessary to the security of a free state, the right of the people to keep and bear arms, shall not be infringed'. In 1792, amending the constitution of the new country they had just brought into being, the founding fathers of America, in the First Amendment, sought to guarantee its citizens' freedom of speech, religion and the press. What was their second overriding concern? Surely beyond question it was to protect the security of the nation they had created. The new USA had no regular or standing army. And many of the founders were against the creation of one, believing that a federal army could easily become a source of tyrannical power in the land. Yet across the Atlantic Ocean, the war-torn world of the 1790s was a dangerous place. How was American freedom to be protected? The answer of course was by the maintenance of a militia – a people's army. The functions of the federal government, defined in Article 1, Section 8 of the American constitution, include the organizing, arming, and disciplining of the Militia to execute the 'Laws of the Union, suppress Insurrections and repel Invasions'. The Second Amendment with its specific reference to national security and the role of the militia seems largely to reinforce the meaning of the original article: the need to maintain the militia clearly remains the heart of the matter.

Today however, America's politicians, commentators, lawyers, and the public in general, believe that the Second Amendment means something entirely different: the right of all Americans to keep and bear arms. This is the meaning that that now is automatically and slavishly reiterated whenever the issue of guns in America is raised in any form. But the truth is that this interpretation became the orthodox one only in the very recent past. For over two hundred years the American legal system ultimately rejected the idea that the Second Amendment guaranteed the right of individual Americans to bear arms. It was only in 2008, in the case of the District of Columbia v. Heller, that the Supreme Court, in a 5-4 vote, supported the opinion, written by the late judge Antonin Scalia, which overturned past legal history – 'two centuries of precedent' in the words of Michael Wardman in his 2014 book *The Second Amendment* – and set up the new orthodoxy concerning the right to bear arms.

Of course, as we shall see, the campaign in favour of this interpretation has a history of its own, but just how revolutionary it was in legal terms is suggested by a comment made by one of America's most illustrious Supreme Court Chief Justices back in 1991. In that year Chief Justice Warren Burger suggested that the gun lobby's interpretation of the Second Amendment 'is one of the greatest pieces of fraud, I repeat the word fraud, on the American people by special interest groups that I have ever seen in my lifetime. The real purpose of the Second Amendment was to ensure that state armies – the militia – would be maintained for the defence of the state. The very language of the Second Amendment refutes any argument that it was intended to guarantee every citizen an unfettered right to any kind of weapon he or she desires'. So how could an interpretation of the Second Amendment dismissed as rubbish by the Chief Justice of the Supreme Court in 1991 become accepted as the correct one by the Supreme Court in 2008?

A recent article in the *New York Times* provides a convincing answer. In the 1970s members of America's National Rifle Association began to campaign in a range of states for changes in their constitution that would protect the right of individuals to keep and bear arms. Over the following years these campaigns became more and more successful. The result was that by 2008 – when the Supreme Court had to rule on the meaning of the Second Amendment – most states had already legislated in favour of protecting gun ownership. In these circumstances it seemed reasonable to argue that the federal government should endorse what was already happening in many states. Then the NRA's strategy also involved the setting up of generous research grants and prizes available to scholars prepared to provide legal and academic arguments for the reinterpretation of the Second Amendment as protecting the right of individual Americans to keep and bear arms. Finally, the US Congress, and the presidency, had to be persuaded to endorse the same understanding. Just how successful this campaign was is indicated by the appointment of John Ashcroft as the country's attorney-general in 2001. Ashcroft was a member of the NRA, and under him the Justice Department changed its position in favour of the association's interpretation of the Second Amendment. The verdict in the Heller v. the District of Columbia case in 2008 thus was the result of a well-organized and well-funded campaign supported both by enthusiastic gun owners and gun-manufacturers.

The question remains of how Judge Scalia was able to persuade another four Supreme Court judges that his revolutionary interpretation of the Second Amendment was the correct one. Appointed to the court in 1986, Scalia quickly emerged as a deeply conservative legal voice. He consistently opposed all laws that made distinctions on the basis of race or gender or sexual orientation. Above all he rejected with considerable animus what he saw as politically liberal attempts to regard the American constitution as evolving alongside changes in society at large. Rejecting any form of 'updating the constitution', Scalia adopted the view that the only valid interpretations of the constitution should be based on the notions of 'originalism' and 'textualism'. The only factors that mattered were the intentions of the original framers – and if it was impossible to be certain what those intentions were, then the original public meaning of the words used provided the only reliable source for interpreting the constitution's meaning. A 'nothing but the words on the page' approach became the defining characteristic of the legal philosophy of Scalia and all those who shared his views.

Antonin Scalia no doubt was convinced that his new and revolutionary reading of the Second Amendment – that it did after all guarantee the right of all individual Americans to keep and bear arms — was wholly consistent with his commitment to originalism and textualism. In fact his opinion is nothing of the kind. 'Faux originalism' is how one senior judge described it. On the central issue of the relationship between the original sentence's two clauses — the state's security requiring a well-regulated militia, and the right of the people to keep and bear arms — he has almost nothing to say. And what he claims to be the original, hyper-literal meanings of all the key words in the amendment are far from being self-evidently true. Ultimately too there is an element of intellectual incoherence in his opinion. Towards its end, Scalia seems to forget about originalism altogether and writes as follows: 'nothing in our opinion should be taken to cast doubt on long-standing prohibitions on the possession of firearms by felons and the mentally ill, or laws forbidding the carrying of firearms in sensitive places such as schools and government buildings, or laws imposing conditions and qualifications on the commercial sale of arms'. If the right of the individual to keep and bear arms can be denied in all such cases, why is it unconstitutional for the District of Columbia to deny Heller the right to keep an unlocked, loaded handgun in his home? The truly revolutionary impact of the Supreme Court's 2008 ruling is still emerging. Despite Scalia's qualification, the carrying of firearms in such sensitive places as schools and university campuses and government buildings is becoming increasing common in many states. Guns are now allowed in psychiatric hospitals in Texas; in Florida hospitals have to put up signs saying the carrying of guns is forbidden. Deadly mass shootings, whether in the workplace, schools or colleges, cinemas, or anywhere else, seem to happen on so regular a basis, that they no longer take us by surprise. Of course, the Supreme Court decision in the case of the District of Columbia v. Heller is not responsible for this situation. But the impact of that ruling on gun controls in general is surely a significant factor.

Writing on the Second Amendment a few years ago I suggested that there was a neglected 'Scottish' dimension to the 1792 debate. In his 2008 opinion Judge Scalia does make fleeting reference to the English Bill of Rights of 1689 which said that 'the Subjects which are Protestants may have Arms for their Defence suitable to their Conditions and allowed by Law'. But inevitably he makes no reference to the in my view much more relevant historical fact that in 1792 Scotland was still denied the right to raise a militia. In 1708 the post-Union parliament passed a Scottish Militia Bill. But on the advice of her ministers, Queen Anne vetoed the bill because of doubts over Scottish loyalty. Even more significantly, in 1757 the British government's Militia Bill did not apply to Scotland. Scottish intellectuals deeply resented this decision: the Select Society in Edinburgh, to which nearly all the leading figures in the Scottish Enlightenment belonged, was renamed the Poker Club in order to promote the cause of a Scottish militia. Key figures in the debate over the Second Amendment in America in 1792 would certainly have been familiar with this history. James Madison, for example, a major architect in the framing of the American constitution and deeply committed to the role the militia should play, had been educated at the College of New Jersey in Princeton by its president John Witherspoon, one of the two Scottish signers of the Declaration of Independence. Thomas Jefferson, the original drafter of that declaration, had also been taught by a Scot. In his autobiography he tells us that at the College of William and Mary, it was from William Small, a graduate of Aberdeen University, he got his 'first views of the expansion of science, and of the system of things in which we are placed'. James Wilson, the other Scottish-born signer of the Declaration of Independence, taught law at the College of Philadelphia and went on to become a member of the very first American Supreme Court. Wilson too was an active participant in all the debates over the American constitution. All of these men would have been familiar with the fact that Scotland had been denied a militia. In passing the Second Amendment they were declaring their commitment to America's maintaining its militia. That was the only reason why the people's right to bear arms should not be infringed.

So what can be done to restore some degree of sanity to the debate over gun controls in America? As readers will know, the death of Judge Scalia means that the remaining eight Supreme Court judges – assuming none of them have changed their minds – are split four against four over the interpretation of the all-important Second Amendment. As the constitution empowers him to do, President Obama has nominated District of Columbia Circuit Judge Merrick Garland to fill the vacancy on the court. All observers agree that Garland is very much a middle-of-the road non-partisan nominee. In normal times his nomination would win Senate approval almost without opposition. But these are not normal times. The current Republican-controlled Senate is choosing to renege on its constitutional duty to debate and vote on the President's nominee. Many of us will be hoping that this behaviour will only help the election of another Democratic president in November. Should that be the case, we can begin to hope that the 2008 ruling on the Second Amendment will in due course be revised, and the long slow process of re-imposing sensible gun controls over American society be set in motion. Would James Madison and the other 'originalists' who passed the Second Amendment approve? Of course they would.

14 Gun Controls Yet Again

April 17th, 2013 was a black day for American democracy. That was the date on which the United States Senate voted to deny any strengthening of gun controls across America: no ban on military-style assault rifles; no ban on magazines holding more than ten bullets; no extension of background checks on gun buyers to include purchases made at gun shows or on the internet. No change of any kind. And this in the face of a powerful and moving campaign by members of the grieving families of Newtown, Connecticut, pleading for some kind of response to the Sandy Hook primary school massacre – and so many other similar outrages in recent history. But the Senate refused to budge. There would be no new legislation.

President Obama reacted angrily. It was 'a pretty shameful day for Washington'. Former congresswoman Gabrielle Giffords, grievously wounded in a shooting in Texas in which six others died, agreed. Seconds after the litany of negative votes in the Senate, she emailed: 'Over two years ago, when I was shot point-blank in the head, the U.S. Senate chose to do nothing. Four months ago, 20 first-graders lost their lives in a brutal attack on their school, and the U.S. Senate chose to do nothing'. Those senators who had voted against action of any kind had, she said, 'brought shame on themselves and our government itself by choosing to do nothing'.

The president's and the ex-congresswoman's outrage may well have been intensified by the fact that a week earlier, there had been just a faint glimmer of hope that this time progress on gun control might actually be made. A group of Republican senators, including Mitch McConnell of Kentucky, leader of the Senate Republicans, chose to introduce a motion which, if passed, would have meant there would be no debate and no vote on any form of gun legislation on the Senate floor. End of story there and then. Given the fact that opinion polls were unanimously indicating that the vast majority of Americans were in favour of new legislation – over 90% favoured extending background checks – I in Florida must have been merely one of millions of people across the country waiting disbelievingly for the result of the vote on this proposal to shut down debate of any kind. (In the case of this, and all subsequent votes – a result of the Byzantine procedures of the U. S. Senate – 60 senators, rather than a simple majority, had to vote in favour for any proposal to succeed.)

In the event, the attempt to cut off debate was defeated by 68 votes to 31. 16 Republicans voted in favour of debate, while 2 Democrats voted against. (One Democrat was too ill to vote.) Interestingly, of the 68 voting in favour, 21 turned out to have 'A' ratings from the NRA (the National Rifle Association, the hugely powerful pro-gun lobbying group, hostile to any form of gun legislation). More ominously, many of the 'yes' voting Republicans were soon making it clear it was one thing to vote in favour of debate, quite another to vote actually in support of new gun controls. So it turned out that those who had doubted there would be 60 votes in favour of changes in laws over guns proved right. The amendment banning assault weapons (which had actually been in place for ten years after 1994) was defeated 60-40; that banning magazines holding more than ten bullets fell 54-46; and even the attempt to extend background checks went down by the same 54-46 margin.

Given that President Obama was personally strongly committed to new legislation, and given too that there are only 47 Republican senators, how is it that the vote in favour of any of the proposed amendments never got above 46? The answer is simple. Too many individual Democratic senators, up for re-election in 2014 in such states as Alaska, Arkansas, Louisiana, Montana, North Carolina, and Virginia, voted in favour of self-preservation rather than preservation of the lives of fellow-Americans. They are largely senators in states which did not support Obama in 2012, and many of which have relatively small, rural-based, gun-carrying populations. Hence they no doubt felt vulnerable to the kind of attacks that the NRA, with its almost unlimited financial power, would inevitably launch against them, should they vote in favour of new gun controls.

The only winner then on April 17th was the NRA. The $500,000 it paid out on attack ads that single day, proved money well spent. So what — apart from its unlimited financial backing from the gun-making industry — is the source of the NRA's power? The answer, I'm afraid, is what has become the holy writ of the Second Amendment to the American constitution. Opponents of gun control endlessly repeat the shibboleth that nothing should be allowed to infringe the constitutional rights of citizens. What they mean is the right to bear arms allegedly guaranteed by the Second Amendment. Hard line Republican senators, texting in triumph after their success in the Senate votes, constantly referred to it as a victory for the Second Amendment. And the reality is that a large majority of Americans do honestly believe that that amendment gives them the inalienable right to bear arms. In fact, as I have argued here before, it doesn't.

Article 1, section 8, of the American constitution includes among the functions of the federal government, the organizing, arming, and disciplining of the Militia to execute the 'Laws of the Union, suppress Insurrections and repel Invasions'. The Second Amendment – 'A well-regulated militia being necessary for the security of a free State, the right of the people to keep and bear arms shall not be infringed' – seems in no way to alter or refute the original article. Rather it appears to reinforce it. In both formulations, the maintenance of the militia is clearly the heart of the matter.

A recent writer in the New Yorker suggests that 'as a nation, we're a little vague on what the Second Amendment's protections of a citizen militia mean for gun ownership today'. The trouble is, as the writer acknowledges, there is nothing vague about the NRA's take on that amendment: what it means is more or less unlimited access to firearms for Americans in all times and all places. Hence the organization's drumbeat insistence that gun controls amount to an attack on Second Amendment rights.

What should be emphasized, however, is that this is not an interpretation accepted by even the most conservative members of today's Supreme Court. Even the arch-conservative Antonin Scalia, who wrote the opinion in 2008 that led to the overturning of the District of Columbia' s ban on the carrying of handguns, agrees that the Second Amendment does not confer 'a right to keep and carry any weapon whatsoever and for whatever purpose'. Long-standing prohibitions on who may possess firearms, and where they may be carried, he said, should remain in place. But these qualifications have been to no avail. The NRA, alongside all the gun manufacturers and lobbyists, and the politicians they support financially (of the 45 senators who voted against all the proposals for new legislation, 42 had received financial support from the gun lobby) go on endlessly repeating the mantra that Americans have a constitutional right to bear arms.

Between the Newtown massacre last December 14th and April 17th, 3628 Americans have died in gun-related incidents. Every day, according to the *New York Times*, 270 American are killed or injured by gunshots. Given such frightening and tragic statistics, that those in charge of the governance of a nation should decide to take no action is scarcely credible. To my mind, a crucial first step would be a massive and relentless campaign to re-educate American citizens in the actual meaning of the Second Amendment.

15 March for our Lives

March 24th was one of the most extraordinary days in the history of American democracy. On that day between 1.2 and 2 million American children took part in eight hundred March for our Lives demonstrations across the country. They were protesting about the recent shooting of seventeen students and staff in the Douglas High School in Florida, and calling for the institution of new gun controls in their country. As we all know, lethal outrages of this kind have become an all too regular in the world's most iconic democracy. And the consequences have always been the same: anguished cries of outrage, horror, and revulsion. But nothing changes and no action is taken. The American legal and political system seems paralysed — to the bewilderment of the rest of the civilised world.

Has all this changed on March 24th? Yes and no. For the first time the victims have found a way of fighting back. The scale of the protest has been amazing and uplifting. And the fact that the marchers — as well as the speakers and organisers — have been high school students is quite extraordinary and surely ground breaking. The television pictures of the streets of Washington D.C. filled to overflowing with the vast mass of young marchers were unforgettable — and the thousands who turned their backs on the White House for seventeen silent minutes — one minute for each of the victims-made a dramatically powerful point.

However, a few days later, a *New York Times* reporter spoke to a seventy-seven year old man in a small Virginian town forty miles away. The man was the owner of some seventy-five guns. 'Every time something happens, everybody is hollering' he said. 'A couple of months it's in the news, and then it's gone'. Recent history suggests he has a point. But the seventeen-year old junior high school student in a nearby town disagrees: 'We're not going to get bored'. And across America the thousands of young people who agree with her are apparently quoting this lyric from the hugely successful musical 'Hamilton': 'This is not a moment, it's the movement'.

For the movement to succeed what is needed is a new willingness among young voters to get out and use their vote. In the last midterm elections only 20% of those between eighteen and twenty-eight actually did so – whereas 40% was the figure for those between forty-five and fifty-nine. Still more important is what the March for our Lives should aim to achieve. To my mind, minor changes in existing gun controls — raising the age at which individuals can buy guns, slightly more demanding background checks, a ban on military-style assault weapons, etc. are no longer the answer. What is needed is something much more radical and more dramatic. Something that in the end will amount to a transformation of American society's attitude towards the owning of guns.

Is such a change even conceivable? Or merely a hopelessly liberal dream? Well, former Supreme Court judge John Paul Stevens does not think so — and I agree with him. Stevens was one of the four Supreme Court judges who in 2008 voted against Antonin Scalia's interpretation of the Second Amendment – the interpretation that continues to prevail today. And in a recent contribution to the *New York Times* he proposed what I believe should become the rallying cry of the March for our Lives — backed by all the millions of Americans moved to tears by the sight of the young marchers. So what is the proposal? Nothing less than the repeal of the Second Amendment.

Is such a development even possible? Yes. There is a precedent. The 18th Amendment – meant to restrict the availability of alcohol in the US — was passed in 1919. Because it was doing more harm than good, it was repealed by the 21st Amendment in 1933. Today the existence of the Second Amendment is the fundamental source of the problem over the proliferation of guns in American society – which in turn leads to the gunshot carnage which shocks and appals so many of us. (Since just 1970 more Americans have died from guns –1.4 million — than in all the wars in American history — 1.3 million.) How has this come about? Because the amendment contains the phrase 'the right of the people to keep and bear arms shall not be infringed'. This has become the endlessly repeated mantra of those who resist all attempts to legislate for meaningful gun controls in America. Without it, they would have no case.

Are there grounds for repeal? Once again the answer is yes. Discussing gun controls in the past, I have more than once explained why the 2008 Scalia interpretation of the Second Amendment is both revolutionary and wrong. Because it takes no account of the amendment's opening phrase — 'A well regulated militia being necessary to the security of a free state' — the Scalia interpretation flies in the face of over two hundred years of American judicial history. Prior to 2008, the Supreme Court had always recognised that the Second Amendment had been about the maintenance of militias. The security of the new United States of America in the dangerous world of the 1790s was the issue the amendment addressed. Lacking a regular army, and reluctant to create one, local militias were the answer. This – and not some permanent right of citizens to bear arms – is the meaning of the amendment. Hence before 2008, as one scholar puts it 'there was no more settled view in constitutional law than that the Second Amendment did not protect an individual right to own a gun'. What is astonishing is how quickly since 2008 this historical reality has been forgotten. Over and over again, listening to or reading in today's media, I've heard it assumed that all Americans have always believed they have the right to bear arms. Nothing could be further from the truth.

In the course of his dramatic proposal, Judge Stevens quotes the words of Chief Justice Warren Burger in 1991 which are well worth repeating. Addressing those who were supporting what would become effectively the Scalia interpretation of the Second Amendment, the impeccably conservative Burger said: 'The Gun Lobby's interpretation of the Second Amendment is one of the greatest pieces of fraud, I repeat the word fraud, on the American People by special interest groups that I have ever seen in my lifetime'. And he goes on to say that the language of the amendment 'refutes any argument that it was intended to guarantee every citizen an unfettered right to any kind of weapon he or she desires'. Stevens clearly regards Burger's words as true today as they were in 1991. But that is not the grounds on which he bases his argument that now is the time to repeal the Second Amendment. Rather it is that the amendment is no longer required. The USA has the world's most powerful armed forces. It no longer needs militias. So it no longer needs the Second Amendment. So repeal it.

To change American attitudes towards gun ownership in the necessary radical fashion will take a generation or longer. The Second Amendment will not be repealed in my lifetime. But those who March for our Lives are very young. For them it could become a life-giving reality. They should go for it.

16 The Referendum

Will 2012 be the year of the referendum? Probably not. I suspect that the betting man's choice is 2014: conveniently late in the government's term of office, and on June 24th, the seven hundredth anniversary of the Battle of Bannockburn which, as we all know, sent the English home to think again. Braveheart Scotland in a blaze of patriotic emotion will vote overwhelmingly for restored independence. Still, that is more than two years away. In the meantime I suggest that 2012 is a good time to launch a debate on the independence referendum itself.

Initially at least most of us are inclined to regard referendums as archetypically democratic. They make it possible for the voice of the people to be heard directly. Whatever the issue, a referendum, we assume, clearly establishes the general will. In relation to questions of constitutional change in particular, however, referendums have had a somewhat chequered history. In the past bad people – Hitler and Mussolini among them – have exploited them to consolidate their power. Today dictators, heads of one-party states, and elected leaders determined to remain in power, continue to use referendums to give a veneer of democracy to their usurpation of power. Referendums, that is, may well be manipulated by governments for their own ends.

Perhaps more relevant to the Scottish case are other possible objections to the use of referendums to settle constitutional issues. James Madison's identification of the danger of 'the tyranny of the majority' is particularly relevant in the case of referendums. A yes/no referendum is undeniably a somewhat blunt decision-maker, unresponsive to the rights of minorities. More serious are the issues of timing and wording. In our present circumstance, both of these will be in the hands of the Scottish government. Our first minister continues to insist that referendum legislation will not be introduced until late in the current parliamentary session. Why? Because he wishes to hold the referendum at the time when he has the best chance of winning it. And the same circumstance applies to the wording of the question (or questions) asked. The issue here is whether this is an appropriately fair and democratic way of proceeding?

Most serious of all is the enormous gap between the consequences flowing from a 'yes' or a 'no' vote in the referendum itself. A majority 'yes to independence' vote, however narrow, produces change on a monumental scale: three hundred years of Scottish history are reversed and the United Kingdom is no more. If on the other hand the majority of voters reject the independence option, what is the consequence? Virtually nothing. The Scottish National Party suffers a setback, a loss of momentum, but that is all. It continues its campaign for independence, and hopes for a better result next time round. In 1980 the Parti Quebecois' referendum on Quebec's secession from Canada was defeated by a margin of 59% to 40%. However, fifteen years later, a second referendum was lost by the narrowest of margins, 50.58% to 49.42%. (Since then the Parti Quebecois seems to have imploded.) A constitutional referendum, that is, readily morphs into a 'never-end-um'. To my mind at least, this lack of finality in a constitutional referendum is an issue that has to be recognized and addressed.

How can these difficulties surrounding the referendum issue be overcome or mitigated? I suggest the following proposals are worth debating. 1. The Scottish Government should agree to discuss the timing of the referendum and the wording of the question (or questions) with a representative body similar to the old Scottish Constitutional Convention. 2. Given that the issue is of such revolutionary importance, consideration should be given to requiring something more than a simple majority of those choosing to vote, for independence to be endorsed. A majority of registered voters might be a more appropriate requirement. 3. If a majority for independence is achieved, a second referendum confirming that decision should be held within six months by which time a detailed account of everything involved in the dissolution of the United Kingdom will have to have been laid out. 4. If the initial referendum results in a 'no to independence' vote, then the issue should be legally off the table for at least another generation – say forty years.

Of course the reconstituted Scottish Constitutional Convention could make recommendations on these and no doubt other points. But the debate should begin now.

17 Mr Cameron in Scotland

I am no fan of David Cameron. On the central issue of the British economy and the deficit I agree with those who argue that the Cameron/Osborne austerity plan has failed. The budget cuts are, as Ed Balls has maintained all along, too deep and too fast. It's time for Plan B. However, I have to say I found the prime minister's performance on his recent visit to Scotland not unimpressive. The debate over the referendum issue has at last been raised to something nearer the intellectual level which its importance demands.

The knock-on effects were immediately clear. On Newsnight Scotland, Joyce McMillan and the peerless Professor John Curtice of Strathclyde University were somewhat grudgingly prepared to admit that Mr Cameron had done well. The jokes were timely, and the tone was measured; the argument was lucid and well-presented; there was no scaremongering and no slip-ups. Even the personal, emotional case on behalf of maintaining the union was hinted at. Joyce McMillan was right to contrast this polished performance with the abysmal shortcomings of the leaders of the Scottish unionist parties. But what struck me most about the Newsnight discussion itself was the altogether more adult level at which it was pitched. The real issues of the referendum were at last under intelligent and serious discussion. Of course there will be those who say that has nothing to do with the prime minister's intervention. I'm not so sure.

So in terms of the disputed issues, where was the Cameron contribution most significant? Clearly over the issue of whether there should be one or two questions on the referendum ballot-paper. The case for a single in/out question was made simply and forcefully. The central question is about independence: does Scotland wish to remain in or withdraw from the United Kingdom? That and that alone is what the referendum should decide. But it was here that the prime minister made his new and most provocative contribution. If the Scottish people vote in favour of the union, then according to Cameron, the whole issue of further devolution would be immediately up for discussion. Mr Cameron insists he is a friend of devolution, supports it, and thinks it could be made to work better. 'Devo-max', he suggests, would remain on the constitutional agenda.

It seems to me at least that the prime minister has played a skilful game here. For once he has wrong-footed Scotland's first minister. Mr Salmond's response was rather weak. The prime minister, he suggests, has to tell us what exactly 'devo-max' would mean. But Mr Salmond and his party have a problem here. They are in favour of independence and so are against 'devo-max'. But failing independence, they are in favour of 'devo-max' — which is why, whatever it is, they want it on the ballot-paper. And in any event how explicit have the first minister and the SNP been about what exactly independence itself means? The Scottish people, it seems to me, has only the vaguest of ideas of what a vote for independence, and the disentangling of Scotland from England, Wales, and Northern Ireland, would really involve.

Having had time to digest David Cameron's intervention, commentators sympathetic to the SNP position have come up with a response based on events in the 1970s. Writing in the *Guardian*, for example, Lesley Riddoch complained that Cameron had not 'promised' increased tax-raising powers for the Scottish parliament in the event of a 'no' to independence. And she goes on to argue that his plan 'overlooks Scottish history'. What she means is that at the time of the 1979 devolution referendum, the then prime minister, Sir Alec Douglas-Home, promised a better devolution bill than the one then on offer. A promise of course on which he did not deliver. Ms Riddoch ends by apparently agreeing with a blogger who describes the Cameron offer of further but unspecified powers as 'insulting'. That, she writes, 'may be the conclusion of many Scots.' On the other hand it may not. How many Scottish voters today are actively recalling the Douglas-Home promise? I have to admit that, involved as I was in the 1979 debate, it is not exactly something that springs readily to mind. How many of Scottish sixteen and seventeen-year-olds, whom the SNP are so anxious to enfranchise, will have even the slightest idea of who Alec Douglas-Home was? The challenge of Mr Cameron's intervention is in no way damaged by this appeal to a forgotten past. It deserves serious attention at least.

18 The Union

A recent issue of *The Observer* included a three-page feature entitled 'What future for the Union?' The subheading read as follows: 'Following the dramatic triumph of Alex Salmond's SNP in May's Holyrood elections, the future of the 200-year link between England and Scotland has never been more hotly debated. Here, some of Scotland's best-known writers reflect on the state of this sometimes-vexed marriage and wonder what independence might mean for their beloved country'. You would have thought that someone on the paper's editorial team might have noticed that the writer of this introductory statement had managed to lose a whole century of Anglo-Scottish history, but despite this inauspicious opening, the feature itself does raise some interesting questions.

The five 'best known' Scottish writers who contribute to the 'hotly debated' subject are: Iain Banks, Janice Galloway, Shena Mackay, A.L. Kennedy, and David Greig. Given the prominence of the marriage metaphor as a key to defining the Anglo-Scottish relationship, it is perhaps just as well that concern has been shown over gender balance among the contributors. But isn't it at least probable that in choosing authors the editorial team would have been concerned about achieving balance of a different kind. Debates always have two sides. So surely the feature would include authors inclining to favour the case for independence, alongside others leaning towards the view that the union should be maintained?

So what in fact do we find? Well, all five contributions are undeniably serious, thoughtful, and carefully considered. Iain Banks comes first. He suggests it was Thatcherism, embraced by the English, rejected by the Scots, that marked a growing divide within the United Kingdom. 'Suspicious', as he says, 'of the populist, divisive appeal of nationalism', and still prepared to 'sacrifice an independent Scotland for a socialist U.K', he is nonetheless prepared to be a 'pragmatic voter' for an SNP more left-leaning than the Labour Party. So while recognising all the problems of 'poverty, ill health and religious tribalism' facing an independent Scotland, his conclusion is that having 'our destiny at least largely back in our own hands again' is something we could do — 'And that we should'.

Janice Galloway comes next. She confesses 'that being asked "what being Scottish means to me" makes me break into a sweat'. 'Britishness', on the other hand, is easy to understand in geographical and cultural terms: 'I like it here. I feel I belong'. Nevertheless, 'it never occurs to me that Scotland an England are one.... We were separate countries with different political make-ups'. So political separation under the SNP is 'a serious alternative'. Like Iain Banks, she has reservations: 'If Scottish self-esteem... is reflected in our statistics for liver disease, drug-addiction, obesity, young male suicide and domestic abuse, we're not in great shape'. But 'Scottish priorities for solutions to health, education and social mobility might be different'. Finally the SNP 'needs to establish that its motivation has more in common with *Small is Beautiful* than "Scotland the Brave" if it is to be the credible answer'. But 'if it can — and that's a big if — the risk of secession will be worth taking'.

Sheena Mackay, though born in Edinburgh, has spent most of her life in England. She sees much in the U.K. that makes her despair, but, as she puts it, 'at a time in history when everything everywhere seems to be getting worse, should it be broken up? I don't know'. Sometimes, she says, she has wished she could belong to 'a Scottish community of writers' — because 'it would be nice not to feel an outsider'. But at least in terms of the arts, her conclusion is that 'separation from England' wouldn't 'make much difference to the Scots'.

A.L. Kennedy seems to share something of Sheena Mackay's ambivalence, her contribution making frequent use of the word 'perhaps'. An independent Scotland could flourish, but she's far from sure. She admires Mr Salmond, but she is much less confident about the party he leads. She holds the view that 'few would represent the SNP landslide as an endorsement of independence'. But given Westminster's poor performance, 'the more attractive and untraumatic independence may seem'. Her conclusion is that perhaps the marital relationship between Scotland and England 'has had its day'.

David Greig agrees. An 'old-fashioned social democrat', a former Labour Party supporter, once inclined to equate nationalism with 'racism, xenophobia, inward-lookingness and militarism', he now believes that Scottish Nationalism is a 'civic, social-democratic, multicultural movement'. So he tells us that, like a majority of Scots, he will vote for independence — including independence "lite". And here the marriage metaphor makes its final appearance: 'The Union is an unhappy marriage. I think it's time we both sat down and said it out loud — it's over'.

So at the end of the feature where are we? Well, if we score Sheena

Mackay as a fence-sitter, then the result is Independence 4 ½, the Union ½. Of course we have no idea how the contributors were selected, but should we be surprised by this perhaps 'unbalanced' outcome? In my opinion, probably not. In the half-century covered by James Robertson's novel *And the Land Lay Still*, (1945-1995), Scotland's political nationalism has always been deeply indebted to Scotland's cultural nationalism. How many of today's 'best known' Scottish writers and artists are not cultural nationalists? 'Damn few' is perhaps the right answer. And if Scotland's chattering class is indeed persuaded that independence is now more or less inevitable – as Kenneth Roy and Walter Humes have recently been suggesting in the *Review* – then it would not be surprising if the surviving few Unionists choose to keep their heads down – and out of *The Observer*.

19 Glasgow Referendum

'Do you agree that Scotland should be an independent country?' Invited to answer the 2014 question in a mock referendum on 21st February, 967 students at Glasgow University answered Yes, 1614 answered No. I was surprised by this result. Walking around the campus on referendum day, I noted that the Yes campaign was clearly winning the poster war. Resources from supporters of the Yes campaign nationally had clearly been forthcoming. The desire to get the kind of result they were looking for also meant that, on voting day and earlier, major figures in that campaign were out on campus rallying support. No less a figure that Nicola Sturgeon, architect of the SNP's Yes campaign, and deputy leader of the party in the Edinburgh parliament, turned out – as did Patrick Harvie, leader of the Scottish Green Party. The novelist Alan Bissett presumably represented the commitment of Scottish artists and writers to the cause of independence.

However, the best efforts of the great and the good proved unavailing. In a turnout of 10%, 62% of students voted No, only 38% voted Yes. The referendum had been organized by the Dialectic Society at the university, aided by the range of political parties, and by both the Glasgow Student Union and the Queen Margaret Union. Unlike me, the organizers were delighted by the level of student participation. On reflection, however, I think they were right and I was wrong. In my mind had been the turnout at actual elections. In that context, 10% would have been a pitiful figure. (Though something close to it was apparently achieved at some of the recent elections for police commissioners in England!) But this was only a mock referendum – an elaborate game, not a serious undertaking. To get two and a half thousand students to make their way to one of the unions to take part in such a game was a considerable achievement.

Why then was I surprised by the result? An Ipsos Mori poll carried out in the same week as the Glasgow referendum revealed that among 18 to 24 year-old Scots, 58% would vote Yes in 2014. So solace there for the SNP despite its Glasgow defeat – but my surprise at the Glasgow result had nothing to do with this poll. Speaking to some students before the referendum took place, I got a clear impression of the major consideration that might lead them to cast a Yes vote. In question was the direction of U.K. politics in the post-Thatcher era — specifically, a perceived rightward shift in all three mainstream political parties. Crucially, Tony Blair's New Labour party is seen as having turned its back on its socialist origins.

So given that even a victory for Labour in the 2015 U.K. election does not guarantee any move away from free-market politics and all that that implies, what is the left-leaning young person — and are not most young people left-leaning — going to do? The answer of course is to follow a left-of-centre SNP into an independent Scotland. In an independent Scotland, market forces will no longer be allowed to determine public policy. In an independent Scotland a traditional form of the welfare state will remain in place. In an independent Scotland ordinary people will live in a society committed to the values of fairness and justice for all. Surely an appealing prospect, particularly in the context of the now generally accepted premise that Scotland has always had a greater commitment to a kind of democratic socialism than the rest of the U.K.

Why then did the prospect of an independent Scotland fail to appeal to 1614 Glasgow students? Of course not all of those who bothered to vote were necessarily Scottish? Could students from England and other parts of the U.K. have taken this opportunity to dissent from the break-up of a union that has lasted over three hundred years? Could the local politics involved in Glasgow's two separate student unions have been somehow involved? Did politically active Glasgow students — Labourites, Lib Dems, Tories — simply follow their party's line and vote No? I really don't know. Do we perhaps need to remember that in democratic Scotland in 1955, the Conservative Party won 36 of the 72 Scottish seats? (Even in the famous 1945 Labour landslide, Scotland elected 30 Tory MPs.) Again, I don't know.

In the wake of the referendum's outcome, the vice-convenor of the SNP's youth wing was critical of the Yes campaign's involvement in the campus contest. As a result he was expelled from his post — allegedly because of pressure from senior party members — but subsequently reinstated. This does hint — perhaps not surprisingly — at a degree of panic within the party. I suspect that the Yes campaign — like me — expected it would win the Glasgow student referendum. Perhaps Alex Salmond was wise to postpone the national referendum for as long as possible.

20 Halfway There

The first half of the referendum campaign is almost over. Will it turn out to be a game of two halves? My view is that it certainly needs to be, because so far at least the whole thing has been more or less a non-event. Spending time in London recently – and meeting a wide range of people from academics to artists and simply old friends – I was expecting to be cross-examined about what was going to be the outcome. But not a bit of it. No one seemed the least interested, and the issue never seemed to be worth a mention in the local media. (To be fair, in the course of the hours of screen-time given over to the royal baby, one commentator did remark that he might grow up in a United Kingdom constitutionally different to the present one.)

What about within Scotland itself? I certainly have no sense that the constitutional debate has grabbed people's attention. Newsnight Scotland does its best to keep us interested, but the rest of the Scottish media seems less than enthusiastic. If it's in the kitchen at all, independence remains very much on the back burner. Only once in my lifetime have I experienced real political excitement over the outcome of an election: the contest over the Glasgow Hillhead parliamentary seat in the by-election of March, 1982. This was the occasion on which Roy Jenkins gained the seat for the recently formed S.D.P. in a close, three-way struggle with the Tory and Labour parties. (Hillhead had always been a Tory seat since its creation in 1918.) The turnout at 76.4% – slightly higher than at the previous General Election – reflected the enormous interest the by-election produced. Public meetings were crowded, posters sprouted everywhere, canvassing was intense – this was political engagement and political excitement of genuine intensity. Okay there is still a year to go: plenty of time for the independence debate really to catch fire. But 2014 has other multiple distractions – elections to the European Parliament in May, Glasgow's Commonwealth Games in July, the World Cup in June-July (admittedly without a Scottish team competing), the 100th anniversary of the opening of WW I on August 4th, the Ryder Cup at Gleneagles later in September. Will the 600th anniversary of Bannockburn on June 14th be enough to ensure that the referendum will take centre stage in the public mind? Time will tell.

So halfway through, what is noteworthy about the existing campaign? Most striking perhaps is just how little movement there appears to be in the polling figures. The Yes campaign seems to be stuck at just over 30% – which suggests they are the ones who have the greater work to do to win on 18th September, 2014. Clearly there are on both sides a substantial number of voters whose minds are already made up. There are those for whom the case for Scottish independence is just self-evident. Scotland should be an independent country – end of story. Equally, there are those for whom the idea of breaking up the United Kingdom after more than three hundred years of togetherness is simply silly. Devolution is fine; separation a non-starter.

Then the pollsters tell us there is a category of voters who will vote wholly on the basis of self-interest. Which option they support will depend on the answer to the £500 test: if they believe they will be at least £500 better off in an independent Scotland they will vote accordingly – if they believe that independence will cost them £500 a year they will vote against it. (One suspects that at the end of the day neither side will have come up with an economic argument of such unimpeachable authority as to deliver a knock-out blow on this issue.)

So what of the undecided voter? Has either side so far come up with an argument that might win over a floating voter? The 'Yes' campaign of course accuses 'Better Together' of running an entirely negative one: what the SNP dismisses as 'scaremongering'. There is some truth in the charge. But I'd suggest understandably so. 'Better Together' is basically about defending the status quo. It really doesn't have to come up with some new vision of a very different Scotland. Its case is that we are better off more or less as we are: the future of an independent Scotland is full of doubts and uncertainties – a gamble not worth taking. The Yes campaign is in a very different position. It really does need to persuade us that the future of an independent Scotland is an attractive and irresistible one. To my mind at least it has come up with just one solid argument that some voters might find convincing.

What that argument arises from is the increasingly right-of-centre tendency of today's national Conservative Party. Scotland's rejection of the post-Thatcher Tory party has long been evident. So there is a case to be made that Scotland's electoral preference can no longer be reflected by the Westminster government. Add the rise of UKIP and the Conservative Party's increasingly anti-Europe stance, and the case that the SNP makes that only independence can guarantee a left-of-centre Scottish government is an increasingly persuasive one. If you are pro-Europe, anti-Trident, against economic austerity, and in favour of a just welfare state, your only option is to vote for Scottish independence.

However, whether the majority of Scots actually share such views is perhaps open to question. Many of us would like to believe that Scotland has a kind of built-in democratic bias. The idea is a widely-held and frequently-expressed one. In the recently published *Unstated: Writers on Scottish Independence*, 27 Scottish writers discuss the meaning of independence in anticipation of the coming referendum. (Alasdair Gray's now notorious settlers and colonists essay appears in the collection.) It's hardly a surprise to discover that the contributors are broadly in favour of independence – the chattering class of writers, artists, actors and academics have long been the most clearly pro-independence section of Scottish society. What is striking is the frequency with which the idea surfaces of Scotland being a naturally – or historically – a left-of-centre country, one 'predisposed to communality'.

Is this idea true? Is it worth remembering that in 1955 50.1% of the Scottish popular vote went to the Conservative Party? Then current figures for the circulation of newspapers in Scotland hardly suggests a notable left-wing preference among regular readers. Murdoch's Scottish Sun sells approximately 272,000 copies daily; the *Daily Mail*, 99,000; the *Daily Express*, 55,000; the *Daily Telegraph* and *The Times* both 18,000. So 462,000 right-wing supporting newspapers are sold daily in Scotland – almost exactly double the number of the left's popular Daily Record (234,000). Meanwhile the *Guardian*'s Scottish circulation reaches only 11,000 – *The Independent* a mere 3,000.

In any event the SNP clearly believes that there are 'Yes' votes to be won by reminding us that what 'Scotland opposes', 'Westminster imposes'. In its latest mailing to voters it tells us that 76% of Scottish MPs voted against more austerity cuts, 82% against higher VAT, 81% against welfare cuts, 91% against the bedroom tax. (Without of course mentioning that nearly all of these negative votes were cast by their major opponents – Scottish Labour Party MPs.) Still the political point is a good one and I'm sure the 'Yes' campaign will continue to make much of it in the coming year.

On the other there will be those who, while sharing the commitment to a communal Scotland, do not believe that the exact nature of political policy in the next few years is the real issue. For better or worse, the referendum will answer an altogether bigger question: whether 300 years of union should be rolled back to create a separate, independent Scotland. That for the long term is what is at stake.

21 SNP and SLP

Alex Wood argues with some passion in *The Scottish Review* 561 that Scottish Labour Party supporters should vote for independence in the coming referendum. The case he makes is a carefully considered one. He is anxious to be seen to be fair, accepting that a 'devo-max' option should be on the ballot paper even though he disapproves of it. Not everyone, however, will agree with the parallel he sees between the 'great historical issues' of Scottish independence and the Second World War. The issue in 1939-40 was stark, black and white — the British Labour Party had to decide either to resist fascism or stand aside and effectively capitulate to it. Scottish Labour supporters today surely see the independence issue as a hugely more complex one.

However, my own dissent from Mr Wood's case is based on the other central element of his argument. He seems to me to assume that the SNP would run Scotland in a manner wholly acceptable to the Scottish left. Indeed we are virtually asked to believe that in a post-independence Scotland, the SNP would shed its nationalist identity and emerge as the true Scottish Labour Party. Mr Wood believes that, compared to the present U.K, an independent Scotland would enjoy a more equal and less divided society, would be characterised by a less market-oriented social order, would maintain a high level of tax-supported public services, and pursue a less aggressive foreign policy.

Well perhaps so. But then again, perhaps not. As things stand, I'm not aware of the SNP campaigning, as it should be doing if Mr Wood is right, in favour of the centre-left Scotland he wishes to see created. Such signs as there are — are not particularly encouraging. Mr Wood mentions Britain's outdated feudal institutions — but an independent Scotland will apparently retain the monarchy. He tells us that the British economy has been in decline for the last sixty years. But if an independent Scotland is going to remain within the sterling area, ultimately controlled by the Bank of England, how will things change? Finally it is a touch disappointing to see Mr Wood referring to the 'long imperialist history' of the British state without acknowledging that Scotland profited immensely from its more than willing participation in the British Empire.

22 Post-Referendum Blues

A few weeks back I was suggesting that the long drawn out referendum campaign we are experiencing is doing more harm than good. My point was that the effect of the increasingly bitter exchanges and accusations between the two sides is the entrenching of division, the driving of the two sides further and further apart, and that it is difficult to see how after September 18th, whatever the result, Scottish society can return to any kind of working togetherness. In recent days, a similar view has been expressed by other observers.

A few nights ago, I heard a supporter of the Yes campaign arguing in a television interview that the growing bitterness was all the fault of the destructive negativity that characterised the No campaign. Supporters of the union were constantly implying that Scotland was too weak to stand on its own feet – this was the source of the bitterness problem. The speaker may have a point, but it is clearly one a long way short of the whole story.

A voice that cannot be accused of bias of any kind is surely that of the Rev Sally Foster-Fulton, head of the Church of Scotland's Church and Society committee. Concerned over the tone of the referendum debate and its consequences, she recently suggested that 'regardless of whether it's Yes or No, on 19 September there are going to be some elated people and some devastated people'. What needs to happen, she believes, is that even before the referendum result is known, efforts should be made to rebuild some sense of national unity. Invited to comment, spokesmen for the two sides in the campaign were characteristically bland. Better Together said 'our job is to persuade people and not berate those who don't' [agree with us]. The Yes response was that 'debate should be free from hostility and negativity'.

The trouble with these platitudinous responses is that they do not address the problem. The campaign so far has been full of 'berating' and not short of either hostility or negativity. The evidence is so blatant that it does not need repeating. Suffice it to say that we are already in a situation where individuals – particularly individuals with any kind of public profile – are unwilling to express a view on the referendum because they know all too well what kind of reaction their opinion – whatever it is – is likely to provoke. The Scottish government makes much of how the Scottish referendum campaign – apparently like most things Scottish – is in a class of its own, showing the rest of the world just how large issues of constitutional change can be handled by a mature democracy. Unfortunately so far it has had little to say about how freedom of expression in that same campaign is seen by many voters to be under serious threat.

Of course it's possible that those of us concerned about the long term consequences of the polarising of public opinion over the future of the United Kingdom have got it wrong. Gerry Hassan, in his 'Sceptical Scotland' article in last week's *Review* (April 9th) clearly thinks so. He does not deny there is a problem, and reminds us of the various kinds of division which seem always to have characterised Scottish society. But he thinks we exaggerate: 'the vociferous, combative, almost quasi-militaristic Scotland is a tiny minority. Most of our nation is not currently divided into two warring camps, and nor will it be post-18 September'. The point is a fair one, but I would be a lot less confident about the post-referendum situation — particularly if the result is a close one. Gerry himself, in the conclusion to his article, does not play down the scale of the possible problem: '...bringing about change', he writes, 'requires building alliances, listening and empathising with people we disagree with. Never have such qualities been more required than in the Scotland of 2014'. The problem surely is that in the current situation such qualities seem to be in very short supply.

Still perhaps the great majority of voters will wake up on September 19 and think, win or lose, thank goodness that's all over, now let's get back to normal. Alistair Carmichael, however, currently Secretary of State for Scotland, is the latest big name to express concerns overt the lasting damage to Scotland's sense of shared, communal identity which this referendum campaign may be causing. But he too seems simply to be hoping for the best: 'one thing must be the same the day after the referendum' he says, 'we must all still be friends and family'. The question is, will willing it — however strongly — actually make it happen?

At the time of the Treaty of Union of 1707, easily the most popular way of describing the new relationship between Scotland and England involved the metaphor of marriage. In the pamphlet wars of the period, both those in favour and those against the union, reverted again and again to the marital analogy. In terms of gender it was universally agreed that a feminized Scotland was the bride, England the suitor. For those in favour of the union, the marriage was a happy one based on shared affection and companionship; for opponents the marriage meant a patriarchal loss of Scotland's freedom and power.

Given the long history of the marriage metaphor, it is not surprising to find 'divorce' deployed to describe what the Yes campaign really means. The first minister and his party are reluctant to accept the relevance of the term. (Even 'separation' is not their vocabulary choice.) Mr Salmond insists it is only the political union that will go — the social union, and more or less everything else, will remain just as before. Perhaps it will, but my inclination is to side with the eighteenth-century pamphleteers in this context: marriage or divorce is what is on offer on September 18th. Of course a divorce can be amicable. But with so much at stake, it often turns out to be very much the reverse. I am fearful that the combative, aggressive tone of the referendum campaign is going is making reconciliation in any future situation increasingly difficult to achieve.

23 Looking Back

A student at Edinburgh University in the early 1950s, I knew there were a few people who were committed to a movement called Scottish Nationalism. Its leading figures were the poets Hugh MacDiarmid and Sydney Goodsir Smith. But like all my student friends, I did not take it seriously. In both political and cultural terms, it was very much a fringe activity. If you had told me then that in the 21st century the Scottish National Party would become the government of a devolved Scotland – and that in 2014 no fewer than one and a half million Scots would vote to secede from the United Kingdom — I would have thought you were deluded or crazy.

But no delusion, last week it actually happened. So there is no denying the extraordinary success of the nationalist movement. The tiny, insignificant band of believers in the Scottish nationalism of my student days, has become a great army that came close to occupying and creating a new independent Scotland outside the United Kingdom. And inevitably there are many voices arguing – as, anticipating the situation we are now in, they argued throughout the campaign — that failure to actually win this time is in no way the end of the story. Mr Salmond himself, in his resignation speech, made it clear he is of their number. 'The campaign continues', he said, and 'the dream shall never die'.

Well, this may be so, but I'd like to suggest there is an alternative scenario. In October 1995, in a second referendum on the issue, the supporters of an independent Quebec came fractionally close to winning. The margin by which this Yes vote for an independent Quebec was defeated, was a tiny 1.16 percent. But what has happened to that independence movement in the years after that marginal defeat? Given the even greater degree of autonomy that Quebec has been allowed — what we are calling 'devo max' — the case for independence appears to have lost its appeal. It is no longer high on the political agenda, and there is no prospect of another referendum.

Could this pattern be repeated in Scotland? If the extra powers promised to the Edinburgh parliament are duly delivered, it seems to me to be entirely possible. If so, in historical terms, the result of the current referendum may turn out to have been the high point of the Scottish Nationalist movement.

There are other reasons why this might be so. September 18th 2014, was an ideal day for achieving a Yes vote in favour of Scottish independence. It really was a golden opportunity. And I don't just mean minor matters such as the recent 700th anniversary of Bannockburn, and the successful Commonwealth Games in Glasgow. A whole range of circumstances made this a perfect moment on which to hold a referendum on the independence issue.

The U.K's coalition government in Westminster, for example, has been responsible for a whole series of 'austerity' measures which have been deeply unpopular in Scotland (and of course elsewhere as well). The farcical bedroom tax has been only the most egregious example of this folly. But the existence of such legislation provided Yes campaigners with all they needed to prove that the only way forward towards a fairer and more compassionate Scotland, was to break the link with Westminster altogether. The U.K's commitment to so-called 'illegal wars', the huge sums to be poured into retaining Trident, the threat to our continuing membership of the European Union — these and other issues played into the hands of those arguing that achieving an independent Scotland was the only way to repudiate all such eventualities. And of course the fact that there is only a single Scottish Tory MP in the House of Commons made it easy for the Yes side to argue cogently that we are ruled by a party for which we did not vote. In short, the current political situation across the U.K, was almost an ideal one in which to persuade many disaffected Scottish electors that voting for independence was the only way to show their total rejection of the politics of Westminster. In last Saturday's *Guardian*, Ian Jack made exactly this point in a colourful image: 'From the separatist position, the referendum could hardly have had a more fortuitous context; there was so much bad stuff to leave behind. Here was a lifeboat...'

Then, in addition to this general circumstance, the Yes campaign had going for it, in a big way, the particulars of the referendum arrangements. In what sense? First, the concession that the vote on independence would be postponed for over two years. The SNP and the Yes campaign made brilliant use of the opportunity so carelessly afforded by this decision. Over two years a grass roots campaign of unparalleled strength was efficiently built up. So it was that in the closing weeks before voting day, the streets of much of Scotland seemed so firmly in the hands of Yes supporters that a victory for them seemed inevitable.

Second, for reasons that remain uncertain, Westminster tamely agreed that for this one election, 16- and 17-year-olds would be allowed to vote. The SNP undoubtedly imagined that such a concession would be to their advantage. How far it actually was, is not entirely clear, but the chances are that at least a majority of young voters will have voted Yes.

Third, and even more extraordinary, was Westminster's agreement to the referendum question: 'Should Scotland be an independent country?' When the Yes campaign learned that this was to be the question on the ballot paper, they must have hardly believed their luck. It might well have been the question they themselves would have chosen. No mention of separation, division, disunion. Just independence. How many people are in favour of not being independent? What is the opposite of independence? Subservience? Colonialism?

What I'm suggesting is that the combination of the factors I've been describing meant that the Yes campaign was ideally placed to win. Why did it peak at 45%? I really don't know. There were many people like me – with a father from Gloucestershire, whose whole working life was spent in Scotland, a wife from Cambridge, who until her untimely death did her selfless best for her students at a Scottish university, and a son working and living in London – for whom it was simply unthinkable that Scotland and England should become foreign countries. And then of course there was Gordon Brown....

In any event it is just possible that September 18th's 45% will prove to have been Scottish nationalism's greatest achievement. Of course some time in the future another referendum is possible – that is the nature of (and the problem with) the referendum scenario. But I cannot imagine that the context and arrangements will ever again so favour a positive outcome. Lessons will have been learned in Whitehall. The hubris and stupidity of 2014 will not be repeated. It may well be true that the dream of independence will never die. But the day on which that dream could have been transformed into reality, may already be in the past.

Part Eight

Cultural Moments

The contents of this section do not really need any introduction. The cultural moments I describe and assess here concern most standard forms of artistic creation. I've tried to arrange them according to genre. Thus the Section begins with TV and radio, and goes on through film, drama, music, art, and literature. The final entries concern the Nobel prize-winner William Faulkner and his possible visit to Gatehouse of Fleet. If any reader can throw any light on Phyllis Falkner (1895-1991), please contact me.

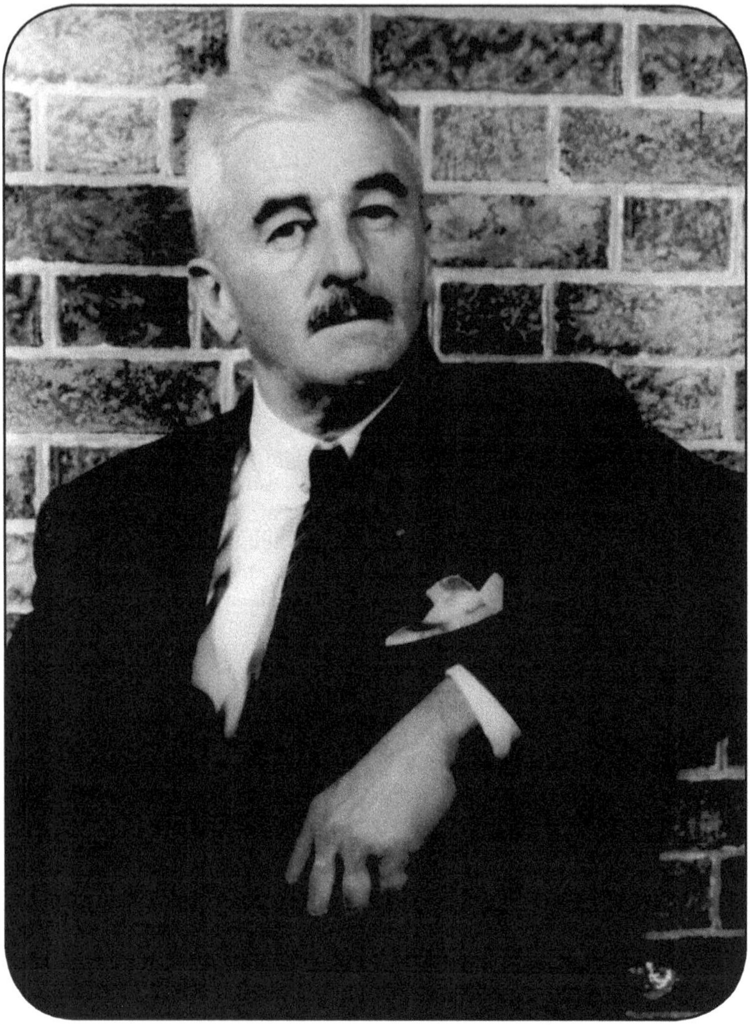

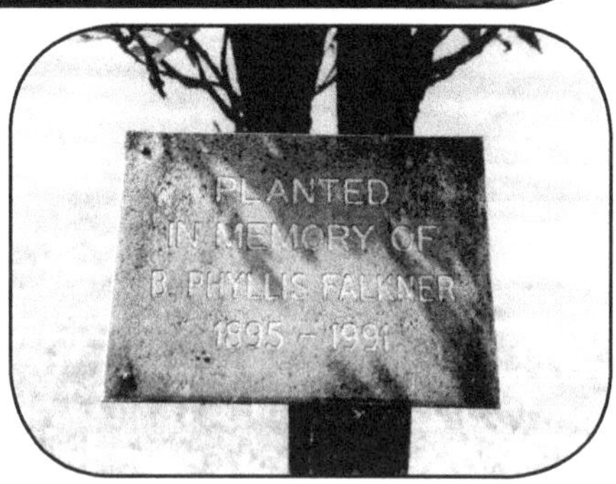

William Faulkner, and, right, tree plaque in memory of Phyllis Falkner

1 Jettison Top Gear

How I wish Steve Coogan (aka Alan Partridge) had it right when in a recent *Observer* he told the BBC's Top Gear team: ' big viewing figures don't give you impunity – they carry responsibility'. But unfortunately all the evidence is against him. As far as the BBC's top brass is concerned, big viewing figures do indeed give Clarkson and his sidekicks both impunity and the freedom to go on dismissing 'responsibility' as a weasel word used only by 'sandal-wearing vegans with beards and no sense of humour'.

Our media critics and commentators routinely tell us that in this country we are happily free from anything equivalent to America's shock jocks on radio and television. Glenn Beck, Russ Limbaugh, and Bill O'Reilly are given free rein on Fox News to rant and rave, defaming and abusing those they regard as their 'liberal' enemies. Well that's America for you. It couldn't happen here. But it does. On the BBC. On Top Gear. Three middle-aged white men can rant and rave, defame and abuse Mexico and Mexicans. And the BBC bosses tell us there's no problem. Just joking. (Odd that the Mexicans don't seem to get the joke.)

In recent times a range of broadcasters have lost their jobs having been caught out using offensive or demeaning language or articulating deeply prejudicial points of view: Carol Thatcher, Russell Brand, Jonathan Ross and, more recently still, the Sky Sports commentators, Gray and Marks. To my mind Clarkson has a record of offensiveness that far outstrips any of them. This is the man who thought it was acceptable in 2009 to tell Australia that the British prime minister was a 'one-eyed Scottish idiot'. Having got away with that, perhaps it's not surprising that a few months later, during a recording of the Top Gear show, he called Gordon Brown 'a silly cunt'. I could go on, but there's no need. Clarkson's self-preening stupidity is breathtaking, but the BBC goes on pretending he's a cuddly national treasure.

Why? Because of course viewing figures do provide impunity. Top Gear is popular world-wide. It makes money. Should the BBC have any concern over the version of contemporary British culture the programme communicates? Apparently not. The world can take a joke. (Apart from Mexico that is.) Well I disagree. In my experience the BBC does have a great reputation across the world: but not for the kind of macho posturing on show in Top Gear.

Post-Mexico, the time has come to say enough is more than enough. The BBC should scrap Top Gear. And here's a thought. Why not use the programme's no doubt enormous budget – along with the no doubt still more enormous salaries of its presenters – to preserve the BBC's international reputation by maintaining its threatened World News Service.

2 A History of the World

A History of the World in 100 Objects on BBC Radio 4 has been trumpeted to us as a major cultural event. Fronted and largely narrated by Neil MacGregor, Director of the British Museum, the programme was heralded by an hour-long special on BBC 2's Culture Show on January 18th, 2010. This we are assured is no less than 'a landmark project', Radio 4 at its best, and both radio and television continue to bombard us with previews of the unmissable next fifteen-minute episode. Critical comment has been unanimous in its praise, and I have no doubt at all that the programme will not lack acclaim over coming weeks and months.

Facing all this positive enthusiasm, one hesitates to ask even the mildest of questions about the intellectual viability of such a hugely hyped programme. But however far out on a limb I may be, I'd like to make two comments on the episodes so far broadcast: one general, one specific. First, what kind of history of the world can be produced on the basis of 100 objects? Not, I'd suggest, history as it is normally understood: history based on documentary evidence, on records and written sources. Rather what we have here is history as speculation. The single object exists, but what the pre-historian makes of it is largely speculative. There is no other evidence. Archaeologists and pre-historians find and detail tiny fragments of human activity that may date from the remotest of pasts; but the conclusions they come to about the people or society that used them are not, in my view at least, strictly historical. Not historical at least in the sense that the work of historians of the French Revolution or the American Civil War is historical. Admittedly the thinkers of the Scottish Enlightenment, seeking to understand how human society developed and progressed, invented what they called 'conjectural history' — conceding by the term that hard historical evidence in support of their theories was difficult to come by. Before speculating about the emergence of a sense of beauty in prehistoric man — on the basis of the Olduvai Handaxe and its appearance — Neil MacGregor and the participants in his programme should have made a similar concession.

The hand-axe is also relevant to my second comment. Episodes two and three of the programme focused on the Olduvai Stone Chopping Tool and the Olduvai Hand-axe, both found in the Rift Valley in Africa. The hand-axe, we were told, is 1.4 million years old. The object focused on in episode four was the carving of the Swimming Reindeer, dated at 13,000 years BC. Self-evidently the consequences for human development of the creation of tools, on the one hand, and of a work of art, on the other, are immense. But I am hugely puzzled by the time scale. Compared with the eternities of time between 1.4 million years ago and 13,000 BC, all the other 90 odd objects that define the history of the world have been produced in the blink of an eye. What happened in the enormous black hole between episodes three and four? What about evolution? Should not such questions have been addressed?

3 'The Killing'

In 2011 I'm a member of a cult. Unwittingly of course. Because I've always thought of cults as very bad things. People sitting on a peak in Darien, waiting for the world to come to an end at the appointed hour. (I always wonder what they say to each other when the time has come and gone and nothing has happened.) Or more horrifically I remember Jonestown in Guyana in 1978 and the murder/suicide of nine hundred ordinary Americans, members of the so-called People's Temple. Or the Moonies and their mass marriages. Or Scientology. Or many, many more.

But of course the cult I'm a member of is something entirely different. Five or six weeks ago I was at home on a Saturday night casually checking on what the television had to offer in the way of entertainment. I belong to the generation that used to have at most four TV channels to choose from, and when all programme-makers regarded the Saturday night audience as looking for the lightest of light entertainment. So my expectations were not high. But something on BBC4 caught my eye: the first episode of a Danish detective mystery called 'The Killing'. Danish? A Danish thriller? Surely not I thought. But then I remembered that Copenhagen is only a bridge away from Sweden and illumination blazed in. Everyone knows that in the last few years Scandinavian writers have become top of the pops in the genre of detective fiction. Ten years ago a departmental colleague recommended to me the Wallender novels of Henning Mankell, so more recently I've been able to look on with a sense of knowing superiority at their growing popularity, and the huge success of the TV adaptations including the BBC's version with Kenneth Branagh as Wallender. Then came the quite extraordinary worldwide success of the Stieg Larrson trilogy 'Millennium'. The character of Wallender has much in common with that of Ian Rankin's Rebus. But neither Mankell nor Rankin had been able to create a female character as intriguing as Larsson's Lisbeth Salander. More recently still, Norway has enlisted in this Scandinavian takeover with the crime novels of Jo Nesbo taking their place in the bestsellers' list.

Given all this, I thought, why shouldn't BBC4 have reasonably decided that Denmark had something good to offer? So I settled down to watch.. And I was right to do so. 'The Killing ' is great television. The format is unusual. At 9 and 10 o'clock BBC4 shows two consecutive episodes of the programme. So next Saturday episodes eleven and twelve – out of twenty in total – will be broadcast. Twenty hours devoted to the investigation of a single crime: the kidnap, rape and murder of an adolescent girl. It is only halfway through, so who can say what one's final verdict will be? But its power to grip is beyond question. Obviously it moves slowly, but it's all the more realistic as a result. Avenues of investigation open up, and a result seems close. But then some detail emerges which means that we are back where we started. The city of Copenhagen – particularly Copenhagen at night – is a sombre presence. City politics, at first only on the fringe of the action, slowly move closer and closer to the centre of the intrigue. The characters, and the tension between them, are beautifully realized. What seems to be happening is that the violence of the original crime has set in motion a cycle of failure and disintegration in the lives of all of those touched by it: the politicians, the police investigators, the victim's friends, the stricken family members. Will any of them be able to put their lives back on track? We'll have to wait and see.

In any event, the media is now reporting that 'The Killing' has become cult viewing. We band of viewers, however small, have become the latest cultural elite. And despite the fact that I'm not particularly intrigued by Sarah Lund's Fair Isle jumper, this is a cult of which I'm pleased to be a member. Why not join it?

4 'The Killing' is over

Early in March, I wrote (in *The Scottish Review* 375) of a cult composed of dedicated viewers of BBC 4's extraordinary Danish crime series 'The Killing'. That was then. By time the series ended on March 27th, the cult had become a full-blown religion. Everybody was watching it — no less than half a million of us per episode. And everybody who was anybody in the world of media comment and criticism felt the need to let it be known they were among the believers. Look at today's *Guardian* (March 31st): a four-page article trying to answer the question 'why is everyone talking about a grim 20-part crime series with subtitles?'

Well, *Review* readers already know the answer. Barbara Millar provided it in her excellent piece on just how 'The Killing' kept her rooted to her seat every Saturday night for the last two months (*Scottish Review* 385). I agree with almost everything she says about the series' fascination in terms of plotting, characterisation, acting, filming, and setting. But we do have one disagreement. Barbara was disappointed by the show's closing episodes. She found them jarring and unsatisfactory. Specifically she felt that there were 'too many loose ends needing to be tied up'; that the reason offered by the murderer for his crime was unconvincing; that Sarah Lund, the investigating officer had become too detached and peripheral; and that the high standard of acting and writing had not been maintained. I'd concede that in terms of plotting Vagn's decision to 'kidnap' Theis and drive him to the woods where the murder had been committed was less than self-explanatory. (Or did he know that the game was up and wanted to die where he had killed?) But about the other points there is certainly room for disagreement.

Writing when the series was only halfway through, I suggested that what we were seeing was a bleak cycle of disintegration and failure in the lives of all those caught up by an initial act of brutal violence. I wondered whether any of the characters in the story would be able to put their lives back on track. Nothing in the episodes that followed made me see things differently. And in fact no one in 'The Killing' survives unscathed. The lives of the main characters are hopelessly shattered. The consequences of violence are unpredictable and uncontrollable. It is no surprise to learn that Soren Sveistrup, the writer of the series, says he had Nietzsche in mind in the creation of Sarah Lund. Nietzsche wrote, 'When you stare at the abyss, the abyss stares back at you'. Lund, he says, has stared into the abyss, and that is what makes her what she is. But I would suggest that what is true of Lund is true of all the main characters in the story. The murder of Nanna Birk Larsen has made all of them look into the abyss. All suffer as a result. That is why loose ends remain untied up. There is no 'solution' to a crime like this. And to attempt to provide a comfortably logical one is simply to distort (and evade) the reality which is Nietzsche's abyss.

What are we to make of 'Uncle' Vagn's confession? Barbara says she is not convinced by it. I would ask whether we are meant to be? Vagn is providing only a self-serving, rational gloss for what he has done. The truth is very different, and we know what it is because we have seen the photographs of Nanna's tortured and sexually-abused body. And Sarah Lund? In these final episodes she is 'detached' and 'peripheral' because she has been traumatised by the events that have occurred — above all by the death of Jan Meyer for which she feels responsible, though of course not in the sense in which she is cruelly accused by the 'justice' system. By this stage her life has fallen apart: her son has left her and gone back to his estranged father: her relationship with Bengt seems not to have survived the devastating pressures produced by the investigation. But she is not alone in suffering such personal disintegration.

Pernille and Theis Larsen, Nanna's parents, are brilliantly portrayed throughout the series. Theirs is an almost wordless relationship. But for all the moving sense of irreparable grief, the unspoken truth is that Theis is a man familiar with the abyss of violence — however hard he tries to be the loving husband and father. His shooting of Vagn in the end is inevitable, and Pernille, protected from but denied the truth throughout, is helpless to prevent it. There will be no redemption for the Larsens. The high-minded politician Troels Hartmann is finally equally undone. He may survive politically but now in as flawed and corrupt a condition as any of his opponents. He has destroyed the woman he loves — not realising that Rie is the victim of the manoeuvrings of his campaign manager Morten Weber, a closet homosexual who resents her relationship with his boss.

The ending of 'The Killing' is as bleak as its setting in a dark and dismal, rain-soaked Copenhagen. Will the follow-up series show us the different Copenhagen of Hans Christian Andersen's Little Mermaid and the Tivoli Gardens? Somehow I doubt it.

5 The Reith Lectures

Delivering the 2013 Reith lectures on Radio Four, Niall Ferguson certainly lived up to his reputation as a public intellectual occupying a position well to the right on the political spectrum. Insisting that the West — effectively meaning the U.K. and the USA — is in a state of declining achievement and influence, he identified the causes of that decline with largely leftist ways of thinking. If the western economy is in sorry straits, that is the result of excessive public sector debt (which penalises future generations) and misguided attempts by the state to regulate market forces and the banking system in particular. If the rule of law is no longer respected as it once was, that is because an excess of state-inspired petty rules and regulations has led to its being replaced by the rule of lawyers. If civil society is in terminal decline that is because our welfare system, however well-intentioned, has led to a culture of welfare dependency, while our system of public education, controlled by local authorities, has led to under-achievement and decline in comparison with our economic competitors in the Far East and elsewhere.

In his final lecture, delivered before an audience in the Royal Society of Edinburgh, Professor Ferguson frequently sounded on the defensive — anticipating, that is, that his views would not go down well in a Scottish context. He admitted, for example, that the Reith lecturers were meant to be non-political. Responding to the ironical laughter of his listeners, he suggested that if his 'historical' analyis of our failing institutions sounded 'conservative' then that was just the way things were. As it happens, when question time was finally reached, some of Scotland's finest public intellectuals — Professors Haldane, Curtice, Kidd and Conroy among them — did indeed challenge many of the lecturer's assumptions just as he had anticipated they would. (Incidentally the professor, an Ayrshire-born pupil of Glasgow Academy, was determined to insist on his own Scottish credentials.)

My own guess is that many Scottish listeners to the Reith lectures would indeed have quarrelled mightily with much of what they were hearing — however confidently Professor Ferguson delivered his rightist polemic. Indeed it would be no surprise to learn that radios were shouted at — or quickly switched to off! For my money, it was that last lecture in Edinburgh that was least persuasive. Its theme was civil society — which the professor believes in, but which in his view in recent years has been in unfortunate decline. Figures were quoted which were meant to prove that fewer and fewer of us take part in any form of social involvement. But equally telling apparently was the torrent of abuse that had greeted Prime Minister Cameron's attempt to persuade us to join in the 'big society'. To the lecturer's chagrin, in recent days even the Archbishop of Canterbury has sided with the critics, dismissing the 'big society' as 'aspirational waffle'.

Civil society, as Professor Ferguson knows full well, was an idea much attended to by the thinkers of the Scottish Enlightenment. Indeed, in the course of his lecture, he recognized that Edinburgh was the ideal place in which to make the case for the importance of such a society, and inevitably he made reference to Adam Smith and David Hume. But what was striking — and even in my view puzzling — was that he seemed to be arguing that civil society could somehow exist independently of the state. Surely Smith, Hume, Adam Ferguson and the rest, saw good government as playing a crucial role in the development of civil society. That civil society could ever be the creation of individuals and voluntary organizations working outside civil government is in no way their understanding. Professor Ferguson here, I believe, is the prisoner of his right-wing ideology. He is convinced that the state and the public sector, including trade unions and publicly-funded schools, are bad; private and voluntary organizations and independent schools are good. Therefore the answer to our contemporary problems is for the state somehow to withdraw from civil society. It is the same argument that makes right-wing American politicians endlessly repeat that big government is bad and small government – or no government — better.

Professor Ferguson ended his lecture by asking us to consider what Adam Smith and David Hume would make of the state of Scotland today. It may well be true that much about our contemporary world would disappoint them. The question is where would they place the blame? On the state and its governance? Or on the workings of contemporary Anglo-American capitalism which Professor Kidd in his question identified as the true enemy of civil society?

6 TV Criticism

Critical controversy is par for the course. My masterpiece is your disappointing failure. At the famous Cannes festival, films that are booed and walked out on by half the audience, subsequently win prizes for their excellence. (The hyper-violent *Only God Forgives* is a recent example.) No contemporary British artists are more celebrated (and rewarded) than Damien Hirst and Tracey Emin, but many of us remain unconvinced that pickled animals, or the intimate details of the artist's private life, have much to do with art.

Currently, however, it is the state of TV criticism that strikes me as of particular interest. Over the last year or so, the critical ratings of TV programmes have seemed to soar to unprecedented heights. So much so that we constantly read that this is a golden age of television. Today's television drama, we are assured, is outperforming the best of Hollywood in artistic and aesthetic terms.

This new emphasis on TV's superior status no doubt originated in the huge popular and critical success of such HBO productions as *The Sopranos* and *The Wire*. More recently it is the emergence of Scandinavian TV drama on our screens that has confirmed TV's artistic superiority. Series such as The Killing, The Bridge, and Borgen have been greeted with almost universal acclaim. And of course it is true that such programmes have indeed set new standards for small screen success.

However, TV's new critical status is perhaps beginning to create its own problems. The expectations of critics, commentators, and viewers of new productions have never been higher. Inevitably the publicity machines of all the different channels do their best to crank up such expectations. Every new series is 'unmissable' viewing. What we are about to see is always the season's finest. And to my mind at least, TV critics and commentators have become all too easily swept up in all this enthusiasm.

In 2013 there have been a series of productions, all heralded as outstanding viewing, the opening episodes of which have been reviewed enthusiastically by TV critics. Homeland, The Americans, Broadchurch, The Fall, The Returned, The Top of the Lake, Southcliffe, come readily to mind. Now I'm happy to agree that most of these are pretty good – certainly above average TV viewing. But I do wonder whether they're nearly as wonderful as all the surrounding hype suggests. And I would argue that the opening episodes of several of these – the episodes that garner the hugely flattering reviews – set a standard that the series as a whole fails to sustain.

Some become victims of their own success. Critical enthusiasm plus good viewing figures lead to the commercial decision to commission a second series – with devastating impact upon the artistic integrity of the original. The French import The Returned, on Channel 4, is a good example. Initially intriguing, intelligent and engrossing, what turns out to have been only a first series ended as just another routine 'zombie' horror film, with a fearful community surrounded by a threatening mob of the apparent 'dead'. Similarly, the initially excellent Belfast-set thriller The Fall reached no kind of aesthetically-satisfying conclusion – because the final episode, however unconvincingly, had to prepare the way for a second series. Even the outstanding Homeland became less and less compelling as its brilliant opening situation had to be adapted to make further series plausible.

However, the most egregious example of what strikes me as over-praise concerns a programme the (probable) final episode of which has just been shown: Channel Four's Southcliffe – about the impact upon a small English town of an apparently motiveless shooting spree by a local man. Here are some examples of critical reactions to the programme: 'frighteningly good, literally'; 'a mesmerising tragedy'; 'rare and brilliant Sunday-night viewing'; 'confident, suffused with a dark, masculine desperation'. Euan Ferguson in the *Observer* was even more enthusiastic: 'stupendous'; 'Channel Four's more dodgy output over the past 31 years is forgiven... by giving us this one sublime drama, they are almost wholly redeemed'; 'the TV event of the year'. 'Sublime drama', 'the TV event of the year'? Really? My view is closer to the anonymous member of the public who blogged 'frankly this is dreary stuff'.

From beginning to end Southcliffe remained monotonously flat, undramatic, and dismal. We were being invited to admire its rejection of anything approaching entertainment. At the same time narrative coherence was wholly disregarded. The 'story' consisted of what were largely random short scenes in which virtually nothing was said and in which virtually nothing happened. The post-shooting paralysis, which had apparently overtaken the town, seemed to take over the work itself. But perhaps this was the dreary, tasteless, postmodern intention.

Finally, it is not only TV drama that has recently been suffering from a form of grade inflation. The same applies to TV comedy.

Recently I read a preview in the *Guardian* of the return to E4 of a comedy programme called the Phone Shop. It sounded like something quite 'unmissable'. *The Guardian* preview writer alleged that 'this riotous opening has been worth the near two-year wait'. (Who waits two years for the return of a comedy show on E4?) In any event the real thing was rather different. Of course I am no doubt not the target audience. (Does true comedy require a target audience?) The Phone Shop was silly, puerile, wildly over-acted, and badly written. But wait. According to Sam Wollaston in next day's *Guardian*, the programme is yes, silly and puerile, but nonetheless 'bloody funny', 'hilarious', 'brilliantly performed' and 'brilliantly written'. Truly 'a sitcom for the 21st century'. Oh dear, can we please go back to the 20th or skip on to the 22nd?

7 Old Tricks

I recently watched episodes of two of BBC 1's most popular and longest-running crime series. The contrast between them could not have been more striking. The first was 'Gently in the Cathedral' in series 5 of 'Inspector George Gently'. The second was 'The Girl Who Lived' in series 9 of 'New Tricks'.

In 'Inspector George Gently', the Inspector is played by the experienced Martin Shaw with Lee Ingleby playing the other leading role of Sergeant John Bacchus. Set in the north of England in the 1960s, over the years this has been a reliably entertaining series, frequently exploiting to good effect the generational gap between Gently and Bacchus. Experienced and careworn, Gently is no Dixon of Dock Green, but nonetheless does seem to belong to an older world of unshakable integrity, loyalty, and total commitment to the rule of law. For Gently, however complex the situation, the law, and the social order it protects, will always be upheld. The younger Bacchus comes over as representing a new, changing, less deferential world – the world perhaps created by the Labour Party's sweeping victory in 1945. But even so there is absolutely no question that 'Inspector George Gently' remains a world away from that of the recent 'Life on Mars' series, with its deliberate creation of a no-holds-barred, politically-incorrect, style of law enforcement back in the 1970s. The prime-time, Sunday night audience of 'Inspector George Gently' never expects to be upset.

'Gently in the Cathedral' was billed as 'last in the series'. We should have been warned. The programme began well, promising perhaps an episode of above-average quality. A big-time criminal whom Gently, back in his days in the Met in London, had been responsible for sending down for twenty years, has come up with a fiendish plot to prove that the oh so upright Gently is in fact a bent cop. The case against Gently is made up by a group of Met detectives all of whom have been successfully corrupted by the criminal. Sergeant Bacchus – seduced by hints of a future glamorous career in London's Met — seems to waver in his support for his boss. Writer and director have created a genuinely absorbing situation. But resolving it proves altogether another matter.

From about halfway through, the programme lurches from one absurdity to another. Realism is utterly left behind. The London Met is apparently staffed by loads of corrupt policemen, most of whom are up here in the north framing the hapless Gently. But never mind. Soon they are all gunned down by the inspector and his sergeant in a kind of sham OK Corral shoot-out. Then it's on to what we are expected to believe is Durham Cathedral where the arch villain is inside popping away at all and sundry with a rifle a big as himself. Only Gently can close him down. The job is done, but both the inspector and his sergeant – who gasps that really he never doubted Gently — are down on the cathedral floor. And the credits roll.

Of course we know what is going on. If a new series is commissioned by the money-men at the BBC, it will turn out that Gently and Bacchus — or at least Gently — will have survived their wounds. If not, we are expected to mourn the loss of two such admirable upholders of law and order. But we don't — because we can't take such a put-up job seriously. What a miserable ending — watched would you believe by over four million people — to an entertaining series!

My second crime programme is even more of an established BBC1 favourite. 'New Tricks' has been running since 2003 and in 2012-13 it is currently in its ninth series. For all these years its cast has been made up of popular, long-term TV stars: Amanda Redman, (the boss), James Bolam, Dennis Waterman, and Alun Armstrong. Retired detectives, they are back solving old cases. But of course the entertainment value of the show lies in the interchanges, tensions, and back-chatting between the three, familiar, ageing ex-detectives. In fact James Bolam seems to have bowed out of the current series, and there are reports that both Alun Armstrong and Amanda Redman are suggesting that the current set of programmes will be their last. It would hardly be a surprise, then, if the programme I watched – admittedly alongside well over 7 million viewers — had shown signs of flagging energy and declining dramatic impact.

In the event, 'The Girl Who Lived' was a minor triumph. The new potential third member of the team proved to be the Scottish actor Denis Lawson. Down in London because of his previous involvement in the case of a girl disappearing in Glasgow, his presence made possible a couple of amusing Scots/English misunderstandings or exchanges. Only the idea that Jack (Dennis Waterman) had to be taught by his new colleague how to drink malt whisky sounded unconvincing and stereotypical. However, the real strength of the episode lay in its excellent storyline. Roy Mitchell's script was realistic and convincing. Brilliantly acted by Daniel Ryan, the villain of the piece — a smooth-talking conman who preyed on vulnerable women — was all too believable. The exchanges during his interrogation were dramatic and compelling. And the downbeat ending suggesting that such a nasty piece of work would get away with at best a minor penalty was once again all too disturbingly believable. The contrast with the inanity of the ending of 'Inspector George Gently' could not have been greater. 'New Tricks' is no doubt rightly described as light entertainment. But it can produce a winner all the same.

8 *The Artist*

In Scott Fitzgerald's novel *The Last Tycoon* – unfinished at the time of his death – there is a rather strange scene in which Monroe Stahr, the Hollywood mogul, and Kathleen, the English girl with whom he is involved, meet a man described in the text as a 'Negro'. The couple are walking at night on a beach in California when they come upon this nameless figure. He is collecting pails of tiny silver fish called grunion being washed ashore by the incoming tide. What he really likes to do out here, however, is read the copy of Emerson he carries under his shirt. He asks Stahr what he does and learns he works in Hollywood. 'Oh', says the man. After a moment he added, I never go to movies. Why not? asked Stahr sharply. There's no profit. I never let my children go.' And filling his pails with fish, he disappears from the novel, 'unaware that he had rocked an industry'.

What does Fitzgerald expect the reader to make of this encounter? That Hollywood and the movie industry were not doing enough to produce the kind of art Emerson had hoped America would bring to the rest of the world? Fitzgerald is not named in Michel Hazanavicius's Oscar-contending film *The Artist* (2011), though a Fitzgerald look-alike does make an appearance as a 'toy' boyfriend of the film's female protagonist, Peppy Miller. Hollywood and its history, on the other hand, are precisely what the film is about.

The Artist is neither more nor less than an extended 'homage' to mainstream Hollywood and its history. Its director is quite explicit about this. The film, he tells us, is 'a love letter to cinema and grew out of my (and all of my cast and crew's) admiration and respect for movies throughout history'. When I was a student, Film Studies was at least a generation away from becoming an academic subject, so I'm no expert on the history of Hollywood. But this lovely film is clearly a richly inter-textual montage of Hollywood movie-making. Its matinee-idol hero is called George Valentin, but he is as much Douglas Fairbanks and Gene Kelly as Rudolph Valentino. Its central love story is Chaplinesque in its heart-warming sentimentality. The benignly attractive world it creates is one of happy film fans, starry luxury mansions, chauffeur-driven limousines, and peaceful neighbourhoods in which friendly policemen seem always ready to help. It is shot in old-style black and white. And most strikingly of all, it is an old-world silent film making minimal use of on-screen passages of dialogue.

Set in the period 1927-1931, *The Artist* focuses significantly on the very years when the mode of production in which it so imaginatively made, is on the way out. 'Talkies' are replacing silent films. George Valentin, star of the silent screen, cannot survive the change. For him sound is a disorienting nightmare. Walking out of his former studio, he risks everything on making his own silent film – another romantic epic, *Love and Tears*. Inevitably it flops. We glimpse the final frames in which the hero is literally disappearing into some kind of deadly quicksand while his lover helplessly stretches out her hand from the side. Meantime of course, Peppy Miller, the beautiful young woman George has brought into the studio, is becoming a peerless shooting star in the new world of talking films.

So *The Artist* embodies that greatest of American themes: the rise and fall of the American Dream. The decline of George is matched by the rise of Peppy. But this is Hollywood. The two stories come together in a loving, redemptive finale that lets us leave the cinema in a mood of Emersonian hope. Still there is a degree of irony here. The perspective on all of this is a purely European one. Shot in Los Angeles, this is a wholly French film, with a French director and French stars. This I think is why its 'homage' is so total, so uncritical, so unconcerned about Fitzgerald's African American fisherman's comment, which Monroe Stahr, the last tycoon, found so unsettling. This is Hollywood unashamed. (At one point, would you believe, George's life is saved by his ever-present – and quick-thinking – little dog Jack: a star more Rin Tin Tin than Greyfriar's Bobby or Lassie Come Home.)

Will *The Artist* sweep the boards at this year's Oscars? Probably. Hollywood is unlikely to give thumbs down to its own past.

9 *Midnight in Paris*

Woody Allen's career has had its ups and downs. Writer and director of over forty films from the 1960s to the present, he has always remained something of a cult figure with a cult following. In the 70s and 80s early films such as *Annie Hall*, *Manhattan*, and *Hannah and Her Sisters* mapped out what became familiar Allen territory: smart-talking, intellectual New York; screwball, Jewish-inflected comedy; neurotic, angst-driven characters; a witty and knowing cynicism seemingly reflecting Allen's own rather tortured personality. The audience Allen built up loved every bit of it.

That audience, however, remained pretty selective. None of Allen's films were big box-office hits. Outside the Hollywood mainstream, his films remained very much his own thing; he was writer, director, and often star. Into the 90s Allen's career continued to flourish, new films appearing with astonishing frequency and regularity. But then something began to go wrong. Too many films seemed to be misses rather than hits. And one factor in particular began to worry even Allen's most loyal supporters: despite his advancing years, Allen continued to play the role of the oddball protagonist who in the end wins over the young and beautiful female lead. Increasingly a less than happy ending.

Worse was to follow. In the 90s, Allen's personal life began to imitate his art. This is the unpleasant period of the break-up of his relationship with Mia Farrow and his involvement with (and eventual marriage to) Farrow's adopted daughter, Soon-Yi Previn. His reputation inevitably suffered.

The good news – and the only reason for writing this account – is that with his latest film, *Midnight in Paris* (2011), Allen is very much back on form. In a radio interview he explained that he now recognises that at his age (he's in his mid-seventies) he cannot possibly play the guy who gets the girl – so he has chosen not to appear. Owen Wilson plays the role in *Midnight in Paris* that in the past would have been Allen's own, and one of the minor pleasures of the film is to register how as the film goes on he begins to sound more and more like Allen himself.

The new film continues Woody Allen's love affair with European cities. (Could this itself be a consequence of the fact that his most loyal audience is now in France, Spain and Italy?) Match Point celebrates London; Vicky Cristina Barcelona does the same for the fashionable

Spanish city – and the next film will apparently be set in Rome. *Midnight in Paris* is a seductively fulsome tribute to the splendours of the French capital – including Paris in the rain. Better still, the film lightly and charmingly evokes the Paris of the 1920s – the Paris which in the post-World War I period attracted so many American artists and writers. And here they all are: Zelda and Scott Fitzgerald, Hemingway, Gertrude Stein, Cole Porter, Josephine Baker, T.S.Eliot – not to mention locals like Picasso and Salvador Dali.

Beautifully acted, the film is intelligent, witty and satirical. Tea-party supporters, and other neo-con Republicans, will continue to regard Allen as an enemy alien. The pedantic, know-all contemporary academic is an ironical treat. The time-shift device is elegantly devised, and the whole film is beautifully written and imagined. Never taking itself too seriously, its central theme is the notional one of a golden age that seems to offer itself as a desirable alternative to all the problems of the present. With this film, Allen has achieved his biggest box-office hit in the US. So I suspect I'm not the only one who has loved this 90-minute escape from today's painful world into that amazing Paris of James Joyce and Sylvia Beach's 'Shakespeare and Company ' bookshop.

10 *Twelve Years a Slave*

In 2014 Steve McQueen's film *12 Years a Slave* will win a host of prizes, and deservedly so. Since its initial screening at the Telluride and Toronto film festivals, it has been received with almost universal critical acclaim. Chiwetel Ejiofor's performance as the film's protagonist is brilliant; Michael Fassbender, the young Lupita Nyong'o, and a range of others are equally good. McQueen's direction confirms his major status. The odd American voice has apparently complained that a film, on a quintessentially American subject, has been made by a British director with British actors – despite the fact that McQueen himself is not white. And there have been a few suggestions that the film is guilty of exploiting a 'pornography of violence'. Any such notion is utterly wrong. As I have argued on previous occasions, gratuitous violence is all too common in contemporary cinema, but the brutal reality of violence here is never remotely gratuitous or merely sensational. Rather, such disturbing and horrifying scenes as the audience witnesses, compel us to look on at the grim reality that lies at the heart of the institution and meaning of slavery.

In the chorus of praise with which the film has been greeted, one theme constantly recurs. Hollywood has failed abjectly to handle the topic of slavery in American history. One of the most admired of early classic films – D. W. Griffith's *Birth of a Nation* – is a deeply racist celebration of the Ku Klux Klan and the old South. The hugely successful *Gone With the Wind* naively romanticizes the South, and glosses over the evils of slavery. In the eyes of many critics at least, Quentin Tarantino's recent *Django Unchained* is no more than a 'spaghetti Western' version of slavery in America. With *12 Years a Slave* all this has changed. As David Simon – of 'The Wire' fame – puts it: the film 'marks the first time in history that our entertainment industry... has managed to stare directly at slavery and maintain that gaze'.

There is much that is true in this view. The film forces audiences in America and elsewhere to recognize the horrifying levels of pain and suffering that slavery entailed. We look on as enslaved families are torn apart, their children sold on to new masters. Inevitably we see the sexual exploitation of slave women – victims both of plantation owners and their offended wives. The hanging of runaways, the horrifyingly brutal, random beatings of male and female slaves — it is all here in distressingly graphic reality. The so-called justification of such brutality too is spelled out. Chattel slavery denies its victims their human reality. As Fassbender's Epps, the most brutal of the film's protagonist's 'masters' explains, slaves are not people; they are not individuals. They are pieces of property to be traded in, bought or sold, like any other possession. That is why there are no legal limits of any kind over how slave-owners can behave. In their own eyes they can do what they like with the property they have bought.

In a sense then *12 Years a Slave* is an educational film, documenting the realities of slavery for audiences — perhaps especially American audiences — who have never been shown the most shocking aspects of the crime that slavery was. But it is precisely here that issues begin to emerge which, while in no way diminishing the power and impact of a major film, are at least worthy of debate. As most readers will know, McQueen's film is closely based on a memoir or slave narrative published in 1853 by a man called Solomon Northup. Northup was not a slave. Rather he was a freeborn African-American, a well-respected, educated, middle-class musician, who lived in New York State. However, having travelled to perform in Washington, D.C., he is kidnapped, drugged, and sold into slavery in 1841. Such kidnappings did of course occur, but Northup — or Platt, as he is renamed as a slave — cannot in the end be seen as a typical or representative slave. On the other hand, having to take on a new name, Northup suffers the same fate as countless thousands of Africans carried off into slavery. Losing one's liberty means losing one's human individuality, means losing one's name.

So, yes I can see how the film can be interpreted in a way that does make Northup's sudden loss of liberty absolutely characteristic of the fate of every slave sold into perpetual bondage. The scenes, for example, on the paddle steamer carrying the kidnap victims down the Mississippi to New Orleans, can readily seen as an image of the middle passage across the Atlantic suffered over almost two centuries by the vast number of human beings caught up in the atrocious slave-trade. As Peter Bradshaw in the *Guardian* puts it, 'Northup is conned, captured, chained, bound in a slave ship — just as normal... History is happening to him and us in microcosm'. 'McQueen', he goes on, 'is making us see the point is (sic) that they are all free — or should be — they are all dignified human beings with families. Northup's sensational situation is only an amplification and distillation of the whole crime'. As I say, this is a possible reading of the film, but it's not the whole story.

In fact the film keeps underlining the point that 'Platt' is not really a slave. His owners all notice there is something different about him. His 'good' owner (played by an over-exposed Benedict Cumberbatch) fears that no good will come of his obvious superiority. His 'evil' owner and his employees are infuriated by it. Then he is special because he can play the violin – and even make money from doing so. Forced to pretend he cannot read or write, we are still left in no doubt about his intelligence and abilities. For most of the film it is his un-slave-like qualities that are emphasised, his difference from those among whom he finds himself. That is why, for me at least, the high point of the film comes late on, in a scene soon after a fellow-slave collapses and dies while picking cotton.

After his hasty burial, all the other slaves gather round and led by an older woman begin to sing a kind of spiritual – 'Roll Jordan, Roll'. The scene is a brilliant counterpoint to an earlier one where Epps' sadistic overseer sings mockingly 'Run Nigger Run' in the faces of the slaves over whom he has absolute power. In the later scene, Northup/Platt is there among the group of slaves, his face etched with conflicting emotions of rage and sorrow. At first he does not sing, but as the simple words – Roll Jordan Roll – are repeated over and over, his lips begin to move, and the soundtrack catches his voice as it joins in with ever-growing power until it is his voice above all we are hearing. It is a scene of enormous emotional intensity because it is the moment in the film when Northup's identity with the routine world of suffering slavery is absolute and unequivocal. Could it be because of this he afterwards breaks in pieces his precious violin? He will no longer stand apart from those around him.

But such solidarity is not the note on which the film ends. Northup's status as a kidnap victim finally saves him. After years of slavery, his friends in the north are informed of his fate and come to his rescue. But given that what we have here is a film of the utmost seriousness, perhaps it is not unfair to suggest, as one American critic has done, that *12 Years a Slave* suffers from its 'hero problem'. 'We're more interested in one hero than in millions of victims'. What will be the fate of young Patsey and all the others left behind on the Louisiana plantation? I suppose it could be argued that in Northup's restoration to his family there is an image of the apparently new and better world that emancipation and the abolition of slavery will shortly bring about. But what cannot be altered is the dark truth that from the later seventeenth century until well into the nineteenth, for an immense number of human beings, seized from their African homes and shipped across the Atlantic to work as slaves on the sugar or cotton plantations of Barbados or Jamaica or America's southern states, there would be no rescue, no restoration, and no redemption of any kind.

11 Cinema Noise

I always look forward to reading Ian Jack's weekly column in the *Observer*. I'm not sure why that is – a shared Scottish background, and shared status as senior citizens perhaps – but he and I seem to see the world today from a similar perspective. That he turns out to read the *Scottish Review* is also reassuring. But the reason I'm writing about him is because he and I in the recent past shared an identical experience and reacted to it in identical ways. I had considered writing about that experience myself, but decided it was no more than an unfortunate one-off that had no wider significance. I was wrong.

In a column in 2012 Ian Jack described a visit to the cinema to see Quentin Tarantino's new film *Django Unchained*. Early in the piece he vividly evokes the film's endless tsunami of violence which is of course Tarantino's trademark as a film-maker. 'Bullets rip into flesh, which flies out in messy chunks as blood spatters walls and falls like crimson rain on nicely arranged white flowers – on and on it goes, bang-bang-bang, spatter-spatter-spatter, mercilessly, while we, a grey-haired audience on a Wednesday afternoon, break open our foil-wrapped carrot cake and drain the dregs of our cappuccinos.'

I have not seen *Django Unchained*, nor do I intend to. I have watched the clips on TV, listened to the views of film critics on the radio, and listened to the director's unconvincing response when asked on TV a perfectly reasonable question about the possibility of a link between filmic and real-life violence. If I did see it, I'm certain my reaction would be exactly like Ian Jack's. Like him, I don't 'get' Tarantino. Like him, I'm puzzled by the admiration and respect afforded the film maker by the *Observer* and the *Guardian*'s own estimable film critics, Peter Bradshaw and Philip French. All this, however, is incidental to what I want to write about here.

What that is emerges from the sentence that Ian Jack writes immediately after the one quoted above. Here it is. 'From the moment we sat down, we've been softened up for these scenes. First came the Pearl and Dean adverts, and then the trailers, all of them an assault on the senses full of dizzying cuts and deafening noises, as if their makers wanted to pull you from your seat, slap you around the head and make you surrender to their juvenile interpretation of the world.' In a cinema in London I recently had exactly the experience that is described here.

The film we had gone to see was *The Hobbit*. But inevitably the adverts and trailers had first to be endured. And 'endured' this time carried its full weight of meaning. The sound level was shattering. It really was an assault on the eardrums. More torture than entertainment. Like Ian Jack I felt slapped around the head. To what end? My cynical response was that we were being driven into the foyer in the hope we would buy even more wildly overpriced drinks and popcorn...

More recently still, I went to see Steven Spielberg's *Lincoln* in Glasgow's West End cinema. I waited with interest to find out what the Pearl and Dean sound level would be like. It turned out to be not quite at the deafening height of the London cinema, but still many, many decibels above what was necessary. So what is going on here? A little investigation revealed that there is a long-running issue over the sound level in TV advertising. Rules are in place to try to control this. But the technology is complex and the advertisers are adept at ensuring that their product assails the public ear at the top end of the listening scale. In all of this there is no mention of any kind of regulation of advertising in cinemas. There clearly ought to be. I guess that I and Ian Jack, and cinema audiences in general, are suffering because the latest business manuals have decided that the soft sell no longer works. Ear-splitting loudness rules. For some of us at least, a huge mistake.

So what finally of the films themselves? Near the opening of Tolkien's *The Hobbit* the following passage occurs: 'Old Took's great-grand-uncle Bullroarer ... charged the ranks of the goblins of Mount Gram in the Battle of the Green Fields, and knocked their king Golfimbul's head clean off with a wooden club. It sailed a hundred yards through the air and went down a rabbit-hole, and in this way the battle was won and the game of Golf invented at the same moment.' This is an extreme example of the kind of comic whimsy that characterises *The Hobbit* throughout the adventurous tale of 'there and back again'. Peter Jackson's film in its opening sequences retains something of this arch humour as the growing band of dwarves assemble and take over Bilbo Baggins' house. But once the intrepid band set off on their quest to recover their lost treasure, the mock-heroic note is lost. *The Hobbit* simply morphs instead into *The Lord of the Rings* mark two: endless scenes of epic struggles, mighty battles, and heroic endeavour. All well done and certainly entertaining. But to my mind at least, *Lord of the Rings*, alongside its epic scale, retains a moving human reality sadly lacking here.

And *Lincoln*? *Lincoln* is distinguished by a quite stunning performance by Daniel Day Lewis. It is Lincoln himself, not an actor, we seem to be in the presence of. Lewis has already won the BAFTA award for best actor. He will surely win an Oscar as well. The film's focus on the closing weeks of the Civil War, and the struggle to get the House of Representatives to pass the 13th Amendment with the required majority to abolish slavery in the US, works extremely well. The compromises required, the double-dealing, the lies and deception, and the lost ideals, come across as all too real. Perhaps Spielberg does provide too positive a gloss to American history. The final, wild celebration of the passing of the amendment as a triumph of American democracy, for example, does not quite tally with the film's earlier hintings that emancipation and the 13th amendment's abolition of slavery will in no way resolve the issue of race relations in America. Still *Lincoln* is a film well worth seeing.

12 Walkouts

There's no denying Ian Jack is a brave man. To write about walking out of the current (2010) production of 'Men Should Weep' in London's National Theatre in – of all publications – the *Scottish Review*, must have taken a lot of nerve. Whatever its past history, there is no question that Ena Lamont Stewart's play has come to be regarded as a Scottish classic. The playwright is at last receiving the critical acclaim she was denied for most of her lifetime. The London production has been an acclaimed success, winning at least four stars from all the critics. The trials of its working-class family in the 1930s have even been seen as relevant to the post-cuts, welfare-slashed, society of contemporary Britain. Setting the success of 'Men Should Weep' beside the current enthusiasm for the Glasgow Boys exhibition now on at the Royal Academy, some commentators have been talking of a Scottish near take-over of London's cultural scene. In the midst of all this excitement, how could Ian Jack and his family have opted for pizzas rather than returning to their seats for the second half of 'Men Should Weep'?

Well, in his contribution to *The Scottish Review* 333, Mr Jack does try to explain and in doing so criticises aspects of this particular production and of the play itself. Not having seen the London production – nor for that matter the Glasgow one of 1982 – I am in no position to comment. But as it happens Ian Jack and I do have something in common. We have both effectively walked out on plays at the National Theatre. In fact we could even have walked out on the same night! Let me explain. I recently went down to London with a friend to meet another friend who had recently announced her forthcoming marriage. Our friend and her future husband had decided to celebrate by arranging to meet us for dinner in the Lyttelton Theatre's Mezzanine restaurant on the South Bank and taking us to see that night's play.

We had an excellent dinner and took our seats in the Lyttelton with high expectations. The play proved to be 'Blood and Gifts' by an American called J.T. Rogers. Rogers, I find, is a successful contemporary playwright with a long list of prizes and awards to his name. Probably his most admired play is 'The Overwhelming' set in Rwanda; 'Blood and Gifts' is about Afghanistan in the 1980s. The main character proves to be a rather high-minded CIA agent who is surrounded by a clearly unreliable cast of Brits, Russians,

Afghans, and Pakistanis. Nothing much happens. Scene after scene consisted of nothing but talk apparently designed to let us see just how complex the political situation in Afghanistan really is. But as the long first half wore on, I came increasingly to feel I was being instructed rather than entertained. Mr Rogers' anticipated audience seemed to be all those Americans who had failed to keep up with the *New York Times*'s dispatches about the politics of the war in Afghanistan. My mind was soon wandering to Graham Greene's account of the dangers of American idealism in *The Quiet American* – and to the highly entertaining chutzpah of *Charlie Wilson's War*, a film set in exactly the same period of Afghanistan history. Meantime the play meandered its tedious way to a welcome interval.

In the theatre bar we began to talk a bit tentatively about the play. No one seemed very enthusiastic. It was okay, a bit unexciting. I think I was the first person to use the word boring. But it was all downhill thereafter. And before long our host was suggesting we could either go back in for the second half, or stay where we were and enjoy another bottle of wine. That was the option we went for. Now for me – just as much as for Ian Jack or George Gunn (in *The Scottish Review* 334) — to walk out of a play was almost unprecedented. Still feeling guilty, I asked my friend to look for reviews on her iPhone. The first few she found were unanimous in their praise. The play is an 'exciting political thriller'; 'it illuminates Afghanistan in brilliant new light'; 'a slick production'. I began to feel even more guilty. But then she finally read a review in *The Independent* which elegantly and effectively made the case against the play, responding to the whole evening exactly as I had done to the first half. I really began to enjoy my wine. 'Remember that we saw only the half of it' warns Ian Jack. I suppose I should say the same — but my heart isn't in it.

13 Great Expectations

I am not invariably a fan of Suzanne Moore's journalism. Perhaps some readers will recall her highly personal spat over shoes and other matters with Germaine Greer in the 1990s. Just the kind of exchange to give the sisterhood a bad name. However, last week she ended her *Guardian* column on celebrity shoplifting with this comment on a recent visit to the theatre (in London one has to assume): 'Not a big deal for some but, as usual, disappointing for me. I can only conclude that there is some mathematical equation between the low standards of theatre critics and audiences and the ridiculous price of the tickets'.

On this subject at least Suzanne and I are in complete agreement. Recently in London in 2011 I attended a show that has received universal acclaim from the city's theatre critics. Every single newspaper from the *Times*, *Telegraph*, and *Guardian* to the Mail, Sun, and Metro has joined in the chorus of unstinted, five-star praise. Originally a National Theatre production, the play soon moved to the Adelphi theatre in the West End, and that run over, a new move to the Theatre Royal, opening on March 2nd, has just been announced. Richard Bean's 'One Man, Two Guvnors', a new version of Carlo Goldoni's 1743 play 'A Servant of Two Masters' is by any standard a smash-hit.

Given this background, I went along to a matinee in the Adelphi with the highest of expectations. Before proceeding though, I have to admit that a special circumstance attended the performance I was about to see. Even my ticket told me in bold type that James Corden – who has been celebrated as the star of the show – would not be performing that afternoon. Best known to audiences as the writer of, and actor in, the TV series 'Gavin and Stacey' – the huge success of which is demonstrated by its move from BBC3 to BBC2 to BBC1 – Corden's presence has clearly had a lot to do with the play's popularity. But the packed matinee audience, of which I was part, loved his understudy, Owain Arthur. His performance, including all the comic business, timing and gesture, is surely modelled on that of Corden, and in fact his curtain call at the end of the show was greeted with thunderous applause. The role of the 'servant' is of course at the comic heart of the play, but even so 'A Servant of Two Masters' (and so 'One Man, Two Guvnors') is in no sense a one-man show.

I cannot believe, in other words, that Corden's presence on stage would have converted what was at best a mildly entertaining afternoon into a sublime, theatrical experience. For my money – and Suzanne Moore is right to describe the price of West End theatre tickets as ridiculously high – 'One Man, Two Guvnors' was a long way short of a five-star show. The opening ten minutes were almost embarrassingly bad: woodenly stagey, with not very funny dialogue between not very funny characters. The rest of the first half gained some pace with the entry of the Corden/Arthur servant, but after the interval there was just more of the same: lots of knockabout, farcical, slapstick action. Nothing more. Goldoni's play can be seen as having a subversive subtext: the clever servant outwitting his socially superior masters. But Bean's version offered no hint of that.

Suzanne Moore's comment links the low standards of critics to the low standards of audiences. I think she has a point. The audience that afternoon was determined to be entertained. It wanted to get its (big) money's worth. It was ready and willing to laugh. Huckleberry Finn really doesn't know that the drunk man on the circus horse is a ringer; we were happy to pretend to believe that the members of the audience brought up on stage to be made fun of were the real thing. *The Guardian* has told its readers to go along to 'One Man, Two Guvnors' and 'forget your cares at the funniest show in town'. As you can tell, I failed to forget mine.

A postscript. The Royal Shakespeare Company's 'Matilda the Musical', which has also transferred to the West End, is worth every penny. Imaginatively staged, musically exciting, and brilliantly performed – by the children in particular – this is an unforgettable theatrical experience. Roald Dahl's Matilda – the little girl who loves to read – is worth every word of the praise she received on the *Guardian*'s editorial page on January 12th.

14 Two West Ends

In London's West End in 2013 a friend and I saw a play. For two seats near the back of the stalls, the cost was £114. The theatre was Wyndham's in Charing Cross Road, and the play was 'The Weir' by Conor McPherson. The production had opened in the Donmar Warehouse some months ago, and thanks to critical and popular success, had transferred to the West End for a twelve-week run.

I had opted for this play because I knew that McPherson, now generally recognized as one of Ireland's finest contemporary playwrights, had launched his career with The Weir back in 1997. Having had no previous experience of his work, but well aware of the success he has enjoyed ever since, I settled into my seat in the packed theatre with the highest of expectations. An added bonus was that the cast included one of Scotland's most acclaimed actors: Dundee's Brian Cox.

The curtain went up on the interior of a small Irish pub. This proved to be the play's only setting — and one had already gathered from the programme (another four pounds) — that it would last for an hour and three quarters without an interval. All five members of the cast kept the bar's cash machine rolling by buying – and downing — successive rounds of drinks. It did not take long before I was wishing I could buy one of my own.

A review I'd read spoke of how the play 'slowly smoulders into life'. For me the problem was that in the long, slow-moving hour and three quarters, it never got past the smouldering stage. The lives these characters lead are dreary to the point of dolefulness but that level of dullness seemed unfortunately to take over he play itself. Then there was a communications issue. In today's dominant school of naturalistic acting, clarity of diction is not always a priority. But it's still a help if one isn't struggling all the time making out what is being said. Irish accents were not the main issue — though to my ears at least Brian Cox's 'Irish' did not echo that of the other characters. Rather the problem was that at key moments in the play — moments meant to be of emotional depth and intensity — characters spoke at breakneck speed or so quietly as to be barely audible.

Of course it's possible to identify serious issues beneath The Weir's comic Irish banter. All of these characters have been damaged by past experiences which, more or less in turn, they take centre stage to describe. These experiences all seem to have a spiritual, or other-worldly, or even ghostly dimension. Or do they? Can they all be explained away?

In any event, on the night I saw it, this tired production of The Weir never seemed to suggest it was a play of creative originality. More disappointingly still, it never managed to explode into the dramatic life characteristic of the best of modern Irish theatre.

A week earlier in Glasgow's West End I saw a very different play. 'The Friends of Miss Dorian Gray', by Marcella Evaristi, was staged by the Oran Mor in its long-established 'a play, a pie, and a pint' series. Lasting exactly one hour, it proved to be a richly entertaining rewriting and updating of Oscar Wilde's Gothic tale of the increasingly dissolute young man whose beauty appears unaffected by the passage of time. In her witty and sophisticated version, Ms. Evaristi successfully weaves together contemporary society's obsession with celebrity, youthfulness and ageing, and contemporary culture's feminist concern with beauty, art, women's bodies, the male gaze and other fashionable theories. All of this achieved with the lightest of touches, hints of sadness – and a succession of one-liners which the past master Wilde himself would surely have appreciated. 'Not only very funny', a friend e-mailed, 'but perceptive, well-observed, and poignant'. I could not agree more.

London's West End's hour and three quarters cost, as I mentioned, £114 for two. Glasgow's West End's hour cost £20, also for two – and that included a pie and a pint, or a glass of wine and a slice of quiche. And in terms of theatrical entertainment and aesthetic value? My money at least was better spent in Glasgow.

15 Riverside Museum

Here in 2011 Glasgow's new transport museum is up and running, but as one approaches the site all that surrounding empty space creates a less than vibrant setting. As a result Zaha Hadah's new building has something of an outpost air about it. Why exactly is it located here one asks oneself? OK, the Tall Ship is located alongside, but once again why has this particular Clyde mooring been chosen? The Clyde here is quiet, serene, tranquil, and placid. Why? Because on and beside the quiet water nothing is happening. Inside the museum one is reminded again and again of a very different Clyde. A Clyde of enormous activity, of enterprise and production, of success (and occasional tragic failure), of ships and ship-building towering above the surrounding streets. A Clyde bursting with life and activity. The contrast with the empty, pastoral quiet surrounding the new museum could not be greater.

No doubt the planners are hoping the very existence of this riverside museum will attract new life to the surrounding area: that in due course it will become the hub of a new Clydeside world of social and cultural activity. But meantime there's no getting away from the irony that the focus of such regenerative hopes should take the form of a museum – a museum memorializing a world that belongs to an increasingly distant and irrevocable past.

Still the building itself is strikingly new. Surely the modernity of its architecture makes the point that the city that built it is looking to the future rather than dwelling in the past? I find it hard to be certain. The zig-zag of the facade, and its black marble-looking material is undeniably dramatic. The point is made that this is a building with a meaning in itself. But does the rest of the building, extending behind the facade, quite confirm that meaning? I'm not sure that it does. The plain grey bulk of its body is perhaps too reminiscent of a huge Clydeside warehouse to maintain that sense of challenge.

I know there has been considerable criticism of the pistachio-green colour in which the entire interior of the building is decorated. The day I visited the sun was shining and the colour inside seemed fine, the pale green perhaps echoing the pastoral exterior and contrasting the dark, shifting colours of the water of the Clyde. Most striking though was the boldness of the shaping of the interior, the striking irregularity of the perspectives from different levels and elevations. I hope it does not sound pretentious to say I was reminded of the interior of Frank Gehry's Guggenheim museum in Bilbao. There the sweeping and curving perspectives seem even more dramatic, but that is perhaps because, in the absence of crowded content, they are more able to speak for themselves. The windows and interior window spaces are among the finest aspects of Hadah's building, but there were occasions when I wished one were given more space to register and enjoy the drama of the architecture within. I at least would have been willing to give up (say) some of the motor cars or pelatons of bicycles to make that happen.

As far as the contents of the museum is concerned, not a great deal has changed . This is still a museum of transport. The railway engines are huge and hugely impressive. The vast range of model ships tells the story of the Clyde and shipbuilding. The old style tramcars and buses speak eloquently of a past Glasgow. And for me — and I suspect for many of the mums and dads, grannies and grandads — that is really the point. This is a museum of memory, a museum of nostalgia. (Hey! That's a model of the Queen Mary. Could that have been my cabin — many decks down of course – when I sailed in her from Southampton to New York in 1957, one of many young British scholars on a Senator Fulbright travel grant?) And the curators, with their recreation of the streets of 1895-1930, 1930-1960, and 1960-1980, don't hesitate to indulge our bitter-sweet taste for that lost, older world. Almost the first vehicle I saw was an ancient coal delivery van, number plate BS something or other. BS I wondered, wasn't that Orkney? And yes, on the side door, there it was — a name and Coal Merchant, Kirkwall. But already my mind was remembering our own first family car: a 10 hp. Hillman Minx, ST 9147. ST was Inverness. We were living in Wick, Caithness. Caithness was SK. Sutherlandshire was NS. Wasn't AS Nairn?

Today's number-plates are a meaningless jumble of letters and figures — or occasionally someone's ostentatiously 'personalized' (hideous word) plate. ST 9147 belonged to a world so much denser with meaning. Visit the new Riverside Museum — if you want to catch many other glimpses of that older and, in some respects at least, richer world.

16 Musical Moments

Recently I have enjoyed two very different musical experiences. The first was in London. In 2007 the iTunes London Festival was held in the Institute of Contemporary Arts, but its venue soon switched to the Roundhouse in Camden Town. Built in the mid-nineteenth century as a railway engine turning shed, the Roundhouse began its life as a centre of the performing arts in the early 1960s when it hosted Arnold Wesker's Centre 42 theatre group. Since then it has become something of a London cultural icon providing over the years a location for a range of pop concerts and singers, (including the Rolling Stones, Jimi Hendrix, Pink Floyd, David Bowie and Led Zeppelin), musicals, dance, radical theatre (the RSC staged its complete cycle of Shakespeare's history plays there), and other forms of avant garde or experimental cultural events.

The format of the iTunes Festival is simple: 31 nights (July 1-31) of single performances by individual artists or groups. The Roundhouse auditorium has room for around 3000 people most of whom stand – Proms or Globe Theatre style – in the space in front of the wide proscenium stage. This year's programme featured one night stands by many of popular music's currently most celebrated performers: Artic Monkeys, Adele, Coldplay, Glasvegas, Moby, Manic Street Preachers, and the not quite so young Paul Simon. However, the night on which I had been invited had been carefully chosen because it seemed to offer something completely different: Two Cellos followed by the evening's main event – a performance by the world-famous Chinese classical pianist Lang Lang.

The interior of the Roundhouse auditorium is impressive enough. The vast sense of circular space, the spectacle from the balcony seating looking down on the mass of mostly young people filling the promenade arena, the batteries of elaborately constructed stage lighting sweeping across the scene, and – strange this – the periodic outbursts of clapping as the waiting audience apparently thinks it's time for the action to begin.

Finally on to the stage come the Two Cellos. (Their names are Luka Sulic and Stjepan Hauser.) Dressed in dark leather jackets, black t-shirts and jeans, they are young and fashionably handsome. Their opening number sounds like a resonant, mainstream nineteenth-century cello duet, even if the volume of sound seems to be filling the auditorium to a surprising degree. In fact what they are playing are electric cellos with the kind of amplification required of most pop-group instruments. Soon the sound they are creating leaves behind any suggestion of the classical cello: the music is faster, louder, increasingly wild and frenetic. The audience is swaying, arms aloft, in time with the driving, pulsing rhythm. The Two Cellos are joined by a jazz-style drummer, and the volume of sounds grows even louder and more mind-blowing. The transformation of the Roundhouse into, say, T in the Park, is complete.

This is only the warm-up for Lang Lang. The pianist arrives on stage in a rainbow of changing spotlights and –yes – in a slowly uncurling bank of stage mist or smoke. He too is dressed for the occasion: a shiny black jacket, t-shirt and jeans. He plays Liszt. On each side of the proscenium arch huge screens show close-ups of his hands on the piano keys. (They had been there for the Two Cellos too.) Meantime the entire wall at the back of the stage becomes a vast film screen. So as our ears listen to the piano, our eyes are dazzled by an endless sequence of brightly coloured images of ever-changing streets and buildings and traffic and people, seascapes and cityscapes, shopping malls and neon advertisements, a bright kaleidoscope of a fast-moving and bustling world.

And the music? Well, Lang Lang performs the most difficult of Liszt's demanding pieces with incredible panache. This is virtuoso piano-playing at its virtuosic best. We are swept away by the brilliance of it all – the brilliance of the performance perhaps, more than of the music itself. Apparently 40 million Chinese children have been inspired by Lang Lang's example to take up the piano. The Roundhouse audience is equally ready to celebrate a star. After one of his several encores, Lang Lang, now dressed all in white, begs his enthusiastic audience to support classical music. But what we have just experienced is something not entirely unlike the so-called 'classical-pop crossover' represented by the Two Cellos.

My second and so different musical experience took place in Glasgow. In Glasgow University's Randolph Hall where the opening reception for the British Association of Romantic Studies biennial conference took place. In the course of the reception, Kirsteen McCue, who lectures on Scottish literature, sings a selection of songs by Burns and James Hogg, accompanied on the university's beautiful forte-piano by her husband, David Hamilton. In the grand setting of the nineteenth-century hall, the audience, just as in the Roundhouse, remains standing. But that is the only similarity between the two occasions. Here only the simplicity of voice and piano are on offer. The voice is pure and eloquent and richly moving.

Words and music are performed with classical power and classical restraint. The sound and fury of the Roundhouse suddenly seem a very long way away.

17 *That Guy Fae the Corries*

On the last page of his book Ronnie Browne writes that he has 'had a long, interesting and rewarding life'. The autobiography he has just published confirms that this is indeed the case. 'Successful' might well have been added to the list of adjectives, but it is characteristic of the author's modesty that he chooses not to include it. Nonetheless the narrative of the Browne life is in reality one of almost uninterrupted success. As a result, his book is sometimes in danger of becoming somewhat flat and unexciting. Of course we learn that at certain times Ronnie Browne made mistakes or bad decisions; that occasionally he behaved badly, hurting people he cared for; that schemes and plans he set up sometimes went badly wrong; and that, as for all of us, the passage of time inevitably meant he had at different times to cope with the illness and death of friends and family. But despite all this, the life of that guy from the Corries described in these pages – as the author fully recognizes — is a life of quite remarkable achievement and personal fulfilment.

When in the late 1950s at the Edinburgh College of Art, Ronnie Browne met the man destined to be the other half of the legendary Corries — Roy Williamson — he was acutely aware of the differences between them: they played for opposing rugby teams and competed for different Edinburgh athletic clubs, but more importantly, 'socially, as well, we were at opposite ends of the scale. I was working class and he was from a moneyed, professional background, his mother a pianist and his father a prominent attorney'. (p. 72) His father a long-distance lorry driver, Ronnie grew up in Edinburgh in what was clearly in most respects a fairly typical working-class family — though Browne's mother did develop a strong commitment to spiritualism, finally becoming a séance-holding medium herself, and persuading her husband and son to share her beliefs.

At both Preston Street primary school and Boroughmuir High School Ronnie proved to be an able student, frequently competing to be the 'dux' of his class. However, from an early age he showed an unusual aptitude for drawing and painting. So much so that when two reporters from the *Edinburgh Evening News* happened to see him –at the age of eleven — outside drawing Edinburgh's Black Watch Memorial, they arranged for him to be photographed and featured in the newspaper. About the same time, however, taken by his mother to see a spiritual healer over a minor sore, mother and son were told by the spiritualist 'this boy isn't going to make his name from drawing, you know, but from music'. (p. 41)

Despite this message from the spirit world, post-Boroughmuir Ronnie decided that Art College was where his future lay. Completing his four-year course in 1959, followed by teacher training at Moray House, for the next two years he did actually become a high school art teacher. In fact, despite the major change in the direction of his life that was about to happen, Ronnie never gave up drawing and painting, and indeed at different periods in his life, he enjoyed great success as a portrait painter in particular. It is not too much to say that, had he never sung a note, he would still have made his name as an artist in the world of Scottish culture.

But of course it was indeed from music that he was destined to make his name. *That guy fae the Corries* from childhood on had always been something of a singer. Yet there is nothing in the book to suggest that Ronnie ever had any sense — not to say expectation — that singing rather than painting would come to define his life. In making this happen, the meeting and growing friendship at college with Roy Williamson was crucial. 'Then,' as he puts it, ' in the early months of 1962, fate took a hand'.(p.90) Sitting with their wives (Ronnie had married his childhood sweetheart Pat in 1959 after a courtship and engagement which had lasted for several years), one night Roy picked up his guitar and the two men sang a few songs together. 'My goodness', said Roy's wife, 'they could easily be another Hall and MacGregor'. (p.90) (Robin Hall and Jimmy MacGregor were of course already famous as Scottish folk-song singers.) Soon afterwards a folk-singing group, including Paddie Bell, which Roy had joined, found itself missing a male singer. Ronnie agreed to take part and immediately became a regular member. The result was the creation of 'The Corrie Folk Trio and Paddie Bell'. Success was immediate. The new folk group was soon receiving invitations to appear at venues all around Scotland. Ireland and England followed suit before long, and perhaps more importantly, appearances began to occur on BBC television programmes such as the 'Hootenanny Show' and the 'White Heather Club'. Roy and Ronnie had already become professional performers, but by late 1963 Ronnie had a bigger decision to make. Should he resign his teaching post and become a full-time performer? The answer of course was yes.

In the years of the Corrie Folk Trio, Ronnie Browne's role was exclusively that of singer. Roy Williamson and Bill Smith played the various instruments the group employed. However on New Year's Day, 1966, everything changed. Relations between Smith and the others had become increasingly fraught, and on that day the breach became final. As Ronnie puts it: 'on January 1st, 1966, The Corrie Folk Trio was no more'. (p. 116) Ronnie and Roy were now The Corries — and Ronnie had to begin learning how to help with the instrumental accompaniment to their songs. Nervously at first, but in time with growing confidence, this he succeeded in doing.

For the next twenty-four years, the story that this autobiography tells, is quite simply that of how the Corries went from local and national to world–wide folk-singing success. Ronnie writes: 'I have painted the picture of my earlier professional life as one of unbridled progress and unqualified success'. (p.185) He goes on to suggest that in the period that followed, he had to face serious problems as a result of business and property ventures that did always go according to plan, but such problems had nothing to do with his life as a performer. Inevitably there were critics — of the status of the Corries as folk singers. 'Some people on the folk scene, club organisers and columnists, didn't entirely hold with our performances, thinking we should present a more serious blend of what they considered to be authentic...' (p.154) But Ronnie is reluctant to take such criticism seriously — the Corries provided the kind of programme their audiences wanted to hear, and some element of light-hearted entertainment in their shows was necessary. In any event, Ronnie, even if he is unwilling to try to analyse the reasons for their immense success, is confident of the integrity of the Corries' music. When Roy Williamson died in 1990, Ronnie said in a TV tribute: 'I think that what we managed to do was capture the eternal essence of Scottish music and Scottish-ness. That is certainly what I felt, and I know Roy did too'. 'Obviously', he goes on, 'we had to follow certain patterns, but the motivation was mainly feeling: feeling for the songs, the country, and the music'. (pp. 255-6) That is as much in the way of analysis that the surviving Corrie singer is prepared to offer.

After Roy Williamson's death, Ronnie Browne went on to continuing success as a solo performer, as a portrait painter, and even as an after dinner speaker, and the closing chapters of his book take us on his travels to participate in St Andrew's Day celebrations, Burns nights, and major sporting events, in countries around the world. Much of this of course had to do with the impact of the most famous of the Corries' songs: 'Flower of Scotland'. Let me end with a comment or two on this phenomenon.

First of all Ronnie is characteristically scrupulous in insisting that he played no part in the creation of 'Flower of Scotland'. Both words and music were exclusively the work of his partner, Roy Williamson. The only credit that Ronnie takes is that, after Roy's death, he became what he calls the song's 'guardian'. February 2nd, 1968, was the date of the Corries' first public performance of the song, and Ronnie tells us it became 'an instant hit with our audiences'. (p.137) However it was 1974 before it 'caught on' with the wider public — in Ronnie's view because of the publicity that resulted from its being adopted as their team song by the British Lions rugby players touring South Africa that year. A few months later the Corries cashed in on their success by releasing the song as a record single — which sold 8,000 copies in a week. Despite all this, I still feel it's true to say that it was only at the beginning of the 1990s — when Roy Williamson was dying — that 'Flower of Scotland' finally attained the status of Scotland's unofficial national anthem which it still holds today. Crucial here, as Ronnie Browne proudly explains, were the decisions by first the Scottish Rugby Union, and a few years later, by the Scottish Football Association, to make 'Flower of Scotland' Scotland's pre-kick-of national anthem — an accolade confirmed when Ronnie's own final personal rendition of the song took place at the opening of the Commonwealth Games in Scotland in 2014. So perhaps the history of 'Flower of Scotland' may be seen as supporting the theory that Scottish cultural nationalism preceded or anticipated the rise of Scottish political nationalism.

Finally, Ronnie Browne acknowledges there were those who were unhappy about the song's adoption as Scotland's anthem — because of its anti-English dimension. (I admit I'm one of them.) Ronnie's answer is that 'Flower of Scotland' is no more anti-English than 'God Save the Queen' is anti-Scottish. To prove this he quotes a verse, written in 1747, just after the end of the 1745 Jacobite Rebellion, which is certainly anti-Scottish. But this will not do. The verse in question disappeared almost as soon as it was written, and never appeared in the version that was adopted as the British national anthem much later in the eighteenth century. 'Flower of Scotland', on the other hand, in all of its verses, oddly, and in my view, inappropriately, chooses to define Scotland's identity by referring only to an ancient battle fought with its neighbour. Never mind. Ronnie Browne's understandable enthusiasm for the current status of the Corries' song will, I know full well, be shared by the vast majority of the readers of his quietly entertaining book.

18 Hockney

If you are in London any time between now and April 9th 2012, do not miss the David Hockney exhibition at the Royal Academy. It is a spectacular experience. Called 'A Bigger Picture', the exhibition focuses exclusively on versions of landscape. The vast majority of works on display depict scenes in Hockney's native Yorkshire and have been created between 2004 and 2011. However, some early examples of the painter's portrayal of scenes in the America where he lived for many years are included to suggest how, throughout his long career, Hockney has been preoccupied with the depiction of landscape space.

From the outset, two features will strike nearly every viewer. First the sheer scale of these works: bigger pictures indeed. Four huge works occupy the walls of the opening room. Called 'Thixendale Trees', they depict an identical tree-lined landscape over the four seasons of spring, summer, autumn, and winter. Works on a similar grand scale, often composed of an integrated grid of up to six large canvases, recur in many of the succeeding rooms. The second striking feature of the entire exhibition is the extraordinary, flamboyant vividness of Hockney's use of colour. The brilliance of light and shade transforms the familiar elements of the Yorkshire countryside – grass, fields, flowers, bushes, trees, leaves – into a symphony of explosive colour. East Yorkshire becomes as dramatically exotic as Tahiti.

Despite the concentration on landscape alone, the exhibition is multifaceted in a variety of ways. The earliest Yorkshire paintings, from the 2004-05 period, are watercolours painted outside from direct observation. In 2006 Hockney produced seven large oil paintings, called 'Woldgate Woods', featuring the same scene at different times in the year, all produced at an easel fixed at the same spot. On the other hand, many of the landscapes are the work, not of direct observation, but of memory and imagination combined. Then there are earlier examples of Hockney's amazing photo-collages of landscapes such as that of America's Grand Canyon – which captures the very texture of the layered strata of rock. In a recent development the artist has been producing new works using visual and technological aids – such as the iPad. Finally, near the end of the exhibition, a room is dedicated to showing Hockney's films of the Yorkshire landscape he has made by controlling nine cameras mounted on the bonnet of a Jeep. In a technically complex manner, the films flow and blend together in strange and fascinating detail. Some art critics have been prepared to see a greater or lesser degree of success in Hockney's use of these various techniques. No expert, I can't. Every work is impressive, and the variety of approaches suggests only the continuing energy and creativity of the not-so-young artist.

One factor above all, I believe, ensures Hockney's success as a landscape artist: his ability — so evident in this exhibition--to draw the viewer into the scene at which he is looking. Several large works depict woods. Standing in front of them, one's eyes are stretched to take in the entire scene. The result is that the gap between you and the trees seems to disappear. You no longer are outside, but rather inside the wood. Still more important is Hockney's inclusion in so many of these pictures of roads or pathways. I have no idea of the exact percentage, but over and over again these landscapes contain a road of some kind. The pattern is established in the American examples on display here. 'Pearblossom Highway' (1986) is a wonderful photo-collage of an empty road with litter, road-signs, and one or two stunted cactus trees. 'Mulholland Drive: the Road to the Studio' (1980) has the curving ribbon of the road at the heart of the picture. Such roads feature in almost every Yorkshire landscape, and the effect is always the same: the viewer's eye is drawn in by the road, following its direction, seeking its destination. Inevitably you are there, part of the scene at which you are staring. And what do you see? Nothing human, usually not even a human artefact. The road remains empty — except for you and the landscape of which you have become part.

Enjoying this exhibition and the world it creates so vividly, I'm reminded of some of Robert Frost's poems about the landscapes of New England: 'The Road Not Taken', 'Stopping By Woods on a Snowy Evening', and, especially in the context of Hockney's paintings of piles of cut and stacked logs, 'The Wood-Pile'. But for Frost the focus is always on man's presence and role within the natural world. For Hockney, the landscape of the natural world speaks for itself.

19 Scottish Women Artists

That the Glasgow Girls Exhibition, about which he writes so vividly, is being held in 2014 in Kirkcudbright Town Hall, while the Glasgow Boys appear in Kelvingrove Art Gallery, leads Kenneth Roy to conclude that ours is a society that continues to undervalue the work of women artists, and if Scotland is indeed 'the land of the forgotten sex', the role of women in society more generally. Of course, there will be those who will argue that the status of more recent Scottish women artists has been widely recognised: Joan Eardley, Anne Redpath, Elizabeth Blackadder, Barbara Balmer, Bet Low, for example, are admired names. Others, however – such as Germaine Greer – will agree that in the orthodox history of art the role and contribution of women continue to be seriously neglected if not completely denied.

Not so long ago I myself wrote here about just how difficult it is to alter received opinion about the status of male and female artists in a different field: that of Romantic poetry. I noted how all seven of the writers in *The Guardian*'s give-away series called 'The Romantic Poets' were men. So despite the best efforts of a whole generation of critics and commentators arguing that the work of women poets in the Romantic period should be more widely recognised, nothing seems to have changed.

In his article, Kenneth is rightly much exercised by the neglect and denigration of Joan Ure, perhaps the twentieth century's most outspoken critic of our culture's treatment of women artists in the field of theatre. And Joan Ure had every reason to feel that her work had been undervalued and even rejected by the Scottish theatrical world of her time. (She died in 1978.) But perhaps in this area at least there has been a change for the better. In the decades after the Second World War the Scottish playwrights who gained general recognition were almost all men: one thinks of Robert Kemp, Robert McLellan, Ronald Mavor, C.P. Taylor, Stewart Conn, Bill Bryden, John Byrne and John McGrath. In more recent decades, however, there has been at least something of a change. Liz Lochhead, Marcella Evaristi, Anne Marie Di Mambro, Rona Munro, Sue Glover, have all enjoyed some degree of recognition and success. Ena Lamont Stewart's 1947 play 'Men Should Weep' has been successfully revived, and Kenneth I hope will be pleased to hear that, outside Scotland at least, his friend Joan Ure is not entirely forgotten.

Italy has recently become a centre of Ure studies. Professor Valentina Poggi, formerly of the University of Bologna, has both translated and written on Ure. Dr. Gioia Angeletti, teaching at the University of Parma, has just published a book containing a long introduction on Ure's writing career, followed by translations of two of Ure's plays: her own translation of 'I see Myself as this Young Girl' plus Professor Poggi's version of 'Take your old Rib back, then'. In addition Dr Angeletti has written on three of Ure's 'Shakespearean' plays: 'Something in it for Ophelia', 'Something in it for Cordelia', and 'Seven Characters out of The Dream'. I suspect that Joan Ure herself would find it both unsurprising and deeply ironic that she should be better known in Italy than in the land of the forgotten sex.

20 *A Chasm in Time: Scottish War Art and Artists in the Twentieth Century*

The title of this remarkable book comes from a letter to his brother by the Scottish poet Charles Sorley. An admirer of German culture, Sorley was actually studying in Germany when the First World War began. Back home, he enlisted to join the fight for his country, but unlike so many of his fellow-countrymen, never regarded the enemy as anything other than equally civilised opponents. From the beginning he had no illusions about what the war meant. His letter makes this abundantly clear: 'The war is a chasm in time. I do wish that all journalists etc., who say that war is an ennobling purge etc., etc., could be muzzled... All illusions about the splendour of war will, I hope, be gone after the war'. Sorley was to die in the Battle of Loos in October 1915.

In fact as late as 1916 the general run of British art had scarcely been affected by the reality of the war or its meaning. Lady Cynthia Asquith records visiting the Royal Academy's annual exhibition in June that year and being appalled by what she saw. 'Amazing to see it just the same as ever,' she writes. 'The old sheep by lakes, historical pictures, etc. It gave an extraordinary sense of stability unaffected by cataclysm.' A reviewer in *The Studio* agreed. 'Certainly there is no hint given by the show that this country is going through an experience almost without precedent in its history, and is engaged in what is actually a struggle for existence.' However, the one picture that both observers admired was a piece of war art: John Lavery's 'The First Wounded, The London Hospital, August 1914.' Cynthia Asquith's conclusion was that 'Certainly war does not seem to incubate art'.

The truth is that war has always stimulated the creative imagination in every form of art--including painting. But as Patricia Andrew shows in her opening chapter – 'From Colour to Khaki' – in the century preceding 1914, British art had been inclined to celebrate only the heroism and splendour of war, helping to create the kind of illusions that Charles Sorley hoped to see abandoned. And in that older patriotic and glorious tradition, no soldiers and regiments were more prominent than the Scottish ones. Scots in scarlet tunics and kilts had indeed attained iconic status in such late nineteenth-century pictures as Elizabeth, Lady Butler's hugely popular 'Scotland for Ever!' depicting the charge of the Scots Greys at Waterloo, and Robert Gibb's equally famous Crimean War picture 'The Thin Red Line'. In the extraordinary range and scope of Scottish war art of the twentieth century, however, which this book so effectively reveals, it is very much khaki, not scarlet, that becomes the dominant colour.

In her Introduction, Patricia Andrew explains that 'war art' and 'war artists' have been given 'generously wide definitions'. Her book, that is, covers much more than just painters and paintings; 'both fine and applied art, together with memorial sculptures, and some propaganda work and ephemera' are all included. The definition of 'Scottishness' is equally generous. Scottish-born artists predominate, but work produced, while they were based in Scotland, by artists from England and a range of other countries, is also well represented. Some familiar names appear: Muirhead Bone, John Lavery, Stanley Cursiter, Charles Rennie Mackintosh, D. Y. Cameron, J.D. Fergusson, Stanley Spencer (who 'did Scotland proud' with his fine variety of works depicting the Clyde shipyards during the Second World War), and (perhaps surprisingly) Robert Colquhoun and Robert MacBryde. But represented here are over 150 artists – the vast majority of whom I imagine will be unknown, not only to me, but to most readers. Again the majority are trained professionals, career artists who turn for a time to the subject of war. But a few are non-professional, self-taught figures successfully producing powerful images of war. A fine example is Hiram Law Sturdy's ink and watercolour sketch of the Western Front in the First World War called 'Blowing Bodies to Smithereens'. Sturdy, from Lanarkshire, a miner and house painter, was an amateur artist but, unlike the large number of professionals who, from 1916 on, acquired official status in either or both world wars as designated war artists, he was free to record exactly what he saw. The official artists on the other hand, though able to record the desolation and destruction of trench warfare, were not permitted to portray killing and death. (Sturdy survived the first war and went on to produce sketches of the Home Guard in the second.) Another amateur was Fred Farrell, a civil engineer who became a self-taught painter and etcher. So impressive was his work that, after his discharge from the army on medical grounds, the city of Glasgow uniquely appointed him its official war artist in 1917 and 18. Many of his simple and direct, but atmospherically powerful, sketches were published in 1920 as 'The 51st (Highland) Division War Sketches' with an introduction by Neil Munro.

In her Introduction once again, Patricia Andrew insists that her book 'is aimed at the general reader, not the academic art historian'.

What this means is that *A Chasm in Time* is refreshingly free from theory-ridden jargon and over-intellectualisation. Equally there is a welcome absence of naïve political point scoring over the horrors of capitalist warmongering or imperialist propagandising. No attempt is made to find underlying structures or themes that will handily explain away all we need to know about Scottish war art and war artists. What we have instead is an immensely comprehensive account of the amazing range of forms (including posters and cartoons), styles, and objects, through which Scottish and Scotland –based artists, major or minor, have documented two world wars and subsequent conflicts in the twentieth century. Many readers I feel sure will be reminded of realities we should never forget — the bombing of Clydebank in 1941 for example — evoked so dramatically in the work of Ian Fleming, Hugh Adam Crawford, and Tom McKendrick. And how many of us knew that Charles Rennie Mackintosh's final piece of architectural design in Glasgow was for an extension to Miss Cranston's Willow Tea Room in Sauchiehall Street in 1916/17? The basement extension was specifically intended to be both a celebration and memorial of the ongoing war. Lacking any kind of natural light, it became known as the 'Dug-Out'.

In the Second World War Kenneth Clark devised a scheme he called 'Recording Britain'. The idea was to record the kind of Britain the war was fighting to preserve, and watercolour was to be the sole medium employed. More artists took part than in any other war-artist scheme. Despite its success, however, the scheme had a major flaw. 'Recording Britain' in fact recorded only England and Wales. The result was that in 1942 a separate 'Recording Scotland' scheme was set up in which artists could work in any medium, and the organising committee was free to purchase works already completed. A single volume 'Recording Scotland' was finally published in 1952.

A Chasm in Time is a Scottish record in itself. This book tellingly and vividly preserves, restores and represents the link between war and the painterly or visual imagination throughout the twentieth century. Better still, the book is a work of art in its own right. The writer, publisher, designer, and all those individuals and trusts that have contributed to its production for only £30, deserve the highest possible praise. The quality of illustration is a joy in itself. Appointed the official British war artist for Bosnia in 1993, the Glasgow painter Peter Howson described his role in the following terms: 'My job is to do the things you don't see, that the army doesn't even get to see, not to be an illustrator, not to tell stories, but to produce strong images of things'. Some of Howson's fellow war artists do indeed provide illustrations and tell stories, but readers of this beautiful book will find 'strong images of things' on almost every page.

21 Two Cultural Moments

Two recent (2014) newspaper articles have helped to focus some thoughts of my own. The first took the form of a book review in the *Observer*. The book being discussed is called *Narrative and Identity in the Ancient Greek Novel*. The reviewer thinks well of Tim Whitmarsh's academic work, but what really struck me were two general observations he makes about the overall state of literary studies on the basis of his reading of this particular work. He suggests that literary scholars are suffering from a sense that their area of expertise is not really of much importance. Poetry and fiction are no more than forms of entertainment, hence what they do, in the words of the reviewer (the novelist Tibor Fischer), makes them no more than 'high-class usherettes of an auditorium of mere entertainment'. That is why the theories of literary criticism – Fischer cites post-colonialism in particular – currently so much in fashion, all involve large helpings of history, politics, economics, race and issues of identity. In my opinion there is a large measure of truth in this observation. Literature courses today rarely focus on the aesthetic value of texts. All texts are equal in the light they may cast on the post-colonial, new-historical, feminist, deconstructive, psychological – or whichever paradigm happens to be in question.

Fischer's second observation makes me laugh as much as it does him. Here is how he puts it: 'It seems now impossible to publish an academic work without mentioning Foucault, Derrida or Lacan..'. One might add a few other names – Benjamin, Althusser, Kristeva, Baudrillard – but Fischer's point is spot on. Young scholars, whatever the topic they are writing on, clearly feel it is an absolute imperative to find a way of making one or other of these masters of 'theory', relevant to their narrative. I recently listened to a perfectly sensible paper on James Robertson's wonderful novel *Joseph Knight* But whether any fresh light was thrown on the text by invoking at length Julia Kristeva's theory of abjectness was another matter. But I quite understand that the chance of the paper appearing in an academic journal will be enhanced less by the presence of James Robertson than by the appearance of Kristeva and her theories.

The second article that helped to clarify my own response to its subject appeared in a recent *Guardian*. The paper's art critic, Jonathan Jones, had been on a lightning visit to Glasgow to take in the exhibition of work by this year's graduating class at the city's School of Art. For Jones, Glasgow's degree show turned out to be 'the most enjoyable and gripping' he has seen this year, reinforcing the School's international reputation, underlined, as he sees it, by the fact that the last two winners of the Turner prize were its graduates. (He does not mention that he was a Turner prize judge for one of those years.) Inevitably then, the artists and works he chooses to praise are such as might be in competition for future awards of that much-debated prize: Amy Dolan's powerful video in which a young woman describes what Jones calls 'unspeakable violence'; John Kellock's 'excellent and spookily comic paintings' (but apparently not his 29-hour digital photograph performance); and an outrageous video by Max Prus 'involving scenes of celebrity sex, defecation, and a man who claims to be John Lennon's killer'.

On my visit to the exhibition I somehow missed that particular video — and I cannot honestly say I much regret that. But my main point is that my own purely personal response to the show was really the opposite of Mr Jones. I was pleasantly surprised by the number of Glasgow graduates who, despite the continuing enthusiasm of many metropolitan critics, and Saatchi-style collectors, are clearly not interested in the Turner Prize. Of course, as Jonathan Jones's piece indicates, there were numerous installations, videos, and mixed media presentations; fashionably conceptual art, that is, was inevitably present in a range of forms. But there were also a large number of what could be called more traditional works of art: oils on canvas and board, water-colours, different forms of prints. Some young artists remain interested in portraits and landscapes. I enjoyed a variety of paintings by Garry Brander, Amelia Barratt, Dominika Majowicz, and Mary Stephenson. And I have to admit it was reassuring to learn that on graduation day the Chairman's Gold Medal was awarded to the large, bold, and richly-coloured oil paintings of Gabriella Boyd.

22 Swan Lake

Late in 2013, eighteen years after its original 1995 Sadler's Wells production, a revival of Matthew Bourne's 'Swan Lake' began touring the U.K. On a recent Saturday night, I attended Glasgow's King's Theatre's final performance. It was a fabulously overwhelming experience. Like I suspect many other theatre and concert-goers, I've become irritated by the way in which, at the end of any kind of half-decent performance, it's become fashionable for people to get up from their seats trying to ensure a standing ovation. Not on Saturday night. I was out of my seat — damp-eyed — wildly applauding like everyone else. Let me try to explain why.

I should say that I make no claim to any kind of particular expertise on either classical ballet or modern dance. But the intriguing opening moments of this production in which a young man (the royal prince) seems to be possessed in his sleep by some kind of terrible nightmare, while at a window high above his bed, a ghostly swan-like figure seems to be struggling to get in, are immediately followed by a series of scenes of a wholly different kind. These scenes are professionally brilliant: hugely entertaining, and danced with stunning polish, speed and vividness. The stage seems to be constantly in motion. Situations and characters are established and identified; comedy and wit abound — especially in the trendy Swank Bar, disco-style segment. A form of 'dance within a dance' even allows some gentle parody of classical ballet. And throughout Tchaikovsky's great music drives the performance forward.

However, half an hour in, with the beginning of Act 2, all this changes. Making one, crucial imaginative innovation, Matthew Bourne transforms 'Swan Lake', and lifts his production to an entirely different level of aesthetic and artistic achievement. The lonely and confused young prince finds himself confronted by the swans of the lake. But these swans are not the delicate, tutu-clad, young women of the classical ballet tradition. Bourne's swans are muscular young men, bare-chested and bare-backed, their lower bodies covered in swan feather-like costumes. In a series of scenes they take over the stage, dominating it in a dauntingly physical choreography of movement and power. These swans are challenging, aggressive, threatening — but also brilliant, thrilling and exhilarating.

At the centre of these scenes — indeed at the imaginative heart of the entire production — come the confrontations between the young prince and – most challenging of all — the principal swan, towards whom he finds himself irresistibly drawn. As these two command the stage, facing and taunting each other, circling, colliding, breaking apart, and redoubling their challenge, the emotional power and intensity of their dancing — and Tchaikovsky's score — are heart-stopping and spellbinding to the degree one wishes there should be no end. This is art offering us an insight into the very essence of life and experience — the life and experience of sensuality, passion, emotion and love — at a level of transcendent genius.

Writing of a pre-Glasgow performance (in Milton Keynes Theatre), a reviewer admitted that what she hadn't expected was that 'the sheer beauty and power of the dancing between Mower [the prince] and Trenfield [the principal swan] would reduce me to tears by the end'. In Glasgow the roles were played by Simon Williams and Jonathan Ollivier with exactly the same emotional outcome — so no doubt the ultimate credit for the work's final impact lies with Matthew Bourne himself, and his inevitable decision to follow the original Swan Lake story down to its tragic conclusion.

Which brings me in conclusion to the possibly controversial issue that Bourne's version of 'Swan Lake' raises. Near the end of the production there is a brief scene in which the young prince, made even more troubled and confused by his latest encounter with the all-powerful, all-conquering swan, appears to be incarcerated in some kind of mental institution. The common assumption since 1995 appears to be that we are to see this as evidence of his breakdown into madness. Perhaps. But it is surely possible in 2014 to suggest that we are to see the scene as representing his being desperately treated for a different 'illness'.

In a *Guardian* interview last October, Matthew Bourne talked interestingly about his original design for 'Swan Lake'. The decision to cast the swans as men, he maintained, arose from his observation of actual swans and their natural aggressiveness — and he had also been strongly influenced by Hitchcock's film *The Birds*. His portrayal of the young prince, he tells us, was partly suggested by his sense of how restricted members of the royal family found their lives to be. But he also recognized Tchaikovsky as 'a troubled man who, partly because of his homosexuality, couldn't be the person he wanted to be'. On the other hand, on the crucial question of the role of homosexuality in the production as a whole, Bourne was somewhat defensive. 'It's been interpreted as a homosexual story,' he said, 'but that wasn't the explicit intention'. It was 'more about a repressed young man's need to be loved, rather than about any sexual desire'.

How far a homosexual theme is explicit or implicit here is for audience members to make up their own minds. But as far as the history of gay rights is concerned, there can be no question that Bourne's Swan Lake ballet should be seen in the context of two equally successful works in differing artistic forms which had appeared at almost the same time: Tony Kushner's play 'Angels in America' (1993), and Jonathan Demme's film *Philadelphia* (1993) starring Tom Hanks and Denzil Washington. The difference is that while both the play and the film effectively and movingly explore the moral, legal and social issues arising from the homosexual theme, it is the dance that displays, above all, the power and passion of love that transcends gender.

Much of the world of course continues to deny even the possibility of such an experience. (No fewer than 36 countries in the African continent ban and persecute same-sex relations as illegal.) No doubt it is merely fanciful to ask whether Ugandan president Museveni and his like, as members of the audience, would join in the standing ovation at the end of the next performance of Matthew Bourne's 'Swan Lake'?

23 London Life

The American actor Kevin Spacey, artistic director of the Old Vic since 2004, is stepping down next year. However, he is planning to stay on in London which he regards as 'a very energising place to be'. 'It's been incredible to be in London,' he tells us, 'at a time when it's developed into the cultural centre not just of Europe, but arguably the world'. Such comments set beside many others from a range of perspectives – economic, financial, social, as well as cultural – suggest that London stands apart from the rest of the country, making the great wen sound more and more like a city state in its own right. In medieval and renaissance Italy, Florence, Siena, and Venice were powerful political entities, in the end more distinguished for their artistic and cultural achievements than anything else. Contemporary London in 2014 certainly buzzes with material energy and activity: the scale and range alone of new building and reconstruction going on apace are astonishing. Whole areas of the city appear to be undergoing transformation. Is Spacey right, and does that transformation extend to the city's artistic life?

Obviously any visitor's report is strictly limited, but for what it's worth here is mine. First the English National Opera's 'Cosi Fan Tutte' in the Coliseum theatre. This was a spectacular production which my American companions loved. Enjoying it, I was rather less enthusiastic. A joint production with New York's Metropolitan Opera, London seemed determined to show that it could dress up a classic work in entirely new clothes. The basic concept behind this version of Mozart's text was that the story was taking place within some kind of amusement park or fairground. I was thinking Vauxhall Gardens, but with a nod perhaps towards the New York staging, it was in fact supposed to be Coney Island. The result was that much of the time the stage was crowded with incidental fairground performers: acrobats, jugglers, fire-eaters, sword-swallowers, dwarves and others. All good fun, but in the end too much of a good thing, distracting from rather than enhancing the opera's main focus on love, fidelity and betrayal.

The same degree of over-production appeared in the very elaborate stage effects: seedy motel rooms with lots of farcical business, swan boats slowly floating across the stage, a metallic Faberge-style egg (with a singer inside) descending from above. All just a bit too much, turning Mozart's comic opera – which is widely seen as not without its darker side – into very light entertainment indeed.

The Royal Ballet's production in the Royal Opera House, Covent Garden, was a show of a very different kind. Consisting of three separate, short ballets, it opened once again on an international, American note: a performance of 'Serenade', the very first work choreographed by George Balanchine, founding father of modern American dance. Danced all in white against a richly blue background, 'Serenade' was stunningly beautiful. Movement and music (by Tchaikovsky) blended perfectly to produce a transcendent experience of aesthetic purity. The second work – 'Sweet Violets', with music by Rachmaninoff – proved more problematic. The story it was telling, involving the English painter Walter Sickert, his prostitute models, 'Eddy', Queen Victoria's son and heir, the British prime minister Salisbury, and Jack the Ripper, was a highly complex one. Music and dance alone, however fine, struggled to get it across.

However, given the third work, 'DGV: Danse A Grande Vitesse', choreographed by Christopher Wheeldon, with music by Michael Nyman, the evening ended with renewed brilliance. Driven by Nyman's pulsating, minimalist music, the speed and athleticism of the Royal Ballet dancers in this performance were breathtaking. Against a background of curving metallic shapes (the work was originally composed to celebrate a new section of France's TGV railway system), the speed and violence of movement gained an impressively radical beauty of its own. Once again the power of dance was transforming.

My final report from London involves the iconic setting of Tate Modern, a location about which I have in the past had mixed feelings. Immediately opposite, in full view just across the Thames, rises St. Paul's Cathedral – and Wren's masterpiece – I sometimes feel, represents a classical challenge to the modern art that Tate Modern celebrates. Not this time however. The current exhibition of Henri Matisse's 'cut-outs' is extraordinary.

Late on in his long life, when health problems meant he was largely wheelchair-bound, Matissse found a new way of creating works of art by cutting out painted paper shapes. As his secretary and studio-assistant recalled: 'Matisse had cut out a swallow from a sheet of writing paper and, as it distressed him to tear up this beautiful shape and throw it away, he said, he put it up on this wall also using it to cover up a stain, the sight of which disturbed him. Over the following weeks other shapes were cut out and put up on the same wall'. In subsequent years, the shapes he cut out from paper of every colour became more and more elaborate, and what was created grew in scale and variety. 'It is no longer the brush that slips and slides over the canvas, it is the scissors that cut into the paper and into the colour.'

The current exhibition is displayed in 14 rooms – some with only a handful of large works, others in which every wall explodes with a mass of smaller ones. But every room is ablaze with creative energy, vivid colour, and imaginative power. There is even a film with the artist at scissors-wielding work. Cutting out in this manner clearly provided Matisse with an extraordinary new lease of creative life. Sitting in his home and studio, the shapes he made came to reflect what he had seen and known in his past life. 'It's as though my memory had suddenly taken the place of the outside world.' 'I don't think that I have ever found such balance as I have in creating these paper cut-outs.' This exhibition is an experience not to be missed.

I had gone to Tate Modern with an old Glasgow friend now living in London. Sitting in a sandwich bar close to St. Paul's, our post-Matisse thoughts moved on to the absorbing political issue of the day – the referendum. As we chatted away, we were interrupted by a young man who explained he couldn't help hearing what we were discussing. It turned out he had lots of Scottish friends and relatives, and was fascinated to hear the issue being discussed. His enthusiasm in turn made me wonder whether Matisse's cut-outs, Balanchine and the Royal Ballet, and Mozart's opera could have any relevance to Scotland's political debate? Perhaps one point is worth making. London's culture is clearly confident enough to be totally international and transnational. Is there a message for Scotland there?

24 The Romantic Poets

These days it's not only charities that bombard us with 'free gifts' in order to persuade us – or should that be blackmail us – into supporting them. Very frequently now newspapers too try to boost their sales by accompanying each copy with a free something or other. Normally I find these freebies have little appeal but recently *The Guardian* had on offer something I found irresistible. On seven successive days the paper was sold along with a contribution to a pamphlet-style series called 'The Romantic Poets'. Each little publication consisted of a short introduction to that day's poet by a well-known contemporary writer – Andrew Motion, Margaret Drabble, Germaine Grier, for example – followed by a selection of poems and extracts from poems, rounded off by some form of autobiographical comment by the poet in question. What interested me most about the series was not its contents – the selection of poetic material included – but just who the 'Romantic Poets' were deemed to be. Here they are in the order in which they appeared: Keats, Byron, Burns, Wordsworth, Coleridge, Shelley, Blake.

Most readers of *The Guardian* – and of the *Scottish Review* – will find nothing surprising in that list. Nor do I. Nonetheless it did set me thinking. What if the *Guardian*'s sister paper *The Observer* had published a similar series not in 2010 but in 1810 – when the Romantic movement was sweeping all before it in Western culture. Would the names have been the same? I think not. By 1810 Blake had produced most of his best work but he remained virtually unknown: it would be late in the nineteenth century before his importance as a Romantic poet would begin to be recognized. By 1810 Wordsworth and Coleridge too had produced the best of their poetry, but their status and popularity were distinctly limited. They would not have made an appearance. Keats and Shelley of course were too young in 1810 to be included – but even if their later work had been available, I don't think they'd have made the list. As compared with 2010's series, in 1810 only Burns and Byron – just launching his hugely successful poetic career – would have been sure to appear. Who else? 2010 is in fact the bicentenary of 'The Lady of the Lake' – a poem that proved even more successful than Scott's earlier narrative poems. Scott would undoubtedly have been there. A fourth Scot would probably have appeared: Thomas Campbell, author 'The Pleasures of Hope',

'Gertrude of Wyoming', and immensely popular war-songs and ballads. Only one Englishman would have been sure of appearing; the hugely successful Samuel Rogers, author of 'The Pleasures of Memory', a work which went into four editions in its first year. So Byron, Burns, Scott, Campbell, and Rogers would have been the newspaper's choice in 1810 – with the Irishmen Tom Moore and James Montgomery possibly also appearing.

What if we move on a hundred years to 1910? The answer then is clear. The 'Romantic poets' had become the famous five: Wordsworth, Coleridge, Byron, Keats and Shelley. No one else really mattered. Blake was still a somewhat eccentric poetic figure, and Burns had disappeared into the Scottish ghetto where he would remain stranded for several generations. (A year or two back, Professor Murray Pittock delivered a British Academy lecture in which he demonstrated just how far Burns had disappeared from conventional accounts of British Romanticism.) So one's first reaction to today's *Guardian* series of 'the Romantic poets' is to applaud the inclusion of the former outsiders: Blake and Burns. Whatever the shortcomings of the year of Homecoming and the Gathering, the bicentenary celebrations of Burns's birth – including nine international conferences on his work – should be seen as an unqualified success. Burns is back.

One's second response to the *Guardian* list is more equivocal. For many of us today what is the most striking thing about the Romantic roll call of Keats, Byron, Burns, Wordsworth, Coleridge, Shelley, Blake? Surely the fact that the Romantic poets remain exclusively male. For well over a generation now a host of literary critics and scholars have argued the case for a revision of the traditional literary canon of major English writers. Why? Because the canon is the creation of a dead, white, middle-class, male, world. Minorities have never stood a chance of admission, and the biggest minority of all is that composed of women. So in the case of the Romantic period, enormous efforts have been made to rediscover and re-evaluate a range of women Romantic poets. Anthologies of their work have been published; data-bases and web-sites have been established; catalogues and electronic text collections and editions compiled; critical studies produced. No literary historian today, writing about British Romanticism, would fail to acknowledge the importance of Mary Robinson, Charlotte Smith, Joanna Baillie, Mrs Barbauld, Hannah More etc. Growing up in Wick, I remember my grandfather reciting 'The boy stood on the burning deck' (Casabianca) by Felicia Hemans: today Mrs

Hemans is the subject of serious scholarly study. But has all this academic investment and endeavour in redefining the Romantic poets delivered the longed-for change? *The Guardian*'s choice of an all male cast of the famous five plus two has to suggest that the answer is no. The boys still rule OK?

25 A Big Book

In James Kelman's Booker Prize-winning novel *How Late It Was, How Late* (1994), there is a scene in which the incarcerated Sammy, the novel's protagonist, comments on a cell-mate using a personal stereo: 'ye knew he was coming a cropper: he had gave up the ghost; sitting there backed into the wall with his eyes shut, his knees up and his chin down, the earplugs, dreaming his fucking dreams'. This image of the personal stereo prisoner – eyes shut, ears plugged – is a defining one for the kind of novel that in recent years has come to dominate Scottish fiction. In novel after novel writers have succeeded brilliantly in focusing on and creating characters who, for a variety of reasons – social, political, psychological – find themselves ignored, shut out, disconnected from any meaningful contact with the surrounding world. The resulting self-enclosed, limited consciousness is evoked for the reader with astonishing intensity, immediacy and vividness. *How Late It Was, How Late* is the classic example of the genre, well worth the Booker and every other prize.

What defines the so-called 'Glasgow' school of contemporary novelists – Kelman himself, Alasdair Gray, William McIlvanney, Jeff Torrington, Janice Galloway, Agnes Owens, and of course Irvine Welsh – is a commitment to giving a voice, to a greater or lesser degree, to the Scottish working or under-class, to the ignored , the neglected, the dispossessed. And in a general sense, the job has been done. No account of contemporary Scottish culture, and of Scottish literary culture in particular, could possibly ignore the impact of the Glasgow school. But they are not the whole story. Alongside their familiar names, there exists another group of Scottish novelists working within an alternative tradition of Scottish writing. Their immediate antecedent is the unjustly neglected James Kennaway, but today's Allan Massie, Ronald Frame, Iain Banks, William Boyd (if we can lay claim to him as Scottish) and Emma Tennant continue to create fictions in which plot and character are able to engage with that wider world of society, history, politics, art and culture that Sammy and the other oppressed and victimized characters of the Glasgow school are inevitably excluded from.

Is it possible for a writer to bring together in some way these two traditions of the contemporary Scottish novel? Well in my view that is exactly what James Robertson has achieved in his splendid new novel *And the Land Lay Still*. Robertson is of course already an established and admired contemporary writer. His 2003 novel *Joseph Knight* gained both prizes and critical praise – and deserved even more. Its evocation of life in enlightened eighteenth-century Scotland , and on the Scottish-owned and run slave plantations in Jamaica, is compelling. It proves that in the right hands the historical novel is very much alive and well. (That is why it is so surprising to learn that, in terms of sales, *Joseph Knight* is the least popular of Robertson's novels: what are all those American professors with their literature courses in colonialism, slavery, and racism thinking about?)

The new novel is a big book — and not only in the sense that it's almost 700 pages long. It is big as Grassic Gibbon's *Scots Quair* is big. It is big as McIlvanney's *Docherty* is big. It is big as Gray's *Lanark* is big. *And the Land Lay Still* charts the movement of fifty years of Scottish history from 1947 to 1997, evoking a changing society, economy, morality, and political world — including the story of the emergence of the SNP, a story handled with a Scott-like even-handedness. Its settings range as widely: from the remotest north-west of Sutherlandshire, through mining villages and provincial towns, to Edinburgh and Glasgow. Its characters, created with an almost Dickensian richness, emerge from and define every level of the class structure of Scottish society. Readers may find such range and variety of characters hard to keep up with. (There's no harm in checking back...) And Robertson does not choose to bring them all together through the kind of complex plotting that a Victorian novelist might have chosen to invent. Most of these characters act out their own story — inside or outside a family structure. But as in a Faulkner or Dos Passos novel, the story of one character will fleetingly intersect with that of another.

The narrative structure is not a simple linear one. There are many flashbacks, recollected memories, surreal moments, interminglings of past and present. Does Robertson succeed in unifying such a country-wide sweep of material? I think he does. His sense of an ending has always been keen. Joseph Knight, the actual slave brought from Jamaica to Scotland by his owner, and finally freed by the Court of Session in Edinburgh in 1778, thereafter disappears from history. James Robertson finds him in a brilliant flight of the creative imagination. *And the Land Lay Still* ends with parallel brilliance. In allowing one of his main characters — a photographer — to explain how he has arranged a retrospective exhibition of the work of his father — a more successful photographer — Robertson is able to comment on the nature of his own work as a novelist, forming and structuring a picture of the Scotland of the recent past. The intellectualism of these pages then fades into an electrifying account of the link between the photographs on the gallery's wall and the lives of some of the characters with whom we have become involved. It is an ending that is emotionally powerful and extraordinarily moving. A big book indeed.

26 Witch Wood

As an eager young reader growing up in Wick, I began to collect the 'Best of the Best Books' published in the once popular Nelson Classics series. Each volume cost two shillings and sixpence and recently I was pleased to see that still sitting on my bookshelf was a Nelson Classics edition of *Prester John* by John Buchan. My pleasure in the acquisition is made clear by the neatly written inscription on the volume's flyleaf: 'Bought by Andrew Hook, on the 10th day of November 1944' (when I was eleven years old).

Whether I enjoyed reading *Prester John* as much as or more than the second Nelson Classic title I acquired on that very same 10th of November in 1944 – *Rob Roy* by Sir Walter Scott – or for that matter the R. L. Stevenson titles in the series I bought in Glasgow in April, 1945 – *Treasure Island, The Master of Ballantrae*, and *Travels with a Donkey in the Cevennes* – I'm afraid I really can't remember. What I do know is that as a student and teacher of English literature, I stopped thinking of John Buchan – if I thought of him at all – as a 'classic' author. Rather I came to think of him in what I suppose came to be the standard, or taken-for-granted, manner of recent years. He was the popular author of a great many adventure stories, entertaining and easy to read, but regrettably celebrating a time – now deeply unfashionable – when the values of a still imperial, establishment Britain were accepted without criticism of any kind.

Aware of Buchan's Scottish background, I nonetheless would never have thought of him as a Scottish writer. Rather than emerging from any Scottish literary tradition, his many novels seemed to align him with other contemporary writers of popular adventure stories such as Rider Haggard, A.E.W. Mason, or fellow-Scots, Andrew Lang and Conan Doyle. Scottish landscapes may have occurred in *The Thirty-Nine Steps*, and other stories, but that was the extent of their Scottishness. With Scott and Stevenson there is indeed a Scottish tradition of fiction involving travel and adventure, but Buchan had chosen not to follow it – or so I thought.

In fact I was entirely wrong. Like many others I suspect, the problem was I had not read the right novels. Early in his career Buchan wrote a historical novel *A Lost Lady of Old Years*. Published in 1899, it was written when he was scarcely twenty-three years old – the same age as Scott Fitzgerald when he launched his career with *This Side of Paradise*. The American's novel was an instant success — clearly much more so than *A Lost Lady of Old Years* (the somewhat clumsy title comes from a poem by Browning). But Buchan's attempt at writing a historical novel is full of interest. Set in the years of the Jacobite rebellion of 1745, and including a persuasive account of the inevitable defeat at Culloden, the novel's most striking feature is the characterization of its protagonist — Francis Birkenshaw. Birkenshaw is an early example of what we would call an anti-hero. He is a deeply flawed character, violent, impetuous, selfish, and uncaring. Almost from moment to moment, his emotions swing wildly from hope to despair. His behaviour is unpredictable and irrational. Neither a Jacobite nor a Hanoverian, he seems to be without principles or beliefs. He struggles only to survive in a stricken Scotland — literally, in impressive passages in which Buchan describes his solitary trek through the Scottish Highlands at their most hostile, desolate and forbidding. Perhaps it is a step too far to see in the conflicted and ambiguous, but finally conformist Birkenshaw, an image of mid-eighteenth Scotland itself, yet even to suggest as much is to point to the quality and promise of this early tale.

That promise was emphatically realised in 1927 when Buchan published what he himself came to regard as his finest novel: *Witch Wood*, another Scottish historical novel, set this time in the mid-seventeenth century. The Scottish historical figure for whom Buchan appears to have had the highest regard was James Graham, the Marquis of Montrose: so much so that he published two biographical studies of a man he saw as a truly heroic figure. The first appeared in 1913, the second, a revised and more mature study, appeared in 1928. In other words Buchan was writing *Witch Wood* almost exactly at the time when he was back at work on Montrose. It is then no surprise to find Montrose actually appearing briefly in the novel.

In *A Lost Lady of Old Years* Buchan chooses not to become involved in providing any kind of analysis of the issues at stake in the 1745 Jacobite rising. The focus of the novel is very much on Birkenshaw's adventures, and his complex relationship with the doomed Jacobite leader Simon Fraser, Lord Lovat — and as we have seen, Birkenshaw's motivations have little or nothing to do with religious or political beliefs. The historical context of the civil wars involving Scotland and England in the 1640s is more fully addressed in *Witchwood*, but even here the main focus is not on historical event. In fact the central theme of *Witchwood* is one that links it to another major tradition of Scottish historical fiction: Calvinist extremism as a feature of Scottish religious, political and social experience.

In the debate surrounding the recent referendum, questions were frequently asked about the role of Scottish literature in relation to nationalism and the union. Where, one historian asked, was the great novel about 1707 and its consequences? For me the answer – if there is one — has to be Scott's *Waverley*, published exactly two hundred years ago in1814. Its closing powerful image of the magically restored estate of Tully-Veolan — devastated in the conflict of the '45 — points to the reconciliation and unification achieved 'sixty years since'. But it is true that the era of the union has proved less amenable to the Scottish novelists' imagination than has the religious strife and violence of the decades that preceded it. Calvinism has in one way or another stimulated some of the most admired works in Scottish fiction: Scott's *Old Mortality*, Hogg's *Justified Sinner*. Galt's *Ringan Gilhaize*, and more recently, James Robertson's *The Fanatic* and his *The Testament of Gideon Mack*. Buchan's *Witch Wood*, however, should certainly be added to this list.

The protagonist of *Witch Wood* is David Sempill, a young, idealistic Presbyterian minister in the Scottish borders, who finds himself locked in a bitter confrontation with leading members of his congregation whose Calvinist extremism, he comes to suspect, coexists with a secret commitment to the practices of an ancient pagan world. This social and religious confrontation in the parish of Woodilee is set in the context of the Scotland-wide political and religious strife of the 1640s. Montrose, originally a supporter of the National Covenant and the Presbyterian party in the early years of the English Civil War, having become disillusioned by the behaviour of the leaders of the Kirk, switches to the Royalist side. Initially successful at the battles of Inverlochy and Kilsyth, Montrose is finally defeated at Philiphaugh.

This background is foregrounded when Montrose and a few followers briefly pass through Woodilee. But Buchan's interest in Montrose remains the true source of his novel's power. Writing his Montrose biography, Buchan had immersed himself in seventeenth-century sources. As a result he is able brilliantly to catch the biblical-rich rhetorical language and style in which the contemporary religious debates were conducted. Equally fine (and equally surprising) is his use of Scottish vernacular speech — the young minister's housekeeper, and a range of other local characters, speak a Scots of such density and richness that most readers, including Scottish ones, will frequently be checking a glossary or reaching for a dictionary of Scots.

Finally Montrose is crucial for another reason. As I have indicated, Buchan admired Montrose and sympathized with his attempt to remain a supporter of the Covenant while repudiating the politics of the Presbyterian party. The historical figure makes only two brief appearances in the text of the novel, but the impression Montrose makes on David Sempill proves unforgettable. Ultimately, I would suggest that Buchan finds a way of keeping Montrose, and crucially the values he stands for, in his novel, by creating Mark Riddel, a companion-soldier, who is effectively Montrose's double. It is the voice of Mark that Buchan deploys to confront and demolish the attitudes and arguments of Calvinist extremism. In a great chapter called 'The Witch Hunt', it is Mark Riddel who dramatically defeats a 'pricker's' cruel attempt to identify an old woman as a witch, and it is Riddel who is Sempill's key defender against his Calvinist critics in the novel's dramatic closing scene. Buchan seems to have written thrillers ('shockers', he called them), with consummate ease. With *Witch Wood* he wrote what deserves to be better known as a major Scottish novel.

27 Two Novelists

In their different ways, James Robertson and Ian Rankin are two of our finest contemporary novelists. In terms of convention of course, they are not the same kind of writer. Robertson, author of four highly-regarded novels, is identified as a 'literary' author – which means he is seen as a novelist writing within the cultural mainstream of English and Scottish fiction. Rankin, on the other hand, author of over twenty novels, is identified as a 'genre' author – meaning he is regarded as working within the boundaries (or expectations) of one specific kind of novel: in Rankin's case, of course, detective fiction. (The Inspector Rebus series ended after seventeen appearances.) Robertson and Rankin both write to entertain the reader, but in Robertson's case entertainment can involve seriousness of purpose, the imaginative illumination and interpretation of human experience in all its forms. Rankin has above all to satisfy the reader's expectations of the detective fiction genre: crime of some kind has to be committed, investigated, and finally resolved. If the genre writer has anything to say about the complexities of life and experience, it has to be achieved within the limits imposed by the genre's requirements. Of course I recognize that the divide between the two kinds of writing can come under pressure. We live at a time when we are regularly told that the old barrier between high culture and pop culture no longer exists – that in such art forms as music, dance, painting, and cinema, such traditional discrimination survives only as cultural snobbery. In terms of literature, however, genre writing for whatever reason continues to be seen as existing; all bookshops keep separate shelves for 'crime', 'sci-fi', 'horror', 'chick lit' etc., etc.

James Robertson's 2011 novel *And the Land Lay Still* (which I have praised here on a previous occasion), provides us with a wonderfully detailed but panoramic sweep of social and political change in Scotland between 1955 and 1995. As part of his analysis of that political change, Robertson charts the ups and downs of the Scottish nationalist movement throughout the period. This leads him to create characters who emerge from the shady world of semi-official counter-espionage and counter-terrorism. Their interest is in the surveillance and even penetration of fringe nationalist groups, which, unlike the SNP itself, believe in what they call direct action. However small and unrepresentative, such groups certainly did exist within the nationalist movement, and few would doubt today that Special Branch, for example, did take an interest in their existence. Key to Robertson's account of this problematic episode in Scottish political history is the case of William McRae.

Some readers — I suspect not too many — may recall the McRae case. McRae was a Glasgow lawyer with a long history of involvement in nationalist politics. He had been an SNP parliamentary candidate on several occasions. He had a considerable reputation as a political activist, campaigning effectively on the issue of the disposal of nuclear waste in Scotland. There is some suggestion that he was a member of the direct action Siol nan Gaidheal group. Robertson doesn't think he was an actual member, but suggests he sympathised with such groups and knew 'where they were coming from'. Another of these groups, the so-called Scottish National Liberation Army, insisted that McRae, if not a member, was a supporter and a source of funding. In any event, in April 1985, McRae crashed off the road in his Volvo car between Fort William and Dornie, where he had a holiday cottage. Taken to hospital in Inverness, and transferred to Aberdeen, he died without ever regaining consciousness. The exact circumstances of his death have remained an issue ever since. A host of questions surrounding his accidental death/suicide/ murder are still disputed. Unsurprisingly, the theory that McRae was the victim of some form of state-sponsored conspiracy is widely believed.

Robertson uses the historical reality of McRae's death to lend credibility to the existence and behaviour of his characters who are linked to the murky world of counter-terrorism agencies and their possible involvement in this controversial area of Scottish politics. We never know for sure that Robertson's imaginary character was responsible for McRae's death. But recognition that McRae was a real person who did die in questionable circumstances moves this section of Robertson's complex novel out of the world of Gothic mystery and into the mainstream of the Scottish story he is telling. Robertson doesn't mention the case of Hilda Murrell, the 78-year-old anti-nuclear campaigner who died a year before McRae in circumstances which have led conspiracy theorists to link the two cases over the issue of possible MI5 involvement. (Michael Mansfield, the well-known human rights lawyer, is currently asking for a fresh police investigation into Hilda Murrell's death.)

Should there be a demand for a new investigation of William McRae's death, Ian Rankin might well be among those supporting it. Rankin's latest novel, *The Impossible Dead* (2011) belongs of course to the post-Rebus world. Its main character is Malcolm

Fox, who heads 'the Complaints' — detectives whose job it is to investigate allegations of police corruption or improper behaviour. The novel opens in fairly leisurely fashion as the bad behaviour among the Fife constabulary the Complaints are investigating does not seem of great interest. The unresolved suicide or murder of a retired officer, however, changes everything, and Malcolm Fox's investigation enters new and more dramatic territory.

The dead officer turns out to have been re-investigating the case of Francis Vernal, a politically-active lawyer, who had died in problematic circumstances in his Volvo car in 1985. Vernal had been involved with the (historical) Dark Harvest Commando, a fringe nationalist group campaigning in 1981 for the decontamination of Gruinard Island which had been used for the testing of an anthrax biological weapon. Fox finds himself drawn more and more into an exploration of the Vernal case – which, despite the change of location to Fife, emerges in every detail as being modelled exactly on the narrative once again of the historical William McRae.

In the end, the Vernal/McRae story becomes what *The Impossible Dead* is about. In James Robertson's novel, the McRae material is linked to what becomes only a disturbing sub-text of its comprehensive Scottish narrative. And Robertson offers the reader no final answer to the issues involved in McRae's life and death. The presumably coincidental use of the same material in *The Impossible Dead* (both authors must have been working on their 2011 novels at more or less the same time) is very different. Rankin here is on excellent form, writing at a level as high or perhaps higher than in his hugely successful past. But inevitably the mechanics of the genre of detective fiction remain in play. Inspector Fox finally successfully unravels the mystery of the Vernal case. Readers may well disagree over the implications of the novelist's solution. Its political dimension is not really explored. Perhaps Ian Rankin did not fancy sailing far into such choppy waters.

28 *The Professor of Truth*

James Robertson's bold and extraordinary new novel — *The Professor of Truth* — has already sparked controversy. Hardly surprising given that its prime subject-matter involves the most controversial episode in the modern history of Scottish justice: the conviction and imprisonment of the late Abdelbaset-al-Megrahi as the terrorist responsible for the destruction of Pan Am Flight 103 over Lockerbie in December, 1988.

Robertson sticks closely to the circumstances and characters involved in the Lockerbie tragedy and its aftermath, but what he has written remains a novel, a work of fiction. The book's central character is closely based on that of Jim Swire, the English doctor who lost his daughter on Flight 103, but who has subsequently become celebrated for his public and outspoken rejection of the validity of the trial and conviction of Megrahi. Dr Swire here becomes Alan Tealing, a lecturer — significantly not a professor — in the Stirling University Department of English Literature. He has lost his wife as well as his daughter in the disaster. Likewise Megrahi has become Khalil Khazar.

In the first section of the novel, entitled 'Ice', the setting remains a wintry Scotland, and Robertson creates a full and moving imaginative account of Tealing's response to the loss of his family and the existential freezing of his life and experience that follows. But in the book's second and final section – called 'Fire' — the scene shifts to a wholly imaginary experience of Australia where Tealing tracks down a Maltese character called Parroulet, clearly based on the real-life Maltese clothes shop owner, Tony Gauci, whose evidence was crucial in the trial and conviction of Megrahi.

Given this context, the novel inevitably raises a series of familiar quasi-philosophical questions: about the relationship between life as it is lived and how it is depicted in a work of art, about fiction and reality — not to mention others about how far the ideals of truth and justice actually operate in the practice of the law, and the validity of realistic or idealistic visions of human experience. So much so that one reviewer has referred to the Scottish section of the novel as a 'tutorial' on such issues. Perhaps there is a potential problem here for the novelist, but to my mind at least, the particulars of Alan Tealing's predicament, which we never lose sight of, prevent any descent into mere abstraction. Issues surrounding the meaning of truth and justice have come to define Tealing's life.

Another reviewer – Alexander Linklater in the *Observer* – raises a more central issue. He argues that the book is at its best when it is most fictional: it 'feels most real at the points where it is clearly fictional'. I agree. Again and again James Robertson's creative imagination provides the tiny, telling detail which confirms the human reality of what is being described. Over the years, Tealing's relations with his wife's family in America slowly deteriorate. They cannot understand his rejection of the court's verdict. Their phone calls become infrequent; they have less and less to say to each other. 'When we spoke', Tealing tells us, 'I pictured the ocean rolling between us, vast and grey and cold'.

But the novel's closing scenes, in which Alan Tealing's original experience of struggling unauthorized through the Scottish landscape over which the exploded fragments of Pan Am 103 have been scattered, is clearly paralleled by his finding himself in a dangerous bushfire in the Australian countryside, culminate in a situation that Linklater finds unsatisfactory. He argues that Tealing's joining with Parroulet in fighting off the fire around the Maltese witness's house is too 'contrived' to be convincing. But is it?

For Linklater the problem stems from Robertson's over-commitment to the truth and accuracy of Swire's rejection of the Scottish court's verdict. In his view the novel would have been more satisfying had Tealing been less sure that, say, Parroulet's withdrawing or qualifying his original evidence would lead to 'Khazar's' acquittal. In fact, Tealing is frequently shown struggling with doubt over the usefulness and value of his total commitment over so many years to the pursuit of the truth behind what he calls 'The Case'. Like the governess in Henry James's *The Turn of the Screw*, he is even ready to entertain – momentarily – the horror of his being entirely wrong.

What is actually in question here is a larger issue. Linklater's position (or preference) is very much a current, postmodern one. Contemporary art in all its forms prefers the uncertain, the problematic, the unresolved, the fragment. For the majority of today's artists there are no finalities, no absolutes, no firm or unchallengeable truths of any kind. But when in 1898 Emile Zola took on the French legal and political establishment with the publication of *J'Accuse*, a man – Alfred Dreyfus – was in prison for a crime he did not commit. A great wrong existed which could and should be righted. Eight years later, it was. Writing *The Professor of Truth*, even if he chooses not to challenge the Scottish legal establishment head-on, James Robertson is clearly on Zola's side. Will the Lockerbie story be a different one eight years from now?

29 *The Blade Artist*, by Irvine Welsh

What would be an appropriate TW rating for this novel? In case you happen to be unfamiliar with this particular abbreviation, let me explain it stands for 'Trigger Warning'. And what does it mean? Here is a recent dictionary definition. The term is used 'to alert people when an internet post, book, article, picture, video clip, or some other media could potentially cause extremely negative reactions (such as post-traumatic flashbacks or self-harm) due to its content'. Surprisingly a body of opinion has arisen across university campuses in Britain and America that contends that today's students need to be protected from unexpected exposure to attitudes, values, opinions, on social or political issues, that they do not share. Thus we now are living in a world (despite or because it's a world in which organisations such as ISIS or Boko Haram see nothing wrong in making young children into killers or suicide bombers) in which *The Great Gatsby* – would you believe – earns a TW for its depiction of 'suicide, domestic abuse and graphic violence'.

I think we can take it for granted that the author of *Trainspotting* (1993) and *Filth* (1998) would be deeply offended if the TW rating for his books was anything other than totally off any scale meant to assess their offensiveness. After all that was what they were about. Here is how Welsh puts it in one of his more successful rants in *Trainspotting*: 'Choose us. [His group of young doped-up characters.] Choose life. Choose mortgage payments; choose washing machines; choose cars; choose sitting oan a couch watching mind-numbing and spirit-crushing game shows, stuffing fuckin junk food intae yir mooth. Choose rotting away, pishing and shiteing yersel in a home, a total fuckin embarrassment tae the selfish, fucked-up brats ye've produced. Choose life'. Some readers –and I'm one of them – may be inclined to feel that the 'selfish, fucked-up brats' mentioned here include the speaker and his pals, and that 'choosing life' is not exactly what they seem to be doing – but in this context that is not the relevant point.

Welsh's early novels only work if they offer a convincing onslaught on conventional orthodoxies of every kind – social, moral, political, religious. If they are not offending they are not succeeding. *Trainspotting* does the job pretty well. Here for example is Renton – the novel's main narrative voice – on Anglo-Scottish politics:

'Ah don't hate the English. They're just wankers. We are colonised by wankers. We can't even pick a decent, vibrant, healthy culture to be colonised by. No. We're ruled by effete arseholes.... Ah don't hate the English. They just get oan wi the shite thuv goat. Ah hate the Scots'. There's no denying that *Trainspotting*'s diatribe against the status quo is delivered with a kind of frantic verbal energy that is often successfully offensive. Whether the novel really merited the critical enthusiasm with which it was received in the 1990s is another matter. Its explosiveness seems now to have succeeded in disguising its flaws. It's much too long and boringly repetitive. One vividly disturbing and brutally detailed account of a beating-up turns out to be all too similar to the next one. Welsh obviously enjoys writing such scenes, but readers tire of reading them.

Then there is something seriously flawed about the demotic language which on the face of it is the book's major success. Renton turns out to have been a history student at Aberdeen University for two years before dropping out. Hence his use of the demotic is a choice, a ploy; he can revert to orthodox English on demand. The point is underlined if *Trainspotting* is set against James Kelman's prize-winning *How Late It Was, How Late* published just a year later in 1994. The dense Scottish vernacular language of Kelman's protagonist Sammy — initially just as deeply offensive to some readers as Welsh's expletive-laden prose — is in the end not only authentically vivid but humanly true to the world in which he lives. Hence Kelman's novel explores and illuminates the human condition and its moral universe in a manner that is well beyond Welsh's reach.

To be fair, the Welsh of *Filth* would no doubt retort that even the idea of the human condition — not to mention a moral universe--is just another sentimental delusion. This is a work of such negativity and cynicism that it makes *Trainspotting* seem like light entertainment. All the first novel's sexism, misogyny, racism, homophobia — and of course extreme violence and cruelty — are here in spades. And this time there is no relief. Renton, Begbie and the rest in *Trainspotting* seem to celebrate the life-style they have chosen — and occasionally at least they reveal a flicker or two of normal human feelings. The corrupt policeman who is the protagonist of *Filth* is utterly alien – beyond redemption. *Filth* is an entirely appropriate title. D.H. Lawrence would have described this book as doing dirt on life.

With his latest novel, however, Welsh has made the interesting decision to move back to the world of *Trainspotting*. The central character in *The Blade Artist* is an older, as it were, 'grown-up' version of *Trainspotting*'s Francis Begbie. Remember him? The most unreconstructed, threatening, dangerously violent of all of Welsh's characters. 'That Begbie, man, it's like say ... that's a fuckin jungle cat. We're just ordinary funky feline types. Domestic cats, likesay.... Keep these claws in catboy. Show the world some soft pads. This is a bad cat, a big, bad panther.' But keeping his claws in in 1993 is exactly what Begbie – an expert at kicking faces in or going crazy 'wi the bladework' – chooses not to do. But all has changed in 2016. Francis Begbie is now Jim Francis. Married to Melanie – young, good-looking, intelligent, from a wealthy family – a former art therapist in his jail, he now lives in California with his wife and two young daughters. More than that, he has turned his life around becoming a successful sculptor, planning his next exhibition which he hopes Rod Stewart will attend. His violent past? Well, as he tells his wife, he used to be 'addicted to violence'. 'But I've got that nonsense under control now, cause it doesn't take me anywhere interesting. Just jail. Done too much of that.'

But this is an Irvine Welsh novel, not an essay on how art can therapeutically transform the life of violent prisoners. The death of a son he hardly knew back in Edinburgh brings the apparently reformed Jim back to Scotland on a trip to find out what had really happened. Of course what he has returned to is his old Begbie life. Sunny California is replaced by a dank and dismal Edinburgh. And soon he is encountering all his old friends and – more ominously – old enemies. With all of them he maintains that he has changed utterly. The bad cat has apparently been declawed. As long as the reader even half-believes this, the novel remains reasonably interesting. And Welsh encourages us to take Begbie's transformation seriously. 'Increasingly', the character tells us, 'his life seems fractured, as if his past had been lived by somebody else. It isn't just that the place he now resides in [California] and the people around him [in Edinburgh] are poles apart, it's like he himself is an entirely different person. The overriding obsessions and foibles of the man he'd once been now feel utterly ludicrous to the current resident of his mind and body. The only bridge is rage; when angered he can taste his old self. But in California, the way he is currently living his life, few things can vex him to that extent. But that's over there'.

But in fact it's all a lie. Jim may talk Californian but Begbie acts Edinburghian. And despite what Welsh extraordinarily tells us in this passage, it is even a lie in California. Only days before returning to Edinburgh, 'Jim' — or rather Begbie — has secretly battered to death two ne'er-do-wells who had made the mistake of threatening his wife and daughters on their Californian beach. It emerges that he believes in vengeance as he has always done. So the rest of the novel follows an all too predictable pattern. Back in Scotland, Begbie returns to his violent roots and eventually sees off his range of enemies in what readers should be warned is horrifyingly graphic Irvine Welsh style.

It was in 1991, a couple of years before the publication of *Trainspotting*, that the so-called Young British Artists made their initial mark on the cultural scene with such deliberately controversial works as Damien Hirst's formaldehyde shark, Marc Quinn's head made from frozen pints of his own blood, and Tracey Emin's disorderly bed. But 25 years on the artistic rebels of the 1990s have become something very different — not just members of the cultural establishment but vastly rich cultural celebrities. Has not something similar happened to the rebellious rejectionist Irvine Welsh? Today we are expected to listen respectfully while in interviews and articles he gives us his views on literature and society like any other establishment figure. This is why it is worth asking whether there is a bizarre link between Begbie the creative artist living in California and Welsh the controversial Scottish writer now living in Chicago. Near the end of *The Blade Artist*, Melanie suggests that her husband lives 'in a parallel moral universe to the rest of us'. Begbie agrees, but says he wants to get out of it. Does Irvine Welsh? Given the disturbing ambiguity that readers will discover in the title of his latest novel, the answer in the end is no.

30 *Trainspotting*

Irvine Welsh's first novel *Trainspotting* has recently been named Scotland's most popular novel of the last fifty years. I thought it might be interesting to go back and re-read it – now twenty years after its first appearance. I remember reading it then without subscribing to the wild enthusiasm with which in many circles it was being greeted. Perhaps I was over-influenced by my colleague Philip Hobsbaum – a leading figure, as many readers will recall, in helping the emergence of what has become known as the Glasgow novel. Philip was pretty dismissive of Welsh's book — and not because it was set in Edinburgh.

Twenty years ago *Trainspotting*'s huge, popular success was undoubtedly due to its wild, excessive, and shockingly untraditional, language and subject matter. Its apparent celebration of the world of drug and alcohol abuse, of totally amoral, uninhibited sexual freedom, and above all its constant, unlimited, page after page, reiteration of a demotic language of relentless obscenity, seemed to prove that it was giving voice to a class of people previously denied any kind of even fictional life. This at last, it seemed, was the real thing — the truth beneath the façade of routine, dull, dreary, conventional, middle-class life. Conventional, middle-class Scottish life in particular.

When I ask American students – as I regularly do both at home and abroad — what and where they have learned about Scotland, *Trainspotting* always comes up, though admittedly it's the film they have seen (along with *Braveheart*) rather than the book they've read. But I suspect the reference to the film is fair enough. The fifty-year accolade is at least in part to be explained by the enduring popularity of Danny Boyle's film which caught quite a lot of the book's demotic energy. A vote for the book may well have been really a vote for the film.

But what was the outcome of my own re-read? Nothing particularly surprising. Twenty years ago I was already too old to have been part of Welsh's anticipated audience. And the passing of the years has hardly changed that. As I've said, the success Welsh's book undoubtedly had, owed everything to its shock effect. Now take that away and not much is left. There's very little here in the way of story. There is no plot to unwind, indeed no narrative energy of any kind. And the railway line between Edinburgh and London is hardly enough to impose any kind of meaningful structure upon the random events of the novel. Interviewed after his success, Irving Welsh (in Chicago) stressed the importance of his characters. Renton, Begbie and Sick Boy were archetypes whom every reader would recognize. Really? Archetypes of what exactly? In fact for most of the novel it is difficult to tell them apart, because they choose to speak in the same relentlessly offensive demotic language. And when Renton, the student who has dropped out of his history course at Aberdeen University, chooses in court to show off his ability to debate the finer points of existentialism in a very different kind of discourse, what kind of archetype has he become?

In the course of his interview, Welsh paid tribute to other Scottish writers including Alasdair Gray and James Kelman. Well he might. Without Kelman's example, would Welsh have been able to write *Trainspotting*? I doubt it. But the difference is that Kelman does not use the demotic language of *How Late It Was, How Late* simply to shock. That language is an integral part of the essential, convincing, and moving human reality that Kelman creates — at a level far beyond anything Irving Welsh can reach.

Finally there's no denying that for better or worse things have moved on since 1993. What was shocking then is less so now. How many people still believe that *Trainspotting* deserves to sell more copies than the Bible? In today's art world, a recurring emphasis on pain, suffering, violence and horror has moved centre stage. Novels struggle to compete with art forms that have a more immediate sensory impact. Read any group of reviews of recent films and you will come across warnings that film-goers must be prepared to watch scenes — in one film or another — of horrifying pain and torture. I know nothing of the world of computer games, which apparently so many of us now buy into, but the adverts I see appear to involve nothing but endless scenes of violence, mayhem and murder. In, say, the films of Lars Von Trier, or the exhibitions of the smugly self-satisfied Chapman brothers (see their current one in London's Serpentine Gallery), there seems to be a kind of competition in seeing how far one can go in the name of so-called art. As far as you choose seems to be the answer — because there will always be those willing to go along with the curators of the Chapmans' show when they assure us that it compels us 'to confront the nagging fears that lie at the dark heart of the western psyche'. I don't buy it. 'The western psyche'? So the Chinese have nothing to be afraid of? It's just too glib. Real suffering and real pain lie in the world outside art galleries, and outside the pages of novels. Readers won't be surprised to hear I'm not proposing to pay up to see the film of Irving Welsh's *Filth*.

31 *Moscow Calling, Memoirs of a Foreign Correspondent* by Angus Roxburgh

These days we frequently hear of the declining number of teachers and students of foreign languages. English, we are told, is becoming a world language, so what's the point of taking the trouble to master the language of any other country? Well any young person hesitating over whether to take up the study of a foreign language would do well to read this book. Born in England but brought up in Scotland, Angus Roxburgh became fascinated by Russian at school, and went to study the language for five years at the universities of Aberdeen and Zurich. That decision was the key to the remarkable and hugely rewarding life he went on to lead as a foreign correspondent. His book, an excellent example of a professional autobiography, explores in detail that fascinating life. By describing it as a 'professional' autobiography I'm indicating that while the book is rich and full in evoking Roxburgh's depth of feeling about his Russian experience, there is nothing here of a Rousseau-esque, emotional, confessional kind. (I suspect that there will be many readers who share my surprise in learning late on that the author's marriage to Neilian, with whom he shared his life in Russia, had come to an end.)

Soon after completing his Russian studies at university, Roxburgh got himself a job in Moscow. In October, 1978, he arrived there to work as a translator at Progress, the Soviet Union's largest foreign language publishing house. Two years later he decided against extending his job into a third year, and returned to Glasgow. Teaching Russian, Neilian became the main breadwinner while Angus enrolled as a doctoral student at Glasgow University working on Pravda and the Soviet mass media, but his ambition was to establish himself as a journalist with a special expertise in Russian affairs. *The Glasgow Herald* helped by publishing a few articles, and later *The Economist* did likewise, but otherwise these years in the early 1980s were the most difficult of Roxburgh's professional life. His attempt to establish a career for himself as a journalist seemed to be going nowhere. However in 1984 he got a job with the BBC Monitoring Service where he listened in to Soviet news bulletins, transcribing anything of interest. Soon his work involved monitoring Soviet TV as well. None of this was exactly journalism but it got him a coveted NUJ card – and he continued to have the odd article published.

The big breakthrough seemed to come in 1985. Roxburgh had been working on a profile of the short-lived Russian general secretary Konstantin Chernenko for *The Sunday Times*. When he died and was succeeded by Mikhail Gorbachev, the paper asked Roxburgh at short notice to produce an account of the new Soviet leader. His piece duly appeared on *The Sunday Times* editorial page. Roxburgh described it as 'the most thrilling moment of my life'. But once again his career as a journalist seemed to stall. In 1986 he moved to the BBC Russian Service and the following year 'Newsnight' sent him to Russia with the senior correspondent Charles Wheeler to do a series of reports on the reforms that Gorbachev was beginning to put in place. Not long afterwards a meeting with the foreign editor of *The Guardian* led to a job on that paper's foreign desk, but a mere three months later the big moment finally arrived: Roxburgh was appointed *The Sunday Times* Moscow correspondent. He held that post from 1987-1989; in 1991-97 he was the BBC Moscow correspondent; and in 1998-2005 he was BBC's Europe correspondent. These jobs all involved returning to Russia on many occasions, and sometimes for lengthy periods. Roxburgh had become a recognised Russian expert.

To my mind Roxburgh's success had two main sources. One was simply a matter of good luck: his time in Russia happened to coincide with one of the most momentous events in twentieth century European history: the slow disintegration of Stalin's Soviet Union under Khrushchev, Brezhnev, Gorbachev and Yeltsin — leading finally to the emergence of Putin. To witness and report on such a dramatic story would have been any foreign correspondent's dream.

The second source of Roxburgh's eventual triumph was his initial decision to take up a job with the Moscow publisher Progress. For these first two years in Russia, Roxburgh worked and lived the life of an ordinary Russian citizen. He tells us that in these two years in Moscow he had no contact with any western official. He soon became friendly with a range of Russians — and many of them became friends for life. On his many later returns to Moscow he always made a point of catching up with them. This meant that all the time he was hearing what ordinary Russians were making of the momentous changes they were caught up in. Most expert commentators, academic historians, or western officials were reporting on Russia from the outside. Roxburgh had earned the right to be an insider.

As a result, among the finest chapters in his book are those detailing just what it was like to live under the Soviet regime. Here is the first sentence of chapter four: 'Sadly the quest for Russia's soul usually took second place to the search for food'. This establishes the tone – gently ironic – of much that is to follow. Russia turns out to be a bureaucratic nightmare. Soviet planning of every aspect of daily life is farcical – the simplest transaction involves endless form-filling and being passed from one bureaucrat to another – none of whom are able to make a final decision. 'At times like this', Roxburgh writes, 'one seriously pondered whether the Soviet way of life had been devised by raving lunatics'. 'The iron rule of Soviet life', he suggests, 'was: if there isn't a rule, invent one'. Then shop shelves are frequently entirely empty. News that a food delivery has arrived means that enormous queues immediately form. A two-hour wait to reach a check-out is quite normal. And of course such food as was available was abysmal – at least by western European standards.

How then did Roxburgh's Russian friends survive? He seems frequently to have mulled over that question. They rarely complained – rather 'they seemed resigned to the raw deal that was their unfortunate birthright'. 'They "emigrated" to an inner world of poetry or science, philosophy and longing, and animated discussions at their kitchen tables' – while invariably drinking vast quantities of vodka. Roxburgh's conclusion was that 'taking everything together – the hardships, the good times, and the comfort brought by acceptance of one's lot – the Russians were probably no unhappier than Americans or Britons or any other people in the affluent and free West. Worrying about mortgages, muggings, high prices, and finding a job, was not necessarily less of a burden than the particular cares that marked the Soviet way of life'. (The implication is that Russians at least were free from that list of worries.)

Roxburgh's first-hand knowledge of life under the old regime gives an added spice to his account of its demise. It's as if he is reacting exactly as ordinary Russians were. But by any standard his account of every twist and turn in that history is vivid and compelling – including his description of how under Yeltsin, the switch from socialism to unconstrained capitalism, which allowed the emergence of that band of oligarchs who now seem to own half of London and its football teams, made most Russians in the early years of their 'freedom' worse off than in the past.

I suspect that my account may have given the impression that *Moscow Calling* is exclusively about Moscow. Nothing could be further from the truth. Roxburgh at different times was able to travel the length and breadth of the Soviet Union including those areas that quickly reclaimed their independence when Russia returned to its original boundaries. His reporting is always immensely informative. Never more so than in his later account of the war in Chechnya. That war raged from December 1994 to the autumn of 1996. His chapters evoking its horrors are the most moving in an absorbing book.

A footnote. Some readers may recall that Roxburgh got himself into trouble over his decision to accept a post in the public relations department of Putin's Kremlin in 2006. He defends that decision here, but not everyone will be persuaded that it was the right one to make.

32 William Faulkner and Gatehouse of Fleet

In March 1958, the Nobel Prize-winning American novelist, William Faulkner visited the campus of Princeton University in New Jersey. Throughout his writing career, Faulkner had chosen to steer well clear of the American academy, but a year earlier he had finally accepted a position as writer-in-residence at the University of Virginia. Influenced by Saxe Commins, his editor at Random House — who happened to live in Princeton — he subsequently accepted an invitation from that university's Council on Humanities to spend two weeks living on the campus. He would give readings from his work, and have informal meetings with undergraduate and postgraduate students.

I happened to be one of them. Summoned by the Dean of the graduate college where I was living, I was told that Mr Faulkner would join the graduate students one night for dinner in Procter Hall. Afterwards he would have drinks with a small group of students in the Dean's own rooms. Would I be willing to organize the group of students? Back in the 1950s, life in Princeton's graduate college was a very formal affair — closely modelled on the traditional Oxbridge college example. Procter Hall had a (rarely used) high table, and at dinner in the evening we students were required to wear black gowns. Latin grace was said before the meal could begin. Wearing his gown, Faulkner sat with us with what seemed to be a faintly bemused air, not having a lot to say, enjoying his dinner, but apparently surprised by the eager attention with which he was being received by all these bright young men. (There were only men. It would be the 1970s before Princeton began to admit women students.)

Upstairs after the meal, the situation was much the same. Faulkner seemed reluctant to talk about his role as artist or writer. However when he learned I was actually from Edinburgh, the conversation took a different turn. Relevant here is a comment by the novelist which Joseph Blotner cites near the opening of his standard 1974 Faulkner biography in support of his contention that his subject was always conscious of his Scottish ancestry. Talking to a friend, Faulkner is supposed to have said, 'my great-grandfather Murry had his grandfather's claymore which he had carried at the battle of Culloden. My aunt has it now'. (Faulkner's father's name was Murry Cuthbert Falkner, and his paternal grandmother was

Sallie McAlpine Murry.) However readers of *The Sound and the Fury* will perhaps remember that the claymore carried at Culloden also has a kind of fictional existence.

In the original version of *The Sound and the Fury*, published in 1929, there is no mention of a claymore. However, when Malcolm Cowley was preparing *The Portable Faulkner* for Random House in 1946, he learned that Faulkner wanted to add a new section to the novel's text: 'When you reprint *The Sound and the Fury*, I have a new section to go with it'. This is the *Appendix Compson 1699-1945*, now included in all editions of the wonderful novel, and what it consists of is biographical details concerning all the main characters in the narrative. Among them is: 'Quentin Maclachan. Son of a Glasgow printer, orphaned and raised by his mother's people in the Perth highlands. Fled to Carolina from Culloden Moor with a claymore and the tartan he wore by day and slept under by night, and little else.'

Now in 1958 in Princeton, Faulkner told me the story of how he himself had been shown this claymore and told of its history by one of his aunts. He may or may not have mentioned the ancestral Murry, but he was certainly insisting that his family history had Scottish roots in the eighteenth century. Encouraged by his evident interest in Scotland I asked the great man whether he had ever been able to visit Scotland. His answer was yes. 'Where had he been?' I asked. 'Gatehouse of Fleet' he replied.

To say I was taken aback is an understatement. I'd heard of Gatehouse of Fleet, and remembered vaguely it was in the Galloway area of southwest Scotland, but how on earth could William Faulkner have heard of it — not to mention actually having been there? But the occasion was hardly one on which a young student could cross-examine a world-famous author, so that was the end of that particular exchange. Inevitably however, I never forgot it, and years later made a serious effort to find an explanation.

Blotner's biography tells us that on May 31, 1952, Faulkner, despite being unwell, flew from Paris to London, saying he was determined to set off for England, 'and, he said, for Scotland as well, the land of his ancestors'. According to the biographer, however, he did not make it to Scotland. Might he be wrong? Gatehouse is not far from Carlisle. Could Faulkner have been determined enough to settle for just crossing the border? But the problem of why Gatehouse remains. Could it be that the novelist had heard Gatehouse mentioned by painter friends as being in an area of Scotland that had gained something of a reputation as an artistic colony?

Still puzzled, I decided a visit to Gatehouse was necessary. It proved to be necessary indeed. Gatehouse seemed to me to have something of the quality of a traditional English village, and on a kind of village green beside a street I struck what looked like remarkable gold. There on the green was a single, slender but thickly leaved tree. At its foot was a memorial plaque with the following inscription: 'Planted in Memory of B. Phyllis Falkner 1895-1991.' A stunning moment in so many ways.

Faulkner scholars in particular will be struck by the spelling 'Falkner'. This is the spelling of the Falkner family who in the nineteenth century moved from Missouri and Tennessee to settle finally in Ripley, Oxford, and New Albany, Mississippi, where in 1897 William Cuthbert Falkner (the novelist) was born. It was Faulkner himself who changed the spelling of his name. In 1918, rejected in an attempt to enlist in the US Army, Faulkner travelled to Canada hoping to join the Royal Air Force. Knowing that 'Faulkner' was the standard spelling in England and Scotland, he made the change to increase the likelihood of his application to join being successful.

B. Phyllis Falkner in Gatehouse of Fleet, and William Faulkner's statement that he'd been there: it is surely inconceivable that merely coincidence is involved here. Faulkner must have known of this Scottish B. Phyllis Falkner and surely assumed that she and his Mississippi family were connected. Given an opportunity to meet her, he would have been certain to take it up. I think I now know when it happened.

Faulkner's Nobel Prize for Literature was for the year 1949. But it was in 1950 that he attended the award ceremony in Stockholm and made his magnificent acceptance speech. (Even though it was unintelligible at the time.) So it was in December, 1950, that he flew from New York to Stockholm but his aircraft found it necessary to land in Prestwick en route. There was an overnight delay, and he did not fly on to Stockholm until the following day. How far is Gatehouse of Fleet from Prestwick airport? Sixty-one miles. So that has to be the visit to Scotland about which William Faulkner talked to me in Princeton's graduate college in 1958. Where had he been? Gatehouse of Fleet.

Puzzles remain. Who was B. Phyllis Falkner? Who planted the memorial tree? How had Faulkner become aware of her existence? When I was there no one seemed to know. And no one knew anything at all of a visit by a famous American author. However, more recently I have established that Phyllis Falkner was the wife of a Major Basil Falkner, born in Brighton in 1892. Falkner's cousin was Elizabeth Murray Usher, owner of the Cally Estate in the Gatehouse area. The Falkners farmed at the Murrayton farm on the Cally Estate in the 1920s. Having built a holiday home there, the Falkner family, children and grandchildren, continued to holiday in Gatehouse for many years. They erected the plaque in memory of Phyllis Falkner. The question remains whether William Faulkner could have been in touch with this Falkner family.

33 Gatehouse Revisited

In last week's *Scottish Review* (November 5th) Professor David Wasserstein dismisses my attempt to find an explanation for William Faulkner's remark that yes he had been in Scotland – and specifically in Gatehouse of Fleet. Re-reading Joseph Blotner's account of the novelist's trip to Stockholm in December, 1950, to receive the Nobel Prize, I have to concede that the stopover at Prestwick does seem not to have been long enough for Faulkner to have visited Gatehouse. Mind you the biographer's account of the Prestwick experience is more than a little odd. 'At 5 A.M. in the airport restaurant', he tells us, they [Faulkner was travelling with his daughter Jill] 'were served strong steaming Scotch tea by waiters wearing white tie and tails'. What exactly is 'Scotch tea'? And waiters at five in the morning in Prestwick airport wearing white tie and tails? Could the novelist's well-known lack of patience with facts, to which the professor refers, be in evidence here?

Exactly how many hours elapsed on that December day before the Faulkners' flight took off for Oslo and Stockholm, Blotner does not tell us. But as I say, I'm prepared to accept that logistically it seems impossible that Faulkner could have squeezed in a visit to Gatehouse. But that is the only concession I'm prepared to make. I find the rest of Professor Wasserstein's attempts to explain away Faulkner's remark to me in 1958 – that he had been in Gatehouse of Fleet – wholly unconvincing. The key piece of evidence linking Faulkner and Gatehouse – apart that is from his actual statement – is of course there in the photograph I provided of the memorial plaque in the village to B. Phyllis Falkner.

The professor asks us to believe that this is no more than 'some sort of coincidence'. Some sort indeed! What an incredible coincidence that would be. To justify this lame explanation we are told 'Falkner and Faulkner are variations of the same name, and it is not an uncommon name in that part of Scotland'. This is quite simply wrong. 'Falkner' is a very uncommon name in all parts of Scotland. The Glasgow North telephone directory has one or two Falconers and Faulkners. Not a single 'Falkner'. The one and only time I personally had encountered the 'Falkner' spelling was in the context of William Faulkner's deciding to add the 'u' to his family's Falkner name. The odds against a mere coincidence here must be beyond computation.

'But was Faulkner ever really in Gatehouse of Fleet?' writes Professor Wasserstein. 'How could he have known of this B. Phyllis Falkner? Did he ever meet her? A negative answer to the first question implies negative answers to the rest.' No it doesn't. We don't need to meet someone to know that she exists. I shall say a little more about B. Phyllis Falkner below, but how Faulkner might have known her is exactly something that a keen graduate student in Faulknerian studies might well explore.

Professor Wasserstein goes on to make some suggestions that could explain how the mistaken idea of a Faulkner/Gatehouse link could have arisen. None of them is convincing. His first proposal is that I am some kind of unreliable narrator. Faulkner didn't say he had been in Gatehouse. It never happened. I'm misremembering. Well despite the passing of the years I can assure him that this oral tradition remains utterly reliable. It did happen. Take my word for it. (My first account of this story appeared in my book *From Goosecreek to Gandercleugh,* published in 1999.)

The next suggestion is that Faulkner was fibbing. Asked where had he been in Scotland, he simply out of nowhere came up with 'Gatehouse of Fleet'. Of course I know that Faulkner distrusted journalists and commentators, and often fobbed them off with answers that were not always true. All I can say is that in the course of that memorable evening in Princeton's graduate college, none of us gained the impression that William Faulkner had decided graduate students were in the same category as journalists. The tone throughout was always one of mutual respect. But even if he was embellishing the truth in his reference to Gatehouse, Professor Wasserstein is clever enough to see a problem remains. If he was making up a story, how out of all the place-names in Scotland, could he have come up with Gatehouse of Fleet — a place name by no means sure to be recognized by Scots, and presumably known to one in a million Americans.

Well, the professor suggests Faulkner had come upon the name either in Scott's *Old Mortality* or in Dorothy L. Sayers' *The Five Red Herrings*, and had oddly decided it was a name 'too good to pass up'. So he was able to trot it out when I asked my question. Compared with the hard fact of a Phyllis B. Falkner living in Gatehouse until 1991, this surmise carries absolutely no weight at all.

I recently learned from a correspondent, who had read my original *Scottish Review* article, that Phyllis Falkner was the wife of Major Basil Falkner. In the 1920s they farmed on the Cally Estate outside Gatehouse. Subsequently the Falkner family, children and grandchildren, had for many years a holiday home in Gatehouse — they were responsible for the Phyllis Falkner memorial plaque I photographed. Basil Falkner was a cousin of Elizabeth Murray Usher, the owner of the Cally Estate. The name 'Murray' as it happens is also one familiar to the world of Faulknerian scholarship: it was Faulkner's great-grandfather who changed his name from 'Murray' to 'Murry' so that the name 'Murry' became part of Faulkner's genealogy. John Murray of Broughton — a place not that far from Gatehouse — was in 1745 one of Bonnie Prince Charlie's closest aides. That night in Princeton Faulkner told me the story of his aunt's possessing the claymore their ancestor had carried at the battle of Culloden — the story he fictionalises in the *Appendix Compson 1699-1945* section of perhaps his most famous novel — *The Sound and the Fury*. Gatehouse of Fleet, the Scottish Falkner family, the Murray connection, and William Faulkner are perhaps all connected. Despite Professor Wasserstein's sceptism, I continue to think there is a story here well worthy of serious investigation.

Part Nine

Further Dispatches from the *Scottish Review*.

The *Scottish Review* began publishing online in February 2008 under the editorship of Kenneth Roy. Kenneth had been its editor in its previous incarnation as a regular magazine, and I had become a frequent contributor of articles – some of which are reprinted elsewhere in this book — in the years between 2003 and 2007. That of course explains why I have been a regular contributor to the online version since its inception up until the present. Much earlier, before Kenneth took over, the magazine had been edited by Maurice Lindsay and Alexander Scott and as long ago as 1984 it contained an article I had written on 'Ossian' Macpherson. (It now appears in the Scott and Scottish Romanticism section.) And reviewing recently Ursula Buchan's new biography of her grandfather John Buchan, I learned that Buchan had brought into being an earlier *Scottish Review* in 1907-08. Buchan hoped it would become a Scottish version of *The Spectator*. Today's version, I like to think, offers a similar challenge. The pieces I include here simply represent a selection of those I enjoyed writing.

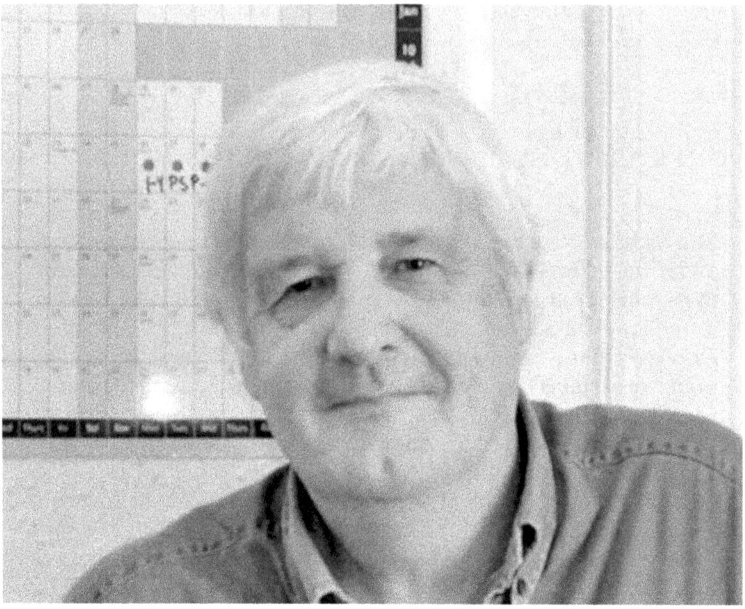

Kenneth Roy

1 Marx Is Back?

Today's students of American literature are surprised when I suggest to them that in the 1920s and 30s Marxism was the ideology of choice for perhaps the majority of American artists and writers. I remind them that with the stock-market crash of 1929, and the long years of depression that followed, capitalism as an economic system appeared to have failed. What was the alternative? A handful of Southern writers – the so-called Fugitive group – argued for a return to a more agrarian society in which a concern for traditional community values would replace the alienation and rootlessness inherent in the western world's industrialized society. But for a great many American intellectuals the answer lay not in a romantic 'back to the land' approach, but in the apparent success of the increasingly powerful Soviet Union. Capitalism was failing, Communism was succeeding. Perhaps Karl Marx could be the new founding father.

Of course Roosevelt's New Deal, and the outbreak of World War II, changed everything. Both in western Europe and the US capitalism revived, and any prospect of a re-ordering of western society along Marxist lines disappeared. But Marx's ideas, and the Marxist analysis of the capitalist economic system, did not. In countries like France and Italy, Marxism remained in the forefront of intellectual life and debate. And in Britain and the US, a Marxist approach to the study of history and related subjects remained a powerful presence. It was only with the fall of Stalinism, and the now undeniable revelation of the true horrors of the Soviet system, that Marxism seemed to be consigned to the dustbin of history. Meanwhile in the post-war decades, two Marxist historians stood out in the U.K. One was Ralph Miliband (father of course of David and Ed), the other E.J. Hobsbawm.

Professor Hobsbawm, author of some fifteen studies of modern European and British political and economic history, has just published another book: *How to Change the World: Tales of Marx and Marxism*. According to the reviewer Stefan Collini, himself a distinguished intellectual historian, Hobsbawm argues that the financial collapse of 2008, with which we are all still trying to cope, marks the end of the period in which Marx was no longer believed to be relevant: 'Once again', writes Hobsbawm, 'the time has come to take Marx seriously'. Is he right I wonder?

All our politicians chorus endlessly about the need to create a juster , fairer, and freer society. We are urged to join in a debate about what terms like freedom and fairness really mean. Well I'd suggest that a central tenet of Marxism is one to which, in this context, all our politicians should be invited to respond: 'freedom is the recognition of necessity'. (Friedrich Engels in 1878) Is it possible to talk about the freedom of an individual who is imprisoned by poverty, ill-health, and unemployment? Is not the freeing of that individual more important than cutting the budget deficit at whatever social cost? On a recent Newsnight Scotland programme, Joyce Macmillan argued forcefully for the view that the time has come for Britain and America and other major powers to act together to limit the powers of the banks and the markets to determine the fiscal and economic decisions of the elected governments of individual countries. I think she's right, but will it happen?

The omens are not good. Gordon Brown argued for the imposition of a tiny tax on every transaction in the financial sector world-wide. Such a Robin Hood tax would raise billions of pounds. Why are we not demanding of our governments that it be put in place? Leaving things as they are only means that the banks continue to rule OK? What better evidence could there be than the abject failure of governments to deal with the issue of bankers' bonuses? The Liberal Democrat Treasury spokesman Lord Oakeshott is reported as saying: 'I have pinched myself in recent weeks and asked who is really running the country – the banks or the elected government?' It's a good question. Sir John Vickers, chairman of *The Independent* Commission on Banking, is about to deliver his report. Will he recommend the complete separation of investment banking from High Street banking – the position once favoured strongly by Vince Cable (remember him)? Apparently not. Will the government be ready to impose on the banks the less radical changes he may suggest? Don't bank on it, might well be Marx's comment.

2 A World Gone Wrong

From time to time events happen in our world that make me despair. Not natural disasters, not accidents, not acts of madness by unbalanced minds. But wilful, calculated acts of horrific, unimaginable violence carried out against fellow human beings. On the heath in *King Lear*, Edgar encounters his now eyeless father Gloucester being led by an old man. Believing himself a moment before 'The worst,/ The lowest and most dejected thing of fortune', he now realises that there is no horror that cannot be overtaken by something still worse: 'the worst is not / So long as we can say ,'This is the worst'. In similar vein, in one of his 'terrible' sonnets, Gerard Manley Hopkins writes 'No worst there is none. Pitched past pitch of grief, / More pangs will, schooled at forepangs, wilder wring'.

Over a lifetime most of us will remember moments when we thought something that had happened was the worst that could be imagined. Let me choose just two such moments happening in close proximity in 1992. The deaths of two brave men: Giovanni Falcone and Paolo Borsellino. Remember them? They were judges in Sicily appointed to crack down on the local mafia. But on May 23, 1992, the mafia murdered Judge Falcone, alongside his wife and three bodyguards, by blowing up the car in which they were travelling. A few weeks later, on July 19, Judge Borsellino, with five accompanying policemen, suffered an identical fate.

But now the problem is that – as I see it at least — such 'worst' moments are happening with ever-increasing frequency. Let me cite four since the beginning of 2011 alone: two in Pakistan, one in Afghanistan, and one in Northern Ireland. On January 4th, Salman Taseer, the Governor of Punjab, was murdered in a hail of bullets fired by one of his own bodyguards. His crime? Being critical of his country's absurd blasphemy law. Worse, and providing even more reason for despair, the perpetrator has been lauded as a hero by masses of his countrymen, and showered with rose petals on his appearance in court. Then on March 2nd, the only Christian member of the government of Pakistan was gunned down in an attack on his car. What crime had Sharaz Bhatti committed? He had dared to defend the rights of Christians and other religious minorities in the state of Pakistan. Official condemnations of these murders have been lukewarm at best. And Mr Bhatti was apparently denied the extra security he had asked for from the authorities.

Then on April 1st, in Mazar-e-Sharif in Afghanistan, after Friday prayers, a frenzied mob attacked the United Nations headquarters in the town killing three UN diplomats and four Gurkha security guards. Why? Because on March 20th in Florida, 'pastor' Terry Jones had burned a copy of the Koran. (In fact at least 24 people have died in Afghanistan in similar protests.) Finally, on April 2nd in Omagh, Northern Ireland, a young policeman was murdered by an explosive device placed beneath his car. What was Ronan Kerr's crime? He was a Roman Catholic who had joined the new Northern Ireland Police Service.

What can one say of those who carried out, or rejoiced in, these murders? Only that they exist and act in a world utterly alien to the post-Enlightenment one in which most of us do our best to live. Theirs is a world beyond reason, beyond debate, beyond logic, beyond argument. Is the fact that their world now looms so large out there a reason for despair? I have to say that I find it hard not to say that it is.

3 The Beautiful Game

The ugly side of football – and of Scottish football in particular – has been vividly on display in recent weeks. The beautiful game appears to have lost whatever right it may once have had to that description. In a previous issue of the *Review*, Kenneth Roy had good reason to question whether, in light of letter bombs, death threats, sectarian chanting, and violent behaviour on and off the pitch by both players and their coaches, first minister Alex Salmond was justified in continuing to use the phrase as if it still had any kind of relevance to Scottish football. However, is it fair to see this problem as am exclusively Scottish one? Well just a few days ago there was a match in Madrid between two of the best teams in the world. What did this 'clasico' encounter tell us about the beautiful game at its highest level?

Before trying to answer that question, and prompted by two recent television programmes, I want to look back to the world of football half a century ago. The programmes in question were 'United' – about the Munich air crash in which most of the then Manchester United team died – and a documentary about Sir Bobby Charlton, one of the survivors of that disaster. On February 8th, 1958, I was a postgraduate student in Princeton University in New Jersey, so I have no memory of the impact of the crash upon the British public at the time. But for me, as for many others alive at the time, it was an event that one never forgot. The BBC dramatization was measured and controlled, but its impact – almost inevitably – was intensely moving. Manager Matt Busby's young team – the so-called 'Busby Babes' – had already achieved so much, establishing the reputation of their English club at a European level. But of the eleven who had faced Red Star Belgrade in the European Cup a day or two earlier, seven died when their BEA aircraft failed to take off at its third attempt from a snow and ice-affected Munich airport. (The pilot, Captain Thain, would take ten years to clear his name by proving that it was the state of the runway, not pilot error, that caused the crash.) And an eighth team member – Duncan Edwards, already a legendary figure at the age of 21 – died in a Munich hospital about two weeks later. Bobby Charlton, on the other hand, after a few days in the same hospital, made a complete recovery. Initially traumatised by the loss of his team-mates, he soon rejoined Manchester United and went on to enjoy an immensely successful career for both club and country.

What emerged from these two programmes, however, was the hugeness of the gap between then and now in the world of football. The footballers of 1958 and the footballers of 2011 play the same game but in ages and cultures that are worlds apart. The Busby Babes were ordinary young men trying to make a decent living by being good footballers. Bobby Charlton, from a working-class family in Ashington in Northumberland, had two choices in his life: he could become a local miner like most of the men in his family, or a footballer – he had six uncles who played professional football. When her son was in hospital in Munich, Charlton's mother couldn't visit him. She couldn't afford the fare. (And anyway, like most of those around her, she didn't have a passport.) In 1958, Bobby Charlton's weekly pay-packet had been allowed to rise to the princely sum of £20. £20 a week was the maximum a footballer was allowed to earn as a result of the salary cap then in place in the English League. (The cap was finally abolished in 1961.) Eight years later, when Charlton was a member of the English team in the final of the World Cup, he sent his miner brother Tom a ticket for the Wembley final. But Tom couldn't afford the trip to London. He gave his ticket to his foreman in the mine – who rode his bicycle to London to see the game. A different world indeed.

What would the Busby Babes make of their contemporaries in Manchester United today? What would they make of the obscenely expensive sports cars they drive to the training ground, of the mansion houses in which they live, of their celebrity wives and girlfriends, of their vast salaries? Remember £200,000 a week rather than £20! Well no doubt all would be amazed, many envious, some perhaps dubious – but they would be unanimous in agreeing that today's world of football is simply unrecognisable as compared to that in which they played the beautiful game.

Just how unrecognisable, both off the pitch and on it, is suggested by that recent 'clasico' match between Real Madrid and Barcelona. Individual brilliance from Barcelona's Lionel Messi, but otherwise little more than a catalogue, as one commentator put it, of 'cheating, diving, sneaky fouling and blatantly attempting to trick, confuse or otherwise control the referee'. For me at least, it is the attitude of players and coaches towards the game's referee that is increasingly transforming football into a boorish spectacle. How today's soccer referees must envy the status and authority of their peers in rugby union football! Help for the soccer referee is available in the technology that a range of other sports, including rugby, have successfully adopted to remove the pressure over split-second decisions. Unless the dinosaurs who run world football move quickly to introduce that technology, the beauty of the beautiful game — so wonderfully represented by Bobby Charlton and the Busby Babes — will become an increasingly distant memory.

4 Privatisation

It was Mrs Thatcher I suppose who popularised the idea that privatisation was the answer to all our economic woes. Public ownership was bureaucratic, wasteful, and unenterprising. Private ownership was dynamic, efficient, and profitable. The Thatcherite battle-cry was: private sector good – public sector bad. As a form of economic policy, then, privatisation was always deeply ideological. It was driven by a fundamental distrust of the state. State ownership was a form of socialism, whereas free enterprise and the market lay at the heart of capitalism. For political conservatives, privatisation had to be the holy grail.

It is no doubt this background that explains my uneasiness over what is going on in Greece today. I just cannot see privatisation simply as an economic policy. Its right-wing, ideological trappings are all too prominent. Yet the IMF and the European Central Bank are making a programme of wholesale privatisation a condition of the provision of further loans to the Greek government. What gives these bodies the right to dictate to a sovereign people the politically-charged fiscal and economic policies they should follow? Should not international bodies – whose funds derive from a range of countries with governments of different kinds – refrain from direct political interference of this sort? Surely it is up to the Greek people to decide how far their public sector should or should not be privatised?

No doubt the scale of privatisation being demanded of Greece would in the short-term help to reduce the country's burden of debt. But then short-termism is one of the fundamental flaws of market capitalism in general. Instant profit always prevails over long-term investment. Already there are widespread suggestions that the rush to privatisation will mean that Greece's assets will be sold off at absurdly low prices. Recent history teaches a lesson here. What happened in Russia when the old communist state economy was sold off to the private sector? We all know the answer, and the group of Russian billionaires who were the beneficiaries of that example of unrestrained privatisation, are still throwing their weight around. What an irony it would be if the outcome of the policy now being inflicted upon the Greek people by bankers and their credit rating agency allies, was no other than the creation of a new generation of tax-avoiding, Greek shipping entrepreneurs!

Nearer home, we recently have had a series of examples which cast doubt on the dogma of public bad, private good. Tell that to the elderly living in care homes being run for profit rather than their well-being. The dogma itself, it seems to me, is well past its sell-by date. We struggle to live with the legacy of the 1980s. How depressing it is that our coalition government frequently seems not to realise this. We still hear far too much about deregulation, the rolling back of the state, the wonders of competition, the evils of the public sector, and the glories of more and more privatisation. Is there a think-tank somewhere working on an analysis of the actual effects of privatisation in the U.K. from 1980 to the present? There certainly ought to be.

5 Brown and Murdoch

What looks increasingly like the decline and fall of the Murdoch empire has implications for the reputation of various public figures. Gordon Brown is an excellent case in point. Whether he knew it or not, it is becoming perfectly clear that even in the period when he was Chancellor of the Exchequer, Brown was already the target of the darkest arts of News International.

As long ago as 2003, police in Plymouth learned that an Exmouth commercial investigations company called SAS Investigations was able to acquire information held in official data bases from a corrupt local police officer. Information from this illegal source on three Labour politicians – one of whom was Gordon Brown – was passed on to a private investigator in Newcastle. This man's files were seized in a police raid in February, 2003, but he was never charged, and he continues to refuse to identify the journalists who had contracted him to pursue investigations into Brown and his Labour Party colleagues. On the other hand, after a three-year investigation, the boss of SAS Investigations and an Exeter detective constable were eventually charged with offences of misconduct in public office. However in 2005 a local judge decided that the misconduct charges were not sufficiently serious to warrant proceeding with the case, and that a trial would be a waste of public money. As a result the defendants were acquitted, and none of the evidence made public.

Then there is evidence of other (successful) attempts by conmen and investigators, directly linked to News International, to gain access to Brown's financial, tax, and legal records – not to mention of course the hacking of his voice-mail. In 2000, lawyers at Abbey National informed *The Sunday Times* that 'someone from the *Sunday Times* or acting on its behalf has masqueraded as Mr Brown for the purpose of obtaining information from Abbey National by deception'. Similar trickery was used in 2000 to obtain information about Brown's purchase of a flat in London. (The conman employed on this occasion was later jailed for fraud.) Two years earlier, in 1998, Gordon Brown's tax records were obtained illegally from his accountants. No doubt to the chagrin of all those involved, the record proved to be completely above board.

All water under the bridge, you may say, and anyway does any of it really matter? Well it gives a kind of wry satisfaction to all of us who have argued that, particularly in the period when he was prime minister, Brown was subjected to an unprecedented level of hostile scrutiny by all the London-based media. Incidents such as 'Top Gear''s Jeremy Clarkson's disgraceful personal abuse of the prime minister – which a pusillanimous BBC let him get away with – were in fact a product of that relentlessly negative environment. What is now clear is that these consistent public attempts to discredit Brown had actually been underpinned by secret and underhand attempts to trawl into his private affairs in the (failed) hope of finding other kinds of damaging material.

More than personal satisfaction is involved here however. Gordon Brown himself seems to believe that but for News International's determination to use every possible tactic to bring him down, his defeat in last year's election might not have been on a scale to rule out a possible coalition with the Liberal Democrats. And if history does indeed prove that, while not publicly challenging the Murdoch empire, Brown did resist all its attempts to extend its control over the British media, then the reasoning behind the tycoon's decision to switch his support to David Cameron becomes sufficiently obvious.

But let me end by turning to what may well turn out to be a truly damaging consequence of the campaign to discredit Gordon Brown. Brown's name had long been associated with a future presidency of the International Monetary Fund. And why not? Who was better qualified for the post that the man universally recognized to have timeously driven through the policies necessary to prevent the catastrophic collapse of the world's economic and banking system in 2008? But when the opportunity arose, a mean-spirited and narrow-minded David Cameron was able to prevent his name even being considered. And he could do this with hardly a squeak of protest from Britain's supposedly well-informed and critical commentariat. News International had won. It was as if Brown's role in saving the world economy had been airbrushed out of existence. Instead we had all been bullied by the Murdoch press, and all their Conservative party adherents, into believing that Brown himself was solely responsible for Britain's budget deficit, as though Lehman Brothers and the world banking crisis had never occurred.

So we are left with Christine Lagarde in charge of the IMF. Known as 'austerity woman', Lagarde is of course a strong supporter of the Cameron/Osborne solution to the world's economic and fiscal problems: cuts in public spending followed by still more cuts. While the British economy continues to flat-line, is this policy working in Greece — or Portugal, or Ireland? In the year after 2008, the economic policies of Brown/Darling in the U.K. were beginning to produce results. There is reason to believe that a Brown-led IMF would have been in the world's best interest.

6 In Defence of Professionals

When I read the heading to Walter Humes's contribution to June Ist's *Scottish Review*, I have to admit I misunderstood it. I took the phrase 'the word "professional" is now as suspect as the word "banker"' to mean that the conjunction of "professional" and "banker" was unfair and unacceptable. But of course I was completely wrong. Professor Humes is fully persuaded that today's professionals deserve as much opprobrium as is heaped on today's bankers.

Well, I disagree. Of course some of the points made in the piece are fair enough. No doubt Edward Said is right to complain about the limitations of professional organizations. It is true that bodies set up to protect the public from bad professionals sometimes prove to be defensive bastions of self-serving conservatism. Professionals on occasion may well be arrogantly complacent. But what is one to make of Humes's conclusion that 'the discourse of professionalism' is used for dubious purposes, including the assertion 'that "experts" always know best'?

My response is to suggest that all too often experts do indeed know best. To deny this is in my view to be complicit with one of the most nauseating shibboleths of contemporary politics: the notion that power should be taken away from 'them' and given to 'us'. 'They' are the state, the government, Whitehall, the civil service in general, local authorities, local councillors, and more or less anyone who is committed to making civil society function. We of course are 'us'. Politician after politician, of every party, bangs on interminably about how we all want more power: power to set up our own schools; power to run our police forces; power to pick and choose a hospital to treat us; power to decide how often our rubbish-bins are emptied. We know best about all these things. Utopia is ours for the taking: once we thumb our noses at all those Whitehall experts and professionals.

I don't believe a word of it. What we want is that the 'professionals — the teachers, doctors, civil servants, administrators — do a good job'. What we want is a good local school, a good local hospital, and a good local administration. We want those who make decisions that affect our lives to be educated, informed, knowledgeable, expert. We want them to be professional. If they are falling short in any way, we want them to be more professional, not less. The man in the street, or on the Clapham bus — like the reader of the *Daily Mail* or the *Sun* — doesn't know what's best. We need to encourage professionals to hone their professionalism. What we don't want to do is denigrate them.

In the middle of the nineteenth century American politics boasted a 'Know Nothing' party. In today's anti-expert, anti-professional, anti-'them' climate, that is the party to which all our politicians seem to belong. I at least find that more than a little worrying.

7 Enough is Enough

Enough is enough. Unemployment in the U.K. stands at 2.57 million – 8.1% of the workforce. 991,000 under 25s are out of work. The British economy has effectively been flat-lining for almost a year. Nobel-prize winning economists Paul Krugman and Joseph Stiglitz have long been warning us that the deficit-reduction-at –all-costs policy of our coalition government would make a bad situation worse. The *New York Times* has chosen to publish a leader (October 14th) specifically rejecting the British government's behaviour. The hard facts show how right these critics are. Here is Stiglitz: 'advocates of austerity believe that mystically, as the deficits come down, confidence in the economy will be restored and investment will boom'. But now the evidence is in showing that business confidence has collapsed, there is no investment boom, unemployment is at its highest for seventeen years, and the threat of a return to recession is increasingly great.

Surely it is time for a change. The Cameron/Osborne austerity policy has been in place for over a year. It has failed to deliver. So what has been the response of our leaders? The first is something of a joke. Yes, they admit, all the economic figures are disappointing. But it's not our fault. It's all because of world-wide economic problems and the difficulties of the Eurozone. Government ministers and their spokesmen repeat this mantra over and over again. They must imagine — or hope — we have very short memories. But in fact we don't. We remember all too clearly how in their opposition days after 2008, they mocked and derided any suggestion from Brown/Darling that Britain's economic problems, including the size of the deficit, had anything at all to do with a world-wide economic problem. If they continue to deploy this argument, perhaps it's time they apologised for their previous rejection of it.

Their second response is much more serious. The austerity policy must be rigidly adhered to because it is delivering a borrowing facility at a mere 2%. But is this really a good enough reason for effectively doing nothing about soaring unemployment and a declining economy? And anyway where is the hard evidence that a modest change in policy in the direction of growing the economy would lead to a massive loss of confidence in the British government's ability to control its budget deficit? After all even Christine Lagarde, the head of the IMF, has been telling European governments that deficit reduction has to be balanced by economic expansion. Yet Cameron/Osborne go on telling us that the slightest deviation from austerity will turn us into another Greece/Ireland/Portugal. (And of course they remain almost the only government heads who continue to take seriously the opinions of the utterly discredited rating agencies.) Is it going too far to suggest that they are virtually telling the markets how to react should even a modest policy change be initiated?

My own opinion is that the reason Cameron/Osborne stick so stubbornly to their failing policy has nothing to do with economics. It is a purely political decision. They feel they cannot admit to having been even marginally wrong. They are afraid of accusations of u-turns. They cannot face a difficult time at prime-minister's questions in the House of Commons. But it's the lives of real people we're talking about. Political point-scoring is irrelevant. Surely it's time for the government to act – and to act in a more imaginative way than changing planning regulations. A big reduction in VAT? Changes in taxation policy making it less costly for employers to take on new staff? Rather than the deficit, it is cutting unemployment that should be our government's first priority. And a final point. Why oh why is the British government failing to support the rest of Europe in pushing now for the implementation of an immensely lucrative Robin Hood or Tobin tax? Surely if ever there was a tax that smacks of natural justice, this is the one.

8 Herbert Hoover

I suspect I was not the only reader to be struck by the angry and rancorous tone of John Cameron's contribution – 'The hand-out generation' – in the October 20th issue of the *Review*. Intended to be an account of the inadequacies and inanities of those protesting, in London, New York, and other cities around the world, against the current failure of our capitalist system to support the 99% of us who are not already rich, it would not win many prizes for fairness or judiciousness. And given its resort to what is no more than a series of reductive, right-wing, stereotypical dismissals of today's students (and universities) – exemplified by its title – I find it difficult to believe that anyone could find the writer's views on the issues involved persuasive.

What really struck me, however, was an assertion made near the beginning of the article. We are told that one Herbert Hoover was an intellectual giant. The current American president is apparently 'hardly in the same league as such intellectual giants as Jefferson, Adams, Wilson and Hoover'. Well most of us would have no problem over that description of the first three: Jefferson and Adams were distinguished Enlightenment intellectuals, and founding fathers of the new republic; Woodrow Wilson was a scholar and academic, and president of Princeton University, before becoming president of his country.

But Herbert Hoover? What kind of intellectual giant was he? Occupying the White House from 1929 to 1933, Hoover's presidency was a failure. In his inauguration speech he said: 'we shall soon with the help of God, be in sight of the day when poverty will be banished from this nation'. The truth proved to be otherwise. The stock-market crash of 1929 brought the roaring twenties to a catastrophic end. In the following years the USA slumped deeper and deeper into depression. Unemployment would rise to almost 25%; the numbers of the poor and the hungry would reach unparalleled heights; and the tented cities and shanty-towns of the homeless, spreading across the country, would become known as 'Hoovervilles'.

A true Republican at heart, Hoover believed in the gold standard and a balanced budget; he distrusted state or government intervention in the economy; voluntary co-operation between the public and private spheres, he believed, was the best way forward; and he forcibly repatriated half a million Mexican workers.

Initially a tax-cutter, he was finally forced to raise taxes on the rich, and tentatively to introduce some of the programmes of state intervention in the economy which would be massively expanded under his successor's New Deal. But such change in direction came too late. The American people rejected this intellectual giant. Franklin D. Roosevelt swept to the presidency with a vote of 472 to 59 in the electoral college.

It is hard to believe that Mr Cameron's other intellectual giants among American presidents would have found much to admire in the policies of Herbert Hoover. (Nor for that matter in the behaviour and beliefs of today's Republican party leaders, or their candidates for the nomination in 2012.) After losing office, Hoover went on to write a great many books, and over the years consistently accused FDR of leading America into Bolshevism and socialism. This may help to explain why today's neo-cons in America and elsewhere, helped on by sympathetic revisionist historians, admire Hoover. But does that make him into an intellectual giant? I think not.

8a Herbert Hoover Again

In his original article (20 October), John Cameron did not argue, as he now suggests, that Herbert Hoover was an intellectual. He said that Hoover was an 'intellectual giant' alongside presidents Adams, Jefferson and Wilson. Not unreasonably I took this to mean that, as president of the United States, Hoover deserved to be rated as highly as the other three. For Mr Cameron (and Anthony Seaton) now (9 November) to argue that Hoover achieved a great deal in other parts of his career is thus entirely beside my point. As a president, Hoover was no kind of giant.

I am happy to agree that Hoover deserves enormous credit for his work, for example, in famine relief in Russia and elsewhere after World War I. I wonder whether Mr Cameron is equally prepared to agree that those involved in the Occupy Wall Street protest around the world deserve better than to be blindly dismissed as a rabble, with or without a cause?

9 Public Intellectuals

At a recent convivial dinner sponsored by a charitable organization, I found myself in earnest conversation with a fellow-academic and a guest from the world of television and film. Perhaps inevitably we two retired professors were soon being asked about the current state of our universities. We were in complete agreement about this. The policies being pursued by the coalition government were wrong-headed and deeply dispiriting. Our universities were being transformed into just another set of business organizations. The role of the universities was ultimately a commercial one: teaching and research should be geared towards economic development and wealth creation; students were our customers concerned to get value for their money – which means only studying those subjects that will get them a well-paid job. In other words, we were repeating the increasingly familiar narrative of academic disillusionment over, and hostility towards, the path down which our university system is being driven.

Our dining companion was happy to agree with the thrust of what we were saying. So, he asked, what were we doing about it? Couldn't a case be made, to the Scottish government at least, in favour of radical change? Who, he went on, were the public intellectuals who could influence public opinion in the way we would like? We looked at each other, and a second or two passed; then we both came up with the same name. The case against the coalition's university policy had been put most effectively by Stefan Collini of the English Faculty of the University of Cambridge. I added that an equally devastating critique of the Browne report — upon which the government's entire policy is based — had been delivered by Stanley Fish, a leading American public intellectual. (And I would now add to the list an equally challenging article in the current *London Review of Books* by Professor Keith Thomas of All Souls College, Oxford). But what about a Scottish voice our dinner companion pressed? After a longer pause, my friend hesitatingly suggested Lindsay Paterson, professor of education in Edinburgh University. But that was as far as we got — it was time for the after dinner speeches.

This episode, and specifically the issue of Scottish public intellectuals, reminded me of an exchange in the *Observer* some months ago in which different figures were asked to comment on the status of intellectuals in British society. The London-based historian Lisa Jardine suggested that public opinion today has little respect for intellectuals. 'If you look at America', she wrote, 'the Ivy League universities and their professors are regarded with an amount of esteem that is reserved in this country for surgeons and judges'. (Is Professor Jardine overstating our respect for surgeons and judges I wonder?) And she concluded that what the current debate over the universities has demonstrated is that 'we have little respect for what would pass for an intelligentsia anywhere else in Europe or North America'. Undaunted by the generally negative tone of this and other exchanges, the *Observer* journalist John Naughton was bold enough to go ahead and publish 'Brains of Britain' – his 'suggested list of 300 public intellectuals'.

What is the most striking thing about Naughton's list? In the present context, the answer is an unsurprising one: the remarkable paucity of Scottish names. The esteemed 300 are divided into a series of categories: Academics, Activists, Authors, Classicists, Critics, etc., etc. Ten academic public intellectuals are listed. The Scottish representation? None. Among 54 authors, three Scots appear: A.L. Kennedy, Tom Nairn, and Andrew O'Hagan. Of 42 historians, two are Scots – but only in the sense that both were born in Glasgow: Niall Ferguson and Norman Stone. Of 62 Journalists/ Editors Naughton seems to come up with only three Scots: Neal Ascherson, Ian Jack, and Andrew Marr. Out of 12 poets and 7 politicians only two Scots qualify: Carol Ann Duffy and Gordon Brown. Of 11 philosophers, none is Scottish.

How should one respond to such a derogatory level of Scottish representation among the so-called brains of Britain? Dismiss it out of hand as ludicrous? Well, yes. Regard it as just another example of the narrowness of outlook, the English bias, the unthinking, blinkered ignorance of the metropolitan elite who run our media? Probably. And yet, and yet, I'm troubled. The *Observer* newspaper was launched on December 4th, 1791 – exactly 220 years ago. Had that first edition – or an edition twenty years earlier or twenty years later – included a feature on the then brains of Britain, it is surely indisputable that Scottish academics, authors, critics, historians and philosophers – and perhaps poets and politicians as well – would have been there *en masse*. No London journalist could possibly have ignored them. So what has happened now? Have metropolitan blinkers simply become bigger? Or is it indeed the case that in today's Scotland intellectuals of any kind are distrusted rather than attended to? If so, perhaps it is not surprising that Scottish public intellectuals are so thin on the ground.

10 Robin Hood

Why on earth is our coalition government so opposed to the introduction of a Tobin or 'Robin Hood' tax on transactions made in the world of high finance? Not of course that Cameron, Osborne and Cable are honest enough to admit that they are. Oh no, they say, we're all in favour of such a tax at a global level. But anything less than global – across Europe, say? No, no, no – quite out of the question. So we are invited to believe that they are in favour of the tax – as long as no serious attempt is made to introduce it.

Why do I find such a position so surprising? Not because of its typical disingenuousness, but rather because if ever there was a tax that seems fair, reasonable, and in accord with natural justice, this is it. What would the imposition of a Tobin tax actually mean? It would mean that a tax amounting to 0.01% of their value would be paid on financial dealings – the buying and selling of stocks, bonds, securities, derivatives, etc., and all the activities of investment banks and hedge funds – within the city. Every time a high-flying dealer or trader pressed that button on his computer in Canary Wharf, and sent however many pounds flashing around the world, the taxpayer would get 0.01% of the total involved. The financial market, that is, would at last be seen to be contributing something to alleviate the damage it caused by its reckless and irresponsible behaviour in the years leading up to the crisis of 2008.

Why on earth shouldn't the City pay up? Without government intervention – meaning the use of vast amounts of taxpayers' money – Canary Wharf would have fallen into the Thames. But what in fact has happened since 2008? Politicians of every persuasion have talked endlessly about how steps are being taken to ensure that casino banking and the kind of financial free-for-all that accompanied it are things of the past. Yet as time passes, nothing seems to change. Bankers still walk away with their extraordinary bonuses. CEOs and other top executives in major companies are awarded ever more stratospheric salaries. The rich get richer while the other 99% of us get poorer.

Given this scenario, who can doubt that the introduction of some form of this 'Robin Hood' tax would be immensely popular? In a situation where we seem to be teetering on the brink of a return to recession – if not to a 1930s style depression – some degree of financial reparation from those largely responsible for the crisis we are in is not a lot to ask for. (Not that I'm suggesting that this tax should necessarily be used for deficit reduction alone.) So I repeat my question: what have our leaders got against Robin Hood?

Well George Osborne tells us – presumably with a straight face – that a 0.01% tax on financial transactions would be a 'bullet aimed at the heart of London'. His backer, ex-prime minister John Major, uploads the weapon image by suggesting that the tax would be akin to directing a 'heat-seeking missile at the City of London'. What fatuous hyperbole! They want us to believe that the fact the tax would raise more money in London than in any other European city proves it is unfair. More nonsense. As people like Osborne and Major are constantly boasting, London is one of the financial capitals of the world. More transactions inevitably mean more tax revenue.

The real reasons for the Cameron/Osborne rejection of the tax surely lie elsewhere. One of them undoubtedly relates to the composition of today's Tory party in the House of Commons. Eurosceptics rule – and Mr Cameron knows it. In his recent Mansion House speech he had to make it clear whose side he was on – so he chose to identify himself with the sceptical majority. The introduction of a Tobin tax in the Eurozone is now strongly backed by both Angela Merkel and Nicolas Sarkozy. So the issue has become a European one. For most Tories now there could be no better reason for saying no. And their leader will not dare to disagree.

Finally there is a still more powerful reason why our leaders will remain on the side of the Sheriff of Nottingham rather than supporting Robin Hood. The audience listening to the Mansion House speech was full of sheriffs. They accept no responsibility for past mistakes, falling living standards, growing unemployment, the widening gap between rich and poor, or any of the other ills our country is experiencing. A tax on the City? No chance. The Tory party supporters with the deepest pockets expect to get value for their money – not a new tax. If the Chancellor of the Exchequer talks about tax in his forthcoming autumn statement it will not be about Robin Hood. Rather the chances are it will be about a promise to abolish as soon as possible the 50% income tax level the sheriffs currently are paying. Why? Because the City rules/OK?

11 Bad Language

Kenneth Roy's recent piece (November 2nd) on the egregious use of the f-word in supposedly entertaining after-dinner speeches – and what it tells us about the coarseness of Scottish life – struck a very resonant chord with me. However, I'd suggest that in this context it is not only Scottish life that is in question. I have been a diligent reader of the *Guardian* newspaper for many more years than I like to remember. Proud of its position as the flagship liberal broadsheet, the paper has inevitably always been careful to avoid linguistic usages that could be seen as offensive in terms of race, gender or any other sensitive category.

However, in recent years I've noted a very clear shift over the use in the paper of what once upon a time would have been regarded as bad language. Here there has been an obvious relaxation of prior editorial practice. Particularly in the paper's G2 section, where the same group of columnists regularly appear, what in my old-fashioned way I'm calling bad language is used with such regularity that it can be fairly called standard procedure. The f-word, in its range of grammatical forms, is commonplace, while not even the c-word is banned. Words of the 'shit' and 'arse' category make regular appearances. In other words, the paper appears to have decided that the language of the street or the pub – or the after-dinner speech – has *carte blanche* to appear in its columns.

Now I absolutely agree that such language is used all the time by large sections of contemporary society. For proof look no further that the *Guardian*'s magazine section on Saturday, November 5th. There is an interview there with the famous Ricky Gervais, and the language in which he talks is peppered with just the kind of usages we are describing. But because this is the real 'real language of men' (in Wordsworth's phrase) should it become acceptable as the standard language of expression in a 'quality' newspaper? I'm not convinced. Like Kenneth Roy, I think there's at least an element of macho display in the use of such language. Using this kind of vocabulary, the writers perhaps believe they are proving their 'street' credibility. What they are actually demonstrating is that bad language and good taste are incompatible.

The bigger question is how far the change I have registered in the *Guardian* is symptomatic of a change in our society as a whole. Unfortunately, I fear the answer is quite far. Coarseness – at least in terms of what is regarded as acceptable in linguistic usage as compared with days past – is all too familiar. Let me end with one example. An exhibition of art works in some sense inspired by Lewis Carroll has just opened in Tate Liverpool. One assumes that the curators will be expecting their show to attract large numbers of families with children of all ages who have read the Alice books. Well what are such children supposed to make of a sculpture called 'Humpty Fucking Dumpty' – or a poster for a porno movie called *Arsewoman in Wonderland?* Coarse indeed.

12 Shakespeare's Pronunciation

I was pleased to read in yesterday's *Guardian* (March 19th) a short piece by Michael Billington, the paper's senior drama critic, expressing a degree of scepticism about a newly-released British Library CD which gives us what claims to be Shakespeare in his original pronunciation. I was pleased because a few nights earlier I had listened to an item on Radio Four's 'Front Row' which gave what amounted to a puffing advertisement for this project. Mark Lawson interviewed a Shakespearean actor called Ben Crystal, one of the authors of the CD in question. His name rang a bell, and a quick check revealed that he is indeed the son of Professor David Crystal, who is one of our leading experts on the English language, and certainly the guru the BBC calls upon whenever some issue about the present state of English becomes a news item. (He can be relied upon to remind us that all languages evolve and change over time so that new words or developments in English usage are nothing to get worried about.)

Unsurprisingly it turns out that it is Crystal senior who is the author of the Shakespeare's original pronunciation theory. Having been less than convinced by Ben Crystal's radio account of what is involved, I listened to the video in which Crystal father and son explain in detail the reasoning behind the new CD. Professor Crystal does try to give a scholarly gloss to the enterprise and offers some justification for the idea that we can recapture how English was pronounced in Shakespeare's day. But the case he makes is far from conclusive. Also while it may well be true that Elizabethan and Jacobean English did not sound like the 'received pronunciation' of English today, I remained unclear over whether all English speakers are supposed to have used what the Crystals call Shakespeare's 'original pronunciation' – which comes across more or less as a west-country regional accent. In the interview with Ben, Mark Lawson failed to question the degree of certainty we can have about how exactly Shakespeare spoke, but did manage to ask when it became normal for our actors to deliver Shakespeare's lines without any regional accent. Ben suggested only in the last hundred years. So in the eighteenth and nineteenth centuries Shakespearean actors all spoke as though they were auditioning for minor roles in 'The Archers'? Is this credible? In the interview Mark weakened the case by making the intellectually lazy suggestion that it was only snobbery that made generations of Shakespearean actors speak in something other than a regional accent. Rather than an upper class establishment plot, could that decision not have much to do with a range of considerations both inside and outside the plays themselves?

Surely Shakespeare's original pronunciation is at best a question of supposition – however well-informed and scholarly. The regional accents of members of London's Elizabethan and Jacobean acting companies are bound to have been diverse. Is it likely that Shakespeare would have expected them to sound like him?

Ben Crystal made two points in support of the original pronunciation case. In Sonnet 116, Shakespeare rhymes 'proved' with 'loved'. Received pronunciation does not make this a true rhyme, while original pronunciation does. Well perhaps so, but Shakespeare's sonnets were meant to be read and the two words do make an eye rhyme. Then Crystal suggests that a speech by Jacques in Act 2, scene seven, of *As You Like It* contains a pun on the word 'hour' – when it is pronounced to rhyme with 'whore'. (Similarly, in the video we're told that in the Prologue to *Romeo and Juliet*, original pronunciation reveals a pun on 'loins/lines'.) Such readings are plausible – but far from certain. If the Globe and other theatres want to give a try to Shakespeare in what the Crystals assure us is original pronunciation, that's entirely up to them. But like Michael Billington, I think it would be 'perverse' if what is only a scholarly experiment became standard practice in the delivery of the language of Shakespeare.

13 A Future for Books?

The Edinburgh Book Festival recently celebrated the fiftieth anniversary of the original, pioneering International Writers' Conference of 1962 (in which I played a small part), by organizing its own World Writers' Conference as part of the 2012 Edinburgh International Book Festival. The idea was to replicate as exactly as possible the structure and content of the 1962 event. Hence on each of the five conference days, versions of the same topics that were debated in 1962 – different approaches to the novel, contemporary Scottish writing, political commitment, censorship, and the future of the novel – were discussed by a range of writers from twenty-six countries. In 1962 the episode that earned the greatest publicity was the confrontation, on the Scottish day, between the fiery nationalist poet Hugh MacDiarmid, and Alexander Trocchi, the voice of the emerging trans-national, Euro-American counter-culture. Nothing that happened this August – not even Irvine Welsh on national literatures--matched this encounter. But that is not to say that the 2012 conference lacked controversy.

On the final day battle was joined on what is fast becoming easily the most fundamental and divisive issue in today's literary culture: the future of not just the novel, but of the book itself. Because this is the issue that the continuing explosion of the market for the so-called 'e-book' is beginning to raise. The English writer China Miéville played the cat among the pigeons on this occasion. In a rambling and sometimes confusing speech, he certainly challenged both his fellow-writers and the audience, saving his most extraordinary suggestion for the conclusion of his lecture: novelists, poets, and writers should be paid a salary equivalent to the 'wage of a skilled worker'. (Typically, Miéville seemed unclear about who would actually pay the writers' wages: 'we shouldn't trust the state', he said, apparently suggesting that the existing social order could be replaced by some more ideal form of democracy.) Nonetheless he was being entirely serious – and there was no denying a kind of logic to his position. Fundamentally he was arguing that writing and writers will soon be in the same position as music and its creators already find themselves. Young people today, he said, no longer believe they have to pay for the music they listen to. Now that music is out there in cyber-space all attempts to regulate it in a traditional sense are failing. You hear something you like, you download it, and pass it on to your friends.

Rather than trying desperately to find effective ways of preventing the computer-led piracy of their work, writers should welcome the new freedom that advancing technology allows both writers and readers. Miéville even applauds the disappearance of writers' control of their texts. Music can be remixed at the listener's choice. Texts of every kind – classical, popular, or genre fiction – can be similarly treated by readers in the form of 'enhanced' e-books – the equivalent of musical 'mashups'. Having lost the power to 'own' their texts, writers will no longer receive an income from royalties, and thus need a new way of earning a living. Hence the apparently crazy suggestion of writers' wages.

Miéville is far from being the only contemporary writer who is delighted by the literary revolution that e-books represent. The recent Festival of Crime Writers in Harrogate devoted a session to a debate on e-books and the future of crime writing. The panel consisted of two crime writers, a bookseller, a literary agent, and the current Chair of the Publishers' Association. Once again most of the audience, and his fellow panel-members, seemed to listen incredulously to the views of the writer Stephen Leather. I have to admit I'd never heard of Stephen Leather. But so what? He happens to be only the second highest seller of books on Kindle worldwide – second only to Lee Child, whose name I do know. In 2011 alone, Leather sold 500,000 e-books: three times as many as he sold in paperback format. What he told his fellow-panellists amounted to saying that they were surplus to requirements: e-books require no delivery or distribution charges, no warehousing – and no publishers. E-book authors can be their own editors, designers, salesmen, and advertisers. Leather sells short stories for 70p, novellas for £1.99, 100,000 word novels for £2.99. But that is still profitable because 70% of these prices come straight to him. Sometimes he distributes stories free of charge, and he goes in for methods of self-promotion that eighteenth-century Grub Street would have been proud of. Like Miéville, he has no concerns over piracy. Piracy is no more than a form of free publicity. Of course, the other panel members challenged much of what Leather had to say and he agreed, for example, that the lack of a traditional editor could be a drawback particularly for new self-publishing writers. On the other hand, his own huge success as a professional writer, increasingly working in the new e-book world, is proof of its utility.

Not all successful contemporary writers are as happy as Miéville and Leather about self-publishing and the e-book. The American crime writer Sue Grafton recently denounced self-publishing as fatally lacking in professional discipline: 'self-publishing is a short cut and I don't believe in short cuts when it comes to the arts'. Grafton was supported by the hugely successful Jodi Picoult and Richard Russo, but she found herself subjected to a barrage of criticism, including accusations of elitism, from supporters of the new world of self-publishing. Scotland's Catherine Czerkawska, for example, insisted that e-books and 'the indie publishing movement' amounted to 'nothing less than an inspirational and creative godsend'. Grafton was forced to concede she had not understood 'how it works' and had meant 'no disrespect for e-publishing and indie authors'.

There is no question that e-books' sales have risen enormously in recent years. In the USA, in the first quarter of 2012, their sales overtook those for all hard-cover books. On Amazon, e-book sales now exceed even those of paperbacks. Given this, and all the possible implications of the self-publishing movement, are we, as some of its proponents believe, only at the beginning of a cultural change as massive as that produced by the invention of printing almost six hundred years ago? I don't know. But the possibility is a real one.

14 Conference Speeches

The political conference season is over for another year. I guess few people will regret its passing. The general opinion now is that these events are even less important than they used to be. Once upon a time the annual conference provided party members with an opportunity to make their views known on the pressing policy issues of the day – even if this meant their disagreeing with the party line adopted by their leaders. Admittedly at this year's Liberal Democrat conference, ordinary members did vote down coalition policy on a couple of issues, but in this age of image, sound bite, spin-doctors, and political management, such occasions are increasingly rare. So much so that many commentators regard party conferences as empty, stage-managed spectacles, well past their sell-by date and largely ignored by the voting public.

Then it seems that fewer and fewer of those attending the conferences actually are ordinary party members. (It cost over £700 to attend this year's Conservative Party do.) The numbers are largely made up of lobbyists and special interest groups, political aides and researchers, aspiring MPs, and those manning the various exhibition stands and shops. And it is also worth remembering that the number of ordinary voters who are members of any political party – and thus theoretically in a position to attend the conferences – continues to decline. Apparently the combined total membership of our three main political parties now stands at 421,000: a figure below that for the number of us who have joined the RSPB.

So do the party conferences offer all of us anything at all? Well this year perhaps the opportunity to listen to the under-threat party leaders attempting to put their best foot forward. First up was Nick Clegg. Headlines were certainly achieved by his well-publicized apology announcement. The vote-catching pledge not to raise university tuition fees had been a serious error – which he now regretted. Will this admission mean a massive return to the fold of former Lib Dem supporters? Somehow I doubt it. My own decision to quit the party had little or nothing to do with the tuition fees fiasco. What outraged me – and I suspect most left-leaning former members – was the party's decision to go on supporting the Osborne/Cameron policy of austerity, austerity, austerity as the only solution to the fiscal deficit. Even now, more than two years on, when the critics of this approach have been proved wholly correct, Lib Dem ministers, including even the saintly Vince Cable, go on endorsing the 'no turning back' Thatcherite nonsense of Mr Osborne.

Ed Miliband's pitch to the Labour party – and the country – was widely regarded as a success. Invoking the 'one nation' idea associated with the Tory Benjamin Disraeli, Miliband dispelled all doubts about his status as party leader and potential prime minister. But I'm not sure that Miliband was as clear as Disraeli either about the crisis the nation was facing or about how precisely to resolve it. When the young Disraeli published his most successful novel in 1845 he entitled it *Sybil, or The Two Nations*. In other words, he was accepting Thomas Carlyle's ominous analysis of the condition of England in this crucial period. In his 1839 pamphlet *Chartism*, Carlyle had asked the question: 'Is the condition of the English working people wrong; so wrong that rational working men cannot, will not, and even should not rest quiet under it?' In the gap between the rich and the poor, the haves and the have-nots, Carlyle saw the potential for social upheaval. Disraeli agreed. In 1840 he wrote: 'None but those devoid of the sense and spirit of Englishmen can be blind to the perils that are impending over our country'. Hence the 'Two Nations' subtitle to 'Sybil'.

Disraeli's novel succeeds pretty well at portraying the nature of the problem dividing English society. It contains vivid scenes of urban poverty and deprivation, of ruthless economic exploitation of the working class, and the cruel consequences of the free-market utilitarianism underpinning what Carlyle called the cash nexus. But like the other contemporary novelists who contributed to the 'condition of England' debate – Dickens in *Hard Times*, Mrs Gaskell in *Mary Barton* and *North and South*, and Charlotte Bronte in *Shirley* – Disraeli had no interest in radical political change, or in the emergence of working-class movements or combinations such as trade unions. The future Tory prime minister's only solution is a new union between the working class and a renewed and regenerate aristocracy accepting its social responsibilities and loyally committed to traditional conservative and religious values. Not in other words a 'one nation' position that Ed Miliband could endorse – even if he might envy its lucidity and simplicity.

David Cameron's speech to the Conservative Party conference was described by the party chairman as 'serious'. Did he mean worthily boring? Lots of straight talking about the difficult world we are facing, of the need to confront global challenges, of making tough choices., etc. etc. But no straight talking and no apology over the rising deficit and the failing economic policies for which he and

George Osborne are responsible. And no explanation of how, while the gap between the rich and the poor continues to grow, further huge cuts in the welfare budget is compatible with the notion that we are all in this together. Cameron would do well to read Disraeli's novel and match its author's deeply-felt concern over the perilous gap between the two nations.

So who was the winner in the party leader's best conference speech contest? In my view, none of the above. That accolade goes instead to the leader of the Scottish Labour Party, Johann Lamont. The speech she gave in Scotland and repeated at the Labour Party conference is easily the bravest performance by any party leader in recent years. Daring to raise the issue of the continuing affordability of highly desirable universal benefits was an act of real political courage. No doubt the vast majority of us would like to retain in perpetuity free care for the elderly, free prescription charges, free bus passes for the over sixties, free TV licences for the over seventy-fives, free tuition for Scottish university students, and a freeze on council tax. All of these are popular, vote-catching policies — but they come at a price. And the SNP government and its many supporters among the Scottish commentariat have to do a great deal more than arrogantly dismiss the Lamont position as no more than an endorsement of the Westminster's government's cuts programme. The first minister and his colleagues have to get serious and tell us where, in or out of an independent Scotland, the money will be found to maintain these policies. Like Gerry Hassan (*The Scottish Review*, October 11), I am dismayed by the abject failure of the Scottish political class to respond seriously to the crucial issue Johann Lamont has raised.

Take the university tuition fees issue. We are constantly assured that the Scottish university system is world-class. The education minister is also determined that no matter what is happening elsewhere in the U.K, a university education will remain free for Scottish students. What will that mean for the resourcing and future status of the Scottish universities? Indeed has Mr Russell taken note of the latest *THES* world university rankings? Of the world's top 100 universities, 61 are American (students pay fees at all of these), 10 are English (and have the benefit of an income stream from their students), only 2 are Scottish: Edinburgh, ranked 36th, and St Andrews, ranked 85th (both of these have substantial numbers of English fee-paying students). Even as things stand, is it honest to go on insisting that Scotland is funding a world-class university system?

15 Risk Aversion

In a recent *Guardian* article Simon Jenkins deplores what he sees as the disproportionate media reaction to the Jimmy Savile case. He argues that 'the BBC, the NHS and some charities' do indeed 'bear a portion of culpability for the harm [Savile] caused to young people'. But he insists that no good will come of suggesting that George Entwistle, the new director of the BBC, is the 'manager of a paedophile ring' or even 'an appeaser of sexual harassment'. 'The case', he writes, 'is awash in malice, vilification, exaggeration and litigation'.

In the rest of his article, Jenkins argues that the Savile case and the reaction to it provide a perfect example of a deeper contemporary malaise. What that is can be defined as the rise and rise of what is called 'risk aversion'. Risk aversion began life in the world of business, finance, economics, and psychology. It involves a cautious habit of mind that prefers the certainty of a small financial return to the gamble that might lead to a greatly enhanced one. But today the phrase has gained much wider currency covering all those habitual attitudes and forms of behaviour that attempt to insulate society from dangers or risk-taking of any kind.

From December 1st this year, the Vetting and Barring Scheme, managed by *The Independent* Safeguarding Authority, comes into force. Around 11.3 million citizens in the fields of education, care, and health will be required to register – for a fee of £64 – on a national database. As it is, we are all familiar with such developments as the disappearing habit of children walking to school, of schools choosing to limit outdoor activities which put children at any kind of risk, of authors requiring criminal clearance before being allowed to read in the classroom. Jenkins mentions the practice of university teachers leaving their office door open when engaged in individual tutorials. (I started doing this in the 1980s.)

Of course there are powerful arguments in favour of all such developments, but what concerns Jenkins is what he calls 'the paranoia of the modern state'. Risk aversion has seeped into 'every factory, office and profession, stifling enterprise, "reassessing" risk, clogging decision'. On the other hand, when failures or mistakes involving the vulnerable or young do occur, those responsible are automatically regarded as criminals to be denounced and pilloried. 'This can only lead', concludes Jenkins, 'to ever more defensive behaviour in every sphere of public life'.

Writing his piece, Jenkins was not to know that news was about to break with the potential to send 'risk aversion' to new heights of tragi-comic ludicrousness. A court in Italy has sentenced a group of Italian seismologists to six years in prison for giving wrong assurances to the people of the city of L'Aquila over the dangers they were facing hours before the fatal earthquake of April 6, 2009. The six scientists – Italy's top earthquake experts — were members of what is called the Major Risks Commission. But on this occasion their risk assessment proved to be hopelessly wrong.

The reaction of the world's scientific community to this Italian verdict has been exactly as one would have expected. The court's decision is utterly irrational: Italy has reverted to the Dark Ages; the persecution of Galileo in the seventeenth century has been repeatedly invoked. But the key point is that risk aversion will now overtake those who are best placed to provide rational risk assessment. Those who assess risk now feel themselves at risk. In consequence, scientists will from now on be reluctant to participate in hazard prediction of any kind. One of the Italian six reports: 'From what I hear... no one wants to join commissions'. Roger Musson of the British Geological Survey says: 'One can imagine that next time there are rumblings heard from Vesuvius, Italian volcanologists are going to be reluctant to make any statement, because they have no guarantee that they won't find themselves arrested if they say one thing and it turns out to be another'. And of course it's not only earthquake experts who could be in the firing line. Will future Michael Fishes be sent to prison if they fail to warn us of impending hurricanes?

Well it turns out that Simon Jenkins, who has just published a piece on the L'Aquila court decision, thinks they should. Science and scientists — our new gods — he thinks deserve to be taken down a peg or two. What crusty old Simon fails to note, however, is that in the highly unlikely event that the L'Aquila six ever do go to prison, the 'defensive behaviour in every sphere of public life,' which he bemoaned in his previous article, would soar to new and stratospheric heights.

16 George Square

The citizens of Aberdeen were allowed to have the final say on the City Gardens Project that would have replaced the historic Union Terrace Gardens in the city centre. The citizens of Glasgow are currently being denied any similar right over the extraordinary scheme to transform the equally iconic George Square in the heart of the city. Why is this the case? Who has made this decision? Politicians of all political parties now talk endlessly about devolving choice to the people, about curtailing the role of officials and experts, and above all about highlighting transparency in relation to how exactly decisions are made. Over the issue of George Square, Glasgow City Council has a golden opportunity to transform all this rhetoric into reality.

Last year a decision was made (by whom?) to begin consultations on the future development of George Square. A council spokesman has said: 'We carried out an exercise last year involving resident focus groups and in-depth stakeholder interviews. This played a role in establishing what the future vision of the square should be, as well as priorities in terms of the redevelopment'. As always, the language used makes it clear where this 'exercise' is coming from: we are instantly in the PR world of focus groups and 'stakeholder' interviews – inevitably 'in-depth' ones. Less clear though is what exactly the 'priorities' were that these interviews apparently established. What we do know is how many people were interviewed: 42, and not all of them were in favour of the major changes to George Square being proposed. On the other hand, we also know exactly who the seven so-called 'stakeholders' were — all of whom turned out to be enthusiasts for a radical redevelopment of George Square. The list makes interesting reading: the Glasgow Hoteliers' Association, the Glasgow Restaurateurs' Association, Glasgow Chambers of Commerce, the Glasgow Marketing Bureau, the Royal Incorporation of Architects in Scotland (RIAS), and perhaps more oddly, Strathclyde Passenger Transport and Strathclyde Police. George Square's 'stakeholders' turn out not to be the ordinary people of Glasgow, but more or less exclusively those involved in the business, commercial, and entrepreneurial life of the city. Who has decided that the 'priorities' of this narrow section of the city's population should have such privileged status?

In any event, the planning report based on last year's 'consultation' led to the decision to set up an architectural competition — only major companies need apply — organized by RIAS, and designed to create a brand new, up-to-the-minute George Square, fit for the 21st century. Council Leader Gordon Matheson has been an enthusiastic proponent of this scheme. According to him, 'it is absolutely essential we choose the very best designer-led team to create a new George Square fit for the 21st century. I look forward to working with the winning design team, and the people of Glasgow, to give the city the George Square it deserves'. An alternative version of Mr Matheson's comments has him saying he looks forward to working with the winning design team 'to develop their design and give the people and businesses of Glasgow the George Square they deserve'. In any event, exactly how Mr Matheson will be working with the people of Glasgow is left unexplained.

If nothing is done to stop or delay the process, what the people of Glasgow will see in the next few weeks is the fulfilment of the planning report's principal objective: the creation of a new George Square based on 'a wholesale re-examination of its image and functions in order that it can be regarded as a place fit for the 21st century'. The winner of the architectural competition will be announced in the next few days. And the £15 million programme of work will begin immediately — because the spruced-up square has to be ready in time for the Commonwealth Games!

The most controversial aspect of all six designs submitted to the competition – they are currently being exhibited for a few days in Glasgow's Lighthouse gallery — concerns the status of the dozen memorial statues that are at present a major component of George Square. As far as one can make out, a decision was taken in advance (by whom?) that the existing statuary (other than – surprise, surprise — the Cenotaph) could be either shifted around within the square or simply permanently removed. As a result, all six of the competing schemes involve the moving or removing of some or all of the existing statues. Why was this decision taken from the outset? Well, according to at least one report, Glasgow city's council leader believes that the statues are no more than 'unknown, lifeless relics from a bygone era'. Clearly unfit then for an up-to-the-minute 21st century.

Presumably not all of those involved in the creation of a new George Square agree that the statues of such figures as Robert Burns, Sir Walter Scott, and James Watt have no relevance to the 21st century. But the universal agreement that the existing statues cannot be left exactly where they are gives the game away over what the proposed modernisation of George Square is really about. The existing statues are clearly seen as blocking the entry of George Square into the brave new world of 21st century free-market, capitalist entrepreneurship. The anticipated image and function of the proposed new square emerge exclusively from the world of business and commerce, marketing and selling, enterprise and wealth creation. A George Square fit for the 21st century is a George Square given over to the commercialised world of shows, fairs, exhibitions, promotions, pop concerts, and sporting events. The statues belong to a different world – so sideline or dump them.

The truth is rather different. George Square, with its statues, is at the heart of Glasgow's reputation as one of the world's great Victorian cities. The statues in George Square speak of the literary, scientific, military, and political history of Glasgow and the whole of Scotland. They symbolise and represent the kind of achievements that gave Glasgow and Scotland their worldwide identity and reputation. To remove them is to demean the city and betray its past.

Will the judges of the planning competition agree? Somehow I doubt it. Who are they? (And who chose them?) One is the current organizer of the 'T in the Park' pop concerts. Another was the designer of the Barcelona Olympic village. Two are modernist academics linked to the Mackintosh School of Architecture. Gordon Matheson is also a judge, while the secretary of RIAS – best known in Glasgow as the planner of a night club in the city's Botanic Gardens – has a role as an observer on the judging panel. At the very least a mechanism should be created that allows the Glasgow public to react to this panel's verdict. Anything less would mean that Mr Matheson's promise that the redevelopment of George Square would only proceed with the involvement of the people of Glasgow was utterly meaningless. Of course, action of some kind is required over George Square. If nothing is done, it will follow the example of once proud Sauchiehall Street into increasingly shabby and dismal decline. But a reckless rush into a modernising 'fitness for the 21st century' is not the answer. Council leader Matheson and his colleagues might like to ponder this question: what would Boris Johnson say to a planning proposal for a 21st century Trafalgar Square that involved the immediate removal of Nelson's Column?

17 Hebrides

Did you watch the first part of 'Hebrides, Islands on the Edge' on BBC 1 Scotland on May Bank Holiday evening? It was a fascinating, if somewhat surprising, programme. About the natural world of the inner Hebrides — mainly Islay and Rhum, with Jura, Colonsay and Oronsay in the background — it was a brilliant example of how much can now be achieved by the makers of today's nature films. They can bring us close-up camera shots beyond anything that could be seen by the naked eye. Comfortable in our sitting-rooms, we can watch every detail and manoeuvre of Hebridean animals and birds and fish as they live their lives in their natural habitat. All this of course set in the context of stunning, wide-angled shots of the ever-changing skies and seas surrounding the different islands with their beaches and rocks, mountain peaks, fields and streams.

So as we seem to fly with eagles, swallows, hooper swans and barnacle geese, swim with otters, seals and basking sharks, and watch the battles of rutting stags, what exactly do we feel? Well for me at least the overwhelming impression was one strangely at odds with the vision of the Hebrides (and indeed of the Highlands in general) promoted by VisitScotland and the tourist industry. Of course there was a kind of beauty here on land and sea, a vision of an unspoiled and natural world remote from the overcrowded, urban reality in which most of us live. But entirely missing here was any kind of sentimental, escapist appeal – however temporary — to an apparently calm, or seductively serene, more natural way of life.

Key here, perhaps, was Ewan McGregor's commentary. His tone of voice was measured, sober, almost flat. Not a hint of promotional enthusiasm. More information and facts than rhetorical flourishes. The programme was cleverly structured around a set of stories within stories. One story – say about swallow chicks living in one of Islay's distilleries — would be set up but not resolved. Rather the chicks would be left behind and another topic — say the arrival of migrating swans and geese — would be addressed. Only then would we hear what had happened to the swallows. Similarly with the story of a seal pup washed away from its mother by storm-driven waves. Or that of the contest for mating supremacy between rutting stags — presented almost as a shoot-out between rivals in a western film. Each would be set in motion — then left — then returned to, and finally resolved.

But most striking about all these stories was their enforcing of the sense of a natural world very much on an edge. Throughout this programme, the Hebrides came across as indeed an edge, a frontier, where Scotland (and Europe) confronts the vastness of 3000 miles of Atlantic ocean. Shots of the sea were invariably imbued with a sense of immense, destructive power as wave after wav smashed against Hebridean rocks and beaches. The skies above were more often slate-grey than blue, full of gale-driven clouds, thunder and rain. Animals endured as best they could. In interludes of calm deer shake and wiggle their bodies and rainwater sprays from their skin. A baby otter separated from its mother fights for its life amid the crashing waves. Swans and geese – exhausted after their epic flights from Iceland and Greenland — settle down to rest and feed, but only to face new danger in the shape of predatory eagles.

Admittedly the film did offer a glimpse of the people of the Hebrides leading a more familiar and rewarding way of life. Sheep farmers successfully brought their lambs to the auction ring. And afterwards there was whisky to drink and music to be played in the local pub. But such positive human resilience co-existed with the reality that the rocks and seas on the western coast of the island are the last resting place of many a wrecked ship. A reality brought home by a shot of an isolated memorial on the island's edge dedicated to the hundreds of American soldiers who lost their live in two forgotten troopships wrecked there in the last weeks of World War I in 1918.

Rather than any kind of Hebridean idyll, what this film brought us was a vision of a Darwinian struggle for survival in a hostile and dangerous environment. And this was merely autumn in the Hebrides. What will winter have in store?

18 Rockall

Rockall is a chunk of volcanic rock rising some 70 feet far out in the Atlantic Ocean. In stormy weather waves crash right over it. It is located 162 miles due west of Soay Island in the St Kilda archipelago; the nearest human beings live on the island of North Uist in the Outer Hebrides, 198 miles away.

Despite its unremarkable and nondescript (rocky) appearance, Rockall has quite a colourful history. Its ownership is disputed between no less than four nation states: the Danish Faroe Islands, Iceland, Ireland, and of course the United Kingdom. One might well ask why any of these countries bother, but no doubt there are issues over fishing rights, under water potential, and posturing national prestige.

The U.K's claim goes back at least as far as 1811. In that year, a British Navy frigate –*HMS Endymion* — landed sailors on the rock to claim possession. Scholars of Scottish literature will be interested to learn that the landing party was led by Edinburgh-born Captain Basil Hall. After retiring from the navy in 1823, Hall became a successful author, writing a series of travel books based on the journals he kept while voyaging to different parts of the world. *Travels in North America* (1829), a typically Tory critique of American society and manners, helped to stoke up the so-called 'literary quarrel' between Britain and the US in this period, while *Fragments of Voyages and Travels* (1831-33), included an account of the Rockall landing.

In 1862 a member of the crew of *HMS Porcupine* – which was surveying the seabed prior to the laying of the first transatlantic cable — managed to land on Rockall, but failed to get to the top. After that, the rock appears to have remained unremarked until well into the twentieth century. However in 1955, for reasons to do with the establishment of a nuclear weapon testing range in the Outer Hebrides, the British government decided to reaffirm its formal ownership of Rockall. A landing party was duly dispatched, the Union Jack was raised, and a brass plaque was secured on the rock proclaiming British sovereignty over it. In the context of the declining days of the British Empire, this episode inevitably raised some satirical eyebrows. Flanders and Swann, for example, produced a song in which 'Rockall' rhymes with 'sweet (something else) all'. And the brass plaque soon mysteriously disappeared — and has still not been replaced.

In recent weeks, Rockall has been back in the news, and it seemed that throughout the summer of 2013, it would be the focus of the closing, heart-warming story of many a news bulletin. Why? Because the adventurer Nick Hancock, from Ratho, near Edinburgh, was planning to become the next Basil Hall.

What Hancock had in mind was to set a new record as the longest solo (human) occupier of Rockall, beating the 40 day stay of an SAS veteran in 1985, and the 42 day record of three Greenpeace protesters against oil exploration, set in 1997. Backed – and presumably funded – by the BBC1 TV programme, 'The One Show', Hancock planned to reach Rockall in a leisure vessel called *Orca III*, land on the rock, and set up the personal survival pod in which he would live for the following 60 days. The point of the exercise? To raise money for that most unimpeachable of current causes – the Help for Heroes charity.

Sad to say, however, as of yesterday (June 3rd) we learned that the show will not go on. The seas around Rockall have been so rough that Hancock has been unable to land. So he has been forced to postpone his attempt on the record until next summer. Here is what he had to say: 'At least we could get out to the rock and get a proper look at the conditions and they just weren't there.... That's the unfortunate thing with expeditions like this. It's like sitting at Everest base camp for a couple of months and not getting a break in the weather'.

Without wishing to sound hyper-critical, I do have to say I find this comment slightly odd. At 70 feet, Rockall is hardly Everest. On the other hand, Everest is clearly not what it used to be. Nowadays so many hundreds of people want to make it up and down that there's a proposal to install a ladder near the top to increase the speedy throughput of climbers. But perhaps Rockall does raise a more serious issue. Are we all being taken in by the publicity surrounding the whole notion of setting records? Why is it so important to beat someone else's record? Is this a true measure of human achievement? That famous Guinness volume surely has a lot to answer for. Perhaps it's time it became a closed book – and that Rockall is left in all its lonely splendour to the gannets and guillemots, fulmars and kittiwakes that sometimes land on it.

19 Westminster Now

In recent days, Westminster politicians have been doing their best to ensure that their reputations sink even lower than they did at the time of the expenses scandal. I have in mind not only the latest sleaze allegations involving members of both the House of Commons and the Lords – shocking as they are – but also the appalling response to these allegations adopted by the Tory half of the coalition government.

In fact the new scandal over lobbying provided our politicians with a golden opportunity to show how they could come together and act effectively over an issue proving highly damaging to the reputation of every member of parliament. Conservatives, Lib Dems, and Labour Party members, could have confronted the issue of lobbying and quickly agreed on new legislation to impose some degree of control on the activity of lobbyists in general. Parliament would have emerged as united behind the need for new levels of transparency and tighter regulation.

But what in fact has happened? The Tory half of the coalition has decided to include in the proposed bill a section designed to make it impossible for trade unions to go on supporting the funding of Labour Party election campaigns. The problem here is that the funding of election campaigns – by trade unions in Labour's case, by rich individuals and big business in the case of the Tories – has absolutely nothing to do with the issue of sleaze and corrupt lobbying practices.

Understandably the Labour Party is outraged by this development. Jack Straw – on this issue at least – has it entirely right: 'There was a good chance of party consensus on these matters, but the government has thrown a firecracker into this proposal by including a totally extraneous matter of trade unions…'.

Downing Street must have known full well that tacking the matter of union funding of the Labour Party on to the proposed bill would make it quite impossible for any kind of cross-party consensus to be achieved. So why has the prime minister agreed to it?

The re-emergence of the parliamentary sleaze issue recently came up (June 6th) in Andrew Neil's late-night BBC1 political programme 'This Week'. The programme's regular heavy-hitters – Alan Johnson and Michael Portillo – were in agreement that what was being proposed, including a new register of lobbyists, would do nothing to prevent the murky wheeling and dealing currently under investigation. They were also in agreement over their amazement about the failure of he politicians in question to realise this time that they were being set up by journalists. (Neil himself asked the most challenging question. Could it be that meetings with lobbyists were so frequent for most politicians that discrimination between pretence and the real thing was difficult? Perhaps inevitably both former and current MP dismissed the idea.)

Surprisingly, however, the late-night discussion did not address the Tories' disgraceful decision to muddy the water by conflating sleaze with the funding of the Labour Party. To my mind at least, what that decision amounts to is a descent to a new level of political cynicism.

The Labour Party is bound to oppose legislation which, while allowing big business and the rich to continue supporting the Conservative Party as of now, contains a direct attack on its own sources of funding. When Labour rejects the proposed bill, the Tories and their media supporters, will of course chorus that the Labour Party is soft on sleaze. Meantime, despite their leader's now famous remark that corporate lobbying is 'the next big scandal waiting to happen', (as a former lobbyist he should know), the Conservative Party will once again kowtow to its backbenchers and do nothing to change the status quo over corporate lobbying.

Will Nick Clegg find it possible to go along with such shabby and disreputable political opportunism? Watch this space.

20 Eurostar

A few weeks ago I was able to fulfil a long-held ambition. I travelled by Eurostar between St Pancras in London and the Gare du Nord in Paris. Ever since the opening of the Channel Tunnel I've looked forward to one day making this trip. For me there was a real hint of romance about the idea of simply boarding a train in London and arriving in Paris – an impression enhanced by a couple of occasions on which I enjoyed a glass of champagne (what else?) at what is apparently the longest bar in Europe while watching St Pancras passengers making their way to join the Paris-bound train. Henry James, I used to think, would have approved of this new form of Anglo-French cooperation.

So did the real journey match the romance of the imagined one? Well yes – but not without qualification. What turned out to be the downside was the process of actually getting on the train. Both in London and Paris there were just too many people. Masses and masses of them, mostly young, many dwarfed by their enormous backpacks; long lines of excited schoolchildren, surrounded by their luggage, stationary, or barely moving. Do I wait? Is there a way for ordinary (and elderly) passengers to move on?

What soon became clear was that boarding the Eurostar was like checking in at an international airport. The hassle was identical: a line to show one's ticket; another for passport checking; yet another for luggage security; and, particularly in Paris, another incredibly slow-moving one, controlled – of course – by everyone's favourite in capital letters: U.K.BORDER CONTROL. By the time I managed to slump into my seat on the train itself, the romance of Eurostar was struggling to survive.

But survive it did. The trip itself was a delight. I was travelling 'standard premier' – and it was worth the money. The accommodation was excellent – quiet, comfortable and cool. The green and pleasant land of Kent and northern France slipping quickly by was easy on the eye. The light lunch served in my seat had at least a hint of real French cuisine. I had imagined there might be some announcement that we were now passing under 'la Manche', but nothing was said. A remarkable achievement, but now just routine. A little over two hours after leaving St Pancras there I was in Paris – my romantic expectations of Eurostar travel more or less intact.

I was in Paris to attend the 26th annual conference of the Eighteenth-Century Scottish Studies Society which, this year, was held in association with the Adam Smith Society. The conference theme was 'Scotland, Europe and Empire in the Age of Adam Smith and Beyond', and it took place in Paris's original university — La Sorbonne. Established in the thirteenth century, La Sorbonne was reconstructed in the same period that saw Glasgow University move from its medieval site in the old merchant city to its present location on Gilmorehill. The Sorbonne remained in its original location, but in terms of grandeur and scale, its late nineteenth buildings are even more splendid than those of Glasgow.

The beautifully domed, seventeenth-century Chapel, associated above all with Cardinal Richelieu, and recognized as one of the masterpieces of Paris's classical architecture, stands at one end of an imposing, stone-cobbled, courtyard containing the main university buildings. All around are reminders of France's great tradition of culture and learning: statues and medallions memorialising philosophers, mathematicians, scientists, and classical scholars. A statue of Louis Pasteur symbolises Science, while Victor Hugo represents Literature. Inside the main building there is a library of several million books, grandly ceremonial salons and halls, monumental galleries, and a series of lecture theatres, most of them decorated with allegorical paintings relevant to the subjects taught in the university. Once again these are named in honour of great figures from France's past: our conference sessions took place in the Amphitheatre Richelieu, the Amphitheatre Descartes, and the Amphitheatre Guizot.

So what were the conference highlights? The first was a concert by the Sorbonne Scholars of 'musique anglaise and ecossaise'. The group, composed of both amateurs and professionals, proved to be of outstanding quality. Dedicated to the performance of Renaissance music and song, their programme for us included on the English side work by William Byrd, John Dowland, and Orlando Gibbons, while the conference's Scottish theme was echoed by wonderful nineteenth-century arrangements of 'My love is like a red, red rose', 'Annie Laurie', 'Loch Lomond', and 'Blue Bells of Scotland'. Their encore was a Renaissance-sounding version of 'Auld Lang Syne'!

The second was the conference's closing dinner held in Le Procope — apparently Paris's oldest restaurant. A satisfyingly elegant and stylish experience.

You may be noticing that my highlights have not featured any of the conference's many lectures or papers. There is a reason for this. Just as there was a downside to the Eurostar, so there was a downside to the Sorbonne. The seating in the university's grand lecture theatres proved to be the opposite of student friendly. The lecture rooms' wooden rows or benches were hard, straight-backed, and unyielding. No nodding-off permitted. Much more problematic were the rooms' acoustics. Even with all the usual modern microphone aids, speakers' words seemed to be swallowed up by the empty space in these lofty rooms. The result was that arguments were hard to follow, points were obscured, and conclusions missed. I have no doubt at all that Amartya Sen's plenary lecture on 'Smith's and Hume's Critique of Imperialism' — like many other conference talks — was of outstanding quality. But I'll have to await the publication of the conference proceedings to fully appreciate it.

21 G2

I've been a regular *Guardian* reader for more years than I care to remember. If someone chose to put me down as 'just a typical *Guardian* reader' I wouldn't protest very loudly. And that includes my views on art and culture – old or new. Thus I normally read not only the paper's main news section but also the more magazine-like section called G2.

Almost exactly two years ago the editorship of the paper changed hands. After his twenty-year stint, Alan Rusbridger was succeeded by Katherine Viner. At first I noticed little or no change. But more recently I've been finding G2 in particular less and less to my taste. Now I accept that in terms of age I am very far from being an average reader. So perhaps that's all that's to it. Perhaps G2 is just aiming at a younger readership with tastes and interests that I'm too old to share. In the area of contemporary art and culture, for example, I am ready to admit there is much that is lauded and celebrated – in G2 and of course elsewhere — which I find impossible to admire. Does that make me an old fogey? Not necessarily.

The G2 for Monday, May 8th, is a case in point. Allow me to share its contents with you — and make up your own mind.

Page five, as normal, is given over to the thoughts of either a regular or specially invited contributor. Today it's by a recovering alcoholic who had decided to dramatise her break with the past by shearing off all her hair. The piece refers to other women who have chosen to do likewise (I recognise hardly any of the famous names) and goes on to comment on how people react; head-shaving in the past; and so on. Marginally interesting at best.

Next is a long, four-page extract from a new book. It is a memoir concerning Caitlyn Jenner's 'journey to trans-gender womanhood'. Before her transition, she had been married three times — including to a member of the Kardashian family — had fathered six children, and had won an Olympic gold medal in the decathlon. OK, I suppose it is striking that she waited until she was 65 before switching genders, but at a time when stories on the trans-gender theme are no longer a surprise, I'm far from persuaded that G2 should be giving free publicity to such a vastly profitable and self-serving book.

Over the page is the headline 'The New Opium of the Masses' — a piece by a lecturer at the Hebrew University of Jerusalem who argues that the solution to what to do with all those made unemployable in a work-free future is the opium of computer games. But the real reason we are hearing about this is, I suspect, what follows. We are told there is nothing new about the idea that living in a 3D virtual reality world would provide 'far more excitement and emotional engagement than the "real world"'. Why? Because 'for thousands of years, billions of people have found meaning in playing virtual reality games. In the past, we have called these virtual reality games "religions"'. Is it only because I have never played a computer game that I find this preposterous?

The Health page that follows concerns postpartum psychosis. At least with this I was learning something new. The following three stories make up the Arts section – and for me this is where problems really begin. The first one is headlined 'Leviathan: how one artist created a monster'. My instinctive reaction is that art is not about creating monsters. 'The giant squid, democracy, mental health, migration – big beasts one and all. And each plays a role in Leviathan, a cycle of ten films by artist Shezad Dawood'. Conceptual art indeed. Described by 'a fellow artist' as 'Grindhouse Derek Jarman', (what does that mean?) the films are described by their maker as 'punkish' and 'freaky'. Given that one apparently involves 'monkey-men masturbating to internet porn', his description is no doubt accurate. The good news is that we shall have to wait until 2020 for the "box set."

A second art piece concerns an actor called Mat Fraser who was born with underdeveloped arms because of thalidomide. The headline is 'I'd begun to feel like yesterday's cripple', and the subtext runs 'He's staged Thalidomide! A Musical, stormed American TV and starred in an explicit fairytale with his wife. Now, Mat Fraser is raising hell as Richard III – without the hump'. Fraser's comment on Shakespeare's play: 'Richard's a nasty, vicious piece of work and he loves it', no doubt deserves a hearing, but in fact much of the article concerns Fraser's storming of American TV – in a drama called 'American Horror Story: Freak Show'. Under his freak-show alias, Sealo the Seal Boy, he also performs in summer season vaudeville shows in Coney Island. 'I treat it' (his act) he tells us, 'as a form of brutalist performance art.... The sideshows attract a fascinating mix of blue-collar New Yorkers, tattooed lesbians and the occasional British tourists who wander in, recognise me from the television, and react with absolute horror because they think it must be the only work I can get'. The recent fairytale with his wife is a version of Beauty and the Beast. We gather it's 'a scabrously funny, true-life fairytale that climaxes in a riotous parody of an Amsterdam sex-show'. I think I'll give it a miss.

But then I also won't be rushing out to buy a ticket for the forthcoming European tour of Argentinian lesbian artist Chocolate Remix. (I'm not making this up.) The third and final arts feature in the G2 of 8th May concerns "lesbian reggaeton" and "Choco" is described as its 'swaggering pioneer', one of a rising number of female reggaetoneras 'changing the male-dominated genre from within'. 'Choco keeps reggaeton's defining dembow rhythm and perreo (the doggy-style grinding dance culture) but uses the lyrics to satirise machismo and bust the taboos of female pleasure and lesbian sex.' Just how this is done – with or with out 'dembow rhythm' (whatever that is) is made explicit in the rest of the piece.

Despite this bombardment of the outlandish, bizarre and unbalanced in G2, I didn't decide to cancel my lifelong subscription to *The Guardian*. But I did feel like sitting down to a nice cup of tea.

22 Customer Service?

I think the rot set in well over a generation ago. I'm old enough to remember the good old days when, needing petrol, all you needed to do was turn in to the station forecourt, wind down the driver's window, chat to the petrol assistant – while he was probably wiping your windscreen – telling him how many gallons you wanted – and sit tight. Only when all was done and dusted, did you have to get out of the car and settle up. The good old days indeed.

The principle was a simple one. Whoever had something to sell – no matter what its nature – employed someone else to do the selling. It was called customer service, and thousands upon thousands of us were employed as clerks, shop-assistants, secretaries, or office-workers, to provide it. Employers, the employed, and customers worked happily together. So what happened?

Someone, somewhere – some bright spark of a business guru – looked at the standard business set-up I've described. OK it was working well and his business – like business in general – was doing well. But how much bigger would its profit be if the threesome of employer, employed, and customer could be reduced to a twosome? And how could that outcome be achieved? Simply by dissolving the distinction between the customer and the employed.

Looking back, I'm amazed at how quickly the self-service petrol pump took over. In no time at all car drivers were not only paying the oil companies for their petrol, but doing all the work of obtaining it: drive in, get out, unscrew the petrol cap, find the hose and push the correct button, watch the quantity indicator tick over – and hopefully stop at the required amount – then remember to replace the hose and refit the petrol cap. Then all that remains is to pay for the privilege. What is astonishing is the meekness of the motoring public in accepting this disappearance of customer service. With soaring profits, the oil companies could hardly have believed their luck. And the guy who used to provide the service? He probably lost his job.

What is the relevance of all this to today's world? The answer is provided by something I recently saw on Facebook: 'Never Self Check out', it boldly announced 'You are not a store employee... Stop being one for free.' The point is that in recent years in an extraordinary and still growing range of contexts, it has become the norm for the customer not only to pay, but also do most of the work. In almost every kind of business or trade, the pattern is the same: the customer has become an unpaid employee.

Of course the widest open door to this development has been what used to be called the new technology. Not being online is being left behind — a relic of the old way of doing things. Recently I was in the refurbished Queen Street station in Glasgow, trying to buy a ticket to Edinburgh with my rail card. I was confronted by a battery of machines which made no mention of rail cards — and a slogan proclaiming 'Paper tickets are so 2017'. Quite so — that puts me in my place. (Happily I was finally able to find a small ticket office, managed by actual people, in a nearby side street.)

The point remains however. The online, machine-driven way is the smart way. Anything else is old-fashioned, out of date — and preferring it defines you as a hopeless fuddy-duddy. Nonetheless I see no reason to go quietly. A London theatre wants me to buy a ticket — online of course. But does that give it the right to tell me I have five minutes within which to complete the transaction? Inevitably I'm not smart enough to pull it off, and remain ticket-less. OK, I'll call the theatre and speak to someone. But that proves to be impossible — a box-office telephone number is no longer available. Soon afterwards I try to get a ticket for a concert in London — once again online. This time all seems to go smoothly. I click 'Proceed to check-out', and provide all the details of my Visa Debit card. What immediately flashes up is 'Your Card is out of date' — despite the fact that it is valid until 09/21. Once again I give up.

To my mind, human beings interact with each other better than with machines; live voices are much more efficient than bodiless, recorded ones. What we are constantly told is a faster, more efficient way of doing things, over and over again proves to be exactly the opposite. Asking the simplest of questions on my PC and I'm confronted with the usual rigmarole: What is my user name (is that me?) What is my email address? (Surely you already have that) And most dismaying of all — What is my password? (I didn't know I had one). 'Forgotten your password' simply leads to further incomprehension.

I know I'll be told that the world has changed and I just need to get on with it. But surely it's worth asking whether particular changes are for the better. The maintenance of individual customer service is a cause worth fighting for, and its preservation is all the more important at a time when automation in all its forms is eroding the job market. If it is no longer ridiculous to consider instituting a four-day working week — or of thinking in terms of providing a basic living wage for us all, then it is perfectly reasonable to demand a return to a traditional level of customer service. Never self-check-out. Exactly.

23. *Beyond the Thirty-Nine Steps, A Life of John Buchan*

There may be a reader out there who remembers that some years ago, discussing Buchan's novel *Witch Wood,* I mentioned that on my bookshelf is a Nelson Classic edition of *Prester John* bearing the inscription 'Bought by Andrew Hook, on the 10th day of November 1944'. Well, in this hugely impressive biography of her grandfather, Ursula Buchan explains that by 1910, when *Prester John* appeared, Buchan had already published three novels – the first in 1895 when he was twenty years old and still a student at Brasenose College, Oxford.

These largely forgotten novels made no impact. *Prester John*, on the other hand, set in South Africa where Buchan had spent two years in 1901-03 working for the Lord High Commissioner of the colony, was at least a minor success. It was his next novel that changed everything. *The Thirty-Nine Steps* was published in October 1915, in the middle of the Great War, and in Ursula Buchan's view was 'an obvious piece of British war propaganda'. Soldiers on the Western front were certainly among its early readers but this fast-moving 'shocker', as Buchan called it, quickly became a best-seller. By the end of 1915, it had sold 25,000 copies. Buchan immediately became known as 'the famous novelist and war correspondent', and never lost his reputation as the writer of un-put-downable thrillers. *The Thirty-Nine Steps* itself received still greater popularity after the appearance of Alfred Hitchcock's hugely successful film version in 1935. (Characteristically, Buchan having viewed the film, said it was better than the book.) The book has never been out of print since its 1915 publication. By 1960 it had sold 355,000 hardback copies, and after appearing in Penguin and Pan paperback versions in the 1950s, double that number were sold. In 1965 it was calculated that total sales amounted to 1.5 million in English – while there were translations in a range of languages including Arabic and Persian. Buchan's work is now out of copyright so it is impossible to keep track of the sales of *The Thirty-Nine Steps* and his many other best-sellers such as *Greenmantle*, *Mr Standfast*, *The Three Hostages*, and *Huntingtower*.

John Buchan died in 1940 at the age of sixty-five. His last novel – *Sick Heart River* – appeared posthumously in 1941. Ursula Buchan insists that her book is not a study of her grandfather's fiction – though she does provide illuminating evidence of how often aspects of his own life fed into his fiction. Commenting on *Sick Heart River* she sounds ready to agree with those readers who see this, his twenty-seventh, novel as his best. (My own favourite is the 1927 *Witch Wood* – about Calvinist Scotland in the seventeenth century.) But novels were far from being Buchan's only writing genre. He also wrote six substantial biographies, including those of Cromwell, Montrose, and Scott. He wrote an immensely long history of the First World War while it was going on – which eventually appeared in 1921 as a four-volume *History of the Great War*. He published dozens of poems and short stories, books about political thought and the law, and wrote around a thousand articles for periodicals and newspapers. In all he published over one hundred books.

On the face of it this is an astonishing writerly output. It becomes even more so if several other factors are taken into account. Throughout his life, Buchan's health was always a problem. When he was four or five, he suffered a serious accident while travelling in a coach. Left with a broken skull, he spent almost a year in bed before making a full recovery. As an adult he was eventually diagnosed as suffering from a duodenal ulcer. This resulted in several operations, and his digestion remained a permanent problem. Frequently he was bedridden for months at a time, though fortunately that did not prevent him from continuing to write. Buchan loved the outdoors – walking, riding, climbing, fishing, shooting – but his health remained an issue. Still more important in relation to his career as a professional writer is the fact that throughout his life – as this magisterial biography makes abundantly clear – John Buchan engaged in a range of activities that he pursued so effectively that they amounted to alternative careers.

In a recent issue of the *The Scottish Review*, John Lloyd compared Rory Stewart to John Buchan: 'though Buchan was born in a Glasgow Free Kirk manse and made himself into what Stewart was born to'. The Free Kirk manse in question was actually in Perth, but there is considerable truth in this observation. Buchan did grow up in such a manse in Glasgow, was educated at Hutcheson's Grammar School, and attended Glasgow University. However, in his third year he sat an entrance examination for Brasenose College, Oxford, was successful, and left Glasgow without completing his degree. His four happy years at Oxford determined the rest of Buchan's life. His rather modest background was very different from that of his fellow-students, but he seems to have settled into their way of life with little difficulty (in his final year he was elected President of the Oxford union), and membership of the Oxford world would remain his for the rest of his life. Marriage to Susan Grosvenor in 1907 consolidated his status, as the Grosvenors were very much an upper-class English family with aristocratic connections.

Post-Oxford, Buchan decided that a future as a barrister was his best bet, and in due course he was called to the bar. Soon afterwards however he accepted the High Commissioner of South Africa, Lord Milner's offer to become a colonial administrator in that country. On his return to the U.K, he was uncertain of what to do next. The law was not proving profitable, so in January 1906, he left the bar in order to accept the position of assistant editor of *The Spectator* on a salary of £800 a year. Soon afterwards he accepted another position at the publisher Thomas Nelson and Sons, and continued to work there for over twenty years. (In 1919 he would also become a paid director at the Reuter's agency.) However, in 1910, now reasonably secure financially, he began to think of yet another career – as a member of parliament. Accordingly, in February, 1911, Buchan was able to have himself adopted as the Conservative and Unionist candidate for the Peebles and Selkirk constituency – then held by the Liberal party. In the following year or two he spent a considerable amount of time in the constituency – an area he had known well since his boyhood holidays spent there – giving speeches, holding meetings, trying to make his candidature well known. The outbreak of World War I in 1914 of course changed everything.

Forty-two years old, and suffering from his duodenal ulcer condition, there was no question of Buchan's fighting in the war. (His youngest brother Alastair would be killed in 1917). Nevertheless in a variety of ways he played an extremely important part: first as a newspaper reporter sending back reports from positions dangerously close up to the western front line, then as an historian writing a two million word account of the war as it went on, and finally working for the national government – including the Foreign Office – becoming Director of the Department of Information, a kind of high-powered public relations position controlling how the outside world learned of the progress of the war.

Post-war, he did finally enter parliament as the occupant of one of the Scottish Universities seats in 1927. He never achieved cabinet rank but did become a highly respected and influential member, on extremely close terms with both the former Labour prime-minister Ramsay MacDonald and the long-serving Conservative prime-minister Stanley Baldwin. Other public appointments followed. In both 1933 and 1934 he fulfilled the role of Lord High Commissioner of the General Assembly of the Church of Scotland. In 1938 he won the election to be the Chancellor of Edinburgh University. By then however, ennobled as Lord Tweedsmuir, he had become the Governor General of Canada – where he would spend the last five years of his life.

The point of this account is to emphasise how extraordinary it is that such an amazingly prolific writer could also achieve so much in so many other ways. The highly ceremonial years in Canada are perhaps something of a disappointment. But as always Buchan played his role superbly. Always addressing French Canadians in French, he and his wife were greeted enthusiastically in every region of Canada. More important perhaps, at a time when the threat of another war with Germany was growing, was the effort Buchan put in to strengthening the special relationship between the U.K. and the US. Visiting Washington, receiving honorary degrees from Harvard and Yale, and becoming the first Briton to address the US Congress, Buchan established close and enduring relations with the US President Franklin D. Roosevelt and the Secretary of State Cordell Hull. Just as his views were sought by three British prime-ministers, so they were sought by the most powerful opinion-formers in the US.

Two closing footnotes. In this monumental tome I found one mistake. At the bottom of p.176 the naval base at Scapa Flow is located in the Shetland Islands rather than the Orkneys! Much more intriguing is to learn that in 1907 Buchan took control of Nelson's weekly journal *The Scottish Review*. His aim was to make it a Scottish version of *The Spectator*, and he became a major contributor. After two years however Buchan's aim had not been achieved, and publication ceased. What would he make of the present version? I'm inclined to believe he would approve.

Postscript

In the opening sentence of the Preface to this book, I refer to Alasdair Gray's memoir 'Of Me And Others'. That is why I've chosen to close 'From Mount Hooly to Princeton' with an extended – and I hope entertaining – response to Alasdair's book.

Inevitably much more about 'me' than the 'others', this is an extraordinary ragbag (Gray's own word) of a book. Yet it is a work entirely characteristic of its author and his work. In his foreword, the author tells us that the potential 'ragbag' turned out to have a kind of unity because the story it tells of his entire career mirrors that of Scottish artists in general throughout the period of his lifetime. How true this is, is debatable – after all, few other Scottish writers or painters have gained anything like the success and status of Alasdair Gray. What is true, however, is that in its apparent randomness, range and oddity, the book does reflect major aspects of Gray's artistic career.

For Gray's superfans – and I don't doubt there are many of them – the book will be a treasure-trove over all its 471 pages. For his scholars and critics, there will turn out to be passages and occasional insights which will prove valuable in their analyses of some of Gray's 18 published books. For the general reader, however, this will be at best a tome to dip into rather than read through. In fact, I suspect there will be readers too irritated by its repetitions and tricksiness to go on reading. And whatever the topic he happens to be writing about, Gray's insistence on making the same sweeping generalisations, from a socialist point of view, on Scottish history – religious, social, economic and artistic – may well lead to the same outcome. Only reviewers like me will read every page.

More than once in the book Gray objects to the term 'postmodern' being applied to his work. I share his dislike for much of the language of contemporary academic literary criticism. But on this point he is wrong. Of all contemporary Scottish writers, he is the one most deserving of the description. Post-modernists inherit the modernism of such writers as James Joyce and T S Eliot, but pushing their rejection of more traditional literary forms and subjects in radical new directions, Gray is unquestionably one of them. Even this collection of autobiographical essays, commentaries on his fiction, accounts of his plays for radio and the stage, descriptions of his murals, and a lengthy list of obituaries and tributes to fellow Scottish writers and artists, has something of the postmodern about it.

In the first place, like nearly all of Gray's books, *Of Me And Others* is a work of art in its own right: its visual and typographical aspects, its illustrations and lino-cuts, its variety of type-faces and its cover, are all carefully designed. The work of writer and painter overlap. A feature of postmodernism is its blurring of the distinction between fiction and reality. Such a blurring lies of course at the heart of Gray's first ground-breaking novel *Lanark* (1981) with its dramatic juxtaposition of conventional literary naturalism on the one hand, and phantasy or a Kafkaesque surrealism on the other. I still remember discussing the novel in Glasgow, not long after its publication, with the poet Iain Crichton Smith, and discovering that we were on opposite sides – the poet admired the phantasy but found the realism boring, while I was uncomfortable with the purely fictional but admired the realism.

There is nothing so radical about *Of Me And Others*, but it is not always clear what we are to make of some of its contents. Was this obituary ever published? Alasdair can't remember. Why are 21 pages of the so-called epilogue of *Lanark* reprinted here? Stranger still is the decision to print what Gray tells us is 'a new fictional conclusion' to his novel *Something Leather* – all 22 pages of it. All I can say is that for someone like me, who decided that *Something Leather* was not my kind of novel when it appeared, this new epilogue does nothing to make me feel I was wrong.

And finally, there is the inclusion of what is called 'Sidney Workman's Epilogue' to Gray's most recent novel *Old Men In Love*. Workman is a fictional character who makes a brief appearance in *Lanark*. Here he is writing from an address in Kirkcaldy – 17 Linoleum Terrace – what quickly becomes a savage, blistering indictment of Alasdair Gray's entire writing career. Gray has previously adopted similar tactics to outfox his critics by getting his own boot in first. This time I do wonder if he has made the correct decision.

Alasdair Gray and I are very much of an (advanced) age. Growing up, we had similar reading habits enjoying boys' weeklies such as the *Hotspur*, *Rover*, *Adventure* and *Wizard*. We both took full advantage of public libraries. Gray tells us he 'visited Riddrie Public Library four or five times a week, never taking much more than a day to read a whole book'. Likewise, I remember taking a book out of the public library near Kenmure Street in Glasgow, and having finished it, being told I could not return it the same day.

Where we differed was over health: Gray was a sickly child suffering from asthma and eczema. What happened to him as a young man is strikingly revealed in an entry called 'A Report to the Trustees', written in 1959. Having completed his studies at Glasgow's School of Art, he was awarded a scholarship to travel and paint in Spain. Sailing from Liverpool to Gibraltar, his trip soon turned into a nightmare of illness. Recurring asthma kept him in his cabin and then the ship's hospital. Arrival in Gibraltar led to no improvement. The following weeks were spent largely in hospitals and hostels. He eventually returned to Glasgow having seen nothing of Spain, and reading between the lines, lucky to be alive. Perhaps there is more than a hint here of the source of the tenacity with which he went on to pursue his artistic career no matter what.

Readers will have gathered that this is a quirky book so I'm going to end with a postmodern quirkiness of my own. I've mentioned that there is a great deal of repetition here. The stories of two individuals in particular come up again and again. One is about the Glasgow museum curator Elspeth King – and what Gray regards as her disgraceful treatment by Glasgow's cultural bosses. I know nothing of Elspeth King, but the subject of Gray's second recurring story I certainly did know.

When I came down from Aberdeen to take up the Bradley Chair in the Glasgow University English department in 1979, Philip Hobsbaum was already a senior member of the department – but not a professor. Arriving from Belfast in the 1960s, Hobsbaum in a year or two began repeating the striking success he had made in Belfast – and before that in London, and before that in Cambridge. In all these locations he proved able to bring together and encourage groups of young writers – many of whom would go on to become major figures in the contemporary literary world. In Glasgow, that group included James Kelman, Tom Leonard, Liz Lochead, Aonghas MacNeacail, Agnes Owens, Marcella Evaristi, Jeff Torrington – and, of course, Alasdair Gray.

Over and over again in this book Gray tells the story of Hobsbaum's meetings and how important they were. But there was another side to Hobsbaum. He could be ill-tempered and opinionated to an extraordinary degree. Within months of arriving in Glasgow from Belfast, he gave an interview to the student magazine GUM (Glasgow University Magazine) in which he launched an unbelievably violent and vitriolic attack on everything about the city – and his new colleagues. (Inexplicably, given his huge admiration for the man, Gray chooses to reprint the entire article here.) One of its consequences was that many of his new colleagues never forgave him.

Soon after arriving in Glasgow I became head of department, and remained in that position for nearly 10 years. I knew that as far as the wider literary and academic world was concerned, Philip Hobsbaum was easily the best-known figure in my department. Yet strangely Glasgow had never promoted him to a professorship. There was still opposition, but I decided 1968 was a long time ago and that it was time to let bygones be bygones. So I made it happen. A few weeks later I was entertained to dinner by the new professor and his brother. Given how much Alasdair clearly enjoyed the title of 'professor' of creative writing, I think he owes me a tiny footnote the next time he tells the Hobsbaum story.

Lightning Source UK Ltd.
Milton Keynes UK
UKHW021016150922
408911UK00012B/291

9 781849 211895